Gateway to Heaven

Gateway to Heaven

Marian Doctrine and Devotion
Image and Typology
in the Patristic and Medieval Periods

Volume 1
Doctrine and Devotion

Brian K. Reynolds

New City Press
Hyde Park, New York

To my wife, Ching-Yi,
my daughters Róisín and Aisling,
and my beloved mother, Bláithín,
born in heaven September 10, 2008

Published in the United States by New City Press
202 Comforter Blvd., Hyde Park, NY 12538
www.newcitypress.com
©2012 Brian K. Reynolds

Cover design by Leandro De Leon

Library of Congress Cataloging-in-Publication Data:
A catalog record is available from the Library of Congress

ISBN 978-1-56548-449-8

Printed in the United States of America

CONTENTS

ACKNOWLEDGMENTS

The final period of research for this book was supported by a grant from the Fu Jen College of Foreign Languages, which enabled me to reduce my teaching load and make a brief foray to the Marianum in Rome, for which I am most grateful. I have had the benefit of much help and support from colleagues, friends and family which I am delighted to be able to acknowledge here. I should like to begin by thanking my colleagues in the Italian Department, Paolo Cumin, Francesco Nati, Catello Crisscuolo and Theresa Tu who have generously allowed me the maximum flexibility possible to carry out research in a system that is not always sympathetic to the needs of the scholar, by taking on duties and teaching hours that might otherwise have been mine. In particular my thanks go to the Head of Department, Antonella Tulli, who has been unstinting in her support. I am also very grateful to Annabella Chang, my teaching assistant, for lightening my burden. For invaluable help with Latin translations I thank Fabrizio Tosolini and Michael Skupin. Thanks also to Sonia Huang and Dorina Altimonti. I am grateful to Bernard McGinn and Brendan Purcell for reading chapters of the book and offering valuable advice and corrections. Such inadequacies and errors as remain are entirely mine. Many friends, far and near, have supported me. In particular I thank Manfried Kögler, Philipp Hu and Joe Ting for being themselves! For their unwavering support and kindness I thank Santina, Geni, Karin and Marilen. I should like especially to acknowledge the inspiration of Chiara Lubich and Igino Giordani. Thanks to the Deasy family who offered constant encouragement, particularly Donal, who helped with proofreading. I am above all grateful to my family, my mother who liked me to read passages that I had translated to her over the phone, my father, who has sent 'vibes' across the wires, my wife, who has continued to love and support me in a thousand ways, my two daughters, who have never failed to remind me of what life is truly about.

Introduction

Haec Virgo Verbo gravida
Fit paradisi janua,
Quae Deum mundo reddidit
Coelum nobis aperuit.
(This Virgin, heavy with the Word, was the gate of paradise, who gave back God to the world and opened heaven for us) *In annuntiatione BVM, Ad nocturnum, 1-4*[1]

These four short lines from a hymn attributed to Peter Damian († 1072) effectively synthesise what Mary had come to mean for the Church and the faithful by the later Middle Ages: she, the Virgin Mother, was the means whereby God had restored a fallen world, and it was thanks to her that humanity, long blinded to God's immanent presence in his creation, could once again have access to the grace that leads to heaven. The Mary that we shall meet in these pages is an infinitely complex figure. She is daughter, mother, bride, virgin, humble woman and hieratic queen, a fitting mother and consort for Christ the king, a figure of popular devotion and affective piety, the subject of abstruse theological debate, a mother to be called upon in need, an inspirational and aspirational model of the virtues, an icon of ineffable beauty, a powerful taliswoman against the wiles of the devil, a channel of graces, a mediatrix and intercessor with God, mother of mercy and refuge of sinners. As we reach the heights of Medieval devotion to the Virgin, in one sense we are a long way from the simple woman of the New Testament, yet all the accretions of the centuries still depend on one fundamental fact, that Mary, through her unconditional yes to God, became the Mother of the Incarnate Word, the second Person of the Trinity.

This book explores how Christian understanding of Mary's place in the divine economy evolved in the Patristic and Medieval periods, and how these changing perceptions were reflected in doctrine, devotion, imagery and typology. The study is divided into two volumes. The first, on doctrine and devotion, deals with all the major Marian doctrines and provides a survey of devotional developments, in the East up to the end of the Patristic era, and in the West up to the beginning of the fourteenth century. These cut off points have been chosen because Marian theology and devotion reached its height in the East with the late Byzantine Fathers, Germanus of Constantinople († c. 733), Andrew of Crete (†c. 740), and John of Damascus († 749), while it was with John Duns Scotus († 1308) and his contemporaries that the theology of the Immaculate Conception, the last of the Marian doctrines to emerge in the Latin

---

[1] *PL* 145, 933C. Unless otherwise indicated all translations of original material in the book are mine.

1

Church, was largely worked out. What is more, by the fourteenth century all the essential lineaments of the sort Marian devotion that was to characterise the Western Church up to modern times were already present, if not always fully developed. The second volume is divided into two sections. The first considers the most important attributes of Mary such as her virginity, obedience and humility, her image as queen and bride, her relationship with the Church and the Eucharist, and so on. As in the first volume, I concentrate principally on original sources and provide extensive quotations. The volume concludes with a lengthy section on Marian typology in which I trace the origin and meaning of all the most important types, such as the ark, the dawn, the rod of Jesse, the burning bush, the star of the sea, the lily, and many more, through an extensive survey of Patristic and Medieval texts. Although a considerable amount of scholarly attention has been paid to Patristic and Medieval exegesis of the Bible since the pioneering work of the likes of Beryl Smalley and Henri de Lubac in the middle of the last century, [2] to my knowledge no systematic study yet exists on Marian typological readings of the Old Testament.[3] This groundbreaking work will, I hope, be a valuable resource for scholars in a variety of fields.

Indeed, this book was born out of my own need to learn more about Medieval Mariology. In carrying out research on the figure of the Virgin in Dante's *Commedia* I found that the sort of information I required on matters such as theology, image and typology was extremely hard to find. What, I asked myself, was the relationship between the humility of the *donna angelicata* in Italian courtly poetry and the Virgin, only to find that virtually nothing had been written on Mary's humility in the Middle Ages. How did Dante's attitude towards the Immaculate Conception and the bodily Assumption compare to the thinking of his time? Again, a virtual blank. Was there a relationship between some of the imagery in the *Commedia* and Marian typology? Nothing. In fact, despite a seemingly exhaustive bibliography on all matters Marian, scholars who are not experts in Mariology are faced with a number of obstacles when seeking

---

[2] Beryl, Smalley, *The Study of the Bible in the Middle Ages,* 3rd edn, rev. (Oxford: Blackwell, 1983), and see the monumental study by Henri de Lubac, *Exégèse médiévale: les quatre sens de l'Écriture,* 4 vols (Paris: Aubier, 1959-64). See also Jean Daniélou, *Sacramentum futuri: Études sur les origines de la typologie biblique* (Paris: Beauchesne, 1950), and Frances Young, *Biblical Exegesis and the Formation of Christian Culture* (Cambridge: Cambridge University Press, 1997), and, of course, the pioneering work by Erich Auerbach, 'Figura', *Archivum Romanicum,* 17 (1938), 320-341, and 'Typological Symbolism in Medieval Literature', *Yale French Studies,* 9 (1952), 3-10.
[3] Some minor observations are to be found in Mary B. Cunningham, 'The Meeting of the Old and New: The Typology of Mary Theotokos in Byzantine Homilies and Hymns', in *The Church and Mary,* ed. by Robert N. Swanson, Studies in Church History, 39 (Woodenbridge: Boydell, 2004), pp. 52-62. There are also occasional in-depth studies such as Margot Fassler's, 'Mary's Nativity, Fulbert of Chartres, and the *Stirps Jesse*: Liturgical Innovation circa 1000 and Its Afterlife', *Speculum,* 75 (2000), 389-434, but they are limited in scope and period.

to access material for the Patristic and Medieval periods. For broad chronological overviews they can turn to the likes of Hilda Graef, Jaroslav Pelikan, or Marina Warner,[4] but surveys such as these, which paint in broad brushstrokes and provide very little source material, are not meaty enough for most scholarly endeavours. Other studies such as Stephen Benko's, *The Virgin Goddess* and Michael Carroll's, *The Cult of the Virgin Mary* are too heavily compromised by an anachronistic critical apparatus to be of much use.[5] One can consult reference works such as O' Carroll's *Theotokos* or turn to monumental studies such as du Manoir's *Maria*, Roschini's *Maria Santissima*, or Carol's *Mariology*, the latter all decidedly dated and intended primarily for a clerical readership (little of significance has appeared in the post-Vatican II period).[6] Alternatively, one can peruse the considerable body of articles and books concerning specific aspects of Mariology, but many of these are too specialised for the needs of the average scholar. A final option is to consult original sources, trawling through collections of Patristic and Medieval writings or anthologies of Marian texts. Until recently, the percentage of original material available in anything other than Latin has been far less than one might expect. The multi-volume set of Marian texts produced by Città nuova is an invaluable resource for Italian speakers, but we still await similar work in English.[7] Luigi Gambero's two volumes on Patristic and Medieval Mariology have the advantage of making quotations from primary texts available in English, though the passages are generally quite short and his choice of a purely chronological approach is of limited usefulness for those who wish to trace the development of specific themes or patterns of thought.[8]

On devotion the situation is very different. Much has been written in recent times regarding the origins and character of the Marian cult, and the motivations behind

---

[4] Hilda Graef, *Mary: A History of Doctrine and Devotion*, 2 vols (New York: Sheed and Ward, 1963-1965), and *The Devotion to Our Lady* (New York: Hawthorn, 1963), Jaroslav Pelikan, *Mary through the Centuries*; Marina Warner, *Alone of all her Sex: The Myth and Cult of the Virgin Mary* (London: Pan Books, 1985).

[5] See below.

[6] *Maria: Études sur la Sainte Vierge*, ed.by Hubert du Manoir, 8 vols (Paris: Beauchesne, 1949-71), Gabriele M. Roschini, *Maria Santissima nella storia della salvezza*, 4 vols, (Isola del Liri: Pisani, 1969), *Mariology*, ed. by Juniper B. Carol, 3 vols (Milwaukee: Bruce, 1955-1961).

[7] The best anthologies, none of which is in English, are: Domenico Casagrande, *Enchiridion Marianum Biblicum Patristicum* (Rome: Cor Unum, 1974); Sergius Alvarez Campos, *Corpus marianum patristicum*, 8 vols (Ediciones Aldecoa, Burgos, 1970-1985); René Lauretin, *Marie, mère du Seigneur: Les beaux textes de deux millénaires* (Paris: Desclée, 1984); *Testi mariani del primo millennio*, ed. by Georges Gharib and others, 4 vols, (Rome: Città Nuova, 1988–1991); *Testi mariani del secondo millennio*, ed. by Angelo Amato and others, 8 vols (Rome: Città Nuova, 1996–).

[8] Luigi Gambero, *Mary and the Fathers of the Church*, trans. by Thomas Buffer (San Francisco: Ignatius Press, 1999) and *Mary in the Middle Ages: The Blessed Virgin Mary in the Thought of Medieval Latin Theologians*, trans. by Thomas Buffer (San Francisco: Ignatius Press, 2000).

the Church's promotion of and devotion to the Virgin, including two volumes that have come out this year, Miri Rubin's stimulating *Mother of God: A History of the Virgin Mary* and the first volume of *Storia della Mariologia*, jointly published by the Pontifical Institute for Marian studies, the Marianum, and Città nuova.[9] It is partly for this reason that I dedicate proportionately less space to devotion than doctrine in this study. Moreover, since excellent material already exists on how social and cultural factors have influenced Marian devotion, in my chapters on the subject I have chosen to concentrate more on primary material and on the theology of intercession and mediation, an approach that is also consistent with the overall focus of the book.

With these considerations in mind, the first volume begins with a chapter on Mary's divine motherhood. I first explore the pivotal role that Mary played in the Christological debates concerning the hypostatic union in the early centuries of the Church. My intention is not to provide a comprehensive guide to incarnational Christology, my focus being on how the theological disputes which swirled around the person of Christ contributed to understanding of the Virgin and her soteriological role. Had Mary's divine motherhood not been so crucial to the debate over the relationship between Christ's humanity and divinity there is little doubt that she would not have become so prominent a figure in the early Church. The declaration which resulted from the Council of Ephesus (431) that Mary was the *Theotokos* (God-bearer) meant that she became the principal guarantor of orthodox doctrine on the mystery of the Incarnation. Thus it is that her divine motherhood continued to be proclaimed as a central tenet of Christian belief by theologians of the Middle Ages, long after the major heresies on the hypostatic union had died down. Recognition of her divine motherhood also meant an exalted place for her in the Christian hierarchy, high above the angels and her fellow humans, as the creature whom God had

---

[9] Miri Rubin, *Mother of God: A History of the Virgin Mary* (New Haven: Yale University Press, 2009), and *Storia della mariologia: dal modello biblico al modello letterario*, ed. by Enrico dal Covolo, and Aristide Serra (Rome: Città Nuova and Marianum, 2009). Other useful studies that have appeared in recent years include *The Origins of the Cult of the Virgin Mary*, ed. by Chris Maunder (London: Burns and Oats, 2008), *Mary: The Complete Resource*, ed. by Sarah Jane Boss (Oxford and New York: Oxford University Press 2007), and by the same author, *Mary* (London: Continuum, 2004), *The Church and Mary* ed. by Robert N. Swanson, Studies in Church History, 39 (Woodenbridge: Boydell, 2004), *Figure poetiche e figure teologiche nella mariologia dei secoli XI e XII*, atti del II convegno mariologico della Fondazione Ezio Franceschini con la collaborazione della Biblioteca Palatina di Parma, Parma, 19-20 maggio 2000, ed. by Clelia Maria Piastra and Francesco Santi (Florence: SISMEL-Edizioni del Galluzzo, 2004), *Stefano de Fiores, Maria sintesi di valori: storia culturale della mariologia* (Cinisello Balsamo: San Paolo, 2005), *Itinerari mariani dei due millenni*, ed. by Ermanno M. Toniolo, 4 vols (Rome: Centro di Cultura Mariana 'Madre della Chiesa', 1996-99), Dominique Iogna-Prat, Eric Palazzo, and Daniel Russo, eds, *Marie: Le culte de la Vierge dans la société médiévale* (Paris: Beauchesne, 1996), Caroline M. Ebertshäuser, Hebert Haag, Joe H. Kirchberger and Dorothee Solle, *Mary: Art, Culture, and Religion through the Ages*, trans. by Peter Heinegg (New York: Crossroad, 1988).

favoured above all others and who was most in his image and likeness. This did not mean that she had become a goddess however, at least in the official teaching of the Church, if only for the simple reason that she had to be fully human for the Word to take his humanity from her, but it did lead to an increasingly fervent and elaborate cult which sometimes spilled over into Mariolatry and threatened to overshadow Christ himself.

The next chapter considers the three aspects of Mary's virginity, before, during and after the birth of Jesus. Here I am less interested in matters such as Mary's image as a virgin and the role she played in promoting virginity, issues that are discussed in the second volume, than in examining the evolution of these three beliefs and the theological justifications for them. Belief in the virginal conception was backed up by Scripture, and was fundamental to Christ's status as the God-man, so that it is defended by all the Fathers from the very earliest times, both against the Jews and the Gentiles. That Mary remained a virgin in giving birth was a less central issue and did not have the solid backing of Scripture. Indeed it is largely in apocryphal sources that we find the earliest evidence for the belief. Although attitudes towards virginity, sexuality, and childbirth undoubtedly played a role in the development of the belief, there were nevertheless important theological reasons for arguing in favour of a painless birth, the most prominent being that Mary, as the new Eve, who had heeded God instead of the serpent, was free from the curse imposed on the ancient mother and her descendents that they would give birth in sorrow (Genesis 3. 16). The virgin birth was therefore a sign both of the uniqueness of Mary and the divine origin of her child. As to Mary's perpetual virginity, although the fittingness of the Mother of God having had sexual relations after the birth of Christ was a major consideration, no crucial theological issues depended on it.

Chapter 3 discusses Mary's remote co-redemption, that is, the role that she played in bringing about God's plan of salvation for humanity through her consent to become the Mother of the Redeemer. This is a fundamental theme running throughout the writings of the Fathers and many of the theologians of the Middle Ages beginning with Justin Martyr (†c. 165) and Irenaeus (†c. 202) who first introduced the notion that Mary was the new Eve. In contrast to Eve, who turned her back on God and brought sin and death into the world, Mary gave life and grace back to creation through her obedience and humility. Mary's yes to God was the opening act in a drama that ended in the redemptive sacrifice of her Son on the Cross in which he offered himself up in expiation for the sin of humanity, something that he could not have done if he had not taken on a human nature from her. Patristic and Medieval writers alike marvel that, though God could have chosen many ways to bring about the Redemption, he chose to do so through the freely-given assent of a woman. Mary's greatness, then, lies in her assent and in her complete openness to God's grace, which allowed her, a finite being, to contain the infinite God. It is in this sense that she is a co-operator in the Redemption.

The two chapters on Patristic and Medieval devotion, intercession and mediation are necessarily but an overview, and are not intended to be a full-blown history of Mary. As noted above, much excellent work has been done in recent years in the field of devotion. It would be foolish to attempt to do in two chapters what others have dedicated books to. As the titles of these chapters suggest, aside from more general information on the development of the Virgin's cult, my main interest is to explore how understanding of Mary's intercessory and mediatory roles evolved through an analysis if contemporary material. My overriding concern here is to present a representative sampling of the ideas as they occur in the material of the time so as to arrive at a better understanding of how Mary went from being an intercessor, similar though superior to the other saints, to the universal Mediatrix of grace and gateway to heaven. Of necessity I have had to be selective in the material I have chosen, concentrating primarily on written sources, especially homilies. I do not dwell at length on liturgy nor have I considered prayers to the Virgin in detail, a subject that has been explored exhaustively by Henri Barré.[10] Likewise, I give only peripheral consideration to art, a field so rich that it would require a volume all to itself. As to music, although I do consider hymns, especially in the second volume, the book does not offer anything like a comprehensive treatment of the subject.

Chapter 6 deals with Mary's part in the Passion and Crucifixion of her Son, one of the more controversial areas of Marian doctrine. The Greek Fathers long believed that the Virgin had suffered a loss of faith on Calvary on the basis of an interpretation, first suggested by Origen (†c. 254), that the sword which Simeon prophesised would pierce Mary's heart (Luke 2. 35) signified a loss of faith that assailed her when she saw her Son being crucified. Alongside these more formal writings are a series of Marian plaints which dramatically portray a highly emotional Mary struggling to accept her Son's fate. In the West, instead, there is relatively little interest in Mary's role in the Passion in the Patristic period. The one major exception is Ambrose of Milan († 397), who rejects the Eastern belief that there was a loss of faith, instead portraying the Virgin as a stoic figure who heroically stood by the Cross while everyone else fled. Though he specifically denied that Mary contributed anything to the Redemption, in the long run Ambrose's view of the *mater dolorosa* set the stage for belief in the Marian co-redemption. In the Medieval West, I believe, these two traditions – the agonised Mary of the East and the stoic Mother of the West – combined with certain elements inherent to Medieval Marian piety to produce a new theology of the co-passion in which the great agony that Mary endured on Calvary was seen as a continuation of her role of co-operating with her Son in the Incarnation. Thus, though Jesus brought about the objective Redemption, she wholly associated herself with his act. Moreover, for many prominent

---

[10] See his monumental *Prières anciennes de l'Occident à la Mère du Sauveur des origines à saint Anselme* (Paris: Lethielleux, 1963). Mary Clayton, *The Cult of the Virgin*, has complemented Barré's work with her study of Marian devotion in England.

Medieval churchmen, most notably Bernard of Clairvaux († 1153), God has chosen to channel grace through the Virgin, rather than pouring it out directly onto humanity, so that she continues to mediate between God and man just as she co-operated in unleashing the grace of the Redemption throughout her life but most particularly on Calvary. Mary's universal mediation of grace and her co-redemption have not, however, been accepted as official Church doctrine. At a more popular level, the Middle Ages saw tremendous growth in Marian plaints, which had previously been confined to the East, as well as the emergence of dramatisations of the Virgin's *compassio*, and devotion to the Seven Sorrows of Our Lady.

Though the bodily Assumption of Mary was only proclaimed as dogma by the Catholic Church in 1950 the roots of the belief stretch back to early Patristic times. In Chapter 7 I examine early apocryphal accounts of the Dormition, discuss early Christian understanding of death and the fate of the soul, survey the different trajectories of belief in the Dormition/Assumption in the Eastern and Western Churches in the first millennium, and consider how and why the Church in the Medieval West went from a position of scepticism to one of almost universal acceptance in a relatively short time. I conclude the chapter by suggesting that official acceptance of the doctrine was delayed so long as there was no agreement on whether Mary had been preserved free from original sin, since only someone who was free from all trace of the original fault could be excepted from the general fate of postlapsarian humanity.

The final chapter explores the Immaculate Conception. Here I consider those Eastern Fathers whose extravagant praise of the Virgin has led some to believe that they were affirming her complete freedom from sin. I argue against this proposition, both on the grounds of internal evidence and on the basis that the Eastern notion of original sin differed too much from the West for there to be an equivalency with Catholic understanding of the Immaculate Conception. The chapter proceeds with an examination of the seemingly insurmountable obstacles posed to the doctrine by the Pauline affirmation of the universal need for Redemption and Augustine's († 430) doctrine of original sin. It was these same obstacles that prevented all the major Medieval churchmen from Bernard of Clairvaux († 1153) to Aquinas († 1274) and Bonaventure († 1274) from accepting the doctrine despite increasing celebration of the feast day and growth in popular belief (*sensus fidei*). It was only with Duns Scotus, who built on the work of previous theologians, most notably his fellow Franciscan and master, William of Ware († c. 1305), that a way around all objections seemed to have been found. Yet, as with the Assumption, although acceptance of the belief was widespread official sanction of the doctrine was long in coming, not least because of the implacable opposition of the Dominicans, who refused to accept the doctrine on the basis that their greatest theologian, Aquinas, had denied it.

Before I finish, a word on my general approach is in order. As I have already stressed, one of my principal concerns has been to focus on original material, for which reason I cite from several hundred texts and translate many passages into English for the first time. In attempting to enter into and interpret the mindset of the time I have tried, insofar as possible, to remain neutral though sympathetic towards the material I discuss, although, in dealing with any religious phenomenon, one is inevitably conditioned by one's own upbringing, culture, education and beliefs. I have avoided imposing any particular theoretical construct – feminist, psycho-social, postmodernist – preferring to deal with the subject on its own terms without imposing anachronistic frameworks on the facts. Throughout the book I have given priority to the role that Christianity itself has played in determining understanding of Mary. While it is indisputable that societal and cultural factors have played an important role in the development of Mary's image, particularly in the area of popular devotion, to focus on these elements while largely ignoring the complex theological issues involved and failing to acknowledge the part played by the internal dynamics of Christianity gives a false and one-sided impression that the figure of Mary is simply the product of some deep collective psychological need within men, or humanity as a whole,[11] that she is merely the inheritor of pre-Christian goddess cults[12] or the construct of a feudal society. Society and culture were crucial factors in the forging of Mary's image but it is equally true that her cult – her image, her theological significance, the symbolism surrounding her, devotion to her – cannot be understood in isolation from the evolution of Marian theology. While not denying the valuable contribution that socio-cultural scholarship can and has made to Marian studies, I hope that this book can provide a somewhat different perspective on the extraordinary figure that is Mary.

---

[11] See, for instance, Julia Kristeva, 'Stabat Mater', in *The Female Body in Western Culture: Contemporary Perspectives*, ed. by Susan Rubin Suleiman (Cambridge Ma. and London: Harvard University Press, 1986), pp. 99-118, and Mary Daly, *Pure Lust: Elemental Feminist Philosophy* (Boston: Beacon Press, 1984), p. 74.

[12] Karl Jung's *Four Archetypes: Mother, Rebirth, Spirit, Trickster* (Princeton: Princeton University Press, 1970), continues to exert considerable influence, and see Erich Neuman's monumental study of the Jungian mother archetype, *The Great Mother: An Analysis of the Archetype* (New York: Pantheon, 1955). Among the most frequently cited proponents of goddess theories are Stephen Benko, *The Virgin Goddess: Studies in the Pagan and Christian Roots of Mariology* (New York: E.J. Brill, 1993), and Michael P. Carroll, *The Cult of the Virgin Mary: Psychological Origins* (Princeton: Princeton University Press, 1986). I am entirely in accord with Jaroslav Pelikan *Mary Through the Centuries: Her Place in the History of Culture* (New Haven: Yale University Press, 1996), who dismisses 'facile modern theories about "mother goddesses"', pointing out that the term *Theotoókos* was adopted by the Council of Ephesus in order to defend Christ's dual nature, not as an alternative to pagan goddesses (p. 58).

Chapter 1 – Divine Motherhood

Psalms 21. 10-11:	For thou art he that hast drawn me out of the womb: my hope from the breasts of my mother. I was cast upon thee from the womb. From my mother's womb thou art my God.
Psalms 131. 11:	The Lord hath sworn truth to David, and he will not make it void: of the fruit of thy womb I will set upon thy throne.
Isaiah 7. 14:	Therefore the Lord himself shall give you a sign. Behold a virgin shall conceive, and bear a son, and his name shall be called Emmanuel.
Jeremias 31. 22:	For the Lord hath created a new thing upon the earth: a woman shall compass a man.
Matthew 1. 18:	Now the generation of Christ was in this wise. When as his mother Mary was espoused to Joseph, before they came together, she was found with child, of the Holy Ghost.
Luke 1. 31:	Behold thou shalt conceive in thy womb, and shalt bring forth a son; and thou shalt call his name Jesus.
Luke 1. 43:	And whence is this to me, that the mother of my Lord should come to me?
Mark 3. 32:	Behold thy mother and thy brethren without seek for thee.
John 19. 25:	Now there stood by the cross of Jesus, his mother.

All the Marian doctrines that have been elaborated over the centuries, as well as the Virgin's many privileges, ultimately depend on Mary being the Mother of God, that is, of the person of Jesus in his human and divine natures.[1] Yet in the early centuries of the Church it was Christ rather than Mary who was main focus of interest in debates on the divine motherhood.[2] Although the Evangelists clearly call Mary the Mother of Jesus,

---

[1] This is a point that the famed Mariologist Henri Barré makes again and again. See, for instance, the opening remarks in his 'Antiennes et Répons de la Vierge', *Marianum*, 29 (1967), 153-254 and his *Prières anciennes de l'Occident à la Mère du Sauveur: Des origines à saint Anselme* (Paris: Lethielleux, 1963).

[2] For a summary of the main debates and the politics surrounding the Christological disputes see Leo D. Davis, *The First Seven Ecumenical Councils (325-787): Their History and Theology* (Collegeville, MN: Liturgical Press, 1983). See also Aloys Grillmeier's *Christ in Christian Tradition*, trans. by John Bowden, 2nd edn, rev., 2 vols (London: Mowbrys, 1975), which covers the period from the Apostolic Age up to Gregory the Great († 604) and John Norman D. Kelly, *Early Christian Doctrines*, 5th rev. edn (New York: Continuum, 2000). For an Eastern perspective see John Meyendorff, *Christ in Eastern Christian Thought* (Crestwood, NY: St. Vladimir's, 1987). For the decrees of the various Councils we shall be discussing see *Decrees of the Ecumenical Councils*, ed. by Noman P. Tanner, 2 vols (London: Sheed and Ward; Washington D.C.: Georgetown University Press, 1990). See also Luigi Gambero, 'Maria negli antichi concili', in *SDM*, I, 451-502,

they were not particularly concerned with defining the nature of that motherhood. But it was precisely this question that became the most burning doctrinal issue in the Church in the first centuries of its existence, because it had a direct bearing on Christological controversies concerning the human and divine natures of Jesus, and the associated question of the relationship between the Son and the Father.

The Patristic Period

The Fathers had to grapple with a variety of opposing positions on Christ's dual nature, many of which persisted in a variety of guises right up to the late Middle Ages and beyond.[3] Some, such as the Ebionites, believed that Jesus was the natural son of Mary and Joseph and denied his divine nature, though they believed that he was the Messiah on whom the Holy Spirit had descended. The Docetic heresy, on the other hand, which arose from the ranks of the Gnostics, argued that Christ was an entirely spiritual being who did not take on a truly human body from the Virgin, but merely passed through her, assuming a human appearance. The Arians, instead, accepted Christ's humanity, but denied his co-eternity and consubstantiality (*homoousios*) with the Father, instead claiming that, though divine, Jesus was created by God as the agent through whom he created the universe.[4] Apollinaris of Laodicea (†c. 490) and his followers denied the complete union of God and man in Jesus, arguing that the Logos took the place of the *nous* or human spirit, which he considered to be inherently sinful.[5] In the fifth century, Nestorianism, which proposed two persons in Christ, rather than two natures in the one person, and Monophysitism, which asserted that Jesus had only one nature, either entirely divine or combined, arose out of the tensions between the schools of Alexandria and Antioch, the former stressing the unity of Christ, the God-man, and the true divinity of his person, the latter emphasising his humanity and duality.

---

both on the early professions of faith and on the councils. For a general overview of Mary in the Fathers see Georges Joussard, 'Marie à travers la patristique: Maternité divinité, virginité, sainteté', in *Maria* 1, 69-157.

[3] For instance, Irenaeus' *Adversus Haereses*, much of which is dedicated to refuting these competing heresies.

[4] By far the most comprehensive study of the Arian controversy is Richard P. C. Hanson, *The Search for the Christian Doctrine of God: The Arian Controversy, 318-381 AD* (Edinburgh: Clark, 1988). For a summary see John Norman D. Kelly, *Early Christian Doctrines*, pp. 226-31.

[5] See Hans Lietzmann, *Apollinaris von Laodicea und seine Schule: Texte und Untersuchungen* (Tübingen, Mohr 1904), and Guillaume Voisin, *L'Apollinarisme: Étude historique, littéraire et dogmatique sur le début des controverses christologiques au IVe siècle* (Louvain: Van Linthout; Paris: Fontemoing, 1901).

The principal dilemma in all these debates centred on how to preserve the unity of Christ while also proclaiming him true God and true man. In order to be the Saviour Christ had to be divine, because salvation could be accomplished by God alone, but in order to redeem human nature he also had to be truly human. Thus it was that the nature of Mary's motherhood became central to soteriology.

Among the most ancient witnesses to belief in the divine motherhood of Mary are the formal declarations of faith, or creeds, known as 'apostolic symbols' which were held to contain the central doctrines transmitted to the Church through the apostolic tradition.[6] Possibly the earliest, dating from the third century, are those of Constantinople and Rome, both of which declare that Jesus Christ was generated *ek*, (Latin *ex*) the Virgin Mary, which may be translated as 'of' or 'out of' or 'from', and from the Holy Spirit.[7] Other symbols vary somewhat, some simply stating that Christ became incarnate, without any mention of either the Virgin or the Holy Spirit, others still using formulae such as 'of' the Virgin Mary, and 'by means of,' or simply 'of' the Holy Spirit, while some merely affirmed that Christ's generation was 'of the Virgin Mary,' leaving implicit the divine origin of the event.[8] What is abundantly clear from these primitive declarations is that the Church held firm from the earliest times to the belief that Mary was truly the mother of Jesus, and that his generation from her came about through the operation of the Holy Spirit, although it awaited the Church councils of the next several centuries to work out the precise nature of the process.

Turning to the writings of the Fathers, as early as Ignatius of Antioch (†c. 115) one finds a vehement condemnation of the 'rabid dogs' who do not accept Christ's dual nature: 'There is but one Physician, both flesh and spirit, both made and unmade, God existing in flesh, true life in death, both of Mary and of God.'[9] Justin Martyr (†c. 165) also defends Mary's motherhood of Christ, primarily against the accusations of the Jews that the Christians were merely imitating Greek mythology.[10] The fact that Mary became pregnant while

---

[6] The standard work on the creeds is John Norman D. Kelly, *Early Christian Creeds*, 3rd edn (New York: Continuum, 2006).

[7] This is a question that is already tackled by Tertullian in *De carne Christi*, 20, 1, *PL* 2, 785A-786B. Basil the Great († 379) will later note that Paul uses the term *ek* and not *dià* (by means of) when he speaks of Christ's generation from Mary (Galatians 4. 4) precisely because he wishes to show that he received a truly human body from his Mother, *De Spiritu Sanctu*, 5, 12, *PG* 32, 85B-C, *TMPM*, I, 295. On the importance of the term see Jean Guitton, *The Blessed Virgin* (London: Burns Oates, 1952), pp. 79-80.

[8] For an excellent and succinct account of the early Apostolic Symbols see *TMPM*, I, 117-18. For more detailed information see the relevant sections in John Norman D. Kelly, *Early Christian Creeds*.

[9] *Epistola ad Ephesios*, 7, *PG* 5, 650-652. See *MF*, pp. 29-31.

[10] See Mario Maritano, 'Giustino martire e gli eretici negatori della maternità di Maria', *Agustinianum*, 37 (1997), 285-301.

remaining a virgin, he argues, shows that Jesus became incarnate through the power of God. This, he adds, is confirmed by the prophecies of the Old Testament, particularly Isaiah 7. 14.[11] Irenaeus (†c. 202), whose *Adversus Haereses* is dedicated primarily to defending Christ's dual nature,[12] condemns both the Ebionites and varying shades of Gnosticism, declaring that those who adhere to the apostolic tradition believe, 'in Christ Jesus, the Son of God, who because of his immense love towards his creatures, consented to be generated from a virgin, uniting God and man in himself, by means of himself.'[13]

Tertullian (†c. 230?) refutes the claims of the Docetists, who maintained that Christ did not have a material body, with arguments that were to be repeated many times over the coming centuries:

> The Son of God was born: I am not ashamed of this, because it is shameful. The son of God died: and this is believable, because it is absurd. He was buried and rose: this is certain because it is impossible. But how could these statements be true in the case of Christ if he himself did not truly exist and did not truly have what he needed to be crucified, to die, to be buried, and to rise, namely, a body, filled with blood, given structure with bones, woven with nerves, shot through with veins, capable of experiencing birth and death? Undoubtedly, then, Christ had a human body, because it was born from a human being. And so this flesh is mortal in Christ, because Christ is man and Son of man. *De carne Christi, 5, 4-5*[14]

Thus, that Jesus truly took flesh of Mary becomes central to the very nature of his redemptive mission: he could not have suffered and died on behalf of a fallen humanity had he not been truly incarnated from the Virgin.[15]

Origen (†c. 254), though he maintained that Christ's human soul existed prior to uniting to his human body (in line with Platonic philosophy), was, in all other respects, an orthodox defender of the true humanity of Jesus:

> In the second place, Jesus Christ, he who has come, was born of the Father before any creature. He, having co-operated as the Father's minister in the creation of the universe – 'all things were made by him' (John 1. 3) – in the last days, making himself nothing, made himself a man, incarnated himself, still being God, and become man, he remained what he was, God. He assumed a body like our

---

[11] See in particular *Apologia*, 1, 12, *PG* 6, 345, and see *MF*, pp. 45-46. See also the chapter in this volume on Virginity.

[12] We cannot yet use the term 'hypostatic union' which appears only in the wake of Chalcedon. For the origins and usage of the term 'hypostasis', see Richard Marcel, 'L'introduction du mot "Hypostase" dans la théologie de l'Incarnation', *Mélanges de science religieuse*, 2 (1945), 5-32, 243-70.

[13] *Adversus Haereses*, 3, 4, 2, *PG* 7, 855-856, *TMPM*, I, 157.

[14] *PL* 2, 761A-B (806), *MF*, pp. 61-62. Unless otherwise indicated all translations are mine.

[15] See *De carne Christi*, 20, *PG* 2, 785B-787B.

body, different only because he was born of the Virgin and the Holy Spirit. Jesus Christ was born, and truly suffered, not in appearance, truly died the death common to all, and he rose from the dead. *De Principiis, Prefatio 4*[16]

Here, we once again see the insistence on the necessity of Jesus being truly human if he is to suffer and die for the redemption of mankind.

Possibly the earliest use of the term *Theotokos* (Θεοτόκος, meaning bearer, or birth-giver of God) is in an Egyptian hymn, known today as the *Sub tuum praesidium*: 'We take refuge in your mercy, O *Theotokos*'.[17] Palaeographic evidence would suggest that it dates from the third century although some commentators insist on a later date on the grounds that there is no evidence of intercessory prayer to the Virgin at this early stage.[18] According to Socrates, the fifth-century Church historian, Origen (†c. 254) used the term in at least one of his lost works, a commentary on the Epistle to the Romans.[19] It most likely is of Coptic or Egyptian origin, a Greek rendering of the title for Isis in her guise as mother of Horus, the god-king.[20] It was certainly preferable as a title to *meter theou* (μήτηρ Θεού), which could easily be confused with the Greek mother goddess.

---

[16] *PG* 11, 117.

[17] Quoted in Stephen J. Shoemaker, 'Marian Liturgies and Devotion in Early Christianity', *Mary: The Complete Resource*, ed. by Sarah Jane Boss (Oxford and New York: Oxford University Press 2007), pp. 130-145 (p. 130). The papyrus is preserved in the John Rylands Library of University of Manchester and may be viewed digitally at <http://rylibweb.man.ac.uk/insight/papyrus.htm> [accessed 10 October 2008]. See *MF*, pp. 69-70 and 79, and Michael O'Carroll, *Theotokos: A Theological Encyclopedia of the Blessed Virgin Mary* (Collegeville, Minnesota: Liturgical Press, 1982), p. 187.

[18] See chapter on Intercession, Mediation and Devotion, 1 for further discussion and for bibliography.

[19] *Historia Ecclesiastica*, VII, 32, 17, ed. by Günther Christian Hansen (Turnhout: Brepols, 2004). See *MF*, pp. 73-74. On the more than sixty pre-Ephesian occurrences of the term 'Theotokos' see Marek Starowieyski, 'Le titre Θεοτόκος avant le concile d'Ephèse', in *Studia Patristica, XIX: Papers Presented to the Tenth International Conference on Patristic Studies*, ed. by Elizabeth A. Livingstone (Leuven: Peeters, 1989), and Lucas Francisco Mateo-Seco, 'El título de "Madre de Dios" en la teología de los Padres anteriores a Éfeso', *Estudios marianos*, 68 (2002), 47-68. See also David F. Wright, 'From "God-Bearer" to "Mother of God" in the Later Fathers', in *The Church and Mary*, ed. by Robert N. Swanson, Studies in Church History, 39 (Woodenbridge: Boydell, 2004), pp. 22-30, Richard Price, 'The *Theotokos* and the Council of Ephesus', in *The Origins of the Cult of the Virgin Mary*, ed. by Chris Maunder (London: Burns & Oats, 2008), pp. 89-103, and, by the same author, 'Theotokos: The Title and its Significance in Doctrine and Devotion', in *Mary: The Complete Resource*, ed. by Sarah Jane Boss (Oxford and New York: Oxford University Press 2007), pp. 56-74 (pp. 56-7). In the same volume, see Stephen J. Shoemaker, 'Marian Liturgies and Devotion in Early Christianity', pp. 130-145.

[20] See Starowieyski, 'Le titre Θεοτόκος', p. 240, Averil Cameron 'The Cult of the Virgin in Late Antiquity: Religious Development and Myth-Making', in *The Church and Mary* ed. by Robert N. Swanson, Studies in Church History, 39 (Woodenbridge: Boydell, 2004), pp. 1-21 (p. 13), Thomas F. Mathews and Norman Muller 'Isis and Mary in Early

It is important to point out that for Christians the meaning of the term *Theotokos* differed radically from the goddess cults of the ancient Near East. While there are undoubtedly coincidences between the figure of Mary and several of the Eastern mother goddesses, the Virgin was not simply the inheritor of these ancient cults. Within the conceptual context of Christian incarnational theology divine motherhood had a very precise meaning unlike its rather fuzzy significance in non-Christian cults.[21] Besides, the principal purpose for Christians in asserting Mary's divine motherhood was to emphasise her humanity since to accord her any kind of divine status would fatally undermine the doctrines of the Incarnation and the Redemption.

It is not until Alexander of Alexandria († 328) that we find the term *Theotokos* being used as an accepted article of faith: 'We confess the resurrection of the dead, the first of whom was our Lord Jesus Christ, having taken his body truly and not in appearance from the *Theotokos*, Mary.'[22] Nevertheless, the Council of Nicea (325), which took place just three years before Alexander's death, did not include any direct mention of the Virgin in its apostolic symbol. The Nicene Creed simply states: 'for us men and for our salvation he came down from heaven, became incarnate and was made man.'

Icons', in *Images of the Mother of God: Perceptions of the Theotokos in Byzantium*, ed. by Maria Vassilaki (Aldershot: Ashgate, 2005), pp. 3-11, and, in the same volume, Elizabeth. S. Bolman, 'The Enigmatic Coptic Galaktotrophousa and the Cult of the Virgin Mary in Egypt', pp. 13-22.

[21] A great deal has been written on the influence of Eastern goddess cults on the cult of Mary, especially in recent decades, much of it methodologically flawed and displaying only a superficial understanding of the internal workings of Patristic Mariology. One such is the oft-quoted volume by Stephen Benko, *The Virgin Goddess: Studies in the Pagan and Christian Roots of Mariology* (New York: Brill, 1993), which, while making some valid points, displays a disturbing lack of familiarity with Patristic theological and doctrinal concerns. Leena Peltomaa, *The Image of the Virgin Mary in the Akathistos Hymn* (Leiden, Boston and Cologne: Brill, 2001), points out the perils of reading too much into symbols that are common to Mary and pagan goddesses: 'When, in Christian usage Mary is called a star, we may assume that the significance of this metaphor is not the same as in the tradition of a pagan goddess, although in both cultural contexts the function of the star as a heavenly body is the same. The use of the same word does not give the right to claim a foreign meaning for the star in the Christian context, making Mary an astral being. The line of influence has to be shown through conceptual systems. Often when the metaphorical language of a Christian text is examined beside the tradition of antiquity it is also interpreted as reflecting that tradition, even though the motivation for its use is to be found in its own context without searching' (pp. 122-23). Rosemary Radford Ruether, *Mary: The Feminine Face of the Church* (London: SCM, 1979), makes a similar point (p. 13).

[22] *Epistula ad Alexandrum*, PG 18, 568.

Later in the century Eusebius of Caesarea (†c. 340) makes use of the term,[23] while Athanasius of Alexandria († 373), who had taken part in the Council of Nicea as a young man, frequently refers to Mary as the *Theotokos*, for instance in these lines on the Visitation: 'The Mother of the Master greets [the mother] of the servant; the Mother of the King greets the mother of the soldier; the *Theotokos* greets the mother of the man'.[24] Indeed Athanasius wrote extensively and effectively in defence of Christ's true humanity, earning the bitter enmity of the Arians. God, he admits, could easily have taken on a human appearance without taking flesh from a woman, but he did not since it would not have fulfilled his purpose:

> If the Son of God had wanted merely to appear, he could certainly have assumed any kind of body, even one better than ours. Instead it was our own kind of body that he took, and not just in any way. He took it from a pure and unstained Virgin, who had not known man. *De Incarnazione, 8*[25]

He argues – as do many of the Fathers – that one of the reasons why God chose to be born of a virgin, in a manner that was outside the laws of nature, was to offer proof of the child's divinity: 'When he came among us, he formed himself a body, taking it from a virgin to offer proof of his divinity which could not be ignored. It had to appear clearly that he who fashioned this body is the maker of all things.' The manner of his conception, then, is unique, and therefore beyond human comprehension: 'No one can describe his bodily generation. No one can point to a father who begot him in the flesh, because his body did not come from a man, but from the Virgin alone.'[26] Moreover, it was necessary for Jesus to take on human flesh in order to restore fallen humanity and guarantee the resurrection of the body: 'They ignore that the Word became flesh, not as an adjunct but in order that the flesh might rise.'[27]

Basil the Great († 379) expresses a similar idea when speaking of the generation of Christ:[28]

> O mankind, what can we do with you? As long as God remains in heaven you do not search for him. Now that he descends to you and stays with you through his body, you do not wish to receive him [...] Learn therefore that God is in the

---

[23] See Richard Price, 'Theotokos: The Title and its Significance', p. 54, and F. Migliore, 'Maria Vergine e Madre di Dio nelle opere di Eusebio di Cesarea' *Theotokos*, 10 (2002), 133-70.

[24] *Homily on the Papyrus of Turin*, in *MF*, p. 105.

[25] *PG* 25, 108, *MF*, p. 102.

[26] *De Incarnazione*, 18 and 37, *PG* 25, 128 and 160 respectively, *MF*, p. 103.

[27] *Epistola ad Epictetus*, *TMPM*, I, 277.

[28] For further comment and bibliography on Basil's understanding of Mary's motherhood see Luigi Gambero, 'La Madre di Dio nella cristologia di Basileo di Cesarea', *Theotokos*, 11 (2004), 41-72.

flesh because it was necessary that this flesh, which had been cursed before, be sanctified, that this flesh which had been enfeebled might be strengthened, that this flesh which was his enemy might be led back to friendship with God, and that the flesh which had fallen from paradise might be brought back to heaven. And what was the workshop of this divine economy? The body of a holy Virgin. And what were the active agents in this generation? The Holy Spirit and the overshadowing power of the Most High. *Homilia in sanctum Christi generationem*, 3[29]

In another passage he writes:

If the Lord did not come in the flesh, the Redeemer did not pay a ransom for us, nor, through his power, did he destroy the kingdom of death. If, in fact, that which was under the dominion of death and that which the Lord assumed were two different things, death would not have ceased to carry out its work. [...] All these effects are eliminated by those who maintain that the Lord came in a celestial body. At this point, what need was there for the holy Virgin, if the flesh that God bore was not drawn from the clay of Adam? *Epistola 262, 2*[30]

Like Athanasius and Basil, Ephrem (†c. 373) repeatedly affirms Mary's motherhood of Jesus, while being equally insistent that he was fully God: 'No one knows what to call your Mother, O Lord! If they call her virgin, her Son seems to demonstrate the contrary; if wife, the fact remains that no-one knew her. But if your Mother is already so incomprehensible, who will comprehend you!'[31] Ephrem writes repeatedly with awe and admiration of the womb of Mary containing the uncontainable God, which forms part of his central theological theme that God has condescended to become man out of love for humanity:

The Power that governs all dwelt in a small womb. / While dwelling there, He was holding the reins of the universe. [...] He dwelt in the vast wombs of all creation. / They were too small to contain the greatness of the First-born. / How indeed did that small womb of Mary suffice for Him? [...] The womb that contained Him, if it contained all of Him, is equal to the wonderful womb that is greater than [the womb] of His birth. / But who will dare to say that a small womb, / weak and despised, is equal to [the womb] of the Great Being? / He dwelt [there] because of His compassion and since His nature is great, / He was not limited in anything. *Hymns on the Nativity, 21, 6-8*[32]

This expression of wonderment that the confined space of Mary's womb could contain the uncircumscribable God was a frequent theme in the Fathers,

[29] *TMPM*, I, 296.
[30] *TMPM*, I, 301.
[31] *Hymns on the Nativity*, 11, 1, *TMPM*, IV, 101.
[32] Translation by Kathleen McVey, *Ephrem the Syrian: Hymns* (New York Paulist Press 1989), pp. 174-75.

especially in the East. One of the primary purposes of the paradox was to highlight the extraordinary mystery of the Incarnation in which the infinite God had taken on finite human nature. The paradox carried an important theological message since it was intended to counter those who claimed that Christ had taken on the appearance, but not the reality of human nature and had merely passed through the Virgin's womb.

The double generation of Christ, eternally from the Father, and historically from Mary, is another recurrent theme in the Fathers in the context of the debate over the hypostatic union. It is one of the most frequent themes in sermons for the feast of Christ's Nativity, which began to be celebrated widely in the fourth century, both in the Eastern and Western Church.[33] Hilary of Poitiers († 367), for instance, writes of Christ's double generation in one of his hymns: 'O Christ, for us the twice-born God! / born once from God unborn; / born twice when the childbearing Virgin / brought you into the world, / embodied and still God.'[34]

In a text ascribed to a close contemporary of Ephrem, Marcellus of Ancyra († c. 374), one finds what is possibly the first direct application of the Jeremian typology to Mary, using a translation that resembles that of Jerome rather than the Septuagint: 'The Lord has created a new thing in the female [Septuagint: 'on the earth'], that is, in Mary. For nothing new has been created in the female except that which was born from the Virgin Mary without intercourse, the body of the Lord.'[35]

The apostolic symbol of the First Council of Constantinople (381), whose primary aim was to condemn the Arian heresy – denial of the consubstantiality of the Father and the Son – and its offshoots, is the first common profession of faith on the part of all the Churches that contains an explicit declaration on Mary's motherhood of Christ: 'For us men and for our salvation he came down from heaven, took flesh from the Holy Spirit and from the Virgin Mary, and became man.'[36]

However, though Mary is now formally declared to be the Mother of Jesus, an even more crucial issue soon arose – whether her motherhood extended to the whole person of Christ or was confined to his human nature. The main issues are neatly summed up in a letter written by Gregory Nazianzen († 390), who was probably the first authoritative Christian writer to assert that belief in

---

[33] See chapters on Patristic and Medieval devotion.

[34] *Hymns 1*, 5-8, *MF*, p. 188.

[35] *Exposition of the Faith*, 3, PG 24, 205B, Hilda Graef, *Doctrine and Devotion*, I, 54-55.

[36] *TMPM*, I, 290. On the Council of Constantinople and later councils see Enrico dal Covolo, 'La maternità di Maria nelle definizioni conciliari di Costantinopoli I, Efeso e Calcedonia', in *Fons lucis: Miscellanea di studi in onore di Ermanno M. Toniolo*, ed. by R. Barbieri and others (Rome: Marianum, 2004), pp. 219-28, and Mario Maritano, 'I primi quattro Concili ecumenici in relazione con la mariologia', *Theotokos*, 12 (2004), 3-23.

Mary's divine motherhood was a criterion of orthodoxy, a generation before the Council of Ephesus, in response the heresy of Apollinaris:[37]

> If anyone does not admit that holy Mary is the Mother of God (*Theotokos*), he is cut off from the Godhead. If anyone claims that Christ merely passed through Mary, as if passing through a channel, but denies that he was formed within her in a divine way (because there was no intervention of a man), and in a human way (that is according to the laws of conception), he is equally godless. If anyone says that a man was formed first, who only afterward was clothed with divinity, let him be condemned. For that would not be a generation of God but a denial of divine generation. If anyone introduces the notion of two sons, one born of God the Father and the other born of the Mother, instead of a single and identical Son, let him be deprived of the adoption of sons, promised to those who believe aright. *Letter 101*[38]

Thus, while it is the Father who generates Christ's divinity, Mary is the human mother of both the divine and human Jesus, because both natures, though distinct, are one.

Gregory of Nyssa (†c. 392) is equally vehement in declaring Mary to be the *Theotokos*, and not the *Anthropotokos*, that is, Mother of the whole person of Jesus, not just of his humanity:

> Are we, perhaps, announcing a different Jesus? Are we, perhaps, indicating a different one? Are we, perhaps, proclaiming a different Scripture? Have some among us dared to call the Virgin Mother of God (*Theotokos*) the mother of a man (*anthropotokos*), which we ourselves have heard say that some people irreverently call her? *Letter 3*[39]

To further complicate matters, Apollinaris of Laodicea († 390) introduced a new heresy regarding Christ's dual natures, stating that the body of Jesus lacked a rational soul, being replaced by the Divine Word himself.[40] For Apollinaris, human nature, mind, will and energy are necessarily sinful so that the sinlessness of the

---

[37] See *TMPM*, I, 303, Francesco Trisoglio, 'La Madre di Dio in Gregorio di Nazianzo', *Theotokos*, 11 (2003), 91-124, and Luigi Gambero, 'Appunti patristici per lo studio della mariologia', in *Gli studi di mariologia medievale: bilancio storico*, Atti del I convegno mariologico della fondazione Ezio Franceschini con la collaborazione della biblioteca Palatina e del dipartimento di storia dell'università di Parma, Parma 7-8 novembre 1997, ed. by Clelia Maria Piastra (Florence: SISMEL – Edizioni del Galuzzo, 2001), pp. 5-17 (pp. 9-11). More generally on Gregory see John A. McGuckin, *St Gregory of Nazianzus: An Intellectual Biography* (Crestwood, N.Y.: St. Vladimir's, 2001).

[38] *MF*, p. 162.

[39] *PG* 46, 1024, *TMPM*, I, 328.

[40] See John Norman D. Kelly, *Early Christian Doctrines*, pp. 289-95 and Frances Young, *From Nicaea to Chalcedon: A Guide to the Literature and Its Background* (Philadelphia: Fortress, 1983), pp. 258-63.

person Christ is possible only if his humanity is excluded.[41] Gregory rejects this hypothesis, reaffirming that Jesus is fully God and man, and pointing out that it is through the co-existence of the two natures in the person of Christ that the gulf between God and humanity is bridged:

> Along with all those who profess the orthodox faith, I too declare my belief that the same [Jesus] is God and man, but not in the manner in which Apollinaris thinks. For the divinity does not become earthly, nor does the humanity become something heavenly, as he maintains; rather the power of the Most High, through the Holy Spirit, overshadowed the human nature and was formed therein; that is to say the portion of flesh was formed in the immaculate Virgin. For this reason, the Child born of her is called Son of the Most High. In truth, the divine power makes possible a certain affinity of human nature with God, while the flesh makes it possible for God to have certain relations with man. *Against Apollinaris, 6*[42]

Cyril of Jerusalem (†c. 397) sets out Church teaching on the two natures with admirable clarity in his *Catecheses*, which, as the name suggests, were written for those who were preparing for baptism:

> It is not holy to worship a mere man, but neither is it pious to state that there is only God, excluding his humanity; for, even if Christ were fully God – as he really is – but had not assumed humanity, we would be estranged from salvation. Let us worship him as God but believe also that he was made man. It is not useful to assert that he is man, while prescinding from divinity; neither is it helpful to salvation to confess his divinity without confessing his humanity. *Catecheses 12, 1*[43]

Jesus truly took flesh from the Virgin and was truly a man, eating, drinking and sleeping as we do, but in addition to this visible nature, he also had an invisible divine one, which revealed itself through his miracles. Had he not truly taken on human nature he could not have saved us: 'For if the Incarnation were a mere appearance, such would be our Redemption as well.'[44] He also speaks of the double birth of Christ:

> And so, almost always everything concerning our Lord Jesus Christ is double: his generation is double, one from God before the ages, the other from Mary at

---

[41] See the brief discussion on Apollinarianism in Demetrios Bathrellos, *The Byzantine Christ: Person, Nature, and Will in the Christology of Saint Maximus the Confessor* (Oxford: Oxford University Press, 2004), pp. 11- 16, and see Hans Lietzmann, *Apollinaris von Laodicea und seine Schule* (Tübingen: Mohr, 1905).

[42] *PG*, 45, 1136C-D, *MF*, p. 153.

[43] *PG* 33, 728A, *MF*, pp. 136-37.

[44] *Catecheses*, 4, 9, *MF*, p. 133.

the end of time; two descents, one almost hidden, of rain on the fleece,[45] the other, his future coming, manifest. *Catechesis, 15, 1*[46]

Epiphanius of Salamis († 403), whose *Adversus haereses* is a veritable encyclopaedia of arguments against the various heresies that were prevalent in his time, does not hesitate to call Mary *Theotokos*, and affirms the divinity and humanity of Christ, who 'is both man and God at once', and is 'truly born of Mary, having been begotten without manly seed.'[47] Nevertheless, in the face of the practices of the Collyridian sect,[48] who, he claims, believed that Mary was divine, and offered her oblations, he is careful to point out that the Virgin was an ordinary woman, not a goddess, and makes it clear that worship is due to God alone.[49] Epiphanius also uses the *topos* of the uncircumscribable God, exclaiming: 'Truly great was the Virgin Mary in front of God and men. How, in fact, can we not proclaim as great she who received the uncontainable within herself, he whom neither heaven nor earth can contain?'[50]

John Chrysostom († 407) writes along similar lines.[51] Commenting that it is impossible for man to understand fully the mystery of the Incarnation, he asks: 'How could he who contains all things be carried in the womb of a woman?' He answers that it was by the work of the Holy Spirit, but that no-one can understand how it was achieved.[52] For John the manner of Christ's conception is utterly beyond human understanding, but since both the prophecies of the Old Testament, and the words of the Evangelists and St. Paul clearly attest to his humanity, we must accept this as an article of faith:

> Based on all these proofs and on many others besides, we establish that Jesus came forth from us and from our human substance and that he was born of the Virgin's womb, but how this happened we do not see. So do not pry into the mystery, but humbly accept what God has revealed, and do not be curious about what God keeps hidden. *On Matthew, 4, 3*[53]

John sees Christ's double birth in terms of a conventional birth from a woman, and a second birth through the work of the Holy Spirit, free from

---

[45] For the meaning of the rain or dew on the fleece which was read as a type of Mary's virginal conception see Dew in vol. 2.

[46] *PG*, 33, 869, *TMPM*, I, 365.

[47] *Adversus haereses*, 78, 23, *PG* 42, 736, *MF*, p. 123.

[48] For further discussion on the Collyridians see the chapter on Intercession Mediation and Devotion, 1.

[49] See *MF*, p. 122, and *Adversus haereses*, 79, 9, *PG* 42, 753D.

[50] *Adversus haereses*, 30, 31, *PG* 41, 460C, *TMPM*, I, 385.

[51] See Sergio Zincone, 'Maria nell'opera di Giovanni Crisostomo', *Theotokos*, 14 (2006), 31-42.

[52] *On Matthew, TMPM*, I, 419.

[53] *PG* 57, 43, *MF*, p. 175.

concupiscence, which is an anticipation of our 'birth' in heaven. The passage should not be seen as supporting dualism however as the issue at hand is not Christ's dual natures but the rebirth of our glorified flesh which the generation of the God-man heralds:

> Therefore, there was a double birth: one similar to ours and another that surpasses ours. In fact, to be born of a woman was what he had in common with us, while to be born, not from blood, not from the will of man, not from the desire of the flesh, but through the work of the Holy Spirit, is a preannouncement of a future birth, superior to ours, which he has given us through the grace of the Holy Spirit. *On Matthew, 2, 6*[54]

In the West, the Church was less directly impacted by the bitter internal controversies over Christ's humanity and divinity that plagued the East, though the Latin Fathers did have to contend with a variety of heretical groups that threatened the Church more from without than within. Arianism, which denied the true divinity of Christ, experienced a resurgence in the fourth century, especially among the Goths, which led Ambrose of Milan († 397) to mount a strong defence of Christ's dual nature:

> Though he remains the eternal God, he undergoes the mysteries of the Incarnation while remaining one and undivided; for the One is both and is present in both, that is, in his divinity and in his body. For there is no difference between the One who proceeds from the Father and is born of the Virgin; no, he is the same who comes from the Father in one way and comes from the Virgin in another. *De Incarnationis, 35*[55]

Ambrose also wrote extensively against the Docetic claim of the Manichees that Christ's body was merely an illusion. He points out that to deny that Jesus truly took on flesh from the Virgin is to deny that he redeemed humanity, since he would not have been able to die for us:

> If one does not believe that he has come, neither will he believe that he has taken flesh; thus, he would have appeared as a phantasm and as such would have been crucified. No, he was truly crucified for our sake; he is truly our Redeemer. Whoever denies this truth is a Manichee, a denier of Christ's flesh; for this reason he will not receive the remission of sins. *Epistola 42, 12-13*[56]

It was only by taking on our nature from her that Christ could save humanity, for only human flesh could redeem human flesh.[57] This, then, is Mary's

---

[54] *TMPM*, I, 418.
[55] *PL* 16, 827C-D, *MF,* p. 193.
[56] *PL* 16, 1128A-B [1176], *MF,* p. 194.
[57] *De incarnationis dominicae sacramento*, 56, *PL* 16, 832C [868].

greatness, that she became the means whereby God restored humanity. Ambrose is also the first of the Western Fathers to call Mary Mother of God (*Dei mater*),[58] a term that many hesitated to adopt because of its associations with the pagan *magna mater*. John Cassian (†c. 435) also uses the term *mater Dei* several times in his *De incarnatione*. Generally, however, in Latin she was called *Dei genitrix/genetrix* (generator of God), or *Deipara* (bearer of God).[59]

Jerome († 419) takes up the Jeremian typology of the uncircumscribable God,[60] as does Augustine († 430) who expresses his wonder at the humility of God in allowing himself to be borne in the womb of a woman: 'The womb of mere woman bore him whom the heavens cannot contain. Mary sustained our king; she bore him in whom we are; she gave milk to him who is our bread. O great weakness and admirable humility, in which divinity completely hid itself!'[61]

In another sermon he writes:

> He is the revelation of the Father and the Creator of his Mother, the Son of God who proceeds from the Father without a mother and son of man who proceeds from his Mother without a father. Great day of the angels, he had become small on the day of man, Word-God before the beginning of the angels, Word-man at the established time, Creator of the sun, a creature under the sun. He determines all the ages in the bosom of the Father where he always remains and he makes this day sacred from the womb of his Mother from which he comes forth. Maker of heaven and earth, come forth on the earth beneath the sky, ineffably wise, wisely a baby, he sucked from the breast of a woman, immense in his divine nature, small in the nature of a servant. But that immensity in not limited by that smallness nor is this smallness crushed by that immensity. When he assumed a human body he did not leave behind his divine operations nor did he cease to extend himself with power from one pole of the world to the other and to govern all things with goodness. When he clothed himself with flesh he was received, not limited in the womb of the Virgin, so that the angels were not deprived of the food of salvation and we tasted the sweetness of the Lord. *Sermo 187, 1*

---

[58] *Hexaemeron* 5, 65 *PL* 14, 233C-D. He uses the same term in *De virginibus*, 2, 7.

[59] See in David F. Wright, 'From "God-Bearer" to "Mother of God" in the Later Fathers' in *The Church and Mary*, ed. by Robert N. Swanson, Studies in Church History, 39 (Woodenbridge: Boydell, 2004), pp. 1-21

[60] *Commentary on Jeremias*, 6, 31, 22. See Graef, *Doctrine and Devotion*, I, 5-6 and 93 and see Luciana Mirri, 'Maria nell'esegisi di san Girolamo', in *L'esegisi dei padri latini dalle origini a Gregorio Magno*, XXVIII Incontro di studiosi dell'antichità cristiana, Roma, 6-8 maggio 1999 (Rome: Institutum Patristicum Augustinianum, 2000), pp. 573-616.

[61] *Sermo 184*, 3. All translations, unless otherwise indicated, are from the Latin and Italian texts in S. Aurelii Augustini, *Opera Omnia, Tutte le opere*, ed. by Franco Monteverde, 45 vols (Rome: Nuova Biblioteca Agostiniana and Città Nuova, 1967), in *Sant'Agostino, Augustinus Hipponensis*, < http://www.augustinus.it/> [accessed 7 July 2008].

He also returns repeatedly to the *topos* of Christ's double birth, which we have already seen in Hilary of Poitiers, and was an important influence in passing it to subsequent writers.[62]

For Augustine the authority of Scripture is sufficient proof that the Word took on flesh from the Virgin, flesh which was subject to death on the Cross, though the reason why God chose this method to save humanity is known to him alone:

> We believe that Christ was born of the Virgin Mary because it is written thus in the Gospel; we believe that he was crucified and died, because it is written thus in the Gospel; and we believe that he was truly born and truly died because the Gospel is the truth. Just why he willed to subject himself to all the weaknesses of the flesh he assumed in the womb of a woman is a hidden design, known to him alone. *Sermo 186, 1*[63]

Augustine was a passionate defender of the co-existence of the divine and human natures in the one person of the Son. He returns again and again to the necessity of Jesus taking on human flesh in order to raise humanity from its fallen state. In a passage that is not without humour, having spoken of Christ's mercy in taking on human flesh, and having reaffirmed the doctrine of the Trinity, Augustine turns to the theory that Jesus did not truly take on a human body but merely the appearance of one in the manner of the Holy Spirit who appeared in the form of a dove:

> And we do not pay any attention to those who claim that Our Lord had a body like that of the dove which John the Baptist saw descending from heaven and alighting on his head in order to signify the Holy Spirit. [...] The reason why the Holy Spirit was not born of a dove in the same way that Christ was born of a woman lies in the fact that he did not come to set doves free, but to show innocence and spiritual love to men, which was visibly represented in the form of a dove. Instead, Our Lord Jesus Christ, who had come to free the human race, in which both men and women pursue salvation, did not despise the former, since he assumed the male sex, nor the latter, since he was born of a woman. *De agone christiano, 22, 24*

Like many of the Fathers, Augustine was also fond of teasing out the contradictions between Mary being both the daughter and Mother of God:

> He who is God and the Lord of heaven and earth came by means of a woman, who is his Mother. Inasmuch as he is Lord of the world, Lord of Heaven and Earth, he is clearly also the Lord of Mary; inasmuch as he is Creator of Heaven

---

[62] See, for instance, *Sermo 140 , 2, PL 38, 773*, and see Mary Clayton, *The Cult of the Virgin Mary in Anglo-Saxon England* (Cambridge; New York: Cambridge University Press, 1990), pp. 25-26 and 203.
[63] *PL 38, 999, MF*, p. 220.

and Earth, he is also Creator of Mary; but inasmuch as he was 'born of a woman, made under the law' (Galatians 4. 4) he is Mary's son. He is at the same time both the Lord of Mary and the son of Mary; at once both the Creator of Mary and created from Mary. Do not marvel that he is both son and Lord, for just as he is called the son of Mary, so is he called the son of David, and son of David because he is son of Mary. *In Evangelium Ioannis tractatus, 8, 9*

Quodvultdeus (†c. 454), friend of Augustine and bishop of Carthage, is among the fiercest defenders of Mary's divine motherhood against the various heresies that were current in the fifth century:

> This Son of God and son of man, Son of God because he proceeds from the heart of the Father and son of man because he was born of the womb of his Mother, is the one and only Christ, who came out of the virginal womb like a bridegroom from his nuptial chamber. In this womb, in fact, the spiritual wedding was celebrated: God joined to flesh and flesh united itself to God so that Christ alone might be God and at the same time a complete man. *Contra Iudaeos, 9, 9*[64]

The *topos* of Mary as the container of the uncontainable God became increasingly popular around the time of the Council of Ephesus (431).[65] Cyril of Alexandria († 444) greets the Virgin as 'you who have contained the Uncontainable in the holy matrix of your virginal womb' and calls her 'the location for the One who is uncontainable,'[66] while Proclus of Constantinople († 446) writes: 'Come then, let us admire the Virgin's womb, a womb wider than the world. For she, without difficulty, enclosed within her him who cannot be contained in anyone, and he who carries everyone in his hands, including his Mother, was carried by her in her womb.'[67] Proclus also uses the double birth of Christ *topos*, in contrasting the heavenly and earthly generation of Christ and in defending Mary's motherhood of God:

> He who was divinely generated by the Father before the centuries, he himself is generated today too by a Virgin for our salvation: above, the only Son of the only Father according to his divinity, below, God, but not only, God and Man, yet not purely a man according to his humanity; above, he is with the Father in an inexpressible way, below, he is born from his Mother in an indescribable way;

---

[64] *TMPM*, III, 465. For translations and commentary on Quodvultdeus' works see Thomas M. Finn, *Quodvultdeus of Carthage: The Creedal Homilies: Conversion in Fifth-Century North Africa*, Ancient Christian Writers, 60 (New York: Newman, 2004).

[65] See Leena Peltomaa, *The Image of the Virgin Mary*, p. 70, on the pervasiveness of the container paradox in the Ephesian context, and for an analysis of the significance of the *topos* in relation to Mary's status as *Theotokos* see pp. 135-39 and 182-83.

[66] *Homily* 4, which was delivered at Ephesus, and *Homily* 11, *TMPM*, I, 490 and 491. See Vasiliki Limberis, *Divine Heiress: The Virgin Mary and the Creation of Christian Constantinople* (London and New York, Routledge 1994), p. 109.

[67] *Fourth Homily on the Birth of the Lord*, 1, PG 65, 708C – 709B, *TMPM*, I, 566.

above, without a mother, below, without an earthly father; above, the Firstborn, before the centuries, and down below the Firstborn too, of a Virgin according to the mystery of the Incarnation. *Homily 24, On the Birth of Christ, 15*[68]

The Nestorian controversy,[69] which led directly to the Council of Ephesus, resulted in Mary being formally recognised as the *Theotokos* or Bearer of God.[70] Nestorius denied the principle that, because the two natures of Christ were united in one person, whatever was predicated of one nature must also necessarily hold true for the other.[71] In denying this understanding of the relationship between the two natures, Nestorius, an Antiochene who was elected patriarch of Constantinople in 428, therefore held that the Virgin should be called Christ-bearer (*Christotokos*) and not God-bearer (*Theotokos*), on the basis that there were two distinct persons in Jesus, the divine and the human, and Mary was mother of the human Jesus alone.[72] For Nestorius, the term *Theotokos* was admissible, though confusing, if it was used in the sense that Mary was the mother of the temple, or body of Jesus which contained his divinity. For this reason he urged that it be avoided altogether by using the term *Christotokos*, or used in combination with the title *Anthropotokos* (bearer of the man):

> In reality, it is the human nature that comes from Blessed Mary; therefore she is the Mother of the man who took his beginning from her, and who afterwards grew and became perfect. This man is not God by nature, although he was so proclaimed as a result of his self-manifestation, which came about gradually. Therefore Mary too, by nature, is only the Mother of the man. *Liber Heraclidis*[73]

Proclus of Constantinople, well-aware of the stance of Nestorius and other Antiochene theologians,[74] provocatively delivered a homily in his presence on the *Theotokos* in 328, which eventually led to the convocation of the Council:

---

[68] *TMPM*, I, 574.

[69] For a fuller account of the Byzantine politics surrounding the controversy, see the chapters on Intercession, Mediation and Devotion. For relevant bibliography and the texts of Nestorius' surviving works, see *TMPM*, I, 540-55.

[70] For a very useful discussion of Eastern understanding of the term *Theotokos* and its implications for the hypostasis see Kallistos Ware, *Mary Theotokos in the Orthodox Tradition* (Wallington: Ecumenical Society of the Blessed Virgin Mary, 1997), pp. 5-7. For discussion and bibliography on the politics surrounding the *Theotokos* declaration, particularly the role of the Empress Pulcheria, see the chapters on Model and on Patristic Intercession, Mediation and Devotion.

[71] See Pietro Rosa, 'Aspetti della mariologia di Cirillo Alessandrino e di Nestorio', *Theotokos*, 12 (2004), 255-85.

[72] For a succinct explanation of the concepts involved see Jean Guitton, *The Blessed Virgin* (London: Burns Oates, 1952), pp. 85-86.

[73] *TMPM*, I, 545.

[74] For a recent in-depth study of Proclus see Nicholas Constas, *Proclus Of Constantinople and the Cult of the Virgin in Late Antiquity, Homilies 1-5, Texts, and Translations*, Supplements

The reason we have gathered here today is the holy *Theotokos* Virgin Mary, stainless treasure of virginity, spiritual paradise of the second Adam, workshop of the union of the natures [of Christ], economy of the saving exchange, bridal chamber in which the Word was wedded to the flesh, living bush that was not burned by the fire of the Divine birth, the true light cloud that bore the One who, in his body, stands above the Cherubim, fleece moistened by the celestial dew, from which the Shepherd put on the garment of the lamb. *Oration 1, 1*[75]

Nestorius, as might be expected, reacted with fury to the provocation by delivering a counter-homily on the spot. Over the next three years all the major religious and civic players became embroiled in the debate. John of Antioch († 441), one of the most respected theologians of the time, supported Nestorius, while Pope Celestine condemned him. However, it was Cyril of Alexandria who took the lead role in opposing Nestorius, canvassing the support of the Pope and the Emperor, and even enlisting the aid of the emperor's sisters.[76] In his *Second Letter to Nestorius* he invokes the authority of Scripture, the teaching of the Fathers, and the declaration of the Council of Nicea in setting out his belief in what was later to be termed the 'hypostatic union'. It is worth quoting at some length since it provides a detailed exposition of the position eventually adopted by the Church and also gives a taste of the extraordinary subtlety of the arguments involved:

> We do not say that the nature of the Word was changed and became flesh, nor that he was turned into a whole man made of body and soul. Rather do we claim that the Word in an unspeakable, inconceivable manner united to himself hypostatically, flesh enlivened by a rational soul, and so became man and was called son of man, not by God's will alone or good pleasure, nor by the assumption of a person alone. Rather did two different natures come together to form a unity, and from both arose one Christ, one Son. It was not as though the distinctness of the natures was destroyed by the union, but divinity and humanity together made perfect for us one Lord and one Christ, together marvellously and mysteriously combining to form a unity. So he who existed and

---

to Vigiliae Christianae, 66 (Leiden: Brill, 2003). See also François J Leroy. *L'homilétique de Proclus de Constantinople*, Studi e Testi 247 (Vatican City: Biblioteca Apostolica Vaticana, 1967). More generally on Byzantine homilies see Mary B. Cunningham, 'The Mother of God in Early Byzantine Homilies', *Sobornost*, 10 (1988), 53-67.

[75] *PG* 65, 681A-B.

[76] For a detailed study of the Nestorian controversy and Cyril's role in it see John A. McGuckin, *St. Cyril of Alexandria: The Christological Controversy: Its History, Theology and Texts*, Supplements to Vigiliae Christianae, 23 (Leiden: Brill, 1994). See also *The Theology of St. Cyril of Alexandria: A Critical Appreciation*, ed. by Thomas G. Weinandy and Daniel A. Keating (London: Clark, 2003), Antonia Atanassova, 'Did Cyril of Alexandria Invent Mariology?', in *The Origins of the Cult of the Virgin Mary*, ed. by Chris Maunder, pp. 105-25, and Paul Imhof and Bernd Lorenz, *Maria Theotokos bei Cyrill von Alexandrien* (Munich: Kaffke, 1981).

was begotten of the Father before all ages is also said to have been begotten according to the flesh of a woman, without the divine nature either beginning to exist in the holy virgin, or needing of itself a second begetting after that from his Father. (For it is absurd and stupid to speak of the one who existed before every age and is coeternal with the Father, needing a second beginning so as to exist.) The Word is said to have been begotten according to the flesh, because for us and for our salvation he united what was human to himself hypostatically and came forth from a woman. For he was not first begotten of the holy virgin, a man like us, and then the Word descended upon him; but from the very womb of his mother he was so united and then underwent begetting according to the flesh, making his own the begetting of his own flesh.

In a similar way we say that he suffered and rose again, not that the Word of God suffered blows or piercing with nails or any other wounds in his own nature (for the divine, being without a body, is incapable of suffering), but because the body which became his own suffered these things, he is said to have suffered them for us. For he was without suffering, while his body suffered. Something similar is true of his dying. For by nature the Word of God is of itself immortal and incorruptible and life and life-giving, but since on the other hand his own body by God's grace, as the apostle says, tasted death for all, the Word is said to have suffered death for us, not as if he himself had experienced death as far as his own nature was concerned (it would be sheer lunacy to say or to think that), but because, as I have just said, his flesh tasted death. So too, when his flesh was raised to life, we refer to this again as his resurrection, not as though he had fallen into corruption – God forbid – but because his body had been raised again. [77]

Mary's motherhood is therefore the explicit guarantee of Christ's humanity, without which he could not have suffered and died, the link between God and creation could not have been restored, and humankind could not have looked forward to the hope of resurrection. The Virgin is worthy of the greatest praise above all because she is the guarantor of the truth of the hypostatic union:

> We salute you, O Mary, Mother of God, venerable treasure of the entire world, inextinguishable lamp, crown of virginity, sceptre of orthodoxy, imperishable temple, container of him who cannot be contained, Mother and Virgin [...] Hail, you who held the Uncontainable One in your holy and virginal womb! Through you, the Holy Trinity is glorified; through you the precious Cross is celebrated and adored throughout the world; heaven exults, the angels and archangels rejoice, the demons are put to flight, the devil, the tempter, falls from heaven, fallen creation is brought back to paradise, all creatures trapped in idolatry come to know of the truth. Through you holy baptism and the oil of gladness are administered to believers; through you churches are established throughout the world; the peoples are led to conversion. *Homily 4*[78]

---

[77] Translation is from *Decrees of the Ecumenical Councils*, ed. by Norman P. Tanner, <http://www.piar.hu/councils/ecum05.htm> [accessed 6 October 2006].
[78] *PG* 77, 992-96, *MF*, p. 247-48.

It was Cyril's view that eventually triumphed as Ephesus. Although the Council did not issue a dogmatic decree on the *Theotokos*, it did condemn Nestorius' position on the humanity of Christ and endorse that of Cyril. Two years after the Council a reconciliation was achieved between the greater part of the Antiochene bishops and the Alexandrians. John of Antioch wrote to Cyril and agreed to confess 'the one Christ' born 'from the Virgin Mary according to his humanity'. On this basis, of a 'union without fusion', he was prepared to concede the title *Theotokos*, since it was the Virgin who had supplied the flesh of Christ. Cyril responded positively and once again set out his position, lest there be any residue of misunderstanding:

> On the matter of how we think and speak concerning the Virgin the *Theotokos* and the manner in which the Only-Begotten Son of God became man, we must [...] state briefly what we have held from the first [...]. We acknowledge our Lord Jesus Christ, the Only-Begotten Son of God, perfect God and perfect man made up of a rational soul and body, begotten from the Father before the ages in respect of the Godhead and the same on the last day for us and for our salvation from the Virgin Mary in respect of his manhood [...]. By virtue of this understanding of the union which involves no merging, we acknowledge the holy Virgin to be the *Theotokos*, because God the Word was enfleshed and became man and from the very conception united himself to the temple taken from her. *Letter 39*[79]

Theodotus of Ancyra († before 446), who had initially sided with Nestorius but later condemned him, offers an interesting argument in favour of the double generation of the Word, likening it to words that are first born in the mind and reborn when they are written down:

> Do not say: since the Only-Begotten was born of the Father, how can it be that he was born again of the Virgin? He was born of the Father by nature; he is born of the Virgin because of the economy [of salvation]: there as God, here as a man. In any case, your word is also born of your mind. But when you want to express this word that the mind has given birth to in letters and characters, and you wish to represent it on paper, you write the letters and, in a certain way, with your hand, you give birth to the word again. Nevertheless, it does not take the beginning of its being when your hand writes the letters but, born of the mind, it receives the beginning of its visibility from the hand that writes the letters. *Second Homily on the Birth of the Lord, 7*[80]

---

[79] Quoted in Richard Price, 'Theotokos: The Title and its Significance', pp. 60-61. Elsewhere Cyril states: 'The holy Fathers do not hesitate to call the Virgin *Theotokos*, not in the sense that the divine nature of the Word took its origin from the holy Virgin, but in the sense that he took his holy body, gifted with a rational soul, from her. Yet, because the Word is hypostatically united to this body, one can say that he was truly born according to the flesh.' *Letter* 4, *PG* 77, 48B, *MF*, p. 237.
[80] *TMPM*, I, 501.

However, the formula of reunion did not achieve a definitive resolution of the differences between Antiochene and Alexandrian positions. On the one hand, both sides agreed that the title *Theotokos* usefully clarified that Christ was both fully God and fully man. Thus the Antiochene theologian Theodoret of Cyrrhus († 466) writes in terms that are perfectly acceptable to the Alexandrians: 'If anyone does not call the holy Virgin *Theotokos*, he is either calling our Lord Jesus Christ a mere man or separating into two sons the one who is both Only-Begotten and Firstborn of all creation.'[81] However, where the two schools differed was on whether it was acceptable to continue using the term *Anthropotokos* alongside *Theotokos*, as Nestorius and the Antiochene Theodore of Mopsuestia († 428) held:

> She was *Anthropotokos* by nature because in the womb of Mary was a man, who also came forth from there, and she is *Theotokos*, because God was in the man who was born, not circumscribed in him according to nature but because he was in him through an affect of the will.[82]

For the Alexandrians, such terminology smacked of dualism. The Council of Chalcedon (451) resolved the problem of how to express the unity of Christ's person while maintaining the distinction of his natures, and added a further clarification in order to combat the Monophysite heresy which claimed that Christ's humanity was absorbed into his divinity at the Incarnation, so that he only had one nature.[83] The Council declared: 'We confess one and the same Jesus Christ, the Son and Lord Only-Begotten, in two natures without mixture without change without division without separation', adding that the Son was 'born of the Father before the ages according to divinity, but, in the latest days, the same born of the Virgin Mary, Mother of God according to the humanity.'[84] For the Monophysites, however, Chalcedon did not sufficiently defend the unity of Christ.

Pope Leo the Great († 461) sets out the orthodox position in response to the Monophysites:

---

[81] Quoted in Richard Price, 'Theotokos: The Title and its Significance", p. 61. On Theodoret's theology of the Incarnation see Paul B. Clayton, *The Christology of Theodoret of Cyrus: Antiochene Christology from the Council of Ephesus (431) to the Council of Chalcedon (451)* (Oxford: Oxford University Press, 2007). On his Mariology see Antonino Gallico, 'Riferimenti mariani in Teodoreto di Cirro', *Theotokos*, 12 (2004), 307-27.

[82] Quoted in Richard Price, 'Theotokos: The Title and its Significance', p. 61. On Theodore's theology see Richard A. Norris, *Manhood and Christ: A Study in the Christology of Theodore of Mopsuestia* (Oxford: The Clarendon Press, 1963).

[83] See Robert V. Sellers, *The Council of Chalcedon: A Historical and Doctrinal Survey* (London: SPCK, 1953), and John Norman D. Kelly, *Early Christian Doctrines*, pp. 338-43.

[84] Quoted in O'Carroll, *Theotokos*, p. 257. See also *MF*, pp. 302-306.

This birth within the confines of time took nothing away from his eternal and divine generation and added nothing to it. He offered it totally for the restoration of man, who had been deceived, in order to conquer death and, by his power, to destroy the devil, who ruled over the world. For we would not have been able to overcome the author of sin and death had Christ not assumed our nature and made it his own. Sin cannot defile him, nor can death hold him. For he was conceived by the Holy Spirit within the womb of a Virgin Mother, who gave birth to him without losing her virginity, just as she remained a virgin in conceiving him. *Epistola 28, 2*[85]

Elsewhere he writes along similar lines:

The birth in human form took nothing from the majesty of the Son of God, and added nothing, since the immutable substance of divine nature could not be diminished nor augmented. The fact that 'the Word became flesh' (John 1. 14), does not mean that the nature of the Word of God changed into flesh, but that the flesh was assumed by the Word in the unity of his Person. It follows therefore that in the term 'flesh' is included the whole man, and to it, in the womb of the Virgin, made fertile by the work of the Holy Spirit, and never deprived of the privilege of virginity, the Son of God so inseparably united himself that, although generated outside all time by the essence of the Father, he was born, within the limits of time, from the womb of the Virgin. *Sermo 27, 2*[86]

A variety of writers continue to use the uncircumscribable God *topos* in the fifth and sixth centuries. A homily attributed to Basil of Seleucia († after 468)[87] imagines the angel Gabriel replying to Mary's objection that she does not know man with a series of questions which show that nothing is impossible to God: 'Could you, perhaps, welcome you own Maker into your womb without the Son communicating his power to you? Have you, perhaps, a womb that is more immense than the heavens? Do you, perhaps, exceed the universe in broadness, which cannot even, of its nature, contain him?'[88] Chrysippus of Jerusalem († 479) exclaims: 'Rejoice, for you received a womb from nature wider than the heavens themselves, since you enclosed within your womb, him whom not even the heavens can contain.'[89] Jacob of Serug († 521) uses the image in one of his hymns: 'Blessed is she: her narrow womb enclosed the infinite Greatness which

---

[85] *PL* 54, 759, *MF*, p. 304-05.

[86] *PL* 54, 217B-C. The The Chalcedonian position was also defended vigorously by many later popes such as Gelasius († 496), *De duabus naturis adversus Eutychem et Nestorium*, *TMPM*, III, Hormisdas († 523), *Epistola 115 ad Anastasium Augustem*, *PL* 63, 379, 525-27, Vigilius I († 555), *Epistola enciclica*, *PL* 69, 56B-57A, Pelagius († 561), *Epistola 7*, 9-10, *PL* 69, 409-410.

[87] Authorship has not been definitively established, with some claiming that it was written by Proclus of Constantinople. See chapter on Patristic Intercession, Mediation and Devotion.

[88] *Homily on the Mother of God*, *TMPM*, I, 598.

[89] *Homily on the Holy Mother of God*, *TMPM*, I, 603.

even the heavens are too small to contain.'[90] One of the earliest occurrences in Latin of the *topos* is in a sixth-century poem for the Nativity, possibly composed in Constantinople by a Roman resident, which speaks of Mary's unique capacity to contain Christ.[91]

Severus of Antioch († 538), one of the more moderate of the Monophysites, makes a statement concerning Mary's divine motherhood in one of his homilies that seems almost identical to the declaration of the Council, but in fact stops short of speaking of Christ's humanity at his birth:

> She belonged to this earth; through her nature she was part of humanity and she had our same essence, no matter how pure from all contamination and no matter how immaculate she was, no matter whether she procreated the God who became flesh with her own womb and thanks to an intervention from heaven, because she conceived and gave birth in an entirely divine manner. Not that she gave the divine nature to him who was born, because he possessed it from the beginning, before all the centuries; but she gave him a human nature without him undergoing any change; and this she herself did thanks to the ineffable and mysterious intervention of the Holy Spirit. *Homily 6, On Mary the Holy Mother of God and Ever-Virgin*[92]

In the centuries after Chalcedon further questions arose concerning the hypostasis, though none posed such a direct threat to the divine motherhood as had the earlier heresies. The Second Council of Constantinople (553) did not deal directly with any Mariological questions, though it once again rejected the title *Anthropotokos*, designating her the 'holy and glorious Mary, Mother of God (*Theotokos*) and Ever-Virgin (*aeiparthenos*)' – the first time that her perpetual virginity was officially proclaimed (see chapter on Virginity).[93]

In the late sixth century the Monothelites proposed that Christ had only one will,[94] but this was rejected by the Sixth Ecumenical Council in 680-681, since, it was argued, Christ would not have been fully human had he not had a separate human will alongside his divine one, in which case he would not have been able to redeem humanity as both God and man. Modestus of Jerusalem († 634) lays out the official position:

---

[90] *Hymn to Mary the Virgin*, quoted from *Early Christian Prayers*, ed. by Adalbert Hamman, trans. by Walter Mitchell (Chicago: Regnery; London: Longmans and Green, 1961), p. 192.
[91] See Averil Cameron, 'A Nativity Poem of the Sixth Century A.D.', *Classical Philology*, 74 (1979), 222-32 (p. 222) for the full text of the poem.
[92] *TMPM*, I, 648.
[93] *Anathemas against the "Three Chapters"*, in *Decrees of the Ecumenical Councils* <http://www.piar.hu/councils/ecum05.htm> [accessed 8 October 2007]. See *TMPM*, I, 679-82 for an account of the Council and the full text of its proclamations in Italian.
[94] For an in-depth discussion of the Monothelite heresy see Demetrios Bathrellos, *The Byzantine Christ*, pp. 60-98.

> Hail, most holy Virgin Mother, who have brought forth Christ, the Son of
> God, made flesh from you by the Holy Spirit! He is perfect in divinity and
> perfect in humanity; in two natures, two wills and two fields of operation, he
> wills some acts as God and wills other acts as a human being, and as one and the
> same subject he possesses full power in both realms, without confusion and
> without division. *Homily on the Dormition of the Mother of God*, 10[95]

In the West, as we have already noted, the impact of the Christological
controversies was felt less severely. Although the Latin Fathers were well aware
of the issues their writings were generally less polemical and passionate and
lacked the linguistic and conceptual finesse of their Eastern counterparts.
Isidore of Seville († 636) sums up the orthodox position:[96]

> Jesus Christ is, at the same time, man and mediator between men and God, but
> he is not one in his humanity and the other in his divinity, but rather is one and the
> same in both natures. He was not conceived purely as a man, nor was he born
> purely a man, nor did he afterwards receive the privilege of being God: instead,
> while the essence that he holds coeternally with the Father and the Holy Spirit
> remained immutable, God the Word took on flesh for the salvation of the human
> race, in which he was able to show himself to be impassible in the face of
> suffering, immortal in the face of death, and, although temporal, eternal before the
> ages. Jesus Christ, mediator between God and men, although one thing proceeding
> from the Father, and another being born of the Virgin, in nevertheless not one
> thing from the Father and another from the Virgin, but he is eternal inasmuch as
> he proceeds from the Father and temporal inasmuch as he is born of his Mother.
> It is he who was made; it is he who proceeds from the Father without a mother
> and from the Mother without a father. *Sententiae, 1, 14, 4-5*[97]

Several take up the *topos* of the uncircumscribable God. Peter Chrysologus
(†c. 450), for instance, says:

> She is truly blessed who was greater than heaven, stronger than the earth,
> vaster than the world. She alone contained within herself that God whom the
> world cannot contain; she bore him who bears the world; she gave birth to her
> Father; she nursed him who nurtures every living thing. *Sermo 143, 7*[98]

The notion of the double birth of Christ is to be found in the declaration of the
First Lateran Council called by Pope Martin I in 649:

---

[95] *EPH*, p. 96.

[96] On Isidore's Mariology see Felipe Mariscal Chávez, *María en las obras de San Isidoro de Sevilla* (Rome: Marianum, 1991).

[97] *PL* 83, 565B-566A.

[98] *PL* 52, 584B. See *MLM*, p. 300.

> If anyone does not, in accord with the Holy Fathers, confess correctly and in accordance with the truth that there are two births of the one and same God, Our Lord Jesus Christ; one from God the Father before all time in an incorporeal and eternal manner; one in the last times, corporeal, from the holy and Ever-Virgin Mary Mother of God; that one and the same is Our Lord and God Jesus Christ, consubstantial with the Father according to his divinity, consubstantial with man and his Mother according to his humanity; that the same is passible in the flesh and impassible in his divinity […], let him be condemned. *Canones, 4*[99]

Maximus the Confessor († 662), a major opponent of Monothelitism, uses very similar language:

> We affirm a double birth of the one and same Christ: the first from God the Father before the ages; the second from the most holy Virgin in recent times for our salvation. […] We confess that the most holy Virgin is properly the Mother of God according to the truth. That is, we confess that she is the Mother not of the pure and simple man, formed, as it were, in the blink of an eye, prior to and separately from the union with the Word, and divinised by the accruement of works and by reaching the maximum level of virtue; rather, that the Virgin is the Mother of the same Word of God, of the only One of the holy Trinity who assumed flesh from her through a mysterious conception and became a perfect man. *Epistola 12*[100]

Maximus offers what is perhaps the most thorough rejection of Monothelitism, arguing that Christ fully possessed a natural human will, but that in him the inclination or *habitus* towards sin did not apply, since the hypostasis, or union without fusion of his human and divine wills allowed him to overcome the deprivation of knowledge of the good which was common to all men as a result of the Fall.[101]

The continuing controversies surrounding the hypostatic union are reflected in two stories of miraculous interventions by the Virgin that the Syrian monk John Moschos (†c. 619) recounts in which she shows her displeasure at heretical

---

[99] *Enchiridion Symbolorum: Definitionum et Declarationum de Rebus Fidei et Morum*, ed. by Henricus Denzinger and Adolfus Schönmetzer, 36th edn (Fribourg: Herder, 1965), n. 504. See chapter on Virginity for further discussion. For a modern take on the question of Christ's two wills with reference to the Monothelite heresy see Ivor J. Davidson, '"Not My Will but Yours be Done": The Ontological Dynamics of Incarnational Intention, *International Journal of Systematic Theology*, 7 (2005), 178-204.

[100] *TMPM*, II, 181.

[101] See Demetrios Bathrellos, *The Byzantine Christ*, especially pp. 99-174, Lars Thunberg, *Microcosm and Mediator: The Theological Anthropology of Maximus the Confessor*, 2nd edn (Chicago: Open Court, 1995), and for further bibliography, Maria Luisa Gatti, *Massimo il Confessore: saggio di bibliografia generale ragionata e contributi per una del suo pensiero metafisico e religioso* (Milan: Vita e Pensiero, 1987).

beliefs regarding her divine motherhood. In one a monk is shown a vision of the punishment that those who have blasphemed against the Mother of God, such as Nestorius, Apollinaris, and Arius, are enduring in hell, while in the other the Virgin appears to an abbot to complain that he has a book in his cell that includes writings by Nestorius. The abbot, who has borrowed the book from another monk, returns it to him immediately and tells him what has occurred, upon which his friend rips out the offending chapters.[102]

Sophronius of Jerusalem († 638), a friend of John Moschos, affirms the truths concerning Mary's divine motherhood in a very different style in his *Homily for the Annunciation*, which takes the form of a much-elaborated dialogue between Mary and Gabriel.[103] In response to Mary's doubts about the veracity of the message, Gabriel assures her that anything is possible to God and that the child that she will conceive will truly be the Son of God. Mary for long remains unconvinced so that Gabriel has to produce more and more proofs that he is not deceiving her and that she will actually become the Mother of God. With this device, Sophronius is able to cover all the doctrinal issues concerning Mary's divine motherhood. Eventually, Mary gives her consent and the angel returns to heaven, at which point Sophronius gives a long exposition on the hypostatic union, the opening lines of which are:

> In her womb she was already carrying the God who had sent the angelic messenger; that God who was glorified in heaven together with the Father, while on earth he was willing to be carried in her womb according to the flesh. The Word and God had descended together to her; by means of the angelic voice he had entered into her divine womb and had become incarnate; he had put on a body without any change in him; he had assumed unsown flesh from the Virgin, truly uniting it to himself, endowed with a rational soul, but it did not subsist prior to its ineffable union with him. It was never the flesh of a man different from us, even more not when it conjoined with the Word of God, and when, together with him it joined together in the formation of the composite. But at the same time it also began to be flesh endowed with a rational soul, drawn from the pure blood of the immaculate Virgin, just as it also agreed to be the flesh of the Word of God, endowed with a rational soul. *Homily on the Annunciation, 46*[104]

Around the same time in the Latin Church, Ildephonse of Toledo († 667) also wrote a lengthy treatise in which he defends Mary's virginity and divine motherhood. In both content and tone it differs somewhat from the more dispassionate work of Sophronius. Addressing the proverbial disbelieving Jew, he writes:

---

[102] *Spiritual Meadow*, 26 and 46, *TMPM*, II, 90-91 and 92-93.
[103] The dialogue extends from numbers 23-44, *TMPM*, II, 143-159.
[104] *TMPM*, II, 159-60.

> And since this Son of hers is God and man he is the Word and flesh at the same time, divinity and humanity; for us he is peace, but for you a scandal, for us he is wisdom, but for the Gentiles he is a foolishness. Rightly therefore the human prerogatives are referable to God and the prerogatives of God are referred to man. It follows that the weaknesses of man are raised to the presence of God and the omnipotence of God is said to be weakened by the presence of man. For this reason the majesty of God lowers itself to earth just as human baseness is raised up to the divine summit. *De virginitate perpetua sanctae Mariae, 3, 3*[105]

In the final part of his treatise Ildephonse emphasises the intimate link between the mystery of Christ's dual nature and the uniqueness of Mary, who is at the same time Virgin and Mother, basing his argument entirely on Scripture rather than resorting to the more philosophical discourses characteristic of the East :

> Since God, inasmuch as he assumes humanity, is called the Son of man, the Evangelist expresses himself thus: 'when the Son of man shall come in his majesty, and all the angels with him' (Matthew 25. 31). Now, this same majesty, which is also recognised by the angels, cannot be attributed to the nature of anyone if not that of the Son of God, who is truly omnipotent. Therefore, since the man that is assumed is called the Son of God, the other Evangelist indicates him to the Virgin with these words: 'He who shall be born of thee shall be called Holy, the Son of God' (Luke 1. 35). It follows that because of the property of the two natures, connected in the unity of the Person, the nature of man and the nature of God, she alone is Virgin and Mother. In this way, in her giving birth to one Son in the two natures, he is at the same time Son of man and Son of God. Therefore this motherhood is more miraculous than all miracles, superior to all works, more august than any other wonder: it transcends the whole of creation, it exceeds the limits of the world, it rises above the excellence of all creatures to the point where the angels also place themselves in the service of this God, in the unity of the two natures, adoring him and exalting him in the wholly peculiar unity of the Person of the Son of God. *De virginitate perpetua sanctae Mariae, 11, 13*[106]

Commenting on the angelic greeting to Mary, Bede the Venerable († 735) offers a straightforward statement on her divine motherhood. Gabriel's words, that Mary will conceive a son, and that he will be the Son of the Most High, 'state in a most clear way that the Lord Jesus, that is, our Saviour, is the true Son of God the Father and the true son of a human mother.' 'You cannot', he continues, 'not recognise that Christ is true man and that he took on the true substance of the flesh from the flesh of the Virgin.' But, he points out, the angel also declares that he will be 'the Son of the Most High (Luke 1. 32), so one must also confess that 'he is true God from true God and that the Son is always coeternal with the Father.' He therefore concludes that: 'The power of divine majesty that the Son of God had from eternity, this same power he assumed as

---

[105] *PL* 96, 65C-66A.
[106] *PL* 96, 104C-105A.

a man born in time, so that in the two natures there would be the one Person of Mediator and Redeemer.'[107]

The last major controversy concerning the hypostatic union in the Eastern Church began in the eighth century with the phenomenon of Iconoclasm,[108] at the instigation of the Emperor Leo III (717-741). The Iconoclasts rejected the veneration of images essentially on two grounds. Firstly, if an image represented the humanity of Christ to the exclusion of his divinity, then this was akin to the Nestorian belief that one could separate his humanity and divinity. If, on the other hand, the image represented Christ in both his divinity and humanity this either implied that his divinity could be circumscribed by his humanity – in this case, the human image of Christ – or that his humanity and divinity were so mixed together that the human image also portrayed the divine. The opponents of Iconoclasm fought back by pointing out that any human being who is a part of history may be represented in an image, so to deny that Christ could be portrayed in an icon was to deny that Christ was true man. Furthermore, they argued, Christ had indeed been circumscribed in the womb of the Virgin. Thus it was that Mary once again took centre stage in a Christological controversy. It was also as a result of Iconoclasm that significant numbers of Byzantine monks fled to the West, bringing their rich tradition of Marian devotion with them.[109] Although the Second Council of Nicea (787) upheld orthodox teaching concerning icons, declaring admissible the veneration of images of divine realities, this did not put a definitive end to the problem. In the West, the Frankish bishops, with the support of Charlemagne, rejected the ecumenicity of the Council in 794, despite the adherence of the Pope, while in the East Leo V (813-20) renewed the controversy, which continued under his successors, Michael II (820-29) and Theophilus (829-42), whose widow, Theodora, who ruled as regent after her husband's death, finally put an end to Iconoclasm in 843.

Ironically perhaps, the Iconoclastic controversy actually led to a new flowering of Mariology in the eighth century, as some of the greatest figures in the Church, most notably the three great Byzantine Fathers, Andrew of Crete (†c. 740), John of Damascus († 749) and Germanus of Constantinople († c. 733), sought to defend the Virgin's divine motherhood.

---

[107] *In festo Annuntiationis beatae Mariae*, PL 94, 11C-D.

[108] For a broad overview see *Iconoclasm*, ed. by Anthony Byer and Judith Herrin, (Birmingham: Birmingham University Press, 1977). For the philosophical and theological background see the magisterial study by Alain Besançon, *The Forbidden Image: An Intellectual History of Iconoclasm*, trans. by Jane Marie Todd (Chicago: University of Chicago Press, 2000), especially pp. 109-46.

[109] On contacts between Rome and Byzantium see Michael Angold, *Byzantium: The Bridge from Antiquity to the Middle Ages* (New York: St. Martin's Press, 2001), p. 101, Jean-Marie Sansterre, *Les moines grecs et orientaux à Rome aux époques byzantine et carolingienne (milieu du VIe s. – fin du IXe s.)* (Brussels: Académie Royale de Belgique, 1983), and Peter Brown, 'Eastern and Western Christendom in Late Antiquity: A Parting of the Ways', *Studies in Church History*, 13 (1976), 1-23.

Andrew of Crete is at particular pains to emphasise the separate natures within the one person of Christ:

> He who needs nothing, who is full beyond measure, who is rich, did not choose to dwell in this realm of existence by leaving the divinity which is above all essence, but kept unmingled within himself, even after the ineffable union, the natural structures of what had come together, with neither confusion nor separation as the key to the relationship between them. *First Homily on the Dormition, 7*[110]

He also uses the uncircumscribable God *topos* to get his point across writing that, 'He, who is containable in no place made his dwelling in a virgin's womb without being constricted,' and again: 'O Heaven, rejoice for her! For, imitating you, without difficulty she contained the Lord who was not contained in you.'[111]

John of Damascus also makes a comparison between Mary and heaven when writing of her Dormition:

> Oh, how could heaven receive one who is called 'wider than the heavens'? How could a grave contain the one who contained God? Yet surely it did receive her, surely it did make room for her; for that body was not 'wider than heaven' in any spatial sense. How, after all, can something three cubits long, something that grows more frail each day, be compared with the breadth and length of heaven? But in grace, surely, she surpassed the measure of every height and depth; for nothing can be compared with what is divine. *First Sermon on the Dormition, 13*[112]

In another passage on the Dormition, John identifies Mary herself as a 'living heaven' since she contains God within herself:

> For who could err in calling her heaven, unless one were to say – and say rightly – that she has been lifted even above heaven in her incomparable privileges? For the maker and preserver of heaven and of everything in and beyond this universe, the craftsman of all that has been made, visible and invisible – he who has no place, because he *is* the place of all other beings (if, indeed, place is defined as what contains the things within it): he has created a child in her, of his own power and without human seed, and has revealed her as the spacious treasure-house of that divinity that fills all things, alone and uncircumscribed. He has gathered himself up completely in her, without suffering diminution, yet he remains wholly beyond her abiding in himself as his incomprehensible home. *Second Homily on the Dormition, 2*[113]

---

[110] *EPH*, p. 112.
[111] *First Homily on the Dormition*, 3, *EPH*, p. 107, and *Fourth Encomium for the Nativity of the Most Holy Mother of God*, TMPM, II, 413.
[112] *EPH*, p. 198.
[113] *EPH*, p. 206.

John offers several lengthy expositions on the Incarnation, one in a homily on the Dormition, which may usefully summarise the official position of the Church at the close of the Patristic Age:[114]

> Then you, the Father's self-defining Word, dwelt in her without being limited, summoning the farthest reaches of our nature up to the endless heights of you incomprehensible divinity. Taking the first-fruits [of our nature] from the holy, spotless and utterly pure blood of the holy Virgin, you built around yourself a structure of flesh, livened by a rational and intelligent soul; you gave it individual existence in yourself, and became a complete human being without ceasing to be completely God, of the same essence as your Father. Taking on our weakness, rather, in your unutterable mercy, you came forth from her a single Christ, a single Lord, one and the same who is both Son of God and Son of man, at once completely God and completely human, the whole God and a whole human being, one composite individual [formed] from two complete natures, divinity and humanity. You are not simply God or merely human, but one who is both Son of God and God enfleshed, God and human at the same time; you have not undergone confusion or endured division, but you bear in yourself the natural qualities of two natures essentially distinct, yet united without confusion and without division in your concrete existence: the created and the uncreated, the mortal and the immortal, the visible and the invisible, the circumscribed and the uncircumscribed, divine will and human will, divine activity no less than human activity; two self-determining realities, divine and human at the same time. *First Homily on the Dormition, 3*[115]

In his *Exposition on the Orthodox Faith*, John goes into considerable technical detail on the generative mechanisms involved in the Incarnation. Firstly, he makes it clear that the Incarnation resulted from a free choice of the Virgin. Then stressing the perichoretic relationship of the Trinity, he describes how the Logos formed a body for itself. Basing his explanation on Aristotelian embryology he states that the active principle was not a male seed but the creative power of God, while the passive material was the Virgin's blood. In order to counter any suggestion that Christ was less than human, he underlines that all these processes took place at the instant of conception: there was no pre-existing embryo to which Christ added his divinity; rather from the very first instant there was a perfect hypostasis of the two natures. He then goes on, in a rather cumbersome and repetitive way, to stress again and again that the two natures, divine and human, subsisted in the one person without in any way being confused:

> So then, after the consent of the holy Virgin, the Holy Spirit came upon her, according to the word of the Lord, as the angel had announced, purifying her

---

[114] For a detailed treatment of John's theology see Andrew Louth, *St. John Damascene: Tradition and Originality in Byzantine Theology* (Oxford: Oxford University Press, 2002), especially pp. 144-78.

[115] *EPH*, pp. 185-86.

and giving her the capacity to receive the divinity of the Word and to generate. And then, the en-hypostatic[116] Wisdom and Power of God descended into her, the Son of God, consubstantial with the Father as of divine seed, and from her chaste and most pure blood he formed a body for himself, animated by a rational and spiritual soul, the first-fruits of our race; not through procreation but by creation through the Holy Spirit; not developing the embryo with a series of small additions, but perfecting it in one instant. He is the same God-Word who became hypostasis of the flesh. For the divine Word did not unite himself with a pre-existing flesh, as to a person, but having come to dwell in the womb of the holy Virgin in an uncircumscribed way, he formed, of his own hypostasis, through the pure blood of the Ever-Virgin, a body animated with a rational and spiritual soul, assuming to himself the first-fruits of our own compound nature, himself the Word, having become a hypostasis in the flesh. So that at the very instant the flesh came to exist, it was flesh of the Word of God, animated, rational and spiritual flesh. Therefore we do not speak of a man being divinised, but of God become man. For, being by nature perfect God, he likewise became perfect man; not changing his nature nor simulating the Incarnation, but without change and without division he united himself through hypostasis with the flesh that he took from the Virgin, animated with a rational and spiritual soul and which has being in itself, without altering the nature of his divinity into the substance of the flesh, nor the substance of the flesh into the nature of his divinity; he did not form one compound nature from his divine nature and the human nature that he had assumed. *Exposition on the Orthodox Faith, 3, 2*[117]

Therefore, John goes on to say (3. 12), the title *Theotokos* contains in synthesis the whole mystery of God's Incarnation: 'Therefore it is right and proper to call holy Mary the Mother of God. For this name constitutes the entire mystery of the [divine] economy: for if she is the Mother [and] Genetrix of God then he who is born of her is necessarily God and likewise man.'[118] Nevertheless John is also extremely careful to avoid the possibility that Mary might be considered a goddess. He makes it abundantly clear that Mary was entirely human and should not be worshipped: 'So we, who recognize this virgin as Mother of God, now celebrate the feast of her Dormition. We do not call her a goddess – we will have none of such pedantic classical fabling – for we proclaim her death. But we recognize her as Mother of the God who became flesh.'[119]

Germanus of Constantinople († c. 733), characteristically, provides one of the most hyperbolic elaborations of Mary being greater than paradise itself because she contained God: '"You are higher than heaven" (Job 11. 8), and wider than the heaven of heavens – even that seventh heaven, which a certain holy man, on

---

[116] That is, the human nature of Christ has its being only in the subsistence of the Incarnate Son.

[117] *TMPM*, II, 486, *PG* 94, 985-988.

[118] *Exposition on the Orthodox Faith*, 3, 12, *TMPM*, II, 488-89.

[119] *Second Homily on the Dormition*, 15, *EPH*, p. 220. See also the chapters on Intercession, Mediation and Devotion where the question of veneration of the Virgin is discussed.

the basis of Scripture, distinguishes from it.[120] 'You are greater than the eighth heaven, and than any other heaven beyond it.'[121]

Iconoclasm marked the last great controversy concerning the divine motherhood in the Eastern Church, and although heretical movements did arise in the Latin Church, such as the Albigensians or Cathars and the Waldensians, the responses of those who defended the official line were not particularly original, relying to a great extent on the teaching of the Councils and the Fathers.

The Medieval West

In the Medieval West, which was far removed from the doctrinal battles of the Eastern Church, statements on Mary's divine motherhood are generally less polemical in tone and lack the highly sophisticated metaphysical language that characterises so many of the Greek Fathers. This is perhaps also a reflection of the difference between the Greeks and the Latins, the latter tending towards a more precise and legalistic tone. Ambrose Autpert's (†c. 781) uncomplicated explanation may serve as an example:

> In the one person of our Redeemer, God and man, we confess the presence of the perfect nature of God and the perfect nature of man. From the one, the Lord, from the other the servant; from the one strength, from the other weakness; from the one he who creates, from the other he who is created; from the one he who nourishes, from the other he who is hungry; from the one, he who sates, from the other he who is thirsty. *In Purificatione S. Mariae, 10*[122]

Ambrose, who was strongly influenced by Byzantine Mariology, also uses the *topos* of Mary containing the uncircumscribable God:

> She of whom we are speaking is higher than the heavens. She whose mystery we are trying to proclaim in [words of] praise is more mysterious than the abyss, for she bore within her immaculate womb that God which the whole universe is not able to contain. *In festo Assumptionis B. Mariae, 4*[123]

However, the Western Church was not entirely free of controversies, one of the more serious being Adoptionism, espoused by Felix of Urgel and Elipandus of Toledo in eighth-century Spain, and in a somewhat modified form by Abelard in the twelfth century, which claimed that Christ, in his humanity, is not the true, but only the adoptive Son of God. This teaching was condemned by Pope Hadrian in two letters to the bishops of Spain, and Charlemagne, and

---

[120] See Basil, *Homiliae in Hexaemeron*, III, 3.
[121] *First Homily on the Dormition*, 10, *EPH*, p. 163.
[122] *PL* 89, 1299B-C.
[123] *PL* 39, 2130. See Graef, *Doctrine and Devotion*, 1, 166-67.

was officially condemned by the Council of Frankfort, summoned by Charlemagne in 794 and another held in Rome in 798.[124]

Alcuin († 804), who was a key figure in combating Adoptionism, reaffirms Mary's divine motherhood in a number of his works.[125] Basing his arguments on a Latin translation of the decrees of the Council of Ephesus, Alcuin uses the original Greek terms *Theotokos* and *Christotokos* in discussing the nature of Mary's motherhood. Having explained how Mary conceived through the Holy Spirit and the power of the Most High he writes:

> In this way the most Blessed Virgin Mary became both *Theotokos* and *Christotokos*. For, even though, before her, there were many *Christotokos* in the population, that is mothers of christs,[126] they were nevertheless neither virgins, nor were they overshadowed by the Holy Spirit and by the power of the Most High so that they might be found worthy of giving birth to God. Instead, Mary is not just *Christotokos* but is also the one and only *Theotokos*. Conceiving by means of the Holy Spirit and through the power of the Most High, she is the only virgin to receive such great glory as to give birth to God: the Son of God, coeternal and consubstantial with the Father. *De fide sanctae et individuae Trinitatis, 3, 14, De Maria Virgine, et incarnatione Verbi Dei*[127]

Shortly afterwards, Haymo of Halberstadt († 853), a pupil of Alcuin's, in a commentary on Ecclesiasticus, condemns the ancient Manichean heresy, that Christ did not assume true flesh from the Virgin, presumably with the Adoptionists in mind:

> Therefore let the heretical presumption of the Manicheans stop grunting, for they dared to affirm that Christ did not assume true flesh from the Virgin. Then let the very Wisdom of God say in the name of the Virgin: 'He that created me, rested in my tabernacle, and he said to me: Let thy dwelling be in Jacob, and thy inheritance in Israel' (see Ecclesiasticus 24. 12-13). *Homilia V, In solemnitate perpetuae Virginis Mariae*[128]

---

[124] See John C. Cavadini, *The Last Christology of the West: Adoptionism in Spain and Gaul, 785-820* (Philadelphia: University of Pennsylvania Press, 1993), and Joseph Sollier, 'Adoptionism' in *The Catholic Encyclopedia*, ed. by Charles George Herbermann, Edward Pace, and others, 15 vols (New York: Appleton, 1907-1912), I (1907), in *New Advent*, <http://www.newadvent.org/cathen/01150a.htm> [accessed 30 July 2008]. See also Leo Scheffczyk, *Das Mariengeheimnis in Frömmigkeit und Lehre der Karolingerzeit*, Theologische Studien, 5 (Leipzig: St. Benno-Verlag, 1959), and Irene Scaravalli, 'Per una mariologia carolingia: autori, opere e linee di ricerca', in *Gli studi di mariologia medievale: bilancio storico*, pp. 65-85, particularly pp. 66-71.

[125] Including two works specifically against Felix, the *Libellus Adversus haeresim Felicis* and the *Contra Felicem libri septem*.

[126] In the sense of mothers of prophets or 'anointed ones'.

[127] *PL*, 101, 47A.

[128] *TMSM*, III, 764-65.

A few decades later Paschasius Radbertus († 865), one of the most influential figures in the early Medieval Church, offers a relatively straightforward, albeit lengthy, restatement of Church teaching:

> Therefore, the Word of the Father, without ever distancing himself from the Father, deigned to become man for us in the secret of his mystery of salvation, which he alone knew. He, since he entirely took on that which is human, is entirely a man; and insofar as he retained everything that is of God, he cannot be other than God, born of Mary.
>
> [...]
>
> He, in fact, will not be limited by time nor will he be separated from the Passion, but God passes entirely into Christ and Christ into God so that whatever is said of the Son of God may be said of Christ; and moreover, [...] it is rightly believed that everything that Christ bore in the flesh was borne by God. Instead, if you trust in reason and human intelligence, you will certainly never understand how the human condition and divinity could come together. And yet, they come together in Christ, and the Emmanuel is one from both. Therefore, it seems to me that those who have thought that there were two sons, or that Christ was other than the Son of God have not diligently examined, nor have they been able to penetrate such a great mystery in depth. Therefore we neither venerate nor adore the man considered in himself, something [that would be] impious, but rather adore the God who took on flesh and united an animated body to himself in such a way that God Word would become flesh, and the unity would come about not just in any person, but in himself, who was from all time the one and true Son of God. *Cogitis me, 5 and 10*[129]

He ends his exposition with this brief summation: 'It is necessary to reflect carefully on all things to the point of understanding that in Christ the fullness of divinity is united to the man and the fullness of humanity was assumed in God.'[130]

Paschasius also speaks of the inability of finite space to contain the infinite God in the context of reaffirming Church teaching on Christ's dual nature:

> He could not be enclosed in a place, he who is in every place, he who is everything everywhere and without whom everything does not exist. Therefore, the Word of the Father, without ever distancing himself from the Father, deigned to become man for us in the secret of his mystery of salvation, which he alone knew. *Cogitis me, 5*[131]

---

[129] *PL* 30, 127B and 133A-C, *TMPM*, III, 794 and 802.
[130] *Cogitis me*, 12, *TMSM*, III, 806.
[131] *PL* 30, 127B, *TMPM*, III, 794.

Hrabanus Maurus († 856) reaffirms the truths of the faith regarding Mary's divine motherhood without adding anything new.[132] Instead he is interested in clarifying another question, namely that the conception of Christ was not just the work of the Holy Spirit but of the whole Trinity. It is through their combined action that the second Person of the Trinity united himself to a human nature so that he became, at one and the same time, the Son of God and the Son of man:

> It is not licit to say that Christ is the Son of the Holy Spirit, because he is the only Son of God the Father Almighty according to his divine and human substance. Indeed all things were made through him (John 1. 3), our Lord Jesus Christ, insofar as he is God; insofar as he is man, and he became man, he was born, as the Apostle says, from the stock of David according to the flesh (Romans 1. 3). Now, the way in which Christ was born, that is, not as a son through the work of the Holy Spirit, but as a son born of the Virgin Mary most certainly introduces us to the mystery of God's grace. Through this [grace] in fact a human being, without any pre-existing merit, and in the same origin of his nature with which he begins to exist, united himself to God the Word in such a sublime unity of person so that the son of man became Son of God and the Son of God became son of man. *Commentariorum in Matthaeum, 12-13*[133]

Peter Damian († 1072), who had a rich knowledge of the Eastern tradition, writes of the mystery of the Incarnation in the familiar terms of the uncircumscribable God being contained in the Virgin's womb. The whole tone of the passage, however, is somewhat different from Eastern texts:

> What tongue could sufficiently explain, and what human mind would not be astonished when faced with these most fundamental reflections: that the Creator arose from a creature, the Maker from that which is made, that that which is conceived in the virginal womb of a young girl is he who cannot be contained even by the great vastness of the whole world, that in the maternal womb lies, as a little child, he who, as the immense One, governs the laws of all things together with the coeternal Father? *Sermo 45, In Nativitate beatissimae Virginis Mariae, 5*[134]

Here alongside the doctrinal issues that he wishes to underscore Peter is concerned with instilling wonder in his listeners at the immense mystery of the Incarnation. The language is less hieratic than that of the Eastern Fathers, painting a picture of a young woman with her child that is intended to inspire affection as much as awe. Indeed he goes one to speak of the Christ-child suckling at the Virgin's breasts, another image designed to inspire both wonder and affection.[135]

---

[132] See, for instance, his *Commentarium in Matthaeum*, 1, 1, *PL* 107, 752D-754C.

[133] *PL* 107, 750D-751B, *TMSM*, III, 775, and 753A-754A, *TMSM*, III, 777-79.

[134] *PL* 144, 742D-743A.

[135] See vol. 2 for discussion on Mary as a nursing mother.

In Godescalcus of Limburg († 1098) the notion of Mary as the container of the uncontainable God has a doctrinal content but is also aimed at emphasising Mary's mediatory role:

> What great glory could suffice for your more than virginal body since it enclosed the uncontainable God, he who contains all things in himself? In you, he reduced his omnipotence to the point where he does not reveal his presence to anyone without you. For, as God he did not come to mankind without you, and in the same way man will never reach God without you. *Sequentia 'Exulta, exaltata'*[136]

Hugh of St. Victor († 1141) sets out all the standard theology regarding the divine motherhood in commenting on Elisabeth's greeting to Mary as the Mother of the Lord, and specifically rejects the Adoptionist position:

> Rightly [did Elisabeth say], Mother of the Lord, for although in the form of a servant, it was the Lord of majesty who had come. For he who was born as a man was also God: son of the Virgin in what had been assumed; Son of majesty in what he assumed. The same [person] however is the son of the Virgin and the Son of majesty. Therefore the man that was assumed is the natural Son of God in virtue of he who assumed him; and he is truly Son of man in virtue of he whom he assumed. Let no-one therefore call Christ an adopted Son because he is a natural son. In fact the man who is assumed and the God who assumes are not two sons but one Son only, God and Man, Jesus Christ. For this reason she who generated the form of the servant is the Mother of the Lord because in the form of the servant was the majesty of the Lord. *De Verbo incarnato, Collatio 3*[137]

Bernard of Clairvaux († 1153), opponent of Abelard, also restates orthodox Church teaching, affirming that Mary was not simply the mother of Christ's human nature or of his flesh, but was Mother of the 'whole' Jesus in his divine and human natures:[138]

> Although there is an infinite difference between the Flesh Which this Son obtains from thee and the Divinity Which He derives from the Father, He shall not be only in part thy Son, and in part the Father's, but wholly and entirely the same Son of both thee and the Father. *Fourth Sermon on the Glories of the Virgin Mother*[139]

His follower, Nicholas of Clairvaux († 1176), apostrophises Mary by expressing his wonderment at her ability to contain God, a less direct if equally effective way of affirming her divine motherhood: 'O womb greater than the heavens, broader

---

[136] *AH*, 50, 343-44, *TMSM*, III, 65.

[137] *PL* 177, 322C-D.

[138] See *Respice stellam: Maria in San Bernardo e nella tradizione cistercense: atti del convegno internazionale, Roma, Marianum, 21-24 October 1991*, ed. by Ignazio M. Calabuig (Rome: Marianum, 1993).

[139] *SBS*, p. 66.

than the earth, more capacious than the elements, which encloses in his entirety him who contains all things and in whom lies the God of glory.'[140]

Peter Lombard († 1160), who had a major influence on Scholasticism,[141] sets out the doctrine of Mary's divine motherhood with his characteristic thoroughness. It is interesting to note how he incorporates the bridal language of Canticles which was very much in vogue in the twelfth century. Note also the repeated insistence on the dual nature of Christ in opposition to the Adoptionist and Cathar heresies:

> Therefore the Son of God became Son of man in the virginal bridal chamber; Bridegroom united to Bride, the Son of God born of God according to the reality of nature, and Son of man born of a human creature according to the truth of nature, and not by adoption nor merely in name; so that, in being born, in both generations he bears full right to the name of Son, and this one Son and one Christ is true God and true man. We do not confess that there are two christs or two sons but a single Son who is God and man, for which reason we say that the Only-Begotten persists in two natures or substances that are not confused or mixed; and we profess that the Blessed Virgin is Mother, not just of the man but also of God, because the Virgin conceived and gave birth in time to him whom the Father generates in eternity. We venerate the two births: one from the Father before the ages and above flesh, time and nature; the other taking place in the last times for us and in conformity with us: for us because it was for our salvation, and in conformity with us because as a man he was born of a woman, respecting the time of conception; but in a superior way to us because he was conceived not from seed but from the Holy Spirit and the holy Virgin outside the law of conception. *In festo annuntiationis beatae Mariae*[142]

Catharism, a new manifestation of an old heresy began to make its presence felt in the twelfth century. The Cathars, also known as the Albigensians, who first came to prominence in the Languedoc region of France in the late eleventh century and flourished in the twelfth and early thirteenth centuries before being crushed by the Albigensian crusade, held a variety of dualistic and Gnostic beliefs and maintained a position similar to the Docetic heresy concerning the nature of Christ, whom they believed to have merely taken on the appearance of a man, thus directly involving the question of Mary's divine motherhood. Some also accorded Mary a semi-divine status, claiming that she possessed a celestial body.[143] The Cathars were

---

[140] *De Annuntiatione, PL* 144, 558C.

[141] All schoolmen were expected to write a commentary on his *Sententiae* before they were allowed to teach.

[142] *PL* 171, 605C-606B.

[143] On the Cathars and Mary see Sarah Hamilton, 'The Virgin Mary in Cathar Thought', *The Journal of Ecclesiastical History*, 56 (2005), 24-49. For a general study of the Cathars see Malcolm Lambert, *The Cathars* (Malden, Mass: Blackwell, 1998). For a controversial view that the Cathar heresy was deliberately exaggerated by the Church see Mark Gregory Pegg, A Most Holy War: The Albigensian Crusade and the Battle for Christendom

anathemised, along with anyone who gave them comfort, by the Third Lateran Council in 1179, which also authorised the taking up of arms against them.[144] As with Adoptionism, this outbreak of heresy did not so much lead to doctrinal innovation as to an insistence on restating age-old truths.

Three important figures in combating the Cathar heresy were Egbert of Schönau († 1184), brother of the famed mystic Elisabeth, Henry of Castro Marsiaco († 1189), who participated in the Third Lateran Council at the invitation of Pope Alexander III, who subsequently sent him to France as a papal legate to combat the heresy,[145] and Alan of Lille († 1203), who was particularly active in refuting the Albigensians. This is evident even in his less doctrinal work such as in this commentary on Canticles 3. 11, 'His mother crowned him in the day of his espousals':

> She crowned him, that is to say, she gloriously conceived him without male seed, and gave birth to him having clothed him in noble flesh. I repeat, look at him 'in the day of his espousals', that is, in the luminous spectacle of his Incarnation, when he wed the Virgin not only in a spiritual union, but also through a union of the two natures. Therefore in this verse the Incarnation is defined as a marriage. *Elucidatio in Cantica Canticorum, 3*[146]

Bonaventure († 1274), in the manner of the Scholastics, dwells at some length on the physiological aspects of Christ's conception, favouring, unusually, Galen's position that the woman plays an active role in conception, rather than Aristotle's teaching that the female merely provides the passive material which is given form by the male seed.[147] Mary's conception of Jesus was both natural in that the process occurred 'as is proper to the female sex', and supernatural because the generative power was 'actuated by the Holy Spirit and elevated above its capacity'. This is a miracle of a higher order than in the cases of Sara and Elisabeth, since Mary conceived while remaining a virgin while they were merely freed from their sterility. Since, according to the doctrine of the hypostatic union and the principle of the communication of idioms,[148] she did not just conceive Christ but true God, generated in eternity from the Father,

(Oxford: Oxford University Press, 2007). For a broader perspective see Walter Wakefield and Austin P. Evans, *Heresies of the High Middle Ages*, (New York: Columbia University Press, 1991). Also useful is Carol Lansing, *Power and Purity: Cathar Heresy in Medieval Italy* (Oxford: Oxford University Press, 1998).

[144] See Canon 27 of the Council, in *All Catholic Church Ecumenical Councils - All the Decrees*, <http://www.piar.hu/councils/ecum11.htm> [accessed 12 December 2008].

[145] See *TMSM*, III, 418.

[146] *PL* 210, 77A-B.

[147] See *Sent.* III, d. iv, a. 3, q. 1-3. For a detailed treatment of Bonaventure's teaching on the divine motherhood see George H. Tavard, *The Forthbringer of God: St. Bonaventure on the Virgin Mary* (Chicago: Franciscan Herald Press, 1989), pp. 29-35, on which I draw extensively.

[148] That is, the two natures do not come together in nature, but in the Person of Christ.

she should not only be called *Christotokos* but *Dei Genetrix* or *Theotokos*. In both the *Sententiae* and more synthetically in the *Breviloquium* Bonaventure explains the mode of Christ's conception. Unlike the normal process, in which, according to the Aristotelian teaching on embryology that he followed, the body of the child is formed progressively in the womb, Christ's body was perfectly formed from the instant of conception: 'At the first instant of conception there was not only the forming of the germ, but also its strengthening, its shaping, its vivification by the soul and its deification by the deity united to it.'[149] Thus, he concludes, the Virgin 'truly conceived the Son of God' through the union of her flesh, made worthy through the medium of her soul, with God.'

Albert the Great († 1280) likewise asserts that the Virgin gave birth to the whole person of Christ, not just his humanity: 'This person is truly the Son of God, existing in two natures, and therefore the Blessed Virgin is the Mother of God, or rather, of the Son of God, and not of a human nature. Therefore she must be called *Theotokos*, not *Christotokos*, and still less *Androtokos*.'[150]

Aquinas († 1274) explains the biological details of Christ's generation according to the theory of Aristotle, who held that it was the blood of the woman that provided the matter on which the active male principle was stamped. In the case of Mary the manner of conception differs in that it is God who supplies the active principle, so that there is one aspect of the conception which is super-natural, but in all other respects the conception abides by the laws of nature:

> As stated above, in Christ's conception His being born of a woman was in accordance with the laws of nature, but that He was born of a virgin was above the laws of nature. Now, such is the law of nature that in the generation of an animal the female supplies the matter, while the male is the active principle of generation; as the Philosopher proves (*De Gener. Animal. I*). But a woman who conceives of a man is not a virgin. And consequently it belongs to the supernatural mode of Christ's generation, that the active principle of generation was the supernatural power of God: but it belongs to the natural mode of His generation, that the matter from which His body was conceived is similar to the matter which other women supply for the conception of their offspring. Now, this matter, according to the Philosopher (*De Gener. Animal.*), is the woman's blood, not any of her blood, but brought to a more perfect stage of secretion by the mother's generative power, so as to be apt for conception. And therefore of such matter was Christ's body conceived. *ST, III, q. 31, a. 5*[151]

---

[149] *Brev*, ch. 3, n. 5, Tavard, *Forthbringer*, p. 53. See also *Sent*. III, d. ii, a. 3, q. 2.

[150] *Tractate 3*, q. 3, a. 9, in *TMSM*, IV, 330.

[151] Translations are from *Summa Theologica*, ed. and trans. by Fathers of the English Dominican Province, 3 vols (New York: Benzinger, 1947-48). See Richard Cross, *The Metaphysics of the Incarnation: Thomas Aquinas to Duns Scotus* (Oxford: Oxford University Press, 2005).

He dedicates two questions specifically to Mary's divine motherhood. In the first place he asks whether she can be called Christ's mother in respect of his birth in time. His answer is again based on the claim that although there was a supernatural aspect to Christ's conception it followed the laws of nature other than in the active principle:

> As Damascene says (*De Fide Orth. 3*): 'The temporal nativity by which Christ was born for our salvation is, in a way, natural, since a Man was born of a woman, and after the due lapse of time from His conception: but it is also supernatural, because He was begotten, not of seed, but of the Holy Ghost and the Blessed Virgin, above the law of conception.' Thus, then, on the part of the mother, this nativity was natural, but on the part of the operation of the Holy Ghost it was supernatural. Therefore the Blessed Virgin is the true and natural Mother of Christ. *ST, III, q. 35, a. 3*

In the second answer, as to whether Mary may be rightly called the Mother of God, Aquinas briefly recapitulates what he has just said regarding the hypostatic union (questions 1-19), namely that since the divine nature united to the human nature in the person of Christ at the moment of conception, according to the principle of the communication of idioms Mary is the Mother of God just as she is mother of the man:

> As stated above (Question 16, Article 1), every word that signifies a nature in the concrete can stand for any hypostasis of that nature. Now, since the union of Incarnation took place in the hypostasis, as above stated (2, 3), it is manifest that this word "God" can stand for the hypostasis, having a human and a Divine nature. Therefore whatever belongs to the Divine and to the human nature can be attributed to that Person: both when a word is employed to stand for it, signifying the Divine Nature, and when a word is used signifying the human nature. Now, conception and birth are attributed to the person and hypostasis in respect of that nature in which it is conceived and born. Since, therefore, the human nature was taken by the Divine Person in the very beginning of the conception, as stated above (Question 33, Article 3), it follows that it can be truly said that God was conceived and born of the Virgin. Now from this is a woman called a man's mother, that she conceived him and gave birth to him. Therefore the Blessed Virgin is truly called the Mother of God. For the only way in which it could be denied that the Blessed Virgin is the Mother of God would be either if the humanity were first subject to conception and birth, before this man were the Son of God, as Photinus said; or if the humanity were not assumed unto unity of the Person or hypostasis of the Word of God, as Nestorius maintained. But both of these are erroneous. Therefore it is heretical to deny that the Blessed Virgin is the Mother of God *ST, III, q. 35, a.4*

Appropriately it is with Aquinas, the greatest theologian that the Middle Ages produced, that we end our survey of the doctrine of Mary's divine motherhood. In the centuries to come many new challenges would face the *Theotokos* and new scientific discoveries would show that Aquinas's Aristotelian understanding of the processes of generation was fatally flawed, but this did not alter the theological fundamentals of his argument which ultimately boils down one question: was Mary truly the Mother of the God-man, Jesus of Nazareth? For those who would uphold the orthodox teaching of the Church, firmly rooted in Scripture and Tradition, Mary's motherhood of God has remained the greatest guarantee of the truth that is Jesus. To deny that Mary is the *Theotokos* is to deny the very essence of Christianity, that God became man in order to unite humanity to and in himself.

Chapter 2 – Virginity

Genesis 3. 16:	I will multiply thy sorrows, and thy conceptions: in sorrow shalt thou bring forth children.
Isaiah 7. 14:	Therefore the Lord himself shall give you a sign. Behold a virgin shall conceive, and bear a son, and his name shall be called Emmanuel.
Isaiah 66. 7:	Before she was in labour, she brought forth; before her time came to be delivered, she brought forth a man child.
Matthew 1. 18-23:	Now the generation of Christ was in this wise. When as his mother Mary was espoused to Joseph, before they came together, she was found with child, of the Holy Ghost. Whereupon Joseph her husband, being a just man, and not willing publicly to expose her, was minded to put her away privately. But while he thought on these things, behold the angel of the Lord appeared to him in his sleep, saying: Joseph, son of David, fear not to take unto thee Mary thy wife, for that which is conceived in her, is of the Holy Ghost. [...] Now all this was done that it might be fulfilled which the Lord spoke by the prophet, saying: Behold a virgin shall be with child, and bring forth a son, and they shall call his name Emmanuel, which being interpreted is, God with us.
Matthew 1. 25	And he knew her not till she brought forth her firstborn son
Luke 1. 26-35:	And in the sixth month, the angel Gabriel was sent from God into a city of Galilee, called Nazareth, to a virgin espoused to a man whose name was Joseph, of the house of David; and the virgin's name was Mary. [...] And the angel said to her: Fear not, Mary, for thou hast found grace with God. Behold thou shalt conceive in thy womb, and shalt bring forth a son. [...] And Mary said to the angel: How shall this be done, because I know not man? And the angel answering, said to her: The Holy Ghost shall come upon thee, and the power of the most High shall overshadow thee.

IN this chapter we shall consider the doctrinal issues surrounding Mary's triple virginity, before, during and after the birth of Christ. The first and most fundamental aspect of Mary's virginity is her conception of Jesus without human intercourse (*virginitas ante partum*), which we have already partially considered in the previous chapter, where we saw that, from the very dawn of the Church, the exact nature of the conception was the subject of passionate debate because it was only by defending the idea that Christ had been conceived without human intercourse, while taking on a truly human nature from the Virgin, that he could be shown to be both fully God and fully man. Here we shall examine the doctrine purely from the perspective of the arguments put forward in favour of the virginal conception.[1] The second doctrine concerns the preservation of Mary's virginity at the birth of Christ, the *virginitas in partu* or virgin birth. That Christ was born without depriving Mary of her virginity is considered both a sign of the divine origin of her child and a consequence of the purity of her conception, which allowed her to avoid the curse of suffering in childbirth (Genesis 3. 16) laid on Eve and all women as a result of original sin. Belief in the *virginitas in partu* was already a prominent feature in the Church from at least the early second century, as is evidenced by the *Protoevangelium of St James* and other apocryphal texts, and, since its formal adoption in 649, has continued to be a binding doctrine to this day in the Catholic Church.[2] The third aspect of Mary's virginity is her *virginitas post partum*, or perpetual virginity. Here it is the fittingness of the Mother of God having had normal marital relations after she had become the sacred vessel of divinity that is at issue, rather than any fundamental matter of doctrine.

Virginal Conception

Unusually for Marian doctrines, which are generally extra-testamentary, the Lucan narrative of the birth of Jesus leaves relatively little room for ambiguity on the question of Mary's virginal conception of Christ.[3] The Lucan text speaks of the angel Gabriel coming to a *parthenos*, corresponding to the Hebrew *bethulah*. While the Hebrew term could mean either 'virgin' or 'young woman', a contextual reading would seem to militate against the latter interpretation.[4] Indeed, Mary

---

[1] For the almost infinite bibliography on Mary's virginity see the relevant headings in Michael O'Carroll, *Theotokos: A Theological Encyclopedia of the Blessed Virgin Mary* (Collegeville, Minnesota: Liturgical Press, 1982). The question of possible cultural and societal influences on Mary's image as a virgin, and her role in promoting the ascetic ideal of virginity are discussed in vol. 2.

[2] The doctrine was officially proclaimed by the First Lateran Council, in 649 which spoke of Mary giving birth 'without loss of integrity' and of her having 'preserved her virginity inviolate'. See below for further discussion. For an overview of Patristic views on Mary's virginity see Georges Joussard, 'Marie à travers la patristique, maternité divine, virginité, sainteté', in *Maria* 1, 69-157. Also useful is Angelo Amato, 'Il concepimento verginale di Gesù: introduzione a una "quaestio disputata', *Theotokos*, 3, (1995), 89-103. See also the thorough treatment by Gabriele M. Roschini, *Maria Santissima nella storia della salvezza*, vol. III, part II, *Il dogma mariano* (Isola del Liri: Pisani, 1969), pp. 338-448.

[3] See Jean-François Baudoz, '"Marie, de laquelle est né Jésus" (Mt 1, 16): La virginité de Marie dans la tradition synoptique', in *La virginité de Marie: Communications présentées à la 53e Session de la Société française d'études mariales*, Issoudun, septembre 1997, ed. by Jean Longère (Paris: Médiaspaul, 1998), pp. 9-23, and in the same volume René Laurentin, 'Singularité significative des textes sur la virginité de Marie et leur omniprésence dans le Nouveau Testament', pp. 35-51.

[4] See Mary F. Foskett, *A Virgin Conceived: Mary and Classical Representations of Virginity* (Bloomington: University of Indiana Press, 2002), particularly pp. 16-20 and 25-9. See

herself declares that she has no knowledge of man whereupon the angel explains that her conception will come about through the power of God, the overshadowing of the Most High (Luke 1. 26-35). We also have the Matthean account of the angel appearing to Joseph to reassure him that the conception of the child is through the work of the Holy Spirit (Matthew 1. 18-23).

For the Christians of the early Church, still closely bound to their Judaic origins, the witness of the Old Testament was equally crucial to that of the New, since it offered proof the Jesus truly was the Messiah foretold by the prophets. The prophecy of Isaiah concerning the virgin who would give birth (7. 14) was the most essential proof, both of Mary's virginity and Christ's divine origin, given that it is mentioned by Matthew himself (1. 23). However, this claim was disputed by the Jews who argued that the Hebrew referred to a 'young woman' (*almah*) not a virgin, and that the sign was purely historical, referring to king Ahaz, who was threatened by enemies and whom Isaiah was seeking to persuade to place his trust in the Lord.[5] To this the early Fathers replied that a normal birth would not constitute a 'sign' from the Lord, but that the virginal conception of Mary was just such a sign. A further essential element in the defence of Mary's virginity was the use of Old Testament types such as the burning bush that was not consumed (Exodus 3. 2), the closed gate (Ezekiel 44. 1-3), the stone cut from the mountain without human hands (Daniel 2. 34-35), etc., which we consider separately in Volume 2. A final and crucial way in which the Old Testament was linked to the New, from the time of Justin Martyr (†c. 165) onwards, was the antithesis between Eve, who had allowed herself to be seduced by the devil, and Mary, who had preserved her virginity even while conceiving.

Turning to extra-testamentary sources, virginity is central to the narrative of the second-century apocryphal *Protoevangelium of St. James*, which played a crucial role in promoting Mary's triple virginity. Unlike the canonical texts, the *Protoevangelium* offers a description of Mary's unique sanctity and purity since childhood as well as providing a detailed account of the events surrounding the Annunciation.[6] It is also here that we find the first testimony to the virgin birth

---

also, for a discussion of the Greek understanding of *parthenos*, Giulia Sissa, *Greek Virginity*, trans. by Arthur Goldhammer (Cambridge, Mass.: Harvard University Press, 1990). See also Peter Brown, 'The Notion of Virginity in the Early Church', in *Christian Spirituality: Origins to the Twelfth Century*, ed. by Bernard McGinn and John Meyendorff, World Spirituality, 16 (New York, Crossroads, 1989), pp. 427-43.

[5] The bibliography on the subject is immense. See Adam Kamesar, 'The Virgin of Isaiah 7:14: The Philological Argument from the Second to the Fifth Century', *Journal of Theological Studies*, 41 (1990), 51-75, J. Coppens 'La prophétie de la "Almah", Is vii: 14-17', *Ephemerides Theologicae Lovanienses*, 28 (1952), 648-78, and P. G Dunker, 'Our Lady in the Old Testament – II', in *The Mother of the Redeemer: Aspects of Doctrine and Devotion*, ed. by Kevin McNamara (Dublin: Gill, 1959), pp. 13-29, among others.

[6] Quotations are from Ronald F. Hock, *The Infancy Gospels of James and Thomas* (Santa Rosa: Polebridge Press, 1995), in *Gospels.net* < http://www.gospels.net/translations/

as well as the first mention of Joseph having had children by a previous marriage, thus offering an explanation for the 'brothers' of Jesus (Matthew 12. 46-50 and 13. 55; Mark 3. 31-35; Luke 8. 19-21).

The *Protoevangelium* tells of how Mary's parents brought her to the temple at the age of three where she remained until her betrothal to Joseph at the age of twelve (7-8). The process whereby Joseph is chosen to be her husband, in which all the widowers are instructed to bring a staff or rod to the temple, with Joseph's rod miraculously producing a dove (8-9), is intended to echo the miraculous events surrounding Old Testament rods such as those of Aaron and Jesse, both of which were interpreted as prophecies of the virginal conception.[7] The *Protoevangelium* also recounts how the high priest calls for the 'pure virgins from the tribe of David' to make a curtain for the temple. Among those chosen is Mary, who is described as 'pure before God'. Later, after the angel has appeared to Mary, Joseph discovers her pregnancy and is devastated. He declares: 'Has not the story of Adam been repeated with me? For while Adam was glorifying God, the serpent came and found Eve alone and deceived and defiled her – so it has also happened to me' (13). Mary vehemently denies Joseph's accusations and that night and angel appears to him confirming Mary's story. However, when the high priest discovers what has happened he accuses Joseph of having violated the trust bestowed upon him, and forces both Mary and Joseph to undergo the so-called water test, in which a suspected sinner was required to drink 'the water of the Lord's wrath' and then go out into the desert. If the person returned unharmed then he or she was innocent. Both Joseph and

---

infancyjamestranslation.html> [accessed 5 October 2007]. See the thorough analysis in his 'Introduction'. For an alternative English translation of the text see *The Apocryphal New Testament: A Collection of Apocryphal Christian Literature in an English Translation*, ed. by James K. Elliott (Oxford: The Clarendon Press, 1993), pp. 48-67, and by the same author, 'Mary in the Apocryphal New Testament' in *The Origins of the Cult of the Virgin Mary*, ed. by Chris Maunder (London: Burns & Oats, 2008), pp. 57-70. See also Mary Clayton, *The Apocryphal Gospels of Mary in Anglo Saxon England* (Cambridge: Cambridge University Press, 1998), especially pp. 1-23 for a comprehensive discussion of the infancy gospels and their origins, Mary F. Foskett, *A Virgin Conceived*, pp. 142-64, Edouard Cothenet, 'La virginité de Marie dans les Apocryphes', in *La virginité de Marie: Communications présentées à la 53e Session de la Société française d'études mariales*, pp. 53-69, Hans Josef Klauck, *Apocryphal Gospels: An Introduction* (London: Clark, 2003), Lorenzo M. Perotto, 'La Vergine Maria nel pensiero di uno scrittore del secondo secolo: la mariologia del Protevangelo di Giacomo', *Marianum*, 16 (1954), 228-65, Émile de Strycker, *La forme la plus ancienne du Protévangile de Jacques*, Subsidia Hagiographica, 33 (Brussels: Société des Bollandists, 1961), Pieter A. van Stempvoort, 'The Protoevangelium Jacobi: The Sources of its Theme and Style and their Bearing on its Date', in *Studia Evangelica*, III, part II, ed. by Frank L. Cross, TU, 88 (Berlin: Akademie-Verlag, 1959), pp. 413-23, *MF*, pp. 35-42, *Apocrifi del Nuovo Testamento*, ed. by Luigi Moraldi, 3 vols (Milan: UTET, 1994), and *Gli apocrifi del Nuovo Testamento*, ed. by Mario Erbetta, 4 vols (Casale Monferrato: Marietti, 1983).

[7] See Rod, vol. 2.

Mary, naturally, are not touched by their ordeal and the high priest believes in the miraculous nature of the conception (13-16).

The *Protoevangelium* was widely accepted in the Eastern Churches in the early centuries, being cited by Gregory of Nyssa, Origen and others, but far less so in the West.[8] The same events are retold in later apocryphal texts, the most important being *The Gospel of the Pseudo-Matthew*,[9] a Latin rendition of the *Protoevangelium* composed between the sixth and eighth centuries,[10] which had an important influence on the Western Church, though it never achieved the same credibility as the *Protoevangelium* had in the East.

Turning to the Fathers, one of the first proclamations of the doctrine of the virginal conception is by Ignatius of Antioch (†c. 115), who praises the faithful for their firm belief that Jesus was truly, 'the Son of God according to the will and power of God, truly generated of a virgin.'[11] A few decades later Justin Martyr (†c. 165) offers a far more extensive exposition, emphatically rejecting the possibility that Jesus was anything other than fully divine and human, and rallying a number of Old Testament passages in support of the virginal conception, the most important being Isaiah 7. 14 ('Behold a virgin shall conceive, and bear a son,'), Isaiah 11. 1 ('And there shall come forth a rod out of the root of Jesse, and a flower shall rise up out of his root') and Numbers 24. 17 ('A star shall rise up out of Jacob and a sceptre shall spring up from Israel'), all of which thereafter became central planks in the defence of the belief.[12] It is from here that the practice of reading an almost endless variety of Old Testament passages, some decidedly outlandish, as types of the virginal conception grew. Over the centuries these types would become a sort of shorthand, especially in hymns.[13]

Justin also answers the objections of the Jewish Trypho that the correct translation of the Hebrew *almah* should be 'young girl' rather than 'virgin' by

---

[8] See Bertrand Buby, *Mary of Galilee*, 3 vols (New York: Alba House, 1994-1997), III, 35-36.

[9] See *Gospel of the Pseudo-Matthew*, trans. by Alexander Walker, in *The Ante-Nicene Fathers*, ed. by Alexander Roberts and James Donaldson, 10 vols, (Buffalo: The Christian Literature Publishing Company, 1885-96; repr. Grand Rapids, MI.: Eerdmans, 2001), VIII, in *Christian Classics Ethereal Library (CCEL)* <http://www.ccel.org/ccel/schaff/anf08.vii.v.html> [accessed 24 October 2007]. Mary Clayton provides text and translation of an English version of the *Gospel* in *The Apocryphal Gospels*, pp. 151-210. The precise date of *Pseudo-Matthew* is still unclear, with dates proposed being anywhere between the sixth and eighth centuries, though the modern consensus tends towards the latter. See vol. 2 for further discussion and bibliography.

[10] See James K. Elliott, 'Mary in the Apocryphal New Testament', pp. 60-61, and Mary Clayton, *The Cult of the Virgin*, p. 13.

[11] *Epistola ad Smyrnaeos*, 1, PG 5, 708.

[12] *Apologia* I, 32-33 and *Dialogus cum Trypho*, 43.

[13] See Vasiliki Limberis, 'Hymns to Mary the Mother of God the Theotokos', in *Religions of Late Antiquity in Practice*, ed. by Richard Valantasis (Princeton: Princeton University Press, 2000), pp. 357-63.

See the relevant sections on types in vol. 2.

pointing out that the Septuagint, a Greek translation of the Old Testament which was widely accepted among the Jews as having been inspired by God, used the Greek *parthenos* (virgin), and not *neanis* (young girl), another argument that was to become standard fare among the Fathers.[14]

Aside from polemics with the Jews, a further concern was to avoid the idea that Mary's conception was in any way like the stories of parthenogenesis that were not uncommon in Greek and other Eastern mythologies. Justin also tackles the question of apparent parallels with Greek mythology and Mithraism. While acknowledging similarities with pagan mythology – Zeus, Bacchus, Semele – he rejects these stories as the fanciful imaginings of poets or imitations of the prophets inspired by the devil.[15]

Justin was also responsible for inaugurating what was to become one of the central features of discussions on Mary's virginity, namely the Eve-Mary antithesis.[16] Eve, it was believed, had been a virgin prior to the Fall, and Justin suggests that it was through listening to the words of the serpent that she had lost her primordial innocence. Mary, on the other hand, paid heed to the words of the angel and was rewarded with the virginal conception:[17]

> In fact, Eve, when still a virgin and incorrupt, conceived the word of the serpent and gave birth to disobedience and death. Instead, Mary, the Virgin, received faith and joy when the angel Gabriel brought her the happy news that the Spirit of the Lord would come upon her and that the Power of the Most High would overshadow her, and that for this reason the Holy One that was to be born of her would be the Son of God [...]. Through him God annihilates both the serpent and the angels and men who resemble him, and brings about liberation from death for those who convert themselves from their wicked works and believe in him. *Dialogus cum Trypho, 43*[18]

Irenaeus (†c. 202), whose influence on the subsequent evolution of Mariology was far-reaching, considerably developed Justin's idea of the antithesis between Mary and Eve by rooting it in the Pauline notion of recapitulation, that is, that just as Christ was the new Adam (I Corinthians 15), so Mary recapitulated, or reversed, the actions of Eve. It was therefore essential that Mary be a virgin if she were to recapitulate the actions of Eve, who allowed herself to be seduced by the words of the serpent:

> And just as through a disobedient virgin man was stricken down and fell into death, so through the Virgin who was obedient to the Word of God man was

---

[14] See Hilda Graef, *Doctrine and Devotion*, I 37.

[15] *Apologia* I, 21 and 54, *PG* 6, 360 and 408-409; *Dialogus cum Trypho*, 69-70, *PG* 6, 636-641.

[16] Although some would argue that Apocalypse 12 portrays Mary as the new Eve.

[17] For a more extensive discussion on the Eve-Mary antithesis see the chapter on Remote Redemption.

[18] *TMPM*, I, 137. Translations are mine unless otherwise indicated.

> reanimated and received life. [...] For it was necessary that Adam should be summed up in Christ, that mortality might be swallowed up and overwhelmed by immortality; and Eve summed up in Mary, that a virgin should be a virgin's advocate, and by a virgin's obedience undo and put away the disobedience of a virgin. *Demonstratio apostolicae praedicationis, 32-33*[19]

Irenaeus also follows Justin in relying on exegesis of the Old Testament to prove that Mary's virginal conception and birth-giving were foretold by the Prophets, writing at length on Isaiah 7. 14 (LXX). He also gives typological interpretations of passages, such as the stone that detached itself from the mountain without aid of human hands (Daniel 2. 34-35), and the rod of Jesse which, he believes, demonstrate that Christ was born of a virgin.[20]

Tertullian's (†c. 230?) vigorous defence of the virginal conception, which takes up a large part of two of his works, *Contra Marcion* and *De carne Christo*, is typical of the arguments put up against the Gnostic claim that Jesus simply passed through Mary but took nothing from her. His arguments are based partly on Scriptural exegesis – he quotes Isaiah 7. 14 and 11. 1 (the rod of Jesse) among other passages – and partly on a cogent use of logical argument, as the following lines illustrate: 'If he proceeds from God the Father then he certainly does not come from a human father; if not from a human father, what is left is that he proceeds from a human mother; if he is from a human mother it seems clear that he is born of a virgin.'[21] He sets out the nature of Christ's conception with considerable clarity, seeking to cover all possible counter-arguments, and laying the foundation for many later Fathers:

> He who was already the Son of God, generated by the seed of God the Father, that is, by the Spirit, desiring also to become the Son of man, decided to assume flesh from the flesh of mankind, but without man's seed. He who had the seed of God did not need the seed of man. Just as, before his birth of the Virgin, he had God for a Father, without having a human mother, in the same way after being born of the Virgin, he had a woman for a mother without having a human father. In short, he is a man who possessed divinity, since he is human flesh possessing the Spirit of God. His flesh was produced from a human, without human seed; his spirit comes from the seed of God. *De Carne Christi, 18-1-3*[22]

---

[19] Adapted from the translation by J. Armitage Robinson, *The Demonstration of the Apostolic Preaching* (London: Society for Promoting Christian Knowledge; New York: Macmillan, 1920) in *The Tertullian Project* <http://www.tertullian.org/fathers/irenaeus_02_proof.htm> [accessed 5 May 2007]. See also *Adversus Haereses*, 3, 22, 9-10, *PG*, 7, 954-956.

[20] *Adversus Haereses*, 3, 21, 1-2, *PG*, 7, 946-948; 21, 7-9, *PG* 7, 953-954; *Demonstratio apostolicae praedicationis*, 59, *TMPM*, I 180.

[21] *Contra Marcion*, 4, 10, 6, *TMPM*, III, 54-55. See also *De Carne*, 23, *PG* 2, 336 and 411-412.

[22] *PG*, 2, 783A. See *MF*, pp. 64-65.

Tertullian also outlines the argument in favour of the virginal conception on the basis of the Irenaean notion of the Eve-Mary antithesis, again with characteristic clarity:

> In fact, just as the word [of the devil], creator of death, had penetrated into Eve while she was still a virgin, analogously the Word of God, edifier of life, needed to enter into a virgin so that what had been damned might be brought back to salvation by means of the same sex. Eve had believed the serpent; Mary believed Gabriel: the sin that Eve committed in believing was cancelled out by Mary, who believed too. But Eve did not conceive anything in her womb after the words of the devil, it may be objected. No, she did conceive. In fact, the word of the devil was a seed for her: abandoned, she was to give birth in sorrow. And, in fact, she gave birth to the devil, killer of his brother. Instead, Mary gave birth to him who would bring salvation to Israel. *De carne Christi, 17, 5-6*[23]

Clement of Alexandria (†c. 215), while not dealing specifically with the question of Mary's virginal conception, makes it clear that it is beyond discussion when he likens the Church's role as Virgin Mother to that of Mary: 'There is also the Virgin Mother, whom I love to call the Church. [...] She is virgin and mother simultaneously, a virgin undefiled and a mother full of love.'[24]

Origen (†c. 254) mounts one of the most sustained defences of Mary's virginity amongst the early Fathers, both before and after the birth of Christ. He warns the faithful not to heed the Docetists, who would deny the virginal conception, and instead rely on the truth of Scripture: 'Therefore, it is wise to accept the meaning of Scripture and not to pay attention to those who say that [Jesus] was born through Mary, not of her.'[25] The distinction is a crucial one since the former implies that Jesus merely used Mary as a conduit whereas the latter (Greek *ek*, meaning 'from', 'of' or 'out of') makes clear that she was truly his natural mother.

To counter the claims of Celsus, who alleged that Jesus was the illegitimate son of Mary and a Roman soldier, Origen offers arguments based on philosophy, Scripture and reason. On a philosophical level, making reference to Plato, Pythagoras and others, he argues that it would be absurd for someone who had lived a great life, carrying out great deeds, as Jesus did, to have been born in ignominious circumstances; rather to a great soul is given a worthy body. He then turns to Scripture, relying principally on Isaiah 7. 14 to rebut the arguments of the Jews that Jesus was far from being the Messiah born to a virgin. He concludes by addressing the Greeks, arguing that since various animals reproduce parthenogenically, and several Greek myths contain stories

---

[23] *TMPM*, III, 67.

[24] *Paedagogus*, 1, 6, *PG* 8, 300-301. See *MF*, pp. 64-65. See Mary and the Church in vol. 2 for further discussion and see Maria Grazia Bianco, 'Riferimenti mariani in Clemente Alessandrino', *Theotokos*, 10 (2002), 33-42.

[25] *Commentary on the Letter to the Galatians*, *PG*, 14, 1298, *MF*, p. 73.

of asexual reproduction, there is no reason not to believe in the truly miraculous conception of Jesus.[26] He also insists on the necessity of a virginal conception, free from any concupiscence, in order for a perfect union to occur between the divine and the human in the person of Christ.[27] In this he is followed by many later Fathers, most notably Augustine.

Eusebius of Caesarea (†c. 340), considered the most important Eastern Father after Origen, offers the by now standard interpretation of Isaiah 7. 14, declaring that the virginal conception 'will be an extraordinary miracle amongst men, a sign never heard of in any generation.'[28] Anticipating the belief that Virgil had prophesised the coming of Christ, which was to become widespread in the Middle Ages, he turns to the fourth *Eclogue* when addressing Constantine on Mary's virginity:

> The great line of centuries begins anew: Now the Virgin returns, the reign of Saturn returns' (*Eclogues*, 4, 5-6). Who, then is that virgin who returns? Is she not perhaps the one who was full and pregnant with the Holy Spirit? What is there to prevent her from being pregnant of the Holy Spirit and remaining still a maiden and a virgin? *Oratio de Laudibus Constantini, 19, 5-6*[29]

Athanasius of Alexandria († 373) offers a variety of arguments in favour of the virginal conception, especially against the Arians, affirming that the prophets of the Old Testament, especially Isaiah (7. 14), had foretold the manner of her generation: 'From the beginning the prophets predicted the marvel of the Virgin and the Son that would be born of her: "Behold a virgin shall be with child, and bring forth a son, and they shall call his name Emmanuel, which being interpreted is, God with us" (Matthew 1. 23).'[30]

Ephrem († c. 373) also defends Mary's virginity: 'With Your pure conception / evil men have slandered me. O Holy One, / be Your Mother's defender. Show miracles / to convince them whence your conception.'[31] He launches into a long explanation of the use of the genealogy of Joseph instead of Mary for Jesus, justifying it on the basis that it was 'for the glory of the race of David' that the male line was used.[32] He goes on to quote from a variety of Old and New Testament passages in order to prove that Mary too was of the line of David. Further on in the same text he cautions against confusion with pagan myths

---

[26] See *Contra Celsus*, I, 34-37, *PG*, 725-733, *TMPM*, I, 200-204.

[27] *Peri Archon (Treatise on First Principles)*, 2, 6, 5-6, *PG* 11, 214. See *MF*, p. 75.

[28] *Commentaria in Isaiam*, 7, 14, *TMPM*, I, 251.

[29] *PG* 20, 1291B.

[30]*De Incarnazione*, 33, *PG* 25, 153A. See also *Oratio 2, 7, PG* 26, 161. See Michel Aubineau, 'Les écrits de S. Athanase sur la virginité', *Revue d'Ascétique et Mystique*, 31 (1955), 140-71.

[31] *Hymns on the Nativity*, 6, 3, translated by Kathleen McVey, *Ephrem the Syrian: Hymns* (New York: Paulist Press, 1989), p. 33.

[32] *Diatesseron*, 1, 25.

which also spoke of unions between the gods and mortals, pointing out that the crucial difference is that Jesus was not conceived through carnal relations:

> 'Now the generation of Christ was in this wise. When his Mother Mary was espoused to Joseph, before they came together, she was found with child' (Matthew 1. 18). The evangelist did not say this as if it were an ordinary fact. The pagans imagine in their legends that their gods were subject to shameful passions and to the procreation of children that is not in conformity to their nature. So that you might not imagine a story of this sort, the evangelist adds: 'with child of the Holy Ghost.' Jesus was not born of a carnal union; therefore, because of his holy conception, the way of chastity was opened, so that it would live in everybody. That Mary was betrothed, that she received her name from a man and that, after this, she conceived, all came about because of the lineage of kings. It was not possible to enrol the child in a genealogy that bore the name of his Mother. Instead, the son of David was placed in the list of kings. *Diatesseron, 2, 1*[33]

For Basil the Great († 379) Mary was chosen to be the Mother of God because of her virginity:

> Since the humanity of that time had nothing to equal Mary's purity, as to be able to accommodate the working of the Holy Spirit, but was totally constrained by marriage, the Blessed Virgin was chosen since her virginity was totally uncontaminated by marriage. *Homilia in sanctum Christi generationem, 3*[34]

Rather unusually, he suggests that one of the reasons why God chose to be born of a married virgin was in order to affirm the righteousness of both states, though he makes it clear that virginity is the higher calling.

Gregory of Nyssa († c. 394) relies heavily on Isaiah in his defence of Mary's virginal motherhood:

> Hear Isaiah crying out: 'A child is born for us; a Son is given to us' (Isaiah 9. 6). Learn from the prophet how the baby was born, how the son is given. Was it according to the law of nature? The prophet denies it. The Master of nature does not obey the laws of nature. But how is the child born? Tell me. The prophet answers: 'Behold, the virgin shall conceive in her womb and bear a son, and they shall call him Emmanuel' (Isaiah 7. 14), which, translated, means: God with us. *On the Birth of Christ*[35]

He goes on to cite the burning bush as another sign that God would enter into the world without damaging Mary's virginity.

Cyril of Jerusalem (†c. 397) draws on Genesis in his rebuttal of those who deny the possibility that Christ could have been born of a virgin. Answering the

---

[33] *TMPM*, IV, 81.
[34] *PG* 31, 1464B-C, *MF*, p. 146.
[35] *MF*, pp. 154-55.

objections of the Jews, he notes that Adam was made from the earth and Eve from his rib, so there is no reason why they should not believe that Christ was conceived without the seed of a man. As to the Greeks, he points out that it is far more reasonable to believe in the virginal conception than to claim that Bacchus was born from the thigh of Jupiter.[36] Interestingly, he links Mary's virginity to that of the priesthood:[37]

> It was fitting, then, that the most Pure One, the Teacher of purity, should have his origin in a pure nuptial chamber. Given that those who hold the office of the priesthood under Jesus abstain from women, how could the same Jesus have been born of a man and a woman? *Catechesis, 12, 25*[38]

Cyril also uses the Eve-Mary antithesis in proof of Mary's virginity: 'Through the virgin Eve death came in; it was necessary that life should come by means of, or rather, of a virgin, so that just as the serpent tricked the one, to the other Gabriel might bring the joyful announcement.'[39]

Ambrose of Milan († 397), a contemporary of Cyril's, also argues that only a virginal conception was fitting for the Son of God and the manner of his conception and birth is itself a sign of his divine origin:[40]

> What generation according to the flesh could be more fitting for God than this one, in which the immaculate Son of God, even in assuming a body, should maintain the purity of the immaculate generation? Surely the sign of the divine event consists in his being born of a virgin, and not in his being born of a woman. *Expositio in Lucam, 2, 78*[41]

According to Ambrose, Mary's virginal conception is a sign of the divine origin of her child. Mary herself was not unaware of this since, he suggests, she would have been familiar with the prophecy of Isaiah:

> Such an incredible and unheard-of birth needed to be announced to her before it could be believed. A virgin giving birth is the sign of a divine mystery, not a human one. And so he says: 'Let this be a sign for you: Behold, the virgin can conceive in her womb and bear a son' (Isaiah 7. 14). Mary had read this passage; therefore, she believed that the prophecy would come true, but she could not have read about how it would happen. *Expositio in Lucam, 2, 15*[42]

---

[36] *Catechesis*, 12, 25-30, *TMPM*, I, 362-63.

[37] See Mary and the Eucharist, vol. 2.

[38] discussion on *TMPM*, I, 361. See also *MF*, pp. 137-38.

[39] *Catechesis*, 12, 15, *PG* 33, 741, *TMPM*, I, 359.

[40] See Goulvan Madec, 'Marie, Vierge et Mère selon saint Ambrose et saint Augustin', in *La virginité de Marie: Communications présentées à la 53e Session de la Société française d'études mariales*, pp. 71-84

[41] *PL* 15, 1581B. See also *De institutione virginis*, 44, *PL* 16, 317 [331].

[42] *PL* 15, 1639, *MF*, p. 192.

Epiphanius of Salamis († 403) employs a variety of arguments in rejecting the claim that Jesus was not truly born of a human mother. He notes, as had others before him, that Gabriel does not speak of Jesus being generated *in* Mary, but *of* (*ek*) her (Luke 1. 35) in order to show that he came from her according to nature. He also believes that the episode that Luke recounts of a woman who cries out to Jesus, 'Blessed is the womb that bore thee, and the paps that gave thee suck' (Luke 11. 27), shows that Mary was truly his Mother, since it would be impossible for a virgin who had not given birth to produce milk.[43] Epiphanius also rallies the standard Old Testament passages, such as Genesis 3. 16 and most particularly Isaiah 7. 14, which were by now universally accepted as prophecies of the virginal conception.[44]

John Chrysostom († 407), in the face of Jewish scepticism regarding the virginal conception, argues that if God could cause Isaac's wife, Rebecca, to conceive when she was sterile, then there is no reason to deny the possibility that he caused the Virgin to conceive. Imagining the conversation at the Annunciation, he has Gabriel tell Mary not to try to understand how the Incarnation will take place since it does not conform to the natural order. 'Indeed', the angel proclaims, 'if you had known man, you would not have been considered worthy.' Not, he goes on to say, because marriage is an evil, but because virginity is superior, and it was necessary that Christ's entry into the world be more majestic than ours. Moreover, by being born like us, Christ showed his equality to us, while, by being conceived without marital union, he showed that he was also of a higher order.[45] In his *Commentary on Isaiah*, he argues that Mary would not have been 'a sign' (Isaiah 7. 14) if she had not been a virgin, since the conception had to supersede the natural order: 'The sign, in fact, has to go beyond the common order of things, exceed the natural course of nature and be new and extraordinary to the point of proposing itself as a distinctive sign for everyone who sees it or hears tell of it.'[46] Chrysostom also uses the Eve-Mary antithesis: 'A virgin caused us to be expelled from Paradise; through a Virgin we found eternal life. Because of those things we were condemned; because of these ones we have been crowned.'[47]

Severian of Gabala († after 408) writes in a similar vein: 'Christ came, he who loosens the chains, and he was met by the Genetrix of the Lord, who defended her sex, the holy Virgin in place of the virgin – in fact Eve was a virgin before sinning – she took away the suffering and groaning of the one who was condemned.'[48]

Jerome († 419) is the most polemical of the Latin Fathers in his defence of Mary's virginity, addressing Jovinian and Helvidius, two fourth-century heretics

---

[43] *Adversus haereses*, 77, 7, PG 42, 649C-D, TMPM, I, 390.
[44] See *Ancoratus*, 32, PG 43, 76A-B, TMPM, I, 373-74.
[45] See *Commentary on Genesis*, 49, 3, TMPM, I, 409.
[46] 7, 5, PG 50, 84, TMPM, 414.
[47] *Commentary on the Psalms*, 44, 7, PG 55, 193, TMPM, I, 409.
[48] *Homily on the Creation of the World*, 4, 10, PG 56, 497, TMPM, I, 427.

who denied the perpetual virginity, with barely disguised venom. His over-zealous opinions on the superiority of virginity over marriage are rather off-putting and have led some to dismiss his writings. Nevertheless, he was a Biblical scholar without equal in the early Church, who knew both Greek and Hebrew, and tackles the question of the meaning of *almah* with considerable authority:

> I know that the Jews are in the habit of objecting that the Hebrew word *almah* does not mean virgin but young woman. And, in effect, virgins are properly called *bethulah*, yet a young girl or maid is not called *almah* but *naara*. So then, what precisely is the meaning of *almah*? It means 'hidden virgin', that is, not only virgin but virgin with *epitasei* [vehemence of emphasis], because not all virgins are hidden and remove themselves from the casual glances of men. Besides, in Genesis, Rebecca, because of her great chastity and her being a type of the Church, a typology that she incarnated in her virginity, is called *almah* and not *bethula*. *Adversus Jovinianum, 1, 32*[49]

In upholding Mary's virginal conception, he deploys a wide range of Old Testament texts, including Isaiah 7. 14,[50] the closed gate of Ezekiel 44, the 'light could' of Psalm 78. 14 and Isaiah 19. 1, which he likens to Mary, 'who was not weighed down by any manly seed', the flower and the lily of Canticles 2. 1, and so on. Jerome also addresses the question of why the angel appeared to Mary when she was already betrothed to Joseph, and not when she was still unquestionably a virgin:

> If anyone is confused by the fact that the Virgin conceived when she was an engaged woman, and not as a maiden who had no fiancé and was not married, as Scripture says, let him know that there are three reasons for this. First, through the genealogy of Joseph, to whom Mary was related, her ancestry is also revealed. The second reason was so that she would not be stoned by people as an adulteress, according to the law of Moses. The third reason is so that, during the flight into Egypt, she would have the comfort of a guardian rather than a husband. *Adversus Helvidium, 4*[51]

Augustine († 430), who believed that original sin was passed on through the inherent concupiscence of carnal relations, laid great emphasis on Mary's virginal conception since any other sort of conception would, in his opinion, imply that Jesus inherited a sinful nature:

> Neither was carnal concupiscence involved, which is responsible for the seed and conception of all other men, heirs to original sin, but absolutely free from it [concupiscence], holy virginity was made fertile by faith and not by joining

---

[49] *PL* 23, 254C-D.
[50] See Francesco Pieri, 'Il concepimento verginale e l'argomento biblico di Is. 7. 14 nell'esegisi di Girolamo, tra polemica ed apologia', *Theotokos*, 11 (2003), 363-84.
[51] *PG* 23, 187, *MF*, p. 214.

together. As a consequence, he who was born of the stock of the first man took on only his human nature and not his fault. *De Trinitate, 13, 18, 23*[52]

In addition, both the virginal conception and birth were proof of God's omnipotence and the divine origin of the child:

> And just as the universe has need of him who remains with the Father, so he who comes to us has need of a Virgin. In fact, the Virgin Mother was the proof of his omnipotence: virgin before his conception, virgin after his birth; found to be pregnant without having been made such by a man; pregnant with child without the intervention of a man, all the more blessed and more unique for having received the gift of fruitfulness without losing her integrity. *Sermo 184, 1*

Moreover, had Christ not been a virgin born of a virgin the Church could not have become his bride. Indeed God anticipated the virginity of the Church by preserving Mary's virginity:

> Christ, who was to reconstitute virginity in the heart of the Church, first conserved it in the body of Mary. In human marriage the woman is given to her husband and loses her virginity; the Church, instead, could not be a virgin had the Bridegroom to whom she is given not been the Son of a virgin. *Sermo 188, 4*

Like Cyril of Jerusalem, he argues that there is no reason why God should not have become incarnate from a woman without the seed of a man since the same God created woman from the rib of Adam.[53]

Another Latin Father, Peter Chrysologus († 451), imagines Joseph's puzzlement in the face of the miracle of the virginal conception:

> His bride was pregnant but a virgin; she was full of promise but not empty of chastity; she was troubled by the conception that had taken place, yet felt sure of her own integrity. She was clothed in her maternal role but not despoiled of the honor of virginity. What should her husband do in such a situation? Accuse her of a crime? But he himself was the witness of her innocence. Reveal her sin? But he himself was the guardian of her good reputation. Charge her with adultery? But her himself was the asserter of her virginity. *Sermo 145, 9*[54]

---

[52] All translations, unless otherwise indicated, are from the Latin and Italian texts in S. Aurelii Augustini, *Opera Omnia, Tutte le opere*, ed. by Franco Monteverde, 45 vols (Rome: Nuova Biblioteca Agostiniana and Città Nuova, 1967–), in *Sant'Agostino, Augustinus Hipponensis*, < http://www.augustinus.it/> [accessed 12 June 2008].
[53] See *De Genesi ad Litteram*, 9, 16, 30.
[54] *PL* 52, 588-589, *MF*, 295.

In the same sermon he declares that Mary's triple virginity is a sign that her conception came about through divine means and cannot be explained by the logic of the philosophers.[55]

With the Councils of Ephesus (431) and Chalcedon (451) debate within the Church regarding the virginal motherhood reached a high watermark.[56] Though it would still prove necessary to combat a variety of heresies that would arise in the coming centuries, most were essentially new manifestations of old controversies, so that on the whole, theologians, exegetes and homilists contented themselves with rehearsing arguments that had been put forward by earlier Fathers.

Theodoret of Cyrrhus († 466), last of the great Antiochene theologians and a central figure in the disputes on the hypostasis that dominated the fifth century, defends orthodox teaching on the virginal conception against a variety of heresies, such as those of Arius, Eunomius, and Apollinaris,[57] though he himself was a figure of controversy because of his refusal to refute fully the teachings of Nestorius and his opposition to Cyril of Alexandria.[58]

Pope Leo the Great († 461) repeatedly affirms the virginal conception while at the same time stressing that this in no way means that Christ had anything less than a fully human nature, as the Monophysites claimed: 'He was engendered through a new kind of birth, since the inviolate virginity did not know concupiscence when it supplied the fleshly material [of his body]. From his Mother, the Lord took [human] nature, not the original fault.'[59] He also argues that it was necessary for Christ to be born of a virgin so that he would be entirely free of any contamination of sin:

> Therefore he was born through a new birth. Because he was conceived by a virgin and born of a virgin without the concourse of carnal concupiscence of a father and without damage to the integrity of the Mother; such origins befitted the future Saviour of mankind, destined to have the nature of human substance in himself, without undergoing the contamination of human flesh. *Sermo 2, 2*[60]

---

[55] For a fuller discussion of Peter's teaching on Mary's virginity see Boguslaw Kochaniewicz, 'Il concepimento e il parto verginale di Maria nella riflessione teologica di san Pietro Crisologo', *Theotokos*, 12 (2004), 197-214.

[56] See chapter on Divine Motherhood.

[57] Eunomius argued that there could be no essential resemblance between God and his creation and therefore no possibility of a dual nature in Christ. He also argued for the utter simplicity of the Godhead, thus denying the doctrine of the Trinity, a position even the Arians regarded as extreme. Apollinaris denied that Christ had a rational human soul.

[58] See *De Incarnatione Domini*, PG 75, 1419-1478, the *Eranistes*, PG 83, 27-336, and the *Haereticarum fabulorum compendium*, PG 83, 335-556. For an English translation of the *Eranistes*, see Gerard H. Ettlinger, *Theodoret of Cyrus: Eranistes* (Oxford: The Clarendon Press, 1975). Selections in Italian are to be found in *TMPM*, I, 585-93. On Cyril's thought see *The Theology of St. Cyril of Alexandria: A Critical Appreciation*, ed. by Thomas G. Weinandy and Daniel A. Keating (London: Clark, 2003).

[59] *Epistola 28, 2, PL* 54, 759, *MF*, p. 305.

[60] *PL* 54, 195A-B.

Jacob of Serug († 521) defends Mary's virginal conception, her *virginitas in partu* and *post partum* against all comers – Jews, pagans, and heretics:

> From those near and far she receives calumnies; by the Jews and the Gentiles her praise is wounded. Strangers gossip about her as do domestics, and according to taste friends and enemies talk about her. Indeed, the Jews censure her [saying] that her conception was not of the Father, that she neither conceived nor gave birth in her virginity, and that the Son who lives in her is not the Power of the hidden Father. Natives, who are far [from God] do not know that she gave birth, nor do they know that she existed and that the Blessed One had a Son. Another fool, who is neither a Jew nor a native, spread gossip that the body of the Son does not come from her. A wicked man denies that she gave birth to God, but that [she gave birth to] the Messiah, since the Messiah is not God. [...] Arise, doctrine and announce the truth without anxiety, openly proclaim the truth which is superior to the dissensions. *Homily on the Holy Generatrix of God and Perpetual Virgin Mary*[61]

He goes on to defend Mary's virginity with a variety of arguments, including Old Testament passages such as Isaiah 7. 14 and Ezekiel 44. Like Cyril of Jerusalem and others, in refuting the Jews he asks the rhetorical question of whether it was more difficult for God to cause Adam to give life to Eve or Mary to conceive without male seed.[62] The basic message of the sermon is that Mary's virginity constitutes a proof and a guarantee of the divinity of Christ.

Severus of Antioch († 538), who adhered to the Monophysite belief that Christ's human nature was subsumed into his divinity, is nonetheless a firm defender of Mary's virgin motherhood. Indeed, he believes that the Virgin is the guarantor of orthodoxy and celebrates her victory over those who claim that Christ was human only in appearance:

> They say that Christ came rather in appearance; that the actual Emmanuel did not, in reality, become man, thus contradicting the divine books and the holy book of the Gospel, according to which the holy Virgin, appearing as the instrument of the divine humanisation, destroyed, all the fiction of their chattering. *Homily 14, In Memory of the Holy Mother of God, 11*[63]

Romanos the Melodist (†c. 560) lists off a variety of Old Testament typologies that he imagines Joseph using in defence of Mary's virginal conception in the opening verse of his *Second Hymn on the Annunciation*: 'Thinking, however, of the rain on the fleece / of the bush that the fire did not consume / of the rod of Aaron that flowered / your spouse and custodian,

---

[61] *TMPM*, IV, 167. For an English translation of Jacob's Marian sermons see Mary Hansbury, *Jacob of Serug on the Mother of God* (Crestwood, N.Y.: St. Vladimir's, 1998).
[62] See *Homilies against the Jews*, 1, *TMPM*, IV, 186.
[63] *TMPM*, I, 644.

bearing witness, declared to the priests: / "The Virgin gives birth and remains a virgin after the birth.'"[64] In his celebrated *Kontakion on the Nativity of Christ* Romanos also asserts both the virginal conception and the virgin birth:

> Tell me, my Child, how were you sown,
> or how were you planted in me?
> I see you, my flesh and blood, and I am amazed,
> because I give suck and yet I am not married.
> And though I see you in swaddling clothes,
> I know that the flower of my virginity is sealed,
> for you preserved it when, in your good pleasure, you were born
> a little Child, God before the ages. *2, 4-10*[65]

A homily attributed to Anastasius of Antioch († 599) affirms the three aspects of Mary's virginity, before, during and after the birth of Christ:

> You conceived without any relationship with a man; you gave birth without being married; you alone are at the same time both Mother and Virgin. In fact, neither did your giving birth exclude your virginity nor did your conception take away your integrity. You kept the treasure of your virginity inviolate even after the birth. *Second Homily on the Annunciation, 2*[66]

Sophronius of Jerusalem († 638), a vigorous defender of the orthodox position on the hypostatic union, writes at length on Mary's divine motherhood and virginal conception. In an imagined dialogue between Mary and Gabriel at the Annunciation, he has the angel reassure Mary that her conception will be unlike any other, since this is within God's power:

> God is he who can will everything. Who can oppose the decrees of God? Therefore, though all women who become mothers always have conjugal relations prior to motherhood, you, since this is the will of God, will become a mother, but nevertheless you will be, and will remain a virgin, because it will be God who will preserve you. *Homily on the Annunciation, 35*[67]

Isidore of Seville († 636), whose writings had a major influence on the Medieval West,[68] asserts both the virginal conception and birth, with such Old Testament prophecies as Isaiah 7. 14[69] and uses typologies such as the 'closed

---

[64] *TMPM*, I, 702.

[65] The full text is reproduced in *On the Life of Christ: Kontakia*, trans. by Ephrem Lash, (Harper Collins: San Francisco, 1995), pp. 1-12.

[66] *TMPM*, II, 77.

[67] *TMPM*, II, 152.

[68] See Felipe Mariscal Chávez, *María en las obras de San Isidoro de Sevilla* (Rome: Marianum, 1991).

[69] See *De fide catholica contra Judaeos*, 1, 10, 4, *PL 83*, 468B-C.

garden' the 'sealed fountain', and Daniel's mountain. In a comment on Mary's conversation with Gabriel he affirms both, emphasising the importance of her virginity through repetition:

> Holy Virgin, pregnant Virgin, Virgin before giving birth, Virgin after giving birth. She received the angel's greeting and knew the mystery of the conception; she asked for details of how the birth would come about; and she did not withhold the obedience of faith. *De ortu et obitu Patrum, 111*[70]

It should be noted that in both these authors, as in many of the Church Fathers, Mary is by no means a passive agent in the events leading up to the Incarnation: she questions the angel, and it is only after he has given a satisfactory explanation that she makes an act of faith and assents to God's plan. It is not God who imposes his will on her but she who freely chooses virginity and motherhood.

Leontius of Neapolis (†c. 650) offers a different angle in upholding both the virginal conception and the virgin birth, pointing out that God is not subject to the Law, which constituted the highest authority for the Jews: 'But the Legislator does not subject himself to the Law: his delivery goes beyond human law just as his birth is without the seed of man.'[71]

The three great Eastern Fathers of the late Patristic period, Germanus of Constantinople, Andrew of Crete, and John of Damascus employ a variety of strategies in their defence of Mary's virginity. Germanus († 319) uses the rather unusual strategy of creating an imagined dialogue between Mary and the angel Gabriel, followed by a tense discussion with a very upset Joseph, to make his point. The text relies heavily on the apocrypha, portraying Joseph as an old man and mentioning such details as the Mary's sojourn in the Temple as a child, her familiarity with angels, and the miracle of the rod whereby Joseph was chosen to be her guardian. In the conversation with Gabriel, Mary is extremely guarded and repeatedly asks him to leave because she is not accustomed to being alone in the company of a male. She is very reluctant to accept his message and questions him at length about how she can become a mother when she is a virgin before finally accepting. The dialogue with Joseph, who has returned to find Mary pregnant, is equally drawn out. Gently but firmly Joseph tells her that she must leave his house and go to her lover since she is no longer the immaculate virgin whom he promised to watch over. With equal firmness, Mary insists on the divine origin of her child and her intact virginity, but to no avail. It is only when an angel appears to him in his sleep that he begins to accept her story.[72]

---

[70] *PL* 83, 148, *MF*, p. 374.
[71] *Homily on Simeon, TMPM*, II, 176.
[72] *Homily for the Annunciation of the Most Holy Mother of God, PG* 98, 320-327. See *TMPM*, II, 340-48 for the full dialogue.

Andrew of Crete (†c. 740) takes a more theological approach. Having explained the reasons behind God's choice of the Incarnation as the means to redeem humanity he asks what would be most fitting way for this to come about:

> And in what way could this [the Incarnation] have been brought to its conclusion if not through a pure and intact virgin who would first make herself subject to the mystery and then carry the Supersubstantial in her womb according to a law that is above the laws of nature? And then who could imagine who this might be if not she who had been chosen before all generations by the universal Creator of nature? This is the Mother of God, Mary, a name pronounced by God, from whose womb the Most Divine came forth in the flesh, and which he himself formed in a supernatural way, building her as a temple for himself, for her womb was not ruined when she gave birth, nor did her offspring require seed. *First Encomium for the Nativity of the Most Holy Mother of God*[73]

Andrew also imagines the dialogue between Gabriel and Mary but his is a divine drama, not a human one, with none of the emotional reactions described by Germanus. In fact, it is more a monologue of praise for the Virgin, with occasional comments on her reactions. Her hesitation is portrayed as prudence in guarding her absolute purity lest Gabriel be deceiving her: 'In reality she was perturbed in her soul by the greeting that was addressed to her because she was without any stain, free from any union or relationship with a man, and was in the habit of setting her soul in the immobile contemplation of heavenly things.'

John of Damascus († 749) affirms the virginal conception in both his doctrinal and pastoral writings. In his *Exposition on the Orthodox Faith* he writes:

> The Only-Begotten Son and Word of God and God, out of his great mercy and because of our salvation, and with the agreement of the Father and the synergy of the All-Holy Spirit was conceived without the work of man and was born virginally of the Holy Virgin and Mother of God, Mary, through the work of the Holy Spirit and from her he became a perfect man. *1, 2*

> And the Word became flesh, without undergoing change, from the Holy Spirit and from Mary, the Holy Ever-Virgin Mother of God, and he became the Mediator between God and man, the only friend of men, conceived in the immaculate womb of the Virgin, not out of the will, desire, or union of a man, or through a generation with the presence of pleasure, but from the Holy Spirit according to the first generation of Adam. *3, 1*

He also gives an explanation of the generative processes involved in the Incarnation, according to the medical knowledge of the time, which is essentially Aristotelian, where the mother played an entirely passive role, providing the prime matter which was acted upon by the active agency of the father:

---

[73] *TMPM*, II, 398.

> Therefore, after the consent of the holy Virgin, the Holy Spirit came on her, according to the word of the Lord which the angel had pronounced, and purified her, giving her the capacity to receive the divinity of the Word together with the generative [power]. And then subsistent Wisdom, the Power of God, the Son of God, consubstantial with the Father descended on her as a divine seed and formed a body for himself, animated by a rational and spiritual soul, from her most pure and chaste blood. *3, 2*[74]

John was not above relying on the apocrypha; he follows the tradition that Joseph was an old man when he married Mary, who could no longer remain in the temple due to the onset of puberty. Thus it was that he was 'the guardian of her virginity' rather than a normal spouse. As for Mary she possessed a 'twofold virginity' since 'she preserved the virginity of her soul no less than that of her body'.[75]

In the writings of the Medieval West at this time one finds little of the liveliness and sophistication evident in the late Byzantine Fathers. Commentators generally limited themselves to repeating the well-established arguments of their predecessors and had little need or desire to resort to polemics. That this should be so is unsurprising for a variety of reasons. Firstly the Mariology of the Latin Church at this stage was still relatively subdued and was almost entirely devoid of sophisticated theological content. Moreover, within the realm of Christendom, which in practice meant virtually all of Western Europe, this was a doctrine that was accepted almost without question. Such challenges as did come were usually from the Jewish communities and could be answered in the same way as they had been by the Fathers. Where there were pagans to be converted and catechised a rehearsal of Patristic teaching would also suffice. One noticeable difference, which is equally true for other aspects of Mariology, is that Churchmen now begin to address the question of Mary's virginity more in sermons for her feast days than in specially dedicated tracts.

Bede the Venerable († 735), writing for the feast of the Annunciation believes that Mary had vowed to remain a virgin prior to the appearance of the angel, like Augustine and others after him:

> The Virgin was truly full of grace if, through a divine gift, it was given to her, first among all women, to offer the most glorious gift of virginity to God. Therefore she, who was entirely intent on imitating the purity of the life of the angels, rightly merited to see and at the same time talk to the angel. *In festo Annuntiationis beatae Mariae, 4*[76]

---

[74] *TMPM*, 2, 485 and 486.
[75] *First Homily on the Dormition*, 7, *EPH*, p. 190.
[76] *PL* 94, 11A.

Ambrose Autpert († 781) writes of Mary's virginity in the context of her purification, which he says was not actually necessary since she had not been subject to concupiscence: 'For she, far from all human concupiscence and carnal relationship, conceived as a virgin and always remained a virgin, and what is more, no male child opened her womb.'[77] Paul Deacon Warnefred (†c. 799) also uses a sermon for the feast of the Purification to affirm the virginal conception – citing Isaiah 7. 14 – and the virgin birth.[78]

Hrabanus Maurus († 846) writes at length on Mary's virginity in his commentary on Matthew's Gospel. There is, he says, 'an enormous difference [...] between the birth of Christ and that of other men', because the birth of ordinary men comes about through the union of a man and a woman, whereas 'Christ came into the world as the Son of God by means of a Virgin.'[79] He goes on to speak of the genealogy of Christ with the standard explanation that Mary and Joseph were of the same tribe. He then turns to the question of Joseph's reaction to Mary's pregnancy, clarifying that she became pregnant during their engagement by the Holy Spirit and that Joseph took her into his home only after the angel appeared to him and revealed that the child was from God. Further on he explains Matthew's citation of the Isaiah prophecy:

> The evangelist refers to the words of the Prophet when he speaks of the virgin birth so that the miracle of such great majesty should be held all the more certain not only because he believes it but above all because it has been foretold by the Prophet. *Commentariorum in Matthaeum, 16*[80]

In the *Cogitis me*, pseudo-epigraphically attributed to Jerome, Paschasius Radbertus († 865) speaks of the unique and wondrous virginity of Mary which was also fruitful. It was out of respect for her virginity, he suggests, that Jesus entrusted her to the virgin apostle, John, at the time of his death. He also speaks of the suitability of an angel appearing to Mary at the Annunciation since 'virginity is always strictly linked to the angels, because it is a 'living beyond the flesh'.[81]

Fulbert of Chartres († 1028) also highlights the relationship between Mary's virginity and the angels, though he does so on the basis of apocryphal accounts of Mary's childhood (probably a version of the *Pseudo-Matthew*), which speak of her being given into the care of the Temple priests at the age of three by her parents because they had promised her to God. He asserts that she took a vow of virginity during the time that she was living in the Temple:

> Afterwards however, in accordance with the promise made by her parents to consecrate her to the Lord, she was conducted to Jerusalem and raised in the

---

[77] *In Purificatione sanctae Mariae, PL* 89, 1293B-C.

[78] See *Purificatione sanctae Mariae, PL* 95, 1562A-B.

[79] *Commentariorum in Matthaeum*, 2, *PL* 107, 747D-748A.

[80] *PL* 107, 752B.

[81] *Cogitis me*, 5, *PL* 30, 126D.

Temple of the Lord until she was fourteen. Mary served day and night with fasting and prayer and consecrated her virginity to him, something that no virgin had ever done before, speaking frequently with the angels. *Sermo 5, De nativitate beatissimae Mariae Virginis*[82]

Peter of Alfonso (†c. 1106), a Spanish Jew who converted to Christianity, whose original name was Moses, wrote a twelve-book dialogue between two characters, Peter and Moses in which he deals with many facets of Christian doctrine, including Mary's virginal conception. The work gives a fascinating insight into the aspects of Christianity which were difficult for Jews to accept. In the case of the virginal conception, however, it proves to be entirely unoriginal, simply repeating the arguments of the Fathers:

Moses: Now I wish you to speak to me about Mary, who, according to your belief, gave birth without carnal relations, and if I can, I shall reply.

Peter: We believe that when the Holy Spirit came into her and the power of the Most High overshadowed her, forces flowed together from her members and so she conceived without seed.

Moses: It is truly surprising and difficult to understand how a son can be generated by the mother without a carnal father. In fact, in the normal generation of men we observe that, if the two natures do not unite, that is, the man's and the woman's, a man cannot be generated.

Peter: Why does this generation seem surprising to you and inconceivable if you have heard something similar already, given that both we and you believe that Eve was procreated by a father without a mother, that is, from the flesh of Adam?

Moses: Certainly, that generation, as this one, could have come about as the result of a miracle. But that the former happened is attested to by the authority of Moses, who is not contested in any way by the Law. As to the latter, however, I do not believe that you will find any authority. If you can find something in the books of the prophets, produce it. Dialogi[83]

Peter goes on to produce the necessary proofs, including Isaiah 7. 14. He discusses at length the meaning of Isaiah's words, especially the meaning of the sign and of the term *almah*.

Anselm of Canterbury († 1109) makes the important point that the fact that Jesus was born of a pure virgin who had not known man was a guarantee that Christ himself was free from all trace of sin, although it would have been possible for Jesus to be born of someone who was not pure, since God can do all things, it was more fitting that Jesus was born of a virgin:

Although the Son of God was truly conceived of a most pure virgin, the thing did not, however, come about through necessity, as if according to reason a holy offspring could not be generated from a sinful mother through a generation of

---

[82] *PL* 141, 324D-325A.
[83] *TMSM*, III, 73-74.

this kind, but because it was suitable that the conception of that human nature should come about from a most pure Mother. For it was proper that that virgin should shine with a purity such that one cannot conceive a greater other than God himself. *De conceptu virginali, 18*[84]

Ivo of Chartres († 1115) uses the example of sun passing through glass without damaging it to explain the virginal conception, an example employed by several other Patristic and Medieval commentators:

> Christian meekness can know this [doctrine] beyond all doubt and can demonstrate it rationally to others too going from the minor premises to the major, and from the a priori to what follows. For if a ray of sun penetrates a crystal it does not perforate it in entering nor does it destroy it in exiting. Is it not all the more reasonable, perhaps, that the virginal womb should remain closed and intact even after the entrance and exit of the true and eternal Sun? *De Annuntiatione*[85]

Hugh of St. Victor († 1141) has Gabriel reassure Mary that she need not be concerned about the loss of her virginity which she had vowed to keep intact, according to a belief that stretched back to Gregory of Nyssa († c. 394):

> The angel says: Do not distrust the promise of the Offspring because of your proposal of virginity. The Holy Spirit will come upon you. You will conceive a son not of man but through the work of the Holy Spirit. My promise will be fulfilled and, on the other hand, your proposal will not be violated. *De b. Mariae Virginitate libellus epistolaris, 1*[86]

Peter Lombard († 1160) turns to a number of Old Testament verses including Isaiah 7. 14 and Jeremiah 31. 22 in his restatement of the doctrine of Mary's virginal conception:

> This is the novelty that the Lord brought about on earth: the Virgin conceived and gave birth without the admixture of male seed. For it was she who 'encompassed the man in the lap of the womb' (see Jeremiah 31. 22), because the Son of God was conceived in the womb of the Virgin by means of her flesh alone, sanctified through an intervention of the Holy Spirit. *In festo annuntiationis beatae Mariae*[87]

Gerhoh of Reichersberg († 1169), a prominent figure in the German Church, uses the rather unusual examples of the worm which, it was believed, was generated directly from the soil, and of an egg to illustrate the manner of Mary's conception:

---

[84] *PL* 158, 451A-B.

[85] *PL* 162, 585B-C.

[86] *PL* 176, 868A.

[87] *PL* 171, 605C. See also his *Liber Sententiarum*, III, dist. 3, where he also affirms the virginal conception.

Suffused and a warmed by the love of the Father, she conceived while remaining integral. Just as a bird is conceived in an integral egg through the heat of another bird, or as a worm is conceived from the earth alone thanks to the heat of the sun, so the Virgin, integral and pure, conceived through the heavenly love of God the Father who, looking on her humility and loving her chastity, introduced the holy Word into her mind and her womb, and with the warmth of his love, through a spiritual rather than a carnal pleasure, he extracted the generative flesh for his seed from her flesh, that is, for his Word which, as we have said, he introduced into the Virgin. *Commentarius in Psalmos, 1* [88]

Richard of St. Victor († 1173) upholds Mary's virginal conception on the basis of Isaiah 7. 14 and Matthew 1. 21: 'There it is said that she would conceive; here it says that she conceived by means of the Holy Spirit. She conceived therefore according to the work of the Holy Spirit and not the intervention of man.' [89]

Gualtier of Châtillon (†c. 1179) vigorously defends the virginal conception in his *Tractate against the Jews*, citing all the usual arguments and Scriptural proofs, such as Isaiah 7. 14 and Jeremiah 31. 21-22. [90] It is important to point out that works which directly addressed 'the Jew' and accused him of heresy or failure to understand were not necessarily intended to be anti-Semitic. In the first place, the tradition of using a proverbial Jew with whom to argue goes back to the early Fathers who often did have to contend with Jewish opposition. Nor was opposition confined to the Patristic period. Jewish scholars in the Middle Ages were equally horrified at the notion that God would have demeaned himself to the extent of being born of a woman. [91] Consequently, the Christian response may not be quite so intolerant as seems at first glance, though it cannot be denied that anti-Semitism was lamentably common in the Medieval Church.

Anthony of Padua († 1231), referring to the closed gate of Ezekiel 44, [92] writes that Mary preserved her virginity intact, consenting only for the Word to enter in:

No man shall pass through it, referring to Joseph, who was to have no knowledge of her. It shall be shut for the prince refers to the devil, the prince of this world. It was closed to his suggestions, because her mind was open to no temptation, just as her body knew no contact with a man. The prince alone means Jesus Christ, who sits in her by the humility of the flesh he took. *Sermon on the Purification of the BVM* [93]

---

[88] *PL* 193, 639A-B.

[89] *On the Emmanuel*, 1, 1, *TMSM*, III, 354.

[90] See *TMSM*, III, 491-92 for the relevant passages.

[91] See chapter on Intercession, Mediation and Devotion, 2, for further discussion.

[92] See Gate, vol. 2.

[93] *The Sermons of St Antony*, trans. by Stephen Spilsbury, in *The Franciscan Archive* <http://www.franciscan-archive.org/antonius/opera/ant-hd00.html> [accessed 28 March, 2006].

With the advent of Scholasticism, the Western Church for the first time began to address the question of Mary's virginal conception with a certain degree of scientific rigour. In his *Summa* Aquinas († 1274) offers four reasons why it necessary that Mary conceive virginally, all of which are drawn from the Fathers, most notably Augustine. Firstly, he repeats the well-established argument that it was not fitting for Jesus to have a human father since he already had a Father in heaven:

> It is fitting for four reasons that Christ should be born of a virgin. First, in order to maintain the dignity or the Father Who sent Him. For since Christ is the true and natural Son of God, it was not fitting that He should have another father than God: lest the dignity belonging to God be transferred to another. *ST, III, q. 28, a. 1*[94]

The next two reasons are based on the notion that postlapsarian sexual intercourse was inherently corrupting:

> Secondly, this was befitting to a property of the Son Himself, Who is sent. For He is the Word of God: and the word is conceived without any interior corruption: indeed, interior corruption is incompatible with perfect conception of the word. Since therefore flesh was so assumed by the Word of God, as to be the flesh of the Word of God, it was fitting that it also should be conceived without corruption of the mother.
>
> Thirdly, this was befitting to the dignity of Christ's humanity in which there could be no sin, since by it the sin of the world was taken away, according to John. 1. 29: 'Behold the Lamb of God' (i.e. the Lamb without stain) 'who taketh away the sin of the world.' Now it was not possible in a nature already corrupt, for flesh to be born from sexual intercourse without incurring the infection of original sin. Whence Augustine says (*De Nup. Et Concup.* I): 'In that union,' viz. the marriage of Mary and Joseph, 'the nuptial intercourse alone was lacking: because in sinful flesh this could not be without fleshly concupiscence which arises from sin, and without which He wished to be conceived, Who was to be without sin.' *ST, III, q. 28, a. 1*

The final reason, which identifies Mary's virginal conception as a type of the Church's virginal generation of the members of the Mystical Body, is strongly rooted in the Ambrosian and Augustinian tradition:

> Fourthly, on account of the very end of the Incarnation of Christ, which was that men might be born again as sons of God, 'not of the will of the flesh, nor of the will of man, but of God' (John. 1. 13), i.e. of the power of God, of which fact the very conception of Christ was to appear as an exemplar. Whence Augustine says (*De Sanct. Virg.*): 'It behooved that our Head, by a notable miracle, should be

---

[94] Translations are from *Summa Theologica*, ed. and trans. by Fathers of the English Dominican Province, 3 vols (New York: Benzinger, 1947-48).

> born, after the flesh, of a virgin, that He might thereby signify that His members
> would be born, after the Spirit, of a virgin Church.' *ST, III, q. 28, a. 1*

In the Responses he deals with all the standard arguments against Mary's
virginal conception. In reply to the objection that Joseph is named as the father of
Jesus he says, citing Bede and Augustine, that this was indicative not of a blood
relationship but of Joseph's guardianship. On the question of the Matthean
genealogy (1. 1-17), he quotes from Jerome's assertion that Mary and Joseph were
from the same tribe (see above). Showing his Aristotelian colours he rejects the
theory, based on Galen, that both male and female seed were necessary for Jesus
to have a truly human body, arguing instead that the matter was supplied by Mary,
but the agent which transmuted that passive matter into the human person of
Christ was divine power, just as God's power had formed the earth into Adam, a
parallel which had been used since the very dawn of the Church.[95]

Albert the Great († 1280), like Aquinas, relies on Aristotelian medical theory
in his explanation of the virginal conception, stating that Mary's only role was to
provide the material on which the power of God acted, taking the place of the
normal active agent, the male seed:

> In the Incarnation of the Son of God the Blessed Virgin had no active role
> since everything took place because of divine operation. Nevertheless, she
> played her won role, that of a mother, which, in the generation, is not that of
> operating in the order of the production of the species, but only of guaranteeing
> availability in relation to that which is conceived, being moved by the other
> cause. As to her, her generative power, which belongs to her insofar as she is a
> mother, was not set into motion by any other than the divine power. *On the
> Divine Names, 2, 53*

He goes on to explain Mary's conception with the rather unusual example of a
blind man seeing while still remaining blind:

> But she was moved although she persisted in virginity and therefore the
> generation of Christ was also miraculous according to its actualization, as if a
> blind man could see while remaining blind. In fact, in the case of a blind man
> who, having become sighted, sees, we are not dealing with a miraculous act even
> if the mode is miraculous. In the case of the Blessed Virgin, instead, the act too
> was miraculous because the generative power cannot be activated without the
> virginity being eliminated.

Conrad of Saxony († 1279), whose work was often attributed to Bonaventure,
makes the same point in less technical language:

> We learn of the excellent chastity of Mary from the witness of the Evangelist,
> from the witness of Mary herself, and the witness of the angel. Mary was chaste

---

[95] See Earth in vol. 2.

in her virginal flesh as the Evangelist testifies, saying: The virgin's name was Mary. Even purer was she in her virginal mind as she herself testifies: How can this be, since I am a virgin? [Lk 1:34], that is, I state that I am a virgin. Mary was chaste in her virginal child, as the angel testifies in saying: Joseph, son of David, do not be afraid to take Mary as your wife, for the child conceived in her is from the Holy Spirit [Mt 1:20]. Mary was pregnant from the Holy Spirit with the divine child, and in no way was her virginity damaged by such a child, but she was wonderfully glorified in such a child. Mary's virginity was approved, consecrated, made noble, enriched, gifted, sealed and confirmed in her child. *Speculum Beatae Mariae Virginis, 4*[96]

Duns Scotus († 1308), the great champion of the Immaculate Conception, is particularly insistent on the question of Mary having taken a vow of virginity. Having first explained that a vow should only be taken on the understanding that it is subject to God's acceptance of it, and that such a vow nevertheless remains absolute, he turns to the question of Mary's vow, the existence of which he believes is demonstrated by her question to the angel, 'How shall this be done, because I know not man?' (Luke 1. 34):

If it were a question of not having known him [man] without having made any firm proposal never to know him, there would be no problem because once having known him, not being sterile, she would have conceived. But the question concerned an even more marvellous event for she had established and made a vow that she would never be known by man. And the explanation of the angel corresponds to this intention: 'The Holy Ghost shall come upon thee, and the power of the most High shall overshadow thee.' (Luke 1. 35) *In IV Sententiarum, d. 30.q. 2*

Though the language, the exegesis and the technical understanding of the virginal conception has changed through the centuries, the teaching of the Church has essentially remained the same as it has been since the earliest Fathers: Mary conceived Jesus without relations with a man through the power of God who suspended the normal laws of nature. To believe otherwise would cause the whole framework on which the doctrine of the Incarnation is based, and therefore also of the Redemption, to collapse.

Virgin Birth

Of less central concern than the virginal conception, at least from a doctrinal point of view, was the question of whether Mary's virginity had been preserved intact at the birth of Christ (*virginitas in partu*). Nevertheless, from the third century onwards, the Fathers expended considerable energy in proclaiming and defending

---

[96] Trans. by Campion Murray as *The Angel's Greeting,* in *Franciscan Friars Province of the Holy Spirit* <http://www.franciscans.org.au> [accessed 3 June 2007].

the virgin birth, primarily because they considered it to be an incontrovertible sign of the divine origin of Jesus.[97] Moreover, based on the Pauline and Irenenean doctrine of recapitulation, which held that Christ was the new Adam who reversed the consequences of the Fall, it was argued that Mary, who recapitulated Eve, should not have suffered from the pangs of childbirth. What is more, for the Fathers Mary's physical integrity was a logical consequence of the virginal conception, and a visible sign of her holiness. At the same time a delicate balance had to be struck between showing that the Virgin's birth-giving was truly unique and divine, as the prophets had foretold, and ensuring that Christ's birth conformed sufficiently to the normal laws of nature for him to be also fully human. In addition, there was the danger that the virgin birth could be confused with Greek and Roman myths of parthenogenesis.

From very early on, both in popular piety and in the official teaching of the Church, we find evidence of belief in Mary's *virginitas in partu*. The earliest known documents that speak of the virgin birth are the *Odes of Solomon*, the *Ascension of Isaiah* and the apocryphal infancy Gospel, the *Protoevangelium of St. James*, all dating from around the beginning of the second century.[98] The latter offers a lengthy and fanciful account, most likely influenced by Old Testament stories concerning the consequences of touching the Ark of the Covenant,[99] of how Salome, disbelieving the midwife's claim that Mary's virginity had remained intact, had her hand withered when she sought physical proof:

> So the midwife went with him. And they stood near the cave and a dark cloud was hovering over the cave. And the midwife said, "My soul glorifies this day, for today my eyes have seen a miracle: salvation has come to Israel. "And immediately, the cloud withdrew from the cave and a great light appeared in the cave so that their eyes could not bear it. And a little while later the same light withdrew until an infant appeared. And he came and took the breast of his Mother, Mary. And the midwife cried out and said, "How great this day is for me, for I have seen this new miracle." And the midwife departed from the cave and met Salome and said to

---

[97] For a survey of Patristic attitudes towards the *viginitas in partu* see P. G. Dunker, 'Our Lady in the Patristic Age', in *The Mother of the Redeemer: Aspects of Doctrine and Devotion*, ed. by Kevin McNamara (Dublin: Gill, 1959), pp. 42-55.

[98] On the influence of early apocryphal texts on belief in the virgin birth, see Graef, *Doctrine and Devotion*, I, 34-37, *MF*, pp. 33-34, and Chris Maunder, 'Mary in the New Testament and Apocrypha', in *Mary: The Complete Resource*, ed. by Sarah Jane Boss (Oxford and New York: Oxford University Press 2007), pp. 11-46. Maunder also cites the *Odes of Solomon* (probably first-century, and therefore the earliest of the three) as a possible source for belief in the virgin birth, though it speaks of Wisdom, not Mary, as the Mother of Jesus (p. 40). For an English translation of the *Odes* see John Davidson, *The Odes of Solomon: Mystical Songs from the Time of Jesus* (Bath: Clear Press, 2005). See alsoRendel Harris, *The Odes and Psalms of Solomon* (Cambridge: Cambridge University Press, 1909. On the narrative in the *Protoevangelium* see Mary F. Foskett, *A Virgin Conceived*, pp.158-59.

[99] For instance, the story of Huzzah who is stuck dead by God even though he touched the Ark accidentally (2 Kings 6. 6-7).

her, "Salome, Salome, I have to describe this new miracle for you. A virgin has given birth, although her body does not allow it." And Salome said, "As the Lord my God lives, unless I insert my finger and investigate her, I will not believe that a virgin has given birth." And the midwife went in and said, "Mary, position yourself, for not a small test concerning you is about to take place." When Mary heard these things, she positioned herself. And Salome inserted her finger into her body. And Salome cried out and said, "Woe for my lawlessness and the unbelief that made me test the living God. Look, my hand is falling away from me and being consumed in fire." And Salome dropped to her knees before the Lord, saying, "God of Abraham and Isaac and Jacob, do not expose me to the children of Israel, but give me back to the poor. For you know, Lord, that I have performed service and received my wage from you." Suddenly, an angel of the Lord appeared, saying to her, "Salome, Salome, the Lord of all has heard your entreaty. Stretch out your hand to the child and lift him up and he will be salvation and joy for you." *Protoevangelium of St. James, 19-20*[100]

With the exception of Tertullian[101] and to a lesser extent Origen[102] the early Greek Fathers, undoubtedly influenced by these texts, did not openly contest the virgin birth, though several remained ambiguous, wishing to avoid the taint of Gnosticism that could potentially arise from claiming that Christ's birth was anything other than normal. Clement of Alexandria (†c. 215), for instance, denies it in a homily on Luke, but later accepts it in a homily on Leviticus, making reference to the apocryphal story of the midwife,[103] while Athanasius of Alexandria († 373) implicitly rejects it in *Against the Heresies*.[104]

However, several of the early Fathers do put a cogent case in favour of the virgin birth, many basing their argument on the Eve-Mary antithesis. According to the Irenean notion, in which Christ and Mary reversed the actions of Adam and Eve, since Mary was entirely free from all taint of sin at the time of the Incarnation (see chapter on Immaculate Conception), and since she did not conceive Jesus according to the order of nature, and the whole transaction was free from any taint of cupidity, she was not visited with the travails of childbirth imposed on Eve and her descendents as punishment for eating the fruit (Genesis 3. 16). Moreover, it was believed that Eve was a virgin prior to the Fall, so that Mary too had to be a virgin in order to reverse her actions. These are the

---

[100] Hock, *The Infancy Gospels of James and Thomas*. See Graef, *Doctrine and Devotion*, I, 35-37.

[101] See Tertullian's outright denial in *De carne Christi*, 23, *PL* 2, 790A-C.

[102] 'As to the Mother of the Lord, her womb was opened at the moment of birth, since prior to the birth of Christ absolutely no man had touched her holy body, worthy of all veneration. *In Lucam*, 14, *TMPM*, I, 220. See Tina Beattie, 'Mary in Patristic Theology', in *Mary: The Complete Resource*, pp. 75-105 (pp. 96-99).

[103] *Homily 14* and *Homily 8*, 2 respectively. See Graef, *Doctrine and Devotion*, I, 43-44, and Mary Clayton, *The Cult of the Virgin Mary*, p. 3.

[104] See Graef, *Doctrine and Devotion*, I, 71.

arguments that Ephrem († c. 373), who returns repeatedly to the theme of Mary's virginal integrity in his hymns,[105] uses when he affirms the virgin birth:

> Thanks to Mary, blessed amongst women, the curses uttered at the beginning of time were abolished, according to which a child is born in pain and shame. A woman who gives birth amongst these sufferings could not be called blessed. The Lord, just as he entered in through the closed door (John 20. 26) came out of the virginal womb, because this Virgin truly gave birth, and truly did not suffer pain. *Diatessaron, 2, 6*[106]

Ephrem also likens Christ's emergence from the sealed tomb at the resurrection with his issuing forth from Mary's sealed womb, a comparison that one also finds in later writers:[107]

> He caused his body to emerge from the tomb even though it was sealed; and the seal of the tomb bears witness in favour of the seal of virginity of she who had borne his body, for although his Mother's virginity was sealed, the Son of God, came out a living man from her womb. *Diatessaron, 21, 21*

> But in your Resurrection you made your birth comprehensible; since the womb was sealed, and the sepulchre closed up; being alike pure in the womb, and living in the sepulchre. The womb and the sepulchre being sealed were witnesses unto you. The womb of the Mother and hell cried aloud of your Resurrection: The womb conceived you, which was sealed; the tomb let you go forth which was closed up. Contrary to the laws of nature did the womb conceive you, and the tomb give you up! Sealed was the sepulchre to which was entrusted the care of the dead. Virgin was the womb which no man knew. Virgin womb and sealed sepulchre resounded like trumpets in the ears of a deaf people. *Hymns on the Nativity, 10, 6-8*[108]

Gregory Nazianzen († 390) expresses an opinion that was quite common among the Fathers when he states that 'where there is that God from whom comes salvation there is nothing sordid.'[109] In fact, the idea that the Son of God had suffered the indignity of normal childbirth was unacceptable to some, despite their willingness to accept that he had died on the Cross. In this they were undoubtedly influenced by Jewish attitudes towards childbirth, based on the Mosaic Law, which regarded the whole process as impure, as is witnessed by the fact that Mary had to present herself and her Son for purification in the Temple (Luke 2. 22-40).

---

[105] See in particular *Hymns on the Nativity*, 12, whose central message is the *virginitas in partu*.
[106] *TMPM*, IV, 83.
[107] See, for instance, Jerome, *In Evangelium Matthei*, 4, 27-60, *PL* 26, 215 and *MF*, p. 265. Theodotus of Ancyra († before 446) offers one of the most extensive expositions on the parallels. *Fifth Homily on the Birth of the Lord*, 1, *TMPM*, I, 506-07.
[108] *TMPM*, IV, 87 and 100-101.
[109] *Oratio 40*, 45, *TMPM*, I, 307.

Among the early Eastern Fathers, Gregory of Nyssa († c. 394) is one the most vigorous defender of belief in the virgin birth, explicitly stating that a pregnancy which was not the result of concupiscence could not have resulted in suffering for the mother: 'Just as her virginity posed no obstacle to her giving birth, neither did her childbearing destroy her virginity. Indeed it was fitting that [the Redeemer], having entered into human life to make us all incorruptible, should Himself originate from an incorruptible birth.'[110]

He is also the first to put forward clearly the argument that Mary did not suffer the pangs of childbirth since she reversed the curse of Eve, basing his argument on an exegesis of Genesis 3. 16 and Isaiah 66. 7:[111]

> The prophet Isaiah also affirms that her labour was without pain, since he says: 'Before she was in labour, she brought forth; before her time came to be delivered, she brought forth a man child.' Therefore he was chosen to introduce a twofold innovation in the order of nature, since neither the beginning of his existence was a result of pleasure, nor was he born through suffering. This came about for an understandable reason, which is in no way absurd. Since she who introduced death into nature by means of sin was condemned to give birth in suffering and travail, it was necessary that the Mother of Life, having conceived in joy at the beginning, should bring the pregnancy to a conclusion in joy too. *In Canticum Canticorum, 13*[112]

In the West, Ambrose († 397) was the first to set forth the reasoning behind the belief fully,[113] arguing that the virginal birth follows logically from the virginal conception, and pointing out that if the God of the Old Testament performed great miracles such as causing the rocks to bring forth water (Exodus 17. 6), then there is no reason why he should not have caused Mary to give birth without damaging her integrity. [114]

For Augustine († 430) the preservation of Mary's virginity, like her virginal conception, is a consequence of grace.[115] How it came about that God took on flesh, that the Virgin conceived and gave birth while remaining a virgin, is beyond human comprehension:

---

[110] *On the Birth of Christ*, MF, p. 155.

[111] See the chapter on the Remote Redemption for further discussion.

[112] *TMPM*, I, 329. See also *Against Eunomius*, 2, *TMPM*, I, 329, and *Homilia in Resurrectionem*, *TMPM*, I, 327.

[113] Zeno of Verona (†c. 380) gives a graphic description of the virgin birth some years earlier, but this was an account based on the apocrypha. See *Tractatus 1*, 54, 4-5, *PL* 11, 414-415.

[114] See, for instance, *Epistola 42*, *PL* 16, 1124A-1128C. See David G. Hunter, *Marriage, Celibacy, and Heresy in Ancient Christianity: The Jovinianist Controversy* (Oxford: Oxford University Press, 2007), pp. 197-204 for an excellent summary of Ambrose's teaching on the *virginitas in partu*. See also John R. Meyer, 'Ambrose's Exegesis of Luke 2, 22-24 and Mary's *virginitas in partu*, *Marianum*, 62 (2000), 169-92.

[115] See *Sermo 291*, 6.

> If you wish to know about his birth according to the flesh, which he took on out of kindness for our salvation, listen and believe that he was born of the Holy Spirit and of the Virgin Mary. Regarding this birth of his, 'who shall tell of his generation?' (Isaiah 53. 8). For who could adequately appreciate a God who wished to be born a man for mankind, a virgin who conceived him without male seed, who gave birth to him without corruption and whose integrity remained after the birth? For our Lord Jesus Christ deigned to enter into the womb of the Virgin, he immaculately filled the frame of the woman, without corrupting her, he made her a Mother; when he was formed, he came out of her and closed her still intact maternal viscera. In this way he enriched her of whom he deigned to be born with the honour of motherhood and the holiness of virginity. Who could ever comprehend this? Who could tell of it? *Sermo 215, 3*[116]

So Mary's miraculous birth-giving is as much part of the mystery of the Incarnation as is her conception of the Word, and should be treated with the same reverence and respect. Not to believe in the preservation of her virginity is to question the very divine origin of her child. Therefore, while no-one can adequately explain it, it should most certainly be believed: 'Even if he had violated her integrity only in being born, he would no longer have been born of a virgin, and the whole Church would confess falsely'.[117]

Jerome († 419) is an exception to the general acceptance of the doctrine. He seems to have been reluctant to accept the belief on the grounds that it had its origins in the Apocrypha, which he despised. In his treatise of Mary's virginity he writes of Mary becoming a normal wife, that is, no longer a virgin, after the birth of Christ: 'If every day the hands of God form babies in their mothers' wombs why blush to think that Mary, after the birth of Jesus, became a real wife?'[118] Even after the Synod of Milan (360), when Jovinian, a Roman layman who upheld the equal value of marriage and virginity, was condemned for denying Mary's *virginitas in partu*, he remained ambiguous on the question.[119] In this passage, where he quotes from Ezekiel and from Luke (who in turn is quoting Exodus 34. 19), he seems to suggest that Mary's birth canal opened for Christ's birth, yet also says it remained closed. This is not entirely in accord with the official line that, as it were, the door never opened since Jesus passed through the hymen without causing any damage:

> All the heretics have erred because they have not understood the mystery of his birth. The affirmation, 'Every male opening the womb shall be called holy to the Lord' (Luke 2. 23), is far more applicable to the special birth of the Lord than to other men. Only Christ opened the closed door of the virginal womb, which continued to remain closed, however. This is the closed eastern gate,

---

[116] [accessed 30 April 2008].
[117] *Enchiridion*, 34, 10.
[118] *De virginitate perpetua*, 19, *MF*, p. 208.
[119] See David G. Hunter, *Marriage, Celibacy, and Heresy*, in particular pp. 187-96, Graef, *Doctrine and Devotion*, I, 89-90, and *MF*, pp. 208-09.

through which only the high priest may enter and exit and which nevertheless is always closed. *Contra Pelagianos*, 2, 4[120]

But Jerome was not alone in using rather ambiguous language as these lines by Nilus of Ancyre (†c. 430) demonstrate: 'At the moment of his birth, Our Lord Jesus Christ opened an immaculate womb. He himself, with his wisdom, power, and capacity to perform miracles, sealed that womb after his birth, without in any way undoing the seals of virginity.'[121]

Leo the Great († 461) insists repeatedly on the truth of the virgin birth, which he ranks alongside the Virgin's miraculous conception as proof of the human and divine natures of Jesus.[122] Theodotus of Ancyra († before 446) declares that it is a lack of faith that prevents the Gentiles from believing in the virgin birth: 'Hearing that a virgin gave birth and remained a virgin, they contend that the doctrine is foolishness because they have not learned to believe in the miraculous power of God.'[123] He also expresses the commonly held view that Mary's virginal conception constitutes a guarantee of the divinity of her child:

> Have you seen how marvelous was the mystery, transcending the law of nature? Have you seen this supernatural occurrence, wrought by the power of God alone? Have you seen the Word beyond words being born? The fact that he did not destroy her virginity plainly shows that the One born is the Word of God. A woman who gives birth to mere flesh ceases to be a virgin; but the Word of God, born in the flesh, maintains her virginity, thus showing that he is the Word. *Homily 2, 8*[124]

Proclus of Constantinople († 446) likewise believes that the virgin birth is proof that the child who was born of Mary truly was God: 'If the Mother had not remained a virgin, the child born would have been a mere man and the birth no miracle.' This he states even more specifically in a letter written to the Church of Armenia, saying that it was necessary 'to preserve the birth-giver as a virgin, testifying that he is God.'[125]

Severus of Antioch († 538) cites Isaiah 66. 7 (LXX) as proof that Jesus came out of Mary without pain and without violating her virginity, and strikes a careful balance between claiming that the birth was both supernatural and natural: 'The word, 'escaped' denotes the extraordinary character of the labour. In fact, though born through nature he came into existence beyond the limits of nature and above the capacity of our intelligence and of our words.'[126]

---

[120] *PL* 23, 538C, *MF*, p. 211.

[121] *Letters*, 1, 263, *PG* 79, 180B-C, *TMPM*, I, 446.

[122] See *Epistola 28, 2, PL* 54, 759, *MF*, p. 304-05.

[123] *Homily for the Birth of the Lord*, 3, *TMPM*, I, 499.

[124] *PG* 77, 1377D-1380A, *MF*, p. 262.

[125] *Homily 1*, and *Letter to the Church of Armenia* quoted in Leena Peltomaa, *The Image of the Virgin Mary in the Akathistos Hymn* (Leiden, Boston and Cologne: Brill, 2001), p. 186, n. 277.

[126] *Homily 108*, *TMPM*, I, 661.

Romanos the Melodist (†c. 560) has Mary proclaim, in a lullaby that she sings to the Christ child, that her unbroken seals of virginity are proof that he is truly the Word become flesh: 'Seeing the inviolate seal of my virginity, I can proclaim that you are the immutable Word become flesh.'[127] Theodosius of Alexandria († 566) writes that that Jesus, 'as God, preserved the seals of her virginity for her in their natural state.'[128] Venantius Fortunatus (†c. 600) affirms the virgin birth as well as upholding the virginal conception in several of his hymns: 'Observe: He wanted to be born from a maiden's womb; / see from whose flesh the high Lord's flesh comes forth. / The venerable Spirit, wishing to dwell in a virginal house, / leaves her womb intact. / God entered her, who did not know man; / the Virgin is known only by the man she bore.'[129]

Gregory the Great († 604) likens Christ passing out of Mary's womb without damaging her integrity and his passing through the closed doors of the Upper Room after his resurrection (John 20. 19-31): 'The body of the Lord went through the closed doors where the disciples were assembled in the same way that he appeared to the eyes of men at his birth, issuing forth from the virginal womb of his Mother.'[130] He also uses the unusual analogy of the parting of the Red Sea as a type of the virgin birth.[131]

Although the Council of Milan had already condemned Jovinian for his denial of the virgin birth it was the First Lateran Council, called by Pope Martin I in 649 to refute the claims of the Monothelites that Christ had only one will,[132] which produced the first definitive statement on Mary's virginal integrity, a doctrine which has been put forward as official Church teaching ever since:

> If anyone does not, in accord with the Holy Fathers, confess correctly and in accordance with the truth that Mary is the holy and Ever-Virgin and immaculate Mother of God, inasmuch as she, in the fullness of time, and without seed, conceived by the Holy Spirit, in a most special but real way, God the Word Himself, who before all time was born of God the Father, and without loss of integrity brought Him forth, and after His birth preserved her virginity inviolate, let him be condemned. *Canones, 3*[133]

The *Life of Mary* attributed to Maximus the Confessor († 662) speaks at some length of the virgin birth, which it links to the reversal of the curse placed on Eve and her descendents as a result of her disobedience. Just as it was God who

---

[127] *Second Hymn for Christmas*, 1, *TMPM*, I, 709.
[128] *Sermon for the Assumption of Our Lady*, 5, *TMPM*, II, 58.
[129] *Carmina miscellanea*, 8, 6 PL 88, 268, *MF*, 364.
[130] *Homiliae in Evangelia*, 26, 1, *PL* 76, 1197C.
[131] *In Ezechielem*, 2, 8, 9, *PL* 76, 1033D.
[132] See chapter on Divine Motherhood.
[133] *Enchiridion Symbolorum: Definitionum et Declarationum de Rebus Fidei et Morum*, ed. by Henricus Denzinger and Adolfus Schönmetzer, 36th edn (Fribourg: Herder, 1965), n. 503. See Michael Hurley, 'Born Incorruptibly: The Third Canon of the Lateran Council (A. D. 649)', *The Heythrop Journal*, 2, (2007), 216 – 236.

cursed Eve, so it is the Lord who preserves Mary's virginity, both in his conception and birth:

> 'The Lord is with thee': no longer does man have power over you, nor do you suffer the pangs of childbirth. In truth, she alone was a virgin above all the other virgins: a virgin before the birth, in giving birth, always a virgin, immaculate. *20*[134]

Ildephonse of Toledo († 667), a major figure in the early development of Marian devotion in the Spanish Church, is one of the strongest defenders of Mary's virginity in the Patristic West.[135] In the context of a society that experienced a long period of Muslim domination and that had a very substantial Jewish population, Ildephonse does not hold back in excoriating those whom he considered to be heretics, addressing his remarks to Jovinian and Helvidius, who denied Mary's perpetual virginity, and the Jews, who denied Christ's divinity and consequently the Virgin's divine motherhood. He writes addressing Jovinian, as had become somewhat of a convention in commentaries on the virgin birth:

> Now Jovianian, try to understand above all with your heart, you fatuous person! Try to understand above all with the assent of your mind, you foolish person! Learn to see and discern well, frivolous person that you are! I will never concede what you dare to allege as a pretext, that the purity of our Virgin was compromised by her giving birth; I will never concede that you destroy her virginal integrity because of her maternity; I will never accept that you lacerate her virginity by making reference to the birth of the Son from her; neither will I allow you to deprive the Virgin of her office as Mother, nor that you deny the Mother the fullness of her virginal glory. [...] For in this way you affirm that God was not capable of preserving her intact in her maternity yet you admit that he could enter into the womb of the Virgin without harming her integrity in the conception. In this way you declare that God could not even accomplish what he intended, since you insist on saying that he had found the Mother intact at her conception but deprived her of her integrity in his birth. Therefore, in you opinion, the divinity of the Almighty did not only not benefit but caused harm to virginity. [...] Instead the Virgin remained such through the power of God and by his wish, when he became man. She was Virgin at the Annunciation, Virgin at her husband's declaration, Virgin before meeting her husband and Virgin when she stayed with her husband; most certainly Virgin when her Spouse expressed no doubt, and Virgin too when her husband nurtured doubts. She was a Virgin before the birth of her Son; Virgin after giving birth to her Son; Virgin during the birth of her Son, Virgin after the birth of her Son. *De virginitate perpetua sanctae Mariae, 1, 4-5*[136]

---

[134] *TMPM*, II, 198.
[135] See Juan Gil, 'El tratado "De Virginitate Beatae Mariae" de S. Ildefonso de Toledo', *Habis*, 6 (1975), 153-66.
[136] *PL* 96, 59B-60A.

Andrew of Crete († 740) speaks of the birth of Jesus as being free from 'the corruption and the pains of childbirth', and of the 'stainless inviolability' of Mary's virginity.[137] In one of his hymns he attributes the extraordinary manner of Christ's conception and birth to his having made himself nothing in order to take on human nature: 'The conception of the Mother of God was without seed, her birth-giving without suffering corruption, because God, performing both miracles, made himself nothing in order to unite himself to us.'[138] John of Damascus († 749) repeats the standard explanation the Mary avoided the pangs of birth because her child was not the fruit of pleasure.[139] He affirms the threefold virginity of Mary in a homily for the Dormition: 'Every virgin, after all, loses her virginity in giving birth; but she, who was a virgin before giving birth, remained so during her labors and even after them.'[140]

The Roman liturgy for Advent unequivocally proclaims Mary's *virginitas in partu*, which it attributes to her virginal conception of Christ: 'Not knowing man the Virgin Mother gave birth without pain to the Saviour of the ages.'[141] Alcuin († 804), who was closely involved with the reform of the liturgy under Charlemagne, lays out Church teaching on Mary triple virginity without undue elaboration:

> Conceiving by means of the Holy Spirit and through the power of the Most High, she is the only virgin to receive such great glory as to give birth to God: the Son of God, coeternal and consubstantial with the Father: a virgin before the birth, a virgin in giving birth, a virgin after the birth. For it was right that, since it was God who was being born, the merit of chastity should increase, so that her integrity was not violated by him who was come to heal that which was corrupt. *De fide sanctae et individuae Trinitatis*, 3, 14, *De Maria Virgine, et incarnatione Verbi Dei*[142]

However some decades later a French Benedictine monk, Ratramnus of Corbie († 875), feeling the need to respond to a rise in a Docetic interpretation of the Virgin's birth-giving in Germany,[143] wrote a detailed treatise which reaffirmed Mary's virginity before, during and after the birth of Christ. His argument is that the birth of Christ was natural, except in that he passed through the Virgin's maidenhood without causing it damage:

> Understand, once and for all, that the birth of Christ could have taken place from any part of the body without causing damage to its integrity; consequently this is what happened in the door of the womb. On the contrary, if he had violated her he would have violated her integrity no matter what part

---

[137] *First Homily on the Dormition*, 2, EPH, p. 105.
[138] *Canon for the Saturday of Lazarus, Theotokion, Ode V*, TMPM, II, 463-64.
[139] *Exposition on the Orthodox Faith*, 6. 14, TMPM, II, 493.
[140] *Second Homily on the Dormition*, 1, EPH, pp. 204-05. See also his *Exposition on the Orthodox Faith*, 6, 14, TMPM, II, 493.
[141] Henri Barré, 'Antiennes et Répons de la Vierge', *Marianum*, 29 (1967), 153-254 (p. 198).
[142] *PL*, 101, 47A.
[143] See *MLM*, p. 81.

of her body he emerged from. Now, the catholic faith with regard to the Virgin Mother of the Saviour confesses that she was a virgin before the birth, a virgin during the birth and a virgin after the birth. It ensures that both things are believed: the virginity of the Mother and the birth of the Son. The Church, indeed, precisely because the chamber of modesty remained intact, preaches the virginity [of Mary], both before, during and after the birth, just as, because of the origin of the true birth, it confesses the true birth-giving of the Mother. For what meaning does the expression 'virgin before the birth' have if not that virginity was made pregnant? What does 'virgin in giving birth' mean, if not that it is a virgin who is giving birth? What sense does it have to speak of 'virgin after the birth', if she did not remain a virgin after giving birth? Now, if the birth-giving is denied, where is the virgin that is giving birth? *De eo quod Christus ex Virgine natus est*[144]

To this claim, his teacher, Paschasius Radbertus († 865), replied, denying that Mary gave birth in the same way as other women, because unlike them, she was not subject to the curse of Genesis 3. 16.[145] However, Ratramnus is fully in line with the teaching of Church Fathers such as Augustine and Gregory the Great, and it is Paschasius who comes closer to denying orthodox doctrine.[146]

Fulbert of Chartres († 1028) uses the occasion of the feast of the Purification, as do many of his fellows, to affirm Mary's absolute purity, writing that, 'when Christ was born of the most Blessed Virgin Mary, she did not have need of purification according to the law because she was pure and holy.'[147] Odilone, abbot of Cluny († 1049), reaffirms the teachings of the Fathers and the Popes on Mary's divine motherhood and virginity, in a sermon for the Assumption. His words are a simple restatement of orthodox belief and a far cry from the polemical writings of earlier times:

> The popes, the confessors and the catholic doctors rejoice because thanks to their teachings those who believe in God venerate and declare their faith in the Son of God who assumed that which he was not without losing that which he was. They preach that the Mother of God gave birth as a virgin and remained a virgin after the birth. *Homily for the Assumption of Mary Mother of God, 12*[148]

---

[144] The full text is to be found in *PL* 121, 81-102. See *TMSM*, III, 820-23.

[145] *On the Parturition of the Virgin*, *PL* 120, 1367D-1368A.

[146] See Georg Söll, *Storia dei dogmi mariani* (Rome: Accademia mariana salesiana, 1981), p. 276 and Irene Scaravalli, 'Per una mariologia carolingia: autori, opere e linee di ricerca', in *Gli studi di mariologia medievale: bilancio storico*, Atti del I convegno mariologico della fondazione Ezio Franceschini con la collaborazione della biblioteca Palatina e del dipartimento di storia dell'università di Parma, Parma 7-8 novembre 1997, ed. by Clelia Maria Piastra (Florence: SISMEL – Edizioni del Galuzzo, 2001), pp. 65-85 (pp 83-85). See also Alfonso Langella, 'La disputa tra Ratramno e Pascasio Radberto sulla verginità di Maria nel parto', *Theotokos*, 16.2 (2008), 39-86.

[147] *Third Sermon on the Purification of the BVM*, *TMSM*, III, 847.

[148] *TMSM*, III, 885-86.

Geoffrey of Vendôme (†c. 1132) uses a variation of the well-known image of the ray of light not taking anything from the sun to explain how Mary could have given birth to Jesus without losing her virginity:

> She is the only one who conceived as a virgin, who gave birth as a virgin and who, after birth, remained inviolate in soul and in body. In fact, just as the ray proceeds from the star, so the Son of God was born of Mary. The star is not corrupted to by the fact that a ray departs from it; just so, neither did the Blessed Mother find herself violated upon the birth of her Son. *In omni festivitate b. Mariae*[149]

Hugh of St. Victor († 1141) sets out a thorough defence of the virgin birth on the basis of the Eve-Mary antithesis. He observes that the reason women suffer the pangs of childbirth does not lie in the fact of having had carnal relations with a man but in the libidinousness that has become an inherent part of the act as a result of Eve's sin. He speculates that had Eve not sinned it could well be that women would neither have lost their virginity nor suffered the pangs of birth as a result of intercourse. He concludes:

> Instead, the Blessed Virgin Mary, so that the second restoration would be above the first condition and the grace of the Lord would win out over the nature of the human race, not only conceived without libidinousness, but she did not receive the seed of the Son to whom she gave birth from a man; and for this reason she brought him into the world without pain and after the birth she remained a virgin with the honour of her integrity. *De b. Mariae virginitate, 3*[150]

In an exegesis of Ecclesiasticus 25. 23, 'As the vine I have brought forth a pleasant odour', Guerric of Igny († 1157), a disciple of Bernard of Clairvaux's uses a rather unusual image to explain the virgin birth:

> You ask how a virgin could have given birth to the Lord: just as the flower of the vine gives off its perfume. If you find a flower that has been corrupted because it has emitted its perfume, then you may believe that her virginity was a violated in the act of giving birth to the Lord. Do you have some objection to the exactness of this comparison? What is virginity if not the flower of an inviolate body? And what is the Son of virginity if not the sweetness of its perfume? *In Nativitate B. Mariae, 3*[151]

Around the same time Peter Lombard († 1160) also affirms the virgin birth, returning to the antithesis between Eve and Mary favoured by the Fathers:

> Eve transmitted three evils to her descendants: the dominion of man over woman, conception in sin, and the travails of childbirth. On the contrary, no

---

[149] *PL* 157, 266D.
[150] *PL* 176, 873A-B.
[151] *PL* 185, 201D.

carnal concupiscence was involved in the conception of the Virgin; she who conceived endured no sadness and had no difficulty at the moment of giving birth. Indeed, he who had come to bring joy to the world ought not to have afflicted the dwelling-place of the womb. Therefore, just as this conception is exempt from every corruption, so, notwithstanding the contrary chatter of the heretics, the Virgin's womb remained intact and undefiled in conception and in giving birth. *In festo annuntiationis beatae Mariae*[152]

Pope Honorius III (1216-1227), likening Mary to the enclosed garden of Canticles,[153] writes: 'She was also an enclosed garden in the birth of her Son, since she was not corrupted and neither did she suffer the pangs of birth, for she was a virgin before the birth, in giving birth.'[154]

According to Anthony of Padua († 1231) the bodily privileges of the Virgin are 'her outstanding virginity, her undefiled fruitfulness, her unburdensome pregnancy, her painless child-bearing.[155] Elsewhere he affirms: 'The Blessed Virgin remained green in the conception and birth of the Saviour, inasmuch as she retained the strength of her virginity: she remained a virgin before and after childbirth.'[156]

Richard of St. Laurence († after 1245), in his *De Laudibus*, a work that was long believed to be by Albert the Great († 1280), numbers a painless parturition among the three curses imposed on Eve that the Virgin avoids. In a wordplay favoured by many in the Latin Church, he contrasts the woe (*vae*) of Eve (*Eva*) with the 'Ave' addressed to Mary:

> One could also say that the first curse consists in the corruption of conception, the second in the pregnancy that follows on the conception and the third in the pains of labour. On the contrary in this greeting [the Ave] Mary received a triple benediction because she became fruitful without corruption, pregnant without being weighed down and a mother without pain. This is what the 'Ave' means, that is, the absence of the triple woe (*vae*) of corruption, of the burden and pain which Eve incurred because of sin and which all women, with the exception of Mary, received from her, almost as an inheritance. *De laudibus beatae Mariae Virginis, 1, 1, 1*[157]

Albert himself argues that it would be illogical for Christ, who came into the world to bring perfection and joy, to do so in a manner which would cause pain.

---

[152] *PL* 171, 607C-D.

[153] See Garden in vol. 2.

[154] *Sermon for the Feast of the Assumption*, TMSM, IV, 128.

[155] *Sermon on the Annunciation of the BVM*, 2, in *The Sermons of St Antony*, trans. by Stephen Spilsbury.

[156] *Sermon on the Assumption of the BVM*, 4, in *The Sermons of St Antony*, trans. by Stephen Spilsbury.

[157] *TMSM*, IV,199.

Like many before him, he believes that the birth pangs which Mary avoided at Bethlehem were hers on Calvary:[158]

> She will give birth without being bothered by pain. For it would be shameful for the Creator and perfect Lord of all nature if the Virgin Mother suffered pain in putting into the world he whom all natural beings welcome with joy and with progress in perfection. In fact, the Virgin did not suffer in giving birth while other mothers suffer great pain. But later, at the moment of the death of her Son, when, that is, she suffered for her Son who was hanging on the Cross, nature reclaimed those moans which the birth-giving Virgin denied it. For then, through the intimate suffering of the Cross in her heart, she learnt what it means to be a mother. *Postilla super Isaiam, c. 7, 14*[159]

In his *Commentary on Luke*, Bonaventure († 1274), like many of his predecessors, links the absence of libidinousness in the conception of Jesus with Mary's pain-free parturition, when he speaks of her experiencing a 'conception without concupiscence, a birth without parturition and pain.'[160]

In a work that was long erroneously attributed to Bonaventure, Conrad of Saxony († 1279), citing the example of Judith, who is said to have been continent in her widowhood, not taking another husband (Judith 10. 10-11), writes:

> In this blessing of chaste Judith, the blessing of Mary is not only prefigured but even proven by a stronger argument. If the chaste widow is blessed, how much more the chaste virgin, and especially such a virgin who is to give birth to God and who certainly merited to give birth in such a way as not to lose her virginity. *Speculum Beatae Mariae Virginis, 15*[161]

Aquinas († 1274), in a departure from the norm, has little to say about Mary in his treatment of the question in the *Summa*. He does not directly address the question of concupiscence and ignores the Eve-Mary parallel. Instead his argument is strictly Christological: it is because of the property of the Word, and as a sign of his purpose in becoming incarnate that the Virgin remains incorrupt, while Mary's purity, though implicit, is peripheral:

> Without any doubt whatever we must assert that the Mother of Christ was a virgin even in His Birth: for the prophet says not only: 'Behold a virgin shall conceive,' but adds: 'and shall bear a son.' This indeed was befitting for three reasons. First, because this was in keeping with a property of Him whose Birth is in question, for He is the Word of God. For the word is not only conceived in the

---

[158] See chapter on Immediate Redemption.
[159] *TMSM*, IV, 333.
[160] Quoted in George H. Tavard, *The Forthbringer of God: St. Bonaventure on the Virgin Mary* (Chicago: Franciscan Herald Press, 1989), p. 63.
[161] Trans. by Campion Murray as *The Angel's Greeting*, in *Franciscan Friars Province of the Holy Spirit* <http://www.franciscans.org.au> [accessed 3 June 2007].

mind without corruption, but also proceeds from the mind without corruption. Wherefore in order to show that body to be the body of the very Word of God, it was fitting that it should be born of a virgin incorrupt. [...] Secondly, this is fitting as regards the effect of Christ's Incarnation: since He came for this purpose, that He might take away our corruption. Wherefore it is unfitting that in His Birth He should corrupt His Mother's virginity. *ST*, III, *q. 28, a. 2*[162]

The third reason that Aquinas gives, that Jesus wished to honour his Mother in accordance with the fifth commandment, is also not part of the usual array of arguments put forward in favour of the virgin birth: 'Thirdly, it was fitting that He Who commanded us to honour our father and mother should not in His Birth lessen the honour due to His Mother.' Aquinas is careful to avoid any hint of Gnosticism, stating clearly that the virgin birth of Jesus did not mean that his body was any different from the rest of humanity. His passing through the hymen without damaging it was, as it were, a once-off miracle, and is not to be confused with the ability he demonstrated after his resurrection to pass through solid objects, an ability that is a property only of a glorified body resulting from 'an overflow of the soul's glory on to the body'.

Mechthild of Magdeburg (†c. 1285), a German mystic who experienced visions from the time she was a child, provides a rather poetic description of Mary's pregnancy and confinement:

> The longer the pregnancy went on, the more radiant, beautiful and wise she became. She arose and said: 'Lord, Father, I give you praise because you have raised me up and my child will become great in heaven and on earth.' When the time came in which other women become listless and move around heavily, Mary was at peace and happy even though her body was full, since she kept within herself the well-formed Son of God. [...] The omnipotent God in his wisdom, the eternal Son in his human reality, the Holy Spirit with his delicate sweetness, slid joyously and without effort through the body of Mary. It happened suddenly, as when the sun causes its ray to fall on dew, in loving peace. When Mary hugged her beautiful baby she bent her head over his face and said: 'Welcome, O my innocent child and my powerful Lord, to whom all things belong.' *The Flowing Light of the Godhead*[163]

The contrast with Aquinas could not be greater. Where the one is interested purely in the Christological implications of the virgin birth the other concentrates on Mary's maternity, appropriately reflecting the two sides of this Marian privilege – the unique worthiness of Mary to give birth to the Lord, and the extraordinary nature of the child born to her.

---

[162] Translations are from *Summa Theologica*, ed. and trans. by Fathers of the English Dominican Province, 3 vols (New York: Benzinger, 1947-48).
[163] *TMSM*, III, 363.

Perpetual Virginity

Unlike the virginal conception and the virgin birth, Mary's perpetual virginity (*virginitas post partum*)[164] has no direct bearing on Christology. Rather, it was a question of fittingness: could Mary have permitted her womb, the sacred vessel that had borne the Messiah, to have been violated by common sexual commerce? Here, two elements combine. The first is reverence towards sacred spaces, such as temples or vessels, present in Greek and Latin culture, but particularly marked in the Hebraic tradition. In this regard it is no coincidence that two of the more prominent Marian typologies among the Fathers are the Ark of the Covenant and the burning bush, both *loci* made sacred by the presence of God.[165] Thus it is that one finds in apocryphal accounts of the Virgin's Dormition the story of the Jew whose hand is withered when attempting to assail Mary's funeral bier, just as Uzzah is struck down by God for having touched the Ark of the Covenant (II Kings 6. 6-7).[166] Secondly, the doctrine reflects the generally negative attitude towards sexuality and the strong tendency in the early Church to promote the ideal of virginity, which was (and continues to be) regarded as the primary expression of a radical choice of God which anticipates the life of Heaven.[167] It was primarily for these reasons that the Fathers dedicated so much time to providing a firm Scriptural basis for belief in Mary's perpetual virginity, which remained one of her most discussed attributes in both the Patristic and Medieval periods.[168]

Although the title Ever-Virgin (*aeiparthenos*) did not come into common usage until the fourth century, the first known use of the title being by Peter of Alexandria († 311),[169] for most of the Fathers it was inconceivable that the body of Mary, which had contained the living Word of God, should have remained anything but inviolate. Aside from the fact that belief in Mary's perpetual virginity was particularly important if she were to serve as a model for the life of

---

[164] The terminology here can be rather confusing in that Mary's perpetual virginity is also used with reference the preservation of her virginity in giving birth to Christ. The sense in which I use it here is with reference to her complete abstinence from sexual relations throughout her life.

[165] For further discussion see the Ark and the Burning Bush in vol. 2. On the sacredness of vessels and for further bibliography see Sarah Jane Boss, 'The Development of the Virgin's Cult in the High Middle Ages', in *Mary: The Complete Resource*, pp. 149-72 (pp. 157-58).

[166] See chapter on the Assumption.

[167] For further discussion see vol. 2.

[168] In fact, no theologian of note in the first millennium of the Church fails to deal with the question. See Leena Peltomaa, *The Image of the Virgin*, who states that the only two attributes associated with Mary in the early centuries of the Church were virgin motherhood and antitype of Eve (p. 126). On the pervasiveness of the ascetic ideal of virginity in late antiquity, even beyond Christian circles, see Jaroslav Pelikan, *Mary through the Centuries*, pp. 113-16.

[169] See Mary Clayton, *The Cult of the Virgin Mary*, p. 6.

asceticism and monastic chastity, the idea that she might have gone on to have a normal married life was seen to threaten her status as the true Mother of Jesus since it would suggest that she was something less than the sacred and untouchable vessel that has enfleshed the Word. In fact, Tertullian (†c. 230) is the only Father of note to deny explicitly Mary's perpetual virginity: 'She was a virgin who gave birth to Christ, but after his birth she was married to one man, so that both ideals of holiness might be exemplified in the parentage of Christ, in the person of a mother who was both a virgin and married to one husband.'[170] The principal arguments that were raised against Mary's *virginitas post partum* were her marriage to Joseph and the fact that the Gospels make reference to the 'brothers' of Jesus (Matthew 12. 46-50 and 13. 55; Mark 3. 31-35; Luke 8. 19-21). As with belief in the virgin birth, the apocrypha played an important role in bolstering the argument in favour of her perpetual virginity. The *Protoevangelium of St. James* explicitly speaks of the sons of Joseph being by a previous marriage, and was cited frequently, particularly in the Eastern Church, as proof that the brothers of the Lord were, in fact, half-brothers:[171]

> And the priest said to Joseph, Thou hast been chosen by lot to take into thy keeping the virgin of the Lord. But Joseph refused, saying: I have children, and I am an old man, and she is a young girl. I am afraid lest I become a laughing-stock to the sons of Israel. And the priest said to Joseph: Fear the Lord thy God, and remember what the Lord did to Dathan, and Abiram, and Korah; how the earth opened, and they were swallowed up on account of their contradiction. And now fear, O Joseph, lest the same things happen in thy house. And Joseph was afraid, and took her into his keeping. *Protoevangelium, 9*

Origen (†c. 254) embraces the explanation offered by the apocrypha that the 'brothers' of Jesus were sons of Joseph by an earlier marriage.[172] He offers two reasons for Mary's marriage to Joseph, which were subsequently adopted by many writers, the first being that it avoided the scandal of a virgin being with child, and the second that God wished to hide the birth of Christ from the devil.[173] Origen also explicitly links Mary's perpetual virginity to her dignity as the Mother of the Word:

> Those who speak thus mean to safeguard Mary's dignity in the virginity she conserved until the end, so that the body chosen to serve the Word [...] did not know any relations with a man, after the point that the Holy Spirit came down

[170] *De monogamia*, 8, 3, *PL* 2, 939B, quoted in *MF*, p. 65. See also *De virginibus velandis*, 6. 1-1, *PL* 2, 897B-898B.
[171] See Bertrand Buby, *Mary of Galilee*, 3 vols (New York: Alba House, 1994-1997), III, 35-36 and Chris Maunder, 'Mary in the New Testament and Apocrypha', pp. 20-23 and 39-44.
[172] See *MF*, p. 75.
[173] See *In Lucam*, 6, 3-4, *PG* 13, 1814-15, *MF*, pp. 75-77.

upon her and the power of the Most High overshadowed her. *Commentary on Matthew, 10, 17*[174]

Hilary of Poitiers († 367) couches the question of Mary's marital relations with Joseph in the language of Roman law, stating that Mary gave birth while betrothed to Joseph, after which he recognised her as his wife, but without ever consummating the marriage. He too believes that the ''brethren' of Jesus were children of Joseph by a previous marriage.[175] Athanasius of Alexandria († 373) explicitly states that one of the reasons that Mary remained a virgin was in order to be a model: 'Mary, who gave birth to God, remained a virgin to the end [in order to be a model for] all who come after her.'[176] He is one of the first Fathers to use Christ's words from the Cross to his Mother and John, 'behold thy son. [...] Behold thy mother' (John 19. 27), as proof that Jesus did not have brothers to whom he could entrust is Mother: 'With these words he affirms that Mary did not generate another son apart from the Saviour. If, in fact, she had had another son the Lord would have taken this into account without having to entrust her to others.'[177] He goes on to point out that if Mary had abandoned her own family to become the mother of others, this would have been a punishable offence under Jewish law.

Ephrem († c. 373), rather unusually, places his argument in favour of Mary's perpetual virginity within the context of the Eve-Mary antithesis. How, he asks, would it be possible for Mary to become subject to the curse of the pangs of childbirth, having been the abode of God:

> Many dare to profess that Mary behaved as the normal wife of Joseph after the birth of the Saviour. But how would it have been possible for she who had been the abode of the Spirit, and covered by the shadow of divine power, to become the woman of a mortal man and to give birth in pain, according to the first curse? *Diatessaron, 2, 6*[178]

Basil the Great († 379) believes that Joseph and Mary lived the loving and caring life of a married couple, but that they abstained from conjugal relations, and appeals to a tradition that was already well-established by the time he was writing: 'Since those who love Christ refuse to hear that the Mother of God ceased to be a virgin at a particular moment, let us rate their testimony as sufficient.'[179] Basil, like many of the Fathers, also tackles the meaning of 'till' (Greek: *eos* Latin: *donec*) and 'firstborn' in the words of Matthew, 'And he knew

---

[174] *PG* 13, 876, *MF*, pp. 75-76.

[175] *In Matthaeum*, 1, 3 -1, 4, *PL* 9, 921A-922B.

[176] *De Virginitate, MF*, p. 104.

[177] *De Virginitate, TMPM*, I, 279.

[178] *TMPM*, IV, 83.

[179] *Homilia in sanctum Christi generationem*, 5, *TMPM*, I, 299.

her not till she brought forth her firstborn son,' which Tertullian[180] had interpreted as implying that Mary had normal conjugal relations with Joseph after the birth of Jesus. He notes that Matthew also writes that the Lord said that he would be with us *until* the end of time (28. 20), but this does not mean that Jesus will cease to be with us after the end of the world. Furthermore, the term 'firstborn' does not necessarily imply that Jesus had siblings; rather he was the first to come out of the maternal womb.

The notion that Mary took a vow of virginity was most likely first proposed by Gregory of Nyssa (†c. 394). Writing of the Virgin's reaction to Gabriel's announcement, he observes:

> What is Mary's response? Listen to the voice of the pure Virgin. The angel brings glad tidings of childbearing, but she is concerned with virginity and holds that her virginity should come before the angelic message. She does not refuse to believe the angel, neither does she abandon her convictions. She says: I have renounced every contact with man. 'How shall this be done, because I know not man?' The words of Mary herself are a confirmation of certain apocryphal traditions. If, in fact, she had been betrothed to Joseph for the purposes of conjugal union, why would she have marvelled when faced with the announcement of maternity, since she herself would have accepted becoming a mother according to the law of nature? *In Nativitate Domini*[181]

Gregory was followed by many of the Fathers both the East and the West, most notably Augustine.

Epiphanius of Salamis († 403), in response to the Antidicimarianites, a sect that denied Mary's perpetual virginity, offers a vigorous defence, which he bases both on Scripture and tradition. Like Athanasius, he uses the argument that Jesus would not have entrusted Mary to John had she had other children, and says that the 'brethren' were sons of Joseph, who was an old man of eighty when he married Mary.[182] He argues, with a clear undertone of distaste, for the inappropriateness of the Mother of God having engaged in relations with Joseph: 'We must affirm with certainty that Joseph and Mary never had matrimonial relations. Far be it from us to make such an affirmation!' He then goes on to use an argument that we have already seen in the Fathers, namely, that Jesus would not have entrusted his Mother to John as he was dying on the Cross, if she had had other children.[183] Epiphanius also deals with the issue of the meaning of 'until' and 'firstborn' in Matthew 1. 25, largely repeating the arguments of earlier Fathers.[184]

---

[180] *De virginibus velandis*, 6, 1-3, and *De monogomia*, 8, 2.

[181] *TMPM*, I, 320-21. See, *MF*, p. 157.

[182] See *MF*, pp. 123-24.

[183] *Adversus Haereses*, 28, 7, *TMPM*, I, 383.

[184] *Adversus Haereses*, 78, 21, *TMPM*, I, 401.

John Chrysostom († 407) also uses all of the standard arguments in support of Mary's perpetual virginity: the 'until' of Matthew 1. 25 does not imply that Mary had marital relations with Joseph after the birth of Christ, and Jesus entrusted Mary to John since she had no other children.[185]

In the West, Ambrose mounts a spirited and wide-ranging defence of Mary's perpetual virginity, rallying all the standard arguments drawn from Scripture.[186] He sets about tackling some of the difficulties that arise from Scripture, such as the 'brothers of the Lord', and the meaning of *donec* (till). Unlike the Eastern Fathers, he does not claim that the brethren of Jesus were sons of Joseph, instead arguing that the term was not limited merely to siblings.[187] He demonstrates with a variety of examples from the Old Testament that 'till' does not necessarily mean that something happened afterwards; besides, Jesus would not have entrusted his Mother to John (John 19. 26) if the had had other sons to take care of her.[188] The most powerful and heartfelt of all his arguments is that it is absurd to think that Mary, who had received God in her womb, would have allowed her virginity to be compromised, especially when others, who did not receive the fullness of grace that she did, preserved their virginity:

> Would the Lord Jesus, perhaps have chosen a Mother who contaminated his heavenly chamber through contact with a man, as if it were impossible to her to preserve her virginal integrity intact? And would she, whose example invites love of virginity, have deviated from that perfection which is proposed for others to imitate? [...] He promises others that they will not fail and he allows his Mother to fail? But Mary did not fail; she who is the mistress of virginity did not fail; she who had carried God in her womb could not have resolved to carry a man! Nor would Joseph, a just man, have fallen into such madness as to unite himself in a bodily union with the Mother of the Lord. *De istitutione virginis, 44-45*[189]

Jerome († 419) responds robustly to the claims of Helvidius and Jovinian[190] that virginity and marriage were of equal merit, and that Mary had consummated her marriage with Joseph after the birth of Jesus:

> We believe that God was born of the Virgin, because we read it. That Mary was married after she brought forth, we do not believe, because we do not read it. Nor do we say this to condemn marriage, for virginity itself is the fruit of

---

[185] *On Matthew*, 5, 3, *PG*, 57, 58.

[186] See *De istitutione virginis*, 32-48, *PL* 16, 313A-319A [328-333].

[187] *De istitutione virginis*, 43, *PL* 16, 317A.

[188] See *De istitutione virginis*, 35-48, *PL* 16, 315-318 [328-33].

[189] *PL 16*, 317A-C [331].

[190] See David Hunter, 'Helvidius, Jovinian, and the Virginity of Mary in Late Fourth-Century Rome', *Journal of Early Christian Studies*, 1 (1993), 47-71.

marriage; but because when we are dealing with saints we must not judge rashly. *Adversus Helvidium, 1, 21*[191]

Despite lapses into intemperate language and an excessive zeal for the superiority of virginity over marriage, Jerome's arguments in favour of Mary's perpetual virginity carry particular weight owing to his expertise as an exegete and Biblical translator, as we have already noted. In his formidable rebuttal of Helvidius he offers a detailed analysis of the Scriptural passages concerned. Like Ambrose, he firmly rejects the theory that the brethren of Jesus (Matthew 12. 46-50; Mark 3. 31-35; Luke 8. 19-20) were sons of Joseph and sets about giving the doctrine a stronger Scriptural basis, showing that the Hebrew and Greek terms for 'bother' could equally be translated as 'cousin', an argument that is still used by the Church today.[192] In like manner, he shows how a number of other Scriptural passages that Helvidius quotes do not necessarily suggest that Mary had marital relations with Joseph. Regarding Matthew's statement, 'before they came together, she was found with child, of the Holy Ghost', he says that 'before' does not necessarily mean that they came together afterwards, but rather that the conception occurred prior to their intended union. He concludes:

> It is not necessary that the things one was planning to do should really happen, should something else intervene to prevent them from happening. Thus, when the Evangelist says, 'Before they came together', he means that the time of the wedding is near and that things have reached the point that she who had been considered engaged was about to become a wife. *Adversus Helvidium, 1, 4*[193]

He goes on to refute Helvidius' claim that Matthew 1. 25, 'And he knew her not till she brought forth her firstborn son', shows that Mary knew Joseph after the birth Jesus. Using a variety of Scriptural examples he shows that the meaning of 'until' (*donec* or *usque*) is ambiguous and need not imply that something necessarily occurred *after* a designated period of time. Elsewhere he also addresses the question of whether the use of 'firstborn' proves that Mary had other children:

> Based on this passage, some perversely suppose that Mary had other children, maintaining that a son is not called 'firstborn' unless he has siblings. To the contrary, the divine Scriptures are accustomed to call someone 'firstborn', not because other siblings come after him, but because he is born first. *In Evangelium Matthei, 1, 1, 25*[194]

---

[191] This, and subsequent quotations are adapted from the translation provided in *The Catholic Encyclopedia*, <http://www.newadvent.org/fathers/3007.htm> [accessed 4 September 2007]. For the original Latin see *PL* 23, 183A-206B.
[192] *Adversus Helvidium*, 1, 15, *PL* 23, 198C-199C. See also his *In Evangelium Matthei*, 12, 50.
[193] *PL* 23, 186B, *MF*, p. 206.
[194] *PL* 26, 25C, *MF*, p. 207.

In Augustine († 430) we find a very different approach to the question of Mary's virginity than in previous Fathers. He shows less interest in the sort of arguments that delighted Jerome, centred on technical interpretations of Scripture,[195] and does not indulge in diatribes against the married state, although he does consider virginity the higher vocation.[196] Instead, in speaking of Mary's lifelong commitment to virginity he emphasises that she freely chose this path in response to God's promptings. God chose Mary to be the Mother of Jesus because she had consecrated her virginity to him, and it was he who showered on her the necessary grace for her to make this choice, but this she did of her own free will and not because God commanded it of her. The reason she chose Joseph as her betrothed was because consecrated virginity was not an acceptable choice in Jewish custom and she knew that he would respect her choice:

> Mary's virginity was certainly most pleasing and dear to the Lord. After his conception he was not content simply to protect her from any violation on the part of man and thus keep her forever intact. Already before he was conceived he wished to choose for himself, in order to be born, a virgin who was consecrated to God, as is indicated by words with which Mary responded to the angel, who was announcing her imminent motherhood: 'How shall this be done, because I know not man?' (Luke 1. 34). And she certainly would not have responded in such a way if she had not already made a vow of virginity. She had become engaged because virginity had not yet become a custom among the Jews, but she had chosen a just man who would not have used violence to take away what she had vowed to God [...]. The obligation to remain a virgin could have been imposed on her from without, so that the Son of God might assume the form of a servant through a miracle worthy of the event. But this is not what happened: it was she herself who consecrated her virginity to God when she did not yet know whom she would conceive. *De sancta virginitate, 4, 4*[197]

Isidore of Pelusium († c. 435) provides a series of examples of the use of the term 'until' in the Old Testament to show that Matthew 1. 25 does not imply that Mary engaged in conjugal relations after the birth of Christ.[198] Peter Crisologus († c. 450), Metropolitan of Ravenna, defends Mary's lifelong virginity, arguing that the 'brothers' of Jesus are the children of Mary's sister.[199] Jacob of

---

[195] This is not to say that he ignores such matters. For instance, he deals with the question of the 'brothers' of Jesus in his *In Evangelium Ioannis tractatus, 10, 2, PL 35,* 1467-1468.

[196] See, for instance, *De Sancta Virginitate, 7, 7, PL 40,* 399-400, where he argues that mothers cannot compare themselves to Mary in the same way that virgins can since the former do not give birth to Jesus but to human children while the latter give birth to Christ spiritually. He continues, however, by saying that mothers may also give spiritual birth if they ensure that their human children become good Christians.

[197] [accessed 8 August 2008].

[198] *Epistola 1*. 18, *PG* 78, 192B-193A.

[199] *Sermo 48, PL* 52, 335B.

Serug († 521) paints a picture of Joseph as a faithful servant of the Virgin, who treats her with immense respect and admiration once he has learned the truth about the Child she is bearing:

> He loved her, he admired her, he adored her, he treasured her, he respected her, he served her, he gazed on her as the cloud on Mount Sion, because the power of divinity dwelled within her. Pure was his heart and holy were his thoughts too. He gave thanks and adored because he had been made worthy of being a priest for the Son. Like a spiritual angel he served her, and he was not taken by canal thoughts. Pure was the Virgin and upright her spouse, of one mind. *Homily on the Annunciation of the Generatrix of God, 345-353*[200]

By the beginning of the reign of Justinian (527) use of the term 'Ever-Virgin' seems to have been well-established since it is found several times in the imperial profession of faith.[201] Severus of Antioch († 538) dwells at some length on the question of Mary's virginity before and after the birth of Jesus. He offers the standard explanation of Matthew 1. 25, and also argues against the possibility of Mary having had sexual relations following her conception of the Son of God: 'She who conceived in a way so worthy of God, could not subject herself afterwards to the reception of the male seed.'[202]

The Second Council of Constantinople (553), although it did not deal directly with matters concerning the Virgin, marks the first time that Mary's perpetual virginity is proclaimed as an official doctrine of the Church:

> If anyone will not confess that the Word of God has two nativities, that which is before all ages from the Father, outside time and without a body, and secondly that nativity of these latter days when the Word of God came down from the heavens and was made flesh of holy and glorious Mary, Mother of God and Ever-Virgin, and was born from her: let him be anathema. *Anathemas against the Three Chapters*[203]

Cassiodorus († c. 583), commenting on Psalm 88. 28, 'And I will make him my firstborn, high above the kings of the earth', asserts that Mary had no other child except Jesus:

> We must examine carefully why the Psalmist said 'firstborn', as if the Father had substantially generated this Son and another son had followed him. In truth it is evident to everyone that this way of expressing oneself is typical of divine Scripture. In fact, we find a similar expression in the Gospel when, with

---

[200] *Homily on the Annunciation of the Generatrix of God, TMPM*, IV, 162.
[201] Leena Peltomaa, *The Image of the Virgin Mary*, p. 127.
[202] *Homily 96, TMPM*, I, 658-59.
[203] In *Decrees of the Ecumenical Councils: From Nicaea I to Vatican II*, ed. by Norman P. Tanner (Washington DC: Georgetown University Press, 1990) <http://www.piar.hu/councils/ecum05.htm> [accessed 8 October 2007]. See *TMPM*, I, 679-82 for an account of the Council and the full text of its proclamations in Italian.

reference to Joseph and Mary it says this: 'And he knew her not till she brought forth her firstborn son' (Matthew 1. 25). Is it not consequential to believe that the Ever-Virgin Mary did not give birth to another child after the Lord Jesus Christ? The term 'firstborn' is therefore exact even if it is proved that Christ is the only one to be generated from the substance of the Father. *Expositio psalmorum, 88, 28*[204]

Venantius Fortunatus (†c. 600) portrays Mary as the leader of myriad virgins who now share the joy of heaven with her. Thus he sees her, in a certain sense as both the founder and inspiration of the virginal life:

> If then she shines forth, the Mother of God, the Virgin Mary,
> And she leads the virgin sheep of the Lamb's flock.
> She, surrounded by a bevy of maidens,
> With the light of her chastity leads on the splendid ranks.
> In the banquets of paradise basing their vows;
> One collects violets, another gathers roses;
> With their fingers they pick the buds and lilies of the lawns.
>
> *Carmina miscellanea*, 4, 26 [205]

The *Life of Mary* attributed to Maximus the Confessor († 662) asserts that the Virgin had never intended to wed: 'Not only did the Virgin not have any knowledge of the reality of marriage, but she also did not even have the intention of desiring it in her heart, since, from the beginning, she had grown up entirely holy in soul and body.'[206] Like a number of earlier writings, the author dismisses the possibility that the Virgin and Joseph had marital relations with a tone of distaste: 'The angel called him to whom she was promised 'spouse', but, in truth she had not been given to him as a bride in the manner of other women – far from it! She had become engaged to him so that he might guard her like a divine treasure, dedicated to the Lord.'[207]

John of Damascus († 749) defends Mary's perpetual virginity with reference to Matthew 1. 25:

> The Ever-Virgin, therefore, remains a virgin even after the birth, never uniting herself to any man in any way up to her death. For, although it is written, 'And he knew her not till she brought forth her firstborn son,' it should be known that the firstborn is called firstborn even if he is the only child. The term 'firstborn' only means that he was born first and does not at all suggest the birth of others. And the word 'till' signifies the limit of the established time, without adding anything regarding the subsequent situation. The Lord too says, 'Behold I am

---

[204] *PL* 70, 636D. Cassidorus also deals in like manner with the question of 'till' with reference to Psalms 109, 1: 'The oracle of the Lord said to my Lord: Sit thou at my right hand: Until I make thy enemies thy footstool. 109, 1, *PL* 70, 794A-B.
[205] *PL* 88, 175, *MF*, p. 364.
[206] *Life of Mary*, 23, *TMPM*, II, 200.
[207] *Life of Mary*, 30, *TMPM*, II, 206-07.

with you all days, even to the consummation of the world' (Matthew 28. 20), not because he will be separated from us. Indeed, the divine Apostle says, 'And so shall we be always with the Lord' (I Thessalonians 4. 17), meaning after the general resurrection. *Exposition on the Orthodox Faith, 6, 14*[208]

With characteristic vigour Ildephonse of Toledo († 667) rebuts the argument that Mary went on to have other children after the birth of Jesus, addressing his remarks to Helvidius, a heretic of an earlier age, though they are clearly intended for contemporary ears:

> Why do you put yourself forward, filled as you are with shame? Why do you approach, unworthy as you are of all respect? Why do you bustle about, deprived as you are of all modesty? For what reason do you attempt to dishonour the initial state of our Virgin, destining her to a conclusion of corruption? Why do you try to debase the roots of her virginity by referring to the reality of her being mother to another? And why do you attempt to undermine her integrity, consecrated to God, through recourse to purely human arguments? I will never permit you to insinuate yourself abusively into the rights of divine majesty, to despoil the possessions of God with your impudence, to cause damage to the dwelling place of the Lord with your corrosive insults, to maintain that the door of God's house, which remained shut during the birth, was violated by any other person. *De virginitate perpetua sanctae Mariae, 2, 1*[209]

Hrabanus Maurus († 846) is representative of many of his fellow churchmen in the West in that he essentially repeats all of the traditional arguments in favour of Mary's perpetual virginity although he does add some insights of his own, such as Jesus being the 'firstborn' to the life of Heaven. His is also one of the more thorough restatements of traditional teaching in the Medieval Church. He begins by tackling the meaning of the Matthean, 'And Joseph rising up from sleep, did as the angel of the Lord had commanded him, and took unto him his wife. And he knew her not till she brought forth her firstborn son' (Matthew 1. 24-25). Joseph, he says did not 'know' his wife because of what he had learnt from the angel. Repeating the argument of the Fathers he notes that 'till' does not necessarily mean that Joseph knew Mary after the birth of Jesus. Rather it means that he knew or recognised her as his wife: 'therefore she is known, not united carnally.' The 'brothers of the Lord' are his cousins while 'firstborn' does not automatically imply that more children came afterwards but simply that Mary had not had children before. Moreover Jesus is called the 'firstborn' since all those who accepted him became children of the Father and his brothers: 'as many as received him, he gave them power to be made the sons of God (John 1. 12). What is more, he is the firstborn in the sense that he is the first to have been resurrected to the new life of Heaven: 'He is therefore called the firstborn of the dead because, although he became incarnate after many brothers, he was

---

[208] *TMPM*, II, 493.
[209] *PL* 96, 61A-B.

the first among all to rise from the dead, and from death he opened the way to heaven to believers.'[210]

Fulbert of Chartres († 1028) extols Mary's virginity and urges his listeners to follow her example:

> Rejoice as much as you can, all you who are virgins, you who know that one day you will be enriched by such a holy and most bright gift of God. Put your hope in her who has become the true mistress of the gift of virginity, both before and after the birth [of Christ]. Magnify her, incessantly demonstrating holy conduct in life, because persevering in virginity you will rejoice in the presence of the Mother of the Lord. *Sermo 5, In Ortu almae Virginis Mariae inviolatae*[211]

In condemning those who would deny Mary's *virginitas post partum* John of Fécamp († 1078) makes reference to the ancient heresy of Helvidius. It was a common practice to highlight old heresies both as an excuse for condemning those who might repeat the error and in order to show that the author had the authority of Church Tradition to back him up:

> The Mother of this Lord of ours, Jesus Christ, Blessed Mary, most certainly gave birth as a virgin, and remained a virgin after the birth. And we must not assent to the blasphemy of Helvidius who says [that she was] a virgin before the birth but not after. On the contrary, we must believe with intact faith that the integrity of such a great Virgin remained always intact. *Confessio fidei, 3, 8*[212]

Rudolph the Ardent († 1101) declares his admiration for Mary, who preserved her virginity despite being married, for which reason she was chosen to be the Mother of God:

> Although she was married and tender maiden she did not allow herself to be ensnared by the allures of marriage, but rather preserved her virginity in marriage too. For this reason, even in her virginity she was worthy of a singular fruitfulness to the extent that she gave birth, not to an ordinary individual, but to the Son of God. *Sermo 16, In Annuntiatione*[213]

Herbert of Losinga († 1119) speaks of Mary offering turtledoves when she presented herself and her Son at the temple for purification to symbolize their virginal integrity. Mary, he goes on to say, with reference to the Bride of Canticles, did not give herself over to bigamy by having relations with another husband:

> So, the most Blessed Virgin, whose immaculate flesh had been espoused to the Word of God, did not know another husband, either before or after [the birth],

---

[210] See *Commentariorum in Matthaeum*, 19-23, *PL 107*, 747-754, *TMPM*, III, 776-79.
[211] *PL* 141, 330D,
[212] *PL* 101, 1059A.
[213] *PL* 155, 1359B.

totally excluding the odiousness of bigamy. She conceived as a virgin, gave birth as a virgin, and a virgin she remained, and she preserved intact the seal of her virginity for the High King who was born of her. *Sermon for the Purification of Holy Mary*

Bruno of Asti († 1123) repeats the reason given by many of the Fathers for Mary marrying Joseph, namely that she would have been stoned as an adulteress had she not, and that she would have need of the protection of a man for herself and her Son in the vicissitudes that she would have to face.[214] Bernard of Clairvaux († 1153) also relies on the Fathers, asserting that God inspired Mary to make a vow of virginity and declaring that 'she undoubtedly must be ranked over all who was the first among mortals to conceive the design of emulating upon earth the life of the angels'.[215]

Peter Comestor († 1178) defends the triple virginity of Mary, before during and after the birth:

> And the Lord said to me: this gate shall remain closed and man shall not enter in by it (Ezekiel 44, 2). This is the third time that this affirmation is repeated. Certainly the term man does not mean gender but rather husband, so that the thing would be more expressly stated, as if he were saying: not even her husband, that is, Joseph had conjugal relations with her. Therefore he opportunely recalls for the third time that the gate was shut, because there is no doubt that the Virgin was such before the birth, during the birth, and after the birth. *In festo Assumptionis Beatae Mariae 2*[216]

Adam of St. Victor (†c. 1192) also proclaims Mary's triple virginity, in verse:

> Say, O nature, by changing things, where are your laws? A Virgin bore a Son, but, conceiving by means of the truth, she did not cast aside the lily of uncorrupted chastity. She was virgin before, during, and after birth, virgin in mind and in body; made a Mother without father she bore in time the Word of the Father who had no mother. A branch bore a flower, a star bore the sun, the Virgin Mother bore a child coeternal with the Father *In Assumptione BVM, 37*[217]

Martin of León († 1203) affirms that Mary was the first to choose the 'angelic life' of virginity by taking a vow:

> Certainly she is the most blessed among all women because she was the first among all women to offer the most glorious gift of her virginity to God. It is

---

[214] See his *Commentaria in Matthaeum*, PL *165*, 73-74.
[215] *Fourth Sermon for the Feast of the Assumption*, in *SBS*, p. 202. See Eva Cariota Rava, 'Verginità perpetua e maternità divina di Maria', in *Respice stellam: Maria in San Bernardo e nella tradizione cistercense, Atti del convegno internazionale*, ed. by Ignazio M. Calabuig (Roma, Marianum 21-24 October 1991), (Rome: Marianum, 1993), pp 125-41.
[216] *PL* 171, 632B.
[217] *AH* 54, 326-327, n. 206.

said she is the first in the court of the High King because on earth she dedicated herself to imitating the angelic life. *In Assumptione sanctae Mariae* [218]

Adam of Dryburgh (†c. 1212) comments on the revolutionary choice that Mary made in choosing to remain a virgin in a society that regarded sterility as a curse from God. He notes that not only did she go against the practice of the Jews, but having received the extraordinary gift of becoming the Mother of God, she chose not to keep it for herself. Here, he is clearly giving the message that virginity for virginity's sake is not the Christian ideal but that only by generating Christ for others is the virgin following the example set by Mary:[219]

> What woman, at that time, would have been capable of, or would have been willing to make a statement of this nature: 'I know not man' (Luke 1. 34)? You would most certainly answer that there was no-one if you fully understood the meaning of these words. What does this assertion, 'I know not man' mean if not that she did not intend to know man? Not only was she ignorant of man at that moment but she had made a firm proposal not to know him throughout her life. Was not the sterile woman considered accursed at that time? And this was true to the degree that the daughter of Jephte felt she had to grieve and cry because she was about to bring her flesh to the grave in a virginal state and not because she was about to be butchered by her father's sword. But you turned to Christ with an interior intent. You looked to the East, that is, to the virginity of the flesh, during a life that was lived in purity. I repeat it, you aimed for this before all other women for which reason you have been called blessed amongst women (Luke 1. 48) through the centuries. But you did not wish to keep only for yourself him whom you received then. On the contrary, he who came to you from the bosom of the Father has come to us though you. *Sermon 16, for the Second Sunday of Advent, 3*[220]

John of Ford (†c. 1214) makes the same claim: 'Finally, like a lily that takes its origin in a celestial field, immediately, through divine inspiration, she made a pact with virginity and [was] the first among women'.[221]

Honorius III († 1227) likens Mary's chastity to the walls of a fortified castle which was utterly invincible:

> The wall signifies her chastity because just as the wall defends the castle from its enemies chastity defends the soul from the temptations of the demons and from all their insidiousness, because the demons never leave anything un-tempted. [...] That castle, that is to say, the Virgin Mary, was furnished with an impregnable wall, that is, an invincible chastity, to the point that libidinousness

---

[218] *TMSM*, III, 502.
[219] On the spiritual generation of Christ see Model in vol. 2.
[220] *PL* 198, 187B-D.
[221] *Sermon 70, On the Canticle of Canticles, TMSM*, IV, 76.

never touched her senses, nor did the slightest thought pollute her mind. *First Sermon on the Assumption*[222]

The mid-twelfth-century *Vita rhythmica*, a hugely popular work that draws on canonical and extra-canonical texts as well as the writings of the Fathers to build up a portrait of Mary's life, and which inspired many imitations, offers an elaborate and convoluted explanation of the 'brothers of the Lord' which relies heavily on *Pseudo-Matthew*. According the *Vita*, Anna, the mother of Mary, married twice more after the death of Joachim and had two more daughters both of whom were also called Mary – hence the different Marys present at the Passion. These two Marys had a number of children who were the cousins of 'brothers' or Jesus.[223] Such an account, of course, blatantly contradicts the belief – also apocryphal – that Anna was already well-advanced in years and sterile when she miraculously conceived the Virgin, but such contradictions do not seem to have been of concern either to the author or his readers.

Anthony of Padua († 1231) mentions Mary's vow of virginity, which he considers her first and best defence against the devil: 'Blessed Mary crushed the 'head', the beginning, of the devil's temptation, when she made her vow of virginity'.[224]

Bonaventure († 1274) uses forceful language in his condemnation of those who would claim that she had normal marital relations, saying that it is, 'totally irrational that the most Blessed Mother of God, after being the temple of the Holy Spirit, would have performed the work of the flesh.' Reflecting the abhorrence with which such a prospect was regarded, he continues: 'To believe such an indignity of the Mother of God can only enter a soul that is impious and stupid; therefore it is erroneous and pernicious.'[225] Like his predecessors he considers the brothers of Jesus to be cousins, and counters the argument that 'firstborn' implies that Mary had further children by pointing out that Jesus entrusted her to John on Calvary. Speaking of Mary's resistance to any form of desire, he says: 'This was done by a vow of strictest virginity to which, from divine inspiration, the Virgin Mary totally gave herself and among others she was the first to do this.'[226]

---

[222] *TMSM*, IV, 126-27.

[223] See *Vita Beatae Mariae Virginis et Salvatoris rhythmica*, 3, 3764-3799, ed. by Adolf Vögtlin, Bibliothek des litterarischen Vereins Stuttgart, 180 (Tübingen: Laupp, 1888), pp. 132-33. For extracts from the poem in Italian see *TMSM*, IV, 137-145.

[224] *Sermon on the Purification of the BVM*, 4, in *The Sermons of St Antony*, trans. by Stephen Spilsbury.

[225] *Dubia circa litteram*, IV, d. 30, dub. iv, quoted in Tavard, *The Forthbringer*, p. 7.

[226] *Third Sermon on the Annunciation of the Blessed Virgin Mary*, in *Sermons on the Blessed Virgin Mary*, trans. by Campion Murray, in *Franciscan Friars: Province of the Holy Spirit* <http://www.franciscans.org.au > [accessed 26 August 2006]. See also *Sent*. IV, d. xxviii, a. un, q. 6, where he again asserts that the Virgin took a vow of virginity and that her consent to marriage did not imply agreement to sexual relations. See Tavard, pp. 35-37.

Aquinas († 1274), like Bonaventure is vehement in his defence of Mary's perpetual virginity, indicative of the passion stirred by the very notion that the Mother of God could have allowed her body to be sullied by a man. To suggest that Mary had had carnal relations with Joseph, he declares, 'is derogatory to Christ's perfection' as well as being 'an insult to the Holy Spirit' whose temple she was. Moreover, it 'is derogatory to the dignity and holiness of God's Mother', who would seem ungrateful for the privilege she had received, and 'would be tantamount to an imputation of extreme presumption in Joseph', who full knew that she had conceived by the Holy Spirit.[227] Despite the vehemence of his language, however, Aquinas does not dwell on Mary's personal purity here, preferring to stress her status as the Mother of God rather than her sanctity. Aquinas does not accept that Mary took an absolute vow of virginity before the Annunciation, as this would have gone against the Law of the Old Testament. Instead, he believes that Mary made a vow that was conditional on God's favour, and only later, once the new Law had been instituted by the advent of Christ did she make an absolute vow, together with her husband, Joseph.[228]

Albert the Great († 1280) writes of Mary's perpetual virginity in less technical language than was his wont, paraphrasing from the Septuagint version of Canticles:

> 'I saw my bride like a dove who was rising above the rivers of waters; flowers of roses and lilies of the valley surrounded her like the days of spring.' Adorned with simplicity, the dove was most beautiful also because of her virginity. To her is applied what was said of Judith: 'All this dressing up did not proceed from sensuality, but from virtue' (Judith 10. 4). Above the rivers of the waters, she rose up to the summits of virginity, treading under foot the flow of concupiscence and practicing every virtue. [...] She was always a virgin, before the birth, in giving birth and after the birth, as Ezekiel says: 'The gate that you saw will remain closed; it will not open for anyone and no man shall pass through because the Lord God of Israel has entered in' (See Ezekiel 44. 2). *On the Sacrifice of the Mass, tr. 2, c. 8*[229]

The anonymous *Mariale Super Missus Est*, attributed until 1952 to Albert the Great, speaks of the imperfection of the women of the Old Testament who did not understand virginity. Mary was the first to comprehend its true value in the eyes of God, for which reason it was to her that the angel came:

> For this reason no figure could in fact fully express the Annunciation to the Virgin because no other virgin would have ever conceived, and until this Virgin, virginity was considered as a curse and a shame. Instead this Virgin cancelled out the opprobrium of virginity and made virginity itself sacred, so that the beatitude of virginity began from her, and she is the Virgin of virgins who, without any command, without any counsel, and without any example offered the glorious

---

[227] *ST*, III, q. 28, a. 3.
[228] *ST*, III, q. 28, a. 4.
[229] *TMSM*, IV, 340.

gift of virginity to God. *Mariale sive quaestiones super Evangelium: Missus est Angelus Gabriel*, q. 11, 4[230]

This passage expresses well the fundamental reason behind the Church's constant and consistent insistence on Mary's perpetual virginity namely the sacredness of virginity as a radical choice which leads to union with God which generates Christ and which frees the person to become a mother and father of souls. It was because of Mary's complete and exclusive giving of herself to God, in mind, body, spirit and will, that he had chosen her amongst all women to be the Mother of his Son. Why should she reverse a choice that had led her to a union with her Maker like no other? How could any other choice give her such joy and fulfilment, she whom all generations would call blessed?

---

[230] *TMSM*, IV, 346.

Chapter 3 – Mary Co-Redemptrix: Remote Co-Operation

Genesis 3. 15:	I will put enmities between thee and the woman, and thy seed and her seed: she shall crush thy head, and thou shalt lie in wait for her heel.
Genesis 3. 20:	And Adam called the name of his wife Eve: because she was the mother of all the living.
Ecclesiasticus 24. 14:	From the beginning, and before the world, was I created.
Luke 1. 38:	And Mary said: Behold the handmaid of the Lord; be it done to me according to thy word.
Apocalypse 12 5-6:	And she brought forth a man child, who was to rule all nations with an iron rod: and her son was taken up to God, and to his throne. And the woman fled into the wilderness, where she had a place prepared by God

Theologians make a distinction between Mary's remote co-operation in the work of Redemption, whereby, by consenting to the Incarnation, she provided Christ with the humanity that he offered in sacrifice on Calvary,[1] and her immediate co-operation in the Passion through her willingness to unite herself completely with her Son's suffering for the sake of humanity. From an etymological point of view, the term Co-Redemptrix derives from the Latin *cum* (with), which does not necessarily imply equality in status.[2] In Mary's case, her role in the Redemption is totally subordinate to that of her Son, since she is a creature wholly dependent on him. Nevertheless, though God could have brought about the Redemption in any number of ways, he chose to do so through Mary. It was through her that he took on human flesh, and she co-operated fully with his redemptive mission, in the first place by accepting to become his Mother, and thereafter by remaining faithful to him throughout his life, and in a special way, during his Passion and death. The consequences of Mary's *fiat*,[3] viewed in terms of the history of salvation, were seen as immense. From the moment of her assent, not from the moment of Christ's birth, the plan of redemption went into operation on earth. From her assent flowed consequences reaching right back to the dawn of history in terms of the

---

[1] See Paul Haffner, *The Mystery of Mary* (Leominster, Herefordshire: Gracewing, 2004), pp. 191-93.

[2] See the classic study by Gabriele M. Roschini, *Problematica sulla Corredenzione* (Rome: Edizioni Marianum, 1969), and see Mark Miravalle, *'With Jesus': The Story of Mary Co-Redemptrix* (Goleta, Ca.: Queenship Publishing, 2003), particularly pp. 7-14. Also useful is Juniper B. Carol, *De corredemptione beatae Virginis Mariae* (Vatican City: Typis Polyglottis Vaticanis, 1950) and René Laurentin, 'Le titre de Corédemptrice: Étude historique', *Marianum*, 13 (1951), 399-402.

[3] '*Fiat mihi secundum verbum tuum*' ('Be it done to me according to thy word') (Luke 1. 38).

redemption of Adam, Eve and all the Old Testament figures, as well as future events such as the Second Coming, the Resurrection of the dead, the Last Judgement and the glorification of creation (a new Heavens and a new Earth).

She is therefore the new Eve who is instrumental in restoring the bridge between God and humanity destroyed by the sin of the first Eve.[4] This is why the Fathers confer titles on her such as 'true mother of all the living' (see Genesis 3. 2), 'gate of heaven' (see Ezekiel 44. 1-3) and 'ladder of heaven' (see Genesis 28. 12). In this chapter we shall consider the question of how Mary's co-operation in the Incarnation contributed to the Redemption of humanity.

The Patristic Period

For the early Fathers, Mary's essential function was to generate Christ, the Redeemer, and by extension, the Church, which they saw as the body of her Son.[5] It was largely in this sense that she was perceived as playing a role in the economy of salvation. In the very earliest writings, one finds claims that the Virgin is already foretold from the beginning of history in the prophecy of Genesis 3. 15[6] She is seen as the fulfilment of a variety of Old Testament prophecies and the great Hebrew women of old foreshadow her.[7] Some of the

---

[4] The bibliography on the Eve-Mary antithesis is immense. See in particular the studies in the three issues of *Études mariales* entitled 'La nouvelle Ève', 12, 13, 14 (1954-57) See also André-Marie Dubarle, 'Les fondements bibliques du titre marial de la nouvelle Ève', *Recherches de science religieuse*, 39 (1951), 49-64. Lino Cignelli, *Maria, nuova Eva nella patristica greca (sec. II-V)* (Assisi: Porziuncola, 1966), and Kathleen N. Nyberg, *The New Eve* (Nashville: Abingdon, 1967). Also useful is Celestino Corsato, 'La tipologia "Eva-Chiesa-Maria" nella tradizione patristica prenicena", *Theotokos*, 9 (2001), 153-90 and Ernst Guldan, *Eva und Maria: Eine Antithese als Bildmotiv* (Graz and Cologne: Böhlaus, 1966). For further bibliography see Michael O'Carroll, *Theotokos: A Theological Encyclopedia of the Blessed Virgin Mary* (Collegeville, Minnesota: Liturgical Press, 1982), p. 141. For brief syntheses of theological developments regarding Mary in the Patristic period see the two chapters by Elio Perotto, 'Primi abozzi di riflessione teologica su Maria', and 'Maria nell'area culturale greca: da san Giustino († 165 ca) a san Giovanni Damasceno († 749 ca)', in *SDM*, I, 257-62 and pp. 293-305. In the same volume, for the Latin area, see Mario, Maritano, 'Maria nell'area culturale latina: da Tertulliano († 240 ca) a sant'Ildefonso di Toledo († 667), pp. 306-27. See also *La mariologia nella catechesi dei Padri (età prenicena)*, ed. by Sergio Felici, (Rome: Libreria Ateneo Salesiano, 1991) and Davide M. Montagna, 'La lode alla Theotokos nei testi greci dei secoli IV- VII', in *Marianum* 24 (1962), pp. 453-543.

[5] For further discussion see Mary and the Church in vol. 2.

[6] See Hilda Graef, *Doctrine and Devotion*, I, 1-6.

[7] See Angelo M. Gilo, 'La Vergine Madre e l'Antico Testamento secondo i primi Padri della Chiesa', *Theotokos*, 9 (2001), 83-128.

Fathers, in addition to believing that the Old Testament foretold the Virgin, also saw her foreshadowed in pagan mythology and literature.[8]

The Fathers did not see Mary merely as the passive recipient of Gabriel's message at the Annunciation (Luke. 1. 26-38). Rather, heaven awaited her choice and by uttering her *fiat* she freely cooperated in God's salvific plan, providing the Word with his humanity, which was the very instrument of Redemption. In so doing, she reversed the actions of Eve and opened up the way for humankind to be restored. The Eve-Mary antithesis, based on Genesis 3. 15, was one of the earliest and the most enduring of the themes in Mariology, and is the foundation for the notion of the co-redemption.

Justin Martyr (†c. 165) was the first to speak of this central soteriological role, playing off the Virgin Mary's reception of Gabriel's message against the virgin Eve's response to Satan's words (it was believed that Eve remained a virgin until after the Fall).[9] Just as Eve had brought death to the world by listening to the voice of the serpent and disobeying God, the Virgin Mary had rescued the world from its bondage and opened the way to salvation by her *fiat*. It is precisely in this free consent that she reverses Eve's choice and sets in motion the process whereby humanity is restored to grace:

> He became man by the Virgin, in order that the disobedience which proceeded from the serpent might be destroyed in the same manner in which it derived its origin. For Eve, when she was still a virgin and undefiled, conceived the word of the serpent, and gave birth to disobedience and death. But the Virgin Mary received faith and joy, when the angel Gabriel announced the joyful news to her that the Spirit of the Lord would come upon her, and the power of the Most High would overshadow her: so that the Holy One born of her would be the Son of God; and she replied, 'Be it done to me according to thy word.' And from her was born he of whom so many Scriptures refer, as we have shown. Through him God destroys both the serpent and those angels and men who are like him, and he brings about deliverance from death to those who repent of their wickedness and believe in Him. *Dialogus cum Trypho, 100, 4-5*[10]

An important theme in this passage, which was to form a central plank in the understanding of Mary's role in the economy of salvation, is the enmity between her and the devil. Although most of the early Fathers speak of the enmity between the serpent and Christ, and not Mary, in the context of Genesis 3. 15, since the Greek Bible as well as early Latin versions correctly translated the Hebrew *hu* (it) as a masculine pronoun (as opposed the Latin feminine *ipsa* in the Vulgate), so that it was the seed, and not the woman who crushed the

---

[8] Eusebius of Caesarea (†c. 340), for instance, asks, having quoted Virgil's *Eclogues* (IV, 7), 'Who then is that virgin who returns? Is it not perhaps the one who was full and pregnant with the Holy Spirit?' *Oratio de Laudibus Constantini*, 19, 5-6, *PG* 20, 1291B.

[9] See Alfonso Langella, 'Il vangelo di Maria in Giustino martire', *Theotokos*, 9 (2001), 329-52.

[10] *PG* 6, 709-712. See *MF*, pp. 46-48.

serpent's head,[11] by no means do they exclude Mary's role in defeating the devil.[12] Since the rupture between God and humanity came about as a result of Eve and Adam, who allowed themselves to be tempted by the devil, it was necessary that another woman (Mary) and man (Jesus) should reject his attempts at seducing them. Had Mary not rejected Satan, which she was seen to do above all in her obedience to God's will and in her chastity, God's plan of salvation would have failed.

It was Irenaeus (†c. 202) who gave Justin's idea theological depth through his development of the Pauline notions of recapitulation. Irenaeus' extensive reflections on the Eve-Mary parallel led him to the realisation that the Virgin is no mere cipher, because her freely-given consent was an essential element in God's salvific plan.[13] While it is Christ, the new Adam, who is the formal cause of salvation, Mary, the new Eve, also plays an instrumental role in undoing the damage caused by original sin and in restoring creation. Christ and Mary not only restore humanity, and creation as a whole, to their prelapsarian state, but actually complete the process cut short by original sin, bringing humanity and the created universe to maturation thereby fulfilling the original *telos* established by the Father.

For Irenaeus, recapitulation (*anakaphaiosis*) involves the restoration of what has been lost through original sin, which is not simply a return to the *status quo ante*, a restitution of the lost perfection of Eden, but a fulfilment of creation itself. According to Irenaeus, Adam and Eve were created in the image and likeness of God, specifically in the image and likeness of the Son, the Logos. Prior to the Fall, man was fully in God's image because he possessed unsullied free will and reason. However, likeness to God was incomplete because Adam and Eve were still childlike, so their will and reason had yet to mature towards a perfect likeness of their Creator. He uses the example of a mother who does not give solid food to an infant, though she could if she so chose. Similarly, God could 'have endowed man with perfection from the beginning, but man

---

[11] See Graef, *Doctrine and Devotion*, I, 1-2, Jaroslav Pelikan, *Mary through the Centuries*, pp. 26-27 and 91-92, and P. G. Dunker, 'Our Lady in the Old Testament – I', in *The Mother of the Redeemer: Aspects of Doctrine and Devotion*, ed. by Kevin McNamara (Dublin: Gill, 1959), 1-12 (pp. 4-5).

[12] On the history of Marian interpretations of Genesis 3. 15 see René Laurentin, 'L'interprétation de Genèse 3.15 dans la tradition jusqu'au début du XIII siècle', *Études mariales*, 12 (1954), 79-156.

[13] See Antonio Orbe's *Antropología de San Ireneo* (Madrid: Biblioteca de Autores Cristianos, 1969), Matthew C. Steenberg, 'The Role of Mary as co-Recapitulator in St. Irenaeus of Lyons', *Vigiliae Christianae*, 58 (2004), 117-137, Mary Ann Donovan, *One Right Reading? A Guide to Irenaeus* (Collegeville, MN: Liturgical Press, 1997), José María Canal, 'María, nueva Eva en Justino, Ireneo, Tertuliano y Agustín', *Ephemerides Mariologicae*, 46 (1996), 41-60, and Fernando Rodrigo Polanco, 'La mariologia di sant'Ireneo', *Theotokos*, 9 (2001), 359-400. See *MF*, pp. 52-56.

was as yet unable to receive it, being still an infant'.[14] Had they not sinned, Adam and Eve would have been perfected and would have become immortal both in body and soul. Irenaeus is very insistent that the body, and not just the soul, is in the image and likeness of God, mainly because he was countering the Gnostic notion that the material world is corrupt. For him, part of the reason for Adam and Eve's weakness in giving in to the devil's temptation was that they had no visible model of perfected humanity to follow:

> For in times long past, it was said that man was created after the image of God, but it was not [actually] shown; for the Word was as yet invisible, after whose image man was created. Wherefore also he did easily lose the similitude. When, however, the Word of God became flesh, He confirmed both these: for He both showed forth the image truly, since He became Himself what was His image; and He re-established the similitude after a sure manner, by assimilating man to the invisible Father through means of the visible Word. *Adversus Haereses 5, 16, 2*

It is Christ, then, by being the visible image of humanity perfected, who opens up the possibility for all to deify themselves (*theosis*), to become perfect images and likenesses of God both in the flesh and in the spirit. The Son had to 'recapitulate,' to take on himself, the whole of mankind's sinful nature and redeem disobedience through his obedience. Having recapitulated the sinful history of mankind on the Cross and having transformed it through this supreme act of sacrificial love, the resurrected Christ restored and perfected humanity. A logical sequela to this is that only resurrected humanity fully manifests the divine likeness to the Father that is the *telos* of human nature. The Incarnation and Resurrection, then, are not only a divine response to human sin, but the planned culmination of creation. Thus creation, Incarnation and Redemption are intimately linked. For mankind, they manifest themselves sequentially but in God, who exists outside time, they are all part of one eternal movement of his love, though accomplished in history.

Closely linked to Irenaeus' doctrine of Christ's recapitulation is his teaching on Mary, the new Eve, the universal Mother of the new creation. For Irenaeus, Mary is the 'cause of salvation', while Christ is salvation. It is in this sense that Mary is the fixed point, on whom the whole history of salvation depends. Mary's obedience to God's plan opens the way to salvation and brings life, just as Eve cut humanity off from God and brought death:

> Likewise the Virgin Mary is found obedient, when she says, 'Behold the handmaid of the Lord; be it unto me according to thy word.' But Eve disobeyed, and she was disobedient when she was still a virgin. [...] Therefore, just as Eve, by disobeying, was made the cause of death, both to herself and to the entire human race, so Mary, who although betrothed to a man, was nevertheless a virgin, by obeying, became the cause of salvation, both to herself and the whole

---

[14] *Adversus Haereses*, 4, 38, 1. For a fuller range of passages from the *AH* that deal with Mary, see *TMPM*, I, 156-176, and for the *Demonstratio apostolicae praedicationis*, 176-181.

> human race. [...] In fact, what has been tied cannot be untied unless one loosens the knot in reverse order. [...] And thus also it was that the knot of Eve's disobedience was loosed thanks to the obedience of Mary, for what the virgin Eve had bound fast through unbelief, the Virgin Mary set free through faith. *Adversus Haereses, 3, 22, 4*[15]

Mary does not simply put right the damage caused by Eve's sin. She recapitulates her, that is, she fulfils what Eve, and therefore all of humanity, was to be in God's eternal plan: 'And thus, as the human race fell into bondage to death by means of a virgin, so is it restored by a virgin.'[16] Nor does he consider her role passive; the fulfilment of God's plan for the salvation of humanity required her active consent.

> And just as through a disobedient virgin man was stricken down and fell into death, so through the Virgin who was obedient to the Word of God man was reanimated and received life. The Lord, in fact, came to search for the lost sheep, that is, mankind who had lost his way. Therefore he did not form a different body for himself, but through her who had descended from Adam he preserved the likeness of that body. For it was necessary that Adam should be summed up in Christ, that mortality might be swallowed up and overwhelmed by immortality; and Eve summed up in Mary, that a virgin should be a virgin's intercessor, and by a virgin's obedience undo and put away the disobedience of a virgin. *Demonstratio apostolicae praedicationis, 32-33*[17]

Irenaeus' doctrine exerted a powerful influence on Mariology in the coming centuries, with writers assigning an increasingly exalted role in the restoration of creation to the Virgin.[18] Tertullian (†c. 230?), for instance, follows Irenaeus in drawing a parallel between Eve and Mary, and in attributing an active role in the restoration of humanity to Mary, as it was through her belief that God became incarnate: 'God recovered his image and likeness, which had been stolen by the devil. [...] Eve believed the serpent; Mary believed Gabriel. The fault that Eve introduced by believing, Mary by believing, erased.'[19] Tertullian also appears to be the instigator of the idea that the dates of the Annunciation and the

---

[15] *TMPM*, I, 171. Translations are mine unless otherwise indicated.

[16] *Adversus Haereses*, 5, 19, 1

[17] Adapted from the translation by J. Armitage Robinson, *The Demonstration of the Apostolic Preaching* (London: Society for Promoting Christian Knowledge; New York: Macmillan, 1920) in *The Tertullian Project* <http://www.tertullian.org/fathers/irenaeus_02_proof.htm> [accessed 7 May 2007]. See also *Adversus Haereses*, 3, 22, 9-10, *PG*, 7, 954-956.

[18] See *MF*, p. 117

[19] *De carne Christi*, 17, *PL 2*, 782B (828), *MF*, p. 67.

Crucifixion were aligned, signifying the intimate bond between the Incarnation and the Redemption.[20]

Ephrem (†c. 373) sees the Annunciation as the moment when the reconciliation of humanity with God was set in train: 'God appointed as intercessors the Angel and the Maiden, that by their mutual words they might settle the difference, so that reconciliation should be made between those on high and those here below, and the handwriting of the debts be torn up.'[21] Ephrem returns repeatedly to the Eve-Mary antithesis in his writings, making it abundantly clear that he believes the process of Redemption began with the Virgin comparing Satan's conquest of Eve with Mary's crushing destruction of his schemes:

> In Eden Eve made herself guilty. The great author of the fault, because of which her children would be punished with death in the generations to come, the Serpent – perverse scribe, wrote and signed it, sealing it with his perfidy. The ancient Dragon saw that the fault of Eve was growing because of his perfidy. It was the girl who loved the perfidy of her seducer and obeyed her defrauder, driving Adam from his position. Eve made herself guilty of the crime, but to Mary was reserved the expunging of the fault, so that the maid would pay for the faults of her mother and would rip to shreds the writer who had brought about the lament of all generations. *Carmina Soghita in Memory of the Mother of God, 24-25*[22]

Christ's birth is an occasion of joy for Eve, since he will liberate her from Sheol, the realm of the dead, to which he will descend after his death: 'The Son of her daughter has descended as the medicine of life to raise the mother of his Mother. The blessed child crushes the head of the serpent which had wounded her.'[23]

He also identifies Mary as the true Mother of all the living, a notion that one finds repeated in many of the Fathers: 'Eve, mother of all the living, became the source of death for all the living. But Mary caused a new branch to sprout forth from Eve, the ancient vine, and in this new branch the new life made his abode.'[24] It is partly on this basis that the idea of Mary's spiritual motherhood was elaborated in the Middle Ages by the likes of Anselm of Canterbury and Rupert of Deutz.[25]

Basil the Great († 379), in his *Homilia in sanctum Christi generationem*, speaks of the Virgin's body as the 'the workshop of this economy' of salvation, that is, the place in which 'the flesh that had fallen from Paradise' was brought back to heaven.[26]

---

[20] See *Adversus Judaeos*, 8, *PL*, 2, 656, where he performs highly convoluted calculations based on his reading of the Book of Daniel, to show how God had anticipated the two events. See Enrico dal Covolo, 'La dottrina mariana di Tertulliano' *Theotokos*, 10 (2002), 17-31.
[21] *On the Annunciation* 2, 3, quoted in Thomas Livius, *The Blessed Virgin in the Fathers of the First Six Centuries* (London: Burns and Oates, 1893), pp. 436-7.
[22] TMPM, IV, 90. See also *Diatessaron*, 1, 1.
[23] *Hymns on the Nativity*, 13, 2, quoted in Graef, *Doctrine and Devotion*, I, 61.
[24] *Sermon on the Lord*, adapted from the translation quoted in Graef, *Doctrine and Devotion*, I, 61.
[25] See Juniper B. Carol, *Fundamentals of Mariology* (New York: Benziger, 1956), pp. 51-52.
[26] TMPM, I, 296.

Gregory Nazianzen († 390), in explaining how Christ took the place of Adam and, through the Passion returned man to his original state, sees a clear parallel between creation and the Incarnation: 'For this reason the generation [of Christ] took place; for this reason there was the Virgin, the crib, and Bethlehem. Generation came after creation, the Virgin followed on from the woman [Eve], Bethlehem followed Eden, the crib followed paradise.'[27] Gregory of Nyssa († c. 394), like most of the Fathers, contrasts Mary with Eve – 'The woman is defended by the woman. The first opened the way to sin; the second facilitated the arrival of justification. The one followed the counsel of the serpent, the other presented the slayer of the serpent and generated the author of light'[28] – and considers the Virgin, not Eve, to be the 'Mother of life'.[29]

Aside from her obedience, the other aspect of Mary that reflected her strength, according to the early Fathers, was her virginity. Indeed, it was believed that Eve had remained a virgin up until the Fall, so that the serpent's actions were seen as a sort of seduction, to which she succumbed in marked contrast to the impregnable strength of the Virgin in the face of every temptation. Gregory of Nyssa, with characteristic clarity, writes of how death, in this case a synonym for the devil, was defeated by Mary's virginity. It is important to note here that it is not virginity in itself that defeats the devil, but the fruit of that virginity, which is the presence of Christ within Mary, and within each soul that consecrates itself to him:

> But he found in virginity a barrier, which it was an impossible feat to pass. Just as in the age of Mary, the bearer of God, he who had reigned from Adam to her time found, when he came to her and dashed his forces against the fruit of her virginity as against a rock, that he was shattered to pieces upon her, so in every soul which passes through this life in the flesh under the protection of virginity, this strength of death is in a manner broken and annulled, for he does not find the places upon which he may fix his sting. *De Virginitate, 14, 1*[30]

Amphilochios of Iconium († 398) also writes of Mary's defeat of the devil, exclaiming: 'What a great and supremely astute stratagem against the devil! That world, which of old had fallen under the power of sin because of a virgin, is now set free thanks to the Virgin. Through the virgin birth a great quantity of invisible demons has been flung into Tartarus.'[31]

Cyril of Jerusalem (†c. 397) also contrasts Eve and Mary in terms of death and life: 'Death came through a virgin, Eve. It was necessary that life also should

---

[27] *Discourses*, 2, 24, *PG* 35, 433A, *TMPM*, I, 308.

[28] *In Nativitate Domini*, *TMPM*, I, 321. On Gregory's Mariology see Elena Giannarelli, 'Gregorio di Nissa: fili mariani', *Theotokos*, 11 (2003), 125-43.

[29] *In Canticum Canticorum*, 13, *PG* 44, 1052D-1053B, *MF*, pp. 158-59.

[30] Translation by Leena Peltomaa, *The Image of the Virgin Mary in the Akathistos Hymn* (Leiden, Boston and Cologne: Brill, 2001), p. 191.

[31] *Homilia in Natalitia Jesu Christi*, *PG*, 39, 40D, *TMPM*, I, 334.

come through a virgin, so that, as the serpent deceived the former, so Gabriel might bring glad tidings to the latter.'[32] Epiphanius of Salamis († 403) provides a thorough treatment of Mary as the true Mother of the living:

> In fact, Eve had been called mother of the living after she heard the words, 'for dust thou art, and into dust thou shalt return' (Genesis 3. 19), that is, after the Fall. It might seem strange that she received such a grandiose title after having sinned. Looking at the facts, one notes that Eve is the one from whom the entire human race on this earth took its origin. The Virgin Mary, on the other hand, truly introduced life itself into the world, since she generated the Living One, so that it was she who became the Mother of the living. *Panarion, 78, 17*[33]

Peter Chrysologus (†c. 450) offers a similar interpretation in explaining why Mary came to Christ's tomb on Easter morning (Matthew 28. 1): 'The Mother came, the woman came, so that she who had become the mother of the dying might become now the Mother of the living, and so that what had been written might be fulfilled: "She was the Mother of all the living" (Genesis 3. 20)'.[34]

The Latin Fathers tended to be more restrained in their treatment of the Virgin's contribution to the Redemption, though this does not necessarily mean that they accorded her a lesser role. Ambrose († 397) is fully in line with the Eastern Fathers in rooting Mary's role in the Redemption firmly in the Incarnation.[35] Without taking on flesh it would not have been possible for Christ to take on the burden of human sin and to redeem our nature through his suffering and death on the Cross: 'He bore our flesh in his own flesh, bore in his body our weakness and curses, in order to nail them to the Cross.'[36] It was through Mary that salvation came to man, and without taking his humanity from her Jesus could not have died for us:

> The Truth agreed to be born of the Virgin Mary, and in this way he could offer the sacrifice by which man was justified, the sacrifice of the Passion, the sacrifice of the Cross. For, how could he have offered the sacrifice for our sins if he could not die? But how could he die if he did not take from us that which gave him the possibility of doing so? I mean, if Christ had not assumed mortal flesh from us he could not have died. *Enarratioines in Psalmos, 84, 13*[37]

Mary herself is the first beneficiary of God's salvific work, which began when he became incarnate in her womb: 'No wonder that the Lord, wishing to rescue

---

[32] *Catecheses*, 12, 15, *PG* 33, 741B, *MF*, p. 135.

[33] *TMPM*, I, 401. See *MF*, pp. 128-30.

[34] *Sermo 74*, 3, *PL* 52, 409, *MF*, p. 299.

[35] See Celestino Corsato, 'La mariologia in Ambrogio di Milano', *Theotokos*, 11 (2003), 291-336, and Biagio Amata, 'Intuizioni ambrosiane sulla centralità mediatrice di Maria nel "mysterium salutis"', *Marianum*, 59 (1997), 139-57.

[36] *Sermo contra Auxentium, PL* 16, 1015A.

[37] *PL* 37, 1079.

the world, began his work with Mary. Thus, she through whom salvation was being prepared for all people would be the first to receive the promised fruit of salvation.'[38]

For Augustine († 430) Mary is the predestined instrument of God's salvific plan.[39] For this reason Jesus was conceived on March twenty-fifth, the same date on which he would die,[40] just as the sealed womb of the Virgin anticipates the sealed tomb from which he will rise.[41] He writes of God's choice of Mary as his Mother in the context of his doctrine of predestination, which was largely a defence of the absolute gratuity of divine grace in the face of the Pelagian heresy: 'Even before he was born of her, he knew his Mother when he predestined her. He knew his Mother before he, as God, created her, from whom he would be created as man.'[42] So, for Augustine, God foreknew that she would fulfil this role and created her for this purpose, yet it also required an act of free will on the part of the Virgin, since it is because of her faith that he entered into her womb: 'She, with pious faith, merited to receive the holy seed within her.'[43] But this faith itself is a gift of God's grace, so that ultimately, as Luigi Gambero puts it, she 'is a pure grace of the Lord, given to the incarnate Word and to all humanity.'[44]

Both Ambrose[45] and Augustine took up the Irenaean notion of the Virgin as the anti-Eve, which was important in transmitting this idea to later Western writers. Augustine, for instance, writes:

> Just as death came to us through a woman, life is born to us through a woman. And so, by the nature of both one and the other, that is to say, female and male, the devil was vanquished and put to torture, he who had rejoiced in their downfall. It would have contributed little to his punishment if those two natures had been delivered in us without our being delivered by both of them. *On Christian Suffering, 22, 24*[46]

---

[38] *Expositio in Lucam*, 2, 17, *PL* 15, 1559C (1640), *MF*, p. 196.

[39] For a useful recent overview of Augustine's writings on Mary see Lorenzo Dattrino, 'Riferimenti Mariani in Agostino', *Theotokos*, 12 (2004), 161-68.

[40] Tertullian († c. 230?), *Adversus Iudaeos*, 8, already identifies March twenty-fifth as the date if the Crucifixion.

[41] See *De Trinitate*, 4, 5, 9.

[42] *In Evangelium Ioannis tractatus*, 8, 9, *PL* 35, 1455. All translations, unless otherwise indicated, are from the Latin and Italian texts in S. Aurelii Augustini, *Opera Omnia, Tutte le opere*, ed. by Franco Monteverde, 45 vols (Rome: Nuova Biblioteca Agostiniana and Città Nuova, 1967–), in *Sant'Agostino, Augustinus Hipponensis*, <http://www.augustinus.it/> [accessed 15 February 2008].

[43] *Sermo 69*, 3, 4, *PL* 38, 442, *MF*, p. 219.

[44] *MF*, p. 219.

[45] See, for instance, *Epistola* 42, *PL* 16, 1124C.

[46] Quoted in Tina Beattie, 'Mary in Patristic Theology', in *Mary: The Complete Resource*, ed. by Sarah Jane Boss (Oxford and New York: Oxford University Press 2007), pp. 75-105 (p. 93). See also *Sermo* 51, 2 *PL* 38, 335, among others.

The Council of Ephesus (431) when Mary was declared *Theotokos* (bearer of God) marked a new phase in the understanding that Mary was more than just a historic figure, but continued to play a role in giving birth to Christ in the Church. Cyril of Alexandria († 444), a central figure in the *Theotokos* debate at Ephesus attributes a long list of achievements to Mary's motherhood of Christ, ranging from the conquest of hell to the conversion of the nations, summing up Mary's role by stating that 'every faithful soul achieves salvation' through her:

> Through you, the Holy Trinity is glorified; the precious Cross is celebrated and adored throughout the world; heaven exults, the angels and archangels rejoice, the demons are put to flight, the devil, the tempter, falls from heaven, the fallen creation is brought back to paradise, all creatures trapped in idolatry come to know of the truth. Through you holy baptism and the oil of gladness are administered to believers; through you churches are established throughout the world; the peoples are led to conversion. *Homily 4*[47]

Proclus of Constantinople († 446), another of the main movers in the events surrounding the Council of Ephesus, argues strongly that it was necessary for Christ to be truly born of Mary if he were to redeem human nature:

> Do not be ashamed, O man, of this birth: for us it was the principle of salvation. In fact, had he not been born of woman, neither would he have died; and if he had not died he would not have annihilated with his death, 'him who had the empire of death, that is to say, the devil' (Hebrews 2. 14).

Mary is the *locus* where the whole Trinity has acted so that creation might be remade, paradise restored, and human nature returned again to its divine image and likeness:

> The Holy *Theotokos*, the Virgin Mary has called us together here, the unsullied treasure of virginity, the rational paradise of the second Adam, the workshop of the [two] natures of Christ, the market of the salvific transaction, the bridal chamber in which the Word wedded the flesh, the living thorn bush of nature, which the fire of divine labour pains did not consume, the truly light cloud that carried, united with a body, he who is seated above the Cherubim (Isaiah 19. 1), The most pure fleece of the celestial rain, with which the shepherd dressed himself from the ewe, Mary, handmaid and mother, virgin and paradise, God's only bridge to men, the extraordinary tapestry of the Incarnation, on which the tunic of the union was ineffably weaved, whose weaver was the Holy Spirit, spinner, the overshadowing power from on high, wool, the ancient fleece of Adam, woof, the uncontaminated flesh of the Virgin, shuttle, the immense grace of him whom she assumed, artist, the Word that entered through her ear. Who has ever seen, who has ever heard that, without being circumscribed, God dwelled in a womb and the

---

[47] *PG* 77, 992-96, *MF,* pp. 247-48. For a more detailed study of Cyril's thought see *The Theology of St. Cyril of Alexandria: A Critical Appreciation,* ed. by Thomas G. Weinandy and Daniel A. Keating (London: Clark, 2003).

womb of a woman was not [too] narrow to contain he whom the heavens could not contain? *First Homily on Mary, the Mother of God, 1*[48]

It is in her consent to become the *Theotokos*, or God-bearer that her greatness lies, because it is not she herself who brought about the Redemption but the God-man whom she bore:

> Salvation was not within the power of a simple man: in reality man needed someone to save him, as St. Paul says: 'For all have sinned, and do need the glory of God…' (Romans 3. 23). Therefore, given that sin drove the guilty towards the devil, and the devil in his turn sent them to their death, we came to a situation of grave peril and the dissolution of death was impossible. […] Therefore, he who is King by nature did not disdain human nature which had been tyrannised for so long, nor did God, in his mercy permit it to be subject to the devil until the end of time. He who is always present gave his own blood as a ransom for us, and offered his flesh, which he took from the Virgin, for the human race as the price for compensating death. *First Homily on Mary the Mother of God, 3 and 7*[49]

Proclus also speaks of the blessing that all women have received through Mary. Thanks to the grace that descended on her, the curse laid on women as a result of original sin has been removed, not just for those born after the Incarnation but beginning with Eve, and including all the great women of the Old Testament – Sarah, Rebecca, Leah, Deborah, and Elizabeth.[50]

Theodotus of Ancyra († after 446), another important figure at Ephesus, writes in a similar manner of the restoration that took place through Mary: 'Through you the odious state of Eve has been put to an end, through you abjection has been destroyed, through you error has been dissolved, through you suffering has been abolished, through you the sentence has been lifted.'[51]

The *Akathistos Hymn*, possibly dating from shortly after Ephesus,[52] salutes Mary repeatedly as the instrument through whom humanity has recovered its relationship with God. One has the sense in reading the hymn that the entire economy of salvation hinges on the moment when the angel greeted Mary, and set in motion the events that would transform history:

---

[48] *TMPM*, I, 557. See also *Homily on the Birth of the Lord*, 4, 2, *TMPM*, I, 567.

[49] *TMPM*, I, 558 and 560-61.

[50] *Homily* 5, 3, *PG* 65, 720 B. See Jan H. Barkhuizen, 'Proclus of Constantinople: A Popular Preacher in Fifth-Century Constantinople' in *Preacher and Audience: Studies in Early Christian and Byzantine Homiletics*, ed. by Mary B. Cunningham and Pauline Allen (Leiden: Brill, 1998), pp. 179-200.

[51] *Homily on the Mother of God and the Birth of Christ*, *TMPM*, I, 514.

[52] For further discussion, dating and bibliography see the chapter on Intercession, Mediation and Redemption, 1.

Hail, through whom joy shall shine forth; / Hail, through whom the curse shall cease; / Hail, recalling of fallen Adam; / Hail, deliverance of the tears of Eve / [...] Hail since you bear him who bears all; / Hail star causing the sun to shine; / [...] Hail through whom creation is made new; / [...] Hail, celestial ladder by which God descended; / Hail, bridge leading those from earth to heaven. / [...] Hail, atonement for the whole world; / Hail, good will of God towards mortals; / Hail, freedom of approach for mortals before God. / [...] Hail, key to the gate of Paradise; / [...] Hail, through whom Hades was stripped bare; / Hail, through whom we were clothed in glory. [...] Hail, you who closed the furnace of deception; / Hail, you who protect the initiates of the Trinity; / Hail, you who have cast the inhuman tyrant from his dominion. / [...] Hail, elevation of humans; / Hail, downfall of demons; / Hail, you who trampled on the delusion of error. / [...] Hail, beginning of spiritual renewal; / Hail, bestower of divine goodness; / Hail, for you gave new birth to those conceived in shame.[53]

The use of the anaphoric 'through whom' is a typical characteristic of Eastern encomia to the Virgin, which we have already seen in Cyril of Alexandria's sermon. The hymn had a major impact on the Eastern Church, inspiring generations of homilists and hymnodists, and was almost equally influential in the West, after its translation into Latin in the ninth century.[54]

There were no equivalent panegyrics to Mary in the West at this time. The best that Sedulius († c. 440) can rise to is, 'Hail, O holy Mother, you who gave birth to the King who governs heaven and earth through the ages, whose divinity and dominion, which embrace all things in an eternal space, endure forever.'[55] Here the greeting of Mary is perfunctory with the real interest being in praising Christ. This does not mean, however, that there was not an increasing awareness of Mary's role in the economy of salvation. Leo the Great († 461), for instance speaks of Mary's womb regenerating human nature in the same way that baptism expunges original sin, a statement that is particularly significant coming from a figure of his stature.[56]

Chrysippus of Jerusalem († 479), in the typical anaphoric style of the Greeks, urges Mary to rejoice because she is the source from whom salvation comes. One can clearly see the influence of the *Akathistos Hymn* in the imagery that he uses:

Rejoice depository of life. Rejoice, garden of the Father. Rejoice, meadow that gives forth all the fragrance of the Spirit. Rejoice, O root of all goods. Rejoice, pearl beyond all price. Rejoice, O vine laden with beautiful bunches of grapes.

---

[53] Cited from the translation by Leena Peltomaa, in *The Image of the Virgin Mary*, pp. 1-19.
[54] The classic study on the influence of the Akathistos in the Latin Church is Gérard Gilles Meersseman's *Der Hymnos Akathistos im Abendland*, 2 vols (Freiburg: Universizätsverlag, 1958-60). See also Kariofilis Mitsakis, 'The Hymnography of the Greek Church in the Early Christian Centuries', *Jahrbuch der Österreichischen byzantinischen Gesellschaft*, 20 (1971), 31-49.
[55] *Carmen Paschale, 2, Salve, sancta parens*, PL 19, 599A-600A.
[56] *Sermo 24*, 1 PL 54, MF, p. 307. On Leo's Mariology see Lucio Casula, 'Natus ex matre virgine': Maria nei sermoni di Leone Magno,' *Theotokos*, 12 (2004), 215-54.

> Rejoice, O cloud of that rain that offers to drink to the souls of the saints. Rejoice, well of the ever-living water. *Homily on the Holy Mother of God, 1*[57]

In a vivid passage, he imagines the devil lamenting the failure of his original stratagem of corrupting mankind by tempting Eve. Despite his best efforts, Mary, the new Eve, has proved impregnable to temptation, and Christ, whom he attempted to destroy by suggesting to the Jews that he be crucified, has instead liberated mankind from slavery. Who, he asks himself, is the cause of all his woes?

> But what is the cause of all these things that have happened to me? Who if not she who generated the author of these great events? Assuredly, it would have been better for me if I had not deceived the old Eve. It would have been better if I had not seduced her through the serpent. For, what advantage accrued to me from the temptation, if those whom I had reduced to servitude I now seen the gaining their ancient liberty and becoming heirs of the very kingdom of heaven? *Homily on the Holy Mother of God, 3*[58]

In the following century one of the most notable exponents of the Eve-Mary antithesis is the Syrian Jacob of Serug († 521).[59] He imagines a conversation taking place between Gabriel and the Virgin which undoes the evil of the Fall and reconciles heaven and earth:

> A pure virgin and an angel spoke with wonderful words that reconciled heavenly and earthly beings. A woman and the leader of all the Virtues made a pact of reconciliation for the whole world. Between the heavens and the nether regions the two sat and talked and listened and made peace between those who were angry. A maid and an angel met and transacted until they put an end to the strife between the Lord and Adam. The great struggle that took place among the trees was discussed and everything ceased and reconciliation was made. *Homily on the Blessed Virgin Mary Generatrix of God*[60]

He goes on to make a lengthy comparison between Adam and Christ, and Mary and Eve. Adam, he says, produced the 'mother of life', without sexual union, whereas Mary is the Mother who produced Life in virginity.

Romanos the Melodist († c. 560) also uses an imaginary dialogue, this time between Adam and Eve, to explain the restoration brought about through Mary's consent to the Incarnation. In expressing his joy at the news of the Incarnation Adam makes it clear that it is this consent which puts in motion the reversal of the damage caused by the Fall:

---

[57] *TMPM*, I, 603.
[58] *TMPM*, I, 608.
[59] See Costantino Vona, *Omelie mariologiche di s. Giacomo di Sarug* (Rome: Pontificia Univ. Lateranense, 1953).
[60] *TMPM*, IV, 150.

Who is this who has reached my ears with the announcement, long hoped for, of a virgin who gives birth to the ransom for damnation, whose voice alone can put an end to my wretchedness, and whose childbearing wounds him who wounded me? It is she whom the son of Amos foretold as the seed of Jesse of whom is born the shoot whose fruit I will eat without danger of dying, she who is full of grace. [...] Once the serpent surprised me and he rejoiced, but now, seeing my descendent, he will flee screaming. He had raised his head against me, but now he flatters with servility and has no wish to sneer, for fear that the she who is full of grace will strike him. *Second Hymn on the Nativity of Christ, 3-4*[61]

A sermon on the Annunciation attributed to Anastasius of Antioch († 599) which uses the familiar anaphoric 'rejoice' to address Mary, speaks of her as the 'path of salvation', 'the food of life' and the 'font of immortality'.[62] Here Mary is not simply the passive instrument of God's salvific Incarnation; rather she is herself the site or 'tent' as the sermonist puts it in which Redemption begins. He goes on to set forth the reasons why the Incarnation took place on March twenty-fifth, which corresponds, the sermonist argues, to the date of the creation of man, thus highlighting, like Gregory Nazianzen, the close relationship between the two events, so that Mary becomes, as Anselm of Canterbury will put it, 'the Mother of re-creation':

Thereafter begins the Spring, which transforms and moves all things towards beauty and procreation. Since this is so, we believe that the first origin of the visible world may be dated to the twentieth of March. In effect, it was certainly fitting that created things should be formed during the most beautiful season of the year, and this is the spring, as our sensible experience confirms for us. In fact, during this season we see that all things are in motion, in order to multiply and grow, observing that ancient commandment: 'Increase and multiply' (Genesis 1. 28). If then Spring is the most beautiful season of the year and it begins with the equinox, that time when God began to create things, having created man on the sixth day, it is easy to understand how he was created on the twenty-fifth of March, since the sixth day from the twentieth is the twenty-fifth. Since this is how matters were, was it not perhaps supremely fitting that he who had created man in the beginning should choose the same day to unite himself with the flesh? *First Homily on the Annunciation, 6-7*[63]

The sermon goes on to make the standard contrast between Eve who brought death, and Mary, who has bestowed salvation He calls it the day of the

---

[61] *TMPM*, I, 710. On the importance of Romanos as a religious poet and composer see José Grosdidier de Matons, *Romanos le Mélode et les origines de la poésie religieuse a Byzance* (Paris: Beauchesne, 1977) and R. J. Schork, *Sacred Song from the Byzantine Pulpit: Romanos the Melodist* (Gainesville: University Press of Florida, 1995).
[62] *First Homily on the Annunciation*, 1, *TMPM*, II, 71-72.
[63] *TMPM*, II, 74-75.

Annunciation 'the birthday of the whole universe' (8), since the whole of creation has been restored to order and God's image has been renewed in man.

In the West, Venantius Fortunatus (†c. 600), speaks of Mary's role in the redemption of humanity, which he sees in terms of remedying the fault of Eve. The Virgin, he writes in one of his hymns in which he imagines the entire heavenly city singing her praises, is our only remedy, since it is she who has rescued the world from the woes of Eve. He even goes so far as to attribute powers over hell to her, though in the context of her having given birth to the Redeemer:

> O excellent beauty, O woman who are the image of salvation, powerful because of the fruit of your birth-giving and who are pleasing because of your virginity, by means of you the salvation of the world deigned to be born and to restore the human race to which the proud Eve had given birth. For you, O Mother, let thousands of legions, according to their rank, praise this power of yours, with poetry and lyre and in song. Then the angel matchmaker repeats your praises, he who brought you the sacred announcement from heaven, saying: 'O you, happy, inimitable Virgin, whose lamb splits the mouth of the wolf! Destroying hell and returning prisoners to their homeland, you bring back to freedom those who were oppressed under the yoke.' The rest of the angels listen to these praises, repeating them in their turn and the voice, echoing back, resounds from choir to choir. *In laudem sanctae Mariae*[64]

A sermon by pseudo-Epiphanius, most likely dating from the seventh century, speaks eloquently of the transformation that came about through Mary, who has raised womankind from her infirmity and allowed Adam and Eve to return to Paradise:

> The angels had accused Eve; now, instead, they glorified Mary who had made the infirmity of women glorious: Mary, who had lifted up Eve again, who had fallen into sin, and who had returned Adam to heaven, who had been chased out of Paradise. In fact, Mary opened up Paradise which had been closed, and replanted Adam there, who had been chased out because of the thieving serpent. [...] Through you celestial peace has been given to the world, through you the ends of the earth have received the light, through you men have become angels, servants, friends, and they have been called sons of God, through you men have become worthy of conversing with angels and of uniting themselves with them, through you they have knowledge of the things of heaven and a hymn of praise is raised from earth to heaven, through you men acquire trust with the Most High in heaven, through you the Cross, on which your Son, Christ our Lord was hung, gave forth its splendour over the whole world, through you death has been trampled down and hell has been laid bare. *Homilia in laudes sanctæ Mariæ Deiparæ*[65]

Once again we find Mary being spoken of as the means through which creation has been restored in a sermon by John of Thessalonica (†c. 630) who

---

[64] *PL* 88, 283B.
[65] *TMPM*, I, 804.

speaks of her being worthy of all praise because 'through her, in the economy of salvation, all creation has received the great gift of the incarnation of the Only-Begotten Son and Word of God the Father.'[66]

A homily attributed to Modestus of Jerusalem († 634) adds a new element by linking not just the Incarnation but the bodily Assumption with the restoration of creation, so that Mary's mission of reversing the actions of Eve extends beyond her historical life on earth: just as she brought Life into the world by enfleshing the Word, her body is now raised up and glorified, and with her the whole of humanity:

> O most Blessed Dormition of the most glorious Mother of God, through whom a double healing has come to all the world: she has brought to all, health of both soul and body. O most Blessed Dormition of the most glorious Mother of God, through whom the human race has been glorified and called blessed in Christ God, as if it were his invisible body. [...] O most Blessed Dormition of the most glorious Mother of God, through whom all things have been renewed; the things of earth have been united to those of heaven and together with them they exclaim: 'Glory to God in the highest heavens and peace on earth to men of good will' (Luke 2 . 14). *Homily on the Dormition of the Mother of God, 7*[67]

Isidore of Seville († 636) notes the Marian interpretation of Genesis 3. 15, saying that some have explained it in terms of the enmity between the devil and Jesus, the fruit of Mary's womb:

> The inheritance of the devil is a perverse suggestion while the inheritance of the woman is the fruit of a laudable action, with which one opposes the perversity of the suggestion. She will crush his head since she crushed perverse suggestions from her mind from the outset. He will lie in wait for her heel because in the end he will attempt to deceive that mind which he was not able to deceive with his first suggestion. *Quaestiones in Genesin, 2, 18, 5-6* [68]

According to Sophronius of Jerusalem († 638), who is an important exponent of the notion of deification,[69] which was a major theme in Byzantine theology,[70] it is from the moment of Mary's consent to be the Mother of God that the process of our salvation begins. Again we see the typically anaphoric style of Greek rhetoric:

> From here, in fact, proceeds our salvation; from here our liberty shines forth; from here springs our adoption as children of God; from here our invocation is generated; from here, the Word of God, coming to us to save us, from here

---

[66] *Homily on the Dormition of Our Lady*, 1, *EPH*, p. 47, *TMPM*, II, 99-100.

[67] *EPH*, pp. 90-91; *TMPM*, II, 129.

[68] *PL* 83, 221A-B.

[69] See Antonino Gallico, 'Riferimenti mariani in Sofronio', *Theotokos*, 15 (2007), 103-25.

[70] See below Andrew of Crete.

begins his work of salvation. This annunciation constitutes the beginning of his mercy towards us; it constitutes the beginning of our deification. There is nothing more joyful for men, nothing more precious for us who are on earth, nothing more agreeable to mortals. *Homily on the Annunciation, 49*[71]

Significantly, he does not attribute Mary's greatness entirely to God but credits her for having merited so exalted a calling. God has showered her with great gifts but it is she who has used them well: 'No one has ever reached such lofty greatness as you; and all this meritedly so: for no one has approached so close to God; no one has so enriched themselves with God's gifts' (25). Sophronius also introduces the Eve-Mary antithesis in an elaboration of the words of Gabriel to Mary:

> Truly 'blessed amongst women art thou', because you have transformed the curse of Eve into a blessing; because you have caused Adam to be blessed, who before was cursed. Truly 'blessed amongst women art thou', because the blessing of the Father has shone on all men through you, and has freed them from the ancient curse. Truly 'blessed amongst women art thou', because through you your progenitors find salvation since you generated the Saviour, who will prepare divine salvation for them. *Homily on the Annunciation, 22* [72]

He goes on to speak of how the virginal conception and birth defeated all the schemes of the devil: 'Through these things all the expedients of the adversary are destroyed; through these things all the machinations constructed by the enemy fall into ruin together with their instigator' (24).[73] The homily concludes with a powerful affirmation that this day, that is, the Feast of the Annunciation, is the occasion of greatest joy for mankind, since it marks the beginning of salvation and the defeat of evil: 'Now we no longer fear ruin; we are no longer terrified by evils; we no longer fear death; we no longer are in horror of the wickedness of the devil; we no longer fear his hidden snares; we do not allow ourselves to be terrified by his manifest tyranny' (48).[74]

The *Life of Mary* attributed to Maximus the Confessor († 662) offers an explanation for the date of the Annunciation, aligning it with the moment of creation, as had earlier writers. However, in this instance it is not the fifth day, on which man was created but the first, a Sunday, which is also the day of the Resurrection:

> It was the first month, the month in which God created the whole world, so as to teach us that now, once again, he renews the world that had become old. It was the first day of the week, that is, Sunday, the day on which he eliminated the darkness and created the firstborn light, the day on which the glorious resurrection

---

[71] *TMPM*, II, 162.
[72] *TMPM*, II, 143.
[73] *TMPM*, II, 144.
[74] *TMPM*, II, 161.

from the tomb of his Son, the King took place, and with it the resurrection of our nature; and not only was it the first day, but also the first hour, according to the words of the prophet: 'God will help her in the morning early.' 19[75]

Ildephonse of Toledo († 667), who can justifiably considered the founder of Spanish Mariology, makes one of the clearest statements of the Patristic Age regarding Mary's remote co-operation in the Redemption:[76]

> Permit that I may speak of and defend the truth of the faith of your Son, allow me to conform to God and to you, to serve your Son and you, to subjugate myself to my Lord and to you: to him as my Creator, to you as Mother of my creator; to him as the Lord of the powers of Heaven, to you as the handmaiden of the Lord of the universe; to him as God, to you as the Mother of God, to him as my Redeemer, to you as co-operator in my redemption. And truly everything that he accomplished for my redemption, he actuated deriving it from the truth of your person. In becoming my Redeemer he became your son; in becoming the price of my ransom his Incarnation is the fruit of your womb, and in it he healed my wounds; from your flesh he took the body that was destined to be wounded, and with it he destroyed my death; from the body of your mortality he drew his mortal body with which he was able to destroy my sins, which he took upon himself; from the reality of your humble body he took on my very nature which he, preceding me into his Kingdom set in the seat of his Father, above the angels. *De virginitate perpetua sanctae Mariae, 12, 1*[77]

Germanus of Constantinople († c. 733) makes use of the well-worn Eve-Mary antithesis, but does so in the context of the preservation and glorification of Mary's body upon her death, rather than in the more usual setting of the Incarnation.[78] This notion that Mary's bodily assumption was the final and necessary stage in a life that reversed that of Eve was becoming an increasingly important feature of Byzantine thought on the Dormition:

> You are the Mother of a life that is real and true. You are the yeast of Adam's remaking; you are the one who liberates Eve from all shame. She was the mother of dust, and you of light; her womb harbored corruption, but yours incorruption. She became death's dwelling-place, but you release us from death. She made our eyes downcast, weighted towards the earth, but you are the unsleeping glory of eyes awake. Her children are grief, but your Son is joy for all ages. She, who was

---

[75] *TMPM*, II, 197.

[76] See Biagio Amata, 'La "schiavitù mariana" di Idlefonso di Toledo', *Theotokos*, 14 (2006), 57-72 and Juan María, Cascante Dávila, 'La devoción y el culto a María en S. Ildefonso de Toledo', in *Acta Congressus Mariologici-Mariani Internationalis in Croatia anno 1971 celebrati*, 5 vols (Rome: Pontifica Academia Mariana, 1972), III, 223-48.

[77] *PL* 96, 105C-106A.

[78] For further discussion and bibliography on the Mariology of Germanus and Andrew of Crete see Vittorio Fazzo, 'Teologia e spiritualità mariane nelle omelie di Germano di Costantinopoli e di Andrea di Creta', *Theotokos*, 14 (2006), 73-90.

earth, came back to earth in the end; but you have given birth to life for us, and you have ascended to life, you are powerful enough to offer life, even after death, to your fellow men and women. *First Homily on the Dormition, 7*[79]

So Mary, through her Assumption, is a beacon of hope and a prophetic sign that all the faithful will rise again and overcome death. Not only has Mary restored life eternal to humankind, but through giving birth to Christ she has re-established the link between the angels and humanity, which had been broken by the sinfulness of humankind, so that now angels and human beings may once again sing together in praise of God:

> But as wretched humanity began, in past times, to live in error and idolatry, and to contaminate the air with the aroma of sacrifices, the angels broke off their companionship with them for good, and God, in turn, took away from them his Holy Spirit. But when you gave birth, at the end of time, to the one who was 'in the beginning,' the Word of God of the Father, from that very moment of your labor the angels looked down from heaven and sang the praises of God, now born of you. Crying out that glory had been added to the heights of heaven, they also exclaimed that peace had come at last on earth, so that enmity could no longer be called a barrier between angels and human beings, heaven and earth; there was now one reign of harmony, one mutually complementary song of praise sung by both angels and human beings to the God who is one and three. *First Homily on the Dormition, 2*[80]

Later in the same homily, he explicitly states that the Virgin redeemed humanity through the Incarnation: 'For how could fleshly decay turn you back into the dust of the earth, you who have redeemed humanity from death's corruptive power through the Incarnation of your Son?' (6) Indeed, for Germanus the two events of the Incarnation and Assumption are intimately linked, since the latter brings Mary's role of universal motherhood to fulfilment. It was necessary for Mary to pass through death before being assumed into heaven in order that she should fully become the Mother of Life, cancelling out the corruption of death that resulted from the actions of the original 'mother of all living', Eve:

> Since he who emptied himself in to you was God from the beginning, and life eternal, the Mother of Life had to become a companion of life, had to experience death simply as a falling-asleep; you had to undergo your passage from this world as an awakening to your own reality as Mother of Life. *First Homily on the Dormition, 6*[81]

Germanus also credits the Virgin with crushing the devil and setting the faithful on the right path by the example of her obedience: 'Hail, you who with the

---

[79] *EPH*, p. 160.
[80] *EPH*, p.154.
[81] *EPH*, pp. 158-59.

falling of your steps trampled the devil, the diabolical serpent with the tortuous mind who loathes the good, who has been a nefarious guide towards disobedience.'[82] Such statements are not unconnected with the iconoclast controversy during which both sides turned to the Virgin in defence of their stance, the iconoclasts portraying Mary as the destroyer of pagan icons while the iconophiles saw her as the enemy of heresy.[83]

Andrew of Crete († 740), whose writings had an important influence on the West, links the Virgin not only with the redemption of creation but with creation itself since she has given birth to the cause of life:

> O mistress of all men and women, you who received the living Word who is wisdom in person, the first and original cause of all things! O provider of life, life of the living, part of the cause of our life! O holy one, holier than all the saints, supremely holy treasury of all that makes us holy! O woman who as one individual, without division or dissolution, united humanity to God! O kingdom of those formed from earth, drawing your invincible power from the glory on high! O outer bulwark of Christian faith, powerful fighter for those who put their hope in you! *Third Homily on the Dormition, 15*[84]

Drawing on Irenaeus, he speaks of the newly-born Virgin as the person in whom human nature, restored to its prelapsarian state, is deified:

> Today the pure nobility of men receives the gift of the first divinisation once again and thus returns to itself; and the nature that is generated, being united to the Mother of the Beautiful One, receives back the excellent and most divine imprint of refulgent beauty which had been obscured by the ignobility of evil. And this new imprint is truly a re-formation, and the re-formation a divinisation, and this in turn a restoration to the first state. *First Encomium for the Feast of the Nativity of the Most Holy Mother of God*[85]

Here Andrew brings up the notion of divinisation or deification (*theosis*), which was fundamental to Greek understanding of the Incarnation. As Athanasius of Alexandria († 373), so succinctly puts it divinisation means 'God became man so that man might become God'.[86] In other words, by condescending to take

---

[82] *First Homily for the Presentation of the Most Holy Mother of God*, 12, TMPM, II, 328.

[83] See Nike Koutrakou, 'Use and Abuse of the "Image" of the Theotokos in the Political Life of Byzantium (with Special Reference to the Iconoclast Period)', in *Images of the Mother of God: Perceptions of the Theotokos in Byzantium*, ed. by Maria Vassilaki (Aldershot: Ashgate, 2005), pp. 77-89. See also the comments in the chapter on Intercession in the Patristic period.

[84] *EPH*, p. 149-50.

[85] TMPM, II, 397, PG 97, 812A. See also Graef, *Doctrine and Devotion*, I, 151.

[86] *De Incarnazione*, 54, 3, PG 25, 192B. On the notion of divinisation see Jules Gross, *La divinisation du chrétien d'après les pères grecs: Contribution historique à la doctrine de la grâce* (Paris: Gabalda, 1938), translated as *The Divinization of the Christian According to the Greek Fathers*,

on human nature, Jesus has also raised up that nature to God, and has opened up the possibility for all of humanity to share in the life of God. This humanity can do by conforming to its own image in Christ, which is the very image and likeness of God that Adam and Eve lost through the Fall. The notion is therefore closely bound up with the Irenaean doctrine of recapitulation whereby humanity is restored to the image and likeness of God through the Incarnation, as discussed above. Indeed it is Irenaeus who lays the foundations of the doctrine that will be developed over the coming centuries by the Alexandrians, Clement, Origen and Athanasius, by the Cappadocian Fathers, and Maximus the Confessor, among others.[87] Now, given that Mary was the means by which this restoration took place and given that she was united to the Word in a totally unique way, no-one can be more 'divinised' than her. But, according to Andrew, the origins of this process of divinisation may be traced not to the moment of the Incarnation but to the nativity of Mary, suggesting that she already contained within herself the potential to restore humanity that will be actualised at the Incarnation, because, being entirely free from all sin, she is *already* in the image and likeness of God as were her forbears, Adam and Eve in the time before the Fall.

The Incarnation raises Mary to a new level of communion with God far beyond anything that her prelapsarian forbears enjoyed. Ultimately, because of Christ's resurrection, it means that her flesh too will be glorified, as will that of all humanity at the end of time. Writing on the subject of the glorification of the body, he says that Jesus, by taking on human nature in Mary's womb 'remade his own humanity into something divine,' so that the old order of death, which resulted from the Fall, was destroyed and a new creation came into being. 'So, by a new relationship of both natures, he destroyed the old order and brought in a new order that will never

---

trans. by Paul A. Onica (Anaheim, CA.: A and C Press, 2002), and Norman Russell, *The Doctrine of Deification in the Greek Patristic Tradition* (Oxford and New York: Oxford University Press, 2004), and *Partakers of the Divine Nature: The History and Development of Deification in the Christian Traditions*, ed. by Michael J. Christensen, Jeffery A. Wittung (Rutherford N.J.: Fairleigh Dickinson University Press, 2007), in particular the two articles by John McGuckin, 'The Strategic Adaption of Deification in the Cappadocians', pp. 95-114, and Elena Vishnevskaya, 'Divinization as Perichoretic Embrace in Maximus the Confessor', pp. 132-45. See also Lars Thunberg, 'The Human Person as Image of God: Eastern Christianity', in *Christian Spirituality: Origins to the Twelfth Century*, ed. by Bernard McGinn and John Meyendorff, World Spirituality, 16 (New York, Crossroads, 1989), pp. 291-311.

On Byzantine theology in general, including *theosis*, see Hans George Beck, *Kirche und Theologische Literatur im Byzantinischen Reich* (Munich: C. H. Becksche Verlagsbuchhandlung, 1959).

[87] See Adam G. Cooper, *The Body in St. Maximus the Confessor: Holy Flesh, Wholly Deified* (Oxford: Oxford University Press, 2005), who discusses deification in many of the Greek Fathers.

grow old, so that all things might become new – in truth, a new creation – through this new, most praiseworthy incarnation of the Word.[88]

The theme of Mary reversing the damage caused by Eve, and restoring creation is also a frequent one in Andrew's hymns. Here is just one example: 'Today Eve is absolved from a condemnation, as is Adam, the ancient sentence is rescinded through your nativity, O Immaculate One!'[89] In another hymn he also writes of the Virgin as the fulfilment of all the Old Testament prophecies, from whom his own regeneration also derives: 'Hail, first offspring of my regeneration, end of the promises and the predictions addressed to us by God, preannounced sanctuary of divine glory, well-awaited salvation of peoples (see Luke 2. 30).'[90]

John of Damascus († 749) imagines the joy of Adam and Eve as they witness Mary being transported to heaven, since the reality of her bodily assumption demonstrates definitively that the corruption and death that resulted from the Fall have been overcome, and that they too may look forward to the resurrection of their bodies:[91]

> It was then, indeed, that Adam and Eve, the ancestors of our race, cried out piercingly, with joyful lips: 'Blessed are you, our daughter, for cancelling the punishment of our transgression! You inherited from us a corruptible body, but you bore in your womb, for our sakes, the garment of incorruptibility. You took your being from our loins, but you restored to us our well-being. You put an end to our travail, and broke through the swaddling-bands of death. You made available to us again our ancient home.' *Second Homily on the Dormition, 8*[92]

But John goes even further later in the same sermon suggesting that Mary's entry into heaven, in a certain sense, glorifies the whole of creation, both the four elements of earth, air, fire, and water that make up the world, and the fifth element, ether, of which the heavenly bodies were composed according to ancient belief:

> And what happened next? I imagine that the elements of nature were stirred up and altered. [...] The air, the fiery ether, the sky would have been made holy by the ascent of her spirit as the earth was sanctified by the deposition of her body. Even water had its share in the blessing: for she was washed in pure water,

---

[88] *Second [First] Homily on the Dormition*, 6, EPH, p. 123.

[89] *Canon for the Feast of the Nativity of Mary*, Ode V, *Troparion*, TMPM, II, 4, 468.

[90] *Fourth Encomium for the Nativity of the Most Holy Mother of God*, TMPM, II, 409-10.

[91] See Vittorio Fazzo, 'La mariologia di Giovanni Damasceno', *Theotokos*, 15 (2007), 127-36, and Kallistos Ware, '"The Earthly Heaven": The Mother of God in the Teaching of St. John of Damascus, in *Mary for Heaven*, ed. by William M. McLoughlin and Jill Pinnock (Leominster: Gracewing, 2002), 355-68.

[92] *EPH*, p. 212.

which did not so much cleanse her as it was itself consecrated. *Second Homily on the Dormition, 11*[93]

He goes on to speak of how Mary has made it possible for humanity to become divine, just as it was through her that God became human. Her own bodily presence in heaven is a foretaste of what awaits all the just:

> Through her, our age-old war against our creator has come to an end. Through her, our reconciliation with him has been forged, peace and grace have been bestowed on us, human beings join with the chorus of angels, and we who were once without honor have now been made children of God. From her, we have plucked the grape of life; from her we have harvested the flower of incorruptibility. She has become the mediator of all good things for us. In her, God has become human and the human being God! What could be more paradoxical than this? What could be more blessed? *Second Homily on the Dormition, 16*

That creation was restored and divinised through Mary is also a common motif in Byzantine hymns. The eighth-century hymnodist Sergius Hagiopolita, for instance, writes that, 'through her we were divinised and freed from death,' and that when she is born 'the world is restored'.[94] Tarasios of Constantinople († 806) salutes Mary as, 'mediatrix of everything that is under the sun [...] complete resurrection of the whole world.'[95] Theodore the Studite († 826), like his predecessors, sees Mary's passage into glory as a continuation of her historical role in reversing the effects of the Fall:

> Long ago, death took charge of the world through our ancestor Eve; but now it has engaged in combat with her blessed daughter and been beaten away, conquered by the very source from whom it had received its power. [...] Let the whole of creation jump for joy, drinking the mystical flood of its incorruption from that virgin spring and putting an end to its mortal thirst. *Encomium on the Dormition of Our Holy Lady, the Mother of God, 2*[96]

The Medieval West

Although Western Mariology was slower to acknowledge the role of Mary in the economy of salvation, the Latin Church eventually caught up with and even surpassed the East. This was in part a consequence of increasing awareness of the Eastern tradition, with the introduction of Marian feasts and devotions from the Greek Church and, especially from the turn of the millennium onwards, the increasing availability of the writings of some of the Byzantine

---

[93] *EPH*, p. 215.
[94] *Sticherà for the Vespers of the Nativity of Mary, TMPM*, II, 614.
[95] *Homily on the Presentation of Mary in the Temple*, 15, *TMPM*, II, 637.
[96] *EPH*, p. 250.

Fathers in Latin, but it was also a result of developments within the Latin Church as it emerged from the difficult centuries that had followed the collapse of the Western Empire.

Mariology in the West also differed in that it was based on different conceptual and cultural roots. The notion of deification, for instance, was less significant, whereas the Augustinian emphasis on fallen nature and the absolute dependence of humanity on God's grace was of central importance. From a cultural point of view, the panegyric tradition of the Greeks which is so evident in the Marian writings of the East was alien to the Roman world. Instead Latin writers latched on to the lyricism of the Canticle of Canticles, passages of which were used in the liturgy for the feast of the Assumption, so that it became a crucial vehicle for Marian reflection and praise. From the eighth century onwards, Sapiential texts (Proverbs 8 and Ecclesiasticus 24) were also used in the Marian liturgies of the Western Church. Alcuin († 804) seems to have been the first to introduce this practice. Among other consequences of this connection was the association of Mary with the act of creation and the idea that, in some way, she pre-existed creation, because she was conceived in the mind of God before the foundation of the world.[97] These passages were also frequently drawn upon in encomiastic texts.

Many Medieval writers also used the traditional Eve-Mary parallel in highlighting the enmity between Mary and the devil. Bede the Venerable († 735), for instance, writes:

> An angel was sent by God to consecrate a virgin with a divine birth-giving, since the first woman had been the cause of human perdition when the serpent was sent by the devil to ensnare the woman with the spirit of pride. Indeed, the devil himself, once the first parents had been ensnared, introduced himself into the serpent in order to denude the human race of the glory of immortality. So, since death made its entrance into the world through a woman, appropriately it was through a woman that life returned. Eve, seduced by the devil through the serpent, gave man the taste of death; Mary, instructed by God through the angel, generated the author of salvation for the world. *In festo Annuntiationis beatae Mariae, 1*[98]

Ambrose Autpert (†c. 781) declares that the redemption of humanity would not have been possible were it not for the co-operation of the Virgin: 'What praises, then, can human fragility offer you, which only found access to the Redemption through your participation in the divine plan?'[99] He goes on to attribute the activation of God's plan to Mary's humility: 'O truly blessed humility which

---

[97] See Sarah Jane Boss, *Empress and Handmaid: Nature and Gender in the Cult of the Virgin Mary* (London: Cassell, 1999), pp. 80-81 and 139-40 on Mary and the Wisdom texts and the parallels between the creation and Redemption.

[98] *PL* 94, 9B.

[99] *In festo Assumptionis B. Mariae (Pseudo-Augustine, Sermo 208)*, 11, *PL*, 2133-2134, *TMPM*, III, 726. See Luigi Gambero, 'Il contributo di Ambrogio Autperto († 781) alla tradizione mariologica della Chiesa', *Theotokos*, 15 (2007), 257-78.

generated God for men, which returned life to mortals, which renewed the heavens, which purified the world, which opened Paradise and freed the souls of men from Hell.'[100] This is a profound departure from the Eastern tradition which gave almost no importance to the virtue of humility. Although two sides of the one coin, the East tended to concentrate on the ascent of human nature through *theosis*, whereas the West, largely through the influence of Augustine, was more inclined to emphasise the kenotic aspect of the Incarnation, that is, the condescension or self-emptying of the Son. Rather than being raised up through divinisation, it is through the humility of Christ and his Mother that God brings about the transformation and restoration of humanity.[101]

We see the same tendency in a sermon by Haymo of Halberstadt († 853), a pupil of Alcuin's, who gives more importance to humility than obedience or virginity in his comments on the Eve-Mary antithesis:

> 'Because he hath regarded the humility of his handmaid; for behold from henceforth all generations shall call me blessed' (Luke 1. 48). And indeed, when observing the humility of the one, Mary, we justly rejoice that men called her blessed; on the contrary, the contemptible pride of the other, Eve, is condemned, definitively stamped as she was with her own name of woe [Latin *vae*] and calamity. It was right therefore that, just as death made its way into the world because of the pride of the first mother, so the second time the entranceway of life should be opened through the humility of Mary. *Feria sexta quattuor temporum, Homilia 5, 2*[102]

The same emphasis on humility as the key virtue in restoring humanity is evident in a passage by Hrabanus Maurus († 846). Commenting on Genesis 3. 15 – 'she shall crush thy head, and thou shalt lie in wait for her heel' – he begins by identifying the Church as the instrument of the serpent's defeat before turning to a Marian interpretation. In both cases humility is the cause of the proud serpent's downfall:

> She [the Church] will crush the head of the serpent because, humbling herself under the powerful hand of God, she resists the pride by which Eve was deceived. For pride is the beginning of all sin (Ecclesiasticus 10. 15). And the serpent lies in wait for the heel of the woman because the devil, who as a roaring lion, goes about seeking whom he may devour, tempts the Church and seeks to find the way of putting us off the path of good works. [...] Some have understood the expression, 'I will put enmities between thee and the woman', as referring to the Virgin from whom the Lord was born. They interpreted it thus

---

[100] *PL* 39, 2133, *TMPM*, III, 727.
[101] See Humility in vol. 2.
[102] *TMPM*, III, 765.

because at that time it was promised that of her would be born the Lord who would defeat the enemy and destroy death. *Commentarius in Genesim, 1, 18, 1-2*[103]

The ninth century also saw the appearance of the hugely popular hymn, *Ave Maris Stella* (Hail, Star of the Sea), which included a word play on Gabriel's greeting to Mary, 'Ave', and Eve's Latin name, Eva, which was to be taken up by numerous sermonists and hymnists: *Ave maris stella, /Dei mater alma / atque semper virgo, / felix caeli porta. // Sumens illud Ave / Gabrielis ore, / funda nos in pace, / mutans nomen Evae.* (1. Hail, Star of the sea, kind-hearted Mother of God, and ever Virgin, happy gate of heaven 2. Taking that sweet Ave, which came from Gabriel, confirm peace within us, changing Eve's name.[104]

Fulbert of Chartres († 1028) indentifies purity and humility as the two qualities that allowed Mary to overcome the devil, but ultimately it is because she became the Mother of Jesus, that is, of Wisdom, that Satan was defeated:

> First of all let us quote one of the announced prophecies and try to explain it. The Eternal One said to the devil, God to the serpent: "I will put enmities between thee and the woman, and thy seed and her seed' (Genesis 3. 15). In this context, my brothers, what does 'crush the serpent's head' mean if not to resist and overcome the principal suggestion of the devil, which is concupiscence? If therefore someone should ask: 'Which woman brought such a victory?' Certainly, following the line of human generation, no one is to be found until we reach she whom we consider to be the saint of saints. And if someone else should object: 'But in what way did she manage to crush the serpent's head?' The answer is: certainly because she sacrificed her virginity to God together with her humility For the Virgin extinguished the concupiscence of the flesh by preserving her virginity while, by guarding her humility, which makes us 'poor in spirit' (Matthew 5. 3), she destroyed the concupiscence of the mind. So, having overcome the principal temptation of the devil, she crushed his corrupt head with the foot of her virtue. But Mary did not triumph only for this reason, but above all because Wisdom says that he assumed a body from her most pure flesh: 'She reacheth therefore from end to end mightily, and ordereth all things sweetly' Wisdom 8. 1). This therefore was the woman to whom the divine prophet was alluding. *Sermo 4, De Nativitate beatissimae Mariae Virginis*[105]

Odilone of Cluny's († 1049) conception of Mary's Assumption is similar to that of the later Eastern Fathers in that it is the moment when she triumphs definitively over the devil, because, by her arrival in heaven, the Virgin becomes the living demonstration that God's plan of Redemption has been fulfilled and

---

[103] *PL* 107, 495D, *TMSM*, III, 769. See also his *Commentaria in cantica quaedam, Canticum Mariae Matris Domini, PL 112,* 1161D-1162C, where he highlights Mary's humility in the face of so great an honour and contrasts her attitude with Eve's.

[104] Latin text from *The Oxford Book of Medieval Latin Verse* ed. by F. J. E. Raby (Oxford, The Clarendon Press, 1959), pp. 94-95.

[105] *TMSM*, III, 848-49.

that Satan's scheme of closing the gates of heaven to mankind for ever has been foiled once and for all. Not only that, but the prophets and patriarchs, and even those still in Purgatory, give thanks, because it is by means of the Virgin that their hopes of gaining heaven are fulfilled:

> The whole world celebrates this day in a choir of joy. For today the angels rejoice in venerating the Assumption of the Mother of the Lord, the patriarchs and the prophets give thanks to God because they recognise that the portents and the prophecies have been fulfilled through the same Mother of the Lord. The Apostles and the Evangelists rejoice, affirming with true faith in their writings that the Lord came into the world clothed in flesh and was born of the Virgin. [...] Only Tartarus [Purgatory] shrieks, trembles and mutters because, the doors of hell having been closed; the joy and happiness of this day offer a certain relief. I believe that the ministers of Tartarus do not dare to touch their prisoners on this day, for they respect them because they have been redeemed by the blood of him who deigned to be born of the Virgin for the salvation of the world. *Homily for the Assumption of Mary the Mother of God*[106]

Mary's Assumption, therefore, is the concluding act in the plan of Redemption, bringing to fulfilment the prophecies of the Old Testament, and proving true the words of the New Testament. Her Assumption also offers the solace of certain future beatitude to those who must still suffer the penalties of their sins in purgatory, and by implication, encourages those who are still struggling in this life with the prospect that they will gain the life of heaven if only they persist in resisting evil.

Peter Damian († 1072), like several of the Eastern Fathers dates the beginning of salvation from the time of Mary's birth. No-one in the West had yet spoken with such clarity of Mary as the source of mankind's Redemption:

> The Nativity of the most blessed and irreproachable Mother of God, my beloved brothers, rightly brings an extraordinary and unusual joy to men because it constitutes the beginning of the whole history of human salvation. For just as almighty God had foreseen, before he became man, with the ineffable gaze of his providence, that mankind would perish by means of a diabolical machination, so in the depths of his immense mercy before the ages he had prepared the plan for the Redemption of mankind. And in the imperscrutable design of his wisdom God established not only the means and the order of the redemption, but he also predefined the precise time of its actuation. Now, just as it was impossible that the human race could be redeemed without the Son of God being born of the Virgin, so it was equally indispensible the Virgin be born so that the Word might take flesh from her. *In Nativitate beatissimae Virginis Mariae 1, 1*[107]

---

[106] *TMSM*, III, 865-66.
[107] *PL* 144, 752D, *TMSM*, III, 869.

These unprecedented lines mark the beginning of a period in which Mary will be raised to a status equal to if not greater than that attributed to her by the Byzantine Fathers. Peter also takes up the ancient theme of Mary reversing the fault of Eve:[108]

> All the proclamations made by human tongue can never speak sufficiently of her who gave birth to the food of our souls from the womb of her spotless flesh, he, that is, who said, speaking of himself: 'I am the living bread which came down from heaven' (John 6. 51). Through a food we were sent forth from the beauty of paradise, but it is also through a food that we have been readmitted to the joys of paradise. Eve ate a food by which we were condemned to the hunger of eternal fasting; Mary, instead produced a food for us that opened wide the doors to the heavenly banquet. *In Nativitate beatissimae Virginis Mariae 1, 6*[109]

He then dwells at some length on the question of why God chose the route of Incarnation in order to save humanity rather than some other way. He concludes that no other way was possible since the corruption of human flesh could only be remedied by a human, yet no human was free of the stain of original sin so that it was only by taking flesh from the Virgin that he could achieve the Redemption. No other woman could have taken on this office since all were corrupted by the sin of Eve.[110]

In another sermon he speaks of her not only restoring life to mankind through giving birth to Christ but also increasing the beatitude of the angels through her Assumption into heaven:

> Through this most Blessed Virgin not only is life restored which of old had been taken away from men, but the beatitude of the sublimity of the angels has increased, because when she is conducted from earth to heaven their number is made whole again which through pride had suffered a diminution. *Sermo 46, In Nativitate beatissimae Virginis Mariae*[111]

Godescalcus of Limburg († 1098) also sees Mary's restorative work extending to heaven by means of the Trinity who brought about the Incarnation in her:

> O Mediatrix, Mother of the Mediator, in you man was united to God and God to man. In the flesh that was assumed from you the three works of the one Trinity were achieved: that the angels might not fall; that fallen men might rise again; that the Tempter might not rise again. [...] Therefore, O Lady of all,

---

[108] On the Eve-Mary antithesis in the Middle Ages see Henri Barré, 'La nouvelle Ève dans la pensée médiévale, d'Ambroise Autpert au pseudo-Albert', *Études mariales*, 14 (1956), 1-26.

[109] *PL* 144, 743B-C.

[110] See *Sermo 45, In Nativitate Beatissimae Virginis Mariae*, 7-12, *PL* 144, 743D-746B.

[111] *PL* 144, 752B-C. It was believed that the saints took the place of the fallen angels, restoring heaven to its former glory.

placate your Son, aid those who beseech you, since it is only through you that he gives life to all those who are to be saved. *Sequence on the BVM*[112]

The English Church at this time surpassed all in its devotion to the Virgin.[113] An eleventh-century Marian Office, known as *The Portiforium of St. Wulstan*, is unusually effusive in its praises of Mary and her role in salvation, anticipating to some extent the fervour of Anselm of Canterbury in the following century: 'Whatever of good the universe has, therefore, it has from her from whom the beginning of our salvation flows.'[114]

In one of his most celebrated Marian prayers, Anselm († 1109) writes of all creation receiving new life thanks to Mary, in terms that would have been undreamt of a few centuries earlier. Here we reach the same heights that we found in Byzantine Fathers such as Germanus of Constantinople and Andrew of Crete. Despite their length, the relevant passages are worth quoting in full since they mark an important watershed in the Western Church. Anselm's writings had a far-reaching effect on Medieval Mariology, both in terms of the growth of affective piety and in the field of theology:[115]

> Let sky and stars, earth and rivers, day and night, everything that is subject to the power or use of humankind, rejoice that they lost their dignity, because through you, Lady, they are in some sense restored and endowed with an inexpressible new grace. In fact, almost all things were dead, having lost their innate dignity, which consisted in advancing the supremacy and uses of those beings that praised God, which was the purpose for which they were created. They were crushed by oppression, obscured and tainted by the acts of those who served idols, a purpose for which they were not created. Now instead they rejoice as if they had been brought back from the dead, because they are governed by the power of those who believe in God and they are honoured by the use that is made of them. In a certain sense they have been exalted by a new and inestimable grace because they have not only perceived that the same God, the same creator, governed over them invisibly from on high, but they saw him visibly in their midst, sanctifying them through his use of them. These great goods reached the world through the blessed fruit of the blessed womb of the Blessed Mary.
>
> But why do I limit myself, O Lady, to saying the world is filled with your benefits. They penetrate hell and reach up above the highest heavens. In fact, through the fullness of your grace, those who were in hell rejoice in their

---

[112] *AH* 50, 342, *TMSM*, III, 64.

[113] It was in the English Church, for instance, that the theology of Mary's Immaculate Conception was first developed. See chapters on Immaculate Conception and on Intercession, Mediation and Devotion, 1.

[114] Mary Clayton, *The Cult of the Virgin Mary in Anglo-Saxon England* (Cambridge; New York: Cambridge University Press, 1990), p. 79. n. 85. For the full Office see *The Portiforium of St Wulstan*, ed. by Anselm Hughes, 2 vols, Henry Bradshaw Society, 89–90 (London: Faith Press, 1958–60).

[115] See Rachel Fulton, *From Judgment to Passion: Devotion to Christ and the Virgin Mary, 800-1200* (New York: Columbia University Press, 2002).

freedom, and those in heaven exult in their restoration. In fact, through the same glorious Son who was the fruit of your glorious virginity, all the just souls who died before his life-giving death rejoice over the cancellation of their sinfulness, and the angels exult at the restoration of their half-destroyed domain. O woman marvellously unique, and uniquely marvellous, thanks to whom the elements are renewed, hell is healed, demons defeated, men saved, angels repatriated. O woman full and overflowing with grace, every creature, sprinkled with your overflowing fullness, begins to flower once again. O Virgin blessed and overflowing with blessings through your benediction every creature is blessed, not only the creature by the Creator, but also the Creator by the creature. […]

Nothing is equal to Mary, nothing, other than God, is superior to Mary. God gave his own Son to Mary, the only one whom he had generated from his heart equal to himself and whom he loved as himself, and from Mary he created a Son for himself, not another Son but the same one, so that in the order of nature he is the one and the same common Son of God and Mary. Every nature is created by God and God is born of Mary. God created all things and Mary generated God. God, who made all things, made himself of Mary, and thus he re-made everything that he had made before. He who was able to create all things from nothing did not want to remake his ruined creation until he became the Son of Mary. God, therefore, is the Father of all created things and Mary the Mother of re-created things. God is the Father of the creation of all things, and Mary the Mother of the restoration of all things. For God generated him, through whom all things were made, and Mary gave birth to him, though whom all things were saved. God brought forth him without whom nothing would exist, and Mary gave birth to him without whom nothing would be good. Truly the Lord is with you, because he granted to you that all nature should owe its unity with him to you alone. *Oratio 7 (51), 4-7*[116]

Here, Anselm goes far beyond anything that had previously been written in the West, and achieves a theological depth that is virtually unmatched in any of the Fathers since Irenaeus.[117] Essentially, what he is saying here is precisely the same as his doctrine of satisfaction as set out in *Cur Deus homo?*, except that he is viewing the Incarnation from the perspective of Mary rather than God.[118] Thus,

---

[116] *PL* 158, 955A-956B. See also Graef, *Doctrine and Devotion*, I, 213-14, and *TMSM* III, 90-91.
[117] For a somewhat different view on Anselm's teaching on Mary see Atria Larson, 'Passive Instrument and Active Intercessor: Anselm's View of Mary's Role in Redemption', *Cistercian Studies Quarterly*, 41 (2006), 32-50. On Anselm's Mariology see also Joseph Simon Bruder, *The Mariology of Saint Anselm of Canterbury* (Dayton: Mount St. Joseph Press, 1939), Richard William Southern, *St. Anselm: A Portrait in a Landscape* (New York: Cambridge University Press, 1990), and Giles Edward Murray Gasper, *Anselm of Canterbury and his Theological Inheritance* (Aldershot: Ashgate, 2004), pp. 144-173.
[118] In *Cur Deus Homo? (Why God Became Man?)* Anselm begins by examining the nature of the problem created by the Fall. God could not simply forgive Adam and Eve, he argues, because the damage to his honour required atonement. But nor could God, as the upholder of the moral order of the universe, simply forgive the debt. Anselm then goes on to examine the possible solutions. If God intervened and paid the debt himself, or sent one of his angels to do so, this would not provide satisfaction, because God was

he never loses sight of the centrality of Christ in all that is achieved through the Virgin. Mary's *fiat* unleashes a re-creation of the whole of God's original creation, and she herself, in some way, contains all of this new creation within herself, not only because she bore the Creator in her womb, but because she herself is the synthesis of nature perfected and redeemed, through her absolute conformity to the divine blueprint. Though God could have chosen another way, he wished to bring about the restoration of creation in the same manner through which it had been corrupted – the free choice of a human creature – for it was only thus that humanity, and through it the whole of creation, could reacquire the dignity it had lost because of the Fall.

Anselm also uses the Eve-Mary antithesis, like the Greek Fathers, to link the harrowing of hell to Mary: 'But why do I limit myself, O Lady, to saying the world is filled with your benefits. They penetrate hell and reach up above the highest heavens. In fact, through the fullness of your grace, those who were in hell rejoice in their freedom, and those in heaven exult in their restoration.'[119]

Bruno of Asti († 1123), in commenting on the genealogy of Christ, identifies the devil with the gargantuan Leviathan (Job 40. 20) and credits Mary with the defeat of this satanic giant:

> The one was defeated by the devil; the other put him in chains and defeated him. Since the line spooled out from Eve to Mary, it was in the latter, that the Hook which captured the Leviathan (that is, the devil or Satan) became incarnate and the line was secured. In this way, he who entered into the kingdom [of the world] through a woman was crushed by another woman. And he who tricked the woman and bound her with his snares, was himself tricked and put in chains by this woman alone. This is affirmed by blessed Job when he says: 'Canst thou draw out the leviathan with a hook, or canst thou tie his tongue with a cord? (Job 40. 20) [...]. It is as if he [God] is saying [to Job] that it will not be you who ties him up for your handmaids, since not even strong men were able to bind him. I, instead, by means of just one of my handmaids, will bind him and deprive him of his strength. This noble handmaid is she of whom we are talking, the most Blessed Virgin Mary.' *Sententiarum liber I, 5, 2, De Nativitate BVM*[120]

Eadmer of Canterbury (†c. 1124), a disciple of Anselm's, affirms that Mary became the Mother of God for the sake of sinners. This is the role that was ordained for her by God before the beginning of time: 'You were preordained in the mind of God before all other creatures, you, the most chaste among all women, to generate God himself from your own flesh.'[121]

---

not the debtor. A human could not pay the debt since all of humanity was tainted by original sin. The only solution, therefore, was for someone who was both God and man – Jesus – to pay the debt.

[119] *Oratio* 7, 5, *PL* 158, 955B, *TMSM*, III, 90.
[120] *PL* 165, 1022D-1023B, *TMSM*, III, 113.
[121] *On the Conception of Holy Mary*, *TMSM*, III, 119.

Rupert of Deutz († 1130) declares that Mary is both the bride of the Father, as the supreme prophetess of the Old Testament, and bride of the Son, as the type of the new Church. 'In fact', he goes on: 'the Holy Spirit, who in her womb and from her womb operated the Incarnation of the only Son of God, would operate in the womb and by means of the womb of the Church', and would bring about 'the regeneration of innumerable children of God.' It is from Mary, therefore, that the Church is born and it is on her that it models itself, in turn generating many new children. She, he goes on to say citing Isaiah 8. 3 – 'And I went to the prophetess, and she conceived, and bore a son' –, is the source of all the graces received by the prophets, the prophetess *par excellence*, for which reason they all turn to her:

> Should we believe the he [Isaiah] alone approached the prophetess? And should we marvel that he was able to approach her? On the contrary, all the holy prophets approached her, and without doubt Moses was the first. All, without exception, came to her because the graces distributed to all and each one and the particular prophecies are present in this prophetess and flowed together at the moment when the Holy Spirit came upon her. *De operibus Spiritus Sancti, 9*[122]

Rupert, in what is one of the first commentaries on the Canticle of Canticles in a Marian key,[123] makes rather unusual use of the Eve-Mary antithesis, contrasting Eve with the beloved of the Song. Like other Medieval commentators, the two aspects of Mary that he contrasts with Eve are her humility and her chastity:

> 'Arise,' he says, 'make haste, my love, my dove, my beautiful one' (Canticles 2. 10); in everything you are the opposite of Eve. For Eve is like an enemy, a viper; she is deformed and ignominious. She is an enemy for me, a viper for her husband, ignominy and confusion for herself. She is an enemy because of her pride which makes her swell up inside, she is a viper because of the malice that she conceived through the work of the serpent before which, tempted from without, she easily ceded; she is an ignominious creature because of the itch of libidinousness that immediately began to break out, for which reason, knowing that she was naked, she hid her shame with a leaf. But you are my friend, thanks to your humility, my dove, because of your charity, my beautiful, because of your chastity. You did not swell up against God, you were pleasing to the Most High because of your humble mind and therefore you are beloved. You did not listen to the serpent, rather I put enmity between you and the serpent; therefore you are a dove. You did not fall into the nakedness of libidinousness; rather the Holy Spirit will cover you with his shadow and therefore you are beautiful. *In Canticum Canticorum*[124]

---

[122] *PL* 167, 1578D.
[123] See Bride in vol. 2.
[124] *PL* 168, 867B-C.

Geoffrey of Vendôme (†c. 1132) affirms Mary's spiritual maternity with admirable clarity and brevity:

> Mary, truly holy, gave birth to Christ, and in giving birth to Christ she gave birth to Christians. Therefore she is the Mother of Christ and the Mother of Christians. If she is the Mother of Christ she is also the Mother of Christians, and this is clear because Christ and Christians are brothers. *De Purificatione Sanctae Mariae*[125]

Anselm's words on the restoration brought about by Mary are repeated almost verbatim by Hermann of Tournai († after 1147) in his *Tractatus de Incarnatione*,[126] while Peter the Venerable († 1156) expresses the same notion in a prose sequence for Christmas:

> Rejoice, O heaven, and you, earth, applaud; mankind returns to his ancient origin through the Virgin. / Now the guilty rise again from the mud, when God lies in the hay; now the humble stable hides the nourishment of heavenly food. / The breasts of the Mother distil milk, and with milk they mould the organs of the child, while he, through the man that he has assumed, distributes the sweetness of grace. / Hail, O Blessed Virgin, who have put malediction to flight, hail, O Mother of the Most High and Bride of the meekest Lamb. / You, Empress of the heavens, you restorer of the earth; to you sigh human creatures, before you perverse demons tremble. [...] The Virgin gave birth to God, so that the ancient dispute comes to an end, the old discord flees, peace and glory follow. *In honore Matris Domini prosa*[127]

The figure who took up Anselm's mantle most fully, however, was Bernard of Clairvaux († 1153). Though he lacked Anselm's theological sophistication, Bernard's eloquent espousal of the Virgin's pivotal role in the history of salvation had an even more powerful impact on the Medieval Church.[128] The following

---

[125] *PL* 265D-266A.

[126] See Chapter 9, and *PL* 180, 36-37.

[127] *AH* 48, 434-435.

[128] On Bernard's influence see Marielle Lamy, 'L'influence de saint Bernard sur la théologie mariale de la fin du Moyen Âge', in *La Vierge dans la tradition cistercienne, Bulletin de la société française d'études mariales*, 54e session de la S.F.E.M., Abbaye Notre-Dame d'Orval, 1998 (Paris: Médiaspaul, 1999), pp. 193-216. Also useful are the papers in *Respice stellam: Maria in San Bernardo e nella tradizione cistercense, Atti del convegno internazionale, Roma, Marianum, 21-24 October 1991*, ed. by Ignazio M. Calabuig, (Rome: Marianum, 1993). In addition see Claudio Leonardi, 'La Mariologia di Bernardo di Clairvaux nelle "Homiliae in laudibus Virginis Matris", in *Figure poetiche e figure teologiche nella mariologia dei secoli XI e XII*, atti del II convegno mariologico della Fondazione Ezio Franceschini con la collaborazione della Biblioteca Palatina di Parma, Parma, 19-20 maggio 2000, ed. by Clelia Maria Piastra and Francesco Santi (Florence: SISMEL-Edizioni del Galluzzo, 2004), pp. 129-34, Antonio Montanari, 'Maria Vergine negli scritti di s. Bernardo di Clairvaux', in *Maria madre del Signore nei Padri della Chiesa*, dizionario di spiritualità biblico-

passage gives a clear idea of the degree to which Bernard was influenced by Anselm and by the Fathers and also gives a taste of his persuasive eloquence:[129]

> It is to thy mercy that we owe the restoration of the whole world and the salvation of all. For it is manifest that thou wast solicitous for the salvation of the entire human race when it was said to thee, 'Fear not, Mary, for thou hast found grace with God,' the grace, that is which thou wast seeking. Who, then, shall be able to 'comprehend what is the breadth and length and height and depth' (Ephesians, 3:18) of thy mercy, O Virgin most blessed? Its length stretches forward even as far as the day of doom to succour all that invoke it. Its breadth is as broad as the universe, so that of thee too it can be said, 'the whole earth is full of thy mercy' (Psalms. 32:5). Its height reaches up to the city of God the ruins whereof it has been the means of repairing. And its depth goes down to them that 'sit in darkness and in the shadow of death' (Psalms. 106:10) for whom it has obtained redemption. For it is through thee, O Mary, that heaven has been filled, that hell has been emptied, that the breaches in the wall of the spiritual Jerusalem have been repaired (Psalms. 1:20), and that the life they had lost has been restored to miserable, expectant mortals. *Second Sermon for the Feast of the Assumption*[130]

Bernard asserts that Mary was foreseen by God even before the beginning of time: she was 'a virgin not newly discovered nor discovered by chance, but chosen from eternity, foreknown and prepared for Himself by the Most High', thus associating her with the feminised Wisdom of the Sapiential texts. He goes on to declare that proof of this is to be found in the writings of the prophets, who use types such as the rod of Jesse, the burning bush, and the fleece of Gideon.[131] Nevertheless, God's plan cannot be fulfilled without Mary's assent. In a passage that was to exert a powerful influence on understanding of Mary's active role in the Incarnation, he portrays in dramatic fashion, how the whole of creation, and even Christ himself, were waiting with baited breath for her to give her consent, without which all prospect of salvation would be lost:

> We also, O Lady, await from thy lips the sentence of mercy and compassion, we who are so miserably groaning under the sentence of condemnation. For lo! The price of our salvation is now offered to thee; if thou wilt only consent, we shall at once be set at liberty. We have been created by the eternal Word of God, and behold we die: by thy momentary word we must be renewed and restored to life. O Virgin most loving, Adam, now exiled from Paradise with all his miserable

---

patristica, 41 (Rome: Borla, 2005), pp. 317-52, and Aurele Ouimet, 'Marie et notre Rédemption selon Saint Bernard', *Veillée Mariale*, 41 (1953), 3-61.

[129] See Ignacio M. Calabuig, 'Les sources patristiques de la pensée mariale de saint Bernard', *Estudios marianos*, 64 (1998), 515-39.

[130] *SBS*, pp. 203-4.

[131] *SBS*, p. 18. For the typologies, see pp. 18-23 and see also the relevant sections in vol. 2 of this book. See also his *Fourth Sermon on the Glories of the Virgin Mother*, p. 71: 'Thou art she in whom and by whom "God our King before the ages hath decreed to work salvation in the midst of the earth."'

offspring, implores this favour of thee. For this does Abraham entreat thee, for this David, for this all the other holy fathers, thy ancestors, who are now dwelling in the region of the shadow of death. See, the whole world, prostrate at thy feet, awaits thy answer. And not without cause. For on thy word depends the consolation of the miserable, the pardon of the condemned, the salvation of all the children of Adam, of the entire human race. O Virgin, delay not to answer. Speak the word, O Lady, speak the word which all on earth, and all in limbo, yea, and even all in Paradise are waiting to hear. Christ Himself, the King and Lord of all, longs for thy answer with a longing equal to the ardour wherewith He 'hath desired thy beauty,' because it is by means of thy consent that He has decreed to save the world.' *Fourth Sermon on the Glories of the Virgin Mother*[132]

Bernard also speaks of Mary as the new Eve, who acts in consort with the new Adam in restoring creation to a glory even greater than that which pertained in the period before the Fall. In an audacious comparison he likens Christ's need of Mary to that of Adam for Eve, and echoing Anselm and Irenaeus, he suggests that although God could have achieved the Redemption without the Virgin, the method that he chose was more appropriate since it recapitulated the sin of Adam and Eve:

It is true, most dearly beloved, that the first man and the first woman did us grievous harm, but – thanks be to God! – by another Man and another Woman all that was lost has been restored to us, not without the addition of abundant grace. [...] The magnitude of the grace won for us by Christ exceeds beyond all proportion the ruin wrought by Adam. Instead of breaking that which was injured (Matt. xxii. 20), the Almighty Creator in His infinite wisdom and goodness restored it to its original perfection, yea, made it better than it had been before, forming a new Adam from the ancient and giving us a second Eve. Christ alone would no doubt have been sufficient, for even now, 'all our sufficiency is from Him' (2 Cor. Iii. 5); but it was not good for us that the Man should be alone (Gen. ii. 18). It seemed more congruous that as both sexes contributed to the ruin of our race, so should both have a part in the work of reparation. *Sermon for the Sunday within the Octave of the Assumption*[133]

Osbert of Clare († after 1158), an English Benedictine, writes of the Redemption beginning with the conception of Mary in almost exactly the same terms in which earlier writers had written of her birth, or before that, of the birth of Jesus, so that we see a gradual shift in the origin of salvation from the Son to the Mother:

This day is the beginning of all human redemption, it is the novelty of all novelties. On this day the origin of the old nature, corrupt because of the prevarication of

---

[132] *SBS*, pp. 70-71.
[133] *SBS*, p. 206.

disobedience, is surprised by the novelty of reparation, and so, through a growth in the virtues, it is lead to the glory of angelic dignity. *Sermon on the Conception of Mary*[134]

Amadeus of Lausanne († 1159), having contrasted the suffering that Eve introduced into the world with the healing that Mary has brought, writes of the joy of the universe upon the birth of Christ. It is on Mary that the universe smiles as much as on Jesus, so that both are given credit for the restoration:

> Imagine that when this Mother gave birth the face of the universe smiled and the world, full of joy, applauded its Lord. Imagine that the sky, free of any cloud, was clothed with beauty and that the stars said: 'Here we are!' And for her they became brilliant with joy. Imagine that the night too gave out light in the darkness, and instead of shadows it gave forth splendour. That night brought light before the rising of the sun; a light that because of its extraordinary splendour even obscured the light of the sun. *Homilia 4, De partu Virginis, seu Christi Nativitate*[135]

Hidegard von Bingen († 1159) writes of God forearming Mary with the graces she would need to defeat the devil, the very qualities that Eve lacked:

> When God foresaw what he intended to achieve, he recalled that he had said she would crush the head of the serpent. For this reason he filled a woman, that is, the Virgin to overflowing with obedience, with chastity, and with every other good, so that the pride that was found in Eve dried up in her. *Epistula 223R*[136]

Godfrey of Admont († 1165) sees Mary as being fully aware of the responsibility she was taking on at the time of the Annunciation. Her fear, he asserts, was not caused by the unexpected apparition of the angel or the words that he spoke to her – as some of the Fathers had maintained – , but was a result of her realisation that the whole plan of salvation depended on her:

> For she was not afraid only for herself or for the salvation of those close to her but for the liberation of the whole human race; she was afraid, I repeat that this Redemption would either not take place in the measure in which was required by the sin [committed], or that it would be postponed for so long that the greater part of the multitudes would be condemned to the ruin of eternal death. *Festive Homilies, 27, Annunciation*[137]

Aelred of Rievaulx († 1167) makes use of the Eve-Mary antithesis to affirm the Virgin's universal motherhood:

---

[134] *TMSM*, III, 453.
[135] *PL* 188, 1323C. See also, Amadeus of Lausanne, Homilies in Praise of Blessed Mary. Trans. Grace Perigo. Intro. M. Chrysogonus Waddell. Kalamazoo: Cistercian, 1979.
[136] *TMSM*, III, 375.
[137] *TMSM*, III, 312.

As you well know and believe we were all dead and agèd, in darkness and in wretchedness. Dead because we had lost God, agèd because we were corrupt, in darkness because we had lost the light of wisdom, and therefore we were completely perished. But through Blessed Mary, in a much better way than through Eve, we were reborn, since when Christ was born of her, in the place of agedness we regained a new life, in the place of corruption, incorruptibility, in the place of darkness, light. She is our Mother, Mother of our life, Mother of our incorruptibility, Mother of our light. *Sermon 23, On the Nativity, 7-8*[138]

Gerhoh of Reichersberg († 1169), among the most prominent figures in the twelfth-century German Church, attributes the Virgin's defeat of the devil to her humility, reflecting the great importance given to this virtue of Mary's by Medieval commentators:[139] 'O woman blessed among women, who crushed the serpent's head because you, O Virgin, remained humble and nullified the curse of the first woman.'[140] Hildegard von Bingen agrees: 'It was holy humility that, manifesting itself in the Mother and the Son, stuck the first beginning of evil, which is identified with the head of the devil.'[141]

Nicholas of Clairvaux († 1176), like Bruno of Asti and others, identifies the devil as the Leviathan whom Christ reels in with the bait of the flesh which he has taken from Mary. Thus it is the apparent weakness of Mary's flesh which deceives the devil and allows him to be captured and defeated by the hook of divinity:

And following the line of the book of generation he united the rod (Numbers 17. 8; Isaiah 11. 1)[142] to himself, taken from the Virgin as the hook of divinity hidden in the virginal flesh so that the great dragon, attracted by the flesh might experience the iron of the divine will. *Sermon on the Annunciation*[143]

According to Geoffroy of Auxerre († after 1188) the reason Mary is crowned Queen of Heaven is because she alone defeated the devil, unlike Peter who three times denied the Lord. Referring to Canticles 4. 8 he writes:

He did not prevail over you with his snares, not in the least nor in the greatest measure because, with virility, you entirely crushed his head. For this reason you will be crowned from the top of Amana, from the peaks of Sanir and Hermon, from the dens of the lions, because you have fought a just battle and you have triumphed magnificently. *El Marial inedito de Gaufredo de Auxerre*, 238[144]

Henry of Castro Marsiaco († 1189), a French Cistercian who was prominent

[138] *TMSM*, III, 323.
[139] See Humility in vol. 2.
[140] *Commentarius in Psalmos*, 118, *PL* 194, 745A, *TMSM*, III, 338.
[141] *Liber Scivias*, 3, 1, 18, *TMSM*, III, 372.
[142] See the the rods of Jesse and Aaron in vol. 2.
[143] *TMSM*, III, 360.
[144] *TMSM*, III, 412.

in fighting the Albigensian heresy,[145] makes the rather unusual claim that the sacraments have their origin in Mary. Although it was not unusual to draw parallels between Mary's generation of Jesus and the Eucharist,[146] to suggest that *all* the sacraments came from her is exceptional. The graces and charisms that she has unleashed derive, of course, from her Son, but she herself shines with her own light through her unique virtue:

> This twelfth gate of our city [Mary] of which we must speak is the first and supreme with relation to the other gates, first in order and supreme in dignity. From her therefore all the other gates have their beginning; they obtain support from her and are complemented through her. She is placed in the most eminent part of the city. She distributes light to the others and confers on them the dignity of their glory. She contains their completion. For from her all the sacraments came to us, the charisms of all the graces, and, no less delightfully, the examples of all the virtues shone forth. *De peregrinante civitate Dei, 11*[147]

Later in the same tractate we find a good example of the Eve-Mary antithesis using the much favoured Ave-Eva word play:

> Rightly was she [Mary] seen at the right hand of the King; of all the mass of human nature, corrupted and bent by Eve, she was the first and only one capable of changing the inauspicious name of Eve and transforming it into that sweet 'Ave'. For she, definitively abandoning the left, which Eve had chosen, turned herself completely to the right. Despising earthly and carnal delights and laying aside the image of earthly man, choosing heavenly and eternal things, she clothed herself in the image of heavenly man. *De peregrinante civitate Dei, 12*[148]

Martin of León († 1203), in one of the most eloquent passages to be found in the Marian literature of twelfth-century Spain, writes of the transformation wrought through Mary's incarnation of the Word:

> She gave God to the world because she gave birth to the on of God the Almighty for us, who ransomed us from the hands of the enemy with his precious blood and freed us from the danger of eternal damnation. She spread peace because she reconciled men with God and inspired the angels to make peace with men. She gave faith to the Gentiles because, thanks to her birth-giving, men who had served the idols for long years, ignorant of the true God, converted to the faith and to the knowledge of their Creator. She brought an end to vices because through baptism and the mystery of the most holy body of Christ the peoples are loosed from the chains of sin, both original and actual, provided that they renounce the works of the devil and they faithfully place their necks under the sweet yoke of Christ's service. She gave an order to life because

---

[145] See chapter on Divine Motherhood.
[146] See Mary and the Eucharist in vol. 2.
[147] *PL* 204, 331A-332D.
[148] *PL* 204, 343A-B.

Christ gave an organisation to his Church, providing it with heads, and ordering inferiors to obey their superiors. [...] She imposed discipline on habits because Christ, who was born of her, enjoined a penance on sinners, so that after baptism, whoever has abandoned himself to sin and vices and has stained the clothes of his innocence may, through prayers made with a pure heart, tears, fasting, and other good works, once again acquire pardon for his sins. *In Assumptione sanctae Mariae*[149]

Alain of Lille († 1203) speaks of Mary as the moon and a star because she brings Jesus, who is the 'Sun of Justice'.[150] Thus, she illumines the night of sin and is the precursor of the light of Christ's salvation:

Nevertheless this night is lit by the lesser light, that is, the Blessed Virgin, saving star, star that precedes the Sun, star that knows no setting, star that announces the rising of the Sun, star that guides the shipwrecked to port. She illuminates the night of our wretchedness in many ways. She eliminates the shadows by giving birth to the Sun of justice, excluding the darkness of guilt, distancing the shadows of ignorance, offering us a model of life and interceding for us continuously with her Son. She smashes the powers of the devil, exterminates heresy, and negotiates in our favour with God. *Sermon on Blessed Mary, 3*[151]

In another favourite word play on Eve's Latin name, Absalom von Springiersbach († 1205) speaks of the four woes (*vae*) introduced by Eve, which are countered, of course, by Mary's 'Ave':

In me is all grace of the way and of the truth, in me is all hope of life and of virtue (Ecclesiasticus 24. 25). Not such was that other mother who introduced onto the face of the whole earth the decree of malediction and the fourfold woe by which all the children of Adam are oppressed from the day of their birth until that of their burial. [...] O Eve, foolish mother, you who kill all your children even before they were born, why did you do this? Why did you bring down such a grave sin on yourself and on them? On the contrary, from you, O Blessed Virgin Mary, they await relief from this catastrophe, from you who had already been promised by the Law and by the prophets, who were foretold by many signs so that in your birth sinners might place their hope of forgiveness. *Sermon 47, For the Nativity of Mary*[152]

Oglerius of Lucedio, († 1214), echoing Bernard of Clairvaux, also writes of everyone awaiting Mary's response to the angel Gabriel. The emphasis on Mary's ability to medicate the wounds of sin is a typical characteristic of many Medieval texts:[153]

---

[149] *PL* 209, 22C-23D.

[150] See Star and Dawn in vol. 2.

[151] *TMSM*, III, 515.

[152] *TMSM*, III, 523-24.

[153] See the relevant sections in vol. 2.

O Virgin, medicine for our painful illness, you who are all our hope and our refuge of salvation, you have heard that you will conceive and give birth to a Son, not by means of man but through the Holy Spirit, the consoler. But we, together with the angel, are waiting to hear you reply. [For the angel] it is time to return to him who sent him. We wretches too are waiting to hear your words of consolation, and for good reason, because on your virginal mouth depends every consolation of the wretched, the ransom of prisoners, the liberation of the damned, the salvation of the lost. Your servants and your handmaidens are listening. Let us hear your voice. May it resound with sweetness, resound in our ears. *Tractatus in laudibus sanctae Dei Genitricis*[154]

For John of Ford (†c. 1214), as for many commentators, it is Mary and not Eve who is the true 'mother of all the living' (Genesis 3. 20). Where Eve brought death she gave life, not just to Jesus but to the whole body of the faithful:

Therefore, as is said above, that most blessed womb is such a generous distributor of his beatitude, without being a prodigal dispenser, and so, for all those who fear God it brings the Sun of justice, in whose warmth one is heated more than any other, and in whose light one becomes resplendent more than any other. Finally, since every grace and every glory emanate from this womb, it is rightly said that every generation of saints derives from it, through a certain wondrous sacrament of divine fruitfulness. I affirm that the Mother of Jesus is not just the Mother of our glorious Head, Jesus Christ, Mediator between God and men (see 1 Timothy 2. 5), but of all those who love Jesus: Mother of the entire holy Body of Jesus. For if she who gave birth to all through death, and became the mother of wrath for all those who are born of her, is called mother of all the living, with all the more reason is she who generated Life, and was constituted as the Mother of grace for all generations of the faithful, called the true Mother of all the living. *Sermon 70, On the Canticle of Canticles, 5*[155]

Pope Innocent III (1198-1216) likens Mary to the dawn because she 'indicates the end of damnation and the beginning of salvation'.[156] He goes on to contrast Eve with Mary:

Since death entered into the world through woman it was necessary that life should return to the world through woman. And therefore that which Eve had destined for condemnation, Mary saved, and she [woman] of whom death had been born became the font of life. The one assented to the devil and ate the forbidden fruit [...], the other, on the contrary, believed the angel and conceived the promised child. [...] The one was created without fault but caused the fault,

---

[154] *TMSM*, IV, 60.

[155] *TMSM*, IV, 73.

[156] See Dawn in vol. 2.

the other was generated with the fault,[157] but generated without fault. The one was called Eva, to the other was said 'Ave' because thanks to her the name of Eva was changed. *Sermon 28, For the Assumption*[158]

Another pope, Honorius III, (1216-1227) also writes at some length of Mary as the true Edenic paradise contrasting her womb with the earthly paradise inhabited by Adam and Eve, a notion we have already come across in several of the Fathers:[159]

> God placed mankind in Paradise when he brought about the conception of Christ in the Virgin's womb. This womb is called Paradise because it is pure, without stain and overflowing with blessings. God the Father placed the second Man in this Paradise so that he would accomplish our salvation. [...] Behold, Eve believed the words of the serpent and caused the expulsion of the first man, that is, Adam, from Paradise. Instead Mary believed the word of the angel and so in Paradise she nourished the second Man, that is, Christ, true Man and true God, and so in her womb and in her breast she totally gave the lie to the serpent's words. [...] Likewise, Mary was full of grace, contrary to Eve who was empty. We have all received of the fullness of Mary (see John 1. 16), while from the emptiness of Eve we have received malediction. Blessed Mary, as the house of God overflowing with every grace and benediction, she converted the curse of Eve into a blessing, restoring what she had taken away. *Second Sermon for the Annunciation* [160]

Anthony of Padua († 1231), commenting on Ecclesiasticus 43. 10 – 'The glory of the stars is the beauty of heaven; the Lord enlighteneth the world on high' –, writes of the uniqueness of Mary's birth since it was she who brought light into the darkness of the world. Here we again see the beginning of salvation shifting backwards from the birth of Christ to that of Mary:

> The purity of her birth is expressed by 'the glory of the stars'. 'Just as star differeth from star in glory' [1Cor 15.41], so the birth of the Blessed Virgin differs from the birth of all other saints. The illumination of the whole world is expressed by 'enlightening the world'. The birth of the Blessed Virgin gave light to a world covered by darkness and the shadow of death. Hence the words of Ecclesiasticus are apt: 'As the morning star in the midst of a cloud' (Ecclesiasticus 50.6). *Sermon on the Nativity of the BVM, 1*[161]

---

[157] Innocent did not accept that Mary had been conceived without original sin. See chapter on the Immaculate Conception.

[158] *TMSM*, IV, 99-100.

[159] For further consideration of this see Garden in vol. 2.

[160] *TMSM*, IV, 124-25.

[161] *The Sermons of St Antony*, trans. by Stephen Spilsbury, in *The Franciscan Archive* <http://www.franciscan-archive.org/antonius/opera/ant-hd00.html> [accessed 28 March 2006]. See René Laurentin, 'The Virgin Mary in the Works of St. Anthony of Padua', *Greyfriars Review*, 10 (1996), 47-74.

For Stephen of Salley († 1252), who meditates on the joys of the Virgin, the first joy is that Mary brought to an end the exclusion of humanity from heaven. Like Anthony, he traces the beginning of the joy and light that entered the world not to the birth of Jesus but of his Mother:

> Reflect on what a distressing situation of death the world had ended up in from Adam until the coming of Christ. The sin of prevarication reigned which wrapped everyone in the shadows of ignorance and of desperation to the point that there was neither saint, nor just man, nor innocent man, not even the Baptist, who was not destined to precipitate into Limbo. And so for those who were sitting in the shadow, amidst the clouds, there sprang up the Virgin Mary, the morning Star, to chase away that dense fog and light anew in hearts the hope of salvation. [...] Imagine what the birth of Mary meant in such a context: a welcome surprise for the desperate, health for the weak, light for those living in darkness, freedom for those who were oppressed in the squalor of prison. *Meditations on the Joys of the Blessed Virgin Mary, First Meditation*[162]

Richard of St. Laurence († after 1245), in his *De laudibus beatae Mariae Virginis*, long attributed to Albert the Great, contrasts the woes (*vae*), or curses endured by Eve with the blessings of Mary: 'Mary was exempt from this triple curse because she possessed that triple good which is opposed to this triple woe: the good of continence, the good of grace and the good of perseverance.'[163] He goes on to speak of her as the meeting point between the Old and New Testaments. The women of the Old Testaments looked to her for the cancellation of their curse while those of the New Testament looked on her as an example of virginity, motherhood and widowhood.[164]

Bonaventure's († 1274) teaching on the Incarnation is strongly rooted in the Irenaean notion of recapitulation.[165] In the *Breviloquium* he writes of the 'principle of reparation' whereby just 'as God created all things through the Uncreated Word, he would heal all things through the Incarnate Word.'[166] It was proper that the restoration should follow the pattern of the Fall and so it is that the remedy mirrored the disease. Of the Annunciation he writes:

---

[162] *TMSM*, IV, 219-20.

[163] 1, 1, 1-2, *TMSM*, IV, 199.

[164] 1. 6. 5, *TMSM*, IV, 200.

[165] See Christopher M. Cullen, *Bonaventure* (Oxford: Oxford University Press, 2006), particularly pp. 128-152, where he discusses Bonaventure's thought on creation and the Incarnation, and Ilia Delio, *Simply Bonaventure: An Introduction to His Life, Thought, and Writings* (New York: New City Press, 2001), particularly pp. 54-98. See also Peter Damien Fehlner, 'I discorsi mariani di san Bonaventura', *Immaculata Mediatrix*, 4 (2004), 17-65. For an English translation of Bonaventure see *The Works of Bonaventure*, trans. by José de Vinck, 5 vols, (Patterson, NJ: St. Antony Guild Press, 1960-1970).

[166] P. 4, ch. 1, n. 2, quoted in George H. Tavard, *The Forthbringer of God: St. Bonaventure on the Virgin Mary* (Chicago: Franciscan Herald Press, 1989), p. 54.

> Since humankind fell by diabolical suggestion, by the consent of a deceived woman, and by the libidinous generation which transmits original sin to offspring, it was opportune that, on the contrary, there would be here a good angel inciting to good, and the love of the Holy Spirit sanctifying and fecundating her for an immaculate Offspring, so that in this way 'contraries [would be] be healed by contraries.' *Breviloquium, Ch. 4. N. 3*[167]

Just as the Fall involved man, woman and the fallen angels, so all three are represented in the Incarnation indicating the universal nature of the restoration of creation. The threefold hierarchy that is evident in the involvement of God, the angels and humanity mirrors the paradigm of the Trinity, with each of the three Persons playing a role in the Incarnation, as indicated by the Lucan account of the Annunciation. Even the timing of the Annunciation (March 25) corresponds to the month of the creation of the world, a notion that we have come across in earlier commentators.[168]

In arguing that is was congruous that Jesus should be born of woman alone, rather than through a sexual act between man and woman purified by God, he states as one of his reasons that it was fitting that the Fall begun by Eve and completed by Adam should be reversed in a process begun by Mary and completed by Jesus: 'a woman by believing and conceiving began in a hidden way to triumph over the devil, and afterwards her Son in the open conquered him in battle – on the gibbet of the Cross.'[169] He quotes Jeremias 1. 5, 'Before I formed thee in the bowels of thy mother, I knew thee: and before thou camest forth out of the womb, I sanctified thee', as proof that Mary was chosen from the beginning of the world.[170]

Aquinas († 1274), as always, anchors Mary's role firmly within Christology, reminding his readers that Mary's greatness lies in her choice of God over all that was seemingly beautiful and pleasurable, unlike Eve who could not see beyond her own desires. We too, he reminds us, will regain paradise only if we follow Mary's example and seek the fruit that she offers us:

> Eve sought the fruit but she did not find in it that which she sought. Instead, the Blessed Virgin found in her fruit everything that Eve had desired. For Eve desired three things in her fruit. [Firstly] that which the devil falsely promised her, namely, that she and Adam would be as gods, knowing good and evil. That liar said: 'You shall be as gods' (Genesis 3. 5). But he lied, because 'he is a liar, and the father thereof' (John 8. 44). Eve was not made like God after having eaten of the fruit, but rather she became unlike God in that by her sin she

---

[167] Modified from the translation in Tavard, *Forthbringer*, p. 50.

[168] See *Commentary on Luke; On the Annunciation*, 1. c, ch. 1, nos. 40-68, *Opera Omnia*, VII, 20-26, Tavard, *Forthbringer*, p. 61.

[169] *Sent.* III, d. xii, a. 3, q. 2, Tavard, *Forthbringer*, p. 40.

[170] *Second Sermon on the Purification of the Blessed Virgin Mary*, in *Sermons on the Blessed Virgin Mary*, trans. by Campion Murray, in *Franciscan Friars Province of the Holy Spirit* <http://www.franciscans.org.au> [accessed July 2005].

withdrew from God and was driven out of paradise. This, however, is what the Blessed Virgin, and all Christians found in the fruit of her womb him because through Christ we are all united to God and are made like to Him: 'When he shall appear, we shall be like to him, because we shall see Him as he is' (I John, 3. 2). [Secondly] Eve looked for pleasure in the fruit of the tree because it 'was good to eat' (Genesis 3. 6). But she did not find this pleasure in it, since she at once discovered she was naked and was stricken with sorrow. Instead, in the fruit of the Virgin we find sweetness and salvation: 'He that eateth my flesh hath everlasting life' (John 6. 55). [Thirdly] the fruit which Eve desired was beautiful to look upon, but that fruit of the Blessed Virgin is far more beautiful, 'on whom the angels desire to look' (I Peter 1. 12). [...] Eve, therefore, looked in vain for that which she sought in the fruit of the tree, just as the sinner is disappointed in his sins. We must seek in the fruit of the womb of the Virgin Mary whatsoever we desire. *Expositio super salutatione angelica*

Mary became like God because, in an act of kenosis, she opened herself totally to him so that he came to dwell in her and came forth from her to offer himself to the whole of humanity. This is why Redemption came through her and this is why she is the pattern of creation restored.

Chapter 4 - Intercession, Mediation and Devotion 1: The Patristic Period

Isaiah 7. 14:	Therefore the Lord himself shall give you a sign. Behold a virgin shall conceive, and bear a son, and his name shall be called Emmanuel.
Luke 1. 28:	And the angel being come in, said unto her: Hail, full of grace, the Lord is with thee: blessed art thou among women
Luke 1. 41-42:	And it came to pass, that when Elizabeth heard the salutation of Mary, the infant leaped in her womb. And Elizabeth was filled with the Holy Ghost: And she cried out with a loud voice, and said: Blessed art thou among women, and blessed is the fruit of thy womb.
Luke 1. 46-48:	My soul doth magnify the Lord. And my spirit hath rejoiced in God my Saviour. Because he hath regarded the humility of his handmaid; for behold from henceforth all generations shall call me blessed.
John 2. 3-5:	And the wine failing, the mother of Jesus saith to him: They have no wine. And Jesus saith to her: Woman, what is that to me and to thee? My hour is not yet come. His mother saith to the waiters: Whatsoever he shall say to you, do ye.
John 19. 27:	Woman, behold thy son. After that, he saith to the disciple: Behold thy mother.

While the terms intercession and mediation are often used synonymously when speaking of Mary, in the strict sense there are fundamental differences between the two. Intercession may be understood as Mary's intervention with God on behalf of sinful humanity, usually in response to a specific request or need, though she may also act gratuitously on behalf of someone who has not directly sought her aid. It is thus primarily an upward movement from an individual supplicant to God via the Virgin, who responds with a downward movement of grace. Broadly speaking, Mary's intercession falls into two categories. Firstly, the faithful may seek her aid in obtaining an outpouring of grace from God that will help them in living fully according to his will and will prevent them from falling into sin – an early version of the pre-emptive strike. Secondly, by praying for forgiveness through her, the sinner increases his or her chances of receiving a merciful response from God. This is essentially the same role as played by the saints, who may also intercede on behalf of the faithful, although Mary's unique position in the heavenly hierarchy as the Mother of God places her above the angels and the other saints and gives her a unique status in the divine economy.[1]

Mediation (Greek *mesiteia*) can refer either to the objective redemption of humanity by Christ on the Cross, or to subjective redemption, which is the distribution of the grace that Jesus made available to humanity through his Passion and death. It is in this latter sense that the term mediatrix is usually applied to Mary. The notion of the Virgin's mediation differs from her intercession in that it states that God, in view of her co-operation in the Redemption, chooses to use her as his primary instrument in distributing grace rather than dispensing it himself. Conversely, humanity may ascend to God through her, just as the Word descended to humanity through her.[2] In the case of those who believe in her universal mediation, *all* grace, even for those who lived before the Redemption (who received grace in view of her future merits), comes to humanity through Mary. Though the notion of Mary's mediation was already present in some of the later Fathers, it was not until the Middle Ages that the term 'mediatrix' came to be widely applied to Mary and that the theological basis for the belief was put on a firmer footing[3]. Mary's universal mediation has never been accepted as a doctrine by the Catholic Church, though it continues to enjoy considerable support.

---

[1] One of the best expositions on Mary's intercession remains Jean Galot, 'L'intercession de Marie', in *Maria*, VI, 513-550. On Mary's intercession in the Fathers see Gustave Bardy, 'La doctrine de l'intercession de Marie chez le Pères grecs', *La Vie Spirituelle*, 56, Supplément (1938), 1-37, George Augustin, 'Les fondements scripturaires de l'intercession de Marie,' *Études mariales*, 23 (1966), 19-35, Jean-Marie Salgado, 'La maternité spirituelle de la Sainte Vierge chez les Pères durant les quatre premiers siècles', *Divinitas*, 30 (1986), pp. 58-61, and Luigi Gambero, 'Patristic Intuitions of Mary's Role as Mediatrix and Advocate: The Invocation of the Faithful for Help', *Marian Studies*, 52 (2001), 78-101. More generally on the Patristic period see the various chapters in *SDM*, I covering the Greek area, Elio Peretto, 'Primi abozzi di riflessione teologica su Maria', pp. 257-62, and 'Maria nell'area culturale greca: da san Giustino († 165 ca) a san Giovanni Damasceno († 749 ca)', pp. 293-305, and for the Latin Church, Mario, Maritano, 'Maria nell'area culturale latina: da Tertulliano († 240 ca) a sant'Ildefonso di Toledo († 667), pp. 306-27, the Syriac Church, Emidio Vergani, 'Maria nell'area culturale siriaca nel IV secolo: Efrem il Siro, pp. 328-36, and the Copts, Mark Sheridan, 'Maria nell'area culturale copta', pp. 337-49.
[2] See Pelikan's useful overview of Mary's mediation in *Mary through the Centuries*, pp. 130-36. See also E. Druwê, 'La médiation universelle de Marie', in *Maria*, I, 417-572, and Juniper B. Carol, *Fundamentals of Mariology* (New York: Benziger, 1956), pp. 55-7.
[3] Leena Peltomaa, *The Image of the Virgin Mary in the Akathistos Hymn* (Leiden, Boston and Cologne: Brill, 2001), p. 146, n. 115, incorrectly asserts that the term does not occur with reference to Mary before Andrew of Crete in the eight century, when it is in fact already found in Basil of Seleucia († after 468). It was primarily through the influence of the Cluniac reform in the eleventh century that the term entered into common usage in the West. See *TMPM*, III, 35-6.

It is impossible to pinpoint with accuracy at what stage significant numbers of Christians began to turn to Mary as an intercessor. That she is mentioned at least twenty times in the New Testament, most of which was written in the hundred years or so after the death of Christ, is itself evidence that there was a living tradition among the first generations of Christians concerning Mary.[4] Likewise, texts such as the apocryphal *Protoevangelium of St. James* and the *Odes of Solomon*, both dating from around the beginning of the second century, attest to a lively interest in her life and person.[5] That the Eve-Mary antithesis was a central theme in Patristic texts from the time of Irenaeus (†c. 202) on, and that she was an important exemplar of virginity for the early Fathers, offers further confirmation that she was a figure of considerable weight in the early Church. Indeed, the notion of Mary as the new Eve, the instrument of salvation, will become one of the central planks on which the doctrine of her intercession will depend.

However, none of this in itself constitutes evidence of a cult of the Virgin – prayers addressed to her, liturgical formulae, devotions, and so on. Far more prominent, for instance, was the cult of Thecla of Iconium, a semi-legendary virgin often identified with the apocryphal *Acts of Paul and Thecla*.[6] One possible explanation for the apparent late development of the Virgin's cult is the lack of any definitive burial site or relics, such as existed for the martyrs, whose cult

---

[4] The oldest writings are those of St. Paul, written within a generation of Christ's death, in which he never refers directly to Mary. Of the four Gospels, Matthew (c. 80-85 AD), Mark (c. 65-70 AD), Luke (85 AD), and John (50-85 AD), Luke provides the most extensive account of the Annunciation and the birth and childhood of Christ, while John is alone in mentioning Mary's presence on Calvary. The Acts of the Apostles, also authored by Luke, speak of Mary's presence in the Upper Room when the Holy Spirit descended upon the Apostles. See 'Mary in the New Testament', the first volume of Bertrand Buby's *Mary of Galilee*, 3 vols (New York: Alba House, 1994-1997). See also André Feuillet, 'La Vierge Marie dans le Nouveau Testament', in *Maria* VI, 15-69 and the relevant pages in Gabriele M. Roschini, *Maria Santissima nella storia della salvezza*, vol. IV, *Il culto mariano* (Isola del Liri: Pisani, 1969), which also contains valuable material on all the period covered in this chapter.

[5] Chris Maunder, 'Mary in the New Testament and Apocrypha', in *Mary: The Complete Resource*, ed. by Sarah Jane Boss (Oxford and New York: Oxford University Press 2007), pp. 11-46, argues that the *Odes* date from the first century. Most commentators plump for a date somewhere around the beginning of the second century for the *Protoevangelium*. See Marie-Joseph Pierre, 'La Vierge dans les Odes de Salomon, *Études mariales*, 60 (2003), 119-37. For a thorough overview of the apocrypha see Enrico Norelli, 'Maria negli Apocrifi', in *Gli studi di mariologia medievale: bilancio storico*, Atti del I convegno mariologico della fondazione Ezio Franceschini con la collaborazione della biblioteca Palatina e del dipartimento di storia dell'università di Parma, Parma 7-8 novembre 1997, ed. by Clelia Maria Piastra (Florence: SISMEL – Edizioni del Galuzzo, 2001), pp. 19-63 and, by the same author 'Maria nella letteratura apocrifa cristiana antica', in *SDM*, I, 143-254. For further discussion and bibliography see the chapter in this volume on Virginity, and and also vol. 2.

[6] See Stephen Davis, *The Cult of Thecla* (Oxford: Oxford University Press, 2001).

already existed in the second century.[7] It may be that veneration of the Virgin was slow to develop as long as martyrdom was seen as the primary exemplar of holiness. Another explanation that is posited is that the early Church was so wholly concentrated on the figure of Christ that it did not leave much space for Mary, but the existence of the cult of the martyrs would seem to argue against this. A more likely factor is the lack of distinction in the first centuries between Mary and the Church, when, as Breandán Leahy points out, 'the concepts of "virgin-mother-church" and "virgin-mother-Mary" are so intertwined that, in a sense, they cannot be separated.'[8] A further factor may have been the fear of confusion with pagan goddesses, a fear that is voiced by several of the Fathers, as we shall see.

Little of significance has been found in the way of art or architecture that would suggest a formal cult before the fourth century. There is legitimate doubt over whether third-century images in the catacombs of Priscilla actually are representations of the Virgin.[9] This leaves us with the earliest portraits of Mary being of the Adoration of the Magi, which do not necessarily point to a cult of the Virgin since it is Christ who is the subject of adoration. Of course, it is possible that they were intended to convey that the way to Christ is through the Virgin, as the later Hodegetria icons were,[10] but the textual evidence would

---

[7] See Richard Price, 'The *Theotokos* and the Council of Ephesus', in *The Origins of the Cult of the Virgin Mary*, ed. by Chris Maunder (London: Burns and Oats, 2008), pp. 89-103 (pp. 99-100), and Hippolyte Delehaye's classic study, *Les origines du culte des martyrs*, 2nd edn. (Brussels: Société des Bollandistes, 1912). Leena Peltomaa, *The Image of the Virgin*, suggests that third-century prayers to the Virgin should be seen in the context of the intercessory powers attributed to the martyrs (p. 75). She also points out that in the Old Testament those who were obedient to God's Covenant enjoyed greater access to him, and were 'bold' in their requests. This tradition, she suggests, contributes to the notion that the saints, and most especially Mary, have the power to intercede with God (p. 154).

[8] The *Marian Profile in the Ecclesiology of Hans Urs von Balthasar* (New York: New City, 2000), p. 20, and see Mary and the Church in vol. 2.

[9] See vol. 2 and see Fabrizio Bisconti, 'La Madonna di Priscilla: interventi di restauro ed ipotesi sulla dinamica decorativa', *Rivista di Archeologia Cristiana*, 72 (1996), 7-34. See also Geri Parlby, 'The Origins of Marian Art in the Catacombs and the Problems of Identification', in *The Origins of the Cult of the Virgin Mary*, pp. 41-56, who points out that many scholars now believe that these representations are not of the Virgin but of an ordinary mother with her child, and see his 'The Origins of Marian Art: The Evolution of Marian Imagery in the Western Church until AD 431', in *Mary: The Complete Resource*, ed. by Sarah Jane Boss (Oxford and New York: Oxford University Press 2007), pp. 106-29. Umberto Utro, 'Maria nell'iconografia cristiana dei primi secoli', in *Storia della mariologia*, pp. 353-81, however, continues to adhere to the traditional view (pp. 156-58). This article contains a wealth of useful information on other representations of the Virgin in the Patristic period.

[10] The Hodegetria type, meaning 'she who points the way', features Mary holding Jesus on her left arm while she points to her Son with her right hand. Variations may also have her seated. It appears to have Coptic origins and was extremely popular

suggest that this idea was not developed until much later (see Romanos below). Images of the Virgin on jewellery and clothing were rare before the second half of the sixth century.[11] The earliest prominent churches associated with the cult of the Virgin nearly all date to the sixth century or later, an exception being the fifth-century Kathisma, situated between Jerusalem and Bethlehem which was reputed to be the place where Mary had rested on her way to the birthplace of Christ.[12] That said, 'hard evidence' concerning Christian cultic practice of any kind is hard to come by for the early centuries of Christianity, as John McGuckin notes.[13] Only in the late second century did Christian art begin to emerge, much of it still arcane – such as the symbol of the fish – because of the ongoing persecutions.

Let us turn now to such evidence as does exist for the early centuries. The *Protoevangelium* recounts a whole series of miraculous events in Mary's life, from her conception to a sterile mother (it is thanks to the *Protoevangelium* that we know the names of Mary's parents) to her unconventional upbringing in the Temple, nourished by angels, her espousal to Joseph, who guards and defends her virginity, and the preservation of that virginity in giving birth to Jesus.[14] Several of the principal themes of the *Protoevangelium*, such as the defence of her virginity, under attack from Jews and Gentiles alike, and the affirmation of her Davidic ancestry,[15] are reflected in the writings of the early Fathers. All in all, the *Protoevangelium* tells us that Christians of the second century were sufficiently curious concerning the Virgin to move beyond the rather scant information provided by the canonical texts, but it does not provide any evidence of belief in her intercession, not does it show that she was venerated in any formal way.

As we have seen in the previous chapter, the Virgin was already a prominent figure in the writings of the early Fathers. She was perceived to have had an active role in the economy of salvation through her assent to become the Mother of Christ, and, as the second Eve, it was through her that the restoration of humanity and the harrowing of hell had been achieved. Some suggest that

throughout the Byzantine area. The seated Hodegetria in particular was also widespread in the later Medieval period in the West. See Victor Lasareff, 'Studies in the Iconography of the Virgin', *Art Bulletin*, 20 (1938), 26-65 (pp. 46-65).

[11] See Henry Maguire, 'Byzantine Domestic Art as Evidence for the Early Cult of the Virgin', in *Images of the Mother of God: Perceptions of the Theotokos in Byzantium*, ed. by Maria Vassilaki (Aldershot: Ashgate, 2005), pp. 183-193.

[12] See Stephen, J. Shoemaker, 'The Cult of the Virgin in the Fourth Century: A Fresh Look at Some Old and New Sources', in *The Origins of the Cult of the Virgin Mary*, pp. 71-87 (p. 75), Michel van Esbroeck, 'The Virgin as the True Ark of the Covenant', in *Images of the Mother of God*, pp. 63-68 (p. 65), and Igino Grego, 'Il Kathisma o luogo del riposo della Vergine', *Asprenas*, 45 (1998), 231-44.

[13] John McGuckin, 'The Early Cult of Mary and Inter-Religious Contexts in the Fifth-Century Church', in *The Origins of the Cult of the Virgin Mary*, pp. 1-22.

[14] For bibliography and more detailed discussion see the chapter on Virginity, and also in vol. 2.

[15] See Rod in vol. 2.

Irenaeus, who calls Mary 'the advocate of the virgin Eve', is attributing a intercessory role to the Virgin, but it is clear from the context that he is speaking in historical terms, and not of any continuing role in heaven.[16] Origen (†c. 254), as well as embracing Irenaeus' teaching on the recapitulation of Eve in Mary, for the first time puts Mary forward as a unique exemplar of holiness,[17] and, if we are to believe the testimony of the fifth-century Church historian, Socrates, he was also the first figure of importance to use the term *Theotokos*, in his lost commentary on Paul's Epistle to the Romans.[18] But he does not mention any cult surrounding her nor does he speak of her intercession. Ephrem (†c. 373), like Irenaeus, sees Mary as playing a role in the salvation of Eve, for whom Christ's birth is an occasion of joy, because he will liberate her from Sheol, the realm of the dead to which he descended after his death: 'The Son of her daughter has descended as the medicine of life to raise the mother of his mother. The blessed child crushes the head of the serpent which had wounded her.'[19] However, this is again referring to the historical event of the harrowing of hell rather than any continuing intercession. Ephrem is also the principal initiator of the great encomiastic tradition surrounding the Virgin, centred primarily on her virgin motherhood and on her role as the second Eve. Yet, while these texts may contain the seeds of the Virgin's cult, they do not show that she was seen as an effective intercessor.[20] Likewise, Eusebius of Caesarea (†c. 340), Athanasius of Alexandria († 373), Basil the Great († 379), Cyril of Jerusalem (†c. 397), and Ambrose of Milan († 397), to name but a few, write in glowing terms of Mary's virginity.[21] For Ambrose in particular, as a virgin mother she is a type of the Church and a model of all the virtues.[22] Ambrose was also responsible for what may be the first hymns to the Virgin in the West.[23] Nevertheless, none speak of her being invoked in prayer.

The first positive evidence of Marian prayer is an early version of the hymn *Sub tuum praesidium*, a prayer that may date from as early as the third century, which became part of the liturgical office for Christmas in the Coptic Rite: 'We

---

[16] See Michael O'Carroll, *Theotokos: A Theological Encyclopedia of the Blessed Virgin Mary* (Collegeville, Minnesota: Liturgical Press, 1982), p. 5, and *MF*, pp. 55-56.

[17] He calls her *panaghía* (all holy) in several of his works and was probably the first to use the term *Theotokos*. See chapter on Divine Motherhood.

[18] *Historia Ecclesiastica*, VII, 32, 17, ed. by Günther Christian Hansen (Turnhout: Brepols, 2004). See the chapter on Divine Motherhood for further discussion and bibliography.

[19] *Hymn on the Nativity*, 13, 2, quoted in Hilda Graef, *Doctrine and Devotion*, I, 61.

[20] John McGuckin, 'The Early Cult', contends that 'it was from Origenian seed that the later Byzantine tradition developed its teaching that Mary and John the Baptist were the two supreme intercessors of the Church' (p. 10).

[21] For homilies in the Greek area see *La homiletica mariana griega en el siglo V*, ed. by Roberto Caro, 3 vols (Dayton, Ohio: University of Dayton Press, 1971-73).

[22] See Luigi Gambero, 'Appunti patristici per lo studio della mariologia', in *Gli studi di mariologia medievale: bilancio storico*, pp. 5-17 (pp. 12-13), and Mario Maritano, 'I Padri latini e la mariologia nel IV sec.', *Theotokos*, 11 (2003), 215-44. See vol. 2 for further discussion.

[23] See Carl P. E. Springer, 'The Hymns of Ambrose', in *Religions of Late Antiquity in Practice*, ed. by Richard Valantasis (Princeton: Princeton University Press, 2000), pp. 347-56.

take refuge in your mercy, Theotokos. Do not disregard our prayers in troubling times, but deliver us from danger, O only pure one, only blessed one.'[24] The prayer provides evidence that Mary was already considered a protectress in times of distress and contains many of the elements that will come to typify Marian prayers and writings on the Virgin's intercession: she is compassionate, a characteristic that will be particularly emphasised in the Medieval West; she provides protection against danger, whether physical or spiritual; her power to provide aid derives from her prerogatives as the Mother of God; the supplicant offers praise to her before pleading for her favour.

Gregory Nazianzen († 390) offers the first authoritative witness to the practice of calling on Mary's aid in his account, dated to 379,[25] of a virgin martyr named Justina, who requests Our Lady's help in protecting her virginity from Cyprian who, prior to his conversion and martyrdom, attempted to seduce her with the aid of the devil. Though there is no historical evidence for the veracity of the story, it illustrates that Mary was already regarded as a protectress of virgins and as a defence against the seductions of the devil, a pattern that is consistent with the strong emphasis in early Mariology on her virginity and on the Eve-Mary antithesis.[26] It is on the basis of Mary's enmity with the devil and her role in restoring the relationship between humanity and God that much of the subsequent development of belief in her intercessory powers derives.

If the witness of the Church historian Sozomon († 425) is to believed, Gregory was also associated with a Church in Constantinople where the intercessory power of the Virgin frequently manifested itself:

> Gregory of Nazianzen presided over those who maintain the 'consubstantiality' of the Holy Trinity, and assembled them together in a little dwelling, which had been altered into the form of a house of prayer [...]. It subsequently became one of the most conspicuous in the city, and is so now, not only for the beauty and number of its structures, but also for the advantages

---

[24] Quoted in Stephen J. Shoemaker, 'Marian Liturgies and Devotion in Early Christianity', in *Mary: The Complete Resource*, pp. 130-145 (p. 130). Shoemaker notes that the caution of some scholars in dating the prayer to the end of the fourth century is contradicted by the palaeographical evidence. Richard Price concurs in, 'Theotokos: The Title and its Significance in Doctrine and Devotion', in *Mary: The Complete Resource*, pp. 56-74 (pp. 56-7), and his, 'The *Theotokos* and the Council of Ephesus', pp. 89-90. The papyrus is preserved in the John Rylands Library of University of Manchester and may be viewed digitally at <http://rylibweb.man.ac.uk/insight/papyrus.htm>. For further commentary on the prayer see *MF*, pp. 69-70 and 79, O'Carroll, *Theotokos*, p. 187, Anthony M. Buono, *The Greatest Marian Prayers: Their History, Meaning and Usage* (New York: Alba House, 1999), and Henri Barré, *Prières anciennes de l'Occident à la Mère du Sauveur des origines à saint Anselme* (Paris: Lethielleux, 1963), pp. 19-20.

[25] See Leena Peltomaa, *The Image of the Virgin*, p. 75.

[26] *Oratio 24*, 11, *PG* 35, 1177C-1181A. See John A. McGuckin, *St Gregory of Nazianzus: An Intellectual Biography* (Crestwood, N.Y.: St. Vladimir's, 2001), *MF*, pp. 164-167, Stephen J. Shoemaker, 'Marian Liturgies', p. 131, and *TMPM*, I, 310-11.

> accruing to it from the visible manifestations of God. For the power of God was there manifested, and was helpful both in waking visions and in dreams, often for the relief of many diseases and for those afflicted by some sudden transmutation in their affairs. The power was accredited to Mary, the Mother of God, the holy virgin, for she does manifest herself in this way. The name of Anastasia was given to this Church. *Historia Ecclesiastica, 7, 5, 1-3*[27]

Although we cannot be sure of the reliability of Sozomon's account nor of the exact date that the manifestations began, since he only says that it was subsequent to the time of Gregory, this is clear evidence that stories of Mary's miraculous powers were circulating in Constantinople in the late fourth or early fifth century.

An important factor in the growth of belief in the Virgin's intercessory powers in the early Church was that she was seen as a bulwark of orthodoxy, since she was closely bound to heresies concerning Christ's dual natures.[28] Gregory of Nyssa († c. 394), in his *Life of Gregory the Miracle Worker*, written in 380, tells of how his namesake, Gregory Thaumaturgus (†c. 270), was unable to sleep because of his preoccupations about the heretics who were assailing the doctrine of the Church. All of a sudden, Mary and John the Evangelist appear to him and begin to converse on the truths of the faith. By listening to their conversation, Gregory comes to perfect understanding of doctrine.[29] Thus, not only is Mary a guarantor of orthodoxy as the historical Virgin Mother of God, but she continues to intervene from heaven in order to sustain those who uphold the true faith. This account is of considerable importance since it was from these roots that Mary came to be viewed both as a protectress of the Church and of Christendom as a whole.

Of particular interest are the various versions of the *Six Books* apocryphon, most likely dating from the late fourth century, which recount numerous miracles performed by the Virgin in the period leading up to her death, most notably the curing of almost three thousand people with a single prayer. The *Six Books* also mention three feasts celebrated in honour of the Virgin, one two days after the Nativity, another in May, and a third on August 13, close to the date of August 15 which was to become the feast of the Dormition or Assumption. They also provide quite detailed instructions on how the feasts should be celebrated. As Shoemaker notes, these instructions bear certain similarities to

---

[27] Quoted in Stephen, J. Shoemaker, 'The Cult of the Virgin in the Fourth Century', p. 73.
[28] See chapter on Divine Motherhood.
[29] *Vita sancti Gregorii Thaumaturgi, PG* 46, 909D-912C. See Graef, *Doctrine and Devotion*, I, 47 and *MF*, pp. 93-94. Thomas Livius, *The Blessed Virgin in the Fathers of the First Six Centuries* (London: Burns and Oates, 1893), pp. 315-337, provides numerous instances of belief in the Virgin's miraculous powers from the fourth to the seventh centuries.

the practices of a group known as the Kollyridians,[30] whom Epiphanius of Salamis († 403) condemns, claiming that they worship the Virgin in a manner due to God alone:

> Yes, Mary's body was holy, but it was not God. Yes, the Virgin was surely a virgin and worthy of honour; however, she was not given us for us to adore her. She herself adored him who was born of her flesh, having descended from heaven and from the bosom of the Father. *Adversus haereses, 79, 4*[31]

Although some have cast doubt on the veracity of Epiphanius' claims,[32] there is no reason why they should not be true, though perhaps exaggerated, since he disapproved of any form of veneration, even for they martyrs, which he considered idolatrous, and would certainly have regarded a cult of the Virgin as unacceptable.[33]

By the time of Epiphanius' death, feasts commemorating the Virgin were being celebrated in both Jerusalem and Constantinople, and probably in Egypt and Syria.[34] The Church in Jerusalem had begun to celebrate a Memory of Mary on August 15 at the Kathisma by the early fifth century. Homilies for the feast delivered by Hesychius of Jerusalem († 451) in 428 and 431-433,[35] and one by Chrysippus of Jerusalem († 479), delivered around the middle of the century,[36]

---

[30] See Stephen J. Shoemaker, 'Epiphanius of Salamis, the Kollyridians, and the Early Dormition Narratives: The Cult of the Virgin in the Fourth Century', *Journal of Early Christian Studies*, 16 (2008), 371-401.

[31] *PG* 42, 745C-D, *MF* 127.

[32] See Averil Cameron, 'The Cult of the Virgin in Late Antiquity: Religious Development and Myth-Making', in *The Church and Mary*, ed. by Robert N. Swanson, Studies in Church History, 39 (Woodenbridge: Boydell, 2004), pp. 1-21.

[33] Stephen J. Shoemaker, 'Marian Liturgies', pp. 132-34, argues that Epiphanius exaggerates the practices of this sect since he is against any veneration of the saints, Mary included. See also his 2008 article, cited above, and his 'The Cult of the Virgin', pp. 76-80. Much of the discussion below on early feasts of the Virgin draws on Shoemaker's articles.

[34] For an overview of liturgical developments see Eric Palazzo, *A History of Liturgical Books from the Beginning to the Thirteenth Century*, trans. by Madeleine Beaumont (Collegeville, Minnesota: Liturgical Press, 1998). For a brief account see Killian McDonnell, 'The Marian Liturgical Tradition', in *The One Mediator, the Saints, and Mary: Lutherans and Catholics in Dialogue* (Minneapolis: Augsburg, 1991), pp. 177-91. See also Corrado Maggioni, 'Le feste mariane nell'antichità e nel primo medievo', *Theotokos*, 16 (2008), 127-54, and the relevant sections in Michael O'Carroll's *Theotokos*, and Margot Fassler, 'The First Marian Feast in Constantinople and Jerusalem: Chant Texts, Readings and Homiletic Literature', in *Paths and Bridges, East and West. In Honor of Kenneth Levy*, ed. by Peter Jeffery (Cambridge: Brewer, 2001), pp. 25-87.

[35] See Michel Aubineau, *Les homélies festales d'Hésychius de Jérusalem*, Subsidia Hagiographica, 59 (Brussels: Société des Bollandistes, 1978), and Stephen, J. Shoemaker, 'The Cult of the Virgin', p. 75.

[36] See Paul Devos, 'Le date du voyage d'Égérie', *Analecta Bollandiana*, 85 (1967), 165-94, and Stephen, J. Shoemaker, 'The Cult of the Virgin', p. 75.

provide evidence of the importance of this feast. Proof positive of the celebration of a Memory of the Virgin in the Greek Church, most probably on December 26, is provided by Proclus of Constantinople († 446), whose *First Homily on Mary, the Mother of God* was delivered on the feast day, which had probably been established by Atticus, bishop of Constantinople from 406 to 425.[37]

The feast seems to have arisen primarily because it was impossible to celebrate Mary's death, or 'birth in heaven' as the early Christians called it, in the same way as that of the other saints and martyrs. The Memory of the Virgin came to be celebrated in all the Eastern Churches as well as in areas of the West, though the dates varied widely.[38] The Alexandrian Church, for instance, celebrated it on January 16, while in Milan and Ravenna it was held on the Sunday before Christmas,[39] in the Gallican liturgy on January 18 and in Spain on December 18.[40] In Rome, instead, there is no evidence of any Marian feast prior to the second half of the sixth century when a celebration was inaugurated on January 1st, although Christmas day was celebrated as a joint feast of Jesus and Mary.[41] However, by the seventh century, as reported in the *Chronicon Paschale*, the four major Eastern feast days, the Assumption, Annunciation, Nativity and Purification of Our Lady, had become well-established in Rome.

The Purification or Presentation of Our Lord had started life as the Hypapante (Meeting) in the fourth century in Jerusalem, as reported by Egeria:

> The fortieth day after the Epiphany is truly celebrated here with the greatest honour, for on that day there is a procession to the [Church of] Anastasis, in which all take part, and everything is done in the established order with the greatest joy, just as at Easter. All the priests, and after them the bishop, preach, always taking for their subject that part of the Gospel where Joseph and Mary brought the Lord into the Temple on the fortieth day, and saw Simeon and the prophetess Anna, the daughter of Phanuel, and of the words they pronounced upon seeing the Lord, and of the offering which his parents made. Then, when

---

[37] See Nicholas P. Constas, 'Weaving the Body of God: Proclus of Constantinople, the Theotokos and the Loom of the Flesh', *Journal of Early Christian Studies*, 3 (1995), 169-94.
[38] See Sévérien Salaville, 'Marie dans la liturgie byzantine ou gréco-slave', in *Maria*, I, 249-326, Martin Jugie, *La mort et l'assomption de la Saint Vierge: Étude historico-doctrinale* (Vatican City : Studi e Testi, 1944), and I. Cecchetti, 'L'Annunciazione: Il racconto biblico e la festa liturgica', *Bollettino Ceciliano*, 38, (1943), 46-48 and 98-114 (pp. 100-05).
[39] See E. Cattaneo, 'La più antica festa della Madonna e la Chiesa di S. Maria al Circo', *Ambrosius*, 28 (1952), 123-129.
[40] The Council of Toledo (656) decided on this date because it was close to Christmas. They did not wish to celebrate the Annunciation as the principal Marian feast since it often fell during Lent. See Corrado Maggioni, *Benedetto il frutto del tuo grembo: due millenni di pietà mariana* (Casale Monferrato: Portalupi, 2000), p. 135.
[41] See Bernard Botte, 'La première fête mariale de la liturgie romaine', *Ephemerides Liturgicae* 47 (1933), 425-430.

everything has been done according to the customary order, the Eucharist is
celebrated, and the dismissal takes place. *Itinerarium Egeria, 26*[42]

Although the feast was originally largely a celebration of the presentation of
Jesus to the world, in which the people were invited to come and meet the
Light of the world with lighted lanterns or candles, the focus would gradually
shift to the person who was doing the presenting, namely the Virgin, in the
coming centuries. The Nativity of Mary also originated in Jerusalem around this
time, being associated with a church built next to the Probatic Pool (see John 5.
1-16) where, according to tradition, the house of Joachim and Anna stood. The
date of September 8 seems to be connected with the dedication of this Church.
By the sixth century the feast was also being celebrated in the Byzantine area.[43]

Turning back to the Fathers, Severian of Gabala († after 408), a Syrian who
acquired fame as a preacher in Constantinople, and whose writings are marked
by a new intensity of devotion to Mary, provides one of the first examples of
Mary being spoken of as a defender of the faith. Likening the Virgin to
Deborah and Jahel, two Old Testament women who demonstrated great valour
in battle (Judges 4 and 5), he declares that she comes to the aid of those who
uphold the truth:

> We too have the holy Virgin Mother of God, Mary, who intercedes for us. If,
> in fact, an ordinary woman could bring victory, how much more will the Mother
> of Christ humiliate the enemies of the truth? Armed to the teeth, the enemy
> judged the woman to be a worthy of derision, but instead found her to be a
> valiant commander. [...] We have Our Lady, the holy Mother of God! *Homily on
> the Legislator*[44]

Here, as in Gregory of Nyssa, Mary is the defender of those who fight against
heresy. It is significant that these lines use military terminology in speaking of
the Virgin's defence of orthodoxy. This is a pattern that will become more
firmly established in later times as the Byzantine Empire comes under attack by
barbarian and Muslims armies, and Mary's brief is extended to include
protection from physical as well as spiritual foes.

Severian extends Mary's mediatory role beyond that of giving birth to Christ,
linking her intercessory powers with her Assumption into heaven: 'But she most
certainly hears [our prayers], because she is in a splendid place, because she is in
the region of the living, she who is the Mother of Salvation.'[45] This belief that
Mary was in a unique position to intervene on behalf humanity because of her

---

[42] Egeria, *Itinerarium* ed. by Georg Röwekamp (Freiburg: Herder, 1995). For an
alternative translation see John Wilkinson, *Egeria's Travels to the Holy Land*, rev. edn
(Warminster: Aris & Phillips; Jerusalem: Ariel, 1981).
[43] See Corrado Maggioni, *Benedetto il frutto*, p. 158.
[44] *TMPM*, I, 429
[45] *Homily on the Creation of the World, TMPM*, I, 428.

Assumption, which is also to be found in apocryphal accounts of the Dormition,[46] will be a much favoured theme in the Byzantine Church.[47]

Epiphanius was not alone in expressing concern at the cult of the Virgin. Isidore of Pelusium († c. 435), for instance, is careful to distinguish between the burgeoning cult and pagan goddesses:

> You ask me what is different and new in our religion from the beliefs of those who walk in error, and from the Greeks, polytheists who number a mother of the gods among their deities, since we too believe in the Mother of God. [...] The pagans recognised a mother of their gods, even of the greatest ones, who conceived and gave birth in libidinousness and amidst the most nefarious loves, to the extent that this mother was not ignorant of and did not overlook any kind of wantonness. But she whom we confess to be the Mother of our incarnate God, and who conceived an Only Begotten Son in an absolutely unique way, this Mother is truly unknown to all the nations of men, who do not know of the lack of male seed or the absence of any stain. *Epistola 1, 54*[48]

Cyril of Alexandria († 444), the great theologian of the *Theotokos*, hints at the Virgin's intercessory role in his comments on the wedding feast at Cana when he asserts that Christ changed the water into wine against his own wishes out of respect for his mother.[49] He also speaks of Mary as she 'through whom ineffable grace entered into the world', and declares that she is the one of whom the Apostle Paul was speaking when he said: 'For the grace of God our Saviour hath appeared to all men' (Titus 2. 11). It is through Mary that 'light has reached those who were in darkness and in the shadow of death'.[50] However, this refers to her historical role in the Incarnation, not her ongoing mediation of grace.[51]

The increasingly vibrant cult of the Virgin evident in the late fourth and early fifth century was given a major boost by the Council of Ephesus (431), in which Cyril was a major player, when it was agreed that Mary should be termed the

---

[46] See the chapter on the Assumption and O'Carroll, *Theotokos*, p. 186 and Graef, *Doctrine and Devotion*, I, 34-37.

[47] See Martin Jugie, *La mort et l'assomption*, p. 223, where he goes so far as to say that, for the Byzantine Church, Mary's mediation constituted one of the principal reasons for her Assumption.

[48] *PG* 78, 216C, *TMPM*, I, 463.

[49] *PG* 73, 225C. Cana is rarely mentioned in the context of Mary's intercession before the twelfth century. See Henri Barré, 'L'intercession de la Vierge aux débuts du moyen âge Occidental', *Études mariales*, 23 (1966), 77-104 (pp. 78-79). On Cyril's theology see *The Theology of St. Cyril of Alexandria: A Critical Appreciation*, ed. by Thomas G. Weinandy and Daniel A. Keating (London: Clark, 2003).

[50] *Homily 11*, *TMPM*, I, 491.

[51] See chapter on Remote Co-operation, and see Richard Price, 'The *Theotokos* and the Council of Ephesus', who discusses Cyril's (lack of) contribution to Marian piety (pp. 98-99).

Theotokos or bearer of God.[52] The extent to which Ephesus led to a flowering of Marian devotion has been a matter of debate in recent years. The traditional position has been that the Council marked a major watershed in the Virgin's cult, prior to which, it is claimed, she was a relatively minor figure.[53] Some have argued that Ephesus marked the moment when the Virgin 'went public', taking the place of pagan goddesses such as Artemis, Athena and Tyche, largely at the instigation of Pulcheria († 453), sister of the Emperor Theodosius II, and later Empress in her own right.[54]

However, more recently, as we have seen, scholars have begun to unearth evidence that the cult was already beginning to burgeon at least fifty years before Ephesus, if not earlier.[55] Indeed some have suggested that the cult of the *Theotokos* itself was partially responsible for the controversies that led to Ephesus, and that Pulcheria, who played an important role in the manoeuvrings surrounding the Council, was a least partially motivated by her devotion to the Virgin and her desire to be identified as an *alter Mariae*.[56] However, while it true that Pulcheria was a figure of importance at Ephesus, and was an even more instrumental figure at Chalcedon (451), engaging in correspondence with Pope Leo the Great in the period leading up to the Council, recent scholarship would seem to indicate that her role was not as important as later legends surrounding her would have us believe.[57] As to the Nestorian controversy being as much

---

[52] See chapter on Divine Motherhood.

[53] See, for instance, *MF*, 233-38.

[54] Stephen Benko, *The Virgin Goddess: Studies in the Pagan and Christian Roots of Mariology* (New York: Brill, 1993), for instance, proposes that there is a 'direct line, unbroken and clearly discernable, from the goddess cults of the ancients to the reverence paid, and eventually the cult accorded to the Virgin Mary' (p. 4). See also Vasiliki Limberis, *Divine Heiress: the Virgin Mary and the Creation of Christian Constantinople* (London and New York: Routledge 1994), who argues that Mary took the places of the goddesses of Constantinople. Leena Peltomaa, *The Image of the Virgin*, argues convincingly against such a proposition (for instance, pp. 122-23).

[55] See Averil Cameron's 'The Cult of the Virgin in Late Antiquity', where she argues very effectively that the cult of the Virgin 'grew naturally with and out of the self-definition of the Church and formulation of doctrine after the Council of Nicaea, and in the context of an intense debate about both virginity and Christology which gathered momentum in the late fourth century' (p. 14).

[56] See, in particular, Kenneth Holum, *Theodosian Empresses: Women and Imperial Dominion in Late Antiquity* (Berkeley: University of California Press, 1982), Vasiliki Limberis, *Divine Heiress*. Stephen, J. Shoemaker, 'The Cult of the Virgin in the Fourth Century', while admitting that Pulcheria's role has been overstated still argues that Marian piety played a central role at Ephesus on the basis of much of the evidence I have presented above, such as the texts of Nazianzus and Gregory of Nyssa and liturgical developments.

[57] Legends concerning her involvement in bringing Marian relics such as the Virgin's robe and girdle to Constantinople, as well as the belief that she was responsible for the building of the major Marian churches in the city, emerged only later, and do not constitute historical proof, contrary to the claims of Kenneth G. Holum, *Theodosian Empresses* and

Mariological as Christological, there is considerable evidence to the contrary. Firstly, as Price points out, there is no evidence to suggest that the cult of Mary was sufficiently well-developed at the time of Ephesus to hold such sway over the Council fathers.[58] But more importantly, the divergence between the Antiochene and Alexandrian schools on the question of Christ's two natures had been many years in the making – some would say it began with Origen (†c. 254) – and could not possibly be construed as having originated in the nascent cult of Mary.[59] What is more, it will be immediately obvious to anyone who peruses the acts of the Council that Christology was the main focus, the *Theotokos*, as it were, acting simply as a handmaid.[60]

It would seem reasonable to suggest that the *Theotokos* declaration which resulted from the Council acted as a crucial catalyst for a pre-existing cult, and that its rise was a more gradual process, resulting from a complex mix of elements, among which were imperial patronage, a switching of allegiance from pagan protectresses, and increasing fervour among the populace, but with the most significant impetus arising from within the theological dynamics of Christianity itself.[61] What is undeniable is that in the centuries following the

---

Vasiliki Limberis, *Divine Heiress*. See Christine Angelidi, *Pulcheria: la castità al potere (399-455)* (Milan: Jaca, 1998), Richard Price, 'Marian Piety and the Nestorian Controversy', in *The Church and Mary*, 31-38, and also his 'Theotokos: The Title and its Significance in Doctrine and Devotion', in *Mary: The Complete Resource*, pp. 56-74, Averil Cameron, 'The Cult of the Virgin in Late Antiquity', and Liz James, 'The Empress and the Virgin in Early Byzantium: Piety, Authority and Devotion', in *Images of the Mother of God*, pp. 145-152. Kate Cooper, 'Contesting the Nativity: Wives, Virgins and Pulcheria's *imitation Maria'e*, *Scottish Journal of Religious Studies*, 19 (1998), 31-43, and 'Empress and Theotokos: Gender and Patronage in the Christological Controversy', in *The Church and Mary*, pp. 39-51, takes the middle ground, acknowledging the inaccuracies in Holum and Limberis, while arguing from a variety of contemporary sources that Pulcheria did cast herself in the role of defender of the Virgin and was important in identifying the cult of the Virgin with the Imperial household. See vol. 2 for further discussion. Specifically on the Virgin's robe or mantle see vol. 2 and see Averil Cameron , 'The Virgin's Robe: An Episode in the History of Seventh Century Constantinople', *Byzantion*, 159 (1979), 42-56.

[58] See Richard Price, 'The *Theotokos* and the Council of Ephesus'.

[59] See chapter on Divine Motherhood.

[60] As Leena Peltomaa, *The Image of the Virgin*, points out, in the writings of this time Mary is largely devoid of any human personality, being essentially reduced to the *locus* of the hypostasis (p. 135). For an alternative view, that Mariology played a far more central role at Ephesus than has been generally recognised, see Kenneth Holum, *Theodosian Empresses*, Vasiliki Limberis, *Divine Heiress*, and Judith Herrin, 'The Imperial Feminine in Byzantium', *Past and Present*, 169 (2000), 3-35.

[61] This is to argue against explanations that rely solely on socio-psychological factors such as the implausible explanations based on the Jungian theory in Michael Carroll's study of the psychological origins of Marian devotion, *The Cult of the Virgin Mary: Psychological Origins* (Princeton: Princeton University Press, 1986), typical of the anachronistic misapplication of voguish theories. His basic argument is that the cult of the Virgin arises because of a need to dissipate the Oedipal complex, which is typically strongly repressed in

Councils of Ephesus and Chalcedon, especially in the East, Marian devotion flourished: liturgical texts, hymns and homilies were composed, icons painted and churches dedicated to Mary, reinforcing the notion of Mary as a channel between God and mankind.[62] One important factor in this was that doctrinal debates over the hypostasis began to move away from technical discussions on the nature of Mary's motherhood to questions concerning the relationship between the two natures within the person of Jesus, which meant that the term *Theotokos* began to lose some of its theological aura, leaving greater space for the development of an independent cult of the Virgin.

The first great Marian Church of the post-Ephesian period was Santa Maria Maggiore, erected during the pontificate of Sixtus III (432-440) to mark the *Theotokos* declaration.[63] The original apse mosaic of the enthroned Virgin is lost but the accompanying text tells us that she was flanked by Sixtus and five martyrs. On the triumphal arch is a series of images which depict the Annunciation and the Adoration of the Magi. It is here too that we find an icon of the Madonna and Child, known since the nineteenth century as the *Salus populi romani*, which possibly dates from as early as the late sixth century. Traditionally attributed to St. Luke, it may have been acquired by Pope Gregory I (590-604) during an earlier period of residence in Constantinople and later became a major focus of devotion in the Roman procession for the Feast of the Assumption, first recorded during the pontificate of Sergius I (687-701).[64] There was also a fifth-century apse mosaic of the enthroned Virgin flanked by saints in the church of Santa Maria di Capua Vetere.[65] Other Roman churches

---

Mediterranean countries, and that it emerged in the fourth and fifth centuries because of the conversion of large numbers of the Roman poor, whose families were 'father-ineffective', that is dominated by the mother. Stephen Benko's suggestion in *The Virgin Goddess* that the Marian cult came about because of a need to express the feminine in the divine, which was lacking in the exclusively male God of the Judeo-Christian tradition, is slightly more reasonable. Both authors fail to convince not least because they largely ignore primary evidence from within the Christian tradition itself.

[62] See Michel van Esbroeck, 'Le culte de la Vierge de Jérusalem à Constantinople aux 6e–7e siècles', *Revue des études byzantines*, 46 (1988), 181-90, and Graef, *Doctrine and Devotion*, 1, 112. On icons see Cyril Mango, *The Art of the Byzantine Empire, 312- 1453* (Englewood Cliffs: Prentice Hall, 1972), Gertrud Schiller, *Iconography of Christian Art*, 2 vols, trans. by Janet Seligman (Greenwich, Conn.: New York Graphic Society, 1971), and Henry Maguire, Henry, 'The Empress and the Virgin on Display in Sixth-Century Art', in *Proceedings of the 21st International Congress of Byzantine Studies*, London, 21-26 August, 2006, ed. by Elizabeth Jeffreys, Fiona K. Haarer, and Judith Gilliland (Aldershot: Ashgate, 2006), pp. 379-95.

[63] See Mario Sensi 'I santuari mariani', in *Gli studi di mariologia medievale: bilancio storico*, pp. 217-38 (pp. 223-24).

[64] See Gerhard Wolf, *Salus populi romani: Die Geschichte römischer Kultbilder im Mittelalter* (Weinheim: VCH, Acta humaniora, 1990).

[65] See Dorothy Shepherd, 'An Icon of the Virgin: A Sixth Century Tapestry Panel from Egypt', *Bulletin of the Cleveland Museum of Art*, 56 (1969), 90-120 (p. 93).

dedicated to Mary in later centuries include the former Pantheon, dedicated as Sancta Maria ad Martyres under Pope Boniface IV (608-615), the somewhat later is Santa Maria Antiqua (somewhere between 565 and 650), and Santa Maria in Trastevere (rededicated in the eighth century to the Virgin), which also contain important early images of the Virgin.[66] In Jerusalem the 'Nea' Maria, dedicated to the Holy Mother of God, the Ever-Virgin Mary, was consecrated in 543,[67] while in the third great centre of Christianity, Constantinople, there are the three great Marian shrines, the Blachernai, where Mary's mantle was housed, the Chalkoprateia where her girdle was kept, and the Hodegon, home to the famed Hodegetria prototype.[68] These churches were reputedly erected at the instigation of Pulcheria, but it may have been her successor, the empress Verina († 484), who was responsible.[69]

This period was also marked by a number of very significant liturgical innovations which encouraged devotion to the Virgin.[70] By the middle of the sixth century the August fifteenth feast, which had celebrated Mary's motherhood and virginity, had been transformed into a commemoration of her Dormition, which became by far the most significant of the Marian feast days in the Byzantine Church.[71] The sixth century also saw the introduction of several other important Marian feasts into the Eastern Church, including the Annunciation (25 March), which was most likely first celebrated in Constantinople, as is evidenced in a homily by the sixth-century monk Abraham of Ephesus (fl. 530-550),[72] the

---

[66] For discussion on the major Marian images in Rome see Gerhard Wolf, 'Icons and Sites: Cult Images of the Virgin in Medieval Rome', in *Images of the Mother of God*, pp. 23-49 and Eileen Rubery, 'Pope John VII's Devotion to Mary: Papal Images of Mary from the Fifth to the Early Eighth Centuries', in *The Origins of the Cult of the Virgin Mary*, 155-99. See also Carlo Bertelli, *La Madonna di Santa Maria in Trastevere: storia, iconografia, stile di un dipinto romano dell'ottavo secolo* (Rome, Eliograf, 1961).

[67] See Margaret Baker, 'The Life-Bearing Spring', in *The Origins of the Cult of the Virgin Mary*, pp. 127-135.

[68] See Liz James, 'The Empress and the Virgin', pp. 145 and 147-148, and Bissera V. Pentcheva, *Icons and Power: The Mother of God in Byzantium* (University Park: Penn State Press, 2006), especially pp. 109-44.

[69] Stephen, J. Shoemaker, 'The Cult of the Virgin', is representative of those who favour Pulcheria (p. 72), while Cyril Mango, 'The Origins of the Blachernae Shrine at Constantinople', in *Acta XIII Congressus Internationalis Archaeologicae Christinae: Split-Poreč*, ed. by N. Cambi and E. Marin (Vatican City: Pontificio Istituto di Archeologia Cristiana, 1998), 61-76, argues for a later date, suggesting that it was the Empress Verina who founded them.

[70] On liturgical developments in the Eastern Churches see Manuel Nin, 'Maria nelle liturgie orientali', in *SDM*, I, 424-47.

[71] See Kilian McDonnell, 'The Marian Liturgical Tradition', in *The One Mediator, the Saints, and Mary: Lutherans and Catholics in Dialogue* (Minneapolis: Augsburg, 1991), pp. 177-91.

[72] See Martin Jugie, 'Abraham d'Ephèse: Homélies pour les fêtes de l'Annonciation et de l'Ypapante', in *Patrologia Orientalis* (Turnhout: Brepols, 1907-), XVI (1922), 429-441,

Nativity of Mary (September 8), which originated in Jerusalem and was first celebrated by the Church of Constantinople under the emperor Justinian,[73] and the Presentation of Mary (21 November), also associated with Justinian, since it originated from the date of the consecration of the Nea (21 November 543), built in the area of the Temple in Jerusalem at the instigation of the emperor.[74] It should also be pointed out that Christmas was regarded by the Church not just as a celebration of the nativity of Christ but also of the virgin motherhood of Mary, for which reason homilies, hymns and antiphons for the occasion often refer equally to her.[75] In fact, the psalms and antiphons of all the major Marian feasts are linked to the Christmas cycle, indicating that it is from Mary's divine motherhood that all her other privileges derive.[76]

The sixth century was also the period of greatest proliferation of Marian icons which appear in a variety of media including frescoes, painted icons, tapestries, stonework, ivories and metalwork, many of which were later destroyed in the frenzy of iconoclasm.[77] There is also ample evidence of personal devotion to the Virgin from this period in the form of jewellery and clothing that contain her image. Amulets were often used to invoke her aid, especially by women in childbirth.[78]

One of the most significant themes to emerge in post-Ephesian Mariology is the Virgin's role as protector of the faithful from both spiritual and physical perils. While to some extent this was due to the enhanced profile of Mary herself in the wake of the *Theotokos* declaration, it also reflected other factors, such as the growing importance of the cult of the saints and the increasingly important role that Mary was playing in the official life of the Byzantine Empire.[79] The Virgin's official status, which dovetailed with her role in defending against heresy, is particularly evident in her position as patron and protectress of Constantinople.[80] It is reported that the citizens of Constantinople gave thanks to the Virgin by

---

and, for further comment as well as an Italian translation of parts of the sermon see *TMPM*, I, 673-75. See also I. Cecchetti, 'L'Annunciazione", who dates the introduction of the feast to between 530 and 550. (p. 99).

[73] The feast, which originated in Jerusalem, was first celebrated by the Church of Constantinople under the emperor Justinian († 565). See *MF*, p. 328, and *TMPM*, I, 695, n. 1.

[74] See Stephen J. Shoemaker, 'Marian Liturgies', p. 141 and Corrado Maggioni, *Benedetto il frutto*, p. 92.

[75] See Henri Barré, 'Antiennes et Répons de la Vierge', *Marianum*, 29 (1967), 153-254 (pp. 153-54).

[76] See Georges Frénaud, 'Le culte de Notre Dame dans l'ancienne liturgie latine', in *Maria*, VI, 157-211 (pp. 208-09).

[77] See Dorothy Shepherd, 'An Icon of the Virgin'.

[78] See Averil Cameron 'The Cult of the Virgin in Late Antiquity', p. 19.

[79] See Leena Mari Peltomaa, *The Image of the Virgin*, p. 75.

[80] See Christine Angelidi and Titos Papamastorakis, 'Picturing the Spiritual Protector: from Bacharnitissa to Hodegetria', in *Images of the Mother of God*, pp. 209-17, Averil Cameron, 'The Theotokos in Sixth-Century Constantinople: A City Finds its Symbol', *Journal of Theological Studies*, 29 (1978), 79-108.

singing the *Akathistos Hymn* following their deliverance from a siege in 626.[81] According to legend, the Virgin herself appeared, brandishing a sword and urging the people of the city to drive off the enemy.[82] Leena Peltomaa, in her study of the hymn, speculates that it was at this point that the renowned second *Proemium* was attached to the *Akathistos*:

> To you, our leader in battle and defender,
> O Theotokos, I, your city, delivered from sufferings,
> ascribe hymns of victory and thanksgiving.
> Since you are invincible in power,
> free me from all kinds of dangers,
> that I may cry to you:
> 'Hail, bride unwedded' *Proemium* II, 1-5[83]

What is clear here is that the Virgin is not merely a guarantor of military victory, but is primarily a defence against spiritual dangers, and that the power which she possesses is not her own, but derives from her status as the 'bride unwedded', the spouse and mother of God. The relationship between imperial power and the cult of the Virgin became even more intimate in post-iconoclastic Byzantium, when processions of her icons were used to signify the divine protection bestowed on the rulers of Constantinople.[84]

Undoubtedly the most influential Eastern hymn, the *Akathistos* is the oldest continuously performed Marian hymn in the Orthodox liturgy. Although neither its writer nor its date of composition is known, its style and content would suggest that it is from around the time of the Council of Ephesus.[85] The hymn is a celebration of the mysteries of the Incarnation consisting of twenty-four stanzas, which by their initial letter form an acrostic of the Greek alphabet. They are alternately separated by long and short refrains. The long refrains, each thirteen lines, are salutations of praise to Mary. The hymn repeatedly emphasises the intercessory role of the Virgin: 'Hail conciliation of the Righteous Judge; hail forgiveness for the many who have stumbled; hail robe of

---

[81] *PG* 92, 1352B. See Mantle in vol. 2, and see Christine Angelidi and Titos Papamastorakis, 'Picturing the Spiritual Protector', pp. 210-11.

[82] See Averil Cameron, 'Images of Authority: Elites and Icons in Late Sixth-Century Byzantium', *Past and Present*, 84 (1979), 3-35 (pp. 5-6).

[83] Quoted from the translation provided by Peltomaa, *The Image of the Virgin*, p. 21.

[84] See Bissera V. Pentcheva, *Icons and Power*, who argues that these developments occurred as late as the tenth century.

[85] The bibliography on the *Akathistos* is vast. Authorship has not been definitively established, two of the most prominent candidates being Proclus of Constantinople and Romanos the Melodist. See Leena Peltomaa, *The Image of the Virgin*, pp. 77-78 for a summary of the debate and bibliography. She herself argues that the hymn was commissioned by Proclus, but not written by him. Most scholars now favour a date somewhere between the Councils of Ephesus and Chalcedon. See also the useful brief article by Ermanno M. Toniolo, 'Akathistos: temi e problemi', *Theotokos*, 15 (2007), 77-102.

free intercession given to the naked' (13, 13-16).[86] The explicitness of these lines on Mary's intercessory powers is quite striking. If the *Akathistos* does indeed date from the fifth century, this would be the first instance of the notion that the Virgin could aid sinners by placating the just wrath of her Son, which was to become a major theme in the later Byzantine Fathers and in the Medieval West.

Despite all these developments, direct addresses to the Virgin requesting her aid were as yet relatively rare.[87] Mary was still perceived to be a somewhat distant heavenly empress while the saints had a more 'hands on' role in terms of resolving everyday problems. A homily on the *Theotokos* attributed to Basil of Seleucia († after 468), in which he asks for the Virgin's aid in reaching paradise, is a rare exception:

> O, most holy Virgin, those who attribute all venerable and glorious things to you surely do not fall short of the truth, but instead do not reach the height of your dignity. [...] Govern us now in peace, and lead us then without confusion before the throne of the Judge, grant that we may participate in sitting at his right hand. *Homily on the Mother of God*, 6[88]

Basil is also the first to use the term 'mediatrix' (*mesiteuousa*) for Mary, though he does so in the context of her generation of Christ and does not seem to imply that she has any continuing role of mediation: '"Rejoice, O full of grace", for you are the mediatrix between men and God so that the middle wall of enmities might be broken down (see Ephesians 2. 14) and earthly things might be joined to the heavenly.'[89] Around the same time Antipater of Bostra († after 457) uses the same term in an identical context: 'Rejoice, you who without effort carry him who carries creation; rejoice you who without penalty are the mediatrix of humanity, rejoice you who give birth to God'.[90]

In the next century Severus of Antioch († 538) provides evidence of the growing awareness that the Virgin was a particularly efficacious intercessor, stating that, 'she, more than all the other saints, is capable of raising up prayers for us'. He goes on to explain that it is thanks to her that we have Christ as a 'celestial ladder' through whom we can climb up to heaven, thus linking her historical function in bringing Jesus to humanity with her ongoing role in reconciling humanity with God.[91]

The Marian hymns of Romanos the Melodist († c. 560) mark a new departure in the image of Mary's motherhood. In his celebrated *Kontakion on the Nativity of Christ*, which centres around the visit of the Magi, Romanos imagines a mental conversation between the Virgin and her infant Son, in which she acts as a

---

[86] Cited from the translation by Leena Peltomaa, in *The Image of the Virgin*, pp. 1-19.

[87] See Henri Barré, 'Antiennes et Répons de la Vierge', p. 201.

[88] *TMPM*, I, 601.

[89] *Homily on the Mother of God*, 5, *TMPM*, I, 598.

[90] *Homily on the Precursor*, 9 *TMPM*, I, 612.

[91] *Homily 14 in Memory of the Holy Mother of God*, 18, *TMPM*, I, 647.

mediator: 'Jesus [...] secretly touched his mother's mind saying, "Bring in those I have brought by my word, for it is my word which shone on those who are seeking me"'(8).[92] Mary speaks of her role in protecting sinners and restoring to Paradise those who had been exiled:

> For I am not simply your mother, compassionate Saviour;
> it is not in vain that I suckle the giver of milk,
> but for the sake of all I implore you.
> You have made me the mouth and the boast of my entire race,
> and your world has me
> as a mighty protection, a wall and a buttress.
> They look to me, those who were cast out
> of the Paradise of pleasure, for I bring them back.
> May all things understand that, through me, you have been born
> a little Child, God before the ages. *On the Nativity of Christ, 23*[93]

In the same hymn (9) Romanos imagines Mary opening the door of the stable to the Magi at the urging of her Son, and identifies Mary with the door that leads to Christ. He also envisages Mary pleading with her Son to accept the homage of the Magi and the shepherds, and in exchange, to grant three favours:

> When the blameless Virgin saw the magi bringing
> new and radiant gifts and worshipping,
> the star showing him, the shepherds praising him,
> she implored the Maker and Creator of all these, saying,
> "Accept, my Child, a trinity of gifts,
> grant her who gave you birth three requests.
> I pray to you for the seasons
> and for the fruits of the earth and for those who dwell on it.
> Be reconciled to all, because through me you have been born
> a little Child, God before the ages. *On the Nativity of Christ, 22*

Romanos describes Mary as a protectress and defence against the forces of evil, a well-established theme by now, but also goes further by saying that she obtains grace for men:

> Your birth is venerable, O Holy One, because you, valid obtainer of grace for men, brought forth the joy of the world. For she is a wall, a defence, and a harbour

---

[92] The *kontakion*, or canticle, is a poetic form found frequently in Byzantine hymnography. It is essentially a sermon in verse that was accompanied by music and probably derived from Syriac hymnological traditions. On Romanos role in inventing it and his dependence on Ephrem see Petersen, William L., 'The Dependence of Romanos the Melodist upon the Syriac Ephrem: Its Importance for the Origin of the Kontakion', *Vigiliae Christianae*, 39, No. 2 (1985), 171-87.

[93] Quoted from *On the Life of Christ: Kontakia*, trans. by Ephrem Lash (Harper Collins: San Francisco, 1995), which reproduces the full text, pp. 1-12.

for those who hope in her. She, who is your fruit, is the protectress, the defence and the hope of salvation for every Christian. *On the Nativity of Mary, 10*[94]

He also provides a hint of the notion that Mary can soften Christ's justice – an idea which we have already come across in the *Akathistos Hymn*[95] – when he writes: 'Cease your laments; I will make myself you advocate in my Son's presence. [...] Curb your tears; accept me as your mediatrix in the presence of him who was born of me.'[96] In a hymn on the wedding feast of Cana, Romanos graphically portrays the mediatory role of Mary in the form of a dialogue in which Jesus several times refuses his mother's insistent requests before eventually yielding 'since it is necessary that parents be honoured by their children'.[97] In one of his hymns for Christmas, in which he imagines Adam and Eve coming to the crib in Bethlehem and conversing with Mary who reassures them that their sin has been forgiven and that their salvation is at hand, Mary uses the term 'mediatrix' (*mesitin*):

> Her innards were moved by compassion for her relatives for she was a Mother, a Mother of tenderness to the Merciful One. Therefore she said to them: 'Restrain your tears; take me as your mediatrix with the one who is born of me. And now, no more sadness, for I have brought Joy into the world. I came into the world to overthrow the kingdom of suffering, I who am filled with grace.' *Second Hymn for Christmas*[98]

In the West, Gregory of Tours († 594) may be considered the founder of a genre that would enjoy great popularity in the later Middle Ages, namely collections of Marian miracle stories. One of the better known stories that he tells in his *Libri miraculorum* is of a Jewish boy who is punished by his father for receiving the Eucharist along with his Christian friends by being thrown into a furnace. The boy remains unharmed thanks to the Virgin Mary who protects him with her mantle.[99] When the father is caste into the furnace for his cruel actions he immediately perishes. He also recounts the adventure of a man named John, whom he claims to have met. Returning from the Holy Land with

---

[94] *TMPM*, I, 697.

[95] The fact that no other instances of this idea appear prior to the sixth century is a possible argument against the *Akathistos* being from the period immediately after Ephesus.

[96] *On Christmas*, 2, 11, *MF*, p. 327.

[97] See *The Marriage at Cana* in *Kontakia of Romanos, Byzantine Melodist*, ed. and trans. by Marjorie Carpenter, 2 vols, (Colombia, Missouri, 1970), I, 67-72. Reference to Cana as an example of Mary's intercession is rare at this time, as we have already noted in the case of Cyril of Alexandria. See also P. Zannini, 'Romano il Melode e le tematiche patristiche greco-siriache su Gv 2, 1-11', *Theotokos*, 7 (1999), 41-65, and F. Migliore, 'La figura di Maria vergine e madre di Dio negli Inni di Romano il Melode', *Theotokos*, 15 (2007), 37-76.

[98] *TMPM*, I, 711.

[99] See Mantle in vol. 2.

some relics of the Virgin the unfortunate man is set upon by some brigands who, in their anger at finding he has no money, fling the relics into the fire. The relics are, of course, undamaged. Another well-known story is of how Basil the Great resuscitated a dead man with the aid of an angel sent to him by the Virgin.[100] That so many stories about the Virgin's miraculous power existed, and were available throughout the Christian world, is testimony to the strength of Marian piety at this time.[101]

Writing around the same time, Venantius Fortunatus (†c. 600) sees Mary's mediation in terms of her role as a bridge between humanity and Christ, though it is not clear whether he extends this beyond her historical role in giving birth to the Saviour: 'Happy are you who became / the ticket, the way, the gate, the vehicle into heaven / for the human race, once fallen under hell's dominion. [...] receptacle of life, bridge that penetrates the vault of heaven'.[102]

By the middle of the seventh century Marian piety was on the rise in the Latin Church, due in large part to Eastern influences and the increasing sway of the monasteries, from whence piety spread to the general populace.[103] Nowhere is this more evident than in Spain. Ildephonse of Toledo († 667), who was in many respects the initiator of the distinctive Marian piety of Spain, is unusually fervent in his devotion to the Virgin by the standards of the West, as this prayer illustrates:

> My Lady, my Mistress, Mother of my Lord, handmaiden of your Son. Mother of the Creator of the world, I pray you, I ask you, I beg you that the Spirit of your Lord may be granted to me, the Spirit of your Son, that I might have the Spirit of my Redeemer so that I can taste true and worthy things about you, say true and worthy things of you, love everything that is true and worthy about you. You were chosen by God, fore-chosen by God, called by God; you are close to God, obedient to God, joined to God. *Oratio et confessio S. Hildefonsi, 1* [104]

---

[100] See *MLM*, p. 93.

[101] See *Les livres des miracles et autres opuscules de Georges Florent Grégoire, évêque de Tours*, 4 vols, ed. and trans by Henri Bordier (Paris: Renouard, 1857-1864), and *MF*, pp. 352-58.

[102] *In laudem sanctae Mariae, MF*, p. 362.

[103] Luigi Gambero, *MLM*, notes that whereas devotion to the Virgin was widespread in Byzantium, in the West it was initially largely confined to Monastic circles (p. 7). On Western monasticism see Jean Leclercq, 'Dévotion et théologie mariales dans le monachisme bénédictin', in *Maria*, II, 547-78. Despite the increasing gulf between East and West there were still significant contacts between Rome and Constantinople. See East and West see *Relations between East and West in the Middle Ages*, edited by Derek Baker (Edinburgh, Edinburgh University Press), Michael Angold, *Byzantium: the Bridge from Antiquity to the Middle Ages* (New York: St. Martin's Press, 2001), who offers evidence of close ties between Rome and Byzantium in the seventh and eight centuries, and describes the cult of Mary as 'a good example of a Byzantine import into the religious life of Rome'(p. 98). See also Peter Brown, 'Eastern and Western Christendom in Late Antiquity: A Parting of the Ways', *Studies in Church History*, 13 (1976), 1-23.

[104] PL 96, 58A.

A further crucial development in this period was the growing belief, which we already noted when discussing Severian, that one of the principal reasons why God raised the Virgin up to heaven was so that she could act as an effective intercessor on behalf of her fellow humans. The seventh-century Theoteknos of Livias, one of the earliest of the Fathers to affirm the bodily assumption, writes powerfully of Mary's role in interceding with God. In terms that come close to the idea of a universal mediation he declares that 'she has left for heaven as the ambassador of all', and goes on to affirm that, 'since she has secure credit with the God, she procures spiritual gifts for us'. He concludes his homily by asserting that, just as she watched over all on earth, so she intercedes for all in heaven: 'While she lived on earth, she watched over us all, and was a kind of universal providence for all her subjects. Now that she has been assumed into heaven she constitutes an impregnable fortress for the human race, interceding for us with her Son and God.' [105]

A homily attributed to Modestus of Jerusalem († 634) explicitly links Mary's virgin motherhood with her bodily assumption, both of which play a crucial role in spanning the gulf between God and humanity:

> The Virgin was to become, on earth, the bridge between God and humanity beyond this world, by grace of her virginity. [...] Through her, he has made known to us the way to ascend to him by right faith and by the blessed life that leads to heaven. [...] The king of glory, the Lord Jesus, chose you to be his spiritual kingdom on earth, and through you he has bestowed on us his heavenly kingdom; there he has ordained that you become one body with him in incorruption, more glorious than all the others [...]. I salute you, perpetual and divine aid of those who devoutly adore God. [...] For he truly saves from all tribulation those who confess you to be the Mother of God – the God who has initiated you into his mysteries, that you might be with him to intercede for us. [...] I salute you, spring of healing! You have poured forth Christ, who cures every illness. [...] I salute you, refuge of mortals with God! *Homily on the Dormition of the Mother of God*, 9-10[106]

Further on the homilist affirms with unprecedented clarity that God's intention in assuming Mary into heaven was for her to act as an intermediary on behalf of humanity: 'He has decreed that he will take you to his side in order that, through your prayers, he might show himself to be always gracious towards the whole of humanity.'[107] He also speaks of her in military terms as 'a mighty shield' who offers 'safety and protection' to all Christians.[108]

By the seventh century the Virgin had been firmly established as the protector of Constantinople, which was now known by the alternative name of

---

[105] *Homily on the Assumption of the Holy Mother of God*, 31, 32 and 36, *TMPM*, II, 86 and 87.
[106] *EPH*, pp. 94-95; *TMPM*, II, 132-33.
[107] *TMPM*, II, 134, *EPH*, p. 97.
[108] *Homily on the Dormition of the Mother of God*, 6 and 7, *EPH*, p. 90; see *TMPM*, II, 128.

'Theotokoupolis',[109] and there followed a period in which icons of the Virgin (and Christ) multiplied both in the public and private sphere, encouraging ever-greater devotion to Mary. This golden age came to an end with iconoclasm, which began with the accession of Leo III (717-741), who hailed from the Eastern part of the empire where Monophysitism was strong.[110] Ironically, the iconoclast crises, which lasted until the 'Triumph of Orthodoxy' under the Empress Theodora in the year 843, did more to stimulate the Virgin's cult than to suppress it, as iconophile elements in the Church rushed to defend her prerogatives. Nowhere is this more evident than in the three great Fathers of the late Patristic period, Germanus of Constantinople, Andrew of Crete and John of Damascus who rushed to Mary's defence with an outpouring of writing that raised her to unprecedented heights.

Germanus of Constantinople (†c. 733) writes extensively on Mary's role as mediatrix in language that anticipates the fervent devotion of Western Mariology in the later Middle Ages. For the first time, we find an unambiguous affirmation of Mary's universal mediation of grace: 'No one is saved except through you, O All-Holy. No one is delivered from evils except through you, O All-Chaste. No one obtains the grace of mercy except through you, O All-Honourable.'[111] He also sees Mary as the protector of both the ecclesiastical and civic realms: 'Confirm our faith, unite the Churches, give victory to the Empire and fight with our army.'[112] He speaks clearly of the Virgin deflecting God's wrathful justice: 'You turn away the just threat and the sentence of damnation, because you love the Christians.'[113] In a sermon for Mary's Presentation in the Temple he writes along similar lines, adding that she also affords protection from the afflictions of this life:

> To those who celebrate your feast day, give your help, your protection and your assistance, freeing them at all times through your intercession from every necessity

---

[109] See Cyril Mango, 'Constantinople as Theotokoupolis', in *Images of the Mother of God: Perceptions of the* Theotokos *in Byzantium*, ed. by Maria Vassilaki (Aldershot: Ashgate, 2005), pp. 17-25 and Christine Angelidi and Titos Papamastorakis, 'Picturing the Spiritual Protector', p. 209.

[110] We do not have the space here to consider the complex causes of Iconoclasm. See the magisterial study by Alain Besançon, *The Forbidden Image: An Intellectual History of Iconoclasm*, trans. by Jane Marie Todd (Chicago: University of Chicago Press, 2000), pp. 109-48 for an in-depth analysis of the crisis.

[111] *Homily on the Cincture*, PG 98, 380B, quoted in *MF*, p. 387.

[112] *Second [Third] Homily on the Dormition*, 11, *EPH*, p. 178.

[113] Quoted in Graef, *Doctrine and Devotion*, I, 147. In his *Homily on the Cincture* (PG 98, 380D-381A), he writes in a similar vein: 'For, just as in your Son's presence you have a mother's boldness and strength, so do you save and rescue us from eternal punishment, with your prayers and intercessions for we have been condemned by our sins and do not dare even to lift our eyes to heaven above.' John the Geometer (†c. 990) expresses himself in similar terms in his *Life of Mary* (63), two centuries later, showing how pervasive the idea had become. See Graef, *Doctrine and Devotion*, I, 198.

and peril, from serious illnesses, and from misfortunes of every kind, and from the impending just threat of your Son. As the Mother of God set them in the place of joy, where there is light and peace and the supreme gift of things desired. *Second Homily on the Presentation of the Most Holy Mother of God*[114]

Germanus played an important role in further consolidating the link between Mary's bodily assumption into Heaven and her mediatory role. For Germanus the key to this role is that just as Mary lived in solidarity with her fellow humans on earth while living in complete union with God, so she continues to act as a bridge between the two realities now that she has been assumed body and soul into heaven and abides directly in God's presence, offering even greater support and solace to humanity:

> For just as when you led your life in this world, you were no stranger to heavenly ways, so now, after your passing there, you have not been removed in spirit from your associations with men and women. We see you now revealed as the heaven wide enough to hold God most high, in that your bosom was ready to bear him as your child, and we also call you his spiritual earth. As a result, we naturally suppose that when you lived in this world, you were God's neighbor in every way, so now, though you have passed on from human contact, you have never abandoned those who live in the world. [...] For as you associated with our forebears in the flesh, so you dwell among us still in the spirit; your great role as our protector is the chief mark of your presence among us. All of us hear your voice, and all of our voices come to your attentive ears. You know us because you care for us, and we know your constant patronage and protection. For there is no barrier, not even that due to the division of soul and body, to the mutual recognition between yourself and your servants. You have never dismissed those whom you saved, nor abandoned those whom you gathered together; your spirit lives always, and your flesh did not undergo a corruption [...], you watch over all, O Mother of God, and your care is for all people. *First Homily on the Dormition, 4 -5*[115]

For Germanus the intimate bonds of the flesh unite Jesus and his Mother for all eternity, which is why he wants her to be close to him in heaven, not only in spirit but in body and it is because of these same bonds that he is ever ready to accede to her requests:

> For you became, in your body, the home where he came to rest, O Mother of God; and by your migration, O woman worthy of all praise, he is himself now the place of your repose. 'For this,' he says, 'is my place of rest for the ages of the ages (Psalms 131. 14 [LXX]): referring to the flesh which Christ took from you and put on himself, O Mother of God. [...] Because you, then, are his eternal place of rest, he has taken you to himself in his incorruption, wanting, one might say, to have you near to his words and near to his heart. So whatever

---

[114] *TMPM*, II, 335.
[115] Adapted from *EPH*, pp. 156-57.

you desire of him, he gives you with a son's affection; and whatever you ask from him he brings to fulfilment with a God's power. *First Homily on the Dormition, 6*[116]

Shortly afterwards he makes a series of assertions that constitute a remarkable affirmation of Mary's universal mediation, going far beyond anything that had previously be said:

> No one is filled with the knowledge of God except through you, all-holy One; no one is saved but through you, Mother of God; no one is free of danger but through you, Virgin Mother; no one is redeemed but through you, Mother of God; no one ever receives mercy gratuitously except through you, who have received God. Who fights on behalf of sinners as much as you do? Who pleads on behalf of those who need correction, and takes their part, as much as you do? [...] You, whose power before God is that of a mother, bring superabundant forgiveness for those whose sins exceed all bounds. For it is impossible you should be ignored, since God obeys you as his true and immaculate Mother in every way, always, and in all respects. So anyone who is in trouble rightly runs to you for refuge; anyone who is weak clings to you; anyone under attack takes you as his shield against the enemy. You put an end to 'anger and wrath and tribulation, and to assaults by the evil angels (Psalms 77. 49 [LXX]). You turn away from us [God's] just threat, and his verdict of a painful condemnation, because you love so greatly the people called by the name of your Son. That is why your Christian people, rightly recognizing its own situation, confidently puts into your hands the office of imploring God on its behalf. *First Homily on the Dormition, 8*[117]

These extraordinary and unprecedented lines were to have a profound effect on the direction of Mariology in the West, where Germanus' homilies were to become widely available in the later Middle Ages.[118] The language is akin to the fervent Marian devotion that was to characterise that Latin Church in later centuries as is the notion that Mary can appease the wrath of her Son, which was to become a staple of Medieval commentators. No longer is Mary just the historical instrument of Redemption. Rather, the grace of salvation continues to flow exclusively through her and she has the power to save all, even the most wretched of sinners who have abandoned all hope in God's mercy. The language here verges on the idolatrous, especially when he speaks of God obeying the Virgin, but it is important to see this in the overall context of Germanus' argument concerning the bonds that unite Mother and Son. Both in life and in death Mary's union with her Son is such that she cannot want what he does not want.

---

[116] *EPH*, pp. 159.
[117] *EPH*, pp. 160-61.
[118] See Graef's comments in *Doctrine and Devotion*, I, 146-47.

In his final sermon on the Dormition, Germanus calls on the authority of Saint Paul to give weight to his affirmation of the bodily assumption and glorification of Mary, which he links closely to her intercessory role:

> Until yesterday, I have preached to the Gentiles that you have given birth to God in the flesh; from now on, I shall also teach that you have been allowed to pass over into his presence, so that the Gentiles may realize that their own salvation is confirmed by your intercession, so that they, too, might have a permanent patron before God. *Third [Second] Homily on the Dormition*, 7 [119]

For Andrew of Crete (†c. 740), the corporeal reality that Mary shares with humanity, and with her Son, is key to the efficaciousness of her mediation. Moreover in being raised up to heaven, she becomes a universal advocate:

> Depart from your dwelling-place within creation; be an intercessor with the Lord on behalf of the corporeal reality we share. As long as you dwelt among the people of this earth, only a small part of the earth contained you. But since you have been taken from the earth to your new home, the entire universe owns you as its common altar of cleansing sacrifice. *Third Homily on the Dormition*, 9 [120]

Andrew combines, as others had done before him, petitions for military and spiritual aid: 'By your prayers, we will look on the arms of savages as if they were children's arrows; by them, the spear, the helmet, the shot and the bow remain ineffectual, fall short of their mark, by them, finally, all good things are obtained for Christians, even likeness to God.'[121] As well as being amongst the greatest preachers produced by the Byzantine Church[122] Andrew was also one of the finest composers of hymns, many of which are replete with supplications for the Virgin's aid and mercy. In various respects, the tone of these compositions anticipates the attitude of the Medieval Church in the West toward the Virgin. Self-castigation, constant expressions of sinfulness and unworthiness, pleas of help, protection and healing, declarations of service and praise, the setting off of Mary's mercy against the stern justice of her Son, all these elements, typical of Medieval Western Mariology, are present in Andrew's hymns as the following examples illustrate: 'Mother of God, hope and protection of those who sing to you, lift the heavy yoke of my sins, accept me, a penitent, O chaste Lady';[123] 'We present the Mother of God as our mediatrix; through her prayers and those of your Apostles, grant that we may participate in

---

[119] *EPH*, p. 175.

[120] *EPH*, p. 144.

[121] *Third Homily on the Dormition*, 15, *EPH*, p. 150.

[122] See Mary B. Cunningham, 'Andrew of Crete: A High-Style Preacher of the Eighth Century', in *Preacher and Audience: Studies in Early Christian and Byzantine Homiletics*, ed. by Mary B. Cunningham and Pauline Allen (Leiden: Brill, 1998), pp. 278-86.

[123] *Great Canon of Repentance, Theotokion, Ode I, TMPM*, II, 463.

your gifts and make us worthy, O Saviour, of the brilliance of your resurrection';[124] 'Immaculate Virgin Mother of God, alone worthy of praise, intercede for your servants with your Son';[125] 'O Mother of God, hope of those who always honour you, do not cease to pray to him who was born of you, that he might save me from perils and from all temptation';[126] 'Virgin Mother of God, incontaminate tent, purify me, filthy with sin, with the most pure waters of your mercy, and give me a helping hand so that I might exclaim: "Glory to you, O Chaste One, who is glorified by God!"';[127] 'You caused the angels to descend on earth and men to rise up to heaven. O all-Immaculate One, being the mediatrix of the salvation of all';[128] 'The terrible tribunal and the incorruptible judge await me; appease him, O Immaculate One, so that he might become benevolent towards me before the judgment';[129] 'You who are in the glory of your Creator and Son, appease him with your maternal intercession, O Ever-Virgin'.[130]

Like Germanus and Andrew, John of Damascus († 749) sees Mary's bodily assumption as closely related to her mediatory role. Where earlier writers had spoken only in terms of Mary's interventions with God on behalf of humanity being more effective because of her presence in heaven, John goes further, seeing the glorified Virgin as a source of God's grace and light, which flows out on humanity, just as her earthly body had given birth to the source of that grace:[131]

> For just as the all-bright, even-shining sun, when it is hidden for a while by the body of the moon, seems in a way to fail and to be covered in darkness, accepting shadow in place of light, yet nonetheless never ceases to produce its own light – for it has welling up within itself an ever-flowing fountain of light, or rather *is* itself an inexhaustible fountain of light, as the God who created it has ordained – so you, too, the ever-flowing fountain of true light, the inexhaustible treasure of life itself, the abundant spring of blessing, the cause and sponsor for us of all good things, even if your body is hidden for a short space of time in death, still you pour forth light for us in a generous and endless stream: immortal life, unceasing, pure, and inexhaustible waves of true blessedness, rivers of grace, springs of healing, blessings without end. *First Homily on the Dormition, 10*[132]

---

[124] *Triodion for Palm Sunday, Theotokion, Ode IX, TMPM*, II, 464-65.

[125] *Triodion for the Monday of Holy Week, Theotokion, Ode II, TMPM*, II, 465.

[126] *Triodion for the Tuesday of Holy Week, Theotokion, Ode IX, TMPM*, II, 466.

[127] *Canon for the Feast of the Conception of Mary, Ode IX, Theotokion, TMPM*, II, 472.

[128] *Paracletic Canon to the Mother of God, Ode V, Troparion, TMPM*, II, 480.

[129] *Paracletic Canon to the Mother of God, Ode IV, Troparion, TMPM*, II, 479.

[130] *Ode VIII, Troparion, TMPM*, II, 481.

[131] For a discussion of John's writings on the Dormition see Andrew Louth, *St. John Damascene: Tradition and Originality in Byzantine Theology* (Oxford: Oxford University Press, 2002), pp. 243-49 and 274-82.

[132] *EPH*, p. 195. In the same homily he also writes of Mary as the 'Mediatrix of all blessings.' See *MF*, p. 405.

In a passage that recalls the *Salve Regina*'s 'banished children of Eve' John imagines the Apostles, who have gathered around Mary's deathbed entreating her not to abandon them:

> 'Stay with us,' they said, 'our consolation, the only comfort we have on earth! Do not leave us orphans, O Mother, as we face danger in order to share the sufferings of your Son. Let us keep you among us, as rest in our labors and respite in our trials. If you wish to stay, it will surely be possible, and if you prefer to go, nothing will stand in your way. But if you go away, O tabernacle of God, then let us go with you, we who are called your people because of your Son! In you, we have the only consolation left to us on earth.' *Second Homily on the Dormition, 8*[133]

Later in the same homily, John speaks of Mary as the 'mediator of all good things' because of her role in reconciling humanity with God, which opens up the possibility that people can now become divine.[134] With all his fervent devotion to the Virgin, John is still careful to avoid elevating her to the status of a goddess, making a clear distinction between veneration and adoration,[135] an idea that will later be formulated more precisely by Scholastic theologians such as Bonaventure and Aquinas.[136]

John's hymns, many of which still form part of the Orthodox liturgy today, are filled with pleadings for the Virgin's intercession and a profound sense of the supplicant's unworthiness. It is worth quoting one of them in full, since it typifies the tone of Byzantine prayers to the Virgin at this time, and shows how close such supplications are to the style that came to dominate the Medieval West. Of particular interest are the repeated declarations of sinfulness and unworthiness which closely parallel later Western prayers, and the by now familiar motif of the Virgin softening the stern justice of her Son. It is also interesting to note the relationship of servant to Sovereign, which will also be typical of Western Mariology:

> Generatrix of the light that does not set,
> I beg you: listen to my confession.
> For I have begrimed and stained myself,
> and, wretch that I am, I have befouled myself.
> Alas, miscreant that I am, I have sullied the earth
> with numerous faults, O Queen.
> Therefore it cries out and moans against me
> to the incorruptible Judge.
> Alas, it calls as witnesses
> the heavens with the stars and the sun.

---

[133] *EPH*, p. 213.

[134] See *EPH*, p. 220 and chapter on Remote Redemption.

[135] *Orations on the Holy Icons*, III, 27-28, *PG* 94, 1348-1349. See *MF*, pp. 406-08.

[136] See Pelikan, *Mary through the Centuries*, p. 102, and see Sarah Jane Boss, 'The Development of the Virgin's Cult in the High Middle Ages', in *Mary: The Complete Resource*, pp. 149-72 (p. 156).

A whirlwind of thoughts throws me into confusion
and swamps me with desperation.
Alas my soul is prey to trepidation
in anticipation of the sentence.
O Mother of God, I, a miserable wretch,
have put all my hope in you.
See, the face of your supplicant, alas,
is covered in shame,
as I implore your Son without cease,
that he might have compassion on my unworthiness.
You alone loosen the unbreakable cords,
you who brought the Saviour into the world.
Whiten me, who am darkened and made shadow,
with the tears of repentance.
Lift me up again, I who have been mortified
through my great indolence, O you who brought forth life.
Conduct me, who have become a stranger to God and the angels.
It is astounding indeed how much the Lord
put up with my sins,
and how he did not fling me
into the depths of Hades, wretch that I am!
And how he did not command the rod and the sword
to strike me from above.
And you, thanks to your pleadings,
have given me life, O Sovereign.
You who seek my conversion,
procure it for your servant.
O you who are most excellent, are my wall of defence,
you are my harbour, and my rampart too.
Cause the light of your divine face to shine on me
who am asleep in the uncaring night.
Grant me, Sovereign, the grace of repentance,
and sighs that do not fall silent, and tears.
Clean the impurities of my soul
and procure perfect remission for me.
You who are the mortal creature that bore God
And gave birth to God, bearer of humanity,
may I look to you, O Mary immaculate,
with spiritual eyes, and rejoice.
O strength, O unshakeable hope,
O life and sweet light of your servant,
From a profane tongue and a foul mouth
receive this prayer.
It is time now for rescue; free me
from passions, transgressions and afflictions.
O Sovereign, may the angels rejoice for me now,
together with the souls of the just,
that I may glorify your most holy name
with gratitude and joy.
O you who are above praise, I know
that you can do whatever you will

before God, whom you brought into the world.

Kata Stichion to the Mother of God[137]

In one of his discourses, defending the veneration of icons, John quotes from the *Life of St. Mary of Egypt*, a story traditionally attributed to Sophronius of Jerusalem († 638), as proof of the Virgin's intercessory powers. The story of Mary of Egypt seems to have originated as an oral tradition in sixth-century Palestine. It was one of the most important influences on popular belief in the Virgin's ability to save even the most hopeless of sinners and enjoyed widespread popularity in the West after it was translated into Latin by Paul of Neapolis (the Deacon) († c. 870) in the ninth century. Mary, the story goes, led a dissolute life from her youth, driven by insatiable desires. Eventually, she joined a pilgrimage to Jerusalem, not out of desire for reform but instead seeing an opportunity to seduce the pilgrims. But as she attempted to enter the church of the Holy Sepulchre she was repelled by an invisible force. Realising that it was her sinfulness that was preventing her from entering the church, Mary prayed fervently to an icon of the Virgin, begging forgiveness. When she attempted to enter church again her way was no longer barred. Guided by a vision of the *Theotokos*, Mary set out for the desert to live the life of a hermit. On her way there, she built a church, bathed in the river Jordan, thus receiving her baptism, and received the Eucharist, all of which occurred miraculously, since she was entirely on her own. After years of living in the desert, she encountered Zosimas, a monk, to whom she told her story. She asked him to return in a year bringing her the Eucharist, which he did. He was told to return again a year later, but found her lying dead in the sand. According to an inscription written beside her, she had died immediately after their encounter the year before and her body had been transported to their meeting place and preserved miraculously. Zosimas thereupon buried her body, with the aid of a lion, and returned to his monastery, where he related to the story of her life to his brethren.[138] The passage that John of Damascus quotes describes, in the first person, the moment when Mary asks the Virgin's aid in entering the church, and promises to reform her life. Of particular note is the fact that Mary assumes that the Virgin has it within her power to obtain forgiveness and that she can command as she wills:

> O Lady, Mother of God, who gave birth in the flesh to God the Word, you know, you know well that it is neither honourable nor appropriate that I, who am so impure and depraved, should look upon your image, O Ever-Virgin. Rather, it is right that I should be hated and detested by your purity. But if the God who was born of you became man for the very purpose of calling sinners to repentance,

---

[137] Translated from the Italian version in *TMPM*, II, 570-71, which is taken from the Greek text in Panagiotis N. Trembelas, *Antologia dell'innografia greco-ortodossa* (Athens: [n. pub.], 1949).
[138] See *PG* 87, 3697-3726.

then come to my aid for I have no other help. Order the entrance of the church to be opened to me. Do not prevent me from seeing the tree on which was nailed according to the flesh, the Word of God who was born of you, and who gave his own blood in ransom for me. Order, O Lady, that the door of the divine veneration of the Cross may be opened to me too. And to God who was born of you I present you as a worthy guarantee that I will never again defile this body with any shameful deed. Rather, when I see the wood of your Son's Cross, I will abandon the world and all the things that are in it immediately and will go promptly wherever you, my guarantor, lead me. *Apologetic Discourses against those Decrying the Holy Images, 135*[139]

Theodore the Studite († 826) lays particular emphasis on Mary's ability to communicate with God through gesture in fulfilling her mediatory role on behalf of humanity. The lack of her bodily presence on earth does not deprive her of the ability to empathise with humanity. Rather, glorified in heaven, she is all the more capable of interpreting the needs of her fellow humans and of communicating them to God:

> Now the Mother of God shuts her material eyes, and opens her spiritual eyes towards us like great shining stars that will never set, to watch over us and to intercede before the face of God for the world's protection. Now those lips, moved by God's grace to articulate sounds, grow silent, but she opens her [spiritual] mouth to intercede eternally for all of her race. Now she lowers those bodily hands that once bore God, only to raise them, in incorruptible form, in prayer to the Lord on behalf of all creation. *Encomium on the Dormition of Our Holy Lady, the Mother of God, 2*[140]

He also provides evidence that Mary's protection was being sought in a variety of circumstances where appeals would have been made to the relevant goddesses in earlier times:

> O Mother of God, remember to bless the bounds of this earth. By your intercession temper the air, give us some rain in due season, rule over the winds, make the earth fruitful, give peace to the Church, strengthen orthodox faith, defend the Empire, ward off the barbarian tribes, protect the whole Christian people. *Encomium on the Dormition of Our Holy Lady, the Mother of God, 6*[141]

In the period following the defeat of the iconoclasts and the Triumph of Orthodoxy in the mid-ninth century, emphasis on Mary's mercy and her powers of intercession for sinners grew even stronger. Increasingly she was seen as the merciful Mother who counters the harsh judgement of her Son. In the ninth-century *Apocalypse of the Theotokos*, for instance, the Virgin, who descends into

---

[139] *TMSM*, II, 496-97.
[140] *EPH*, p. 250.
[141] *EPH*, p. 256.

hell to see the punishment of the sinners, offers to take on the punishment herself while her Son protests that he cannot have mercy on sinners since they had no mercy towards him while he was on the Cross.[142] Another way in which Mary's image became less hieratic was in the increasingly popular theme of her plaint at the foot of the Cross where she is portrayed as an all-too human mother lamenting bitterly at the death of her child.[143] The same tendency is reflected in the writings of John the Geometer (†c. 990), who remarks in his *Life of Mary* that while Christ died for us once, he has granted that his Mother should die for sinners each hour because of her willingness to sacrifice herself for her children.[144] John is considered to be the first commentator in the East to affirm an active role for Mary in the Redemption,[145] and is also among the first Eastern writers to speak unreservedly of her mediation when he declares that she is 'the second mediatrix next to the first mediator'.[146]

It is abundantly clear that in the first millennium the Eastern Churches reached great heights in Marian devotion and led in all matters doctrinal while the Latin Church lagged far behind in many respects. After the turn of the new millennium, this situation was to be reversed to a considerable extent. The Western tradition, which had slowly developed its own distinctive style of Mariology, would combine with Eastern influences to produce what may be described as the greatest flowering of Marian devotion the Church had ever seen, while the Greek Church saw relatively few innovations in terms of doctrine or devotion. What is undeniable is that Mariology in the Medieval West could not have taken off in the way that it did, and would have had a very different face, had it not been for the rich tradition of the East.

---

[142] See Jane Baun, 'Discussing Mary's Humanity in Medieval Byzantium', in *The Church and Mary*, ed. by Robert N. Swanson, Studies in Church History, 39 (Woodenbridge: Boydell, 2004), pp. 63-72 (pp. 67-69).

[143] See chapter on Immediate Co-operation.

[144] See Jane Baun, 'Discussing Mary's Humanity', p. 70.

[145] 'She, just like the Father, has delivered her own Son and knew him to be delivered unto death', *Life of Mary*, 60, quoted in Graef, *Doctrine and Devotion*, I, 198. See chapter on Immediate Co-operation.

[146] Quoted in Sandro Sticca, *The Planctus Mariae in the Dramatic Tradition*, trans. by Joseph Berrigan (Athens, GA: University of Georgia Press, 1988), p. 22.

Chapter 5 - Intercession, Mediation and Devotion 2: The Medieval West

At the outset of the Medieval period devotion to Mary in the Latin Church was relatively sober and subdued, certainly when compared to the exuberant piety of the East. Perception of the Virgin's role in the divine economy had changed little since the time of Ambrose and Augustine. Most churchmen were content to repeat what they had received from tradition and the Fathers regarding her intercession.[1] Marian pilgrimages and local cults were all but non-existent, few churches were dedicated to her, while prayers to her differed little from those addressed to the other saints.[2] Such innovation as was occurring was generally confined to the monasteries and was primarily the result of Eastern influences. By the fourteenth century this situation had been utterly transformed. Mary had become the principal route by which the faithful could approach God and receive grace and forgiveness from him. Devotions to her were myriad, prayers and hymns had multiplied, her feast days were among the greatest highlights of the Church calendar, stories about her miraculous

---

[1] See Jean Leclercq, 'Grandeur et misère de la dévotion mariale au moyen-âge', *La Maison-Dieu*, 38 (1954), 122-35, who poses the question, somewhat tongue in cheek, of whether the sober devotion of the Fathers was not of more grandeur than the exuberant faith of the later Middle Ages (p. 122). On Medieval Marian devotion, apart from Leclercq, see the seminal study by Leo Scheffczyk, *Das Mariengeheimnis in Frömmigkeit und Lehre der Karolingerzeit*, Erfurter Theologische Studien, 5 (Leipzig: St. Benno-Verlag, 1959), Mary Clayton's *The Cult of the Virgin Mary in Anglo-Saxon England* (Cambridge; New York: Cambridge University Press, 1990), *Marie: Le culte de la Vierge dans la société médiévale*, ed. by Dominique Iogna-Prat, Eric Palazzo and Daniel Russo (Paris: Beauchesne, 1996), Corrado Maggioni's *Benedetto il frutto del tuo grembo: due millenni di pietà mariana* (Casale Monferrato: Portalupi, 2000), *Gli studi di mariologia medievale: bilancio storico*, Atti del I convegno mariologico della fondazione Ezio Franceschini con la collaborazione della biblioteca Palatina e del dipartimento di storia dell'università di Parma, Parma 7-8 novembre 1997, ed. by Clelia Maria Piastra (Florence: SISMEL – Edizioni del Galuzzo, 2001), Gabriele M. Roschini, *Maria Santissima nella storia della salvezza*, vol. IV, *Il culto mariano* (Isola del Liri: Pisani, 1969), Giulio d'Onofrio, 'Il "Mysterium Mariae" nella Teologia e nella pietà dell'alto medioevo latino (secoli V-XI)', in SDM, I, 505-66, Penny Schine Gold, *The Lady and the Virgin: Image, Attitude, and Experience in Twelfth-Century France* (Chicago: University of Chicago Press, 1985), and Jean Hémery, 'La devotion du people chrétien envers Marie du 8e au 13e siècles' *Cahiers mariales*, 8 (1964), 193-207. Further works are cited below.

[2] See Henri Barré's magisterial study of Marian prayer, *Prières anciennes de l'Occident à la Mère du Sauveur: Des origines à saint Anselme* (Paris: Lethielleux , 1963), and his 'L'intercession de la Vierge aux débuts du moyen âge Occidental', *Études mariales*, 23 (1966), 77-104.

powers abounded, the finest churches of Europe were dedicated to her. Marian writings were at least as sophisticated and exuberant as anything that the Patristic East had produced and Scholastic theologians had provided profound theological reflections on Mary's place in the economy of salvation, greatly advancing understanding of her intercession and laying firm foundations for the doctrines of the Assumption and the Immaculate Conception.[3]

Some of the fundamental characteristics of Medieval Marian piety are an absolute belief in the Virgin's mercy,[4] an attitude of self-abasement on the part of the supplicant,[5] repeated declarations of admiration, praise and service, and a sometimes naïve belief in her ability to assuage the wrath of her Son, the just Judge. All of these features, as we have seen, were already beginning to be present in the later Byzantine Fathers. But there are fundamental differences with the East which derive from the distinctive internal dynamics of Latin Christianity and the different social and cultural milieu of the West. Medieval Mariology placed far greater emphasis on the direct, here-and-now relationship between the faithful and Mary rather than on her exalted historical role in the history of salvation.[6] The Mary of the Medieval West was not the clement queen of the Byzantine Church, admired and venerated, but ultimately unreachable because her greatness put her beyond the reach and imagination of ordinary mortals. She was the merciful Mother, infinitely good and understanding, in solidarity with her fellow humans, a source of consolation and hope for those who navigated the perilous waters of this world, and a means of approach to her Son, whose sacrifice for sinful humanity was too awful to contemplate without feeling overwhelming guilt if not through his Mother, who alone had not offended him. Medieval Mary had no hard edges, unless in her steely opposition to the devil. She was humble, modest and pure; her beauty was soft and lyrical, not hieratic and ineffable. She was the beloved of Canticles, and the Mother who had suffered unutterable pain on Calvary.[7] If one word could sum up the nature of Marian devotion in this period it would be affection.

Innovation in Marian devotion and growing awareness of the Virgin's intercessory role are initially evident primarily in the area of liturgy. Prior to the early seventh century the ember days – Wednesday, Friday and Saturday – in the week before Christmas were among the most important occasions for veneration

---

[3] See Henri Barré, 'L'intercession de la Vierge aux débuts, p. 79.

[4] For a wide range of articles on Mary's mercy see *Maria madre di misericordia: monstra te esse matrem*, atti del convegno mariologico, Vicenza, Monte Berico (4-8 maggio 1999), ed. by Piergiorgio Di Domenico and Elio Peretto (Padova: Messaggero, 2003).

[5] This attitude is not confined to Marian prayers. An identical attitude of self-denigration is to be found in all forms of prayer, whether to the apostles, the martyrs, the saints, or God himself. See Henri Barré, 'L'intercession de la Vierge aux débuts', p. 81.

[6] This is a point that Leo Scheffczyk makes in his seminal study of Marian writings from the eighth to the tenth centuries, *Das Mariengeheimnis in Frömmigkeit*.

[7] On motherhood in the Middle Ages see Clarissa W. Atkinson, *The Oldest Vocation: Christian Motherhood in the Middle Ages* (Ithaca: Cornell University Press, 1991).

of Mary in the West.[8] The introduction of the four major Eastern Marian feasts into the Roman Church,[9] the Assumption,[10] Annunciation,[11] Nativity[12] and Purification of Our Lady, may be traced to this time as may be the practice of dedicating Saturdays to the Virgin,[13] although other Churches, such as those in Spain, France, England, and Northern Italy already had somewhat different traditions.[14] The latter feast was the first to be introduced and was initially known by its Greek name of Hypapante. Only in the following century did it take on a truly Marian hue and acquire the new name of the Purification.

By the eight century, stimulated by ideas from the East, Western theology had begun to look anew at Mary's maternal solicitude, while Eastern liturgical practices had begun to make their mark on the Roman Church.[15] Spain was

---

[8] On the origin of the ember days, which were celebrated four times a year, see Thomas J. Talley, 'The Origin of the Ember Days: An Inconclusive Postscript', in *Rituels: Mélanges offerts au Père Gy, OP*, ed. by Paul de Clerck and Eric Palazzo (Paris: Cerf, 1990), pp. 465-72. On the influence of the ember days on the Western liturgy for Marian feasts see Margot Fassler's recent study, 'Mary's Nativity, Fulbert of Chartres, and the *Stirps Jesse*: Liturgical Innovation circa 1000 and Its Afterlife', *Speculum*, 75 (2000), 389-434 (pp. 393-95), which also provides a wealth of useful information as well as relevant bibliography on the introduction of the feast days.

[9] See Corrado Maggioni's very useful chapter on the Marian feasts in *Benedetto il frutto*, pp. 130-64.

[10] The introduction of the Feast of the Assumption largely eclipsed the older Roman feast in honour of Mary which had been celebrated on January 1st. See Henri Barré, 'Antiennes et Répons de la Vierge', *Marianum*, 29 (1967), 153-254 (p. 219) and Bernard Capelle, 'La messe gallicane de l'Assomption: Son rayonnement, ses sources', in *Miscellanea Liturgica in honorem L. Cuniberti* (Rome, Edizioni liturgiche, 1948), pp. 33-59.

[11] See I. Cecchetti, 'L'Annunciazione: il racconto biblico e la festa liturgica', *Bollettino Ceciliano*, 38, (1943), 46-48 and 98-114.

[12] See Fassler, 'Mary's Nativity'.

[13] On the Feast of the Purification, the first Marian feast to be introduced into the West, around 640, which was also known as the Presentation or Candlemas, and its pagan antecedents see Alistair MacGregor, 'Candlemas: A Festival of Roman Origins', in *The Origins of the Cult of the Virgin Mary*, ed. by Chris Maunder (London: Burns and Oats, 2008), pp. 137-53. See also Henri Barré, 'Antiennes et Répons' p. 207). See also Hilda Graef, *Doctrine and Devotion*, I, 142-43, and *MLM*, pp. 17-18. This Presentation should not be confused with the Presentation of Mary in the Temple, widely celebrated in the East from the eighth century and introduced into Southern Italy in the ninth century from whence it seems to have spread to England. See Corrado Maggioni, *Benedetto il frutto*, pp. 92-93 for the Presentation of Mary and 101-03 for the Saturday Mass.

[14] See I. Cecchetti, 'L'Annunciazione', pp. 104-05. On the feasts in England see Mary Clayton, 'Feasts of the Virgin in the Liturgy of the Anglo-Saxon Church', *Anglo-Saxon England*, 13 (1984), 209-33.

[15] Important sources for Marian developments in the liturgy include the relevant entries in, *Bibliografia Mariana*, ed. by Giuseppe M. Besutti (1948-1989), Ermanno M. Toniolo (1990-1993), Silvano M. Danieli (1994-), 12 vols (Rome: Marianum 1948 –), Georges Frénaud, 'Le culte de Notre Dame dans l'ancienne liturgie latine', in *Maria*, VI, 157-211,

particularly advanced in its use of direct prayer to the Virgin. The seventh-century *Orationale visigothicum* contains no less than thirty-five prayers for the feast of Mary (December 18), while Ildephonse of Toledo († 767) opens and closes his tractate *De virginitate perpetua* with invocations to Mary (see above). In Rome at this time direct Marian prayer did not yet exist, though antiphons and responsories which called on her aid were plentiful.[16] The Syrian Pope Sergius (687-701) played an important role in introducing a number of Marian practices from the East, such as processions for the feasts of the Nativity, Annunciation and Assumption, while the Greek-born Pope John VII (705-707) was also a fervent devotee of the Virgin as is evidenced by his commissioning of an oratory dedicated to her, in which he was to be buried, the primary purpose of which was to gain her aid and protection: 'Here Pope John erected for himself a tomb and ordered that he be laid under the feet of the Lady, committing his soul to the protection of the holy mother, the unwedded virgin and parent, who brought forth God.'[17] Later in the century the iconoclastic persecutions under the reign of Leo III (717–741) led to a considerable exodus of Byzantine monks, many of whom took refuge in Italy, spreading Byzantine style Marian devotion.[18]

The various versions of the Sacramentary, a book of texts for the liturgical year, are a rich source of evidence for Marian devotion. The oldest is the *Sacramentarium Veronense*, also know as the *Leonianum*, which is really a proto-sacramentary, being a collection of various *libelli*, booklets that contained formularies for liturgical celebration, compiled during the papacy of John III (561-574) from earlier sources. It may have been used for the celebration of the Eucharist, but it is more likely that it was employed for the Divine Office.[19] Given that the only extant manuscript has been dated to between 600 and 625 it would seem that the Sacramentary was not widely used.[20] The few references it

---

Michael O'Carroll, *Theotokos: A Theological Encyclopedia of the Blessed Virgin Mary* (Collegeville, Minnesota: Liturgical Press, 1982), and Pietro Sorci, 'Maria nelle liturgie latine', in *SDM*, I, 382-421. For an overview of liturgical developments see Eric Palazzo, *A History of Liturgical Books*.

[16] See Jean Longère, 'Le *Orationes ad sanctam Mariam* e il genere letterario del *Mariale*', in *SDM*, I, 567-89 (p. 573)

[17] Quoted in Ann Van Dijk, 'The Angelic Salutation in Early Byzantine and Medieval Annunciation Imagery', *Art Bulletin*, 81 (1999), 420-436 (p. 432). See also Maria Andaloro, 'I mosaici dell'Oratorio di Giovanni VII', in *Fragmenta picta: affreschi e mosaici staccati del medioevo romano*, ed. by Maria Andaloro and others (Rome: Argos, 1989), pp. 169-177.

[18] See Jean-Marie Sansterre, *Les moines grecs et orientaux à Rome aux époques byzantine et carolingienne (milieu du VIe s. – fin du IXe s.)* (Brussels: Académie Royale de Belgique, 1983) and Michael Angold, *Byzantium: The Bridge from Antiquity to the Middle Ages* (New York: St. Martin's Press, 2001), who estimates that in the eighth and early ninth centuries, up to a quarter of monks in Rome were Greek (p. 101).

[19] See *TMPM*, III, 893. For the original text see *Sacramentarium Veronense*, ed. by Leo Cunibert Mohlberg, Leo Eizenhöfer, and Petrus Siffrin (Rome: Herder, 1966).

[20] See Michael Kunzler, *The Church's Liturgy*, trans. by Placed Murray, Henry O'Shea and Cilian Ó Sé (London and New York: Continuum, 2001), p. 90. For the discussion that

contains to Mary include one that speaks of the virgin birth and two that address Jesus as the Son of the Virgin.[21]

The *Sacramentarium Gelasianum*, compiled near Paris around 750, contains a mixture of Gallican and Roman elements. Transcribed from earlier codices it offers precious evidence of the early form of Marian festal prayers. Without exception, the prayers are restrained and never address Mary directly,[22] making it clear that her intercessory powers are entirely dependent on God:

> O Lord, we beseech you, may the merits of the blessed, glorious, and ever Virgin Mary, Mother of God accompany us, and always implore indulgence for us [...]. We beseech you, omnipotent God, that the glorious intercession of the blessed, glorious, and ever Virgin Mary, Mother of God may protect us and lead us to eternal life. *Prayer for Vespers, Feast of the Annunciation*[23]

The ninth-century *Sacramentarium Gregorianum*, which may originate in the papacy of Gregory I (590-604), was presented to Charlemagne by Pope Adrian (772-78). It illustrates the impact of liturgical reforms undertaken during the Carolingian period. The prayers are longer and broader in scope. They display a much more developed sense of the principal Marian doctrines, and elaborate on her wider role in salvation history. Her intercession is linked to her role in the Incarnation: 'O God, who in the virginity of Mary gave mankind the benefits of salvation, grant that we may experience her intercession, given that it was through her that we received the Author of life.'[24] She is the guarantor of orthodox faith: 'O Lord, confirm in our minds the mysteries of the true faith, so that we, confessing that he who was conceived from the Virgin is true God and true man, through the power of his saving resurrection, may be worthy of

---

follows I have drawn on David M. Hope, *The Leonine Sacramentary: A Reassessment of its Nature and Purpose* (Oxford: Oxford University Press, 1971), Bernard Moreton, *The Eighth-Century Gelasian Sacramentary: A Study in Tradition* (Oxford: Oxford University Press, 1976), Cyrille Vogel, *Medieval Liturgy: An Introduction to the Sources*, trans. and rev. by William G. Storey and Niels Krogh Rasmussen (Washington, DC: Pastoral Press 1986), Yitzhak Hen, *Culture and Religion in Merovingian Gaul, A.D. 481-751* (Leiden: Brill, 1995), especially pp. 44-46, and Eric Palazzo, *A History of Liturgical Books*. For further bibliography see Richard W. Pfaff, *Medieval Latin Liturgy: A Select Bibliography* (Toronto: University of Toronto Press, 1982). For original texts see Klaus Gamber, *Codices liturgici latini antiquiores*, 2nd edn, 2 vols, Spicilegii Friburgenis Subsidia, 1, (Freiburg: Universitatsverlag 1968).

[21] See *TMPM*, III, 900, for the texts.

[22] Direct address to Mary is an important measure of the degree to which she was seen as a source of aid in her own right. See Henri Barré, 'L'intercession de la Vierge aux débuts'.

[23] *TMPM*, III, 902.

[24] *Octave for Christmas*, p. 904. All citations from the *Sacramentarium Gregorianum* are translated from the texts in *TMPM*, III, 904-09, which are taken from the critical edition by Jean Deshusses, *Le Sacramentaire Grégorien: ses principales forms d'après les plus anciens manuscrits*, 3 vols (Fribourg: Spicilegium Friburgense, 1971-1982). Page numbering is for *TMPM* III.

reaching eternal joy.'[25] Her Assumption is linked to her intercessory role: 'O Lord, the prayer of the Mother of God is efficacious [in obtaining] your clemency, for which reason you transferred her from this world so that she might faithfully intercede with you for our sins.'[26] There are hints of the notion that Mary's mercy overcomes the harsh justice of God: 'Forgive, O Lord, the sins of your servants; and since we cannot please you with our actions, grant that we may be saved through the intercession of the Mother of your Son, our Lord and our God.'[27] Her role in reversing the actions of Eve is celebrated: 'Through an unspeakable gift you ensured that human nature, created in you likeness but made dissimilar by sin and death, would not perish in eternal damnation. On the contrary, in the very place where sin had attracted death your immense mercy restored life. The fault of the ancient virgin was expiated by the new and stainless Virgin Mary.'[28] In all of these prayers the unmistakable stamp of Eastern Mariology is evident.

Occasional examples of extra-liturgical prayers that directly address the Virgin, combining praise of her with declarations of unworthiness and supplications for aid, are to be found throughout the Carolingian period,[29] such as this anonymous prayer dating from late eighth-century France:

> Virgin and Mother whose merit is unique, O Mary, you alone did the Lord conserve in a condition of mind and body such that you were rendered worthy of the mystery in which the Son of God assumed his body from you as the price of our Redemption. O Most Merciful, through whom the entire world has been saved, I pray to you, intercede for me who am unclean and stained by every form of iniquity; intercede for me who, because of my sins, am only worthy to receive eternal torture. O Most Splendid Virgin, grant that I, saved by your merits, may I attain the eternal kingdom.[30]

A further influence on early Western Mariology was the appearance of a reworked version of the *Protoevangelium of St. James*, now attributed to Matthew (hence its modern appellation, *Gospel of the Pseudo-Matthew*).[31] Though a version of the *Protoevangelium* had circulated in Latin translation from at least the fourth century,[32] it was largely ignored in official circles in the Patristic West (though

---

[25] *Feast of the Annunciation, Super oblata*, p. 905.

[26] *Vigil of the Assumption, Super oblate*, p. 905.

[27] *Feast of the Assumption, Alia ad missam*, p. 905.

[28] *Preface for the Third Sunday before Christmas*, p. 909.

[29] See Barré, *Prières anciennes*, p. 70.

[30] Barré, Henri, Prières anciennes, p. 52.

[31] *Gospel of the Pseudo-Matthew*, trans. by Alexander Walker, in *Ante-Nicene Fathers*, ed. by Alexander Roberts and James Donaldson, 10 vols (Buffalo: The Christian Literature Publishing Company, 1885-96; repr. Grand Rapids, MI., Eerdmans, 2001), VIII, in *Christian Classics Ethereal Library* <http://www.ccel.org/ccel/schaff/anf08.vii.v.html> [accessed 24 October 2007]. See vol. 2 for further discussion and dating.

[32] See Fassler, 'Mary's Nativity', p. 396, n. 26.

its influence is evident in art), mainly as a result of the forceful rejection of its authority by Jerome († 419).[33] This did not, however, prevent apocryphal literature from entering into the tradition. The reworked *Pseudo-Matthew*, for instance, the translation of which was ironically attributed to Jerome, originated between 550 and 750, had achieved wide circulation by the ninth century.[34] Its most notable influence on the liturgy was in the choice of Matthew's account of the genealogy of Christ as the Gospel for the feast of Mary's Nativity in the Carolingian Church.[35] An adaptation of the *Pseudo-Matthew*, known as the *Libellus de Nativitate Mariae*, or *Gospel of the Birth of Mary*, which combined the first twelve chapters of the apocryphon with canonical texts from Matthew and Luke, first appeared in the ninth century, or possibly somewhat later.[36] Readings were sometimes taken from it for the feast of Mary's nativity and it was later used by Jacopo of Voragine for his account of the Virgin's birth in the *Legenda Aurea*.[37] The *Libellus* is not to be confused with the eleventh century *De*

---

[33] See Graef, *Doctrine and Devotion*, I, 89-90.

[34] The precise date of *Pseudo-Matthew* is still unclear, with dates proposed being anywhere between the sixth and eighth centuries, though the modern consensus tends towards the latter. Jan Gijsel, the most authoritative contemporary scholar of the text places it at the end of the seventh century. See *Libri de Nativitate Mariae*, ed. and commentary by Jan Gijsel and Rita Beyers, Corpus Christianorum Series Apocyphorum, 9 and 10, 2 vols (Turnhout: Brepols, 1997). See also Margot Fassler, 'Mary's Nativity' p. 379, Mary Clayton, *The Apocryphal Gospels of Mary in Anglo-Saxon England*, James, K. Elliott, 'Mary in the Apocryphal New Testament' in *The Origins of the Cult of the Virgin Mary*, ed. by Chris Maunder (London: Burns and Oats, 2008), pp. 57-70 (pp. 60-61), Stephen Gero, 'The Infancy Gospel of Thomas: A Study of the Textual and Literary Problems', *Novum Testamentum*, 13 (1971), 46-80, and Roscoe, E. Parker, 'The Date of the Gospel of Pseudo-Matthew', *PMLA*, 45 (1930), pp. 1266-67.

[35] Fulbert of Chartres († 1028) offers first-hand testimony on the introduction of this feast in France towards the end of the tenth century, and not coincidentally, he wrote extensively on Mary's role in providing her son with a priestly and royal lineage, and was not averse to making reference to the apocryphal *Pseudo-Matthew*. See his *Sermo 4, De Nativitate Beatissimae Mariae Virginis*, PL 141, 320B-324A, commonly known by its opening words, *Approbatae consuetudinis*, where he justifies the use of the apocrypha and the celebration of the feast on the grounds that popular piety demanded it. Also see his *Fifth Sermon for the Nativity of the BVM*, TMPM, III, 854. See also vol 2.

[36] Cyrille Lambot, L'homélie du Pseudo-Jérôme sur l'Assomption et l'évangile de la Nativité de Marie d'aprés une lettre inédite d'Hincmar', *Revue Bénédictine*, 46 (1934), 265-82, argued that it was composed by Paschasius Radbertus († 865). This has been disputed in a meticulously researched essay by Rita Beyers, 'De Nativitate Mariae: Problèmes d'origine', *Revue de Théologie et de Philosophie*, 122 (1990), 171-188, who asserts that the *Libellus* may not even have existed at the time of Paschasius. See the second volume of *Libri de Nativitate Mariae*, ed. and commentary by Jan Gijsel and Rita Beyers for the text and further remarks.

[37] See James, K. Elliott, 'Mary in the Apocryphal New Testament', pp. 61-62 and Margot Fassler, 'Mary's Nativity', pp. 400-40.

Nativitate Mariae which was an abridged version of *Pseudo-Matthew* purged of some of its more fantastical stories.

As with liturgical innovation, it was often from the East that early Medieval Latin homilists drew inspiration. This Eastern influence is evident in a homily traditionally attributed to Bede the Venerable († 735), which makes the link between Mary's Assumption and her intercessory role:

> Today, dearest brothers, we celebrate the feast of Mary, the Holy Mother of God, who today has gone up from the earth to heaven to pray for us to her Son, for the world would be destroyed were it not sustained by the prayers of holy Mary. We have read that after having gone up to Heaven she is continuously in the presence of God, pouring forth assiduous prayers for our sins. Mary supports the just so that they do not fall; she comforts sinners so that they do not perish; she loves virgins if they persevere in authentic virginity. *Homilia 59, De sancta Maria Virgine*[38]

Bede also provides valuable evidence of Marian devotion in the monastic liturgy of the English Benedictines stating that the *Hymnus Sanctae Mariae* or Magnificat was sung everywhere at vespers in order to meditate on the comforting example of the Virgin.[39]

Ambrose Autpert (†c. 781) is the first writer to speak clearly of Mary's spiritual maternity since the time of his namesake, Ambrose of Milan, for which reason he is sometimes referred to as the father of Medieval Mariology.[40] Abbot of the southern Italian monastery of Benevento which had close contacts with the Byzantine Church,[41] he is clearly influenced by Eastern ideas, for instance in his linking of Mary's intercession with her role in the Redemption and her presence in heaven. The contrast between Mary's mercy and the stern justice of her Son is also of Eastern origin. As we have seen, Mary was already seen as a source of mercy by the late Byzantine Fathers and this trend continued to develop in the following centuries. Indeed it is to the East that Western art is indebted for the Elousa, or Merciful Mother type, in which Mary holds Jesus to her cheek and which spread throughout Italy, France, Germany and England as

---

[38] *PL* 94, 422B, *TMPM*, III, 715. On the unlikelihood that the homily is authentic see *TMPM*, III, 696-97.

[39] *Homilia 1*, 2, *PL* 92, 22A. On the Benedictines in general and Mary see Tomas Moral, 'Los benedictinos, la teologia mariana, y el culto a la Madre de Dios', *Cistercium*, 40 (1988), 541-57.

[40] This is a valid assessment if one includes Bede among the writers of the Patristic period. Bede's Mariology, however, especially his emphasis on the Virgin's humility, places him firmly in the Middle Ages. See Henri Barré, *Prières anciennes*, p. 45 and Benedict XVI, *Ambrogio Autperto*, General Audience, April 22, 2009, <http://www.vatican.va/holy_father/benedict_xvi/audiences/2009/documents/hf_ben-xvi_aud_20090422_it.html> [accessed 2 May 2009].

[41] See *MLM*, p. 39.

well as Russia (the famous Vladimir Virgin) by the twelfth century.[42] The tone and style of Ambrose's prayer, however, with its restrained praise, lack of typological references, and repeated direct pleas for aid, is typically Latin:

> What praises, then, can human fragility offer you, which only found access to the Redemption through your participation in the divine plan? Accept, therefore, our gestures of gratitude, no matter how modest and above all inadequate they may be compared to your merits. Grant our prayers and, through your prayers, forgive our faults. Accept our prayers in the sanctuary of fulfilment and give us in return the grace of reconciliation. Thanks to you, may what we present through your living voice be pardonable, and may we obtain what we ask for with a mind full of faith. Accept what we present, grant what we ask, forgive what we fear, because in placating the ire of the Judge we have not found anyone whose merits are more powerful than yours, who were worthy to be the Mother of our Redeemer and Judge. Come to the aid of the wretched, help the fainthearted, give strength to the weak, pray for the people, intervene for the clergy, intercede for the throng of monks, plead for the devout feminine sex. Everyone is noticeably aware of your comfort, all those who piously celebrate the feast of your Assumption. *In festo Assumptionis B. Mariae, 11 (Pseudo-Augustine, Sermo 208)* [43]

Ambrose goes on to stress that Mary's intercession is not without conditions affirming that it will be far more effective if the supplicant is adorned with charity and humility.[44] He also provides us with a precious description of the celebration of the Feast of the Purification which shows many similarities with the account of Egeria (see previous chapter):

> On this day the entire population of the city, gathered together in one place under the brightest light of candles, participates in the celebration of Holy Masses. No-one is allowed to join the public assembly if they do not have a light in their hands. It is as if every person were presenting himself at the Temple of the Lord. Moreover with the devotion of his offering it is as if everyone were welcoming and showing externally the light of the faith that illumines him within. *In purificatione sanctae Mariae, 1* [45]

He goes on to say that the faithful should imitate Simeon in welcoming Jesus and Mary in presenting him to the world.

---

[42] See Victor Lasareff, 'Studies in the Iconography of the Virgin', *Art Bulletin*, 20 (1938), 26-65 (pp. 36-42) and Niki Tsironis 'From Poetry to Liturgy: The Cult of the Virgin in the Middle Byzantine Era', in *Images of the Mother of God: Perceptions of the* Theotokos *in Byzantium*, ed. by Maria Vassilaki, (Aldershot: Ashgate, 2005), pp. 91-102.
[43] *PL*, 39, 2133-2134, *TMPM*, III, 726. See also Graef, *Doctrine and Devotion*, I, 167-68, and Henri Barré, 'L'intercession de la Vierge', p. 86.
[44] *In festo Assumptionis B. Mariae*, 12, *PL* 39, 2134.
[45] *MLM*, p. 40.

Some believe that Ambrose was the author of the hymn *Ave maris stella*, which was hugely influential in promoting the image of Mary as a loving and merciful Mother, inspiring many hymnists and homilists, most famously Bernard of Clairvaux, to exhort the faithful to turn to the Star of the sea:[46]

> *Ave maris stella, / Dei mater alma / atque semper virgo, / felix caeli porta. // Sumens illud Ave / Gabrielis ore, / funda nos in pace, / mutans nomen Evae. // Solve vincula reis, / profer lumen caecis, / mala nostra pelle, / bona cuncta posce. // Monstra te esse matrem: / sumat per te precem / qui pro nobis natus, / tulit esse tuus. // Virgo singularis, / inter omnes mitis, / nos culpis solutos / mites fac et castos. // Vitam praesta puram, / iter para tutum, / ut videntes Iesum / semper collaetemur.*

> (Hail, Star of the sea, kind-hearted Mother of God, and ever-Virgin, happy gate of heaven. Taking that sweet Ave, which came from Gabriel, confirm peace within us, changing Eve's name. Break sinners' fetters, give light to the blind, chase all evils from us, pray for blessings for us all. Show yourself a Mother, offer him our prayers, who, born for us, took on your nature. Virgin all excelling, mildest of the mild, free us from our guilt, make us meek and chaste. Keep our life all spotless, make our way secure, until, seeing Jesus, we rejoice for evermore.)[47]

A sermon attributed to Paul Deacon Warnefred (†c. 799), who like Autpert, was well versed in Greek Mariology, links the Virgin's Assumption with her mediatory role, as had many of the later Eastern Fathers. He too makes Mary's aid conditional on a willingness to reform. The sermon is particularly notable for its use of the terms 'mediatrix' and 'Mother of Mercy' and for its typically Medieval affirmation that Mary is sympathetic to human frailty because she herself has experienced what it means to be subject to the weakness of the flesh:

> Let us exult and rejoice therefore in her because in heaven Mary is the faithful Advocate of us all. While her Son is the mediator between God and men, she is the mediatrix between the Son and men. And as becomes the Mother of Mercy, she is mercy for all of us; she knows how to sympathise with human weaknesses because she knows well the material from which we are made. For this very reason she never ceases to intercede for us with her Son, on condition, however, that she sees that we deplore and detest our iniquities. [...] Even if our infirmities are terrible, we must never despair of her mercy provided we are capable of acknowledging our fault in her presence and ask with a contrite heart for her

---

[46] See Heinrich Lausberg, *Der Hymnus 'Ave maris Stella'* (Opladen: Westdeutscher, 1976), R. Weber, 'Ambrose Autpert serait-il l'auteur de l'hymne "Ave maris stella"?', *Revue bénédictine*, 88 (1978), 159-66, who rejects the hypothesis and see the somewhat dated article by Hugh T. Henry, 'Ave Maris Stella,' in *The Catholic Encyclopedia*, ed. by Charles George Herbermann, Edward Pace, and others, 15 vols (New York: Appleton, 1907-12), in *New Advent* <http://www.newadvent.org/cathen/02149a.htm> II (1907) [November 10, 2006]. See also Star in vol. 2.

[47] Latin text taken from *The Oxford Book of Medieval Latin Verse*, ed. by F. J. E. Raby (Oxford, The Clarendon Press, 1959), pp. 94-95.

intervention. We will most certainly see her help descending on us, for many are her mercies, especially for those who invoke her. *Homilia XIV, In Assumptione*[48]

Alcuin († 804) wrote several prayers to the Virgin. This one is tinged by the same tone of self-abasement that we find in the late Byzantine Fathers and that reaches its height in the West in the later Middle Ages:

> You are my sweet love, my jewel, the great hope of my salvation. Help your servant, O glorious Virgin. My voice resounds amidst my tears, my heart burns with love. Pay attention too to the prayers of all my brothers who implore you. O Virgin, you are full of grace, through you may the grace of Christ save us. *Ad ecclesiam et aram beatae Virginis*[49]

Here we already see the beginnings of the affective piety that was to blossom in the eleventh century. Such warm expressions of love for Mary would be inconceivable in an Eastern context. It is also noteworthy that Alcuin sees Mary as a distributor of God's grace and not just as a petitioner on behalf of sinners.

Alcuin's reforms, which included the institution of Saturday Mass in honour of the Virgin, were just one aspect of a wider movement towards greater devotion to the Virgin at this time. The Saturday Mass includes the following prayer for Mary's intercession:

> Grant, O Lord, we pray, that we your servants may enjoy continued good health in mind and body, and through the intercession of the blessed Ever-Virgin Mary, may we be freed from the afflictions of our present life and rejoice in the happiness of the life to come. *Liber Sacramentorum, 7, Sabbato missa de sancta Maria*[50]

In the ninth century, books of prayers which were linked to but not directly part of the liturgy, known as *libelli precum*, grew in popularity, especially in England.[51] Three prayers to Mary in the ninth-century Anglo-Saxon *Book of Cerne*[52] are of particular interest since they are one of the few examples of direct recourse to the Virgin's intercession at this time and manifest a fervour heretofore almost unheard of in the English Church. The first prayer addresses Mary thus: '[You] who are the mediator for the whole world when faced with danger, hear, hear, hear us, holy Mary. Pray and intercede for us and do not disdain to help. For we trust and we know for certain that you can obtain everything that you wish

---

[48] *TMPM*, III, 755-56.

[49] *PL* 101, 771B.

[50] *PL* 101, 455B-C.

[51] See Jean Longère, 'Le *Orationes ad sanctam Mariam*', pp. 577-79, who provides a list of the most important *libelli*.

[52] *The Book of Cerne* ed. by Arthur B. Kuypers (Cambridge: Cambridge University Press, 1902), and see Mary Clayton, *The Cult of the Virgin*, pp. 96-104.

from your Son.'[53] Such fervent pleas for aid, and absolute trust in the Virgin's powers, were by no means unique at this time, being evident in a variety of Spanish, Irish, and even Roman texts, as Mary Clayton notes.[54] A second prayer, which also appears in the earlier *Book of Nunnaminster,* dating to the late eighth or early ninth century, is more restrained in tone:

> Holy Mary, glorious Mother of God and ever-virgin, who merited to give birth to the salvation of the world, and who obtained the light of the world and the glory of the heavens for those sitting in darkness and the shadow of death, be to me a merciful Lady and illuminatrix of my heart, and an assistant before God the Father Almighty, so that I may deserve to receive forgiveness for my transgressions, to escape the darkness of hell, and to gain eternal life. *Sancta Maria gloriosa*[55]

In this prayer Mary's intercessory powers depend entirely from her divine motherhood. She assists the supplicant in obtaining what she or he desires from God, but there is no hint that she is an independent power who can obtain whatever she wants.

Perhaps the most popular and influential prayer was the ninth-century *Singularis meriti,* which appears in a variety of Carolingian collections and was reproduced or reworked in many prayer books for the next several centuries:

> Mary, Mother and Virgin, of singular merit, alone and without compare, whose mind and body the Lord preserved inviolate, so that you would be worthy for the Son of God to take from you a human body, the price of our redemption, I beseech you, most merciful one, through whom the whole world has been saved, intercede for me, most foul and impure in all my iniquities, that I who for my iniquities deserve nothing but eternal punishments, may be saved by you, most glorious Virgin, and follow you into the everlasting kingdom.[56]

Here we find the same attitude of self-abasement that we have already come across in other Medieval writers, and that will become increasingly popular in the West, particularly from the twelfth century onwards. The tone is reserved while stylistically the prayer is entirely lacking in embellishments.

Homilies of significance on the Virgin in the ninth century are few. A rare exception is Paschasius Radbertus' († 865), whose *Cogitis me* enjoyed great popularity, primarily because he pseudo-epigraphically attributed it to Jerome. The text is generally discussed today because of its influential denial of the bodily Assumption but in many respects its primary importance at the time was the fervent devotion it expressed for the Virgin. He urges his listeners to seek Mary's

---

[53] Barré, *Prières Anciennes,* pp. 67-68.
[54] Mary Clayton, *Cult of the Virgin,* pp. 100-01.
[55] Barré, *Prières Anciennes,* p. 65. See Rachel Fulton, *From Judgment to Passion: Devotion to Christ and the Virgin Mary, 800-1200* (New York: Columbia University Press, 2002), p. 206.
[56] Barré, *Prières Anciennes,* p. 75-76.

intercession with her Son, highlighting her privileged role among the saints in defeating heresy and upholding the truth, second only to that of God himself: 'This is the Virgin who alone, after God, destroyed the entire evil of heresy, who strengthens us in every truth, reassures us with her merits and helps us with her prayers so that he may find us worthy of expressing our praise for him.'[57]

Paschasius was also an active player in a debate that took up a great deal of energy in this period over the nature of the Eucharist and the real presence. This debate laterally involved Mary because of the obvious parallels between her generation of Christ's body and blood and the priest's transformation of the bread and wine.[58] Another important development of the ninth century was the translation into Latin by Paul of Neapolis (the Deacon) (†c. 870) of two influential legends concerning the Virgin's powers of intercession. One was the story of Mary of Egypt, which we discussed in the previous chapter, and the other was the fifth-century Greek tale of Theophilus, both of which were destined to have a huge impact on the Medieval imagination. The story of Theophilus, the administrator of the bishop of Cilicia, tells of how the Virgin rescues him from the clutches of the devil.[59] A virtuous man, Theophilus refuses many honours and, upon the death of his master, he humbly refuses to be nominated as his successor. However, the new bishop removes him from his position as archdeacon and strips him of all his dignities, upon which he turns to evil ways. A Jewish sorcerer convinces him to seek out the devil's aid and, upon his appearance, Theophilus makes a pact with him, signing over his soul and renouncing Christ and the Virgin in exchange for the restoration of his wealth and status. For many years he continues in a position of power, respected and feared by all. However, God, recalling his previous virtue, prompts him to repent and make amends for his evil, at which point Theophilus turns to the Virgin to seek her aid in wresting the contract from the devil's hands, uttering a compelling and unprecedented testament to the Virgin's powers of intercession that was to resonate powerfully throughout the coming centuries:

---

[57] *Cogitis me*, 3, *PL* 30, 124C, *TMPM*, III, 790. On Paschasius' Mariology see William Cole, 'Theology in Paschasius Radbertus' Liturgy-Oriented Marian Works', in *De cultu mariano saeculis VI-XI*, Acta congressus mariologici-mariani internationalis, Zagreb, 1972 (Rome : Pontificia Academia Mariana Internationalis, 1972),, 395-431.

[58] See Mary and the Eucharist in vol. 2 and see María Ángeles Navarro Girón, *La carne de Cristo: el misterio eucarístico a la luz de la controversia entre Pascasio Radberto, Ratramno, Rabano Mauro y Godescalco* (Madrid: Universidad Pontificia de Comillas, 1989).

[59] On the history of the Theophilus legend see Karl Plenzat, *Die Theophilus legende in der Dichtung des Mittelalters*, Germanische Studien 43 (Berlin: Ebering, 1926; repr. Nendlem, Liechtenstein: Krauss, 1967). See *TMPM*, III, 815-18. See also, especially for the presence of the legend in art, Michael Cothren, 'The Iconography of Theophilus Windows in the First Half of the Thirteenth Century', *Speculum*, 59 (1984), 308-341.

It is possible that God will have compassion on me if you, O Holy One, pray for me, if you constrain your Son to have pity. I beseech you, urge him who is moved to pity by you to have mercy on me. Your Son will do what you wish; tell him and everything will be done. Besides it is your right to take the hand of whoever is plummeting downwards. By nature you possess a particular sense of mercy and this privilege is, as it were, innate in you. In fact, depending on the particular cases, you come to the aid of the human race sometimes as protectress, sometimes as Mother, and sometimes as Mediatrix. God himself most certainly became man through you. Therefore, the Father, whom the whole universe obeys, chose you, Mary, constituting you as a Mediatrix between God and man. As a right, therefore, you have the possibility of talking to you Son and beseeching him. Now, since you alone can turn to your Son, you alone can pray to his Sacred Heart. *Miraculum Sanctae Mariae de Theophilo poenitente, 3, 11*[60]

Mary severely admonishes Theophilus for his reprehensible conduct, but, moved by his prayers and mortification, she agrees to help him once he has sincerely confessed his sins and made a profession of faith. In Paul's version there is no explanation of how Mary wrests the contact from the devil, but later versions describe the struggle in some detail. The story concludes with the death of Theophilus who expires in the sure knowledge that he will not now be damned.

The legend enjoyed widespread popularity throughout the Middle Ages being quoted by such influential figures as Peter Damian, Fulbert of Chartres, Bernard of Clairvaux, Anthony of Padua and Bonaventure as proof of the Virgin's intercessory powers. Graef notes that the Theophilus tale 'contained many epithets that became popular, among them redemption of captives, refuge of the afflicted, hope of Christians and, very important, mediatress between God and man.'[61] It also functioned as a salutary lesson for those of the ruling class, whether secular or religious, who became overly attached to the privileges of their position. Allusions to the legend appear in many hymns[62] and it also made its way into popular collections of miracle stories such as Jacopo of Voragine's († 1298) *Legenda aurea*[63] and vernacular literature, in France where it was retold by such luminaries as Gautier de Coinci († 1236) in his *Miracles de Nostre Dame*, and Rutebeuf († 1285) in his *Miracle de Théophile*, and Spain in Berceo's († before 1264) *Milagros de Nuestra Señora* and Alfonso X's († 1284) *Cantigas de Santa Maria*.[64] By the thirteenth century the legend was also a popular subject in a

---

[60] *TMPM*, III, 817-18.

[61] See Hilda Graef, *Doctrine and Devotion*, I, 30.

[62] See, for instance, Eusebius Bruno's († 1081) *Oratio ad sanctam Mariam*, *AH*, XLVIII, 80-81, Henri Barré, *Prières anciennes*, pp. 147-48.

[63] For an English translation see Jacobus de Voragine, *The Golden Legend: Readings on the Saints*, trans. by William Granger Ryan, 2 vols (Princeton: Princeton University Press, 1993).

[64] See Moshe Lazar, 'Theophilus: Servant of Two Masters. The Pre-Faustian Theme of Despair and Revolt', *MLN*, 87 (1972), 31-50 (p. 32).

variety of artistic media such as stained glass, monumental sculpture, and illuminated manuscripts throughout Europe.[65]

The tenth century was one of relative paucity when it came to Mary, with little in the way of homilies or prayers. Veneration of the Virgin was still centred on the monasteries with little evidence of a developed cult among the ordinary people. Leclercq suggests that one reason for this may have been, as it was for the early Christians, the lack of any relics of the Virgin which in turn meant a lack of any localised cults.[66] Tenth-century England, under the influence of the Benedictine reform, was somewhat of an exception, with numerous monasteries being dedicated or rededicated to the Virgin under the active support of King Edgar, as Mary Clayton notes.[67] However, cults of the local saints began to dominate once again after the death of Edgar in 975. Clayton theorises that monasteries may have found it more lucrative to promote cults that were well-established among the laity and for which they had relics rather than the more generalised cult of the Virgin. One small but important contribution to the spread of Marian piety at this time was by the abbot of Cluny, Odo († 942), who was in the habit of calling on the aid of the 'Mother of Mercy', an epithet that was soon adopted throughout the Latin Church. According to a *Vita* of the abbot written by John of Salerno around 945, a notorious brigand who had repented and become a monk had a vision on his deathbed of the Virgin who declared that she was the 'Mother of Mercy', which he revealed to Odo, who thereafter popularised the epithet.[68] The epithet is also used elsewhere in the *Vita* including this prayer for the vigil of Christmas which Odo reputedly composed:

---

[65] See Alfred Freyer, 'Theophilus the Penitent as Represented in Art', *Archaeological Journal*, 92 (1935), 287-333, Iona McCleery, 'The Virgin and the Devil: The Role of the Virgin Mary in the Theophilus Legend and Its Spanish and Portuguese Variants', in *The Church and Mary*, ed. by Robert N. Swanson, Studies in Church History, 39 (Woodenbridge: Boydell, 2004), pp. 147-56, and the meticulous study by Michael W. Cothren, 'The Iconography of Theophilus Windows in the First Half of the Thirteenth Century', *Speculum*, 59 (1984), 308-341.

[66] Jean Leclercq, 'Grandeur et misère', p. 125. On Marian devotion in Benedictine monasteries see Bernard, Botte, 'Culte et dévotion à la Vierge Marie dans l'ordre monastique aux VIIIe-IXe siècles : Le Calendrier monastique des fêtes liturgiques de la Vierge d'après les « Initia consuetudines benedictinae' de K. Hallinger', in *De cultu mariano saeculis VI-XI* , Acta congressus mariologici-mariani internationalis, Zagreb, 1972 (Rome : Pontificia Academia Mariana Internationalis, 1972), IV, 203-25.

[67] 'Changing Fortunes: The Cult of the Virgin in Tenth-Century England', in *Gli studi di mariologia medievale: bilancio storico*, pp. 87-96 (p. 91).

[68] See *Vita sancti Odonis Cluniacensis*, 2, 20, PL 133, 72A-B, *MLM*, pp. 79-80 and 97, and *TMSM*, 841-42. The title 'Mother of Mercy' had already been used by Jacob of Serug († 521) in his sermon *On the Burial or Death of Mary the Holy Generatrix of God* (line 29), *TMPM*, IV, 172, and in a homily on the Assumption attributed to Paul the Deacon (†c. 799), *TMSM*, III, 755, and by others, but did not catch on.

O Lady, Mother of mercy, you who gave birth to the Saviour of the world on this night, deign yourself to pray for me. I appeal to your glorious and unique birth-giving, O most merciful, and may you bend your merciful ears to my prayer. I greatly feat that my life may be displeasing to your Son, and since, O Lady, he manifested himself to the world through you, I pray to you that through your action he might immediately have mercy on me.[69]

Under Odilone, who was abbot from 994 until his death in 1049, two main innovations, which also had an effect on the wider Church, were introduced, namely the importance given to the solemn liturgy of the Assumption and the practice of consecrating themselves to the service of the Virgin, which Odilone himself had done as a child in thanksgiving for being cured of an illness.[70] The abbot of Cluny, Peter the Venerable († 1156), who was a close friend of Bernard of Clairvaux's (despite several lively disputes) and a figure of considerable stature in his own right, was a noted devotee of the Virgin. He wrote a series of liturgical hymns dedicated to her and was also responsible for the insertion of a number of regulations in the Cluniac rule requiring greater devotion to the Virgin, including the daily celebration of Mass at Mary's altar, the daily singing of the Marian Office, and, as mentioned above, the singing of the *Salve Regina*.[71] He also wrote a *De miraculis*, which speaks of a variety of miraculous events in the lives of monks including many that involve the Virgin.[72]

Another development, which began in the tenth century and grew in the centuries to follow, was the use of Marian tropes (embellishments of the sung responses of the Mass) for the Kyrie, the Gloria, the Sanctus, and the Agnus Dei.[73] This twelfth-century trope is a good example of the genre:

Ave præclara maris stella, / in lucem gentium, / Maria, divinitus orta. / Euge, dei porta, / quæ non aperta / veritatis lumen, / ipsum solem justitiæ / indutum carne, / ducis in orbem /Virgo decus mundi, / regina cœli, / præelecta ut sol, / pulchra lunaris ut fulgor, / agnosce omnes te diligentes. / Te plenmam fide / virgam almam stirpis Jesse / nascituram / priores desideraverant / patres et prophetæ. / Te lignum vitæ / sancto rorante pneumate / paritarum / divini floris amygdalum / signavit Gabrihel / Tu agnum regem, / terræ dominatorem, / Moabitici / de petra deserti, / ad montem filiæ / Sion traduxisti, /Tunque furentem / Leviathan serpentem / tortuosumquae / et vectem collidens / damnoso crimine / mundum exemisti.

---

[69] *TMSM*, III, 841.

[70] See Alfredo Simón, 'La presenza della beata Vergine nel rinnovamento promosso da Cluny, in *SDM*, I, 593-617, who provides a wealth of information on Cluniac devotion to Mary and a detailed analysis of Odilone's Marian writings.

[71] See *PL* 189, 1040-1048.

[72] Pierre le Vénérable, *Les merveilleux de Dieu*, trans. by Jean-Pierre Torrell and Denise Bouthillier (Fribourg: Éditions universitaire, 1992). See Alfredo Simón, 'La presenza della beata Vergine', pp. 593-617 for further information.

[73] See Corrado Maggioni, *Benedetto il frutto*, pp. 105-07.

(Hail most bright star of the sea, a light for the nations, Mary, divinely arisen. O, gate of God, who unopened, lead the light of truth into the world, he himself, the Sun of justice, clothed in flesh, Virgin ornament of the world, Queen of heaven, outstanding as the sun, beautiful as the flash of the moon, recognise all who venerate you. Those who went before, patriarchs and prophets desired you, full of faith, O gentle rod about to be born of the stock of Jesse. Gabriel designated you the wood of life, by moistening you with the dew of the Holy Spirit, you, about to give birth, are the almond of the divine flower. You brought the lamb who is the king, the Lord of the earth, from the rocks of the Moabite desert to the mountain of the daughter of Sion. And you banished Leviathan, the raging twisting serpent, striking him who was dominating the world with dastardly sin), *De Beata v. Maria,* 1-27[74]

By the turn of the millennium interest in Mary was on the rise as part of a general renewal of the Church. Fulbert of Chartres († 1028), who was responsible for the rebuilding of the great Cathedral at Chartres which had been destroyed by fire, recounts the story of Theophilus in order to convince his readers of the immense power of the Virgin:

> You, Mother of God, cause Satan to render illegible the testament that I signed with my own hand, which constitutes the proof of my grave sin. Such a guarantee in his hands terrifies me to the point of death. As you have well understood, I am begging you to take this pact from him, you who are able to do this. For, he before whom the enemy forces are obliged to yield gave you this power. Show your power, my hope, my defence, my shield. Send your forces into the field and show yourself to be a valiant protectress. *Miraculum Sanctae Mariae de Theophilo poenitente, 3, 12*[75]

He also recounts other Marian miracles, such as the well-known account of St. Basil resuscitating the dead man that we came across already, and concludes by urging the faithful to seek for her aid: 'Let the just therefore come to her together with Basil, praising and blessing [her], because without doubt they will find an immediate answer to the requests of their holy desires'.[76] Part of Fulbert's motivation in highlighting Mary's ability to perform miracles, and in more generally promoting her cult, may have been to encourage pilgrims to visit (and donate to) Chartres, which housed an important relic of the Virgin, her

---

[74] Latin text is taken from *Lateinische Hymnen des Mittelalters,* ed. by Franz Joseph Mone, ed., 3 vols (Freiburg im Breisgau: Herder, 1853-55; repr. Aalen: Scientia, 1964), II (1854), n. 555.

[75] *TMPM*, III, 818.

[76] *Sermo 4, De Nativitate beatissimae Mariae Virginis, PL* 141, 324A.

girdle.[77] In common with many Medieval writers, Fulbert identifies virginity and humility as the two qualities that allowed Mary to crush the serpent's head:

> The Eternal One said to the serpent: 'I will put enmities between thee and the woman, and thy seed and her seed' (Genesis 3. 15). In this context what does 'crush the head of the serpent' mean, brothers, if not to resist and overcome the principal suggestion of the devil, that is, concupiscence? If, therefore, one asks: What woman achieved such a victory? Certainly, following the line of human generation, one does not find anyone until one comes to she whom we consider to be the saint of saints. And if someone were to object: But in what way did she manage to crush the serpent's head? The answer is: Most certainly because she sacrificed her virginity together with her humility to God. *Sermo 4, De Nativitate beatissimae Mariae Virginis*[78]

In another sermon he makes an even more unequivocal statement regarding Mary's ability to obtain whatever is asked of her, although he is careful to stipulate that these requests must come from those who are just, or at least desire to become so:

> It is an ineffable thing to say what grace and glory the Lord has accorded his Mother. Nevertheless, we know with certainty that whatever just men ask of her they will immediately obtain through the intercession of his Mother. Sinners too have very often obtained mercy through her. *Sermo 5, De Nativitate beatissimae Mariae Virginis*[79]

Here, although Fulbert makes it clear here that Mary has the power to obtain whatever she desires, he does not claim universal mediation for her since he does not exclude the possibility that grace may flow through other channels.

Fulbert seems to come closer to the notion of Mary's universal mediation when he writes of the necessity of turning to her to overcome the temptations of this life, a passage that clearly influenced Bernard of Clairvaux's famous sermon on seeking guidance from Mary, the star of the sea, in order to avert the storms of temptation:

> All those who adore Christ, rowing through the waves of this world, need to turn their gaze to this star of the sea, that is, to Mary, who is very close to God, celestial pole of the universe, directing the course of their lives by contemplating her example. Whoever behaves in this way will not be buffeted by the winds of vainglory, will not be smashed on the rocks of adversity, nor will they be

---

[77] See Margot E. Fassler, *The Virgin of Chartres: Making History through Liturgy and the Arts* (New Haven and London: Yale University Press, 2010) and vol. 2 for further discussion and bibliography.
[78] *PL* 141, 320C-D.
[79] *PL* 141, 325B.

swallowed up by the turbulent whirlwind of pleasures, but will happily reach the port of eternal calm. *Sermo 4, De Nativitate beatissimae Mariae Virginis* [80]

We also find reference to Theophilus in a famous prayer for Mary's intercession that is almost certainly by Fulbert:

> Pious Virgin Mary, Queen of Heaven, Mother of the Lord, Mother of the Redeemer, Mother of the Artificer, Mother of the Creator, Mother of the Light, Mother of mercy and piety, I, a supplicant, flee to you and ask for mercy and grace from you and through you, that through you I may make peace with your Son. Holy Mother of God, perpetual Virgin Mary, who has ever been deceived who placed his hope in you? Absolutely no-one. My Lady, be merciful and mild towards me, just as you were to the vicar Theophilus, who denied Our Lord Jesus Christ, yet was worthy of reconciliation through you. Be merciful and mild towards me, just as you were to Mary of Egypt, who stood you as surety between herself and God, and merited to be saved. [There follow further miracle stories]. Holy and Immaculate, perpetual Virgin Mary, receive now my humble petitions and bring them before the sight of Divine Majesty, bringing back to me the grace of reconciliation. Holy and Immaculate, perpetual Virgin Mary, receive me into your confidence, and reconcile me with your only Son, Our Lord Jesus Christ, my Judge and my Advocate, on the Day of Judgement. *Oratio ad Sanctam Mariam Matrem Domini* [81]

The prayer continues on for a further two pages with many other requests, some of them remarkably specific, for instance when he asks the Virgin to protect the various parts of his body from ill-health, listing them one by one, and concludes with a request that he may be a 'pure and useful vessel' so that he may carry out well his ecclesiastical and temporal offices. The length of the prayer and its specificity are not the only aspects worthy of note. Particularly remarkable is the preciseness with which he lays out the mechanics of Mary's intercession. First she must be persuaded to receive his petition, which is achieved through protestations of unworthiness, declarations of praise, and demonstrations of her greatness and mercy. Having accepted the supplicant's prayer, Mary should bring his requests before God, and then return to him bearing grace. Also important is Fulbert's insistence on Mary's role in placating God's judgement, not only in the present but at the time of the Last Judgement. Until the advent of a softer image in the twelfth century, in the wake of Anselm of Canterbury, Bernard of Clairvaux and Francis of Assisi among others, the dominant perception of Christ in the Medieval West was of a terrifying judge,[82] as it had been in the later Byzantine Fathers, as we have seen. It may be, as Rachel Fulton has argued, that fear of judgement was augmented in the West as

---

[80] *PL* 141, 322A-B.

[81] Henri Barré, *Prières anciennes*, pp. 155-56. Translation relies in part on Fulton, *Judgement and Passion*, pp. 219-20. See also her discussion of this prayer, pp. 220-21.

[82] See Jean Leclercq, 'Grandeur et misère', pp. 123-24.

a result of millennial preoccupations with the Second Coming.[83] The Mother of Mercy provided an essential counterbalance to such fears. Later on, as the image of Christ became less fearsome, his Mother was to provide a way of contemplating his sufferings on behalf of humanity through a vicarious participation in her desolation on Calvary.[84]

Peter Damian's († 1072) famous phrase, 'Since it was through you that the Son of God deigned to descend to us, so it is through you that we may attain communion with him,' inspired the celebrated motto: 'To Jesus through Mary' which could be said to sum up the entire dynamic of Medieval Mariology.[85] Damian was an ardent devotee of the Virgin, composing many Marian hymns as well as being an active promoter of Saturday devotions to Our Lady.[86] He also tells of the popularity of the *Little Office of the Blessed Virgin* among the secular clergy of Italy, a version of which he himself produced, writing and selecting many of the hymns, lessons and prayers.[87] There is evidence that devotional offices in honour of the Virgin existed in both the Eastern and Western Churches from the early Middle Ages. The Little Office evolved out of the Hours of the Virgin, which seem to have been developed in the ninth century, possibly by Benedict of Aniane (†c. 821) and were already being recited in a number of monasteries, most notably Einsiedeln, by the following century.[88] Originally appended to the Divine Office or to the Psalter,[89] and modelled on the breviary, which contained the prayers for the eight canonical hours, the Little Office gradually evolved into a compendium of texts expressing devotion to the Mother of God. These include Marian hymns, Psalms, Old Testament passages containing Marian typologies, New Testament

---

[83] *Judgement and Passion.* Where Fulton's argument falls down to some extent is in her specific identification of the justice/mercy divide with this period. She does not give sufficient consideration to the long history in the Greek Church of this *topos*.

[84] See chapter on Immediate Co-operation.

[85] *Sermon for the Nativity of the BVM,* 46, 7, *PL* 144, 761B, *TMPM*, III, 882. See *MLM*, pp. 108 and 113.

[86] See Graef, *Doctrine and Devotion*, I, 208.

[87] See *PL* 145, 933C-941A.

[88] See José María Canal, 'El oficio parvo de la Virgen de 1000 a 1250', *Ephemerides Mariologicae,* 15 (1965), 464-475, who provides a list of the principal personalities who mention it and the monasteries in which it was being recited (p. 464). See also Roger S. Wieck, 'The Book of Hours', in *The Liturgy of the Medieval Church* ed. by Thomas J. Heffernan and E. Ann Matter (Kalamazoo: Medieval Institute Publications Western Michigan University, 2001), pp. 473-513.

[89] On the Divine Office see *The Divine Office in the Latin Middle Ages: Methodology and Source Studies, Regional Developments, Hagiography,* ed. by Margot Fassler, and Rebecca A. Baltzer, (Oxford: Oxford University Press, 2000), and John Harper, *The Forms and Orders of Western Liturgy from the Tenth to the Eighteenth Century: A Historical Introduction and Guide for Students and Musicians* (Oxford: The Clarendon Press, 1991).

accounts of the key events in the Virgin's life, prayers and litanies.[90] By the middle of the eleventh century recitation of the Office had become virtually *de rigueur* in ecclesiastical circles. Innocent III († 1216) included a daily Marian office in the reformed Roman breviary, which also led to it's recital by the Franciscans since the rule written by Francis († 1226) included the requirement that all members of the order use the Roman form of the breviary. It was largely through the third order of the Franciscans that the Little Office also become popular amongst the laity, leading to the development of the Book of Hours.

A simplified version of the breviary, the Book of Hours arose out of growing interest in private devotion among lay people and the rise in lay literacy, combined with increasing devotion to the Virgin Mary. The Books were devotional tools, which borrowed from a number of liturgical texts including the Missal, the Breviary the Lectionary, and the Psalter, and were intended to guide the faithful in their individual meditations. They began with a liturgical calendar listing the feast days of the Church year, followed by short extracts from each of the four Gospels. The central text was a cycle of daily prayers dedicated to the Virgin Mary and organised according to the eight canonical hours, modelled on the Little Office. The Book of Hours was completed by the seven penitential psalms, litanies, and prayers to the Virgin and various saints.

Of particular interest is a short Saturday Marian Office known as *The Portiforium of St. Wulstan*, possibly copied from a Winchester source and written in 1065,[91] in which the Virgin is praised in a manner reminiscent of Byzantine Mariology and attributed powers hitherto almost unheard of in the West:

> She is [...] the consolation of the wretched, the refuge of sinners and the restoration of all believers. Whatever of good the universe has, therefore, it has from her from whom the beginning of our salvation flows. May she deign always to help us, her venerators, and piously by her prayers purify us from all faults and may she grant that we contemplate and praise her highly in heaven.[92]

In its first lection the *Portiforium* also makes an oblique reference to the Theophilus story, proof that the legend was sufficiently well-known at the time not to warrant further explanation.

---

[90] See José María Canal, 'Oficio parvo de la Virgen: formas viejas y formas nuevas', *Ephemerides Mariologicae*, 11 (1961), 497-525, Jean, Leclercq, 'Formes successives de l'office votif de la Vierge', *Ephemerides liturgicae*, 72 (1958), 294- 301, and 'Formes anciennes de l'office marial', *Ephemerides liturgicae*, 74 (1960), 89-102, and Rebecca A. Baltzer, 'The Little Office of the Virgin and Mary's Role at Paris', in *The Divine Office in the Latin Middle Ages*, ed. by Margot Fassler and Rebecca A. Baltzer.

[91] *The Portiforium of St Wulstan*, ed. by Anselm Hughes, 2 vols., Henry Bradshaw Society, 89–90 (London: Faith Press, 1958–60) and see Mary Clayton, *The Cult of the Virgin*, pp. 65-89, on which much of the discussion that follows relies.

[92] Quoted from Clayton, *The Cult of the Virgin*, p. 79, n. 85.

A Psalter written in Winchester in 1060[93] contains a prayer for the Virgin's intercession which relies to an even greater extent on the Theophilus legend, though again he is not directly mentioned. It is worth quoting the final part of the prayer at some length since it shows that Mary was already being invoked with considerable fervour in the West around the turn of the new millennium, and typifies a style that was to dominate Marian prayer over the next centuries, in which the repentant sinner throws himself upon the mercy of the benign yet powerful Virgin, seeking not only her aid in receiving God's forgiveness but her protection from the wiles of the devil:[94]

> For you, after God, are the right way for the erring, the life of the dying, the hope of those in danger, the haven of the storm-tossed, rest for the toiling, a spring for the thirsty, the consolation of the sad, the mediatress between God and man, the most happy virgin and most fruitful mother and safest support of Christians, guardian and a mainstay of those who have recourse to you, readiest and soundest defence of Christians. For I know and I truly know that in you is the true medicine of the infirm, the recovery of the despairing, O deliverer of men, most blessed mother of my Lord, most pious consoler of the afflicted and most prompt supporter of the fallen, who alone was made the door of life, alone swept away the dangers of life, alone suckled the price of life. In you is our refuge, in you our consolation, you are the restoration of our life. Receive, I implore, my prayer and offer it to the Lord my God, because your prayer is more powerful than every prayer, your prayer is more acceptable than every prayer, your request is more pleasing than all sacrifice. *Winchester Psalter*[95]

The use of anaphora, unusual in the West at this time, may indicate that the author had some familiarity with Eastern texts.

From around the same time is a version of the prayer, *Singularis meriti*, written by Maurilius of Rouen († after 1067), though long attributed to Anselm of Canterbury, which lays great emphasis on Mary's mercy, and displays the attitude of self-abasement typical of this period:

> O, most merciful, through whom the whole world has been saved, I beseech you to intercede for me, wretched and stained with every sort of iniquity, so that the Lord might grant my unhappy soul a love of purity, a fondness for modesty and uninterrupted progress in chastity. For, woebegone that I am, I have lost the grace of innocence and holiness; I have violated the holy temple many times. But what purpose does it serve to recall my obscenities to chaste ears. I am horrified, Lady, horrified, and, with the reproof of my conscience, shamefully naked, I blush in your presence. To whom should I, dying, offer my wounds, to whom shall I turn, to whom shall I wail about my suffering? How could I ever

---

[93] See Francis Wormald, *The Winchester Psalter* (Greenwich, CT: New York Graphic Society, 1973).

[94] See Barré, *Prières anciennes*, pp. 140-42 and Mary Clayton, *Cult of the Virgin*, pp. 114-17.

[95] Translation from Mary Clayton, *Cult of the Virgin*, pp. 117, n. 78.

expect the benefits of a cure from someone else if the one source of eternal mercy is closed to me?[96]

In the same prayer Maurilius also makes mention of the story of Mary's self-designation as the 'Mother of Mercy' popularised by Odo of Cluny (see above), which he considers to be conclusive proof that there is no better way of receiving mercy than by turning to her:

> Behold, O Lady, a prodigal son, who, with bare and wounded feet, has come from that place of horrors, from that fog of filth and foetidness, and sighing cries out and calls for his Mother, recalling the many times you took care of him, clothed him and made excuses for him to the Father. Certainly that Father is most pious and benign, but you too are a Mother sweet and gentle.

The prayer goes on to use the by-now standard *topos* of Mary mitigating her Son's judgement, appealing to two powerful images of Mary's compassion, her comforting of the Christ child and her suffering with him in his Passion, which justify the rhetorical: 'Who then is more powerful than you in merit when it comes to placating the wrath of the Judge?' The prayer concludes with a plea for Mary's continuing protection: 'Be close to me in perils, in afflictions, in the beginning of my joy. For if I am worthy of obtaining it [joy] through God's gift and yours, I will certainly not fear complete perdition in the least.'

The liturgy for the Marian feasts also promoted the image of Mary as a powerful protector not just of sinners but of the Church.[97] Just as in the East, the Virgin came to be seen as a bulwark against heresy, as is evidenced by the eleventh-century Roman liturgy for the feasts of the Purification, Annunciation and Assumption, which includes a responsory with this refrain: 'Rejoice, O Virgin Mary, you alone have defeated all the heresies of the entire world.'[98]

Eusebius Bruno († 1081), as a demonstration of the power of the Virgin to rescue even the most desperate from perdition, makes mention of both the stories of Mary of Egypt and Theophilus. For Eusebius, Mary is a sure protection against falling into the clutches of the devil as death approaches:

> The end of days is already approaching. Cruel death is hot on my heels, and aches tell of the imminent arrival of their mistress. Against her [death] there is no moat, no tower, no hope of defence. Only he who knows that he is without guilt does not experience fear. As to me, a scoundrel weighed down with faults, I

---

[96] See *PL* 158, 146B-148B, Henri Barré, *Prières anciennes*, pp. 183-84, *TMSM*, III, 45-47 for the full prayer. On the attribution of the prayer see André Wilmart, *Auteurs spirituels et textes dévots du moyen âge latin: Études d'histoire littéraire* (Paris: Bloud et Gay, 1932), pp. 480-81.
[97] On Medieval Marian liturgy see Ann-Katrin Johannson, 'Jalons liturgiques pour une histoire du culte de la vierge dans l'Occident latin (Ve-XIe siècle)', in *Marie: Le culte de la Vierge dans la société médiévale*, pp. 407-39.
[98] See *TMSM*, III, 136, n. 6.

should despair completely were you not a refuge for me. *Oratio ad sanctam Mariam*[99]

He concludes his hymn by invoking his service of Mary in the cause of his avoidance of damnation: 'May I not enter the gates of the underworld without you having presented me to Christ; then bear witness that I have been your servant since birth.'[100]

Godescalcus of Limburg († 1098) provides evidence of growing belief in the universal mediation of Mary, when he makes it clear that her mediation is not just confined to her historical role but that nobody can go to God except through her: 'In you, he reduced his omnipotence to the point where he does not reveal his presence to anyone without you. For, as God he did not come to mankind without you, in the same way man will never reach God without you.'[101] Like many of the later Greek Fathers, in this sequence he also associates her bodily assumption with her mediation.

Anselm of Lucca's († 1086) writings are filled with pleas for the Virgin's intercession. He sees Mary's mercy as a counterbalance to the stern judgement of her Son, who 'forced, as it were, by your intervention, repeals the sentence of most just condemnation'. He appeals to Mary, because 'the Kingdom of Heaven suffers violence thanks to you (Matthew 11. 12) and by your intercession, the violent take possession of it', in other words, even those who have committed heinous sins are admitted to heaven thanks to the Virgin's intercession.[102] Anselm also links Mary's intercessory powers with her Assumption, though he avoids the issue of the fate of her body. Her Son has raised her, according to Anselm, 'above the glory of all mortals and the dignity of the angels' in order that she might serve as a 'counterweight to his severity', to the extent that he is 'almost constrained' by her intervention to revoke 'the sentence of a most just condemnation'. Elsewhere Anselm is even more explicit about the prerogative that Christ gave to Mary: she has been given the power to obtain forgiveness for sinners so long as time will last. This power is greater than that of Peter, and therefore of the Church, a somewhat subversive sentiment that one also finds in various miracle stories where Mary saves those the Church has condemned. Only at the Last Judgement will Christ make a final pronouncement condemning those who are beyond redemption:

---

[99] Henri Barré, *Prières anciennes*, p. 148.

[100] *Oratio ad sanctam Mariam*, Henri Barré, *Prières anciennes*, p. 147-48. See M. Garrido Bonaño, 'El servicio a la Virgen en los himnos medievales', *Estudios Marianos*, 51 (1986), 65-76.

[101] *Sequentia 'Exulta, exaltata'*, *AH*, 50, 343-44, *TMSM*, III, 65.

[102] *Oratio ad suscipiendum corpus Christi 1*, Henri Barré, *Prières anciennes*, p. 227. The full text of Anselm's five prayers composed for Countess Matilda of Tuscany are to be found in André Wilmart 'Cinque textes de prière composés par Anselme de Lucques pour la Comtesse Mathilde', *Revue d'ascétique et de mystique*, 19 (1938), 23-72 (pp. 49-72).

He ascended into heaven and gloriously left all the inheritance of mercy to his Mother, and he substituted us for himself, as children, in the person of his favourite disciple, with a document confirmed by the apostolic faith and fulfilled with the integrity of a sincere mind, so that she might become all the more well-disposed towards indulgence, in that the visceral charity of a mother would cause her to overcome, through an abundance of piety, every carnal affection. He who is hidden in the bosom of the Father leaves to his Mother's judgement all that space of time in which her forgiveness is not excluded, so as not to see our shame until the definitive judgement on the Last Day. So, he hides our sins 'in his exceeding charity' (Ephesians 2. 4) and the inestimable richness of his mercy. He sends the angels so that they might continuously bring him the prayers and offerings of his Mother, and he himself transmits them to the face of the Father, who cannot refuse the Mother what she asks. Peter, who received the keys of heaven, opens the gates to the Queen of heaven and earth, Mother of her Lord, because he absolves those for whom she obtains indulgence. *Oratio ad sanctam Mariam, 3*[103]

Marian litanies appeared from about the eleventh century, the most celebrated of these being the Litany of Loreto, which already contained seventy-three invocations in a late twelfth-century manuscript.[104] This extract from a twelfth-century sung litany gives an idea of the elaborateness of some of these prayers, similar in style in some respects to Greek *chairetismoí:*.[105]

Sancta Maria, porta cœli, | introitus paradisi, | sacrarium spiritus sancti, ora pro nobis benedictum | ventris tui fructum. | Sancta Maria, stirps patriarcharum, | vaticinium prophetarum, | solatium apostolorum, | rosa martyrum, | prædictio confessorum, | lilium virginium, ora. | Sancta Maria, spes humilium, | refugium pauperum, | portus naufragantium, | medicina infirmorum, ora. | Sancta Maria, imperatrix reginarum, | salvatrix animarum, ora. Sancta Maria, lucidissima | maris stella, | salus mundi, ora. | Sancta Maria, claritas cœlorum, | destructio inferorum, | restauratio | et emundatio | cœli et terræ, ora. | Sancta Maria, terror dæmoniorum, | pavor spirituum immundorum. || Sancta Maria, indulgentia peccatorum, | veniæ gremium, | pacis asylum, ora. | Sancta Maria, aula æterni regis, | lectulus Salomonis, | palatium veri pacifici, | cubile cœlestis sponsi, ora. [...] Sancta Maria, melliflua miseratio miserorum, | dulce solamen afflictorum, ora. || Sancta Maria, virtus fragilium, | constantia trementium, | fortitudo laborantium, ora. | Sancta Maria benedicta protectio | humani generis, portus et susceptio | ad te confugientium | aureum misericordiæ | propiciatorium, ora. | Sancta Maria, via vitæ, | causa viæ, | omnis bona copia. | Sancta Maria, laus animarum | sanctorum, | spes reorum, | pes lapsorum, | indeficiens gaudium angelorum, ora. [...]Sancta Maria quæ Theophilum | diabolo manicipatum | potentur eripuisiti, | et aliis quam pluribus pæne desperatis | succurristi, ora. | Sancta Maria ex qua

---

[103] Henri Barré, *Prières anciennes*, p. 229, *TMSM*, III, 57-58.
[104] It is highly probable that the litanies of the saints, which undoubtedly included Mary, were introduced by the Syrian Pope Sergius (687-701). On the history of the litanies and the influence of the Byzantines, see Meersseman, *Der Hymnos Akathistos im Abendland*, II, 45-60, and Ignazio Calabuig and Salvatore M. Perrella, 'Le litanie della Beata Virgine: storia, teologia, significato', *Marianum*, 70 (2008), 103-202.
[105] See section on Praise and see Meersseman, *Der Hymnos Akathistos im Abendland*, I, 77-79.

salus oritur, / per quam culpa moritur, / spes homini restauratur, ora. // Sancta Maria, quæ castitatis lilium / genuisti miseris in auxilium, ora. / Sancta Maria, tu firmata in Sion, / virga florens Aaron, / madidum vellus Gedeon, ora. // Sancta Maria, quae parvi et magni / salvatoris Christi / templum extitisti / et virgo inviolate permansisiti, ora. / Sancta Maria, tu floris et roris, / panis et pastoris, / virginium regina, / rosa sine spine, ora. / Sancta Maria quam collaudat cœlestis curia, / cujus viscera / contra moris fœdera / ediderunt filium, ora. / Sancta Maria, virgiuium lucerna, / per quam fulsit lux superna, ora. [...]Sancta Maria, cujus mirabilis / et laudabilis / est virginitas, / quam totam possedit / et illuminavit / divinitas, ora. / Sancta Maria, filia Jerusalem, / quæ protulisti in Bethlehem / gloriosam progeniem, ora. // Sancta Maria, quam laudant adolescentulæ, / sponsus vocat in meridie, / invocant miserorum animæ, ora. / Sancta Maria, cujus forma desiderabilis, / virtus ineffabilis, / suavitas inæstimabilis, ora. Sancta Maria, nobilis puerpera, / mater sine macula, / quae lavantem maculum sæculi / genuisti, ora. / Sancta Maria, cujus germen divinum / calcat caput serpentinum, / tergit fletum vespertium / reddit lætum matutinum, ora. / Sancta Maria, tu castitatis lilium, / tuum precare filium, / qui salus est humilium, / ne nos pro nostro vitio / in districto judicio / subjiciat supplicio, / sed nos tua sancta prece / mundans a peccati fæce, / collocet in lucis domo, / quam per te recepit omnis homo.

(Holy Mary, gate of heaven, entrance to paradise, shrine of the Holy Spirit, pray for us, blessed the fruit of your womb. Holy Mary, of the stock of the patriarchs, prophecy of the prophets, consolation of the apostles, rose of the martyrs, teaching of the confessors, lily of the virgins, pray. Holy Mary, hope of the humble, refuge of the poor, harbour of the shipwrecked, medicine of the sick, pray. Holy Mary, Empress of queens, saviour of souls, pray. Holy Mary, most bright star of the sea, salvation of the world, pray. Holy Mary, clarity of the heavens, destruction of hell, restoration and cleansing of heaven and earth, pray. Holy Mary, terror of demons, fear of unclean spirits. Holy Mary, indulgence of sinners, womb of pardon, sanctuary of peace, pray, Holy Mary, palace of the eternal King, couch of Solomon, palace of the true peacemaker, marriage bed of the heavenly Spouse, pray. [...] Holy Mary, honeyed compassion of the wretched, sweet solace of the afflicted, pray. Holy Mary, strength of the weak, constancy of the trembling, fortitude of those who labour, pray. Holy Mary, blessed protection of the human race, harbour and protection of those who flee to you, a golden refuge of mercy and atonement, pray. Holy Mary, the way of life, cause of the way, overflowing with all goodness. Holy Mary, praise of holy souls, hope of the wicked, aid of the lapsed, constant joy of the angels, pray. [...] Holy Mary, you who snatched away Theophilus from the devil and who have given succour to many others who were almost despairing, pray. Holy Mary, from whom salvation rises, through whom guilt dies, through whom hope is restored to man pray. Holy Mary, you who are a chaste lily have generated hope as an aid for the wretched, pray. Holy Mary, you, established in Sion, flowering rod of Aaron, pray. Holy Mary, moist fleece of Gideon, pray. Remaining a virgin intact, you the temple of the great and small Saviour, Christ, pray. Holy Mary, queen of virgins, of the Flower, of the Dew, of the Bread, and of the Shepherd, rose without thorns, pray. Holy Mary, whom the court of heaven praises, whose womb produced a Son contrary to the law of nature, pray. Holy Mary, lamp of virgins, through whom shone the supernal light, pray. [...] Holy Mary, whose virginity is marvellous and praiseworthy, whom divinity entirely possessed and illuminated, pray. Holy Mary, daughter of Jerusalem, who produced in Bethlehem a glorious child, pray. Holy Mary, whom young girls praise, whom the Spouse calls at midday, whom the wretched souls invoke, pray. Holy Mary, whose form is desirable, virtue ineffable, sweetness inestimable, pray. Holy Mary, noble birth-giver, Mother without stain, who generated he who washes away the stains of the world, pray. Holy Mary, whose divine bud crushed the head of the serpent, wiped away the tears of evening, restored the joy of morning, pray. You lily of chastity, may you pray to your Son, who is the salvation of the humble, lest he subject us to punishment for our vice through his harsh judgement, but through your holy prayer, may he cleanse us from the excrement of sin, may he place us in the house of light, that light that every man obtained through you. *Letania de domina nostra virgine Maria*[106]

Another development around this time which led to greater identification of the people with Mary was the use of liturgical dramas known variously as *Offitium, Representatio, Ludus* and *Mysterium* which were performed for the most important feasts of the year including those of the Virgin. The texts were nearly always in Latin, drawn from the Office of the feast day and were generally performed by acolytes.[107] It was only much later, in the late thirteenth century, that performances in the vernacular developed in an extra-liturgical setting.[108] It is also in this period that the genre known as the *Mariale*, born in the ninth century, began to gain in popularity. These were collections of Marian tractates, homilies, hymns, and so on, which were intended for pastoral use and private piety. The term is sometimes also used for a collection of Marian homilies by a single writer.[109]

In the twelfth century the name of Mary first began to appear in the *Confitior*, recited during the penitential rite at the beginning of the Mass. The General Chapter of the Cistercians decreed in 1184, followed by other orders, that the name of Mary be placed before that of the other saints: 'I confess to God and to blessed Mary, and to all the saints…'[110] A further innovation was the use of Marian Psalters, in which the traditional antiphons which preceded the text of the 150 Psalms were replaced with short Christological or Marian exegeses.[111]

Three of the four great Marian antiphons of the Middle Ages came into wide use around this time. By far the most influential was the *Salve regina* (perhaps

---

[106] Latin text from Mone, *Lateinische Hymnen*, II, n. 505.

[107] See, among others, Karl Young, *The Drama of the Medieval Church*, 2 vols. (Oxford: The Clarendon Press, 1933), Hardin Craig, *English Religious Drama of the Middle Ages* (Oxford: The Clarendon Press, 1960), Osborne B Hardison, *Christian Rite and Christian Drama in the Middle Ages: Essays in the Origin and Early History of Modern Drama* (Baltimore: Johns Hopkins University Press, 1965)

[108] See Corrado Maggioni, *Benedetto il frutto*, p. 108.

[109] See Jean Longère, 'Le *Orationes ad sanctam Mariam*', p. 586.

[110] See Corrado Maggioni, *Benedetto il frutto*, p. 104.

[111] See Graef, *Doctrine and Devotion*, I, 232-33, and Anne Winston Allen, *Stories of the Rose: The Making of the Rosary in the Middle Ages* (Pennsylvania: The Pennsylvania State University Press, 1992), p. 15.

eleventh century) with its powerful portrayal of the Virgin as a source of mercy
and consolation amidst the troubles of this life:

> *Salve, Regina misericordiae; / vita, dulcedo et spes nostra, salve. / Ad te clamamus, / exsules*
> *filii Hevae. / Ad te suspiramus, gementes et flentes / in hac lacrimarum valle. / Eia ergo,*
> *advocata nostra, / illos tuos misericordes oculos ad nos converte. / Et Iesum, benedictum fructum*
> *ventris tui, / nobis post hoc exsilium ostende. / O clemens, o pia, o dulcis Maria.*

> (Hail, Queen, Mother of mercy, hail, our life, our sweetness, and our hope. To
> you do we cry, banished children of Eve; to you we send up our sighs, mourning
> and weeping in this valley of tears. Turn, then, our advocate, your eyes of mercy
> towards us, and after this, our exile, show us the blessed fruit of your womb,
> Jesus. O clement, O merciful, O sweet Mary)[112]

Of uncertain attribution, the *Salve* was included in the liturgy of Cluny around
1135 from whence the practice spread to other foundations. In 1218 the
Cistercians began to sing it daily and by the middle of the thirteenth century it
was being sung in all Dominican and Franciscan monasteries, and in the evening
devotions of confraternities and guilds.[113] The *Alma Redemptoris Mater,* possibly
composed by Hermannus Contractus († 1054), was originally a processional
antiphon for Sext in the *Liturgy of the Hours* for the Feast of the Ascension, and
is one of four seasonal antiphons sung or recited in the *Liturgy of the Hours* after
Compline or Vespers:[114]

> *Alma redemptoris mater, quae pervia caeli / porta manes et stella maris, succurre cadenti,*
> */ surgere qui curat, populo, tu, quae genuisti, / natura mirante tuum sanctum genitorem, / virgo*
> *prius ac posterius, Gabrielis ab ore / sumens illud Ave, peccatorum miserere.*

> (Gracious Mother of the Redeemer, you who remain the open gate of heaven,
> the star of the sea, help a people who has fallen yet strives to rise again. To the

---

[112] Latin quoted from Walter Berschin, 'Early Medieval Latin Poetry of Mary', in *The
Church and Mary* ed. by Robert N. Swanson, pp. 112-25 (p. 116). As Berschin notes, the
text was later modified to read 'Salve, *Regina,* Mater misericordiae', and 'dulcis *Virgo*
Maria' (n. 6).

[113] 'The Dominicans at Bologna chanted it daily at Compline after a miracle in 1230,
and the custom was adopted by the entire Order in 1250. The chapter general of the
Franciscans at Metzin 1249 prescribed all of these antiphons for Compline.' See Hugh
T. Henry, 'Salve Regina', in *The Catholic Encyclopaedia,* ed. by Charles George
Herbermann, Edward Pace, and others, 15 vols (New York: Appleton, 1907-12), in *New
Advent* <http://www.newadvent.org/cathen/13409a.htm> XII (1912) [accessed 6 April
2006]. See also Corrado Maggioni, *Benedetto il frutto,* pp 116-19, *MLM,* 12, and Graef,
Doctrine and Devotion, I, 229.

[114] See Walter Berschin, 'Early Medieval Latin Poetry of Mary', pp. 118-20, and Herbert
Musurillo, 'The Medieval Hymn *Alma Redemptoris*: A Linguistic Analysis', *The Classical
Journal,* 52 (1957), 171-174.

wonderment of nature you gave birth to him who made you, yet remained a virgin after as before. You who received Gabriel's greeting, have mercy on sinners.)[115]

The *Ave regina caelorum* (twelfth century)[116] was sung at Nones on the feast of the Annunciation, while the *Regina caeli* (probably thirteenth century)[117] was sung at Vespers on Easter Sunday.

Anselm of Canterbury's († 1109) three prayers to the Virgin, in which he portrays her as a tender and merciful Mother, had a major impact on Medieval Mariology.[118] Above all they introduced a new tone of affection that was to become increasingly dominant in the coming centuries.[119] As Jean Fournée puts it, 'if he did not say everything, one can affirm that he anticipated everything. In the eleventh century, he was at the origin of the Marian current of the twelfth century.'[120] Unlike many of his fellow churchmen he does not make a strict division between the mercy of Mary and the wrath of Jesus, instead seeing both as acting in tandem. Both are offended by sin and both can show mercy. His idea that the sinner can seek refuge in one when the other has been offended is essentially a rhetorical device designed to encourage the faithful to seek forgiveness, since, in reality, any sin offends both equally:

> Seeing myself, O Lady, faced with the all-powerful justice of the severe judge, and considering the unbearable vehemence of his wrath, I ponder the enormity of my sins and the gravity of the torments that they merit. Troubled, therefore, by so much horror, O most clement Lady, and terrified by such a great fear, of whom shall I implore a more instantaneous intervention if not from she whose womb nourished the reconciliation of the world? In whom shall I hope more assuredly for rapid assistance if not from she of whom the conciliation of the world came? O what intercession will more easily obtain forgiveness for guilt if not that of she who gave suck to the just punisher of each and every sin, to the merciful reconciler? Just as it is impossible, O most blessed One, that you would forget these merits, which are so singular for you and so necessary for us, so, O most meek One, it is impossible to believe that you will not have mercy on the wretched who implore you. [...] When I sinned against the Son I irritated his

---

[115] Text from *The Oxford Book of Medieval Latin Verse* ed. by F. J. E. Raby (Oxford: The Clarendon Press, 1959), p 157.

[116] 1. 'Hail Queen of Heaven, / hail Mistress of the angles, / hail root, hail gate / through which the Light of the world arose. 2. Rejoice glorious Virgin, more beautiful than all, / farewell O most graceful, / pray for us to Christ'.

[117] 'Queen of Heaven, rejoice, alleluia, for He whom you were worthy to bear, alleluia, / has risen, as he said, alleluia. / Pray for us to God, alleluia. V. Rejoice and be glad, O Virgin Mary, alleluia. R. For the Lord has truly risen, alleluia'.

[118] See chapter on Remote Redemption for further discussion of Anselm's importance.

[119] See Lawrence Cunningham, 'Mary in Catholic Doctrine and Practice', *Theology Today*, 56 (1999), 307-318, and Graef, *Doctrine and Devotion*, I, 214.

[120] 'Les orientations doctrinales de l'iconographie mariale à la fin de l'époque romane', *Centre international d'études romanes*, 1 (1971), 23-56 (p. 26).

Mother, and nor did I offend his Mother without causing injury to the Son. What will you do then, sinner? Where will you take refuge, sinner? Who will reconcile me with the Son if his Mother is my enemy? Who will placate the Mother on my behalf if the Son is angry? Yet, even though you are both equally offended, are you not also both equally clement? Therefore, whoever is guilty before the just God should seek refuge in the merciful Mother of the merciful God. Whoever is guilty of having offended the Mother should take refuge in the merciful Son of the benevolent Mother. Whoever is guilty of offending both should take refuge in both. *Oratio 6, 1-2*[121]

Eadmer of Canterbury (†c. 1124), Anselm's disciple, identifies Mary as the mother of humanity both because it is through her that Christ became our brother and because Christ assigned her this role on the Cross: 'O Lady, if your Son has become our brother thanks to you, have you not become our Mother thanks to him? In fact, when he was on the point of facing death for us on the Cross, he said to John, that is to a man in whose human condition we were all included: "Behold thy mother!" (John 19. 27)'.[122] Eadmer goes even further than his teacher, Anselm, suggesting that salvation will come more quickly if one prays to the Virgin rather than directly to Christ, because he will instantly grant her prayers.[123] Eadmer also asserts that Mary will come to the aid of anyone who invokes her, even if they don't merit it: 'If the name of his Mother is invoked, her merits have such strong powers of intercession that whoever prays is answered even if their merits are not adequate for the request.'[124]

Geoffrey of Vendôme (†c. 1132), however, sets certain conditions for receiving Mary's aid:

> Blessed Mary, Mother, Virgin and intact Bride, in her great mercy, will obtain everything up above from her most merciful Son so that none of those for whom she has prayed a single time may perish. This is not surprising because, if she wishes, she can save the whole world. And she would certainly be most willing to pray for the whole world, so that the whole world would be saved, if it became worthy of her prayers. It is absolutely true, as we have said, that she, by praying to her omnipotent Son, can obtain everything that she desires. However, she does not pray for those who always wish to sin. *In omni festivitate b. Mariae*[125]

Geoffrey goes on to illustrate Mary's mercy and her power to obtain forgiveness, even in the most desperate cases, by recounting the story of Theophilus.

Hermann of Tournai († c. 1147) repeats the well-worn belief that Mary is capable of softening her Son's ire: 'If, perchance, our judge is angry because of our sins, let

---

[121] *PL* 158, 950B-951C. *TMSM*, III, 86-87. See *The Prayers and Meditations of Saint Anselm with the Proslogion*, trans. by Benedicta Ward (Harmondsworth: Penguin, 1973).

[122] *On the Conception of Holy Mary*, *TMSM*, III, 118.

[123] *On the Excellence of the B.V.M.*, 4, *PL* 159, 570A.

[124] *On the Excellence of the B.V.M.*, *PL* 159, 570B.

[125] *PL* 157, 268B-C.

us not despair because his Mother is also our Mother. May our merciful Mother therefore placate her merciful Son on behalf of her guilty children.'[126]

By far the most celebrated words of the Middle Ages on the protection that Mary affords to those who call upon her are by Bernard of Clairvaux († 1153), whose influence on Marian devotion, both in his own lifetime and in the centuries to come, was greater than any other churchman. It is not so much that he says anything radically new about Mary but that he speaks of her with unmatched eloquence and fervour, justifiably earning the epithet 'mellifluous doctor', though perhaps somewhat less justifiably that of 'Marian doctor':[127]

> When the storms of temptation burst upon thee, when thou seest thyself driven upon the rocks of tribulation, look up at the star, call upon Mary. When buffeted by the billows of pride, or ambition, or hatred, or jealousy, look up at the star, call upon Mary. Should anger, or avarice, or fleshly desires violently assail the little vessel of thy soul, look up at the star, call upon Mary. [...] With her for guide, thou shalt never go astray; whilst invoking her, thou shalt never lose heart; so long as she is in thy mind, thou art safe from deception; whilst she holds thy hand, thou canst not fall; under her protection, thou hast nothing to fear; if she walks before thee, thou shalt not grow weary; if she shows thee favour, thou shalt reach the goal. *Second Sermon on the Glories of the Virgin Mother Mary*[128]

Bernard writes powerfully of Mary's universal mediation, explicitly stating that God wishes us to receive all grace through her:

> Remove from the heavens the material sun which enlightens the world, and what becomes of the day. Remove Mary, remove this star of the sea, of life's 'great and spacious sea' (Psalms 103. 25) and what is left to us but a cloud of involving gloom, and the 'shadow of death' (Job 10. 22), and a darkness

---

[126] *De Incarnatione Christi, 9*, PL 180, 37A.

[127] Gabriele Roschini uses the epithet, in his *Il dottore mariano: studio sulla dottrina mariana di s. Bernardo di Chiaravalle* (Rome: Edizioni Cattoliche, 1953). Jean Leclercq, however, disagrees in his 'Saint Bernard et la dévotion médiévale envers Marie,' *Revue d'ascétique et mystique*, 30 (1954), 361-75, arguing that Bernard did not contribute anything to doctrine. See also his *La femme et les femmes dans l'oeuvre de Saint Bernard* (Paris: Téqui, 1982). Henri Barré, 'Saint Bernard théologien', *Analecti Sacra Ordinis Cisterciencis*, 9 (1953), pp. 92-113, takes the middle ground. Antonio Montanari, 'San Bernardo di Clairvaux e la sua scuola', in *SDM* I, 637-61 (pp. 638-41), largely agrees with Leclercq. See also Lamy, 'L'influence de saint Bernard sur la théologie mariale de la fin du Moyen Âge', in *La Vierge dans la tradition cistercienne, Bulletin de la société française d'études mariales*, 54e session de la S.F.E.M., Abbaye Notre-Dame d'Orval, 1998 (Paris: Médiaspaul, 1999), pp. 193-216, and see *Respice stellam: Maria in San Bernardo e nella tradizione cistercense, Atti del convegno internazionale*, ed. by Ignazio M. Calabuig (Roma, Marianum 21-24 October 1991), (Rome: Marianum, 1993), M. André, *Ombre et splendeur: La foi de la Vierge Mère d'après les écrits de Saint Bernard* (Nicolet, Québec: Centre Marial Canadien , 1954) and chapter 4 of Burcht Pranger's *Bernard of Clairvaux and the Shape of Monastic Thought: Broken Dreams* (Leiden: Brill, 1994).

[128] *SBS*, pp. 37-38.

exceeding dense? Therefore, my dearest brethren, with every fibre, every feeling of our hearts, with all the affections of our minds, and with all the ardour of our souls, let us honour Mary, because such is the will of God, Who would have us to obtain everything through the hands of Mary. *Sermon for the Feast of the Nativity of the Blessed Virgin Mary*[129]

Using the metaphor of the aqueduct, which became one of the most famous Marian images of the Middle Ages, he explains how God's grace flows to all through the Virgin, just as prayers may be directed to him through her:[130]

But, my brother, whatsoever thou hast a mind to offer to the Lord be sure to entrust it to Mary, so that the gift shall return to the Giver of all grace through the same channel by which thou didst obtain it. God of course had the power, if He so pleased, to communicate His grace without the interposition of the Aqueduct. But he wanted to provide us with a needful intermediary [...]. Consequently, unless thou wouldst have thy gift rejected, be careful to commit to Mary the little thou desirest to offer, that the Lord may receive it through her hands. *Sermon for the Feast of the Nativity of the Blessed Virgin Mary*[131]

He also clarifies why it is that we have need of a second mediator after Christ, basing his explanation on a notion that we have already encountered, that Christ is too awesome a figure to be approached directly:

But perhaps thou standest in awe of the Divine Majesty of Jesus? For although He has become man He has not ceased to be God. Perhaps thou desirest to have an advocate even with Him? If so have recourse to Mary. [...] Assuredly the Son will listen to the Mother and the Father will listen to the Son. My little children, behold the sinners ladder, behold the main source of my confidence, the principal ground of my hope [...] Prudent Virgin! She does not ask either wisdom, as did Solomon (3 Kings 3:9), or riches, or honour, or power, but only grace. For it is by grace alone we shall be saved.' *Sermon for the Feast of the Nativity of the Blessed Virgin Mary*[132]

He repeats the idea that Mary is a second mediator in another sermon, where he once again makes clear that Christ alone would have been enough but that it was more appropriate (*congruum*) that both sexes be represented in our renewal

---

[129] *SBS*, pp. 85-86.
[130] See also his *Sermon for the Sunday within the Octave of the Assumption*, where he says: 'To all she opens wide the bosom of her mercy so that all may receive of her fullness (John 1. 16): captives deliverance, the sick health, the sad consolation, sinners pardon, the just grace, the angels joy, the whole Blessed Trinity glory, and the Person of the Son the Substance of His Human Nature: so that "there is no one that can hide himself from the heat" of her charity (Psalms 18. 7).' In *SBS*, p. 208.
[131] *SBS*, pp. 86 and 103.
[132] *SBS*, pp. 86-7.

just as they were in our fall. He goes on to say, once again, that Christ may be too awesome for some sinners to approach, because, in their eyes, his humanity is overshadowed by his divinity, so that Mary, who is entirely human, may present an easier path to forgiveness:

> A truly faithful and powerful 'Mediator of God and men is the Man Jesus Christ' (I Timothy, 2. 5); but the Majesty of his Godhead inspires mortals with fear. His Manhood seems to be swallowed up in His Divinity, not that there is any real confusion of the Natures, but because His human affections are in a manner deified [*absorbta videtur in divinitatem humanitas, non quod mutat sit substantia, sed affection deificata*] So great a Mediator is Christ that we have need of another to mediate between Him and us, and for this we can find none so qualified as Mary. [...] Why should human fragility fear to have recourse to Mary? In her is found nothing austere, nothing to terrify: everything about her is full of sweetness. She has for all only the sweetness of milk and the softness of wool.' *Sermon for the Sunday within the Octave of the Assumption*[133]

Bernard also links Mary's intercessory role with her Assumption, and repeats the familiar *topos* of the division between justice and mercy: 'Our exiled race has sent home an Advocate, who, being the Mother of the Judge and also the Mother of mercy, will be sure to advance the cause of our salvation.'[134] However, he goes further than others, since he sees her proximity to God as a necessary condition for her universal mediation, not just her intercession:

> Good reason therefore had the inspired singer, prophesying of Mary, to cry out in admiration, 'who is she that ascendeth as the morning rising, fair as the moon, bright as the sun, terrible as an army set in array?' (Cant. 6:9). She ascended indeed above the whole human race, she ascended even to the angelic choirs, yea, even these she left beneath her and soared high aloft above the whole celestial creation. For she must needs mount beyond the heavenly host in order to draw that living water which it is her destined office to pour down upon men. *Sermon for the Feast of the Nativity of the Blessed Virgin Mary*[135]

It was also under Bernard that a series of new reforms were introduced into the Cistercian Order, which included new practices in Marian devotion, especially Masses and Offices for her feast days, where a particular emphasis is laid on the Bride-Church-Mary relationship, with extensive use of Canticles.[136]

---

[133] *SBS*, pp. 207-8.

[134] *First Sermon for the Feast of the Assumption*, in *SBS*, p. 167.

[135] In *SBS*, p. 90.

[136] See Crisogono Waddel, 'La Vierge Marie dans la Liturgie cistercienne', in *La Vierge dans la tradition cistercienne*, Jean Longère 54ᵉ session de la Société française d'études mariales, ed. by Jean Longère (Paris, Mediaspaul, 1999), pp. 123-35. See also Goffredo Viti and Malachia Falletti, 'La devozione a Maria nell'Ordine Cistercense', in *Respice stellam: Maria in San Bernardo e nella tradizione cistercense*, pp. 287-348.

Bernard's Marian legacy was of major importance, not just within his own Cistercian order but for the Church as a whole. Although he was not particularly innovative, he consolidated and gave further impetus to the direction Western Mariology had already been taking in the previous centuries and had a profound influence in the realms of popular devotion, homiletics and theology in the generations that followed him. It is fair to say that no writer on Mary in the next several centuries is unmarked by him, but none more so than his immediate followers, who, though they often took somewhat different directions from Bernard, were marked by a similar fervour of devotion.[137]

One such, Amadeus of Lausanne († 1159) writes of the Virgin's power to save souls from damnation and to cure those who suffer from physical or mental ailments. Significantly, he makes mention of Marian shrines as places where cures can be sought, indicative of the growth in devotion to images of the Virgin and to purported relics such as drops of her milk, locks of hair, or items of her clothing, which made up for the lack of any physical remains of her body:

> With merciful solicitude she cares and provides remedies, not only for the salvation of souls but also help with necessities of the body. In effect, in places that are consecrated to the memory of her holiness, she causes the lame to walk, the blind to see, the deaf to hear, the mute to speak, and cures all sorts of sickness offering innumerable benefits to the health. [...] But those whose souls are bitter also prostrate themselves at her feet, the sad, the indigent, the afflicted, the desolate, debtors, and also those who (and this is it even more serious), live in dishonour and are marked by some infamy. She willingly welcomes the prayers of them all, and of all those who implore from the depths of whatever tribulation, and, beseeching her Son, she mercifully banishes all evil from them.
> *Homilia 8, De Mariae Virginis plenitudine*[138]

Another Cistercian, Odon of Morimond († 1161) is among the first to specifically link Mary's mediation of grace to her participation in the events of the Passion. Since the Cross is the source of all grace, and since the faithful may receive whatever they need from Mary, he concludes that her ability to distribute these graces must derive from her unwavering faith on Calvary and that the best way to seek her aid is to ask for it in the name of the crucified Christ:

> I take refuge in you today, O only hope of the wretched. Full of trust, devoutly I recommend myself and all my needs to you. Today I choose you among all women, Mother and Patroness. Do not despise me, O merciful Mother, do not reject me, think of him who is hanging in front of you naked and lacerated. How can you believe that she could refuse the person who turns to her with these words

---

[137] Aside from those I mention here, other close followers of Bernard were Guerric of Igny († 1157), Aelred of Rievaulx († 1167), and Isaac of Stella (†c. 1169). See Antonio Montanari, 'San Bernardo di Clairvaux e la sua scuola'.

[137] In *SBS*, p. 90.

[138] *PL* 188, 1344D-1345A.

while she is standing by the Cross? Since therefore the blessed Virgin immediately shows herself to be a Mother if she is prayed to and solicited next to the Cross, where she was totally absorbed in a kind of maternal love, rightly is she called with the name of Mother where is says: 'there stood by the Cross of Jesus, his mother'. *Homily on John 19. 25-27*[139]

Aelred of Rievaulx († 1167), one of the many Cistercians to be influenced by the fervent devotion of Bernard of Clairvaux for the Virgin, makes several statements on Mary's mediation. She, he says, is like a boat that guides across the perilous seas of this world to Jesus, and she is the path that leads to him. He seems to suggest that the mediation of the Virgin is essential to mankind when he writes: 'Observe that whoever is praised by the Lord (see Psalms 33. 3) merits praise only through the mediation of Mary.'[140] He goes on to repeat Bernard's assertion that she is the Mediatrix of the Mediator, along with the well-established *topos* of Mary placating her Son's fury:

> Such is her love towards the human race that, just as her Son is recognised as the Mediator between his Father and mankind, so she, being the Mediatrix between us and her Son, takes away his ire, stimulates his mercy, beseeches grace, removes punishment, so much so that she herself often puts the sword back in its scabbard which had already been taken out and was about to rage against the human race. *Sermo in Annuntiatione Dominica*[141]

Nicholas of Clairvaux († 1176) feigns concern that the Virgin may have forgotten her servants now that she has been glorified in heaven, but dismisses the thought because of her great mercy. In what is one of the clearest statements of an idea that is found in many Medieval commentators, he declares that this mercy derives from the common humanity that Mary shares with her supplicants. Although Jesus also has a human nature, there is, as it were, a certain conflict of interests, since his divine nature means that he must also be a judge. Nicholas then goes on to affirm the Virgin's universal mediation, daringly using words that Jesus had originally spoken of himself immediately prior to his Ascension, saying that all power on heaven on earth has been given to her:

> O Virgin Mother of God, whose beauty even the Sun and the moon admire, O Lady, come to the aid of those who invoke you continuously: 'Return, return, O Sulamitess: return, return that we may behold thee' (Canticles 6. 12). You, who are blessed and super-blessed, return, first of all because of your nature. Have you perhaps forgotten our humanity because you have been so divinised? Absolutely not, O Lady. You know what a perilous state you left us in, you know where your servants are laid low, and how much they sin. It does not become your great mercy

---

[139] *TMSM*, III, 305-06, José María Canal, 'Dos homilias', p. 414. See also chapter on Immediate Co-operation.
[140] *Sermo in Annuntiatione Dominica, MLM*, p. 199.
[141] *MLM*, p. 200.

to forget our great wretchedness, because even though your glory distances you from us, your nature recalls you. For, you do not only remember the justice of God to the point of not having mercy, nor are you so impassible that you are indifferent in the face of the suffering of others. You have our human nature, not another, and it is right that we are sprinkled with the dew[142] of such great mercy.

In the second place, return because of your power. He who is powerful wrought great things in you (see Luke 1. 49) and all power on heaven and earth has been given to you (see Matthew 28. 18). What will be denied you if you were not even prevented from ripping Theophilus from the very jaws of perdition? […] Nothing is impossible to you if you could raise the desperate to the hope of beatitude. How, indeed could the Almighty oppose your power when his flesh has its origin in you. Indeed you approach that golden altar of human reconciliation, not only pleading but commanding, as Mistress and not as handmaiden. […] In your hands are the treasures of the mercy of the Lord, and you alone have been chosen to obtain such grace. *In Nativitate beatissimae Virginis Mariae* [143]

A sermon by Hélinand of Froidmont († after 1212) sums up the importance given to Mary by the Cistercians in this period and also bears witness to the powerful influence of the feudal model on Marian devotion, through the rather curious device of comparing paradise (and by extension Mary) to a fief:

In this land are planted the Cistercians, who render homage to this great Lady and devote themselves to her in perennial service. Our Order has chosen her as our only advocate and has decreed that all its churches should bear her name. They receive this land as a fief and enter into possession of it, when they die, with a good conscience, Just as at the moment of our profession we assure this queen of our service, so, in her papers, that is in the notices that are made for the deceased, she assures us that we will take possession of our fief. There [in the death notices] the sweet name of Mary and the confirmation of the inviolable seal are mentioned in this way: 'On this day died brother X, monk or lay brother of Saint Mary of Froidment. *Sermo 2, In natali Domini*[144]

The Victorines were also swept up in the fervour of Marian devotion of the twelfth century.[145] With clarity and succinctness Hugh of St. Victor († 1141) sets out the Medieval viewpoint on the division of labour, as it were, between God the Father, Christ and Mary, and explains why it is that sinners often find it easier to approach the Virgin rather than her Son:

---

[142] This is a reference to the Incarnation. See Dew in vol. 2.

[143] *PL* 144, 740A-740C.

[144] Quoted in Maria Francesca Righi, 'La presenza della beata Vergine nel rinnovamento cistercense', in *SDM*, I, 618-36, an article which provides a wealth of information about Mary and the Cistercians.

[145] For a summary of the Marian writings of the main Victorines see Luigi Catalani, 'Il modello scolastico', in *SDM*, I, 673-99 (pp. 684-92)

> Mary is the door, Christ is the entranceway, the Father is the mystery. Mary is a human creature, Christ is man and God, the Father is God. Through Mary to Christ and through Christ to God. In Mary mercy, in the Father majesty, in Christ mercy and majesty. Mercy is born of compassion for the human race, majesty from the excellence of divinity. Mary is the star; Christ is the Sun. Therefore sinners, as if they were in the dark, are consoled by Mary; the just are illuminated by Christ as in full daylight. If you are afraid to approach Christ to beseech him, look to Mary. Here you will find nothing to make you afraid; here you see your own race. She is the mercy that precedes, thanks to which, for you who are in trepidation, supreme majesty is mitigated. May you be protected and nourished by her until such time as you are consoled and crowned. *Mary, the Door* [146]

Hugh is also the author of a commentary on the Magnificat which is a fine example of the careful *lectio biblica* that typifies the Victorines.[147] Achard of St. Victor († 1171) joins the ever-growing ranks of those who affirm Mary's universal mediation of grace in the wake of the pronouncements of Bernard of Clairvaux: 'Whatever is sent to us from heaven must be referred to the glorious Mother of God, because whatever grace we receive is without doubt thanks to her mediation.'[148] Richard of St. Victor († 1173) speaks of Mary as the Mother of mercy, but the essential condition is that those who call on her must have faith: 'Who is more merciful than blessed Mary, who is called the Mother of Mercy by all the faithful? All those who call upon her with true faith experience that she is truly the Mother of Mercy.'[149] Geoffrey of St. Victor († after 1194) explains with admirable clarity why Mary should be called the Mother of grace, both as the historical Mother of the Redeemer and as she who continues to obtain grace for humanity from the Father:

> Rightly have we called Mary Mother of grace, not only because she, through the intervention of her prayer and of her merits, is capable of and willing to obtain grace for us from him who is the Father of graces and the font of mercy, but also for another far more excellent reason: remaining a virgin, in an ineffable way, she gave to the world he who in emphatic, that is, expressive terms, may be defined as grace itself. *In Nativitate BVM* [150]

Adam of St. Victor († c. 1192) takes up the theme of Mary as the placatory intercessor with her Son in one of his hymns:

---

[146] *TMSM*, III, 177. The unedited Latin text appears in Roger Baron, 'La pensée mariale de Hugues de Saint-Victor', *Revue d'ascétique et de mystique*, 31 (1955), 249-71 (p. 271).

[147] *In Canticum beatae Mariae*, PL 175, 413-432.

[148] *Sermon on the Nativity of Blessed Mary*, *TMSM*, III, 347.

[149] *In Nativitate, vel Assumptione beatae Mariae semper Virginis*, PL 177, 1105.

[150] *TMSM*, III, 439. See Johannes Beumer, 'Die Parallele Maria-Kirche nach einem ungedruckten Sermo des Gottfried von St. Viktor', *Recherches de théologie ancienne et médiévale*, 27 (1960), 248-266, which includes the Latin text of the sermon.

Powerful and gentle virgin, worthy of angelic praise, filled with the grace of God, we sing your praises, we pray to you with our hearts, absolve our sins. Penitent, we confess our crimes, because of which we deserve the avenging wrath of God; take pity on your flock, O Queen, Mother of the King, make our Judge gentle with us. *In Assumptione BVM, 37*[151]

Another sequence by Adam gives us an idea of the heights to which Marian devotion had risen by the late twelfth century. Similar in some respects to the great hymns of the Byzantine Fathers, for instance in its use of the anaphoric 'Hail' and its extensive deployment of typology, it nevertheless has a distinctly Medieval flavour, especially in its numerous allusions to Canticles, which give an entirely different impression than the Eastern image of Mary as an ineffable, puissant Queen. Though undoubtedly exalted and without equal, Mary is also humble, sweet and loving, while her beauty is tangible rather than ethereal. The concluding prayer for the Virgin's assistance is also typically Medieval in its emphasis on Mary's protection from the wiles of the devil:

Salve, mater salvatoris / vas electum, vas honoris, / vas coelestis gratiae: / ab aeterno vas provisum, / vas insigne, vas excisum / manu sapientiae! // Salve, verbi sacra parens, / Flos de spinis, spina carens, / Flos, spineti gloria; / Nos spinetum, nos peccati / Spina sumus cruentati, / Sed tu spinae nescia. // Porta clausa, fons hortorum, / Cella custos unguentorum, / Cella pigmentaria; / Cinnamomi calamum, / Myrrham, tus et balsamum, / Superas fragrantia. // Salve, decus virginum, / Mediatrix hominum, / Salutis puerpera, / Myrtus temperantiae, / Rosa patientiae, / Nardus odorifera. // Tu convallis humilis, / Terra non arabilis, / Quae fructum parturiit; / Flos campi, convallium / Singulare lilium, / Christus ex te prodiit. // Tu coelestis paradisus / Libanusque non incisus, / Vaporans dulcedinum; / Tu candoris et decoris, / Tu dulcoris et odoris / Habes plenitudinem. // Tu thronus es Salomonis, / Cui nullus par in thronis / Arte vel materia; / Ebur candens castitatis. / Aurum fulvum, charitatis / Praesignant mysteria. // Palmam praefers singularem / Nec in terris habes parem / Nec in coeli curia; / Laus humani generis, / Virtutum prae caeteris / Habes privilegia. // Sol luna lucidior, / Et luna sideribus / Sic Maria dignior / Creaturis omnibus. / Lux eclypsim nesciens / Virginis est castitas. / Ardor indeficiens / Immortalis charitas. // Salve, mater pietatis / Et totius trinitatis / Nobile triclinium. / Verbi tamen incarnati / Speciale majestati / Praeparans hospitium. // O Maria stella maris, / Dignitate singularis, / Super omnes ordinaris / Ordines coelestium; / In supremo sita poli, / Nos commenda tuae proli, / Ne terrores sive doli / Nos supplantent hostium. // In procinctu constituti / Te tuente simus tuti. / Pervicacis et versuti / Tuae cedat vis virtuti, / Dolus providentiae. / Jesu, verbum summi Patris: / Serva servos tuae matris. / Solve reos, salva gratis / Et nos tuae claritatis / Configura gloriae.

(Hail, Mother of the Saviour, chosen vessel, vessel of honour, vessel of celestial grace, vessel prepared from eternity, famous vessel, vessel cut by the hand of Wisdom. Hail, sacred Mother of the Word, flower born from thorns, flower without a thorn, flower, glory of the thorn bush; we are the thorn bush, we are the thorn of cruel sin, but you know no thorn. Closed gate, fountain of gardens, cell of unguents,

---

[151] *AH* 54, 326-327, n. 206.

cell of perfumes; you surpass in fragrance the stick of cinnamon, myrrh, incense, and balsam. Hail, glory of virgins, Mediatrix for men, Mother of Salvation, myrtle of temperance, rose of patience, odiferous nard. You humble valley, unploughed earth that bears fruit; flower of the field, unique lily of the valley, Christ is born from you. You celestial paradise, uncut cypress, who emanate vapours of sweetness; you possess the fullness of brightness and beauty, of sweetness and fragrance. You are the throne of Solomon, unequalled by any throne in art or material; the celebrations of the mysteries call you shining ivory of chastity and pale gold of charity. You present a unique palm, so that you have no equal on earth nor in the heavenly court; O praise of the human race, more than all others you possess the privileges of the virtues. The sun is brighter than the moon, and the moon brighter than the stars, so Mary is worthier than all created beings. Light that knows no eclipse is the chastity of the Virgin and her immortal love is like an inextinguishable fire. Hail, Mother of piety and noble couch of the entire Trinity; but you prepared special hospitality for the majesty of the Incarnate Word. O Mary, star of the sea, singular in dignity, you are placed above all celestial orders; in the loftiest heaven, commend us to your child, lest fear or the wiles of our enemies overthrow us. Prepared for battle, we are safe under your protection. May the forces of evil, deceitful men, of trickery and of fortune, yield to your virtue. Jesus, Word of the highest Father, save the servants of your Mother. Absolve the guilty, freely deliver us and conform us to the clarity of your splendour. *In Nativitate BVM*[152]

Philip of Harveng († 1183), a Premonstratensian, believes that the Virgin has unlimited power when it comes to her intercession. He speaks of her being not just a Mediatrix but an Empress who commands her Son to turn his anger into 'sweetest love'.[153] Such distortions of the relative status of Mary and Jesus, which raised her to a level equal to or even above her Son, were not uncommon in this period, though it should be noted that all the first rank churchmen, such as Anselm and Bernard, and later Aquinas and Bonaventure, never make such exaggerated claims, and are always careful to portray the Virgin as working in absolute co-operation with and subordination to God. In his commentary on Canticles, Philip also addresses a prayer to the Virgin, which is a good example of the servant-Mistress relationship. The prayer begins with the familiar affirmation that Mary, as a result of her Assumption, is now close to her Son. It then continues by highlighting the relationship between the supplicant and his Mistress, which is one of service in return for patronage, typical of the feudal and courtly mentality. Unlike some of the more self-abasing prayers that we have come across earlier, he barely mentions his own faults and does not hesitate to point out how he has served his Lady by writing his commentary, in the hope of receiving her favour:

---

[152] Latin text available in *The Oxford Book of Medieval Latin Verse*, ed. by F. J. E. Raby (Oxford, The Clarendon Press, 1959), pp. 232-34. See also, Mone, *Lateinische Hymnen*, II, n. 524.
[153] *Commentaria in Cantica Canticorum*, 4, 5, PL 203, 360D. One finds similar sentiments in the Pseudo-Albert's *In Praise of Holy Mary*, in reality the work of Richard of St. Laurent. See Graef, *Doctrine and Devotion*, I, 268-69.

I pray you, O holy Virgin, now that you are next to your Son in the heavens, do not cease to care for and pay attention to him who belongs to you. I am yours, if not because of adequate merits, at least because of a somewhat more willing love. I am yours to serve you, even though I am not yet sure whether I am worthy of love or hatred. I am yours, and I want to please you with homage and gifts, if however, in this regard, you help me to be strong. You, therefore, O holy Virgin, accept a small gift from my hands. It is neither gold nor silver, nor a precious stone as would be suitable for a gift made to kings, but a coarse libation of words, pronounced in a vulgar way, a modest offering, to tell the truth, but the result of long hours and much effort. [...] You, therefore, accept what I am offering now, accept me with mercy who am making you this offering and correct me. Having corrected me, love me and recommend me to your beloved Son. For I know that if I am recommended to him by your benevolence, the poisonous serpent will either not bite me at all or his bite will do me no harm. *Commentaria in Cantica Canticorum, 50*[154]

Egbert of Schönau († 1184), brother of the visionary Elisabeth, provides one of the best examples of the well-worn *topos* of the merciful Virgin protecting sinners from the harsh judgement of her Son. It is due to Mary that the unremitting justice of the God of Israel was tempered with mercy through the Incarnation, and she continues to play this same role in heaven. The contrast between the pitiless Lord and the merciful Mother says everything about the unbalanced view of the respective roles of Jesus and Mary at this time, at least in some sections of the Church:

Behold, we sinners are faced with a terrible judge whose terrifying hand holds the trembling sword of his wrath over us. And who will keep him at bay? No-one, O Lady most beloved of God, is more capable of raising a hand in our favour to oppose the sword of the Lord. Thanks to you we received mercy from the hand of the Lord for the first time on earth. Open therefore, O Mother of clemency, the door of your most benign heart to the sighing petitions of us children of Adam, who from the ends of the earth, take refuge in the shadow of your protection, far from the face of the Lord which inspires fear. In front of you, O Lady, our eyes fill with tears. We implore you with the efficacious cry of devotion, that you might mitigate the ire of you Son in our regards, ire which we have aroused by sinning gravely. With your prayer obtain for us his grace, from which we have been excluded because of our ingratitude. *Homilia 52, In Nativitate beatae Mariae Virginins*[155]

He goes on to mention Theophilus as an example of how Mary, the Mother of Mercy, is not afraid of even the most putrid of sinners. The source of her

---

[154] *PL* 203, 489A-490A.
[155] *PL* 95, 1515A.

infinite mercy, he concludes, lies in her divine motherhood, since it was through her that the author of mankind's Redemption came into the world.

Alain of Lille († 1203) is among the growing ranks of those who offer Marian commentaries on the Canticle of Canticles in the wake of Rupert of Deutz († 1132) and Honorius of Autun († after 1133).[156] According to Alain, the kiss of the Bridegroom (Canticles 1. 2) represents the kiss of the Incarnation, of the Holy Spirit, and of the doctrine of Christ, so that Mary has perfect understanding of the divine mysteries. She therefore represents the path which all Christians must follow if they wish to contemplate the mystery of the Incarnation and to be raised up into God.

Hélinand of Froidment († after 1212) adds to the growing body of miracle stories about the Virgin. He recounts the story of how the Hodegetria icon saved the city of Constantinople from a siege when it was immersed in the sea, by fomenting a mighty storm that drove all the enemy ships away, and tells of the many miracles attributed to relics of Mary's funeral bier at the Church dedicated to her in Laon, France.[157] The multiplication of supposed Marian relics and of miraculous statues of the Virgin in this period was an important factor in the growth of her cult since, as we noted earlier, such objects were an essential element in the Medieval understanding of the intercession of the saints, a tangible link between heaven and earth.[158] Oglerius of Lucedio, († 1214), an Italian Cistercian, is unusual in that he claims personal knowledge of a miracle performed by the Virgin, for a man whom he had met some years previously in a piteous condition, covered in leprous sores. Too afraid to ask for the help of Jesus because of the gravity his sins, he had turned to Mary, who had obtained a cure for him and also preserved him from any further grave sin.[159]

Pope Innocent III († 1216) provides an interesting explanation for the date of the feast of the Purification and the use of candles, which he says is due to the fact that it had proved impossible to eliminate the pagan festival which marked the abduction of Persephone by Pluto, the god of the underworld, a festival in which the whole population carried lit tapers in memory of the search that Persephone's mother undertook for her.[160] Around the same time Sicardus of Cremona († 1215) gives two possible explanations as to why Saturday is devoted

---

[156] See the Chapter on the Assumption in this volume, and bride in vol. 2 where there is a full treatment of the Marian commentaries on Canticles.

[157] *Chronicon*, 1, 45 and 48, *PL* 212, 815 and 1011-1012.

[158] See Peter Brown, *The Cult of the Saints: Its Rise and Function in Latin Christianity* (Chicago: University of Chicago Press, 1981), Richard William Southern, *The Making of the Middle Ages* (New Haven: Yale University Press, 1953), especially chapter 5 which is on the Virgin Mary, and Marie-Madeleine Gauthier, *Highways of the Faith: Relics and Reliquaries from Jerusalem to Compostela*, trans. by J. A. Underwood (London: Alpine, 1983).

[159] *Tractatus in laudibus sanctae Dei Genitricis*, *TMSM*, IV, 57-58. See also Ogier of Lucedio, *Homilies: In Praise of God's Holy Mother, On Our Lord's Words to His Disciples at the Last Supper*. Trans. and annot. by D. Martin Jenni (Kalamazoo: Cistercian, 2006).

[160] See *Sermon 12, In Purificatione*, *PL* 217, 506-507, *TMSM*, IV, 97.

to the Virgin. One reason, he says, may be because the veil over an icon of the Virgin in Constantinople always raised itself up miraculously on a Saturday which the Church took as a sign that the day should be dedicated to her. The other, more reasonable explanation is that just as Saturday precedes the Lord's Day, so Mary, who is the gate of heaven, precedes the Son and helps us to prepare for his coming.[161]

Adam of Perseigne († 1221), a French Cistercian, is particularly insistent on the Virgin's mercy: 'Your mercy is as great as your power. You are merciful in your comprehension towards the miserable, and powerful in obtaining what you ask for. Is there ever an occasion on which you do not have mercy for your miserable children, O Mother of Mercy?[162] He goes on to explain Mary's mediation in terms of her being both the Mother of God and of man, so that she becomes a bridge between sinful mankind and the Judge, since through her Jesus has become our adoptive brother.

Pope Honorius III († 1227) is particularly insistent on the power of Mary over the devil, which he explores above all within the context of the Eve-Mary parallel. She is utterly impregnable to the devil's temptations, and is also a fortress for all those who take refuge in her.[163] In his *Second Sermon for the Feast of the Assumption*, he writes of Mary descending on her Church from Heaven to wrest the souls of the elect from the grips of demons. Though the passage it lengthy, it is worth quoting in full since it is rare fore a Pope to write so extensively on Mary, and it illustrates several important elements of Mariology at this time, such as the link between her Assumption and her active protection of the faithful, her motherly concern for the Church, which she watches over from heaven, the extensive interpretation of Canticles in a Marian key,[164] her power over the devil, and her accessibility for those who have fallen into sin. It is notable that he is very careful to clarify that the Virgin acts 'through her Son' rather than in her own right, unlike some of the commentators we have considered:

> In her Assumption, holy Mary was 'terrible as an army set in array' (Canticles 6. 9). In fact, when she was assumed into Heaven, she was surrounded by ranks of angels, archangels, principalities and powers, for which reason it is said in the Book of Kings: 'David gathered together all the elect of Israel to fetch the ark of God (2 Kings 6. 1-2). The ark of God is the Blessed Virgin; David is the Christ. He gathered together all the elect of Israel when, with all the chosen angels, principalities and powers, he came to fetch the ark of God, that is Blessed Mary.
>
> Thereafter, for the demons, Blessed Mary was terrible as an army arrayed for battle because, descending to visit some souls and bring them back with her to the Kingdom, she advanced with a multitude of angels and with the choirs of the holy virgins. Then the supernal virtues exclaimed: 'Who is she that cometh forth as the

---

[161] See his *Mitrale*, 1, 8, 1, *TMSM*, IV, 79.

[162] *Mariale, Sermo 1, In annuntiatione b. Virginis*, PL 211, 703B.

[163] See his *First Sermon for the Feast of the Assumption*.

[164] For a fuller treatment of Mary and Canticles see Bride in vol. 2.

morning rising?' And she immediately replied: 'I came down into the garden of nuts, to see the fruits of the valleys' (Canticles, 6. 10). It is as if she had said: do not marvel, for if I am terrible as an army arrayed for battle in my Assumption, when I descend too, I am terrible for my enemies.

The garden of nuts is the Church; the nuts are the single elect, because as the nut is bitter on the outside and sweet within, so the elect carry bitterness in their bodies but preserve spiritual sweetness in their minds. Every day blessed Mary descends into the garden of nuts; in other words, she visits the Church in the company of the serried ranks of angles. So, if we pray saying, 'Return, return, O Sulamitess' (Canticles 6, 12), God replies to us: 'What do you see in the Sulamitess if not the ranks of armies?'. This means that she will not come alone, but you will see the ranks of armies with her, that is the ranks of angels and virgins.

As to how the Blessed Virgin descends you will find many examples. She is 'like the morning rising, fair as the moon, bright as the sun, terrible as an army set in array.' The moon shines at night, the dawn at first light, the sun at the height of day. Night means guilt; first light means penitence; day, grace. Whoever lies prone in the night of guilt, let him look upon the moon and implore Mary so that she, through her Son, may illumine his heart with repentance. Whoever has risen with the first light because he is repentant, let him look on the dawn and invoke Mary so that she, through her Son, may illumine his heart and guide him to satisfaction. Whoever walks in the day of grace, let him look on the Sun and pray to Mary so that she, through her Son, may irradiate his heart to conduct him to perfection. 85-86 [165]

A further factor in the development of Mary's image as a merciful Mother was the establishment of the Franciscan and Claretian orders by Francis († 1226) and Clare († 1253). Francis himself wrote relatively little on Mary, though he was not lacking in devotion to her as this prayer, with its typical emphasis on the Incarnation, shows: [166]

> Hail Lady, holy Queen, holy Mother of God, Mary, Virgin become Church and chosen by the most holy Father of heaven, and consecrated by him together with the most holy Son, his Beloved, and with the Spirit, holy Paraclete, in whom was every fullness of grace and good. Hail his palace, hail his tabernacle, hail his habitation. Hail his vestment, hail his handmaid, hail his Mother and hail all you holy virtues which, through the grace and illumination of the Holy Spirit

---

[165] *TMSM*, IV, 130-31. See also his comments on Mary as a fortified castle in his *First Sermon for the Feast of the Assumption, TMSM*, IV, 126-29.

[166] Francis was particularly moved by the poverty and humility of the Nativity, and saw a link between God's condescension in taking on flesh in the Virgin's womb and his descent into the Eucharist. See vol. 2. On the Marian piety of Francis and Clare see Leonhard Lehmann, 'La devozione a Maria in Francesco e Chiara d'Assisi', in *La "Scuola Francescana" e l'Immacolata Concezione*, Atti del Congresso Mariologico Francescano S. Maria degli Angeli, Assisi, 4-8 dicembre 2003, ed. by Stefano M. Cecchin (Vatican City: Pontificia Academia Mariana Internationalis, 2005), pp. 1-54.

are infused in the hearts of the faithful, so that they will change them from [being] unfaithful to [being] faithful to God.[167]

From the outset the link between Francis and the Virgin through the Church of the Porziuncola, which was dedicated to her, was emphasised in the Franciscan tradition, as is witnessed by Tommaso da Celano's *Vita secunda*, written between 1245 and 1247.[168] Celano also claims that Francis declared Mary to be the 'Advocate of the poor'. The spread of Franciscan affective piety contributed to the transformation of Mary, the powerful Queen Mother of the Byzantine period, who can bring her influence to bear on her regal Son, into a tender mother entreating her Child, who can deny her nothing. It was partly due to the Franciscans that Jesus himself also began to take in a more caring, maternal image, as Caroline Walker Bynum has shown.[169]

The Franciscan Order produced some of the most important figures in later Medieval Mariology, among whom were Anthony of Padua († 1231), who devoted a series of fervent sermons to the Virgin and was a key figure in the growth of her cult in Northern Italy,[170] Bonaventure, the greatest theologian the Order produced, Conrad of Saxony, author of the *Speculum* (see below), Pietro di Giovanni Olivi († 1298), who affirms the co-passion of Mary, describing her as having been co-crucified with Christ, Robert Grosseteste († 1253), among the first to argue in favour of the Immaculate Conception, as did William of Ware (†c. 1305), and his student John Duns Scotus († 1308), the famed 'doctor of the Immaculate Conception.

The influence of the Franciscans is particularly evident in popular piety, most notably in the German-speaking area and in England, where they played a central role in the development of religious dramas[171] and the passionate Marian devotion and paralitugical activity of the thirteenth century confraternities of central and northern Italy, above all the *laudese* and the *disciplinati* or

---

[167] Translated from the text in Franco A. dal Pino, C'ulto e pietà mariana presso i frati minori nel medioevo', in *Gli studi di mariologia medievale: bilancio storico*, pp. 159-92 (p. 161). By the same author see 'La presenza della beata Vergine Maria nella vita degli ordini mendicanti (Secolo XIII-XV)', in *SDM*, I, 726-73.

[168] See Franco A. dal Pino, C'ulto e pietà mariana', p. 165.

[169] See Caroline Walker Bynum, *Jesus as Mother: Studies in the Spirituality of the High Middle Ages* (Berkeley: University of California Press, 1982). For a brief summary of these developments see Elizabeth A. Johnson, 'Marian Devotion in the Western Church', in *Christian Spirituality: High Middle Ages and Reformation*, ed. by Jill Raitt, World Spirituality, 17 (New York: Crossroad, 1988), pp. 392-414.

[170] See *The Sermons of St Antony*, trans. by Stephen Spilsbury, in *The Franciscan Archive* <http://www.franciscan-archive.org/antonius/opera/ant-hd00.html> [accessed 28 March 2006], and see René Laurentin, 'The Virgin Mary in the Works of St. Anthony of Padua', *Greyfriars Review*, 10 (1996), 47-74.

[171] See Osborne B. Hardison, *Christian Rite and Christian Drama in the Middle Ages: Essays in the Origin and Early History of Modern Drama* (Baltimore: Johns Hopkins University Press, 1965.

flagellants,[172] which attracted large numbers of lay people and produced a considerable body of vernacular hymns to the Virgin. The oldest extant *Laudarium*, dating from the thirteenth century, is the *Laude di Cortona*, compiled by the Confraternità di S. Maria delle *Laude* in Cortona.[173] The first sixteen *laude* are dedicated to the Virgin, as is the forty-seventh and last. In style and language, they rely heavily on Latin hymnody, drawing to a great extent on well-established Marian *topoi*, though they differ noticeably from their Latin counterparts in their use of courtly language. They are imbued with a deep love of the Virgin, emphasising her status as hope of sinners, mediatrix of grace, and co-Redemptrix.

Perhaps the most accomplished of the Marian *laude* is the *Rayna possentissima*, part of the codex of the Servants of the Virgin, a Bolognese fraternity dating from the first half of the thirteenth century:[174] The *Rayna* follows the same basic format of exaltation followed by supplication that characterises most Marian prayers. At a conceptual level, it contains familiar themes: Mary is adorned with every virtue (*De le vertù altissime tuta ne si' ornata / Donna perfectissima*, Most perfect Lady, you are entirely adorned with the highest virtues, 6-7); she is created with the express purpose of bringing salvation (*Per salvar[e] lo segolo fusti al mondo creata*, You were created in the world to save the ages, 8); awaited through the centuries (*Tanto si' stata, madre, de li miseri aspetata*, Greatly have you been awaited, Mother, by the wretched, 28); source of grace (*Vuy si' fontana de gracia*, You are the font of grace, 21); source of life (*Lo fruto che portasti, madona, in Betelèm, a nu la vita ha data*, The fruit that you bore in Bethlehem, my Lady, is life for us, 18); source of joy and consolation (*Chi a vuy torna cum lagreme, l'anima desperata, / da vuy parte cum gaudio e cum çoia consolata*, Whoever turns to you in tears, his soul desperate, leaves you rejoicing and consoled by joy, 40-41). It concludes with a plea for succour: '*Recòrdive de l'anima che sta mortificata. / L'alma di vostri Servi ve sia recomandada, / chi ha complì questa ystoria per vuy, verçene sacrata* (Remember the soul

---

[172] The *disciplinati* originated with the Perugian Ranieri Fasani, who was inspired by Gioacchino da Fiore's († 1202) teachings to prophesise that the reign of the Spirit would begin in 1260. On Gioacchino see Gian Luca Potestà, *Il tempo dell'Apocalisse: Vita di Gioacchino da Fiore* (Roma-Bari: Laterza, 2004), and on his Mariology, Marco Rainini, 'Maria nelle opera di Gioacchino da Fiore († 1202)', in *SDM*, I, 700-25. See chapter on Immediate Redemption for further discussion and bibliography.

[173] The first part of the *laudarium*, including all but one of the sixteen Marian *laude*, possibly dates from as early as 1250, while the second half is later, most likely the early years of the 1300's. Two recent critical editions are *Il Laudario di Cortona*, ed. by Giorgio Varanini, Luigi Banfi and others, with an introduction and notes by Luigi Lucchi (Vicenza: L.I.E.F., 1987), and *Laudario di Cortona*, ed. by Anna Maria Guarnieri (Spoleto: Centro italiano di studi sull'alto medioevo, 1991).

[174] Rosanna Bettarini, 'Jacopone da Todi e le Laude', in *Antologia della poesia italiana*, ed. by Cesare Segre e Carlo Ossola, 3 vols (Turin: Einaudi-Gallimard, 1997-99) I (1997), 278-332 and 975-979 dates it to before 1254 (p. 279). The full text of the codex has been published online by the University of Pisa, <http://dante.di.unipi.it/ricerca/html/Cod-Servi.html> [accessed 20 August 2006].

that is mortified. Mary the souls of your Servants be recommended to you, those who have composed this story for you, Holy Virgin).

The Servites or Servants of Mary were founded on the feast of the Assumption, 1233 when the Virgin appeared to seven noble Florentines, who were members of a *laudese* confraternity,[175] telling them to abandon the world. On the feast of her Nativity, 8 September, she appeared to them again surrounded by a multitude of angles who held various objects, including the instruments of the Passion, the Rule of St. Augustine, and a scroll on which appeared the title of Servants of Mary. She spoke the following words to them:

> I have chosen you to be my first Servants, and under this name you are to till
> my Son's Vineyard. Here, too, is the habit which you are to wear; its dark colour
> will recall the pangs which I suffered on the day when I stood by the Cross of
> my only Son. Take also the Rule of St. Augustine, and may you, bearing the title
> of my Servants, obtain the palm of everlasting life.[176]

The Servants endured a long struggle, being briefly suppressed by Innocent V in 1276 before being definitively approved by Benedict XI with the Bull *Dum levamus* in 1304. Despite these difficulties they spread rapidly throughout Italy, France and Germany, and had more than one hundred houses by the early fourteenth century. Already in their first unified constitution, dating to around 1290, a whole chapter, the *De reverentii beate Marie virginis* is dedicated to the numerous devotional practices of the Order, including Masses of the Virgin on Saturdays, Wednesdays, and other days of the week, a provision that all churches and major altars should be dedicated to her, stipulations regarding recitation of the *Ave*, the *Salve*, the *Hore de Domina*, and so on. In later centuries the Order was distinguished by its devotion to the Sorrows of Mary and the Passion of Jesus. Another important contribution of the Servites was their patronage of art, their churches being adorned by the works of Ciambue, Duccio and others.

A second order with its origins in Marian devotion founded around this time was the Carmelites. The order grew out of a group of pilgrims (possibly linked

---

[175] For a rich variety of articles on the early years of the Servites see *L'ordine dei Servi di Maria nel primo secolo di vita*, Atti del Convegno Storico, Palazzo Vecchio, Santissima Annunziata 23-24 maggio 1986 (Florence: Biblioteca della Provincia soscana dei Servi di Maria, 1988). See also the extensive study on the early centuries of the Servites by Pacifico Maria Branchesi, 'L'ordine dei Servi di Santa Maria e il culto mariano (secoli XII-XV)', in *Gli studi di mariologia medievale: bilancio storico*, pp. 113-58. See also Franco A., dal Pino, 'La presenza della beata Vergine Maria', pp. 767-72, which contains an exhaustive bibliography on the early history of the Order. For further comments on the *laudesi* see chapter on Immediate Co-operation.

[176] See 'Servants of Mary (Order of Servites)' in *The Catholic Encyclopedia*, IX (New York: Appleton, 1910) <http://www.newadvent.org/cathen/09750a.htm> [accessed 9 March 2009].

to the Crusades) who gathered on Mount Carmel in the second half of the twelfth century. They were attached to the Church of Our Lady on Mount Carmel and given a rule by the Patriarch of Jerusalem but were soon forced to flee to the West where they eventually gained recognition after many vicissitudes in 1247. Despite their foundational link with the Virgin the Carmelites did not place any particular emphasis on Marian devotion in their early years. Their first constitution, for instance, dating from 1281, makes little mention of Mary. By the time that the constitution of 1324-27 was being written, however, Mary, the Lady of Carmel had become the special patroness of the order. In the following centuries the Carmelites went on to play an important role in spreading Marian devotion, particularly to the brown scapular, which, according to later Carmelite tradition, had been presented in a vision to Simon Stock († 1265) by the Virgin with the promise that those who wore it would be preserved from the fires of hell.[177]

By the middle of the thirteenth century the Virgin was playing an increasingly important role in the Dominican order.[178] Although there is no evidence that Dominic († 1221) himself was particularly fervent in his Marian devotion, his successor Jordan of Saxony († 1237) was more active in promoting her cult and mentions several miraculous events concerning her, including the conversion of one of Dominic's companions, Reginald of Orléans, as a result of a vision of the Virgin. Under the leadership of Humbert of Romans, elected Master-General in 1254, this subsequently morphed into the myth that Dominic himself had also had a vision in which Mary presented him with the habit of the order, and she was thus to be considered its co-founder. This retroactive attribution of the foundation of the order to the Virgin may have been inspired by the story of the Servites and was a convenient validation in the face of growing criticism of the Preachers. Humbert was also responsible for the introduction of the 'eight special services' (*octo servitia specialia*) in honour of the Virgin, including prayers in the opening and closing offices of the day and a promise of fidelity to her in the profession of the monks. The Dominicans increasingly came to see their foundation as a fruit of the intercession of the Virgin who wished to bring about the restoration of the Church, for which reason she is frequently proposed, most notably in the *Sermones de beata Virgine* of Bartholomew of Breganze († 1271), as the model for the conversion not just of the faithful but of the institutional Church to which she gave birth and which

---

[177] See Corrado Maggioni, *Benedetto il frutto*, pp. 96-97 and Pablo Maria Garrido, 'Elementos marianos presents en los primeros textos escritos Carmelitas medievales', *Marianum*, 64 (2002), 387-406. On the scapular see Richard Copsey, 'Simon Stock and the Scapular Vision', *The Journal of Ecclesiastical History*, 50 (1999), 652-83.

[178] Much of the discussion that follows is based on the excellent article by Laura Gaffuri, 'La predicazione domenicana su Maria (Il secolo XIII), in *Gli studi di mariologia medievale: bilancio storico*, pp. 193-215. See also Franco A. dal Pino, 'La presenza della beata Vergine Maria', pp. 753-56. William A. Hinnebusch, *History of the Dominican Order: Origins and Growth to 1500*, 2 vols (New York: Alba, 1965-1972).

she continues to animate. Mary is also the supreme *exemplar* of the perfect balance between contemplation and action to which the Preachers aspired.[179] The Dominicans, like the Franciscans, were also active in the promotion of the Virgin's cult in the lay confraternities that emerged in increasing numbers in the thirteenth century, seeing in Marian devotion a guarantee that these groups would not stray into heresy.[180]

Another crucial element in the growth of popular devotion to the Mother of Mercy in the later Middle Ages was the emergence of collections of miracle stories, some of which we have already considered.[181] The first written collections date from the eleventh century, but it was not until the next century that they began to multiply, both in Latin and the vernacular.[182] Among the more significant early compilations were the *De laude Sanctae Mariae* by Guibert, abbot of Nogent-sous-Coucy's († 1124), William of Malmesbury's († c. 1143) *De laudibus et miraculis sanctae Mariae*, Hermann of Tournai's *Miracula Sancte Marie Laudunensis*, the *Libellus de miraculis Beatae Mariae Virginis in urbe Suessoniensi*, composed by Hugo Farsit around 1132, and Nigel of Canterbury's († c. 1158) *Miracula sancte Dei genitricis virginis Marie*.[183] Although some of the miracle accounts, such as the Theophilus story, had been in circulation for centuries, most were new, and reflected the values, beliefs and superstitions of feudal society. Although occasionally cited in official Church circles, they were more often to be found in popular literature, especially vernacular texts such as Gautier de Coinci's († 1236) *Miracles de Nostre Dame*, which contains no less that fifty-eight accounts of miracles attributes to the Virgin.[184] Where such stories were linked to specific Marian shrines which housed, images, statues or items that purportedly belonged to the Virgin they were mainly aimed at encouraging the faithful to visit these sites, bringing prestige and monetary gain to the local church. This overcame the difficulty that Marian shrines had in competing with local saints whose miraculous relics were readily available and, once Marian shrines began to multiply, gave a particular cult an edge over its rivals.[185] Such

[179] See Model in vol. 2.
[180] See Gérard Gilles Meersseman, 'Études sur les anciennes confréries dominicaines, III', *Archivium Fratrum Praedicatorum*, 22 (1952), 5-176, and his *Ordo fraternitatis*.
[181] See Benedicta Ward, *Miracles and the Medieval Mind: Theory, Record and Event, 1000-1215* (Aldershot, Wildwood House, 1987).
[182] See Richard William Southern, 'The English Origins of the "Miracles of the Virgin"', *Medieval and Renaissance Studies*, 4 (1958), 176-216, and Graef, *Doctrine and Devotion*, I, 231.
[183] See Jean Fournée, 'Les orientations doctrinales' p. 30.
[184] See Gautier de Coinci, *Les Miracles de Nostre Dame*, ed. by V. Frederic Koenig, 4 vols (Geneva: Droz, 1955-70), Tony Hunt, Miraculous Rhymes: *The Writing of Gautier de Coinci* (Cambridge: D.S. Brewer, 2007), and Daniel O'Sullivan, *Marian Devotion in Thirteenth-Century French Lyric* (Toronto: University of Toronto Press, 2005), pp. 11-12.
[185] This is a point that Mario Sensi makes in his very informative article 'I santuari mariani', in *Gli studi di mariologia medievale: bilancio storico*, pp. 217-38. See also, in the same

was the case with the collections of Hermann of Tournai, written for the shrine of Laon (hair and clothing), and of Hugo Farsit, written for a rival site at Soissons (slipper).[186] Indeed it is surely no coincidence that the proliferation miracle stories from the twelfth century onwards is mirrored by a marked increase in Marian shrines and pilgrimages.

The image that emerges from these accounts is of someone who is on the side of the common people and who is no respecter of the laws and authority of the Church. She repeatedly comes to the aid of those who are on the margins of society, such as uneducated monks who are despised by their abbots and downtrodden mothers, and is always willing to help the disreputable. Even those who have denied God, blasphemed, and died impenitent, whom the Church refuses to bury in holy ground, are not beyond her reach. Even though they may never have prayed to God, one word to her is sufficient. Indeed, it is God who bends to her authority rather than the other way around, as is illustrated by this rather amusing passage from de Coinci's *Miracles* in which the demons grumble about Mary overturning the proper order:

> Say the devils: "In this lawsuit, since it is a choice of the evils, we had best appeal to the judgment of the high judge who lieth not. His mother will not judge aright plea; but God judges us so fairly that he leaves us all our due. His mother judges in such a way that we always find ourselves down when we think that we are up. [...] in heaven and on earth she is the ruler rather than God. He so loves her and believes in her that he will not contradict or disavow anything that she says or does. She makes Him believe anything she likes. If she said that black was white and muddy water clear, He would say 'It is true; My Mother says so.'" *Miracles de Nostre Dame*[187]

Caesar of Heisterbach († after 1240), whose *Dialogus miracolorum* was the basis for many of Gautier de Coinci's stories, tells a particularly subversive story about a monk who is captured by a brigand, whom he persuades to turn to the Virgin in order to gain salvation. The brigand, however, continues his nefarious activities on every day of the week except Saturday, when he prays to the Virgin. Eventually he is captured – on a Saturday, so he does not resist arrest – and brought to trial. Asked if he wants to see a priest before he is executed, he declares: 'It is not necessary. All of you are Christians; I will confess my sins to

---

volume, Sylvie Barnay, 'La foundation viosionnaire des Sanctuaires, un example de politique mariophanique: Notre Dame du Puy', pp. 239-54.

[186] See Sylvie Barnay, 'Le "leggendae" e i "miracula"', in *SDM*, I, 662-72 (pp. 663-64).

[187] Quoted in Eileen Power, 'Introduction', in Johannes Herolt, *Miracles of the Blessed Virgin Mary*, ed. and trans. by C. C. Swinton Bland (London: Rutledge 1928; repr. New York, Kessinger, 2004), pp. ix-xxxv (p. xxxi). For a fascinating study of Mary as a legal advocate see Our Lady's Lawsuits in *"L'advocacie Nostre Dame" and "La chapelerie Nostre Dame de Baiex"*, ed. and trans. by Judith M. Davis and F.R.P. Akehurst (Tempe, AR : ACMRS, 2011).

you all.'[188] Here devotion to the Virgin undermines both God's law and the Church's authority to forgive sins. Such an attitude is not surprising, perhaps, given the deleterious state of the Church and the low standards of a good part of the clergy.

The influence of Bernard is obvious in John de la Rochelle's († 1245) statement that Mary is a second advocate after the Son: 'The Son is an advocate with the Father, Mary is an advocate with the Son. Therefore, O sinner, you have a certain means of access, for the Queen is working to come to your aid.' He goes on to say that Mary's role is to 'placate the offence, remove the penalty, beg for grace and obtain final perseverance.'[189] Further on in the sermon he likens her to Esther, the Old Testament queen who was able to influence King Assuerus' decisions, mitigating the severity of his sentences: 'Everything that she asks she will obtain, to the point of changing the sentence of the King.'[190]

Richard of St. Laurence († after 1245), in his *De Laudibus Beatae Mariae Virginis*, which was frequently attributed to Albert the Great, explains Mary's mediation as deriving from her motherhood of Christ: just as Christ, the Mediator between God and humanity, came through her, humanity can approach God through her.[191] He goes on to make the exaggerated claim that Mary can 'give orders' to Christ because of her 'maternal authority'.[192] As well as urging the faithful to celebrate the vigils and feasts of the Virgin and to devote every Saturday to her, Richard declares that Sunday also has its origin in her because 'she despised all temporal things and turned to that which is eternal'. He then goes on to list all her major feasts, which are her Sanctification (Conception), the Conception of Christ, the Nativity, the Purification, and the Assumption. In fact, Mary may be called 'the altar of the pacification of the Lord, whom she placates on behalf of sinners, when gifts and sacrifices are made in her name on this altar.[193] In Book IV of the *De laudibus* we find a description of how Mary wrests souls from the hands of the devil and brings them back to life so that they can repent of their evil, clearly inspired by the Theophilus legend.[194]

In 1269 the General Chapter of the Franciscans, presided over by Bonaventure, recommended that the order's preachers should encourage the faithful to pray the *Ave* at the ringing of the evening bell in imitation of St. Francis, a practice that eventually developed into the Angelus.[195] The first part

---

[188] *Dialogus Miraculorum, dist, 7, 58, TMSM*, IV, 179-80.

[189] *Sermon 4, On the Assumption, TMSM*, IV, 185.

[190] *TMSM*, IV, 190.

[191] 2, 1, 17. The work is published among those of Albert the Great, *Alberti Magni Opera Omnia*, ed. by Auguste and Emile Borgnet, 38 vols (Paris: Vivès, 1890-99), XXXVI, 144-165.

[192] 2, 1, 21, *TMSM*, IV, 201.

[193] *De Laudibus Beatae Mariae Virgini*, 2, 5, 12, *Alberti Magna Opera Omnia*, XXXVI, 119-20.

[194] See Graef, *Doctrine and Devotion*, I, 270.

[195] See Franco A. dal Pino, 'Culto e pietà mariana', pp. 188-90.

of the *Hail Mary*, ending with the words, 'blessed is the fruit of thy womb', which is a combination of Gabriel and Elizabeth's greetings to Mary (Luke 1. 28 and 42), had been recited from as early as the sixth century in a number of Eastern liturgies.[196] It first occurs in the West in a seventh-century antiphon of the Mass for the fourth Sunday of Advent, but only began to gain popularity from the tenth century.[197] The evening recitation of the *Ave* was adopted by the Dominicans in 1317 and was given a further boost when, in 1318, Pope John XXII granted an indulgence to those who took up the practice.[198] By the fourteenth century the *Ave* had also become popular among the laity since it was included in the Little Office of the Blessed Virgin Mary.[199] The practice of meditating on the joys of the Virgin, first introduced in the Cistercian order in the eleventh century, is the subject of an extensive commentary by one of their number, Stephen of Salley († 1252), in which he meditates on fifteen joys, divided into groups of five:

> The first five joyful mysteries will be identified in the period that goes from the birth of the blessed Virgin to the birth of the Saviour; the second from the birth of the Saviour to the Passion of the Cross; the third from the Passion to the Assumption into heaven of the blessed Virgin. *Meditations on the Joys of the Blessed Virgin Mary*[200]

Over the next several centuries meditation on the joys (to which were added the sufferings in the fourteenth century) became an important aspect of Marian devotion before the practice was absorbed and eclipsed by recitation of the Rosary.[201]

Another prayer, the *Salve Regina*, was the subject of several commentaries in the thirteenth century, the most popular being by the Franciscan James of Milan, which circulated widely under the names of Anselm and Bernard. Writing of the aid that Mary gives those who turn to her he says:

---

[196] It was not until much later that the second, intercessory half was added. See Herbert Thurston, 'The Origins of the Hail Mary', in *Familiar Prayers: Their Origin and History* (London: Burns and Oates, 1953), pp. 90-114.

[197] See Henri Barré, *Prières anciennes*, p. 19.

[198] See Donna Ellington Spivey, *From Sacred Body to Angelic Soul: Understanding Mary in Late Medieval and Early Modern Europe* (Washington: Catholic University of America Press, 2001), p. 29, and Jaroslav Pelikan, *Mary through the Centuries* (New Haven: Yale University Press, 1996), p. 99.

[199] See Ann Van Dijk, 'The Angelic Salutation', pp. 420-21, Graef, *Doctrine and Devotion*, I, 230. Anne Winston Allen, *Stories of the Rose*, pp. 2 and 13-14, and her 'Tracing the Origins of the Rosary: German Vernacular Texts', *Speculum*, 66 (1993), 616-36 (p. 620).

[200] *TMSM*, IV, 219. See Franco A. dal Pino, 'Culto e pietà mariana', pp. 185-87.

[201] On the origins of the Rosary, which evolved in the fifteenth century out of the practice of reciting the *Ave* and borrowed from the joys and sorrows of the Virgin, see Anne Winston Allen's, *Stories of the Rose*.

Those who know your name place their trust in you, because you, O Sovereign, never abandon those who seek you. Those who hope in you will most certainly have a different kind of strength. They will put on the wings of eagles, they will run without tiring, they will not grow weary and give up before the end. *Meditation on the Salve Regina* [202]

Commenting on the line, 'to you do we turn, poor banished children of Eve' he affirms that Mary alone distributes the grace won by Jesus on the Cross:

To you, who alone generated the Lord; to you, who alone put an end to universal heretical depravity. You alone are the Sovereign Queen of the kingdom; you alone are the distributor of the prize. To you our Mother, to you our Nursemaid, to you our Succour, to you and only to you who wash away the excrement of sins, who console us like babies who cry in the cradle. *Meditation on the Salve Regina* [203]

Later on he exclaims: 'O truly wonderful is God's benignity that he has given you, O Sovereign, as an advocate [...] so that you, who have been designated by you Son as a mediatrix between us and him in the exercise of his judicial functions, might obtain for us what you want.'[204] He asks himself how Mary, such a noble creature, can accept such as stinking wretch as himself, and answers that it is because she is the Queen of Mercy. Thus he is confident that she will obtain mercy from the judge, her Son, who cannot deny her anything.[205]

In a similar fashion pseudo-Bonaventure says that Christ and Mary divide the rule of Heaven between them, with Mary being mercy, where Christ is justice:

She makes the sixth distinction with the Son, with whom she divides the kingdom of heaven of which there are two parts, justice and mercy. The blessed Virgin chose the best for herself because she was made queen of mercy and her Son remained king of justice. Mercy is better than justice because mercy exalts itself above justice [James 2. 5], and his mercies are over all his works [Psalm 144:9]. *Sixth Sermon on the Assumption of the Blessed Virgin Mary*[206]

The more sober writings of the Scholastic theologians went some way towards addressing the egregious imbalances that had crept into Marian commentary in the course of the eleventh and twelfth centuries. Although fully acknowledging the greatness of Mary, Albert the Great, Bonaventure, Aquinas,

---

[202] In *TMSM*, IV, 353.
[203] *TMSM*, IV, 353-54.
[204] In *TMSM*, IV, 356.
[205] *Meditation on the Salve Regina*, in *TMSM*, IV, 351 and 356-7.
[206] In *Sermons on the Blessed Virgin Mary*, trans. by Campion Murray, in *Franciscan Friars: Province of the Holy Spirit* <http://www.franciscans.org.au> [accessed 10 March 2006]. The authenticity of the sermon has been in doubt since the early 1960's. See Graef, *Doctrine and Devotion*, I, 281, n. 2 and 288-90.

Scotus, and others were careful to give their Mariology a firm Christological foundation, insisting that the Virgin's privileges derived entirely from God and underlining that there was no question of a rivalry or conflict between Mary's mercy and God's justice.

According to Albert the Great († 1280), it is because Mary received a superabundance of grace when God came to dwell within her that she has become a source of grace, which overflows from her (he uses Bernard's image of the aqueduct) onto humanity.[207] Her mediation of grace is confined to her divine motherhood and not in any way related to her participation in the events of Calvary. She is our spiritual Mother because she 'conceived us in her heart at the same time as she conceived the divine Word in her womb',[208] but in no way did she contribute to the Redemption, though she suffered greatly.[209] Nevertheless, he believes that in her quality as the Mother of Jesus she continues to act as a co-operator of the Redeemer, intervening on behalf of humanity, and that she is a mediator between the Father and the Son: 'Through the Mother we have access to the Son, and through the Son, to the Father.'[210] However he explicitly rejects the notion that Christ is a harsh judge whom Mary must placate, stating that the love and mercy of Jesus is infinitely greater than his Mother's. Mary's task, rather, is to nourish the image and likeness of Christ in which God has formed each of the faithful.[211] Albert also deals with the question of veneration, stating that Mary is due *hyperdulia* (exalted veneration), but not *latria* (adoration), which is due to God alone, and denies the principal expounded by many Medieval commentators that honour bestowed on Mary necessarily redounded on her Son: 'For even though the honour of the Mother is the honour of the King, yet, because he had a different generation through his Godhead, she has no claim to the divine honours, because her Son did not receive his divinity through her.'[212]

Bonaventure († 1274) deals with the question of the veneration due to Mary in his *Sententiae*.[213] Using the same terms as Albert, *latria*, *dulia* and *hyperdulia*, he distinguishes between the different degrees of honour that are due to God, sacred objects, the saints and the Virgin Mary. He begins by asking whether it is

---

[207] *In Lucam*, 1, 28, *Opera Omnia*, XXII, 61-62.

[208] *In Lucam*, 10, 42, *Opera Omnia*, XXIII, 90.

[209] See *Sent. III,*, d. 3. a. 3, *Opera Omnia*, XXVIII, 45 and *Postilla super Isaiam*, 11. 1.

[210] *De natura boni*, quoted in Luigi Gambero, 'Il XIII secolo e la fioritura della Scolastica', in *SDM*, I, 774-829 (p. 819).

[211] See *In Lucam*, 2. 27.

[212] See *Sent. III,*, d. 9. a. 9, *Opera Omnia*, XXVIII, 182, Graef, *Doctrine and Devotion*, I, 275.

[213] See *Sent.* III, d. ix, a. 1 and 2. The discussion that follows relies on George H. Tavard, *The Forthbringer of God: St. Bonaventure on the Virgin Mary* (Chicago: Franciscan Herald Press, 1989), pp. 95-108. See also Stanislaw Bogusz Matula's privately published, *La dottrina mariana nei commentary ai vangeli e nei semoni di San Bonaventura da Bagnoregio* (Rome: [n. pub.], 2001) and Luigi Gambero, 'Il XIII secolo e la fioritura della Scolastica' (pp. 787-93).

legitimate to offer *latria* to the humanity of Christ, and concludes that it is since the two natures are in the one Person of Christ. He next turns to the question of icons and concludes, against the general trend in the West, that it is legitimate to offer *latria* to images of Christ since they act as signs or conduits that point to the divine Person whom they signify. Such is not the case, however, with the Virgin and the saints, who are human beings in their own right. Though they transfer much of the honour they receive to God, some is legitimately kept for themselves since they are worthy of veneration because of the holy lives that they led. The saints therefore should only be offered *dulia*, whereas the Virgin Mary, because of what God worked in her, because of her proximity to Christ, and because she acts in a unique way as a sign of the Incarnation, should be offered a cult of *hyperdulia*. To sum up, *latria* may be offered only to God, or to inanimate objects that signify him, such as icons or the wood of the true Cross, whereas *dulia* (or, in the Virgin's case, *hyperdulia*) should be offered to the saints insofar as they transmit glory to God and are due honour in their own right.

Bonaventure follows Bernard in asserting that Mary is a Mediatrix between humanity and Christ, just as Christ is the Mediator between humanity and God, even using Bernard's metaphor of the aqueduct. He does not, however, claim that grace must *necessarily* flow through her.[214] On one occasion he adds a third advocate, the Holy Spirit, and underlines that mediation is conditional on the supplicant's willingness to reform:

> Having therefore the Son as our advocate who fights, the Spirit as our advocate who speaks for us, the Queen of virgins as out advocate who intercedes, let us safely entrust our cause to them in regard to the law, if at least we have corrected the fact, for, in what touches the fact, an advocate does not redeem his clients errors. *Collationes in Johannem, 53*[215]

On a more personal note, in one of his letters Bonaventure recommends turning to the Virgin with love and devotion when in need. An important condition, however, is that the petitioner show willingness to imitate the Virgin's virtues:

> At all times, have for the glorious Queen, the Mother of our Lord, the highest respectful love; and in all the details and pressures of your needs turn to her as

---

[214] *Sent.* III, d. iii, q. I, a. 1.
[215] Quoted in Tavard, *The Forthbringer*, p. 89. Subsequent translations are also Tavard's. See also Jacques Guy Bougerol, *Introduction to the Works of Bonaventure*, trans. by José de Vinck (Paterson, NJ: St. Anthony Guild Press, 1964). For translations of Bonaventure's works see *The Works of Bonaventure*, trans. by José de Vinck, 5 vols, (Patterson, NJ: St. Antony Guild Press, 1960-1970) and the ongoing translation of Bonaventure's complete works into Italian, *Opere di san Bonaventura*, ed. by Jacques Guy Bougerol, Cornelio Del Zotto and Leonardo Sileo Bougerol, 14 vols (Rome: Conferenza italiana ministri provinciali O.F.M. and Città Nuova, 1990-).

to a very safe shelter; taking her as your advocate, entrust your case, with devotion and confidence, to her who is the Mother of mercy, trying every day to show her a special and singular veneration. And that your devotion may be accepted and your veneration agreeable, endeavor with every effort to imitate the traces of her humility and kindness, by cultivating in yourself, with every virtue, in soul and body, the spotless integrity of her purity. *Epistola continens XXV memoralia*

Commenting on the Angel's greeting to Mary, in his *Fifth Sermon on the Annunciation*,[216] Bonaventure writes that she was filled to overflowing with a sevenfold grace at the time of the Annunciation, which she will pour out on those who are disposed to receive it. The seventh of these is overflowing grace, 'so that she would be of benefit to the salvation of the human race and no-one might evade her warmth'. As in his homily on John, his explanation of how this grace is to be received is considerably more refined than those who claimed that Mary's aid was essentially unconditional. For the grace to be truly effective, the soul of the petitioner must be rightly disposed: 'The grace of the Virgin can overflow to all in asking for grace, but not by an infusion; it is poured out on all in a sufficient amount, but not on all in its effectiveness, something that happens only on those who prepare themselves to receive it.' The faithful may dispose themselves in seven ways, which correspond to the Virgin's seven graces: by orienting their lives with an upright conscience; by knowing how to wait for mercy and grace with trusting certitude; by giving with great goodness of soul; by exercising prudence and discipline; by reigning in the impulses of concupiscence through temperance; by responding with swift obedience to precepts and counsels; by enduring adversity with patience.

Bonaventure comes close to asserting the universal mediation of Mary in commenting on Isaiah 2.2,[217] when he says that the Virgin's 'mercy is necessary for all and so it is right for all to flow to her.' He goes on to offer a detailed account of how she comes to the aid of the faithful, whom he divides into two basic categories, those who are preoccupied with evil, and those who are practiced in the good. Those who are weighed down by evil may be further divided into three types: either 'they are oppressed and look for her as a place of refuge', or 'they are needy and are looking for a place of abundance' or 'they are afflicted and look for a place of quiet'. Likewise, those who have become practiced in virtue turn to her: 'Some are devout and look for a place of prayer. [...] Others are studious and look for a place of learning. [...] Some are cheerful and look for a delightful place.' He concludes: 'Therefore, since each finds in the blessed Virgin

---

[216] Unless otherwise stated, quotations from Bonaventure's sermons on the Virgin are from *Sermons on the Blessed Virgin Mary*, trans. by Campion Murray, in *Franciscan Friars: Province of the Holy Spirit* <http://www.franciscans.org.au> [accessed 10 March 2006].
[217] 'And in the last days the mountain of the house of the Lord shall be prepared on the top of mountains, and it shall be exalted above the hills, and all nations shall flow unto it.'

what he or she needs, rightly do all people flow to her.'[218] What he does not do here, however, is assert that it is *necessary* for all to flow to her, merely that it is right, so that one cannot affirm a doctrine of universal mediation.

In another sermon on the Assumption, Bonaventure offers as a reason for Mary's proximity to God in heaven the necessity for her to intercede on behalf of humanity, a notion that we have come across already in many commentators:

> Having the duty of intercession and reconciliation, she cannot sit for long but must be close by to help and to approach as it were from one side, in fact she must be closely connected as a confidant, lest perhaps a cruel sentence be passed against those entrusted to her, and should that happen, she is provoked. You have an example of this in Esther 7:2: 'What is your petition, Esther?' Immediately at her word the cruel sentence was revoked, the enemy hung, the enemies perished, the people were freed. So in Canticle 6:3 it is said that she is as 'terrible as an army set in array' to help the world and overcome demons. *Third Sermon on the Assumption*

Some sources suggest that it was under Bonaventure's stewardship that the Franciscan Order, at its General Chapter in 1263, introduced the practice of celebrating of the feast of Mary's Visitation to Elisabeth. However, the first firm evidence of the feast dates to 1386 when the archbishop of Prague, John Jennstein composed texts for the Mass and Office of the fest which was celebrated on April 28.[219] The feast was not generally adopted by the Church until a century later. This follows a general pattern for the Franciscans who adopted many Marian feasts such as the Conception of Mary (1263) and the Madonna of the Snow (1302) well ahead of the other orders and the universal Church.[220] Bonaventure also bears witness to the increasing popularity of reciting the Hail Mary in his account of a recalcitrant monk who, close to death, was saved from the clutches of the devil by the Virgin because he had recited the *Ave* one hundred and fifty times a day. She tipped the scales of justice in the monk's favour by placing a drop of her Son's blood on them, at which point the devil admitted his defeat, exclaiming: 'It is not good to fight with you.'[221]

Aquinas († 1274) is more reticent on the question of Mary's mediation of grace. Like his teacher, Albert, he believes that the grace she received at the Incarnation overflowed on all, but it was by giving birth to Christ that this grace became available to all.[222] He makes no mention of her intercession from heaven in the *Summa* or in any of his writings, though it is implicit from what he writes in his *Expositio super salutatione angelica*. Here, Aquinas asserts that Mary

---

[218] *First Sermon on the Assumption.*
[219] See Corrado Maggioni, *Benedetto il frutto*, pp. 89-90.
[220] See Franco A. dal Pino, 'Culto e pietà mariana', p. 178, who provides a wealth of information about early Franciscan devotion to the Virgin.
[221] Quoted in George H. Tavard, *The Forthbringer*', p. 180.
[222] *ST*, III, q. 27, a. 5.

was full of grace in three ways: she was free from all sin, and practiced all the virtues to perfection; the superabundance of grace that she received into her soul was so great that it also sanctified her body; indeed, this grace was so great that it sufficed for all humanity:

> The plenitude of grace in Mary was such that its effects overflow upon all men. It is a great thing in a Saint when he has grace to bring about the salvation of many, but it is exceedingly wonderful when grace is of such abundance as to be sufficient for the salvation of all men in the world, and this is true of Christ and of the Blessed Virgin. Thus, 'a thousand bucklers,' that is, remedies against dangers, 'hang there from' [Canticles 4. 4]. Likewise, in every work of virtue one can have her as one's helper. Of her it was spoken: 'In me is all grace of the way and of the truth, in me is all hope of life and of virtue' [Ecclesiasticus 24. 25].[223]

The reticence of the Scholastics, however, was not sufficient to bring about any significant long-term shift in the trajectory of Marian devotion, as is witnessed by the Conrad of Saxony's († 1279), *Speculum*, a work that was often spuriously attributed to Bonaventure. Conrad is among the many commentators who make reference to Theophilus as proof of the Virgin's boundless mercy.[224] He repeatedly speaks of Mary's power over the demons of hell, and quotes a line of pseudo-Bernard where she is called a warrior: 'Our enemies are the demons whom Mary brought low when she broke their power in herself and in many others, as blessed Bernard testifies, saying: "You are a wonderful warrior, every soldier of the evil spirits is put to flight before your face."'[225] Conrad also links Mary to a series of biblical rods in order to demonstrate her power over the devil:

> Mary is Lady of the demons in hell, so powerfully dominating them that a text of the Psalms can be applied to her: The Lord sends out from Zion your mighty sceptre. Rule in the midst of your foes [Psalms 110. 2]. The mighty sceptre is the Virgin Mary; she is the staff of Aaron putting forth buds through her virginity and fruitful through her pregnancy [Numbers 17. 8]. She is the shoot of which Isaiah speaks: A shoot shall come out from the stump of Jesse [11. 1]; this shoot, the Virgin Mary, is a shoot of power against the infernal enemies whom she controls with great power and so she is rightly loved by us as a Lady of such power, rightly praised by us and rightly entreated by us to keep us safe from these enemies. *Speculum Beatae Mariae Virginis, 3*

---

[223] Translation by Joseph Collins, in *The Catechetical Instructions of St. Thomas* (New York: Wagner, 1939; repr. 2000), pp. 173-80, in *EWTN*, <http://www.ewtn.com/library/SOURCES/TA-CAT-5.TXT> [accessed 18 December 2006]

[224] *Speculum Beatae Mariae Virginis*, 9, trans. by Campion Murray as *The Angel's Greeting*, in *Franciscan Friars Province of the Holy Spirit* <http://www.franciscans.org.au> [accessed 6 December 2007].

[225] *Speculum, 14.* The quote is in fact from Egbertus, *Sermon in Praise of the B.M.V*, 5, *PL* 184, 1013.

Further on he compares her mercy to a bright dawn which terrifies the demons and then to the iron rod of Psalms 2. 9 ('Thou shalt rule them with a rod of iron'), because she causes the demons to flee.[226] Conrad also affirms Mary's spiritual motherhood. He writes that 'the two children of Mary are the God-man and men and women, of whom Mary is the mother of one physically and of the other spiritually', and declares that she is 'not only the mother of the individual Christ but she is the universal mother of all the faithful'.[227] He also writes of the grace that overflows from Mary onto humanity from Heaven:

> If the apostles, indeed all who reign with Christ have perfect joy, how much more complete is the joy of the Mother of God? Of this fullness blessed Jerome says:[228] 'Full of grace, full of God, full of virtues, it is impossible that she does not fully possess the glory of eternal brightness.' Is it surprising if she has an overflowing fullness in heaven whose grace was overflowing while in exile? Is it surprising that from her fullness every creature grows, when in heaven and on earth her fullness exceeded that of every creature?' *Speculum Beatae Mariae Virginis, 7*

By the early fourteenth century all the essential elements of Marian doctrine and devotion that were to characterise the Church in the centuries up to the Reformation were already in place. To be sure, there were to be changes in style and emphasis, such as growing concentration on Mary's suffering and a further softening of her image, as well as some devotional and liturgical innovations, such as the Rosary, the use of vernacular religious drama, and the establishment of new feast days, but these were really just further accumulations on top of already established practices and beliefs. If anything, the imbalances and exaggerations already evident in the previous centuries became even more extreme. At a doctrinal level debate continued to rage on the question of the Immaculate Conception, with the Franciscans in favour and the Dominicans opposed. Perhaps the greatest single change was to be in the increasing use of the vernacular in popular devotion and homilies, which would lead to an even greater dichotomy between the 'high' Mariology of the theologians and the fervent devotionalism of the laity.

Let us conclude this chapter with a work in the vernacular that manages to bridge the divide between theology and devotion, Latin and the vernacular, lay and religious culture, like no other, Dante's († 1321) *Divina Commedia*. In the final *canto* of *Paradiso* it is to Bernard of Clairvaux that Dante entrusts the task of presenting his petition to behold the Beatific Vision. It is an exquisitely beautiful prayer that perfectly expresses the exalted position that the Virgin had achieved in the Medieval mind. Whether approached at a purely literary level or treated as the expression of a genuine mystical vision, the prayer surely ranks as one of the highest poetic expressions of Marian devotion. It is both a laud and a love song,

---

[226] See *Speculum*, 11 and 12.
[227] *Speculum*, 3 and 10.
[228] *Epistula* 9, 15, *PL* 30, 139.

in which Dante combines elements from the centuries-long tradition of Marian devotion with language that is clearly rooted in the *fin'amor* lyric style:[229]

'Vergine Madre, figlia del tuo figlio,

umile e alta più che creatura,

termine fisso d'etterno consiglio,   3

tu se' colei che l'umana natura

nobilitasti sì, che 'l suo fattore

non disdegnò di farsi sua fattura.   6

Nel ventre tuo si raccese l'amore,

per lo cui caldo ne l'etterna pace

così è germinato questo fiore.   9

Qui se' a noi meridïana face

di caritate, e giuso, intra ' mortali,

se' di speranza fontana vivace.   12

Donna, se' tanto grande e tanto vali,

che qual vuol grazia e a te non ricorre,

sua disïanza vuol volar sanz' ali.   15

---

[229] There have been numerous studies on *Canto* XXXIII and on the Prayer to the Virgin, although many fall short of the mark. Among the best are Erich Auerbach, 'Dante's Prayer to the Virgin and Earlier Eulogies', *Romance Philology*, 3 (1949-50), 1-26, Mario Apollonio, 'Il canto XXXIII del "Paradiso"', in *Dante nella critica d'oggi: risultati e prospettive*, ed. by Umberto Bosco (Florence: Le Monnier, 1965), pp. 662-673, Mario Fubini, 'L'ultimo canto del "Paradiso"', in Mario Fubini, *Il peccato di Ulisse e altri scritti danteschi* (Milan & Naples: Ricciardi, 1966), pp. 101-136, Mario Casella, 'Il canto XXXIII del Paradiso', in *Letture Dantesche*, ed. by Giovanni Getto, 3 vols, (Florence: Sansoni, 1970), pp. 675-692, Piero Boitani, 'The Sibyl's Leaves: A Study of *Paradiso* XXXIII', *Dante Studies*, 96 (1978), 83-126, Lino Pertile, '*Paradiso* XXXIII: l'estremo oltraggio', *Filologia e Critica*, 6 (1981), 1-21. See also my three articles, 但丁《神曲》中的女性啟蒙角色 台北;《中外文學》('The Feminine as Clarifier in Dante's *Commedia*'), *Chung Wai Literary Monthly*, 32 (2003), 15-42 , 'A Beauty that Transforms: The Marian Aesthetics of Dante's *Commedia*', *Fu Jen Studies*, 35 (2003), 61-89, and Beyond Beatrice: From Love Poetry to a Poetry of Love', in: *Chivalry and Knighthood in the Middle Ages*, Proceedings of the Fourth Annual Fu Jen Medieval Conference (Taipei: Department of French, Fu Jen University, 2004), pp. 130-192.

La tua benignità non pur soccorre
a chi domanda, ma molte fiate
liberamente al dimandar precorre.   18

In te misericordia, in te pietate,
in te magnificenza, in te s'aduna
quantunque in creatura è di bontate.   21
Or questi, che da l'infima lacuna
de l'universo infin qui ha vedute
le vite spiritali ad una ad una,   24

supplica a te, per grazia, di virtute
tanto, che possa con li occhi levarsi
più alto verso l'ultima salute.   27

E io, che mai per mio veder non arsi
più ch'i' fo per lo suo, tutti miei prieghi
ti porgo, e priego che non sieno scarsi,   30

perché tu ogne nube li disleghi
di sua mortalità co' prieghi tuoi,
sì che 'l sommo piacer li si dispieghi.   33

Ancor ti priego, regina, che puoi
ciò che tu vuoli, che conservi sani,
dopo tanto veder, li affetti suoi.   36

Vinca tua guardia i movimenti umani:
vedi Beatrice con quanti beati
per li miei prieghi ti chiudon le mani!'   39

(Virgin Mother, daughter of your Son, lowly and exalted more than any
creature, fixed goal of the eternal counsel, you are she who did so ennoble
human nature that its Maker did not disdain to be made its making. In your
womb was rekindled the love by whose warmth this flower has bloomed thus in
the eternal peace; here you are for us the noon-day torch of charity, and below
among mortals you are a living spring of hope. You, lady, are so great and so
prevailing that whoso would have grace and does not turn to you, his desire

would fly without wings. Your loving-kindness not only succors him that asks, but many times it freely anticipates the asking in you is mercy, in you pity, in you great bounty, in you is joined all goodness that is in any creature. This man, who from the nethermost pit of the universe to here has seen one by one the lives of the spirits, now begs of you by your grace for such power that with his eyes he may rise still higher towards the last salvation; and I, who never burned for my own vision more than I do for his, offer to you all my prayers, and pray that they come not short, that by your prayers you will disperse for him every cloud of his mortality so that the supreme joy may be disclosed to him. This too I pray of you, Queen, who can what you will, that you keep his affections pure after so great a vision. Let your guardianship control his human impulses. See Beatrice and so many of the blest who clasp their hands for my prayers") (*Paradiso* XXXIII, 1-39).[230]

---

[230] The text of the *Commedia* is cited from the critical edition of Giorgio Petrocchi, *La Commedia secondo l'antica vulgata*, 4 vols (Milan: Mondadori, 1966-67; repr. Florence: Le Lettere, 1994). Translation is from *Paradiso*, trans. by John Sinclair, with modifications by Lauren Seem and Robert Hollander (London: Bodley Head, 1948), <http://etcweb.princeton.edu/dante/pdp/index.html> [accessed 5 April, 2006].

Chapter 6 - Mary Co-Redemptrix: Immediate Co-Operation

Isaiah 66. 7:   Before she was in labour, she brought forth; before her time came to be delivered, she brought forth a man child.

Luke 2. 35:   And thy own soul a sword shall pierce, that, out of many hearts, thoughts may be revealed.

John 16. 21:   A woman, when she is in labour, hath sorrow, because her hour is come; but when she hath brought forth the child, she remembereth no more the anguish, for joy that a man is born into the world.

John 19. 25-27:   Now there stood by the cross of Jesus, his mother, and his mother's sister, Mary of Cleophas, and Mary Magdalen. When Jesus therefore had seen his mother and the disciple standing whom he loved, he saith to his mother: Woman, behold thy son. After that, he saith to the disciple: Behold thy mother. And from that hour, the disciple took her to his own.

Apocalypse 12 1-2:   And a great sign appeared in heaven: A woman clothed with the sun, and the moon under her feet, and on her head a crown of twelve stars: And being with child, she cried travailing in birth, and was in pain to be delivered.

Mary's immediate co-redemption is the belief that she willingly consented to Christ's sacrifice and so completely united herself with his Passion that she spiritually participated in his suffering (co-passion or *compassio*), and was thus an associate (*socia*) in, or co-operated with the objective Redemption brought about by him. This does not mean that the Virgin shared the task of redeeming humanity with her Son, but rather that through her willing identification with Christ's sacrifice she underwent a spiritual martyrdom for the sake of humanity which was, within human limitations, akin to the Passion, thereby partaking in, though not adding anything to his redemptive act.[1] Related, though distinct from, the co-redemption is the notion of Mary's universal mediation, which claims that God has ordained that Mary should collaborate in the distribution of all grace in merit of her role as instrument of the Incarnation

---

[1] To the objection that Mary herself was in need of redemption, and therefore incapable of sharing in it, advocates of the co-redemption answer that she was given a preservative redemption in anticipation of her becoming the Mother of God, and then redeemed definitively along with the rest of humanity on Calvary. See Jean Galot, 'Mary Co-Redemptrix: Controversies and Doctrinal Questions', in *Mary Coredemptrix: Doctrinal Issues Today*, ed. by Mark Miravalle (Goleta, CA: Queenship, 2002), pp. 7-23. See also section on Immaculate Conception.

and her unique participation in the Redemption.[2] In sign of this, it is argued, he entrusted humanity to her in the shape of the apostle John, when he spoke to her from the Cross. Unlike many other Marian doctrines, the notions of the Virgin's co-redemption and universal mediation of grace did not emerge clearly until the Middle Ages, nor has either belief been accepted as an official doctrine by the Catholic Church to this day. [3]

Fundamental to the issue of the Virgin's co-redemption is the question of her behaviour on Calvary.[4] The only testamentary evidence that we have are the brief lines from the Gospel of John which mention Mary's presence on Calvary and Jesus' words to her. Two distinct moments may be identified here, the first in which Mary is described as standing by the Cross together with John and the other Marys, and the second when Jesus entrusts his Mother and John to each other.[5] Beginning with Origen (†c. 254) Mary's standing by the Cross was interpreted in the light of Luke 2. 35, where Simeon prophesises that a sword will pierce the Virgin's heart. Origen interpreted the sword in a negative light as foretelling a crisis of faith that the Virgin would have in the face of her Son's Crucifixion and death, a position that many later Eastern commentators

---

[2] See chapters on Intercession, Mediation and Devotion, and see Daniel Lacoutre, *Marie, Médiatrice de toutes grâces: Raisons, enjeux, conséquences* (Saint-Amand, Cher: Béatitudes, 1997), and Juniper B. Carol, *Fundamentals of Mariology* (New York: Benziger, 1956), pp. 55-71.

[3] Older works that deal with the immediate co-redemption include E. Druwê, 'La médiation universelle de Marie', *Maria*, I, 417-572, Juniper Carol, *De Corredemptione Beatae Virginis Mariae: Disquisitio Positiva* (Vatican City: Typis Polyglottis Vaticanis, 1950), Gabriele M. Roschini, *Problematica sulla Corredenzione* (Rome: Edizioni Marianum, 1969). Two more recent, partisan, studies are Brunero Gherardini, *La corredentrice nel mistero di Cristo e della Chiesa* (Monopoli: Vivere In, 1998), and Mark Miravalle, *'With Jesus': The Story of Mary Co-Redemptrix* (Goleta, Ca.: Queenship Publishing, 2003). See also the collection of articles in *Theotokos*, 7. 2 (1999), dedicated to Mary at the foot of the Cross, some of which I cite below and the acts of three symposia entitled *Mary at the Foot of the Cross*, I, II, II. On non-doctrinal aspects of Mary's suffering at the Cross, the bibliography is vast. Here I shall mention two works in particular. Sandro Sticca's *The Planctus Mariae in the Dramatic Tradition of the Middle Ages*, trans. by Joseph Berrigan (Athens, GA.: University of Georgia Press, 1988), though dated and flawed in several respects, most notably in his misattribution of several important Medieval works, is still essential reading. Rachel Fulton's *From Judgment to Passion: Devotion to Christ and the Virgin Mary, 800-1200* (New York: Columbia University Press, 2002) is indispensable, both for its many penetrating insights and the extraordinary range of material covered. See also *Il mistero della croce e Maria*, atti del 4 colloquio internazionale di mariologia, santuario di Polsi-San Luca (RC), 13-14 settembre 1999, ed. by Stefano De Fiores, Giuseppe Strangio, and Enrico Vidau (Rome: Monfortane, 2001).

[4] See Michael O'Carroll, *Theotokos: A Theological Encyclopedia of the Blessed Virgin Mary* (Collegeville, Minnesota: Liturgical Press, 1982), pp. 104-5, 143-4, 305-6.

[5] See Ermanno Toniolo, 'Gv 19, 25-27 nel pensiero dei Padri, *Theotokos*, 7. 2 (1999), 339-86, who provides a detailed analysis of Patristic treatment of these lines, and gives a comprehensive list of all the relevant passages in the Fathers.

followed, as we will see in the chapter on the Immaculate Conception.[6] In the West, a very different interpretation dominated thanks to the influence of Ambrose of Milan († 397), who held that Mary stoically accepted her Son's suffering while undergoing a spiritual martyrdom, symbolised by the sword.[7] As to Christ entrusting his Mother to John, the Fathers attribute no significant theological meaning to this action. Some pass no comment on it at all while others merely see it as an admirable example of filial piety. Still others argue that the gesture offers proof that Mary did not have other children since otherwise Jesus would not have entrusted her to John, who was not a blood relation.[8] By the later Middle Ages, however, many theologians had embraced the idea that by the words he spoke to her and John from the Cross, 'Woman, behold thy son. [...] Behold thy mother' (John 19. 26-27), Christ had assigned Mary the role of universal motherhood.[9]

The tradition in the Eastern Church of portraying Mary on Calvary as an emotional figure who accepts her Son's fate with extreme difficulty, if at all, was obviously an obstacle to any notion of her having willingly associated herself with the Redemption. The Western position, on the other hand, that Mary willingly endured her Son's death, left open the possibility that she had indeed been an associate (*socia*) in the Redemption, having had foreknowledge of God's redemptive plan, and having consented to the immolation of her Son, and spiritually immolated herself. However, her perceived stoic behaviour was less suggestive of the co-passion, in the emotive if not the strictly technical sense, which may be one reason why the Latin Church long neglected the question of her role on Calvary. Only in the later Middle Ages, when Eastern writings on Mary's suffering at Calvary became more widely known in the West,[10] did theologians begin to dwell seriously on her role in the Passion. However, the meeting of two such divergent traditions inevitably led to certain inherent

---

[6] See *In Lucam*, 6, 3-4 and 17, 6-7, *PG* 13, 1814-15 and 1845, *TMPM* I, 222-23. See the section on the Immaculate Conception for a fuller account of the Greek Fathers' treatment of Mary's behaviour on Calvary. Also see Hilda Graef, *Mary: Doctrine and Devotion* I, 45-46.

[7] See Jean-Marie Salgado, 'La maternité spirituelle de la Sainte Vierge chez les Pères durant les quatre premiers siècles', *Divinitas*, 30 (1986), 58-61, and also by Salgado in the same volume, 'La maternité spirituelle de la Sainte Vierge chez les Pères du V⁹ au VIII⁹ siècle', *Divinitas*, 30 (1986), 120-60, and 'La maternité spirituelle de la Sainte Vierge dans la vie de l'Église du IX⁹ au XI⁹ siècle', *Divinitas*, 30 (1986), 240-70.

[8] See Biagio Amata, 'Giovanni 19, 26-27 come prova scritturistica della perpetua verginità di Maria: origine e sviluppo di questa esegesi', in *Arcidiocesi di Capua, XVI Centenario del Concilio di Capua 392-1992*, Atti del Convegno Internazionale di studi Mariologici, Capua 19-24 Maggio, 1992 (Roma, Torre del Greco: Istituto Superiore di Scienze Religiose Capua e Pontificia Facoltà Teologica Marianum, 1993), pp. 107-172.

[9] See Théodore Koehler, 'Les principales interpretations traditionelles de Jn 19, 25-27 pendent les douze premieres siècles', *Études mariales*, 16 (1959), 119-55.

[10] On relations between East and West see *Relations between East and West in the Middle Ages*, edited by Derek Baker (Edinburgh, Edinburgh University Press).

contradictions which were never fully resolved. The problem as it posed itself to the Medieval churchmen was that an extreme reaction of grief on Mary's part would suggest that she did not have foreknowledge of the purpose of the Crucifixion, for she surely would have rejoiced, at least spiritually, that her Son's sacrifice was bringing about the salvation of humanity. But an excessively stoic attitude would suggest a lack of humanity and an unappealing aloofness, unacceptable to an age which saw Mary as the Mother of Mercy. An additional difficulty concerning Mary's co-redemption which presented itself to Medieval theologians was the question of whether she could have participated in the Redemption when she herself was subject to the consequences of the Fall, and therefore just as much in need of Christ's redemptive sacrifice as everyone else, a question that was closely bound up with the Immaculate Conception.

The Eastern Churches

Origen, as we have noted, is the first to suggest that Mary succumbed to doubt on Calvary:

> Then Simeon says: 'And a sword will pierce your soul'. What is this sword which not only transfixes the hearts of others but of Mary herself? It is written clearly that all the apostles were scandalized at the time of the Passion, as the Lord himself had said: 'You will all be scandalized in my regard this night' (Mark 14. 27). All were scandalized to such a degree that Peter, the head of the apostles, denied Jesus three times. What should we think: that the apostles were scandalized while the Mother of the Lord was preserved free from scandal? If she too did not submit to scandal during the Passion of the Lord, then Jesus did not die for her sins but if 'all have sinned and are deprived of the glory of God', and if 'all are justified and paid for by his grace (see Romans 3. 23), then Mary too, at that moment, was subject to scandal. This is precisely what Simeon prophesised. *In Lucam 17, 6-7*[11]

His intent here is not to assail the holiness of the Virgin but to ensure that the principal of Christ's universal redemption is upheld. A similar preoccupation is to be found in the Middle Ages in the debate over the Immaculate Conception. Likewise, the intent of later Greek Fathers in emphasising Mary's anguish at her Son's suffering, and even her momentary loss of faith, was not to denigrate her in any way, but rather to set her up as an exemplar of Christian perseverance in the face of adversity and temptation.

Origen is also the first of the Fathers, with the exception of Tertullian († after 220),[12] to comment on the entrustment of Mary to John:

---

[11] *PG* 13, 1845, *TMPM*, I, 222-23.
[12] *De praescriptione haereticorum*, 22, *PL* 2, 34.

One must dare to say, therefore, that the first among all the Scriptures are the Gospels, and that John has precedence among the Gospels. No-one can perceive the sense unless he has lain on the breast of Jesus and has received Mary from Jesus, so that she has become his Mother too. Indeed, whoever wishes to become another John must become like this, so that Jesus can proclaim he is [another] Jesus, as with John. Since, according to those who heard truly of her, no-one else apart from Jesus is the son of Mary, and Jesus says to his Mother, 'Behold thy son', and not, 'behold, he too is thy son', it is as if he were saying [of John]: 'Behold, this is Jesus whom you generated.' If every perfect person no longer lives, but Christ lives in him (see Galatians 2. 20), and if Christ lives in him, of him one can say to Mary: 'Behold thy Son'. *Commentary on John, 1, 4*[13]

Although the primary focus here is Christocentric, the point being that all should imitate John in allowing Christ to live in them, the underlying and perhaps unintentional implication of this passage is that Mary is the Mother of all those who fully live as Christians. However, it will be several centuries before this interpretation is drawn out.

Ephrem (†c. 373) does not read any redemptive significance into Mary's presence at the Crucifixion, but, following Origen, he does see her as a model for Christians who, deprived of the physical presence of Christ, should see his image in each other. He writes of Mary's great distress as she sees the Son whom she had suckled at her breast being put to death. It is for this reason, Ephrem believes, that Christ gave Mary into the care of his beloved disciple, John. In this way, Ephrem says, they could contemplate the image of Jesus in each other, impressed like a seal in both of them:

He who was the son of your womb gave and entrusted you to the disciple who has reposed on his breast (John 13. 25). You caressed him, holding him to your breast, when he was a baby; he too held his disciple to his breast. [...] As to you Mary, the Son left you, and yet he did not abandon you since he was still present to you in the person of his disciple [...]. When he saw that you could not separate your love from him, you who had breastfed him as a baby, he who was most pure impressed and forged his image in his pure disciple so that you could contemplate him there. This disciple became an eloquent effigy of he who had remained silent and without words even when he was being tried. [...] Mutually admiring each other, with their gaze they saw you, O Lord, in themselves. Your Mother saw you in the disciple, and he, in turn saw you in the Mother. Happy were they, who continuously contemplated each other! By their example, they taught us that each of us, O Lord, should see you in our neighbour. *Hymns on the Nativity, 25, 2-9*[14]

---

[13] *PG*, 14, 32. All translations, unless otherwise indicated, are mine.

[14] *TMPM*, IV, 107-08. See also *Diatesseron*, 20, 27. On Patristic interpretation of Jesus' words to Mary and John see the very useful article by Théodore Koehler, 'Les principales interprétations traditionelles', pp. 119-55. See also Lucas Mateo-Seco, 'María al pie de la cruz en la patrística griega', *Estudios marianos*, 70 (2004), 71-89.

Ephrem makes it clear that he does not believe Mary had any foreknowledge of Christ's resurrection. In commenting on the Gospel of John, he asserts that Mary had doubted when she had heard that Jesus had risen from the dead and, confusing the Virgin with Mary Magdalene, he says that she mistook him for the gardener when she saw him (John 20. 15).[15] Ephrem is the first of the Fathers to compare Christ's virginal conception and birth with his resurrection from the sealed tomb, a motif that will be taken up by many subsequent commentators[16]. In so doing, he establishes a link between the Redemption and Mary's miraculous virginity, of which it is a prophetic sign, and becomes one of the first contributors to a long tradition of linking the Incarnation to the Redemption:

> With your resurrection you made your birth more comprehensible to her [Mary]. The nest was closed; the tomb was sealed. You were pure in the nest and alive in the tomb. The heap of earth and the tomb were your witnesses, since they were closed. The womb of the Virgin and the underworld announce your resurrection with joy: the womb conceived you while it was closed; the tomb released you while it was sealed. Against the laws of nature the womb conceived you and the tomb restored you. *Hymns on the Nativity, 10, 6-7*[17]

A poem attributed to Ephrem, though its style suggests a considerably later date,[18] employs the rhetorical technique of *ethopoeia* (putting oneself in the place of the subject in order to better express his or her feelings),[19] which was to become one of the main traits of later Greek (and subsequently Latin) Marian laments:

> My sweetest son, my dearest Son. [...] How can you hang on the wood, dead and denuded, my Son, you who cover heaven with your clouds? How could you suffer thirst, you, maker of all, who created the waters and all the oceans there are? [...] O wondrous Simeon, look, here is the sword you foretold would pierce my heart! Look at the sword, look at the wound, my Son and my God! Your death has entered my heart: my inner being is rent, my sight has darkened, and the dread sword has passed through my breast. I behold your awesome Passion, my Son, and my God. I see your undeserved death, and cannot help. Where now is your beauty and comeliness, my Son? Have mercy on your Mother, my Son,

---

[15] See *Diatesseron*, 2, 17 and 21, 27.

[16] See, for instance, Augustine, *De Trinitate*, 4, 5,9, and see John S. Custer, 'The Virgin's Birth Pangs: A Johannine Image in Byzantine Hymnography', *Marianum*, 68 (2006), 417-36.

[17] *TMPM*, IV, 100. The same comparison is to be found in the *Diatesseron*, 21, 21.

[18] There are considerable grounds to be sceptical about the attribution, both on the basis of internal evidence and the lack of a manuscript tradition. As Peter Dronke, 'Laments of the Maries: From the Beginnings to the Mystery Plays', in *Idee, Gestalt, Geschichte: Festschrift Fur Klaus von See: Studien zur europäischen Kulturtradition*, ed. by Gerd Wolfgang Weber (Odense: Odense University Press, 1988), notes the *Treni* are only available in Latin translation (p. 99).

[19] See Henry Maguire, *Art and Eloquence in Byzantium* (Princeton: Princeton University Press, 1981), p. 14, and Rachel Fulton, *From Judgment to Passion*, pp. 537-38, n. 56.

now I am desolate and bereft. *Treni, id est Lamentationes, gloriosissimae Virginis Matris Mariae, 1 and 3*[20]

The apocryphal fifth-century *Acta Pilati B* also known as the *Gospel of Nicodemus*, is very similar in tone to the *Treni*, though Mary's frantic grief, which includes tearing at her face,[21] goes beyond what one finds in the more measured texts of mainstream writers:

> Alas, alas! O my sweet Son, the light of my eyes, the king of the universe. Alas, alas! How can I bear to see you hanging on the Cross? Alas, alas! Where now are the glad tidings of Gabriel? Come here, all of you, and bewail my soul, brutally wounded by sorrow, since I see my sweet Son, my only Son led like an innocent lamb to the Cross and like a condemned man his hands are bound. [...] She uttered a great cry and said, 'My Lord and my Son, what has happened to the beauty of your body? How can I bear seeing you suffer so much?' And with these words she tore her face with her fingernails and beat her breast.[22]

Of similar tone are the *Gospel of Gamaliel*, essentially a Marian lament, and the *Christus patiens*, long attributed to Gregory Nazianzen († 390). These laments were intended to produce an emotional response in readers, primarily so that they would identify more closely with the Passion, and were in no way critical of the Virgin's behaviour. Another factor in the negative portrayal of Mary's reaction to her Son's death was the generally low opinion of women's ability to act rationally. Typical of the prevailing attitude towards women at this time is this passage in which Cyril of Alexandria († 444) comments on John 19. 25, speaking of Mary in strikingly negative terms:

> He introduces as standing by the Cross his mother and the other women with her, and it is clear that they were weeping. The female sex is always somewhat tearful and prone to lamentation when it has abundant cause for shedding tears. What is it then that induced the blessed evangelist to go into trivial details and mention the transgression of the women? His reason was to show this – that the Passion in its unexpectedness had caused even the mother of the Lord to fall, as it appears, and that the death on the Cross, being extremely bitter, made her depart to some extent from the thoughts that were fitting, as did the insults of the Jews and the mocking of the one who had been hung by the soldiers stationed by the Cross, and the way they dared to divide up his clothes in the very sight of his mother. For you need not doubt that she admitted into her mind thoughts of the following kind: 'I gave birth to the one who is mocked on the tree. Perhaps in saying that he was the true Son of almighty God he was mistaken. He was apparently in error when he said. "I am the Life." Why was he crucified? Why was

---

[20] Quoted in Rachel Fulton, *From Judgment to Passion*, pp. 215-16, translation Peter Dronke, 'Laments of the Maries', p. 100.

[21] On gestures and grieving see Henry Maguire, 'The Depiction of Sorrow in Middle Byzantine Art', *Dumbarton Oaks Papers*, 31 (1977), 123-174.

[22] Quoted in Sandro Sticca, *The Planctus Mariae in the Dramatic Tradition*, p. 34.

he caught in some way in the snares of the murderers?' [...] In saying this we are not guessing blindly, as someone might think, but proceeding to a surmise on the basis of what is written about the mother of the Lord. For we remember that the righteous Symeon, when he took the Lord as an infant into his arms, as is written, gave thanks [...] and said to the holy virgin, 'Behold this is for the fall and the raising of many in Israel, and a sign to be spoken against. And your own soul a sword shall pierce, so that the thoughts of many hearts will be revealed' (Luke 2. 34-35). By 'sword' he meant the sharp onset of grief that cleaves the mind of a woman and stimulates misguided thoughts. *Commentary on John, 12*[23]

Further evidence of the emphasis on Mary's human suffering in the Syriac Church is to be found in Jacob of Serug († 521), who is among the first Eastern writers to portray Mary as a thoroughly human mother, shedding bitter tears as she witnesses the death and burial of her Son:

> Your Mother endured great suffering for you and was beset by every kind of distress because of your Crucifixion. So much grief, so many tears shed by those eyes when they buried you, placing you in the tomb. So much horror endured by the Mother of Mercy at your burial, when the guardians of the tomb took hold of you so that she could not come near to you. What suffering she endured as she saw you hanging from the Cross, and they pierced your side with the lance on Golgotha, when the Jews sealed the tomb in which your living body was laid, which gives life and absolves offences. *On the Burial or Death of Mary the Holy Generatrix of God, 25-34*[24]

This passage is part of a longer address in which Jacob reminds Jesus of the events of Mary's life at the time of her death, so that, unusually, we are given Christ's perspective on the suffering of the Virgin. There is no mention of the sword of Simeon: rather, Mary's is the natural agony of a mother as she sees her son enduring torture and death.[25]

Shortly afterwards Romanos the Melodist († c. 560), also a Syrian though he wrote in Greek,[26] composed what may be the earliest example of a *planctus Mariae* (a dramatic plaint or lament of the Virgin), *Mary at the Cross*, which is a dramatised dialogue between Mary and Jesus, which he situates before the opening of the events that lead to the Crucifixion. Mary sits alone in a room, conversing with her Son as he attempts to convince her that there is no other

---

[23] *PG* 74, 661B-664A, quoted from Richard Price, 'The *Theotokos* and the Council of Ephesus', in *The Origins of the Cult of the Virgin Mary*, ed. by Chris Maunder (London: Burns and Oats, 2008), pp. 89-103 (pp. 96-97).

[24] *TMPM*, IV, 172.

[25] See M. Hansbury, *Jacob of Serug on the Mother of God* (Crestwood, N.Y.: St. Vladimir's, 1998), and Graef, *Doctrine and Devotion*, I, 122.

[26] For the influence of Syriac literature on Greek hymns see Sebastian Brock, *From Ephrem to Romanos: Interactions between Syriac and Greek in Late Antiquity* (Aldershot: Ashgate, 1999).

way to achieve the Redemption.[27] After much protestation she finally
acquiesces and asks only that she may accompany him rather than waiting in the
room, to which he agrees, provided that she feels she will be able to control her
emotions. By this clever device, Romanos is able to avoid contradicting the
evidence of the Gospel of John, in which there is no mention of Mary's grief,
since Mary has reconciled herself to her Son's fate in advance. This is
fundamentally different from many later laments in which Mary continues to
protest and grieve both during the Passion and after the death of Christ. This
seminal work set important precedents for subsequent Marian plaints, especially
by emphasising the affective relationship between Mother and Son, and by its
use of dialogue. Imitated by later authors too was the motif of a highly
distraught Mary, unable to understand the soteriological purpose of her Son's
redemptive sacrifice, while Jesus seeks to convince her that his suffering is
necessary if humanity is to be freed from sin:

> Come everyone, let us sing a hymn to him who was crucified for us. Mary saw
> him on the Cross and said: 'Even though you endure the Cross, you are still my
> Son and my God.
> 1. The Ewe, Mary, seeing her Lamb dragged to the slaughter (see Isaiah 53. 7),
> was afflicted and followed with the other women, and cried out: 'Where are you
> going, Son? Why are you hastening with such urgency? Is there perhaps another
> wedding feast at Cana, and are you now hastening so that you can change the
> water into wine? May I come with you, Son? Or would it be better for me to wait
> for you? Say something to me, Word; do not pass by me in silence, you who kept
> me pure, my Son and my God!
> 2. I never thought I would see you reduced to this state, Son, nor did I think
> that the godless would ever become prey to such ferocity, unjustly putting their
> hands on you (see Luke 22. 53). For their children are still calling out to you,
> 'Blessed are you', and the roads are still strewn with palms (see Matthew 21. 8-9),
> bearing witness to the acclamations the godless addressed to you then. So what is
> the reason for such evil now? I want to know, alas, why my light is being
> extinguished and why my Son and my God is being nailed to a cross! [...]
> 4. These are the cries, these the laments that Mary wrenched out of her intense
> pain. Turing to her, he who had come into the world through her exclaimed:
> 'Why do you cry, Mother? Why do you let yourself lose your good sense like the

[27] On Romanos' plaint see Elisabeth Catafygiotou-Topping, 'Mary at the Cross: St. Romanos
Kontakion for Holy Friday,' *Byzantine Studies / Études Byzantines*, 4 (1977), 18-37, Gregory
Dobrov, 'A Dialogue with Death: Ritual Lament and the θρῆνος Θεοτόκου of Romanos
Melodes', *Greek, Roman and Byzantine Studies*, 35 (1994), 385-405, Margaret Alexiou, *Ritual,
Religion, and Art: The Ritual Lament in Greek Tradition*, 2nd edn, rev. by Dimitrios
Yatromanolakis and Panagiotis Roilos (Totowa: Rowman & Littlefield, 2002), pp. 62-77,
and, by the same author 'The Lament of the Virgin in Byzantine Literature and Modern
Greek Folk-Song', *Byzantine and Modern Greek Studies*, 1 (1975), 111-40, and Niki Tsironis,
'The Lament of the Virgin Mary from Romanos the Melode to George of Nicodemia'
(unpublished doctoral thesis, University of London, 1998). For further bibliography on
Romanos see vol. 2. See also Peter Dronke, 'Laments of the Maries', pp. 89-116.

other women? So that I might not endure suffering, so that I might not meet death? But then, how will I pay the ransom for Adam? So that I might not lie in the tomb? But how, then, will I bring those who are in Hades back to life? It is true, and you know it too, that I am crucified unjustly. But why do you cry, Mother? Rather, shout out like this: 'Of his own will he suffers, my Son and my God.'

5. 'Be still, Mother, calm your anguish: laments do not become you of whom was said full of grace. Do not abandon such a title to sobs. Do not be like women with no intelligence, most wise Virgin. You are at the centre of my wedding hall, do not behave as if you had been left outside, your soul withered. Call the women who are in the hall; they are you servants. They will all run to you, trembling, and listen to you Holy One, when you say: 'Where is my Son and God?'

6 Do not make the day of the Passion seem bitter, because it was for this day that I, the Sweet One, descended from heaven like manna, not like of old on Mount Sinai, but in you womb. In it I curdled, as David prophesised: understand it, O Holy One, I am the "curdled mountain" (see Psalms 67. 16), the Word who took flesh in you (see John 1. 14). In this flesh I suffer, in it too do I bring about salvation; do not cry therefore, Mother, but instead cry out: 'Of his own will my Son and my God suffers the Passion.'

6a. [...] At these words, the most pure Mother of him who ineffably became incarnate in her and was born of her exclaimed: 'What have you said to me, Son: "Do not allow yourself to lose your wits together with the other women"? Similar to woman am I in that I bore you in my womb and nourished you at my breast. How can you expect me not to cry for you, my Son, as you rush to undergo an unjust death, you who raised the dead, my Son and my God?'

7. 'You, my Son,' she answered', 'see how I drive away the tears from my eyes and my heart breaks even more; I cannot silence my thoughts. Did you not say, flesh of my flesh: "If I do not suffer Adam will not regain his health"? Yet, without having suffered, you gave health back to many: you purified the leper (Matthew 8. 1-14) without having suffered at all; it was sufficient for you to will it.' [...]

8. 'When you brought the dead back to life you did not subject yourself to death, you were not placed in a tomb, my Son and my life. Why therefore did you say: "If I do not suffer, if I do not yield to death, Adam will not regain his health"? Command it, O Lord, and he will wake up suddenly, carrying his own bed (Matthew 9. 6-7). Even though Adam is lying in the tomb, the same will happen to him as for Lazarus, whom you raised with a single cry. Everything is subject to you because you are the creator of everything. Why then this haste, my Son? Do not hasten to the slaughter, do not make yourself the lover of death, my Son and my God!'

9. 'You do not understand, Mary, you do not understand what I mean to say. Open you mind therefore to receive the Word that you hear, and you yourself, within yourself, meditate on what I say. He whom I named, unhappy Adam, is not just infirm in body, but his soul too has been broken, and willingly so, because he did not want to listen to me, and now he is in danger. Can you grasp what I am saying? Do not cry therefore, Mother, but say rather: "Have pity on Adam, have mercy for Eve too, my Son and my God." [...]

11. When she had heard these words the spotless Ewe replied to the Lamb: 'My Son, do not be upset if I speak to you once again. I will say what I have in my heart, so as to learn from you alone what I wish. If you suffer, if you die, will you return to me? If you go to heal Adam and Eve, will I see you again? This is what I fear: perhaps when you emerge from the tomb you will rush to heaven. And I, [longing] to see you will only be able to weep and cry out: "Where is my Son and my God?"'

12. When he heard these words, he who knows all things before they happen answered Mary: 'Take courage, Mother! You will be the first to see me when I come out of the tomb. I will come to you to show you the many punishments from which I will have ransomed Adam, and the travails I will have suffered for him. […]

14. Still, still your pain and grief therefore, Mother, and walk in joy. As for me, I am in haste to fulfil the will of him who sent me (John 6. 38). […] Run therefore, Mother, to announce to all: "With his Passion he strikes the spiteful enemy of Adam and returns victorious, my Son and my God!"'

15. 'I am overcome, Son, vanquished by love, and I cannot bear the idea of being in a room while you are on the wood, or in a house when you are in the tomb. Allow me therefore to come with you because it will be of comfort to me to see you. I will look upon the impudence of those who honour Moses, who, by their account, blindly seek to kill you to vindicate him.' […]

16. 'If you come, do not cry, Mother, nor should you fear when you see the elements shaken, because this temerity will stir up the whole of creation: the heavenly vault will be blinded, nor will it be able to open its eyes again unless at my command (see Matthew 27. 45), the earth will be in flight with the seas; then the temple will rip the veil, a clear accusation for the authors of such a misdeed; the mountains will be shaken and the graves will empty themselves. When you see these things, if you are afraid as is natural for a woman, cry out to me: "Spare me, my Son and God!"'

17. O Son of the Virgin, God of the Virgin and Creator of the World! Yours is the Passion, yours the depths of wisdom (see Romans 11. 33). You know what you were and what you have become. It is you who, in accepting suffering, became worthy to come to the salvation of man. It is you who took our faults on yourself as the Lamb. It is you who saved all by putting these faults to death through your immolation. You are the same when you suffer and do not suffer. When you die you are you, and when you save you are you. You gave this certainty to the Holy One which allows her to cry out: 'My Son and God'. *Mary at the Cross*[28]

The intent here, as in later plaints, is essentially didactic. The reader is drawn into the drama of Christ's passion and instinctively empathises with Mary's struggle to understand the purpose of such a brutal death. Christ's replies

---

[28] The full text of the hymn is in *TMPM*, I, 722-26. See also the lengthy extract from the hymn quoted in *MF*, pp. 333-37, from the translation by Constantine Trypanis, in *The Penguin Book of Greek Verse* (Middlesex: Penguin, 1971). For an alternative translation see *On the Life of Christ: Kontakia*, Trans. and Introd. by Ephrem Lash (San Francisco: Harper Collins, 1995). See also Graef, *Doctrine and Devotion*, I, 122.

provide the answer. As both the refrain and the conclusion to Romanos' lament remind us, despite her difficulty in accepting the Cross, Mary still maintains her faith that Jesus is God, as should we. Far from undergoing a crisis of faith on Calvary, Mary is prepared for what is to come by Jesus himself so that she may bear witness with complete conviction to the redemptive value of the Cross. Ultimately, full understanding and acceptance comes only with this unconditional faith.

Although some continued to state that Mary had suffered a crisis of faith on Calvary, such as Sophronius of Jerusalem († 638), and the belief was still present at the time of Photius (†c. 897),[29] the majority of later Byzantine writers do not entertain the possibility. Leontius of Neapolis (†c. 650) writes of the sword of Simeon: 'I believe that the sword signifies the trial of suffering that the Virgin had to undergo at the foot of the Cross. Indeed, it pierced her, though without injuring her if not in a superficial manner.'[30]

Written around the same time was one of the most significant documents to emerge from the Byzantine Church concerning Mary's participation in the Passion, the *Life of Mary* attributed to Maximus the Confessor († 662).[31] In the course of its lengthy treatment of the Virgin's reaction to the events of Calvary, which is never hysterical, though her grief is bitter, it makes a number of significant statements concerning the depth of her suffering, which come close to the notion that she shared in Christ's Passion. The author begins by linking the Virgin's generation of Christ with her suffering at the Crucifixion, stating that both events exceeded the laws of nature, a notion that we have already come across in Ephrem, though applied differently:

> For just as at the moment of his birth her beloved Son and God revealed her to be Mother and Virgin, so he kept her impassable at the moment of his Passion: for the blessed Mother was immersed in suffering and suffered with him, according to the order of nature, above all because of the love she had for him; but he rendered her impassable through the divine grace with which her soul was filled, and in virtue of the sovereign power that he showed forth in his Mother. *73*

How far we have travelled from the disparaging comments of Cyril of Alexandria! Later he expresses the same notion even more forcefully: 'Just as

---

[29] Sophronius expresses this opinion in his *Homily for the Hypapante*, 4, 16, *TMPM*, II, 165. Photius writes: 'As to the opinion according to which the sword is that doubt that struck her soul and that led her to ask herself if that crucified man was or was not God, some have affirmed that this to be so. I, however, have never said this.' *Ampilochian Questions*, 157, *PG* 101, 832C.

[30] *Homily on Simeon*, *TMPM*, II, 177, *PG*, 93, 1581.

[31] The full text may be found in *TMPM*, II, 185-289; for the section dealing with the Passion see pp. 240-255. See Maria Melli, 'Il mistero della croce in San Massimo il Confessore', in *Il mistero della croce e Maria*, pp. 79-95 , and see the forthcoming (Yale UP, 2012) translation and commentary on *The Life* by Stephen J. Shoemaker.

the generation of the Son transcends the laws of nature so the grief that filled her in accepting the Crucifixion of the Lord cannot be told of by men: she alone knows how she suffered, and only God, who was born of her, knows it entirely' (84). From the outset Mary is shown to identify entirely with her Son's suffering: when he is condemned, 'the Virgin Mary felt condemned and crucified in her heart with her Son' (77). Indeed, in a certain sense, the author affirms, she suffered more than Christ, since his was a voluntary sacrifice to which she had to acquiesce: 'These sufferings crushed you more than your Son, [who was] stronger than all since he was suffering voluntarily and had foretold everything that would happen to him' (78). With the typical feelings of a mother, Mary wishes that she could take the suffering of her Son on herself, yet she is also aware that he has a greater purpose:

> O terrible sight! How is it that the earth trembles and no longer contains the underworld! How is it that the lamps [of the sky] dim and no longer shed any light, how is it that the heavens shake and do not fall upon the earth, how is it that the angels tremble and hold back from destroying the world! But it is clear that everything that is occurring is because of your mercy and forbearance, O my Son and God, because everything is subject to your power and you will not permit what happened to Noah in times past to come upon the world. Ah, my Son, was it not possible for me to undergo these tortures in your place? Alas, would that your wounds could be inflicted on me! O, would that I could die in your place! *81*

Jesus responds to these laments, according to the author, by entrusting his Mother to his beloved disciple, John, and in so doing, he gives Mary to us all: 'He also gave his Mother to the disciple in exchange for his love and his faithfulness, since he stayed standing [at the Cross] at the time of the Passion. He deemed him worthy of a great honour and in his person he left his Mother to us' (82). The act of entrusting Mary to John therefore, is not just one of filial piety, but has the mystical significance of her becoming the Mother of all humanity. The author identifies the spear that pierced her Son's side with the sword that pierced Mary's heart, and asks himself how Mary could withstand such crushing suffering. In answering, he clearly affirms that Mary experienced the Passion in the same measure as Christ, while, at the same time, it is the grace that comes from Christ's redemptive act which gives the Virgin the strength to endure:

> How could the immaculate Generatrix endure this piercing? How was it that she did not give up the spirit? It is clear that the grace and strength of the crucified Lord preserved her. He himself died in the way that he willed; but his strength preserved the soul of his Mother, so that it might be clothed entirely with his same sufferings. *84*

The author goes on to speak specifically of Mary's compassion: 'Look at the heart of the blessed Mother at this moment, pierced by the sword: how great was her compassion then, and even greater her suffering, since she too almost died when she saw her Son die' (85). Her identification with Christ's suffering is such that the words of the psalmist, 'My heart is consumed within me, my sorrow is renewed' (Psalms 38, 3-4) may be applied to her (85). At this moment Mary also became the first, and most perfect, recipient of the Eucharist, as she collected the water and blood that issued from Christ's side. There follows a lament of the Virgin over the body of Christ after it is taken down from the Cross:

> She flooded the earth with her tears as she received in her arms him who had been taken down. In her lap she received the nails and embraced his wounded limbs with tenderness. She washed the blood with her tears and wept bitterly over that Son who was the sweetness longed for by angels and men. But when he had been taken down from the Cross, and the body of him who is higher than the heavens touched the earth, she too fell down suddenly and almost shattered. She washed him with scalding tears and with divine words she uttered the burial eulogy: 'O fulfilment of the unfathomable mystery! O revelation of the divine plan hidden to the ages! O death more admirable than the Incarnation! The Creator of souls lies without a soul; he who dispenses salvation to all reposes like a corpse; the Word of the Father, who made every creature that speaks is without words. [...] Alas, where is your beauty, O my Son and my God? Where is your face, most beautiful among the sons of men, you who ordered every beauty of the earth and who are the only sweetness that is entirely desirable? You who endured blows and wounds, you who heal the incurable wounds of our nature, stains and blows both ancient and new. You, O King, had pity on us and for us you endured wounding; by your wounds we are all cured. Now, behold, thanks to your free disposition and the magnanimity of your grace and of your love for men, the mystery has been fulfilled. Now therefore, show your strength, hasten and come to our aid. I know with certainty that you will rise again and that you will have pity first of all upon your Mother, and then on this Sion and on Jerusalem which has sinned so much. There you will call together all the Gentiles and you will raise up the living temple of the Church of the pagans. Happy the day when you will let me hear your sweet voice again, when I will see your divinely beautiful face again and I will be filled to the brim with your much-desired grace.' *89*

A clearer witness to Mary's foreknowledge of the Resurrection one could not find. She is cast in the role of prophetess and interpreter of the mystery of the Redemption, as she foresees not only Christ's Resurrection but the birth of the Church and the proclamation of salvation to the Gentiles. Nevertheless, though fully cognisant throughout of the meaning and purpose of the Passion, her role is that of a witness and expositor, not an active participant. At no point does the author suggest in any way that she contributed to Christ's Redemption of humanity though she willingly associated herself with it.

Germanus of Constantinople (†c. 733) likewise does not seem to entertain an active role for Mary in the Passion, when he states that, 'she endured his Passion and death in human fashion.' On the basis of this statement one might assume that he is not crediting the Virgin with any higher understanding of events. However, as the homily proceeds, we get a hint through his birthing metaphors that Mary is aware that out of her dark night and that of her Son, new life will come:

> The Mother reaches a peak in her lamentations. She conceives still greater sighs. She gives birth to more extensive weeping. For now she no longer has sight of her Son. The sun knew its setting, going below the earth, and it became night for the mother of the Sun. A night of heavy sorrow and disaster. *In Dominici corporis sepulturam*[32]

As if to confirm that Christ's death cannot be the end, Mary proceeds in her plaint to use a whole series of typologies that foretell the Incarnation, such as the fleece of Gideon, the burning bush, and the gold jar of manna.[33] These prophetic signs have the dual effect of drawing the reader back in wistful remembrance to the joyful time of Christ's birth and of reminding us that he was no ordinary man and will rise again.

The notion that Mary suffered the pangs of labour during his Passion, pangs which she had avoided at Christ's birth – which also draws on the association of womb with tomb found in Ephrem and others – appears in several of the later Eastern Fathers, such as Andrew of Crete (†c. 740), who writes in one of his hymns: 'Your Ewe, handmaid and Virgin, seeing you hasten to the Passion and give your life for us, O Good Shepherd, suffered the pangs of a mother for you.'[34] John of Damascus († 749) writes along similar lines:

> But this blessed woman, made worthy of gifts that are above nature, suffered those pangs that she escaped at the birth, at the time of the Passion, since her innards were lacerated by her motherly affection when she beheld him whom she knew to be God killed as a criminal. Then her viscera were pierced through by the sword. This was in fulfilment of what had been said of her: 'And thy own soul a sword shall pierce, that, out of many hearts, thoughts may be revealed' (Luke 2. 35). But the joy of the resurrection silences the pain, proclaiming him, who died in the flesh, to be God. *Exposition on the Orthodox Faith, 6, 14*[35]

John also fleetingly suggests that one reason why Mary should have been assumed into heaven in body and soul is her participation in the Passion of her

---

[32] *PG* 98 269B, translation by Niki Tsironis, 'From Poetry to Liturgy: The Cult of the Virgin in the Middle Byzantine Era', in *Images of the Mother of God: Perceptions of the* Theotokos *in Byzantium*, ed. by Maria Vassilaki (Aldershot: Ashgate, 2005), pp. 91-102 (p. 93).

[33] See Volume 2 for these types.

[34] *Triodion for Palm Sunday, Theotokion, Ode VIII, TMPM*, II, 464.

[35] *TMPM*, II, 493-94.

Son: 'It was fitting that she who had contemplated her Son on the Cross, receiving the sword of suffering in her heart, which she had avoided when she gave birth, should contemplate him seated next to the Father.[36] Unfortunately he does not develop this fascinating idea further.

Cosmos of Maiuma (†c. 751), an adopted brother of John of Damascus, also writes of Mary's labour on Calvary in a plaint uttered by the Virgin as she witnesses her Son's death: 'I avoided the pangs at your extraordinary birth / and I was supernaturally blessed, / O Son who has no beginning; / But now, seeing you dead, my God, without breath, / I am horribly rent by the sword of suffering.'[37] By linking the two events of the Incarnation and the Redemption and suggesting that Mary suffered the pangs of birth under the Cross all these authors are emphasising that her role in God's plan of salvation did not end with the birth of Jesus, but that she continued to co-operate with him throughout his life and most especially in the Passion when, in some way, she participated in giving birth to the new creation. George of Nicodemia († after 880) offers an emotional rendering of Mary's lament, stressing in particular her complete isolation as she alone associates herself with her Son's Passion. He too identifies her agony with parturition:

> Who wills this, Lord? [...] O most unjust crime! O wicked sentence! The unjust condemn the just. [...] O, Son, that I could take your tortures upon myself! O that those nails could pierce through my limbs! O, that I might bear the torments of your pains in my body! Then perhaps the grief of my heart might be tolerable; but now truly [...] the grief of my soul is so great it is scarcely possible to bear. [...] O Son, sweeter than sweet! [...] Now I alone am crucified [...]: I alone receive your bitter pains in my breast. For there is no one to share in my sorrow with me, no one to share the wounds with me. [...] Pains greater than those of childbirth burn me now as the sword of your passion cuts through my soul. *Homily 8*[38]

As the sermon progresses, however, we begin to realise that this is more than the traditional emotive evocation of Mary's agony. The homilist marvels at the Virgin's ability to withstand the torment of seeing her Son's agony and goes on to speak of how she participates in his Passion, suffering now the pangs of childbirth that she had avoided at his coming into the world. In commenting on Christ's entrustment of his Mother to John, George makes the first unambivalent affirmation of Mary's universal motherhood to be found in either the East or West. Imagining Jesus addressing John he writes:

---

[36] *Second, Homily on the Dormition, 14.* See *TMPM*, II, 530-31. For an alternative translation, see *EPH*, pp. 218-19.

[37] *Tetraodion for Holy Saturday, Ode IX, Troparion, TMPM*, II, 599.

[38] Translation Rachel Fulton, *From Judgment to Passion*, p. 216, and see her extensive note on the prayer, pp. 537-38. The full sermon is available in Italian in *TMPM*, II, 744-73.

> Since she already enjoys my continuous divine presence let her also have your
> solicitous help and may it never be lacking. Both of us, therefore, you with your
> words and I with acts will try to soothe her immense suffering. You comfort her
> adequately while I will infuse her with all the necessary strength of mind. Now I
> constitute her not only as your Mother, but of all the others too. I place her as
> guide to the disciples and I absolutely desire that she be honoured because of
> her privilege as Mother. *Homily 8*[39]

It will take several centuries for Western commentators to posit such a clear link
between John 19. 26-27 and Mary's motherhood of humanity. Henry Maguire
has shown the influence that this sermon had in the emergence of the theme of
the Lamenting Virgin in Byzantine icons.[40] It is also in this post-iconoclastic
period that triumphant and hieratic portrayals such as the Enthroned Virgin and
the Hodegtria ('she who shows the way') were gradually overtaken by the
Eleousa icon (compassionate Virgin), in which Mary clasps the Child to her
cheek, a mournful expression on her face, as if trying to ward off his
predestined passion and death. It was at this time too that *staurotheotokia*
(versified laments of the Virgin) began to be included in the Byzantine
Passiontide liturgy.[41]

A lament attributed to Simon Metaphrastes, a tenth-century Byzantine about
which very little is known, but possibly written as late as the twelfth century,
once again emphasises the link between birth and death, with Mary likening the
funerary apparel of Jesus to his swaddling clothes.[42] Pierced by the agony of her
Son, and crucified by his sufferings, Mary vocalises her woe and recalls the
happier times when Jesus was a child and she held him in her arms, as she now
holds his dead body.[43] This motif of looking back nostalgically to Christ's
childhood was a common one in Eastern plaints and was also taken up by
Medieval writers in the West. Before turning to the West we must mention John
the Geometer (†c. 990) whom many consider the first commentator to draw out

---

[39] *TMPM,* II, 756.

[40] See his *Art and Eloquence* and also his 'The Depiction of Sorrow'. See also Hans
Belting, *Likeness and Presence: A History of the Image before the Era of Art,* trans. by Edmund
Jephcott (Chicago: University of Chicago Press, 1994), 120-23, and Niki Tsironis, 'From
Poetry to Liturgy', pp. 94-96.

[41] See W. Lipphardt, 'Studien zu den Marianklagen', *Beiträge zur Geschichte der deutschen
Sprache und Literatur,* 58 (1934), 390-444, Graef, *Doctrine and Devotion,* I, 263, Pelikan,
Mary through the Centuries: pp. 125-26, Sandro Sticca, *The Planctus Mariae in the Dramatic
Tradition,* and Niki Tsironis, 'From Poetry to Liturgy', pp. 96-98, and John S. Custer,
'The Virgin's Birth Pangs'.

[42] See Margaret Alexiou's groundbreaking *Ritual, Religion, and Art: The Ritual Lament in
Greek Tradition* 2nd edn, rev. by Dimitrios Yatromanolakis and Panagiotis Roilos
(Totowa: Rowman and Littlefield, 2002) and Henry Maguire, *Art and Eloquence,* who
notes the manuscript evidence suggesting that it was in fact written by the twelfth-
century Nikephoros Basiliskis (pp. 98-99).

[43] See Graef, *Doctrine and Devotion,* I, 201.

the theological implications of attributing a more active dynamic to Mary's maternal suffering. Likening the willing offering that the Virgin made of her Son on Calvary to that of the Father, he asserts that, 'She, just like the Father, has delivered her own Son and knew him to be delivered unto death.'[44] However his was to be an isolated voice in the East and it was to be in the Latin Church that the theology of Mary's co-redemption and co-passion was to be more fully worked out.

The Church in the West

Ambrose († 397), the greatest advocate of Mary in the early Latin Church, ensured that Western Mariology would follow a very different trajectory on the Virgin's role at Calvary by decisively rejecting the Eastern belief that she was assailed by doubt on Calvary. In several celebrated passages that had an enduring influence on the Western tradition he portrays the Virgin's stoic endurance as she witnesses the excruciating suffering of her Son in his Passion and death, contrasting her fidelity to the flight of the apostles.[45] Crucially, he asserts that she was fully aware of the redemptive significance of the Passion and wished to associate herself with it:

> His Mother stood before the Cross, and, while the men fled, she remained undaunted. [...] His Mother looked, her eyes filled with pity, on the wounds of her Son, from whom she knew would come the salvation of the world, and she presented an image not unworthy of her Son. The Son hung from the Cross and the Mother offered herself to his persecutors. If she had been there just to be killed before her Son, her maternal affection causing her not to wish to outlive him, this would have been worthy of praise; but if she wanted to die along with her Son, it was because she looked forward to rising with him. Well did she know the mystery, that she had given birth to One who was to rise; moreover, she knew that her Son's death would happen for the good of all. Thus, by her death, she wished, if it was necessary, to add something to the common good. But Christ's Passion had no need of help as the same Lord had foreseen long before: 'I looked about, and there was none to help: I sought, and there was none to give aid: and my own arm will save them (see Isaiah 63. 5). *De institutione virginis, 49*[46]

Ambrose's enduring legacy resulted in two apparently contradictory tendencies. Firstly, since there was no question over Mary's faith and her willing adherence to

---

[44] *Life of Mary*, 60, quoted in Graef, *Doctrine and Devotion*, I, 198.

[45] See Charles W. Neumann, *The Virgin Mary in the Works of Saint Ambrose* (Fribourg, University Press, 1962), Ermanno Toniolo, 'Gv 19, 25-27 nel pensiero dei Padri', pp. 371-86.

[46] *PL* 16, 318B-319A, [333], based in part on the translation in *MF*, pp. 201-203. See also *De Mysteriis*, 3, 13, (*PL* 16, 410), *Epistola* 63, 110 (*PL* 16, 1218C), *De obitu Valentiniani consolatio*, 39 (*PL* 16, 1371B), and *Expositio Evangelii secundum Lucam*, 10, 132, (*PL* 15, 1837C).

God's salvific plan was clear, portrayals of her suffering on Calvary were far more restrained than in the East. Yet, this same belief in her steadfastness left open the possibility that she had in some way participated in the Redemption and eventually led, in the later Middle Ages, to the notions of her co-passion and co-redemption. Nevertheless, as is clear from this passage, Ambrose himself explicitly excludes the possibility that Mary contributed in any way to Christ's redemptive sacrifice on the Cross. He does not interpret Christ's words to his Mother and John from the Cross as a declaration of her universal motherhood but as an invitation to all the faithful to become children of the Church, which is analogous to Mary: 'May Christ also say to you, "Behold thy mother." May he also say to the Church, "Behold thy Son": for then you will begin to be a son of the Church when you see Christ victorious on the Cross.'[47] However the identification of Mary with the Church does hint at her universal motherhood.

Ambrose's view was not accepted immediately, however. Paulinus of Nola († 431) offers a sober and touching portrayal of a mother's human suffering. Although he does not speak of a loss of faith in the same sense as many of the Eastern Fathers understood it – a total giving in to despair – he nevertheless believes that Mary was blinded to the true import of Christ's death by the weight of her human suffering and did not foresee the Resurrection:

> Should we not believe that with these expressions Simeon intended to prophesise the physical suffering of Mary, of which we find no mention? Is it not more likely that he prophesied the maternal love of the Virgin, that love which she felt again and again during the Passion, when she found herself at the foot of the Cross, to which was pinned the Son to whom she had given birth? She too was nailed [to it] because of her maternal and deep love. The lance of the Cross penetrated her soul; that lance, under her gaze had pierced the Son who was born of her according to the flesh. [...] She saw her dead Son and cried out of human weakness, she gathered him up to bury him, foreseeing nothing of his Resurrection, because the suffering of the Passion that had taken place before her eyes prevented her from perceiving faith in the subsequent glory. *Epistola 50, 17*[48]

Augustine († 430) does not consider the role of Mary at the Crucifixion, beyond commenting on the human relationship between Christ and his Mother. In a rather convoluted explanation, in which he links Jesus' apparent rejection of his Mother at the wedding feast of Cana with his words to her from the Cross (on both occasions he addresses her as 'woman'), he underlines both the importance of Christ's divinity, which he first manifested publicly in the miracle of changing water into wine, and of his humanity, which had to render satisfaction to God on the Cross. Underlying this thought, perhaps, is the idea

---

[47] *Expositio evangelii secundum Lucam*, 7, 5.
[48] *PL* 61, 415B-C.

that Mary's mediatory role was central both at Cana and on Calvary, but he does not elaborate on this:

> This was the hour of which Jesus had said to his Mother, when about to turn the water into wine: 'Woman, what is that to me and to thee? My hour is not yet come' (John 2. 4). He had foretold this hour, which at that time had not yet arrived, when, dying, he would recognise her from whom he had received this mortal life. At that time, therefore, when he was about to carry out a divine act he appeared to distance her from himself, as if she were a stranger, she who was the Mother, not of his divinity, but of his human infirmity; but now, when in the midst of human sufferings, he commended with human affection she by whom he had become man. For then, he who had created Mary manifested himself in his power, but now, he whom Mary had brought forth was hanging on the Cross. *In Evangelium Ioannis tractatus*, 119, 1[49]

Augustine goes on to explain, in a passage that is devoid of any profound spiritual sense, that Jesus entrusted his Mother to John out of a sense of filial piety and that John took Mary in, not in order to gain any possessions but as a duty. No hint, therefore, of any spiritual significance to Mary's presence on Calvary, nor any comment on her suffering, whether human or spiritual.[50] The reason behind this, perhaps, is that for Augustine, whose teaching centred so much on the need for Christ's grace in order to redeem the fallen nature of mankind, the very notion that anyone other than Jesus himself could in any way contribute to or participate in the Redemption was unthinkable. He repeatedly affirms the universal mediation of Christ in his writings, making it absolutely clear that all the children of Eve, including Mary, can only be redeemed through Christ's sacrifice on the Cross:

> Every man is separated from God until he is reconciled to God through the mediation of Christ, and no-one can be separated from God except by the sins that keep him far from God; and he can be reconciled only through the remission of sins in virtue of the unique grace of the most merciful Saviour, in virtue of the one victim offered by the most true Priest. In short, all the children of the woman, who believed in the serpent and was thereby corrupted by libidinousness, are not freed from the body of death if not through the work of the Son of the Virgin, who believed in the angel and was therefore made fecund without libidinousness. *De peccatorum meritis et remissione, 1, 28, 56*[51]

---

[49] *PL* 35, 1950. All translations, unless otherwise indicated, are from the Latin and Italian texts in S. Aurelii Augustini, *Opera Omnia, Tutte le opere*, ed. by Franco Monteverde, 45 vols (Rome: Nuova Biblioteca Agostiniana and Città Nuova, 1967–), in *Sant'Agostino, Augustinus Hipponensis*, < http://www.augustinus.it/> [accessed 25 March 2008].
[50] He does fleetingly make reference to Mary's suffering in his *Ennarationes in Psalmos*, 104, 13, *PL* 37, 1397, where he speaks of her being 'gravely wounded' by the loss of his corporeal presence.
[51] *PL* 44, 141.

Christ alone, who is both God and man, whose flesh is entirely free from all taint of sin, can offer a sacrifice to the Father sufficient for the redemption of humanity:

> Who then is so righteous and holy a priest as the only Son of God, who had no need to purge his own sins by sacrifice, neither original sins, nor those which are added by human life? And what could be so fitly chosen by men to be offered for them as human flesh? And what so fit for this immolation as mortal flesh? And what so clean for cleansing the faults of mortal men as the flesh born in and from the womb of a virgin, without any infection of carnal concupiscence? And what could be so acceptably offered and taken, as the flesh of our sacrifice, made the body of our priest? In such wise that, whereas four things are to be considered in every sacrifice – to whom it is offered, by whom it is offered, what is offered, for whom it is offered, – the same One and true Mediator Himself, reconciling us to God by the sacrifice of peace, might remain one with Him to whom He offered, might make those one in Himself for whom He offered, Himself might be in one both the offerer and the offering. *De Trinitate, 4, 14, 19*[52]

Undoubtedly the force of Augustine's teaching on Christ as the sole Mediator and Redeemer, and the fact that he attributed no importance to Mary's presence on Calvary, was a major factor in discouraging further consideration of her role in the Redemption in the Patristic West. In fact, no theologian of note took up the question for several centuries.

Most early Medieval commentators believe that Mary endured tremendous suffering on Calvary, but they do not read a great deal into it. Bede († 735), commenting on the sword of Simeon, essentially repeats what had been handed down to him by the Latin Fathers. His comments nevertheless underline the profound difference in understanding between East and West on Mary's response to the Passion:

> Although not doubting that Jesus, insofar as he was God, would rise from the dead, Mary could not contemplate him crucified and dying without enduring bitter suffering. She indeed felt terrible anguish for him, who was born of her flesh, struck as she was by his death. *In Purificatione beatae Mariae*[53]

Ambrose Autpert's († c. 781) comments are brief and devoid of emotion: 'Now, although many tribulations pierced the soul of the most blessed Virgin, these words of Simeon, however, signify in a special way that suffering that

---

[52] Quoted from *Nicene and Post-Nicene Fathers*, First Series, III, ed. by Philip Schaff, Trans. by Arthur West Haddan, (Buffalo, N.Y.: Christian Literature Publishing., 1887), revised and edited for *New Advent* by Kevin Knight, <http://www.newadvent.org/fathers/1301.htm>, [accessed 4 February 2009].
[53] *PL* 92, 347A.

pierced the maternal viscera at the death of the Lord on the Cross.'[54] Several, such as Alcuin († 804), Candidus of Fulda († 845), and Haymo of Auxerre († c. 855), repeat Augustine's comment on Christ's words from the Cross being an example of filial piety.[55]

In the ninth century, however, there are two notable exceptions to this lack of commentary. Hrabanus Maurus († 856), speculates at length on Mary's feelings as she saw her Son being tortured and put to death:

> How could such a Mother of such a Son bear to stand by, seeing him die thus? Did not the heart of the Mother possess the viscera of pity? What was the Mother of Mercy thinking, who felt everything that her Son was enduring? How could she bear the weight of his death, when many, after the passing of long years, would not be able to endure the memory of his Passion? Where is the mother who is able to see and bear her son hanging from a gibbet, even if he deserved it? Do not mothers so love their sons that they cannot even hear a bad word against them? How, therefore, was the Mother of the Lord able to stand there, and not fall down, beaten one hundred times, or dead? What was she doing, how could she remain there, and stay silent when all around her she could hear people speaking to each other and to her Son? How did she not run to the Cross, crying out and wailing, tearing her Son away from them, or at least begging tearfully that he be given back to her? *Opusculum de passione Domini*, 6[56]

He goes on to ask how she did not protest when Jesus asked his Father to forgive his crucifiers and how she bore being handed over into the care of John, a mere youth. He ends his series of questions by asking how she had borne the sword, which she had known was coming since the prophecy of Simeon, as it pierced her Son's side and her maternal viscera. The answer he provides is that it was the power or grace of God that allowed her to keep her external composure while all the time her inner agony was growing more bitter, piercing her very soul. Here we are midway between the Ambrosian stoicism of the Latin tradition and the emotive *planctus* of the East. Through Mary, the reader is able to approach the horror of the Crucifixion and live its reality vicariously. Her superhuman restraint in the face of such adversity is put forward as a model for trust in God's grace, but it also diminishes her empathetic appeal.

Commenting on Simeon's sword, Paschasius Radbertus († 865) makes one of the most significant statements in the Latin Church since the time of Ambrose of Milan regarding Mary's sharing in her Son's suffering on Calvary. For Paschasius, the Virgin's participation in Christ's Passion surpasses martyrdom, since her soul fully participated in the agony of her Son and, as he puts it, she made his death hers. Although he does not tease out the theological implications of this assertion, it is an important step towards the notion of the co-passion, made all the more

---

[54] *In Purificatione S. Mariae*, 12, PL 89, 1301. He also briefly mentions Mary's suffering in his *De asumptione sanctae Mariae*

[55] See Rachel Fulton, *From Judgment to Passion*, pp. 208-09.

[56] *PL* 112, 1428B-C.

significant by the fact that Paschasius pseudo-epigraphically attributed his homily to Jerome, thus endowing it with great authority:

> The blessed Mother of God was a virgin and martyr, even though she ended her life in peace. For her suffering is witnessed to by the prophet Simeon when he says to her: 'And a sword shall pierce thy heart' (Luke 2. 35). From this it is established that she was above the martyrs. For, although the other saints suffered for Christ in the flesh, they were nevertheless unable to suffer in the soul, since this is immortal. Instead, the blessed Mother of God, since she suffered in that which is said to be impassible [the soul], was then, as it were, more than a martyr because her flesh also suffered in a spiritual way through the sword of Christ's Passion. This shows that the Virgin loved more than everyone and therefore suffered more, to the point where the strength of suffering, in testimony to her sublime love, passed through and possessed her whole soul. She was more than a martyr, therefore, because she suffered with her soul, and certainly her love was by a long measure stronger than her own death, because the Virgin made Christ's death hers. *Cogitis me, 14*[57]

From the turn of the millennium, and particularly from the twelfth century onwards, the figure of the *mater dolorosa* became increasingly prominent in the West.[58] Broadly speaking we can distinguish two distinct strands in this development. Firstly there are prose texts that confine themselves to the narrative third person, mainly sermons and commentaries, in which the actions and emotions of the Virgin during the Passion are described and analysed. It is mainly in texts of this sort that we find theological considerations of Mary's role in the Passion. Secondly, there is the versified *Planctus Mariae*, with its dramatic dialogue between Jesus and Mary, similar in many respects to its earlier Eastern counterpart, which flourished between the eleventh and fourteenth centuries, and finally the narrative *compassio Marie*, also versified, which was at its height between the thirteenth and fifteenth centuries.[59] The *Planctus* was intended to encourage empathetic meditation on the Passion and was little concerned with theological considerations. Nevertheless, even in the *Planctus* and *compassio* care was taken to arrive at a resolution of Mary's grief in her albeit belated acceptance of her Son's sacrifice. Part of the reason for this new interest in Mary's suffering was undoubtedly increased contacts with the Greek Church, where the Marian plaint was already an established tradition, though the precise paths of influence remain to be traced.[60] Others have suggested indigenous

---

[57] *PL* 30, 138A-B, *TMPM*, III, 809.
[58] See *MLM*, p. 149.
[59] See Sandro Sticca, *The Planctus Mariae in the Dramatic Tradition*, especially pp. 71 and 85.
[60] On the role of Byzantine monks in stimulating renewed interest in the Passion see Sandro Sticca, 'The Montecassino Passion and the Origin of the Latin Passion Play', *Italica*, 44 (1967), 209-19, and his *The Planctus Mariae in the Dramatic Tradition*. See also Donna Ellington Spivey, *From Sacred to Angelic Soul: Understanding Mary in Late Medieval and Early Modern Europe* (Washington: Catholic University of America Press, 2001), pp. 79-80 and Jean-Marie Sansterre, *Les moines grecs et orientaux à Rome aux époques byzantine et*

influences, whether Germanic, Celtic or Romance, in the emergence of Marian plaints, but none has given an adequate explanation as to quite why these influences should not have broken through the more restrained Latin tradition earlier.[61] Another argument that is frequently put forward is that the new emphasis on Christ's human suffering, which began in the eleventh century, exemplified in particular by Anselm of Canterbury († 1109), and embraced by subsequent generations, especially Cistercian mystics, most notably Bernard of Clairvaux († 1153), and by Francis of Assisi († 1226) and his order,[62] was also marked by a new interest in Mary's emotional and spiritual participation in the torment of her Son. Rachel Fulton has recently argued in her study of devotion to Christ and Mary in the Middle Ages that none of these theories adequately explains the phenomenon. She argues that the heightened interest in the twelfth century in the bodily assumption of Mary and in her compassion arose out of earlier changes in understanding of the crucified Christ in response to his failure to return, as many anticipated, at the turn of the new millennium. She suggests that the non-appearance of Jesus was a major factor in renewed interest in his physicality, apparent both in fierce doctrinal debates in the eleventh century over Christ's real presence in the Eucharistic, and a heightened emphasis on his human suffering in the Passion. She also posits a link between the rise in the image of Mary as a merciful Mother who intercedes for humanity with Christ, perceived in this period as a harsh administrator of God's justice, and intensification of interest in her *compassio*. By entering into Mary's suffering the sinner is able to approach Christ, who is being crucified precisely because of those sins.[63] What is clear, as with all cultural change, is that the contributing factors were complex. It is more than likely that a combination of all or many of the elements we have mentioned brought about the paradigm shift.

---

carolingienne (milieu du VIe s. – fin du IXe s.) (Brussels: Académie Royale de Belgique, 1983).

[61] Graef, *Doctrine and Devotion*, I, 263, who bases her argument on W. Lipphardt, 'Studien zu den Marianklagen', acknowledges the influence of Byzantine *staurotheotokia* (versified laments of the Virgin used in the Passiontide liturgy) on the development of Marian plaints in the West, although she claims, in my view without sufficient justification, that Germanic laments for the dead were a still more important influence, especially for the extravagant descriptions of Mary's grief which typify many of them. Peter Dronke, 'Laments of the Maries', pp. 104-05, suggests that improvised laments of the Virgin existed in vernacular languages – Greek, Celtic, Romance and Germanic – before breaking through into the literate world of the clerics, but, as Rachel Fulton points out in *From Judgment to Passion*, he gives no reason why they should surface at this particular point and time (p. 215).

[62] On Franciscan thought on the co-redemption see Karl Balić, 'Die Corredemttrixfrage innerhalb der franziskanischen Theologie', *Franziskanische Studien*, 39 (1957), 218-287.

[63] *From Judgment to Passion*, particularly pp. 215-43. See also Chapter on Medieval Intercession, Mediation and Devotion, where I point out that one weakness in Fulton's argument is that she does not give enough consideration to much earlier instances of the harsh judge / merciful mother divide in the Greek tradition.

A prayer written as a preparation for the reception of the Eucharist by Anselm of Lucca († 1086), in which the bishop speaks of Christ's assignation of Mary to the disciple John, shows that John 19. 26-27 was already being interpreted in terms of her spiritual motherhood in the eleventh century. Anselm sees Christ's words as the moment when he assigned Mary the role of Mediatrix, the first time such a firm link was asserted between the Passion and the Virgin's spiritual motherhood, a role that, according to Anselm, she continues to fulfil alongside her Son at the right hand of the Father. Hence, it is fitting that the mind should turn to her before receiving the body of Christ:

> [It is good to contemplate] Christ hanging from the Cross [...], who commends his Mother to the disciple and the disciple to his Mother: 'Mary,' he says, 'here is your son, apostle, here is your mother' (see John 19. 26-27), so that his glorious Mother, in the great affection of her pity might intercede for all sinners and look after with special care those ransomed prisoners whom she has adopted as her children. [...] It is good to contemplate him 'seated at the right hand of the Father (Colossians 3. 1) with you, O glorious Mother, who pray for the salvation of all your servants and with your pious tears wash away the shamefulness of all sinners. *Oratio ad suscipiendum corpus Christi 1*[64]

In another of his prayers Anselm writes that Christ's act of entrusting his Mother to John was a substitution of humanity for himself, one of the clearest assertions of Mary's universal motherhood to date: 'He ascends to heaven and gloriously leaves all his inheritance of mercy to his Mother. And he substituted us for himself, as children, in the person of his beloved disciple, John [...] so that she might become all the more disposed towards indulgence.'[65]

Godescalcus of Limburg († 1098), arguing in favour of Mary's bodily assumption, describes the sufferings that she endured on Calvary, deeming her sharing in the chalice of her Son sufficient reason for her not to fear death. It would be difficult to find a clearer statement of the co-passion, though Godescalcus makes no attempt to explore the theological implications of what he is saying other than to assert that Mary did not have to endure a normal death:

> Therefore, O Mother and Lady of Mercy, you suffered with the Son and in the Son; and your suffering was so much the harder since your Son, who was hanging dead from the Cross before your eyes, is the best, most innocent, most beautiful of all the sons of men. The more dishonour he endured the greater the wounds inflicted on your heart too. With him you drank the chalice of the Passion to such a degree that there was no longer any need for you to fear death or to suffer its harshness. *Sermon on the BVM*[66]

---

[64] Henri Barré, *Prières anciennes*, p. 227. For the full text see André Wilmart 'Cinque textes de prière composés par Anselme de Lucques pour la Comtesse Mathilde', *Revue d'ascétique et de mystique*, 19 (1938), 23-72, texts, 49-72.

[65] *Oratio ad sactam Mariam 3, TMSM*, III, 57, and see note above.

[66] *TMPM*, III, 66-67.

Anselm of Canterbury († 1109), whose teaching on the Redemption stressed the centrality of Christ's humanity, puts greater emphasis on the Virgin's human suffering at the foot of the Cross than had hitherto been the case. His address to the *mater dolorosa* contains none of the exaggerated emotionalism that was to characterise many later prayers, but nor is it excessively restrained. He, and we, weep for and with the Virgin as she gazes on her tortured Son. This, for Anselm, is the primary meaning of Mary's co-passion, that through her participation in Christ's sufferings she draws all humanity into the mystery of the Cross, but there is no hint that she in any way participated actively in the act of Redemption:[67]

> My most merciful Lady, what can I say about the fountains that flowed from your most pure eyes when you saw your only Son before you, bound, beaten and hurt? What do I know of the flood that drenched your matchless face, when you beheld your Son, your Lord, and your God stretched on the Cross without guilt, when the flesh of your flesh was cruelly butchered by wicked men? How can I judge what sobs troubled your most pure breast when you heard, 'Woman behold your son,' and the disciple, 'Behold your mother', when you received as a son the disciple in place of the master, the servant for the lord? *Oratio 2*[68]

A further factor in the new emphasis on Mary's human suffering was the advent of the mendicant orders. As meditations on Mary's *compassio* moved outside the monastic sphere, with the spread of the mendicant orders, and later with the rise of lay confraternities, they became increasingly emotive and devoid of serious theological content. This trend is evident in Pseudo-Anselm's *Dialogus Beatae Mariae et Anselmi de Passione Domini*, a work which enjoyed widespread popularity throughout the later Middle Ages and beyond, in which the focus is no longer purely on the relationship between Mother and Son but is expanded to include the narrator, and by extension the reader, who are drawn into the drama of the occasion by experiencing empathy with the Virgin and thus encouraged to relive the events of the Passion.[69]

---

[67] See Atria Larson, 'Passive Instrument and Active Intercessor: Anselm's View of Mary's Role in Redemption', *Cistercian Studies Quarterly*, 41 (2006), 32-50. Lawrence S. Cunningham, 'Mary in Catholic Doctrine and Practice', *Theology Today*, 56 (1999), 307-318, is among several authors who note the importance of Anselm in the development of Medieval affective piety.

[68] Numbering refers to *S. Anselmi Cantuariensis Archiepiscopi Opera Omnia*, ed. by Francis S. Schmitt, 6 vols (Edinburgh: Nelson 1946-61; repr. Stuttgart: Fromann, 1968). In the *Patrologia Latina*, which includes many spurious prayers, it is numbered IX. Translation taken from Anselm of Canterbury, *The Prayers and Meditations of Saint Anselm with the Proslogion*, trans. by Benedicta Ward (Harmondsworth: Penguin, 1973), p. 96.

[69] *Dialogus Mariae et Anselmi de Passione Domini*, PL 159, 271-86. See Theo Meier, *Die Gestalt Marias im geistlichen Schauspiel des deutschen Mittelalters* (Berlin: Erich Schmidt, 1959), and A. Luis 'Evolutio historica doctrinae de compassione B. Mariae Virginis', *Marianum*, 5 (1943), pp. 268-85. The *Dialogus* is also notable for seven references that Mary makes to the sword of Simeon at various points in her ordeal, an early precursor

Eadmer of Canterbury (†c. 1124) believes that the moment of greatest suffering for Mary was when Jesus gave her into the care of John, depriving her, in a certain sense, of her divine motherhood. Although he speaks of her undergoing a passion, there is no hint that Mary in any way contributed to the Redemption other than by fully acquiescing to God's plan:

> O Lady, I ask you: what thoughts followed each other within you when you heard of the dubious exchange that was to be made by him whom you loved above all things? Truly the sword of suffering pierced your soul, a suffering more bitter than all the pains of a bodily torment. All the cruelties inflicted on the bodies of the martyrs were light, or rather nothing, compared to your Passion, which in its enormity truly pierced all the wounds of your most benevolent heart. O merciful Lady, I do not believe that you could have endured, in any way, the attacks of such a cruel martyrdom without losing your life, had not the very Spirit of life, the Spirit of all consolation, that is, the Spirit of your most sweet Son whose death was so tormenting you, comforted you, consoled you, and helped you to understand within you that what you who were in anguish saw happening in him was not the effect of death which was carrying him away, but rather the result of the triumph which was about to make all things subject to him. *De excellentia Virginis Mariae liber, 5*[70]

Once again in this passage we see a preoccupation with reconciling the unquestionable agony which Mary must have suffered with the Ambrosian belief that she had stood stoically by the Cross, the only possible explanation being that God had given her the grace to cope with her grief.

For Rupert of Deutz († 1130), with the role assigned to her by Christ as mother of John, Mary becomes the Mother of all humanity. In the agonising labour of Calvary she suffers the pangs that she had avoided in childbirth:

> Given that [on Calvary] the Blessed Virgin truly suffered the pangs of birth (Ps. 47.7), and that in the Passion of her only begotten Son she gave birth to the salvation of us all, she is really the Mother of all. Therefore what he said, being

---

to the Seven Sorrows of the Virgin which would become a dominant theme by the fifteenth century. The Office of the Seven Sorrows of the Blessed Virgin Mary focused on the sufferings that the Virgin endured throughout her life, starting with the prophecy of Simeon, continuing with the flight into Egypt, the loss of the child Jesus, the meeting with Jesus carrying the Cross, the Crucifixion, the taking down from the Cross, and concluding with the burial of Jesus. While the Franciscans and Dominicans contributed to the spread of this devotion, it was the Servites (otherwise known as the Order of the Servants of Mary), established in 1233 by seven Florentines who renounced their wealth for the service of God, who took up the Sorrows of Mary as the principal devotion of their order and who were largely responsible for its propagation. See Elizabeth A. Johnson, 'Marian Devotion in the Western Church', in *Christian Spirituality: High Middle Ages and Reformation*, ed. by Jill Raitt, World Spirituality, 17 (New York: Crossroad, 1988), pp. 392-414 and Carol M. Schuler, 'The Seven Sorrows of the Virgin: Popular Culture and Cultic Imagery in Pre-Reformation Europe', *Simiolus*, 21 (1992), 5-28.
[70] *PL* 159, 567A-B.

rightly concerned about his Mother, 'Woman, behold thy son,' and likewise what he said to the disciple himself, 'Behold thy mother,' could just as well have been said to any of the other disciples, had they been present. *Commentaria in Evangelium S. Joannis, 13* [71]

Hugh of St. Victor († 1141) is unusual in his outright rejection of any role for Mary in the Redemption stating categorically that Christ alone redeemed the world through his Passion and death. Mary's role instead is to act as a model for the faithful to follow so that they can avoid sin in the first place:

> The Mother offers an example against future things so that they will not happen. The Son grants a remedy for past things so that they will not threaten the future. In this the Son is superior to the Mother because, with his Passion, he cancelled out the sin of the world. Indeed, it was not Mary who died for the Redemption of the world but her Son. *Et egredietur virga*[72]

Bernard of Clairvaux's († 1153) intense devotion to the crucified Christ, alongside his powerful rhetoric on Mary's central role in the economy of salvation continued the trend towards a more affective piety. Writing on the Presentation in the Temple, he suggests that Mary plays an active role in the Redemption by offering Jesus to the Father as victim for the reconciliation of the world, thus anticipating the Crucifixion.[73] Elsewhere he speaks of Mary welcoming, and not just accepting, the price of Redemption when she utters her *fiat* at the Annunciation, though it is not clear that she understands what this price is.[74] He also uses the term 'compassion' with reference to the Virgin's sharing in the Passion of Christ when he speaks of the sword that pierced her heart at her Son's death:

> Thy soul was transfixed with the violence of sorrow, so that thou art justly proclaimed to be more than a martyr, since the sufferings thou didst endure from the force of thy compassion far exceeded all the pains that could have been inflicted on thy flesh. "Woman, behold thy son" (John xix. 26). Poor Mother! Were not these words to thee as the sharpest of swords, piercing thy soul "and reaching unto the division of the soul and the spirit" (Heb. iv. 12)? O what an

---

[71] *PL* 169, 790A-B, quoted in *MLM*, 149. See Caroline Walker Bynum, *Jesus as Mother: Studies in the Spirituality of the High Middle Ages* (Berkeley: University of California Press, 1982), particularly pp. 129-30. Amy Neff, Amy Neff, 'The Pain of Compassio: Mary's Labor at the Foot of the Cross', attributes the emergence in the Rhineland at this time of paintings depicting the Swooning Virgin partly to the influence of Rupert (pp. 256-57), though she does not seem to be aware of many of the earlier texts describing the Virgin's parturition on Calvary.

[72] *TMSM*, III, 174-75. The unedited Latin text appears in Roger Baron, 'La pensée mariale de Hugues de Saint-Victor', *Revue d'ascétique et de mystique*, 31 (1955), 249-71.

[73] *Third Sermon on the Purification*, PL 183, 370.

[74] *Fourth Sermon on the Glories of the BVM*, PL 183, 83C.

exchange! John is given thee in place of Jesus, the servant in place of the Lord, the disciple for the Master, the son of Zebedee instead of the Son of God, a mere man instead of Him Who is true and very God! […] But perchance some one will say to me, "did not Mary know beforehand that her Son was doomed to die"? Undoubtedly. "Did she not hope that he would speedily rise again from the tomb"? Most firmly. "And nevertheless, in spite of this foreknowledge and this expectation did she sorrow over her crucified Son"? Yea, and with a sorrow exceeding great. Let me ask thee, who art thou, my bother, and whence hast thou derived this wisdom that thou shouldst marvel more at Mary's compassion than at the passion of her Son? Dost thou grant that He could die even the death of the body, and yet deny her the power of participating in His death by the affections of her heart? The Son's death of pain was caused by love greater than which no man hath (John xv. 13), and the Mother's death of sympathy was caused by love the like of which was never felt before in the heart of a pure creature. *Sermon for the Sunday within the Octave of the Assumption* [75]

Here, though he does not explicitly state it, we are very close to the doctrine of Mary's co-redemption. She is fully aware of the purpose of his sacrifice and therefore willingly endures the anguish of witnessing her Son's agony, sharing in it to a degree greater than any other creature.

In a seminal work, Arnold of Bonneval († after 1156), a disciple of Bernard's, is the first to propose formally the doctrine of Mary's co-redemption in the Latin Church.[76] Building on the Irenaean principle of recapitulation,[77] he affirms that not only did the new Eve share in the process of reversing original sin through giving birth to the new Adam, but she freely chose to share in the Passion of her Son, so that the Passion and co-passion – the free act of a man and a woman – became a counter-parallel to Adam and Eve's rejection of God, thus restoring creation. As a creature, Mary is not competent to contribute anything to Christ's redemptive act, but Christ may, and does according to Arnold, accept the Virgin's self-offering and present it to the Father, whereby it can be said that she participates in the Redemption through her Son:

'Lord, where are thy ancient mercies' (Psalms 88. 50). What are you waiting for? The time has already come: before you are your Mother and John, whom you love. You speak to the thief but do not speak to your Mother? She who is blessed amongst women looks at you and, with her eyes fixed upon you, she contemplates your wounds with maternal pity. And although she is not unaware of the good that your Passion is procuring for the world, she nevertheless feels that she is dying with you in her maternal affection while her Mother's heart is crushed by an unspeakable suffering. She sighs within herself and holds back the

---

[75] *SBS*, pp. 226-27.

[76] See *TMSM*, III, 267, *MLM*, pp. 178-80, Eamon Duffy, 'Mater Dolorosa, Mater Misericordiae', *New Blackfriars*, 69 (1988), 210 – 227, and Ricardo Struve Haker, 'Arnoldo de Bonavalle.: primer teólogo de la Corredención mariana', *Regina mundi* (Bogotá), 7 (1963), 48-75.

[77] See chapter on Remote Redemption.

tears that want to burst forth; and the more her anguish swells, the more is she forbidden from showing it and from relieving her feelings with cries and laments. Every now and again sobs slipped out, but they were controlled and stifled so that they went back into the depths of the mind from which they had come out where they clashed against each other. In her soul a strong storm blew up while violent emotions assailed her. [...] Do not marvel if in that tabernacle you could see two altars: one in the heart of Mary, the other in the body of Christ. Christ immolated his flesh, Mary her soul. She truly wished to add the blood of her heart to the blood of her soul, and, raising her hands to the Cross [she wished] to celebrate the vespertine sacrifice with her Son, and with the Lord Jesus, to consummate the mystery of our Redemption, through her mortal body. But this was the exclusive task of the High Priest, to bring, that is, the offering of his own blood to the sanctuary, and he could not let anyone else participate in this dignity. Indeed, in the Redemption of man, no angel and no other man had or could have this power in common with him. Nevertheless, that affection of his Mother, according to her capacity, cooperated greatly in placating God, because the love of Christ presented both his own offering and that of his Mother to the Father, given that what the Mother asked the Son confirmed and the Father granted. The Father loved the Son and the Son the Father; and after the two of them came the Mother in the ardour of her charity, and if the functions were different the objective, which the good Father, the pious Son and the holy Mother sought and which love caused them to work out together, was the same. Contemporaneously, piety, charity and goodness compenetrated each other: the Mother beseeched, the Son interceded and the Father forgave. *De septem verbis Domini in cruce, 3* [78]

Here we have a fully worked out justification of Mary's participation in the Redemption, the key point being that while she, as a purely human creature, could not offer anything to the Father in expiation of humanity's sin, Jesus could incorporate her offering into his own and thus make it worthy. In this way it is possible to say that Mary was co-crucified with Christ and that together they obtained the salvation of the world (though it is Christ alone who brings it about) by offering the same sacrifice to the Father.

Amadeus of Lausanne († 1159) offers a powerful description of Mary's suffering as she follows him on the *Via Crucis* and suffers with him at the foot of the Cross. She drinks from the same chalice which Jesus had prayed might not be his, reminding us that Christ too had had difficulty in accepting the will of the Father. Her suffering, like his, goes beyond the strength of human endurance, but where his strength is drawn from his own divinity hers is drawn from him. He makes no mention of her contributing anything to the Redemption. His main purpose, as with many Medieval writers, is to draw his readers into Mary's suffering so that they may see the Passion through her eyes:

> The downfall of the Jews and the death of her Son burned in her glorious heart with inexpressible suffering; and he, pierced deeply by the dart of pity,

[78] *PL* 189, 1693A-1695A.

sighed amidst his extreme anguish. She drank a chalice more bitter than death itself. That which the human race could not endure, a woman endured sustained by divine help. She overcame her sex, she won out over human nature, and she suffered beyond the limits of human strength. Indeed she suffered a greater torment than if her own body had been tortured, because she loved him for whom she was suffering in an incomparably greater way. *Homilia 5, De mentis robore seu martyrio beatissimae Virginis*[79]

Odon of Morimond († 1161) joins the growing ranks of those offering very human portrayals of Mary's anguish on Calvary. Like others before him, most notably Romanos, he locates Mary's suffering not only in the present tense but in an imaginative future, so that she suffers the agony of the Passion before actually experiencing it, similar, in some ways to Christ's agony in Gethsemane, when he sweated blood. In this way he is able to suggest subtly the prophetic foreknowledge of the Virgin:

> She was used to seeing him dressed in clothes that she herself, perhaps, had made; now instead he appears naked, that most holy flesh drenched in his own blood, completely lacerated and torn to pieces. She had known the integral body of her Son who, in coming out of her womb, contributed so much to the virginity of his Mother that, in being born, he left her intact; and behold, now, having less pity for himself than he had for his Mother, that blessed body is cruelly transfixed and pierced. She had seen those hands always giving blessings or when they touched the infirm and carried out some gesture of mercy; and now behold them, pierced! She was used to hearing supernatural things and words of consolation from that golden mouth; but now, behold, out of anguish he cries in a great voice: 'My God, my God, why hast thou forsaken me?' (Matthew 27. 46). She had avidly admired that face shining with divine rays, which for her was always our most beloved sight, and now, here it was, bowed down, pale and barren: here a bruise, there the traces of spittle or of blood. In this predicament what could that Mother do except stay by the Cross of Jesus? If she had stayed at home while these things were happening her suffering would have been doubled. Therefore, coming to a maternal decision within herself, in her heart she said: I will stay and await the death sentence that Pilate will pronounce against my beloved Only-Begotten; I will follow him, staying behind him, when he goes out of Jerusalem; with eyes full of tears, I will see where they bring him, I will contemplate how they will pierce the hands and feet of my Son; how they will attach him to the scaffold and raise him up on the Cross; how, having done all these things, they will depart and keep their distance, no longer going near him as if he who is hanging from the Cross were someone accursed. Then I will go nearer and will stay next to the Cross of my Jesus. I will hold him in my arms; I will kiss him with my lips; and will bathe him with tears; and given that it is not permitted to die with him, I will fix my eyes on my hanging Son; I will observe how he leaves this world, I who alone know how he came into this

---

[79] *PL* 188, 1328C-D. See Graef, *Doctrine and Devotion*, I, 246.

world. I will not abandon him as he is dying, I who never left him when he was alive. *Homily on John 19. 25-27*[80]

Crucially, Odon specifically links Mary's presence on Calvary with her mediation of grace. Though he does not say she contributed in any way to the Redemption he does state that since it is from the Cross that all grace flows it was necessary that Mary participate through faith in the Passion if she were to become the font of grace:

> It was necessary that Mary should stay by the Cross of Jesus for another reason. Who is not aware that this Lady of ours is the treasury of heaven, capable of meeting all the necessities of mortals, so that all receive of her plenitude? But tell me, I pray: from whence does she draw all those things that she dispenses with such liberality to those who beseech her? From the Cross of Jesus, I believe, for it is from thence that the rivers of grace flowed, from which Mary drew with the vessel of her faith, and which she now pours out from her hydria of mercy. *Homily on John 19. 25-27*[81]

He then goes on to say that it is through Mary that the faithful look on and remember the Passion because the weight of their sins prevents them from directly participating:

> Behold, O merciful and benign Virgin, we are all before the spring of water. We look upon and remember the Passion of your Son, but under the weight of our sins we cannot bend to devotion. Our thirst is great but we do not have the vessels with which to draw, and the well is deep. *Homily on John 19. 25-27*[82]

Here we have in a nutshell the main role of the *mater dolorosa* as the Medieval Church saw it: to draw in the faithful and accompany them in re-living the Passion through a vicarious participation in her own agonised witness of the events of that day, so that they too might be renewed at the source of all grace.

Gottfried of Admont († 1165) attributes soteriological value to Mary's compassion insofar as she fully understood the reason for Christ's Passion and consented to it for the sake of humanity, putting the Father's will ahead of her maternal feelings :

> Finally the sword pierced her soul when the hour of his Passion had arrived and she saw her Son, the Redeemer, endure the torture of the Cross: nailed to the Cross, given gall and vinegar to drink at the very moment when he was about to die, pierced by the lance of the soldier, numbered among the criminals; and thus [she saw him] finish his life miserably, with an ignominious death,

---

[80] *TMSM*, III, 304-05, José María Canal, 'Dos homilias de Odón de Morimond', *Sacris erudiri*, 13 (1962), 377-460 (pp. 404-06).

[81] *TMSM*, III, 305-06, José María Canal, 'Dos homilias', p. 408.

[82] *TMSM*, III, 305-06, José María Canal, 'Dos homilias', p. 409.

according to a purely human evaluation. She was a spectator to such great misfortunes while she stood next to his Cross as he died in front of her eyes, hanging from the Cross. And yet all these things did not succeed in shaking her, for example, by pushing her to anger towards those who had perpetrated such a grave crime against her innocent Son, or to invoke vendetta against them. Nor did she allow herself to be taken over by feelings of hatred or envy towards them. In her maternal compassion she wished that such a Son might not die, if it were possible. But she put divine will above her maternal affection, so that instead she desired the salvation of the human race; nor did she wish to interfere in the plan of God the Father, who had disposed to save the whole world through the death of his Son. *Homilia 85, In festum dedicationis ecclesiae* [83]

Aelred of Rievaulx († 1167), like Odon, sees Mary as the means by which one can approach and identify with the Passion of Christ. Addressing virgins he writes:

As to you, O virgin, who have a lot more confidence in the Son of the Virgin than in those women who keep themselves at a distance (see Luke 22. 27), draw near to the Cross together with the Virgin Mary and the virgin disciple and regard from close up that face suffused with pallor. What, then? Will you remain tearless even though you see the tears of your most beloved Lady? Will your eyes stay dry as the sword of suffering transfixes her soul? Will you listen to him without a tear as he says to his Mother 'Woman, behold thy son'? And to John: 'Behold thy Mother'? *Rules of the Recluse, 31* [84]

Gerhoh of Reichersberg († 1169), commenting on the hymn *Ave Maris Stella*, speaks of the double motherhood of Mary, first when she gave birth to Christ, and then when she gave life to her spiritual children on Calvary. Interestingly, her fruitfulness is attributed not only to her beloved Son but to the disciples, whom Gerhoh also sees as having played a role in the Passion: [85]

It is not with vain hope, therefore, that we say to her not only 'Hail Star of the sea, noble Mother of God', but also what is added afterwards: 'Show yourself a Mother', because of her double maternity, the first when she conceived her Only-begotten without pain, and the second in which, with her great suffering and sadness, she gave birth, of her Beloved and of his disciples to many children, for herself and for the same Only-begotten Son. *De gloria et honore Filii hominis, 10, 2* [86]

A commentary on Canticles attributed to Luke of Mont-Cornillon († c. 1182) speaks of the Virgin's agony at the foot of the Cross, and asserts that she suffered the Passion with her Son, though there is no hint of the notion of a co-redemption:

---

[83] *PL* 174, 1056C-1057A.
[84] *TMSM*, III, 320.
[85] See his *Commentarius in psalmum 21, PL 194*, 1014B-1015D.
[86] *PL* 194, 1105C, *TMSM*, III, 339.

> For, she was not exempt from the suffering and Passion that the Son endured
> on the Cross; indeed we must believe that the anguish she felt at the agonizing
> death of Christ on the Cross penetrated the viscera of the most pious Mother, who
> could only look on him with great suffering as he hung from the Cross, knowing
> that he was God and that he had truly assumed flesh from her flesh. *Moralitate*[87]

Geoffrey of St. Victor († after 1194) is among the first writers of the Latin
West to compose a versified plaint, the *Liber de Passione*, which at one time was
attributed to Bernard of Clairvaux.[88] Also known by its opening words, the
Planctus ante nescia was a major influence on subsequent portrayals of Mary's grief
and actually appears verbatim in several Passion plays. In vivid detail Pseudo-
Bernard tells the by-now familiar tale of Mary's prolonged agony from the
moment she learns of Christ's arrest to his entombment: her frenzied grief, her
swoons and screams, her desire to die along with, or in place of her Son.[89] It is
worth reproducing in full since its style is representative of many plaints
produced around this time. Unlike some of the longer plaints, however, it is a
monologue, and thus has a somewhat less dramatic impact

> Before now I did not know grief, but now, anguished, I am fainting out of my
> grief; I am tormented by pain. The Jews are depriving the world of its ray of light,
> and me of my Son, of joy and of sweetness. / O Son, my only sweetness and
> singular joy, look on your Mother who is weeping; grant her comfort. Your
> wounds are torturing my breast, my mind, and my eyes; what woman, what
> mother has even been so unhappy and wretched! / O flower of flowers, O guide
> in the conduct of life, vein of forgiveness, how onerous the torture of the nails is
> for you! O suffering! From this moment the face loses its colour; from this
> moment the wave of torment rushes headlong. / Too late you entrusted yourself
> to me, and too early you abandon me; you who were born so worthily, in what an
> abject way you die! O with what love the wrapping of your body was prepared;
> what a bitter prize for such a sweet pledge! / O piteous grace of him who dies in
> such a way; O envy, O delight of such an ill-disposed people! O cruel right hand of
> him who crucifies; O soul of the victim, so meek in its torments! / O true words
> of the just Simeon, I feel the sword of suffering that he had foretold. My moans,
> my sighs and my outward tears are the signs of my inner wound. / Spare my Son,
> O death, and not me; only then can you take care of me alone. O Blessed One, let
> death separate me from you, provided that you, O Son, are not tortured. / What
> crime, what evils that ferocious people has committed! Fetters, canes, wounds,
> spits, thorns, and more, he has to suffer even though he is without fault. I beseech
> you, spare my Son; crucify his Mother; or nail the two of us together to the post of
> the Cross; on his own he would die unhappily. / Give back his body, even though
> it is without its soul, to she who is most grief-stricken, so my tortured Son may

---

[87] *PL* 203, 572C-D, *TMSM*, III, 385.

[88] Henri Barré, 'Le "Planctus Mariae" attribué a S. Bernard', *Revue d'ascétique de mystique*,
28 (1952), 243-55.

[89] Partial text at *PL* 158, 903-904. For the full text of the *Tractatus* and discussion on its
provenance see Henri Barré 'Le "Planctus Mariae"'.

grow again to life through kisses and embraces. If only the heavens willed that I might suffer to the point of dying of pain, for it is more painful to die without death than to perish quickly. / O wretched people, why are you amazed that the ground shakes, that the stars dim, that those who languish cry? If you deprive the sun of light, how can it illuminate? If you deprive a sick person of a remedy, how can he get better? / You let a murderer go and you consign Jesus to torment. You tolerate peace badly and therefore sedition will come. You will learn your lesson through hunger and the slaughter of pestilence: Jesus died for you while Barabbas continues to live. / O blind people, O people worthy of pity, do penance to the degree that Jesus is inclined to forgive you. May the waters of the wells you have dug be propitious for you; may they sate the thirst of all; may they wash away all crimes. / Weep, daughters of Sion, grateful for the gift of such a great grace; his agonies are delights that pay for your offences. Rush into his embrace as he hangs from the Cross; with his arms wide open he offers himself in mutual embraces to those who love him. / In one thing alone do I rejoice: to suffer for you; I pray you, give me something in exchange: weep for the injury you have caused his Mother.
Planctus ante nescia (Tractatus in laudibus sanctae Dei genetricis)[90]

Here, unlike in the third person narratives, emotion dominates and Mary's suffering is unrelenting. There is very little in the way of theological content. Not without some bitterness and hints of anti-Semitism, Mary declares that only the fact that she is suffering for her people gives her joy a curious remark at first sight. Yet, as Rachel Fulton has shown, such an ambiguous attitude is not surprising in the context of the times, when Christians were deeply divided in their attitude towards the Jews.[91]

Alain of Lille († 1203) speaks of Mary's ardent love for Jesus, which caused her to remain faithful to him and suffer with him when he was on the Cross, even when everyone else fled. This love he attributes not just to her human relationship to her Son but to the Holy Spirit, for which reason she is able to offer her suffering in an act of co-passion:

> She loved Christ with all her soul because such was the vigour with which the Holy Spirit helped her that it enflamed her with love for Christ, sustaining her in every holy and wholesome thing. Finally, she loved Christ with such strength that, to her praise, it is sufficient to recall the strength of the love that occupied her mind when, while the disciples had fled, she forgot the fragility of her sex and, standing in tears under the Cross, she suffered with her dying Son. If, according to

[90] *AH*, 20, 156-58. See *PL* 182, 1133A-42A for a slightly different version, that attributed to Bernard.
[91] *From Judgment to Passion*, pp. 280-85. She describes a situation in which some Christians attempted to baptise the Jews, willingly or no, while others carried out unspeakable atrocities, and yet others afforded them protection. She also points out that some Jews did not hold back either, albeit often in the face of terrible persecution, one declaring his horror that Christians believed in a god who allowed himself to be born from the 'shameful exit' of a woman, and another scoffing at god who was 'a bastard son conceived by a menstruating and wanton woman' (p. 283).

the plan of the Passion, she could not offer her life in exchange for that of her Son, she nevertheless offered it with her co-passion. *In Cantica Canticorum*[92]

The thirteenth century is marked by even greater interest in the *mater dolorosa*. Performances of the *Planctus Mariae* began to be incorporated into Good Friday ceremonies,[93] while increased interest in Mary's suffering is also reflected in the art of the period. Where Mary had been typically shown, standing at the foot of the Cross in an attitude of stoic acceptance, she was now also portrayed in a state of emotional distress, with John and the women who had accompanied her offering comfort and physical support, a category known as the Virgin's Swoon.[94] In official circles too there was recognition of Mary's role in the Passion. Pope Honorius III († 1227), for instance, reflects the prevailing view of the time when he asserts that the sword of Simeon was a prophecy of the martyrdom that Mary's soul would undergo on Calvary, which was greater than any physical martyrdom.[95]

The highly influential thirteenth-century *Vita rhythmica* almost certainly came from the pen of a Benedictine or Cistercian monk. The principal source of many later vernacular *vitae*, the *Vita* provides a detailed description of Mary's consternation at her Son's arrest and her subsequent anguish on the *Via Crucis* and at the foot of the Cross:[96]

On that night Mary, the Mother of Jesus, was in a nearby town, named Bethany, in the house of Martha, since her beloved Son, Jesus, her Only-begotten and only Chosen One, had been captured by the Jews in Jerusalem. He was bound by them, beaten, and led away as a prisoner. In the early morning, they told her, through a messenger, that her only-Begotten had been arrested. She was immediately distraught in spirit when she learned that her Son had been taken, and experienced an incommensurable suffering in her soul. Seized by anguish, she was totally shaken by the torment in her heart. She collapsed on a seat, almost beside herself and lay there for a long time, immobile and only half alive.

But when she had re-gathered some of her strength and she came around, drawing breath amidst her sobs, she asked the messenger who had brought news of her Son's arrest: 'Do you think they are going to kill him? Do you know what they have done to him and where they have brought him? Were you there when they took him and did you see him when they bound him and bore him away? Do you think I will find him still alive? I shall go to see him at least while he is dying.'

Therefore Mary went, accompanied by Martha, who was also crying because of the Passion of Jesus. Along the way, Mary carried on, crying out in a load voice. Alas, poor me! Why did I not follow my Son yesterday? What stopped me? Yesterday when my Son set off for Jerusalem with his disciples, I should have

---

[92] *PL* 210, 58D-59A.
[93] Sandro Sticca, *The Planctus Mariae in the Dramatic Tradition*, 134-36.
[94] See Amy Neff, 'The Pain of Compassio', p. 254.
[95] *Sermon for the Nativity of Mary*, TMSM, IV, 120-21.
[96] See *TMSM*, IV, 137.

followed him. Alas, perhaps now I will find him no longer living. Indeed, he is already close to death. Alas, who will grant me, wretched as I am, the chance to see my Son alive and to weep over him before he is killed? Alas, what are we waiting for? Let us hasten more quickly; let us go to die with him. Alas, now what I have always feared is happening, because I knew well the envy of the Jews. I always suspected that something of this sort would happen to my Son, that he would be put to death by the Jews. [...]

Continuing along the way, they met Mary Magdalene and the other women who were with her, who had been sent away when he was flogged. Grieving, they were awaiting the end of the Holy One. When the Virgin Mary saw the Magdalene crying, she understood that he Son was suffering. Deprived of all strength and courage, she felt herself fainting, but clapping her hands she just managed to say: 'Where is my Son? Tell me Magdalene, has he been killed, or in which prison is he detained? Where did you leave my Only-begotten? Did you leave him alive of dead?'

Mary Magdalene could barely speak because of her tears. [...] 'While I was watching, your Only-begotten and my Lord, my beloved Jesus, God, the Saviour of the world, was tied to a statue and cruelly scourged, as I was driven away from him. But now he is appearing before the Prefect to be judged and the pitiless Jews are demanding the death penalty for him.'

On hearing this, the Virgin Mary started to say, grieving bitterly: 'Alas, alas, alas, my Son! Her heart gave way and she fell in a faint into the arms of some men. While Mary was lying almost lifeless on the ground, all the other women started to cry, grieving with her and pitying her great suffering. But when her spirit gave voice to her suffering once again, she said: 'I will go and die with my beloved Son.' Then sweet Mary got up from the ground crying and made for her Son. She was followed by her sister, Mary of Cleophas, together with the other women and the Magdalene. [...]

When they reached the Prefect's courtyard they saw a great throng of people and Jesus was walking with them, dragged by a rope and he was carrying a cross on his shoulders. Some, pulling him with the rope, were making a path for him. Others followed behind him, abusing him and striking him. Seeing this, his Mother erupted in cries of grief and a loud wail. Unable to control herself, she tore out her hair, and ripped her cheeks with her nails, as she cried to her Son: 'My Son, where are you hurrying to? Alas, where are you being dragged to? Alas, why are you carrying the Cross? And where are those people bringing you? Alas, I see now that they want to make you suffer and torture you on the gallows of the Cross.'

Crying in this manner, Mary hastened to follow Jesus, and the other women also followed in tears. When they had already led Jesus to the gates and the women reached him there, Jesus, turning to the women who were following him, grieving and weeping because of his sufferings, said: 'Daughters of Jerusalem, weep not over me; but weep for yourselves, and for your children' (Luke 23. 28). [...]

The Mother of Jesus threw herself on her Son's breast and held him in her arms, weeping. She was incapable of speech because of the excess of grief, but Jesus, consoling her, said sweetly: 'O my sweetest Mother, do not grieve so much because of my Passion. Console yourself a little because I am about to die for the salvation of the world. But on the third day I shall arise again to see you.

> At this moment I am more pained by your affliction than by my own suffering.
> *Vita rhythmica, 3, 4818-4949*[97]

There follows a long and equally heart-rending description of Mary's anguish as she stands beneath the Cross, inconsolable despite the best efforts of Jesus. The account of the Passion ends with a dialogue between Jesus and John, who reassures the Lord that he will take Mary into his house and serve her. On Easter Sunday, Jesus appears first to his Mother, who rejoices ecstatically that he has not only has returned in spirit but in body. We once again see the divide between more serious works, which portray a more stoic Mary and emphasise her willing participation in the redemptive work of her Son and more populist works such as this, which have little theological value and portray Mary as lacking in understanding and acceptance of Christ's sacrifice. While such accounts certainly heightened awareness of the Virgin's extraordinary suffering, they could also potentially undermine the notion of the co-redemption since they invariably portrayed Mary as having great difficulty in accepting her Son's agony, not to mention that they distracted from the soteriological significance of Christ's sacrifice by reducing the whole event to a sort of latter-day soap opera. A *planctus* often attributed to Bernard but in fact composed by his fellow Cistercian, Oglerius of Lucedio, († 1214) is of a similar tone, though it is more didactic in its intent and credits Mary with a certain understanding of Christ's purpose:

> Talking she cried and crying she talked: 'My Son, my Son, who will let me die for you? My Son is dying, why does his wretched Mother not die with him? My only love, sweetest Son, do not leave me, 'draw me after you' (Canticles 1. 3), and to you, so that I might die with you too. It is not good that you should die alone. May your miserable Mother be annihilated by death.
> O death, do not spare a wretch like me. I like you alone more than any other thing. Show your strength, slay the Mother and annihilate her together with the Son.
> O Son, only sweetness, singular joy, life of my soul, my complete desire, I generated you out of love, now let me die with you. Do not die without your Mother, recognise me, a wretch, and satisfy my prayer. It is right in fact that a son should satisfy his mother; satisfy me, I pray. Receive me onto your gallows so that we, who live in the same flesh, may die the one death.'

> [...]

> 'O [you who] cry and lament easily, you know that I came for this, that I took flesh from you to save the human race by means of the gallows of the Cross. How would the Scriptures be fulfilled? It is necessary for me to suffer for the salvation of the human race, but on the third day I shall rise again and appear openly to you and to my disciples. Cease you crying, chase away your pain,

---

[97] *Vita Beatae Mariae Virginis et Salvatoris rhythmica*, ed. by Adolf Vögtlin, Bibliothek des litterarischen Vereins Stuttgart, 180 (Tübingen: Laupp, 1888), pp. 164-68. For extracts from the poem in Italian see *TMSM*, IV, 137-145.

because I am going to the Father. I am ascending to receive the glory of the paternal Majesty. Instead, congratulate me because I have found the lost sheep again (see Luke 15. 6) which I had lost long ago. One alone is dying so that the whole world might return to life. Because of the fault of one alone the rest of mankind died, now all are being saved through the merit of one alone. Why, O Mother, should what pleases God the Father displease you? Do you wish me to drink the chalice that my Father has given me? (See John 18. 11) Do not cry woman, do not cry most beautiful Mother. I am not leaving you alone, I am not abandoning you, I am with you and I will be with you in every time in this world. If I subject myself to the power of death in the flesh, according to my divinity I am and always will be immortal and impassible. You know well from whom I cam forth and from whence I descended. *Plaint of the Virgin Mary*[98]

The *Planctus* continues with the Virgin's lament at the death of her Son and the attempts of those who surround her to console her as she weeps bitter tears. The author exculpates Mary for her reaction by pointing out that the angels themselves cried at the death of their Lord. Reading these lines it is clear that one of the principal aims, aside from drawing the faithful into the suffering of the Passion, is to educate them on the purpose of Christ's sacrifice, as it had been as far back as Romanos. Mary acts as a foil to Christ so that he can explain the meaning of his redemptive act. Unlike some other plaints, her grief, though great, is not unreasonable. It is enough to elicit sympathy and encourage identification with her, without falling into pure sentimentalism. When Christ reminds her of the purpose of his sacrifice we get a clear picture of how she must have struggled to reconcile her natural grief with her faith in God. The intent is that through Mary the readers will fully immerse themselves in the emotion of the Passion without losing sight of its deeper meaning.

The Cistercian Stephen of Salley († 1252) also offers a moving account of the conflict that Mary experienced on Calvary as she oscillated between the agony of a mother helplessly watching her Son's tortured death and the joy of knowing that he was accomplishing the salvation of humanity: 'Who can describe the suffering that you experienced witnessing the Passion of your Son, and at the same time the delight which the certain hope of future salvation aroused in your heart?'[99] This contrast between human suffering and spiritual joy was a frequent theme and a convenient way of resolving the conflict between Mary's grief and her stoicism.

Robert Grosseteste († 1253) is typical of the Franciscan outlook in his emphasis on the interior agony of Mary as she united herself with the Passion of her Son: 'In a certain manner, in her Son, she suffered the pains and opprobrium of the Cross with perfect compassion.[100]

---

[98] *TMSM*, IV, 65-66.
[99] *Meditations on the Joys of the Blessed Virgin Mary*, *TMSM*, IV, 230.
[100] *Tota pulchra es*, *TMSM*, IV, 241.

Bonaventure († 1274), presumably drawing on Bernard, brings together the idea of Mary's participation in the Passion with the Irenaean doctrine that the new Eve is instrumental in the restoration of creation. Just as Adam and Eve destroyed the human race, so Jesus and Mary restore it because she, with Christ, paid for the restoration of paradise by co-offering her Son as the divine victim.[101] Bonaventure also sees Mary's agony at the foot of the Cross as a spiritual birth-giving in which she shares in the Passion of her Son:

> On account of childbirth a woman has pain, that is, before giving birth. But the Blessed Virgin did not have pain before giving birth; because she did not conceive out of sin, as did Eve, to whom the malediction was given; but she had pain after birth. Whence she gave birth, before she was in labour. On the Cross she was in labour; whence in Luke: And thy own soul a sword shall pierce (Luke 2. 35). In other women there is pain of body, in this one there is suffering of heart; in others there is the pain of corruption, in this one there is the sorrow of compassion and of charity. Whence He invites us to consider her sorrow in Jeremiah: O all ye, He says, that pass by the way, attend, and see if there be any sorrow like to my sorrow (Lamentations 1. 12). *De donis Spiritus Sancti*, 5, 17[102]

However, while he clearly believes that Mary participated in the Passion this does not mean that she contributed to the objective Redemption. In his *Commentary on the Sentences*, he makes it clear that he believes that Mary is as dependent as any other creature on Christ's Redemption. To suggest otherwise would imply that Mary was not subject to the consequences of the Fall.[103] Bonaventure also dwells at some length on Mary's sufferings at the Crucifixion in his *Lignum vitae*, in the context of his meditation on the seventh fruit, which contemplates constancy in the face of suffering. He details the various levels of agony that her soul endured as she witnessed the tortures inflicted upon her Son and concludes with the affirmation that she 'was more pierced by the sword of her compassion' than if she had endured the tortures in her own body.[104] In one of his sermons Bonaventure also writes of Mary overcoming the devil through her participation in the Passion: 'The Virgin Mary is blessed the

---

[101] See *Third Sermon on the Assumption* in *Opera Omnia*, IX, 695; *Collations on the Gifts of the Holy Spirit*, 6, 14, in *Opera Omnia*, V, 484; *In III Sent.*, dist. 4, a. 3, q. 3, *Opera Omnia*, III, 115.
[102] In *The Franciscan Archive* <http://franciscan-archive.org/bonaventura/opera> [accessed 30 August 2006]. He expresses the same idea in *Collationes de septem donis Spiritus Sancti*, 6. See George H. Tavard, *The Forthbringer of God: St. Bonaventure on the Virgin Mary* (Chicago: Franciscan Herald Press, 1989), pp. 177-79.
[103] See *Sent.* III, d. iii, a. 1 and 2.
[104] See Tavard, *The Forthbringer*, pp. 155-56. For an English translation of the *Lignum* see *The Soul's Journey Into God; The Tree of Life; The Life of St. Francis*, trans. by Ewert Cousins (New York: Paulist Press, 1978).

most because she conquers the world and the devil who was crucifying her Son and piercing her soul.'[105]

His fellow Franciscan, Pietro di Giovanni Olivi († 1298), who belonged to the Spiritual wing of the order, considers the Virgin's suffering at the Passion in his *De Domina*, treating the question according to the Scholastic method of argument and counter-argument. He argues forcefully against those who would claim that Mary experienced joy on Calvary because she knew that her Son was bringing about the Redemption. Notable is the typically Franciscan emphasis on the human bonds between Mother and Son:

> Faced with Christ so horribly martyred and crucified, it would have been rather inappropriate if his Mother had abandoned herself to some kind of joy. Indeed, it would have been even more peculiar if she had not suffered with Christ from the depths of her viscera, from her very marrow, with all her strength, affections, senses and thoughts, and if she had not applied herself totally to that compassion. This is how she was moved by God at that time. *Questiones quattuor de Domina* [106]

Olivi goes on to say that any person can identify with Christ's suffering in the same way as Mary did and like her participate in the merit of the Redemption. Mary, therefore, by associating herself fully with her Son and participating in his suffering, collaborated in the Redemption of the human race:

> This association would not exist if she had not been co-crucified with Christ beyond all comprehension. And so, the glory that she possesses is so much greater than all the saints because her crucifixion with Christ was superior and more acute than all the sufferings of the saints. [107]

So for Olivi, Mary's co-passion consists in her total identification with Christ's Passion, greater than that of any other human being, which allows her to participate in a unique way in the merits gained by her Son on the Cross. However, he makes it very clear that there is a profound difference between Christ's sacrifice, which was that of God for a sinful and undeserving humanity, and the suffering experienced by those who witnessed the Crucifixion. In line with other thinkers of his time he also sees imitation of Mary as the best means to contemplate the Passion and to gain from its merits.

---

[105] *Sixth Sermon on the Annunciation of the BVM*, in *Sermons on the Blessed Virgin Mary*, trans. by Campion Murray, in *Franciscan Friars Province of the Holy Spirit* <http://www.franciscans.org.au> [accessed June 2006].

[106] Quoted in Luigi Gambero, 'Il XIII secolo e la fioritura della Scolastica', in *SDM*, I, 774-829 (p. 796). See also Pedro de Alcántara Martínez, 'La cooperación de María en la obra salvífica según el pensamento di Pedro Juan Olivi', in *Studies Honoring Ignatius Charles Brady*, ed. by Romano Stephen Almagno and Conrad L. Harkins (St. Bonaventure, N.Y.: Franciscan Institute, 1976), pp. 341-55.

[107] Quoted in Luigi Gambero, 'Il XIII secolo', p. 796.

Albert the Great († 1280) rejects the possibility that Mary participated with Christ in the act of Redemption, though he does believe that she experienced a spiritual martyrdom on Calvary and that she is our spiritual Mother in the sense that she conceived humanity in her heart at the same time as she conceived Christ.[108] Albert also believes that Mary suffered the pangs of labour under the Cross, from which she had been exempt at his birth.[109]

The popular *De laudibus beatae Mariae Virginis*, often attributed to Albert, but in reality the work Richard of St. Laurence († after 1245), speaks of the 'compassion' that Mary underwent as she suffered spiritual pains 'corresponding to those which she saw her Son undergoing.'[110] Another celebrated work, the *Mariale super Missus est*, also attributed to St. Albert until quite recently, goes even further. It begins by explaining that Mary became the spiritual mother of humanity through her martyrdom at the foot of the Cross, which it likens to the pains of labour. But she is not simply a martyr. She is called the 'co-helper of the Redemption' (*co-adjutrix redemptionis*). Christ, the pseudo-Albert asserts, willed that his Mother should share in the penalty of the Passion, so that she would become the Mother of all, through re-creation.[111]

The famed *Stabat Mater*, almost certainly written by Jacopone da Todi († 1306) though it has been attributed to numerous authors, is a prime example of approaching the crucified Christ through identification with his suffering Mother. First we are presented with the picture of the grieving Mother and then we are invited to join in her suffering, so that through her we may share in the Passion of Christ. And the purpose of identification with the Passion through Mary? To be saved from sin and condemnation with the aid of Mary, and granted entry into Paradise by Christ, the Judge:

> The grieving Mother stood in tears beside the Cross on which her Son was hanging. 2. Her soul, lamenting, sorrowing and grieving, was pierced by the sword. 3. O how sad and afflicted was that blessed Mother of the Only-begotten! 4. Who mourned and grieved and trembled as she looked upon the torment of her glorious Child. 5. Where is the man who would not weep to see the Mother of Christ in such suffering? 6. Who would not share her sorrow, seeing the loving Mother suffering with her Son? 7. For the sins of his people she saw Jesus in torment and subjected to the scourge. 8 She saw her sweet offspring dying, forsaken as he yielded up the Spirit. 9. O Mother, fount of love,

---

[108] *In III Sent.*, dist. 3, a. 3, *Opera Omnia*, XXVIII, 45; *Commentary on Luke*, 10, 42, *Opera Omnia*, XXIII, 90, *Commentary on Matthew* 1, 18, *Opera Omnia*, XXXVII, 97. *Alberti Magni Opera Omnia*, ed. by Auguste and Emile Borgnet, 38 vols (Paris: Vivès, 1890-99). See Graef, *Doctrine and Devotion*, I, 275-276.

[109] *Postilla in Isaiam*, 7, 14, and *Commentary on Matthew*, TMSM, IV, 333 and 335.

[110] 3, 12, 2, in *Opera Omnia*, ed. by Borgnet, XXXVI, 156.

[111] The *Mariale*, which was only recognised to be spurious in 1952, is published among Albert's works in *Opera Omnia*, ed. by Borgnet, XXXVII, 1-321. See O'Carroll, *Theotokos*, pp. 298-99, Graef, *Doctrine and Devotion*, I, 270-73, and Sandro Sticca, *The Planctus Mariae in the Dramatic Tradition*, pp. 23-6, who inexplicably treats the *Mariale* as genuine.

make me feel the strength of your grief, so that I may grieve with you. 10. Make my heart burn with love for Christ, my God, that I may be pleasing to him. 11. Holy Mother, this I pray, that the wounds of the Crucified One be driven deep into my heart. 12. Share with me the agony of your wounded Son who deigned to suffer so much for me. 13. Grant that I may truly weep with you, and share the suffering of the Crucified, as long as I shall live. 14. To stand with you beside the Cross and willingly share in your grief is my desire. 15. Virgin of virgins most exalted, be not bitter towards me, let me weep with you. 16. Grant that I may bear the death of Christ, the fate of his Passion, and commemorate his wounds. 17. Let me be wounded with his wounds, and with the Cross inebriated, out of love for the Son. 18. Inflamed and alight, may I be defended by you, O Virgin, on the Day of Judgement. 19. May I be guarded by the Cross, armed by Christ's death and watched over by his grace. 20. When my body dies, grant that may my soul be given the glory of paradise.

Jacopone was also one of the first writers to compose vernacular lauds of the Virgin.[112] The quasi-liturgical *laude* grew out of the thirteenth century confraternities of central and northern Italy, above all the *laudese* companies, which were formed for the purpose of holding religious services that honoured Christ, the Virgin Mary, and the saints, using these hymns as the centrepiece of their worship. The *disciplinati* (flagellants' movement, which originated with the Perugian Ranieri Fasani, who was inspired by Gioacchino da Fiore's († 1202) teachings to prophesise that the reign of the Spirit would begin in 1260) also compiled *laude* and sang them in their services, though their principal emphasis was on penitential activities.[113] A central focus in the *laude* is the Virgin's

---

[112] See Mario Aste, 'Energy of Transport and Ectasy in the Vernacular Characters of Mary's Cult in Jacopone's Poetry', in *Maria Vergine nella letteratura italiana* ed. by Florinda Iannace (Stony Brook, New York: Forum Italicum, 2000), pp. 27-37.

[113] On the confraternities see the comprehensive bibliography edited by Marina Gazzini, 'Bibliografia medievistica di storia confraternale', *Reti Medievali Rivista*, 5 (2004) <http://www.dssg.unifi.it/_RM/rivista/biblio/Gazzini.htm> [accessed 20 August 2006]. Gilles Gérard Meersseman's, *Ordo fraternitatis - Confraternite e pietà dei laici nel Medioevo*, in collaboration with G. P. Pacini, 3 vols (Rome: Herder 1977) is essential reading. For a brief historical survey of the *laude* and accompanying bibliography see Rosanna Bettarini, 'Jacopone da Todi e le Laude', in *Antologia della poesia italiana*, ed. by Cesare Segre e Carlo Ossola, (Turin: Einaudi-Gallimard, 1997-99), I (1997), 278-332 and 975-979. Cyrilla Barr, *The Monophonic* Lauda *and the Lay Religious Confraternities of Tuscany and Umbria in the Late Middle Ages* (Kalamazoo, Mich.: Medieval Institute, Western Michigan University, 1988) provides texts as well as much useful background information, particularly on the *disciplinati*. *Il Movimento dei disciplinati nel settimo centenario dal suo inizio (Perugia, 1260)*, ed. by Lodovico Scaramucci (Spoleto: Panetto and Petrelli, 1962), is a collection of essays by many of the foremost scholars in the field – particularly informative is Ignazio Baldelli's 'La lauda e i Disciplinati', pp. 338-67. Ursula Betka's unpublished doctoral thesis 'Marian Images and Laudesi Devotion in the Late Medieval Italy, 1260-1350', University of Melbourne, 2001, though dealing mainly with art, is useful in contextualising *laudese* devotionalism within the broader Marian tradition.

suffering at the foot of the Cross. While several of Cortona *laude*, such as the *Ave vergene gaudente*, as well as the four Urbino plaints that Bettarini attributes to Jacopone,[114] speak of Mary's suffering, no vernacular poem on the Passion can match the direct impact of Jacopone's *Donna de Paradiso*.[115] In many respects *Donna de Paradiso*, which takes the form of a dramatic dialogue between Mary, Christ on the Cross, and an anonymous messenger, is uncharacteristic of the rest of Jacopone's corpus in that it is entirely devoid of autobiographical content and is also his only dramatic poem. It is particularly from the perspective of Franciscan piety that we must consider this masterpiece.[116] This is a poem with a common touch, which is intent on drawing the reader into Mary's highly emotive response to her Son's Passion and death, and with little concern for the deeper soteriological significance of the event:[117]

> Lady of Paradise, your Son the blessed Jesus Christ has been taken. 2. Run, Lady, and see, for the people are beating him; I believe they want to kill him, so harshly are they scourging him.' 3. 'How can it be that he has been arrested, Christ, my hope, who never committed any fault?' 4. O, my Lady, he has been betrayed; Judas sold him out for thirty denarii; he made a great bargain out of it. 5. Come to my succour, Magdalene. A great misfortune has come upon me. Christ, my Son, is being carried away as was prophesised. 6. 'Aid him, O Lady, help him because your Son is being spat upon; they have brought him to Pilate.' 7. 'O Pilate, do not have my Son tormented, for I can show you that he has been wrongly accused. 8. 'Crucify him, crucify him! Whoever proclaims himself king according to our Law is rejecting the power of Rome.' 9. 'I beg you to understand me; think of my suffering; perhaps then you will change [opinion] regarding what you believed.' 10. 'Let us drag out the thieves so that they may be

---

To my knowledge, almost nothing has been written specifically on the image of the Virgin in early Italian vernacular poetry, in relation to the Mariology of the time other than Brian Reynolds, 'L'immagine della Vergine nelle *Laude* del XIII secolo, in relazione alla *Commedia* di Dante' *Fu Jen Studies: Literature & Linguistics*, 43 (2010), 69-93. See also the brief and decidedly superficial analysis by Charles Franco, 'The Virgin Mary in Early Italian Literature', in *Maria Vergine nella letteratura italiana* ed. by Florinda Iannace (Stony Brook, New York: Forum Italicum, 2000), pp. 69-75.

[114] Though Bettarini has shown that four of the Urbino laments most likely come from the hand of Jacopone, it is not necessary to consider them in the context of this study given that the themes they contain are fully represented in *Donna del Paradiso*.

[115] Slightly earlier than the *Donna del Paradiso* is a vernacular *planctus* from the Abruzzi which also dramatises the Passion, but only four verses are dedicated to the Virgin's grief. Sandro Sticca, *The Planctus Mariae in the Dramatic Tradition*, believes that it dates to before 1296 (p. 29).

[116] See Ubertino da Casale, *Arbor vitae crucifixae Jesu*, ed. by Charles T. Davis (Turin: Bottega d'Erasmo, 1961) and Bonaventure *Lignum Vitae*, and *Officium de Passione Domini*, in *Opera Omnia*, VIII, 68-86 and 152-158.

[117] See Mario Aste, 'Energy of Transport and Ecstasy in the Vernacular Characters of Mary's Cult in Jacopone's Poetry', in *Maria Vergine nella letteratura italiana* ed. by Florinda Iannace (Stony Brook, New York: Forum Italicum, 2000), pp. 27-37.

his companions. Let him be crowned with thorns because he proclaimed himself king.' 11. 'O Son, O Son, beloved lily! Son, who will comfort my tormented heart?' 12. 'O Son, whose eyes were merry, why do you not answer? O Son, why do you hide yourself from the breast that gave you suck?' 13. 'My Lady, here is the Cross that the people are carrying on which the True Light will be raised up.' 14. 'O Cross, what will you do? Will you take my Son. And of what will you accuse him who has no sin in him?' 15. 'Come to his aid [Lady] full of suffering, because your Son is being stripped; it seems that the people want him to be martyred.' 16. 'If you are taking off his clothes let me see him, how they have bloodied him in wounding him cruelly.' 17. 'Lady, they are taking his hand and stretching it out on the Cross; with a nail they split it so hard did they drive it in.' 18. They are taking the other hand and stretching it on the Cross; the pain is becoming more vivid since it has grown greater.' 19. Lady, they are taking his feet and nailing them to the wood; opening every joint they have dislocated everything.' 20. 'And I am beginning the funeral lament; [O] Son, my consolation, [O] Son, who has killed you my exquisitely beautiful Son? 21. They would have done better to rip out my heart, for it has been dragged up onto the Cross and there it is lacerated.' 22. 'O mummy, from whence did you come? You are wounding me mortally, for your wailing with such anguish kills me.' 23. Son, [I am crying] for good reason; Son, Father and Husband. Son, who has wounded you? Son, who has stripped you bare?' 24. 'Mummy, why are you complaining? I want you to remain and serve my companions whom I gathered in the world.' 25. 'Son, do not say this! I want to die with you, I do not want to go away before I have drawn my last breath. 26. Let the two [of us] be buried together, [O] Son of the unhappy Mother; let Mother and Son suffer a violent death in the depths of prostration.' 27. 'O mummy, with my heart afflicted, I place you in the hands of John, my beloved; let him be called your son. 28. John, here is my Mother. Take her into your love, have pity on her for her heart is sorely pierced.' 29. 'Son, your soul has left you, O Son of the lost [Mother], Son of the desolate [Mother], Son who has been poisoned. 30. Son, white [skinned] and blond, Son whose face gives joy, why has the world despised you so? 31. Son, white and red, Son, without compare, Son to whom I turn. 32. Sweet and pleasing Son, Son of the suffering [Mother], Son, the people have treated you badly. 33. John, my new son, your brother is dead. Now I feel the sword that was prophesised. 34. May Mother and Son be embraced by the same death. May Mother and the Son who hangs find themselves in an embrace.' *Donna de Paradiso*[118]

---

[118] Translated from the text in Iacopone da Todi, *Laude*, ed. by Franco Mancini (Bari: Laterza 1974). For an alternative English translation see Jacopone da Todi, *Lauds*, ed. by Serge and Elizabeth Hughes, Classics of Western Spirituality, 30 (New York: Paulist Press, 1982). Among the more significant critical works on Jacopone are Natalino Sapegno, *Frate Jacopone* (Turin: Baretti, 1926), Agostino Barolo, *Jacopone da Todi* (Turin: Bocca, 1929), Mario Apollonio, *Jacopone da Todi e la poetica delle confraternite religiose nella cultura preumanistica: appunti delle lezioni di letteratura italiana* (Milan: Vita e pensiero, 1946), Franco Maccarini, *Jacopone da Todi e i suoi critici* (Milan: Gastaldi, 1952), and Rosanna Bettarini, *Jacopone e il Laudario Urbinate* (Florence: Sansoni, 1969). Recent studies include Alvaro Cacciotti, *Amor sacro e amor profano in Jacopone da Todi* (Rome: Antonianum, 1989), Franco Suitner, *Iacopone da Todi: poesia, mistica, rivolta nell'Italia del Medioevo* (Rome:

Two other Franciscans, one Spanish, the other Italian, who lived around the same time as Jacopone, also write of Mary's co-passion. Raymond Lull († 1315), writing in the vernacular, asserts that Mary contributed to the Redemption both through her role in the Incarnation in which she participated both materially and formally, through her consent to be the Mother of God, and in her compassion on Calvary, when she shared in her Son's agony, but also in his joy at the Redemption of the world.[119] In his *Arbor vitae crucifixae Jesu*, written in 1305, Ubertino of Casale († after 1330) suggests that Mary was fully aware when she presented Jesus in the Temple that she was offering him up for Crucifixion. Here we find a full-blow theology of the co-redemption, in which Mary, fully cognisant of the price she will pay, assents to Christ's sacrifice for the sake of sinners, whose spiritual mother she will become through her participation in the Passion. Ubertino is careful, however, to insist that it is through Jesus that redemption is achieved:

> I know what I am doing, what I am giving, and what I shall receive in return. In return I shall receive the prayers of my adoptive children to whom I offer my Only-begotten in expiation [of their sins]. [...] He is the true and unique Lamb who cannot be offered up by anyone other than me, his Mother, most rich in graces, for the redemption of my wretched and unfortunate adoptive children, who are held prisoner by the double moan of the fault [original sin] and punishment. [...] I know what I am giving; indeed, I am the only one who knows it, apart from my Son, because I am the only one to participate, more than all the others, in his immense suffering. And therefore, with the fullest and most perfect love, I offer my most beloved Son, Jesus to those who need to be formed, instructed, redeemed, restored, and glorified.[120]

Later Ubertino speaks of Mary's 'primacy of compassion' explaining that Christ was not only crucified on the Cross but also in the Virgin's heart, so that she became the advocate of humanity, he its Redeemer.[121]

Here we end our survey. By the early fourteenth century the notion of Mary's co-redemption had reached about as far as it could do within the theological framework of the time. Until the problem of the Immaculate Conception was definitively resolved no progress could really be made since the question of her

---

Donzelli, 1999), Jacopone da Todi, *Laude*, ed. and intro. by Gianni Mussini (Casale Monferrato: Piemme, 1999). Many useful essays appear in *Iacopone da Todi: atti del XXXVII convegno storico internazionale* (Spoleto: Centro italiano di studi sull'alto Medioevo, 2001). In English see George T. Peck's *The Fool of God: Jacopone da Todi* (Alabama: The University of Alabama Press, 1980).

[119] See Sandro Sticca, *The Planctus Mariae in the Dramatic Tradition*, pp. 27-29, who discusses Lull and quotes from his works in Catalan.

[120] *TMSM*, IV, 519.

[121] See Chapter 4 of the *Arbor vitae crucifixae Jesu*, ed. by Charles T. Davis, which also contains an excellent example of a Marian lament. See Sandro Sticca, *The Planctus Mariae in the Dramatic Tradition*, p. 109 and Donna Spivey Ellington, *Sacred Body*, p. 83.

freedom from sin is closely bound up with the fittingness of her participation in the Redemption. However, this does not mean that interest in the *Mater dolorosa* was at an end. As the century progressed writings on the Virgin's co-passion multiplied, peaking in the latter half of the fourteenth century, and while little of significance was added in terms of content, the form did undergo further development especially in the expanded adoption of the vernacular for plaints, the increasing use of dramatic performances, and an explosion in devotion to the Virgin's sorrows.[122] Nowhere is this continuing affective piety more evident than in the great artistic representations of the *mater dolorosa*, crowned by Michelangelo's *Pietà*.[123] As we noted at the beginning of this chapter, this devotion is once again manifesting itself today in a campaign within some sections of the Church in favour of a fifth Marian dogma, the co-Redemption.[124]

---

[122] See John R. Secor, 'The *Planctus Mariae* in Provencal Literature: A Subtle Blend of Courtly and Religious Traditions', in *The Spirit of the Court: Selected Proceedings of the Fourth Congress of the International Courtly Literature Society, Toronto, 1983*, ed. by Glyn S. Burgess and Robert Taylor (Cambridge: Brewer, 1985), pp. 321-26.

[123] See Donna Spivey Ellington, *Sacred Body*, pp. 79-81.

[124] See Mark Miravalle, *'With Jesus': The Story of Mary Co-Redemptrix*.

Chapter 7 - The Assumption

Psalms 15. 10:	Because thou wilt not leave my soul in hell; nor wilt then give thy holy one to see corruption.
Psalms 131. 8:	Arise, O Lord, into thy resting place: thou and the ark, which thou hast sanctified.
Canticles 2. 10:	Behold my beloved speaketh to me: Arise, make haste, my love, my dove, my beautiful one, and come.
Isaiah 52. 1:	Arise, arise, put on thy strength, O Sion, put on the garments of thy glory, O Jerusalem, the city of the Holy One.
II Corinthians 12. 2:	I know a man in Christ above fourteen years ago (whether in the body, I know not, or out of the body, I know not; God knoweth), such a one caught up to the third heaven.
Apocalypse 12. 1:	And a great sign appeared in heaven: A woman clothed with the sun, and the moon under her feet, and on her head a crown of twelve stars.

Although the Catholic Church did not officially proclaim the dogma of Mary's bodily Assumption until 1950, when Pius XII declared, in the Apostolic Constitution *Munificentissimus Deus* that, 'we pronounce, declare, and define it to be a divinely revealed dogma: that the Immaculate Mother of God, the ever Virgin Mary, having completed the course of her earthly life, was assumed body and soul into heavenly glory',[1] the belief that the Virgin was translated directly to Heaven upon her death, or Dormition as it was usually called, was already widespread in the Patristic Church. Strictly speaking the Dormition (falling asleep) is a separate event from the Assumption since the one implies the end of Mary's earthly life and the other signifies her rising to heaven (*transitus*), either with or without her body. In fact, as we shall see, some accounts of Mary's passing separate the two events by hundreds of days. While the Catholic Church affirms her bodily Assumption, the issue of whether Mary died and was then resurrected, or was transported to heaven directly without experiencing death has never been definitively resolved, as is evidenced by the deliberately ambiguous 'having completed the course of her earthly life' of the 1950 declaration, though the general tendency is to believe that she died, since Christ also died. Indeed the ancient term 'dormition' shows that from the outset there was a certain ambiguity concerning Mary's death.[2]

---

[1] *Munificentissimus Deus*, 44, <http://www.vatican.va/holy_father/pius_xii/apost_constitutions/documents/hf_p-xii_apc_19501101_munificentissimus-deus_en.html.> [accessed 20 May 2007].

[2] For a fuller treatment of the differences between the terms 'dormition' and 'assumption' and the related questions of whether Mary actually died and of the fate of her body see Simon Claude Mimouni, *Dormition et Assomption de Marie: Histoire des traditions anciennes* (Paris: Beauchesne, 1995), pp. 7-21.

Various theological arguments have been put forward in favour of the Assumption. One is that if Mary is the new Eve, who, through her Son, brought about a new creation, as Justin Martyr (†c. 165) and Irenaeus (†c. 202) first proposed,[3] then she should be exempt from the consequences of the Fall. Moreover, since death and corruption are a consequence of sin, Mary, who was without sin should not have had to endure them. This is an argument that has been used both by those who believe she was entirely free of original sin and those who claimed that she was sanctified in the womb, or at some point prior to the Incarnation. Linked to Mary's freedom from sin is her virginity, which the Fathers saw as intimately bound up with the incorruptibility of her body after death: if God had made an exception to the laws of nature in preserving her virginity both at the conception of Jesus and at his birth (*virginitas in partu*), then he could also preserve her from the corruption of death. Another frequent reason that is proposed is based on her sharing the flesh of her Son (con-corporeality): since the flesh of Jesus, which he received from the Virgin, has been glorified, then that same flesh should also be glorified in Mary. Further justification is found in Mary's sharing in her Son's victory over sin and death on the Cross. Finally, an argument of convenience that has been put forward is that it is inconceivable that Jesus would have allowed his Mother to suffer the corruption of death and since it was within his power to preserve her from this fate he must have done so – *potuit, decuit, ergo fecit* (God could do it, it was fitting that he do so, therefore he did) as the famous Medieval formula, which John Scotus applied to the Immaculate Conception, puts it.

Before beginning our analysis of the evolution of this doctrine in the Patristic and Medieval periods it is necessary to say a word about early Christian perceptions of the fate of the body and soul after death, since there was no clearly defined understanding on this question in the first centuries of the Church. Indeed, it is impossible to understand that the assumption of Mary's soul, let alone her body, directly into heaven upon her death would have been an extraordinary occurrence in the eyes of many of the early Fathers if one does not realise that in the early Church it was widely believed that admittance to Paradise would occur only at the end of time with the universal Judgement. According to Tertullian († c. 230?), for instance, only the martyrs went to heaven directly after death, while ordinary mortals would have to wait in an ill-defined place somewhere under the earth, the *rifrigerium interim*, until the end of time. The wicked instead would be held in a place called the *tormentum*.[4] Similar

---

[3] Additional information on many of the points made here are to be found in the chapters on the Remote Redemption, the Immediate Redemption, Virginity and the Immaculate Conception.

[4] See *De Anima*, 55, *PL* 2, 742C. On the understanding of death in early Christianity see Brian E. Daley, *The Hope of the Early Church: A Handbook of Patristic Eschatology* (Cambridge: Cambridge University Press, 1991), especially pp. 5-43, and Alfred C. Rush, *Death and Burial in Christian Antiquity* (Washington DC: Catholic University Press of America, 1941). For the later period see Frederick S. Paxton, *Christianizing Death: The*

conceptions of life after death were held by many of the Fathers. Augustine (†
430) offers one of the first glimpses of the notion of Purgatory when he writes
of sinners undergoing a period of expiation prior to entry into heaven. But like
earlier Fathers he believes that the souls of the just will also have to await the
end of time to enter into Paradise:

> During the time, moreover, which intervenes between a man's death and the
> final resurrection, the soul lingers in mysterious dwellings where it enjoys rest or
> suffers affliction in proportion to the merit it has earned by the life which it led
> on earth. *Enchiridion, 29, 109*[5]

Only in the sixth century, after a period in which a rather dark view of death
had held sway, did the Church begin to affirm clearly that the souls of the just
could expect to meet their reward immediately. But the conception of Paradise
was still very nebulous, a far cry from the ordered place, with its gradations of
beatitude, envisioned by Dante. Gregory the Great († 604), building on
Augustine, identifies an intermediate place where souls would purge their
sinfulness prior to entry into Paradise, but says little about the nature or location
of this space. It is crucial to take this understanding of the afterlife into account
if one is to gain a clear understanding of the emergence and evolution of belief
in Mary's assumption. Indeed Brian Daley has suggested that the story of
Mary's Dormition and apotheosis served as an effective means in overcoming
fear of death in late Christian antiquity, helping to transform the popular view
of a dark, dull afterlife.[6]

The Eastern Churches

The earliest accounts of the Dormition, or Assumption as it came to be called
in the Latin Church,[7] were written between the fifth and seventh centuries,
though they are almost certainly based on a pre-existing tradition, possibly

---

Creation of a Ritual Process in Early Medieval Europe (Ithaca and London: Cornell University
Press, 1990).
[5] All translations, unless otherwise indicated, are from the Latin and Italian texts in S.
Aurelii Augustini, *Opera Omnia, Tutte le opere*, ed. by Franco Monteverde, 45 vols (Rome:
Nuova Biblioteca Agostiniana and Città Nuova, 1967–), in *Sant'Agostino, Augustinus
Hipponensis*, < http://www.augustinus.it/> [accessed 26 February 2009].
[6] '"Now and at the Hour of Our Death": Mary's Dormition and Christian Dying in Late
Patristic and Early Byzantine Literature', *Dumbarton Oaks Papers*, 55 (2001), 71-89.
[7] The term 'Assumption' was first introduced by the Latin Church in the eighth century
during the pontificate of Adrian I. See Donna Spivey Ellington, *From Sacred Body to
Angelic Soul: Understanding Mary in Late Medieval and Early Modern Europe* (Washington:
Catholic University of America Press, 2001), p. 104, n. 4.

dating back as far as the third century.[8] Broadly speaking, they fall into two families, one of which relates that Mary's body was preserved intact in the Earthly Paradise but was not reunited with her soul in heaven (*Transitus* D

---

[8] For a recent and comprehensive study on the origins of the tradition see Stephen Shoemaker, *Ancient Traditions of the Virgin Mary's Dormition and Assumption* (Oxford: Oxford University Press, 2002). Also fundamental are Simon Claude Mimouni, *Dormition et Assomption* and Michel van Esbroeck, *Aux origines de la Dormition de la Vierge: Études historiques sur les traditions orientales*, Variorum Collected Studies Series, 472 (Aldershot: Ashgate, 1995). For English translations of the apocrypha see *The Apocryphal New Testament: A Collection of Apocryphal Christian Literature in an English Translation*, ed. by James K. Elliott (Oxford: The Clarendon Press, 1993), and *The Complete Gospels: Annotated Edition*, ed. by Robert J. Miller, 3rd edn (San Francisco: Harper, 1994). For a list of early Dormition narratives with proposed dating and categorised according to language see Michel van Esbroeck, 'Les texts littéraires sur l'assomption avant le Xe siècle', in *Les Actes apocryphes des Apôtres: Christianisme et monde païns* (Geneva: Labor et Fides, 1981), pp. 265-288. Martin Jugie's monumental study, *La mort et l'assomption de la Saint Vierge: étude historico-doctrinale* (Vatican City: Studi e Testi, 1944), is still essential reading for the early history of the Assumption. See also Antoine Wegner, *L'assomption de la Tres Sainte Vierge dans la tradition byzantine du Vie au Xe siècle: Études et documents* (Paris: [n. pub], 1955). For an overview of early Dormition accounts as well as English translations of all the most significant early homilies on the subject see Brian E. Daley, *On the Dormition of Mary: Early Patristic Homilies* (Crestwood, N. Y.: St. Vladimir's, 1998). For an excellent short study of the apocrypha see Enrico Norelli, 'Maria negli Apocrifi', in *Gli studi di mariologia medievale: bilancio storico*, Atti del I convegno mariologico della fondazione Ezio Franceschini con la collaborazione della biblioteca Palatina e del dipartimento di storia dell'università di Parma, Parma 7-8 novembre 1997, ed. by Clelia Maria Piastra (Florence: SISMEL – Edizioni del Galuzzo, 2001), pp. 19-63, particularly pp. 35-61, and, by the same author, 'Maria nella letteratura apocrifa cristiana antica', in *SDM*, I, 143-254. For a broad account of the history of the Assumption see Marina Warner *Alone of All her Sex: The Myth and Cult of the Virgin Mary* (London: Pan Books, 1985), pp. 81-102. Warner also dedicates a chapter to the Apocrypha, pp. 25-33. On sources and doctrinal details see Michael O'Carroll, *Theotokos: A Theological Encyclopedia of the Blessed Virgin Mary* (Collegeville, Minnesota: Liturgical Press, 1982), pp. 55-58, Gabriele M. Roschini, *Maria Santissima nella storia della salvezza*, vol. III, part II, *Il dogma mariano* (Isola del Liri: Pisani, 1969), 451-632. Thomas Livius, *The Blessed Virgin in the Fathers of the First Six Centuries* (London: Burns and Oates, 1893), pp. 338-55, , and, though somewhat pietistic, Joseph Duhr, *The Glorious Assumption of the Mother of God*, trans. by John Manning Fraunces (New York: Kenedy, 1950). See also *L'Assunzione di Maria Madre di Dio: significato storico salvifico a 50 anni dalla definizione* dogmatic, atti del 1° Forum internazionale di mariologia, Roma 30-31 ottobre 2000, ed. by Gaspar Calvo Moralejo and Stefano Cecchin (Vatican City: Pontificia Accademia Mariana Internazionale, 2001). Also very informative is Mary Clayton, *The Apocryphal Gospels of Mary in Anglo Saxon England* (Cambridge: Cambridge University Press, 1998), especially pp. 24-100. Luigi Gambero, *MF*, discusses the apocrypha, pp. 33-41. James K. Elliott, Mary in the Apocryphal New Testament' in *The Origins of the Cult of the Virgin Mary*, ed. by Chris Maunder (London: Burns & Oats, 2008), pp. 57-70, provides a very brief summary of the current state of research (pp. 66-67).

texts), while in the other set Christ reunites body and soul (*Transitus* R texts).[9] The earliest extant text is a group of Syriac fragments that date from the latter half of the fifth century in which there is a description of Mary's burial, the reception of her soul by Jesus, and the transferral of her body to the Earthly Paradise, where it is buried under the Tree of Life.[10] The earliest Greek accounts of the *Transitus*, the most prominent of which is the *Pseudo-John*, dating from the late fifth or early sixth century. One of the earliest Latin R-text versions is the fifth-century *Gospel of the Pseudo-Melito*.[11]

The broad outline of these and later apocryphal accounts are that an angel appears to Mary, frequently bearing a palm, to announce her impending death. Thereafter, the apostles and various disciples arrive, the former sometimes being borne on clouds from the various parts of the world in which they have been preaching. They gather around Mary's bed to bid her farewell. Hosts of angels then appear, and lastly, in most accounts, Christ himself descends from heaven accompanied by angels, and in some accounts, by the prophets and patriarchs. Having taken her leave, Mary breathes her last and her soul then departs for heaven. Thus, although she does undergo a physical death, she does not suffer the fate of other faithful Christians in that the passage from this life to the next is seamless, lacking the fear and trepidation that normally accompany death. In some accounts Mary's soul descends to Hades in the manner of Christ before being welcomed into paradise, but on the whole she is translated directly to heaven. After the departure of her soul, a funeral is held and her body is brought to the tomb in an elaborate procession. In many accounts a Jew named Jephoniah, often identified as the high priest, attempts to overthrow her funeral bier, but is punished by the withering of his arms, a clear reference to the story of Uzzah, whom God punishes with death for having touched the Ark of the Covenant (II Kings 6. 6-7). In most versions the unfortunate Jephoniah subsequently repents of his act and is cured, upon which he sets forth to proclaim the good news to his fellow Jews. Accounts vary on the fate of Mary's body. In some stories Thomas, the doubting apostle, arrives three days late and asks to see Mary's body. When the tomb is opened the body is no longer there. In other versions the period before the body rises from the dead is longer, and the bodily Assumption also involves the descent of Jesus, accompanied by angels, and is witnessed by the apostles. In some accounts the Virgin's body is reunited with her soul, while in others, such as the Syriac account mentioned above, her body is preserved intact in the Earthly Paradise, awaiting the resurrection of the dead.

Ephrem the Syrian (†c. 373) provides what may be one of the first references

---

[9] See Mary Clayton, *The Cult of the Virgin*, pp. 8-10. For a comprehensive survey of all the known Dormition texts from Jerusalem in the East to Ireland in the West see Michel van Esbroeck, *Aux origines de la Dormition*, whom Clayton cites extensively.
[10] See *EPH*, p. 7.
[11] See Mary Clayton, *The Cult of the Virgin*, p. 9.

to the glorification of Mary's body in one of his hymns on the Nativity: 'And as I gave birth to him in a second birth, he, too, has given birth to me. His body is none other than the garment of his Mother which he put on. I instead have received its glory.'[12] Though the precise meaning of these lines is rather ambiguous, and cannot be taken as a reference to Mary's bodily Assumption, what is clearly established here is the principle of con-carnality, in which the glory of Christ's flesh is shared with his Mother.

Epiphanius of Salamis († 403) was the first of the Fathers to raise formally the question of the fate of Mary's body.[13] He notes that the Gospels give us no information about the end of Mary's life, and suggests three hypotheses regarding her death. It is possible that God raised her up to heaven. Alternatively, she may have died a martyr's death, if one agrees with this interpretation of Simeon's prophecy regarding the sword that would pierce Mary's heart (Luke 2. 35). It is also possible, he says, that she died a natural death. In any case, what he insists upon most is that we cannot know her fate for certain:

> If anyone holds that we are mistaken, let him simply follow the indications of Scripture, in which is found no mention of Mary's death, whether she died or did not die, whether she was buried or was not buried. For when John was sent on his voyage to Asia, no one says that he had the holy Virgin with him as a companion. Scripture simply is silent, because of the greatness of the prodigy in order not to strike the mind of man with excessive wonder. As far as I am concerned, I dare not speak out, but I maintain a meditative silence. [...] Simeon says of her, 'And thy own soul a sword shall pierce, that, out of many hearts, thoughts may be revealed.' In the Apocalypse, John writes: 'The dragon hurled himself at the woman who had given birth to a male child; but the wings of an eagle were given to the woman, and she flew into the desert, where the dragon could not reach her' (Apocalypse 12. 13-14). This could have happened to Mary. But I dare not affirm this with absolute certainty, nor do I say that she remained untouched by death, nor can I confirm whether she died. In fact, Scripture has remained above the human mind and has left this point in uncertainty. *Adversus Haereses, 78, 11*[14]

This agnostic position was to be reaffirmed by many commentators in both the Patristic and Medieval Church. However, on another occasion, in condemning the Collyridian sect, which he claims showed undue veneration to Mary, Epiphanius shows no such agnosticism about Mary's end, as Stephen Shoemaker has noted.[15] Pointing out that Elijah is not venerated even though

---

[12] *Hymns on the Nativity*, 16, 11. See Hilda Graef, *Doctrine and Devotion*, I, 58, and *TMPM*, IV, 104-05.
[13] See Clayton, *The Cult of the Virgin Mary*, pp. 6-7.
[14] Translation based in part on *MF*, pp. 125-26. See also *TMPM*, I, 395-96, O'Carroll, p. 135 and Livius, pp. 342-45.
[15] Stephen, J. Shoemaker, 'The Cult of the Virgin in the Fourth Century: A Fresh Look at Some Old and New Sources', in *The Origins of the Cult of the Virgin Mary*, ed. by Chris

he was carried up to heaven, he likens the prophet to Mary, saying that he too 'a virgin from his mother's womb, [...] remained so perpetually, was assumed and has not seen death.' It may be that when his focus was on another issue – the condemnation of excessive veneration – Epiphanius let his guard down and revealed his true belief on the Dormition.

Severian of Gabala († after 408) says nothing about Mary's dormition but he is certain that she now resides in heaven, where she intercedes on behalf of humanity: 'But she most certainly hears [our prayers], because she is in a splendid place, because she is in the region of the living, she who is the Mother of Salvation.'[16] This, as we noted when speaking of Mary's intercession, is one of the first instances of the Virgin's presence in heaven being directly linked to her ongoing role as intercessor, a notion that will be expressed by many subsequent commentators.

A homily by Jacob of Serug († 521), dated August 14th, 489, bears witness to the celebration of Mary's death in the Syriac Church. Jacob clearly states that Mary did die. He does not speak of the fate of her body, but he envisions her soul being accompanied to heaven by Jesus and a vast hosts of angels as well as the patriarchs of the Old Testament, while the whole of creation rejoices at her apotheosis:

> Today all the prophets raised their heads from their tombs since they beheld the light shining upon them. They beheld death trembling and fleeing from them, and the gates of heaven and the depths of the earth opened once again. The prophets and the apostles, the martyrs and the priests had gathered, as had the doctors, the patriarchs and the upright of old. On high the angels, on earth men, glory in the heavens, when the Virgin Mary was buried like [all] the dead. A light shone on that choir of apostles, and on her companions too, her relatives and the daughters of her people. Multitudes of angels flew overhead, singing before the glorious soul of this Mother of the Son of God. The Seraphim of fire surrounded the soul that was emigrating, raising their voices in jubilation. *On the Burial or Death of Mary the Holy Generatrix of God, 179-192.*[17]

Theodosius, Patriarch of Alexandria († 566), uses the term 'Assumption' and not 'Dormition' in a sermon delivered shortly before his death, and provides some of the earliest known evidence for the celebration of the feast on August 15th in the Greek Church. The Church in Jerusalem had honoured Mary on this date since about 450, and it was officially designated for the celebration of her death and Assumption in Byzantium by the emperor Maurice around 600, and

Maunder (London: Burns and Oats, 2008), pp. 71-87 (p. 81). Quotation from Epihanius below is his.
[16] *Homily on the Creation of the World*, TMPM, I, 428.
[17] For an English translation of the entire sermon see Mary Hansbury, *Jacob of Serug on the Mother of God* (Crestwood, N.Y.: St. Vladimir's, 1998), pp. 89-100.

was also accepted by the Latin Church.[18] Theodosius claims to have learnt of the circumstances of Mary's death and Assumption, which he describes in great detail, from a manuscript in the library of Alexandria that originated in Jerusalem. His account in which he has Jesus reassure the Apostles that he will reunite her soul with her body, is very precise. This passage illustrates the close relationship between Mary's Assumption and her intercession on behalf of a sinful humanity:

> Once two hundred and six days have passed between her death and her blessed Assumption, an angle will bring her back to you clothed in the same body in which you now see her with you. Then I shall transport her to the heights of heaven, close to the Father and the Holy Spirit, so that she will dwell there and offer entreaties for you all. *Sermon for the Assumption of Our Lady*, 17[19]

A sermon by Theoteknos, bishop of the Jordanian city of Livias, one of the most important early sustainers of Mary's bodily Assumption, dating from some time towards the end of the sixth century, offers theological justification for the belief, arguing that it was only fitting that Mary's body should be assumed into heaven given that Christ had taken his immaculate flesh from hers:

> It was fitting that her most holy body, that body which had borne and contained God, divinised, incorruptible, illuminated by divine light and full of glory [...] should be entrusted to the earth [only] for a short time, and then be taken up into heaven in glory together with her soul which was acceptable to God. *Homily on the Assumption of the Holy Mother of God, 9* [20]

This notion of con-corporeality was to become one of the fundamental planks in Medieval arguments in favour of the bodily Assumption.[21] Theoteknos goes on to argue that if God had prepared a place in heaven for the Apostles, as well as Enoch (Genesis 5. 24) and Elijah (IV Kings 2. 11), how much more should he grant this privilege to Mary. The conviction that Enoch, Elijah and John (John 21. 22-23) shared Mary's destiny was widely held in the Patristic Church and continued into the Middle Ages.[22] Like Theodosius,

---

[18] See Mary Clayton, *Cult of the Virgin*, p. 27, Stephen J. Shoemaker, 'Marian Liturgies', pp. 138-41, Bernard Capelle, 'La fête de la Vierge à Jérusalem au vᵉ siècle', *Le Muséon*, 56 (1943), 1-33, and Bernard Botte, 'Le lectionnaire arménien et la fête de la Théotocos à Jerusalem au vᵉ siècle, *Sacris Erudiri*, 2 (1949), 111-22.

[19] *TMPM*, II, 63. All translations, unless otherwise indicated, are mine.

[20] *TMPM*, II, 82. For alternative English translation see *EPH*, p. 73.

[21] See Graef, *Doctrine and Devotion*, I, 134-36.

[22] Augustine, for instance, accepts the popular belief that John had not truly died, *Tractates on the Gospel of John*, 124. See the *Post Sanctus* of the Mozarabic, *Missa in diem Sancti Joannis Evangelisteae*, PL 85, 204A-C. And see Donna Spivey Ellington, *Sacred Body*, pp. 106-07, and Jaroslav Pelikan, *Mary through the Centuries*, pp. 34-35.

Theoteknos also emphasises that the bodily Assumption has given Mary unrivalled intercessory powers over which nothing can prevail.

John of Thessalonica (†c. 630), in what is generally acknowledged to be the first extant Byzantine homily on the Dormition – thus marking the official acceptance of the feast in the mainstream Greek Church – retells what had by now become generally accepted details of the event, including her bodily ascent after a three-day interval, though he is careful to exclude some of the more fantastical elements of the apocryphal accounts.[23]

A homily attributed Modestus of Jerusalem († 634), though it actually postdates the Third Council of Constantinople (680-81),[24] is of some doctrinal importance since it distances itself from apocryphal accounts, relying instead on more rational arguments, and affirms the glorification of Mary's body with absolute clarity: 'For Christ our God, who put on living and intelligent flesh, which he took from the ever-Virgin and the Holy Spirit, has called her to himself and clothed her with an incorruptibility touching all her corporeal frame.'[25] The author starts by linking Mary's Assumption with her virginal motherhood: the Virgin, who gave birth to Life, has been rewarded with the fullness of eternal life, and she has been preserved from death by her Son, just as he preserved her virginity. Throughout the homily he returns again and again to Mary's divine motherhood as the primary reason for her bodily Assumption. Nowhere is this more clear than in an encomiastic passage in which he begins each sentence by lauding the Dormition and then follows up with the marvellous transformations that have occurred through the birth of her Son: 'O most Blessed Dormition of the most glorious Mother of God, of her who always remained a virgin, even after giving birth, and who did not experience corruption in that life-giving body of hers, even in the tomb, preserved by the omnipotent Christ the Saviour who was born of her.'[26] Like previous Byzantine writers, the author also emphasises the connection between the Assumption and Mary's role as intercessor.

By the end of the seventh century belief in the bodily Assumption, though not part of official Church doctrine, was widely acknowledged in theological circles in the East, as is witnessed by a number of sermons for the Feast of the Dormition, and by an important *Life of Mary*, attributed to Maximus the Confessor († 662), which affirms that Mary's body was transported to heaven and preserved from corruption.[27] Unlike some previous accounts, the *Life*

---

[23] For bibliography and a brief account of early Syriac and Greek Dormition texts, including a summary of John of Thessalonica's *Homily on the Dormition*, see Brian E. Daley, "'Now and at the Hour of Our Death'", pp. 80-85. See *TMPM*, II, 99-116 for an Italian translation of the sermon, and *EPH*, pp. 47-67 for an English version.

[24] See *EPH*, p. 15.

[25] *Homily on the Dormition of the Mother of God*, 5, *EPH*, p. 89; *TMPM*, II, 128.

[26] *Homily on the Dormition of the Mother of God*, 6, *EPH*, p. 90; *TMPM*, II, 129.

[27] The *Life* was translated from Georgian into French by Michel Van Esbroeck, who argues in favour of Maxiumus as its author: *Maxime le Confesseur: Vie de la Vierge*, Corpus Scriptorum Christianorum Orientalium, 478 (Louvain: Peeters, 1986). An Italian

claims that there were no witnesses to the bodily Assumption, but that Mary's tomb was simply found to be empty, thus paralleling the account of Christ's Resurrection. As to reasons for the preservation of Mary's body from corruption, the *Life* says:

> She was buried as one of the dead according to the laws of nature, but as the Mother of God, she was transported so as to confirm and render credible the Resurrection of the Lord her Son, the ascension of the nature with which he had clothed himself from her, and to confirm our future ascension and true incorruptibility. Just as her birth-giving was incorruptible so was her death incorruptible and just as her birth-giving had been superior to all words and all laws of nature, so too did her transition go beyond the natural order. *Life of Mary*[28]

Germanus of Constantinople (†c. 733), a key figure in the history of the doctrine, puts forward a number of reasons why Mary should have been accorded this special privilege by her Son, all of which also crop up in Medieval discussions. For Germanus, it is unthinkable that God would allow the temple that contained the body of the Son to lie in a tomb: 'It was impossible for what had been God's vessel, the temple of the all-holy godhead of the Only-begotten, to be conquered by the lethal confinement of a tomb.'[29] In addition, he argues that it is natural that Jesus would wish for his Mother to share in the glories of heaven and want to repay her for her earthly role. As further reason for the privilege, he cites Mary's absolute purity, which he connects to the beauty of the beloved in the Song of Songs: 'You are, as it is written, "all-beautiful", and your virginal body is all-holy, all-chaste, all the dwelling place of God, so that dissolving into dust is foreign to you.'[30] He also justifies the belief on the grounds that God wished Mary to take on the role of mediatrix in heaven, in language that is reminiscent of Bernard of Clairvaux's († 1153) famed sermon on Mary, star if the sea:[31]

> I will build you up as a rampart for the world, as a bridge for those tossed about by the tides, as an ark for those who are saved, as a staff for those who are

---

translation of the full text is available in *TMPM*, II, 185-289, whose editors remain more sceptical about the attribution to Maximus, believing it to be of a later date (pp. 183-84). And see the 2012 translation into English by Stephen Shoemaker, which in its comprehensive introduction tends towards accepting it as genuine.

[28] *TMPM*, II, 284.

[29] *First Homily on the Dormition*, 5, *EPH*, p. 157. English translations of Germanus' homilies on the Dormition are to be found in *EPH*, pp. 153-81, Italian versions in *TMPM*, II, 351-68. Daley reunites the two sections of the *First Homily*, which had been traditionally divided into two separate homilies, so that his numbering differs from *TMPM* and *PG*.

[30] *First Homily on the Dormition*, 5, quoted in *MF*, p. 384.

[31] See Bernard's *Second Sermon on the Glories of the Virgin Mother* and his *Sermon for the Feast of the Nativity of the Blessed Virgin Mary*, in *SBS*, pp. 37-38 and 87-87.

led by the hand, as an intercessor for sinners, and as the ladder that can conduct men to heaven. *Third Homily on the Dormition* [32]

For Germanus, it was essential that Mary should truly undergo death, just as had Christ, not only because she was subject to the law of death imposed on all the descendants of Adam, but as yet another proof that Jesus was truly human, born of a human mother:

> You have moved on from our earthly life, in order that the awful mystery of God's becoming human might be confirmed in more than mere appearance: in order that, as you are separated in this way from temporal things, we might come to believe that the God who was born of you came forth as a complete human being, the son of a real mother who was subject to the laws of natural necessity, [and that this happened] at the command of God's decree and subject to the temporal limitations of our life. You had a body just like one of us, and therefore you could not escape the event of death that is the common destiny of all human beings. *First Homily on the Dormition, 6* [33]

Germanus is more willing to include details from apocryphal accounts of the Dormition than some of the other Byzantine Fathers – the palm that the angel gives Mary, the miraculous arrival of the Apostles on clouds, and the withering of the Jewish man's hand, all feature. He also gives an unusually prominent role to the Apostle Paul by having him deliver an encomium to the Virgin, in which he declares that by looking on her he can see her Son, whom he had never seen in the flesh. Germanus is also unusual in that he claims that the Apostles witnessed Mary's body being transported to heaven. [34]

Andrew of Crete (†c. 740), a contemporary of Germanus, also supports the belief that Mary was translated to heaven, body and soul, which he, like others, links to the incarnation of Christ :

> She who turned dust into heaven today strips the dust away, lays aside the veil of this world of change, and gives back to the earth what belongs to it. She who bestowed life ascends to the transformation which is rebirth, and enters the place where life begins and never ends, a place far from all the conditions and complications of matter and the passions. Now, finally, her visible frame rises up from the visible world and is joined to the spiritual in a spiritual way: something only he understands who first joined matter and spirit together, then separated them to rejoin them again. *First Homily on the Dormition, 5* [35]

---

[32] *PG* 98, 361D, quoted in *MF*, p. 385.

[33] *EPH*, p. 158.

[34] See *Second [Third] Homily on the Dormition*, 4-10, *EPH*, pp. 172-78. In fact, Germanus contradicts himself in this sermon, since he had earlier stated that Mary's body was not assumed until she had spent a short time in the 'realm of the dead'.

[35] *EPH*, pp. 108-09. See *MF*, p. 397.

In Andrew's opinion, it is fitting that Jesus should honour Mary in this way: not only because she is his Mother but because her glorification will bear witness to the plan of salvation that he has realised through her in that she is a prophetic sign of the resurrection that awaits all of the blessed at the end of time. Andrew also argues that she underwent death, descending briefly to hell (which he believes to be the fate of all souls)[36] in the manner of Christ prior to ascending to heaven.[37] He spells out clearly that the sentence of death to which human nature was condemned as a result of the Fall has not been removed by the Redemption. Rather, as he puts it, we 'have been created anew not in our nature but only by the gift of grace.'[38] Thus, all must submit to death, Mary included, since even her Son was subject to this law:

> Death, natural to men, also reached her; not, however, to imprison her, as happens to us, or to vanquish her. God forbid! It was only to secure for her the experience of that sleep which comes from on high, leading us up to the object of our hope. [...] No man lives, says Scripture, who will not see death. But even though the human creature we celebrate today must obey the law of nature, as we do, she is superior to other humans. Therefore, death does not come to her in the same way that it comes to us. Instead, it comes in a superior way, and for a reason higher than the reason that obliges us to surrender totally to death. *First Homily on the Dormition*[39]

He further argues that it was necessary for her body to be separated from her soul and to undergo dissolution if it were to be transformed from a corruptible to an incorruptible state. But Mary's death is to be distinguished from that of other saints since the Virgin was without sin and therefore did not have to undergo the fear of condemnation and damnation but rather went to heaven without any judgment. Significantly he likens her death to the sleep of Adam when God extracted his rib in order to create Eve. Both Adam and Mary have produced new life through a direct intervention by God, but in the first case this led to corruption and death whereas in the second it led to incorruption and eternal life:

> Indeed, if I must speak the truth, death which is natural to the human race even reached as far as Mary: not that it held her captive as it holds us, or that it overcame her – far from it! But it touched her enough to let her experience that

---

[36] 'How, then, can it be anything but completely and undeniably clear that the souls of people, even those of the saints, go into that place of darkness that are not detained there: none, that is, but those who have brought death on themselves by sinful self-indulgence in this life.' *Second [First] Homily on the Dormition*, 3, *EPH*, pp. 119-22

[37] *Second [First] Homily on the Dormition*. See *TMPM*, II, 428-30, which numbers it as the first homily and see Daley, *EPH*, pp. 119-22, who takes the view that Andrew's three homilies were originally just two.

[38] *Second Homily on the Dormition*.

[39] *MF*, pp.395-96.

sleep that is for us, if I may put it this way, a kind of ecstatic movement towards the things we only hope for during this life, a passage that leads us on towards transformation into a state like that of God. Mary's death was, we might say, a parallel to that first sleep, which fell upon the first human being when his rib was removed to complete the creation of our race, and he received flesh to take the place of what had been taken away. In the same way, I think, she fell into a natural sleep and tasted death, but did not remain held by it; she simply followed the laws of nature and fulfilled God's plan, which the Providence that guides all things laid down for us from the beginning. Her role, surely, was to show us clearly the way she has moved through a transformation from a corruptible state to an incorruptible one – something that is only thinkable if a natural dissolution of these elements of our body should take place first, and if then the life that has melted away should be forged anew. [...] This, then, is how I suggest you understand her descent into the underworld: that period of time for which death and bodily decay held power over her – in my judgment, at least, - was only as long as was necessary for her to move, at natural speed, through unknown regions and to come to know them first-hand, regions where she had never set foot before and which she was now crossing as in a journey through foreign, uncharted territory. *Second Homily on the Dormition, 4*[40]

In Mary, through the Incarnation, the divinisation of both body and soul,[41] which is the *telos* of all of humanity, is realised, since Christ has destroyed the reign of death by taking flesh from her and uniting it with his divinity, and has transformed humanity into something divine. It is primarily for this reason that he has glorified his Mother in heaven, body and soul:

'I magnify the Lord in my soul, and rejoice in my spirit.', while in my body I am changed and take on a new form, sharing by grace in God's own being. And the source and final form of that transformation into God, I confess, is the form taken by him who is God above all, and who became flesh in an indescribable way in my womb, when he remade his own humanity into something divine. Through a share in the Spirit he bestowed this grace on us, whom he had never abandoned, when he ascended from earth to heaven along with that body. Moved by his care for the human race, 'he looked upon the lowliness of his handmaiden' (Luke 1. 47) and decreed an end to the curse of the first Eve. By his appearing in the flesh he has overshadowed 'those who dwell in darkness and the shadow of death', rising 'like the dawn from on high' and he has 'guided our feet into the way of peace' (Luke 1. 78). Though he is truly God, he became human in me, in a spiritual way, from a virgin's blood, bringing about a conception and growth that were unknown to nature. So, by a new relationship of both natures, he destroyed the old order and brought in a new order that will never grow old, so that all things might become new – in truth, a new creation –

---

[40] *EPH*, pp. 121-22.
[41] On divinisation see the seminal work by Jules Gross, *La divinisation du chrétien d'après les pères grecs: Contribution historique à la doctrine de la grâce* (Paris: Gabalda, 1938), translated as *The Divinization of the Christian According to the Greek Fathers*, trans. by Paul A. Onica (Anaheim, CA: A and C Press, 2002).

through this new, most praiseworthy incarnation of the Word. *Second Homily on the Dormition*, 6[42]

So, Mary is, as Andrew puts it, 'blazing a new and unknown path for the inhabitants of the earth,' that is, anticipating the glorification of the body that all the blessed will experience at the end of time, since she is both the source of our Redemption and the first example of humanity redeemed:

> Jesus, the author of life, has made available to us, from this body, the source of divine life; he transformed the first springing-forth of our redemption into a spring of life, shaping it anew for his own purpose in a supernatural way, from the Virgin's womb. 'If the first-fruits are holy,' the Apostle says, 'then the whole mass is as well; and if the root is holy, then the branches are also' (Romans 11. 16). *Second Homily on the Dormition*, 13[43]

Andrew also provides a lengthy explanation as to why Scripture remains silent on the subject of Mary's passing. In the first place, he says, it is possible that any description of the Dormition was excluded since it took place long after the events described in the Gospels. Secondly, the writers of Scripture may have deemed that the time was not right since priority had to be given to the message of the Gospels, and it was not right that other matters should be dealt with at the same time. Finally, it may have been, Andrew speculates, that the divinely inspired writers only wished to deal with events up to the time of Christ's departure from this earth. He then goes on to strengthen his argument in favour of the Dormition with a detailed elaboration on the Pseudo-Dionysius' *On the Divine Names*,[44] (which was considered a work of great authority since its purported author was a disciple of Paul, though it in fact dates from the late fifth or early sixth century), in which the author claims to have been a witness to the Virgin's death, though he in fact says nothing about her translation to heaven.[45]

John of Damascus († 749), one of the most influential figures in the Greek Church, who had a lasting influence in both the East and West[46] is categorical in his insistence that God did not allow the Virgin's body to be corrupted, an argument that he bases on her instrumental role in the Incarnation, the preservation of her virginity in giving birth,[47] her constant accompaniment of Christ throughout his life, and her close association with his Passion and death.[48] The latter notion, that Mary's co-passion justified her bodily assumption, is a new and interesting idea which John unfortunately does not

---

[42] *EPH*, p. 123.

[43] *EPH*, p. 132.

[44] See *De divinis Nominibus*, 3, 2, *PG* 3, 681C -684A.

[45] See *Second Homily on the Dormition*, 8- 13, *EPH*, pp. 126-32.

[46] For an assessment of his importance, as well as a selection of his writings, see *MF*, pp. 400-09.

[47] See *First Homily on the Dormition*, 10, *EPH*, p. 195 as well as the passage quoted below.

[48] See Daley's comments in *EPH*, p. 23.

develop further. In this passage he summarises all the principal arguments in favour of the Virgin's Assumption:

> Just as the holy, spotless body that was hypostatically united to the divine *Logos* – by means of her – rose from the tomb on the third day, so indeed it was right that she, his Mother should be taken from the tomb and restored to her Son. And just he had descended into her so she too, the highly favoured one, should be taken up to 'the greater and more perfect tabernacle [...] to heaven itself' (Hebrews 9. 11 and 24). It was fitting that she who had sheltered the divine *Logos* in her womb should dwell in the tabernacles of her Son. [...] It was fitting that she whose virginity was preserved intact in childbearing should have her body preserved from corruption even after death. It was fitting that she who held the Creator in her lap as a child, should dwell in the divine tabernacles. It was fitting that that Bride whom the Father had chosen for himself should dwell in the bridal chamber of heaven. It was fitting that she who had contemplated her Son on the Cross, receiving the sword of suffering in her heart, which she had avoided when she gave birth, should contemplate him seated next to the Father. It was fitting that the Mother of God should participate in the blessings of her Son and that she should be celebrated as the Mother and servant of God by the whole of creation. *Second Homily on the Dormition, 14*[49]

John makes it clear that Mary was subject to the law of death, since even Jesus did not exempt himself from it: 'Still, she yields to the law established by her own Son, and as the daughter of the old Adam she undergoes the ancestral trial, since even her Son, life itself, did not refuse it.'[50] Nonetheless, it was a painless death, and fear was entirely absent, since Mary was entirely free from sin:

> For her the gloomy path down to the underworld remains untrodden; a straight, gentle, easy path to heaven is opened for her [...] "The death of sinners is burdensome" (Psalms 34. 22 [LXX]); but since in her "the sting of death, which is sin" (I Corinthians 15. 56), was quelled, shall we say that the end of life was nothing but the beginning of a better life, one that will know no end? *Second Homily on the Dormition 3*[51]

John also draws to a considerable extent on apocryphal accounts of Mary's death, repeating such details as the arrival of the Apostles on clouds, the withering of the hand of the Jew who assailed Mary's funeral bier, and the arrival of Jesus and the angelic escort that accompanied her to heaven. Mary's death is accompanied by prodigies similar to those that occurred upon the death of her Son, and like him, her body arose, according to John, on the third day.

---

[49] Translation mine. See *TMPM*, II, 530-31. For an alternative translation, see *EPH* pp. 218-19.

[50] *Second Homily on the Dormition*, 2, *EPH*, p. 206.

[51] *EPH*, p. 208, modified.

However, he is careful to place these details in the realm of conjecture and imagination rather than historic reality.

Cosmas Vestitor († mid-8th century) defends the bodily Assumption on the basis that Mary shared her flesh with her Son, whose body rose from the dead, and therefore he rewarded her with an incorruptible body. His sermons are particularly significant because they were translated into Latin, along with those of Germanus and Andrew of Crete and were also given in summary form in the *Golden Legend*.[52] In his *Encomium on the Dormition* Theodore the Studite († c. 826) provides a brief account of the events surrounding Mary's death based on the *apocrypha*. Like many of his fellow Byzantine commentators, he emphasises the direct relationship between Mary's virgin motherhood and the preservation of her body from the corruption of death:

> By that ineffable act of generation, you have transformed nature; for who has ever heard of the virgin conceiving without seed? O wonder! See, now: the mother giving birth is also still an incorrupt virgin, because God was the calls of her conceiving! So in your life-giving sleep, since you are different from all the rest, you alone have rightly found incorruption for both [body and soul].
> *Encomium on the Dormition of Our Holy Lady, the Mother of God,* 2[53]

Likewise, he too sees a close link between the Virgin's bodily assumption and her ability to intercede effectively on behalf of a sinful mankind and protect it from the wiles of the devil.

In the following centuries nothing of great depth or significance was added by Eastern writers. The baton now passed to the West.

The Church in the West

In the West, acceptance of the bodily Assumption was much slower, largely due to a more circumspect attitude towards the apocrypha, strongly influenced by Jerome († 419), who would have been well aware of these accounts through his knowledge of Greek.[54] Almost none of the early Fathers even considers the question of Mary's death. Jerome limits himself to rejecting the hypothesis that she had been martyred which some took to be the meaning of Simeon's words to Mary about the sword that would pierce her heart (Luke 2. 35).[55] Both Ambrose and Augustine († 430) also reject the notion that the sword of Simeon was a

---

[52] See Graef, *Doctrine and Devotion*, I, 185-87, and *TMPM*, II, 572. Jean Hémery, 'La dévotion du peuple chrétien envers Marie du 8ᵉ au 13ᵉ siècles', *Cahiers mariales*, 8 (1964), 193-207, mentions that nine sermons on the Dormition were translated at the abbey of Reichenau in the tenth century (p. 202).

[53] *EPH*, p. 251.

[54] See Henri Barré, 'La croyance à l'assomption corporelle en Occident de 750 a 1150 environ', *Études mariales*, 7 (1949), 63-123.

[55] See *MF*, p. 376.

prophecy of Mary's martyrdom[56] Ambrose prefers to remain uncommitted on the question of Mary's earthly end, but Augustine states quite clearly on several occasions that she did die, though he does not offer any ideas either as to the when and the how, nor on her fate after death.[57] Neither makes any mention of the apocrypha, possibly due to a lack of familiarity with these stories, which were not available widely in Latin until some time between 550 and 700.

One of the few early Western Fathers to rely on the apocrypha is Gregory of Tours († 594) who draws on Greek apocryphal sources in his account of the Apostles holding vigil over Mary's body, waiting for the Lord to carry it into heaven:

> The course of this life having been completed by blessed Mary, when now she would be called from the world, all the apostles came together from their various regions to her house. And when they had heard that she was about to be taken from the world, they kept watch together with her. And behold, the Lord Jesus came with his angels, and, taking her soul, he gave it over to the angel Michael and withdrew. At daybreak, however, the apostles took up her body on a bier and placed it in a tomb, and they guarded it, expecting the Lord to come. And behold, again the Lord stood by them; the holy body having been received, he commanded that it be taken in a cloud into paradise, where now, rejoined to the soul, [Mary] rejoices with the Lord's chosen ones and is in the enjoyment of the good of an eternity that will never end. *Libri Miraculorum, 1, 4*[58]

More typical of the cautious attitude in the West is Isidore of Seville († 636) who was frequently cited as an authority in the following centuries by those who did not wish to make a definitive statement on the question.[59] He, like many of the Church Fathers, believed that had God wished to reveal Mary's fate, he would have done so:

> Some say that Mary departed this life by passing through the coarse torments of martyrdom, since the just man Simeon, holding Christ in his arms, was prophesying when he said to his Mother: "A sword will pierce your heart" (Luke 2 .35). But it is not certain whether he was speaking of a material sword or if he meant the word of God, which is stronger and more cutting than any two-edged sword. In any case, no particular historical narrative tells us that Mary was killed by the stroke of a sword, since one reads nothing about it and nothing about her death either. However, some say that her tomb is to be found in the valley of Josephat. *De ortu et obitu patrum, 112*[60]

---

[56] *Expositio in Lucam*, 12, 61 and *Epistola 149*, 33 respectively.

[57] Augustine several times speaks of Mary's death. See for example, *In Evangelium Ioannis tractatus*, 8, 9, PL 35, 1456, *Enarrationes in Psalmos*, 34, 2, 3, PL 36, 335.

[58] PL 71, 708B-C, quoted in Livius, p. 360. See also *MF*, pp. 353-54.

[59] See Felipe Mariscal Chávez, *María en las obras de San Isidoro de Sevilla* (Rome: Marianum, 1991).

[60] PL 83, 148D-149C, quoted in *MF*, pp. 375-76. See *TMPM*, III, pp. 939-44 and 951-56.

The mention here of Josephat as the location of Mary's tomb is a relatively new development. This tradition, which first became popular in the mid-fifth century, seems to have derived from the belief that Joseph and Mary had lived in this valley.[61] That it gained currency is evidenced by this passage describing Mary's tomb by the Irish monk, Adamnan († 704):

> In the eastern corner of it is an altar, and at the right-hand side of the altar is the empty stone sepulchre of the holy Mary, where she was once laid to rest. But how, or when, or by what persons her most holy remains were removed from this sepulchre, no one, it is said, can know for certain. *De locis sanctis*[62]

Isidore was also responsible for the consolidation of the *Mozarabic Rite*, which evolved in Visigothic Spain from pre-exiting rites, and which contains an office for the Feast of the Assumption.[63] By the end of the seventh century the feast of the Assumption was being celebrated in the major Roman Churches on August 15th,[64] and in areas where the Gallican rite was used (parts of Spain and France), in mid-January,[65] and in 813, under Charlemagne, the Council of Mayance established August 15 as a day of obligation.[66] Of course this does not mean that the Virgin's bodily assumption had been accepted.

Bede († 735) repeats Adamnan's description of Mary's tomb verbatim and like him declares his lack of knowledge regarding the fate of her body, although he is less dismissive of the possibility of a bodily assumption. Bede is also cutting in his dismissal of the apocryphal *Pseudo-Melito*, pointing out that internal

---

[61] See Mary Clayton, *The Cult of the Virgin*, p. 13. The comments that follow on Adamnan and Bede rely considerably on Clayton, pp. 16-21.

[62] *Adamnan's de locis sanctis* ed. by D. Meehan, quoted in Mary Clayton, *Cult of Mary*, p. 14, n. 57.

[63] See *TMPM*, III, 894-96, Henry Jenner, 'Mozarabic Rite', in *The Catholic Encyclopedia*, ed. by Charles George Herbermann, Edward Pace, and others, 15 vols (New York: Appleton,   1907-12),   X   (1911),   in   *New   Advent* <http://www.newadvent.org/cathen/10611a.htm> [accessed 5 July 2007] and *Le Liber Mozarabicus Sacramentorum et les Manuscrits mozarabes*, ed. by Marius Férotin (Paris: Firmin-Didot, 1912; repr. Rome: Edizioni liturgiche, 1995), and see section on Bride.

[64] See Mary Clayton, *The Cult of the Virgin*, p. 29 and Martin Jugie, *La mort et l'assomption de la Saint Vierge*, pp. 197-98.

[65] Several Missals dating from the eight and ninth centuries have survived that follow the Gallican rite, the most significant being the *Missale Gothicum*, whose liturgy for the Feast of the Assumption, in particular, had an important influence on other liturgies. See Bernard Capelle, *Travaux liturgiques de doctrine e d'histoire*, vol. III, (Louvain: Centre Liturgique Abbaye du Mont César, 1967), pp. 430-55, and *TMPM*, III, pp. 893-94 and 929-33. The critical edition of the *Missale Gothicum* is by Leo Cunibert Mohlberg (Rome: Herder, 1957).

[66] See Jean Fournée, 'Les orientations doctrinales de l'iconographie mariale à la fin de l'époque romane', *Centre international d'études romanes*, 1 (1971), 23-56 (p. 42).

inconsistencies in the dating show that the author is lying and that the whole account is therefore untrustworthy: 'So far as this aforementioned short book on the death of holy Mary is concerned, since it clearly errs on the questions of time, in other respects also its credibility is suspect.'[67] It was around this time that a reworked version of the *Protoevangelium*, the Latin *Gospel of Pseudo-Matthew*, also known as the *Liber de ortu beatae Mariae*, was compiled, to which were added, at a later date, parts of the *Infancy Gospel of Thomas* and of the flight into Egypt.[68] Although they never enjoyed the same degree of acceptance that they had gained in the Eastern Church, these Latin apocrypha did enter into popular devotion and exerted a certain amount of influence in official Church circles. Nevertheless, the attitude of uncertainty expressed by Adamnan and Bede as to the fate of Mary's body, as well as the more scientific approach to the apocrypha and the altogether more reserved tone, are in striking contrast to contemporary Eastern writings but reflect the more cautious view of many, though by no means all, in the Latin Church.

In what is believed to be the earliest extant sermon in the West for the feast of the Assumption, Ambrose Autpert (†c. 781), while defending the introduction of the feast, and declaring that he believes Mary to have been 'assumed above the angels', rejects the apocrypha and argues that it is better to honour Mary as Queen of Heaven instead of entering into futile speculations about the fate of her body:[69]

> But no catholic history tells by what means she passed hence to the celestial realms. For the church of God is said not only to reject the apocrypha but even to be unaware of these same events. And indeed there are many anonymous writings on her assumption against which, as I have said, one is so warned, that even for the confirmation of the truth one is barely allowed to read them. Hence many people are indeed disturbed because her body was not found on earth, nor

---

[67] *Retractatio in Actus Apostolorum*, in Clayton, p. 18, n. 62. See also n. 61 for a translation of a more lengthy passage from the same work where Bede dismisses the author of the *Pseudo-Melito* as a liar.

[68] For an English translation see Elliot's *The Apocryphal New Testament*, pp. 91-99, and his *The Apocryphal Jesus: Legends of the Early Church* (Oxford: Oxford University Press, 1996). See also Hans-Josef Klauk, *Apocryphal Gospels: An Introduction* (London: Clark, 2003), pp. 78-80. For discussion and dating see Mary Clayton, *The Apocryphal Gospels of Mary in Anglo Saxon England* (Cambridge: Cambridge University Press, 1998) and her *The Cult of the Virgin*, pp. 13-14. See also Chris Maunder, 'Mary in the New Testament and Apocrypha', in *Mary: The Complete Resource*, ed. by Sarah Jane Boss (Oxford and New York: Oxford University Press 2007), pp. 11-46, Jean-Daniel Kaestli, 'Le Protoévangile de Jacques en Latin: État de la question et perspectives nouvelles', *Revue d'histoire théologique*, 26 (1996), 41-102 and Margot Fassler, 'Mary's Nativity, Fulbert of Chartres, and the *Stirps Jesse*: Liturgical Innovation circa 1000 and Its Afterlife', *Speculum*, 75 (2000), 389-434 (p. 399).

[69] Fundamental for this period is Henri Barré, 'La croyance à l'assomption corporelle en Occident'.

is her corporal assumption found in catholic history, as it is read in the apocrypha. Besides, neither is it proper for anyone to investigate rashly on the condition of the body of she who, without doubt, has been raised above the heavens and reigns together with Christ. For men it must be sufficient to know that the Virgin is truly believed to be the Queen of Heaven, because she gave birth to the King of Angels.

   Amongst the Latin writers not one is to be found who says anything on the death of the Virgin. In fact, Ambrose, of blessed memory, commenting on that famous verse of the Gospel, in which Simeon says to the Mother of the Lord, 'And thy own soul a sword shall pierce', affirms: 'Neither history not Sacred Scripture teach that Mary died by the sword'. Isidore also says: 'It is not clear whether with this expression he meant to speak of a sword of the spirit or the sword of persecution'. But what should I say of these writers whom I have quoted if not even he who 'took her into his house' (John 19. 27), that is, the Evangelist John, wrote anything for posterity? For no-one could have written with greater fidelity of this fact, if God had wished that it be known [...]. It is therefore indispensable that man does not reveal, falsely rather than openly, what God wished to remain hidden. Therefore, on the Assumption of the Virgin, all that remains is to uphold the truth of this thought: according to the teaching of the Apostle we believe that the Virgin was assumed above the angels, 'although not knowing whether in the body, or out of the body' (see II Corinthians 12. 2). *In festo Assumptionis B. Mariae, 2-3 (Pseudo-Augustine, Sermo 208)*[70]

This cogently argued rejection of speculation regarding the fate of the Virgin's body had a powerful impact on the Latin Church for centuries to come, not least because of the incorrect attribution to Augustine.

   A sermon attributed to Paul Deacon Warnefred (†c. 799) sees the Virgin's Assumption as intimately linked to her mediatory role between her Son and mankind, possible evidence of Eastern influence. The sermonist takes a cautious view on the corporal assumption, merely declaring that Mary has been raised 'above the heavens' and placed on the throne of glory, without further clarification.[71] He does not dismiss the possibility but is not willing to affirm it either.[72]

   Such negative views did not prevent Pope Pascal I († 824) from commissioning a portrayal of the bodily assumption for a side altar of St. Mary Major's.[73] Indeed, opinion on the question was by no means settled, and even those Carolingian churchmen who adhered to the *assumptio animae* school did not hesitate to celebrate her ascent to heaven.[74] Increasingly they drew on

---

[70] *PL* 39, 2139, based in part on the translation in Clayton, *Cult of Mary*, p. 20, n. 66.
[71] *Second Homily on the Assumption of the BVM*, *TMPM*, III, 752.
[72] See *MLM*, p. 57.
[73] *Liber Pontificalis*, ed. by Louis Duchesne, 2 vols, (Paris: Thorin 1886-92), II, 61.
[74] On Marian devotion in the Carolingian period see Leo Scheffczyk, *Das Mariengeheimnis in Frömmigkeit und Lehre der Karolingerzeit*, Erfurter Theologische Studien, 5 (Leipzig: St. Benno-Verlag, 1959).

Canticles in their sermons, inspired primarily by use of the Song in the liturgy of the feast day.[75]

Another major factor in delaying Church acceptance of the Assumption in the West was a letter by Paschasius Radbertus († 865) known as the *Cogitis me*, which he pseudo-epigraphically attributed to Jerome, thus giving it great authority, in which he rejects the *Pseudo-Melito*, negates the possibility that we can know the fate of Mary's body, despite the fact that her purported burial place lies empty, and recommends that the question be entrusted to God alone:

> However, we know neither how, nor when, nor by which holy people that most holy body was taken from that place, nor where it was placed, just as we do not know whether it rose, although some wish to sustain that she, having been resuscitated, was clothed in blessed immortality together with Christ in Heaven. In any case, many affirm the same thing regarding blessed John the Evangelist [...]. The fact is that we do not know what to think of all this. However, we hold that it is best to entrust everything to God, for whom nothing is impossible, rather than wanting to define boldly what we cannot prove. *Cogitis me, 2*[76]

Further on he elaborates a principal that was to guide many churchmen in the coming centuries, namely that it is better to avoid definitive statements on a matter for which there is no irrefutable evidence while still holding to the pious hope that it is so:

> Now, since nothing is impossible to God, neither do we dare to deny the possibility of resurrection when it comes to the blessed Virgin Mary, although out of caution, and without prejudice to faith, it would be better to think of it with pious desire than to define in a rash way that which is not known without running the risk of error. *Cogitis me, 2*[77]

Like many later writers, Paschasius reads Canticles in terms of Mary's Assumption:

> And he who is used to contemplating the heavenly secrets, observing the ascent of the Virgin to heaven with a look of great admiration expresses himself thus in the Canticle of Canticles: 'I saw my beautiful one rising up like a dove on streams of water'. And the Virgin is truly beautiful as a dove, because she

---

[75] See E. Ann Matter, *The Voice of My Beloved: The Song of Songs in Western Medieval Christianity* (Philadelphia: University of Pennsylvania Press, 1990), pp. 152-54, Fidelis Buck, 'The Marian Interpretation of the Song of Songs in the Middle Ages (A.D. 1100-1500)', in *De cultu Mariano saeculis XII-XV: Acta Congressus Mariologici-Mariani, Internationalis Romae anno 1975 celebrati*, 6 vols (Rome: Pontificia Academia Mariana Internationalis, 1979-81), IV (1980), 69-96, and Donna Ellington Spivey, *Sacred Body*, pp. 104-05.
[76] *PL* 30, 123D-124A. See *MLM*, pp. 83 and 122, O'Carroll, *Theotokos*, p. 57, and Graef, *Doctrine and Devotion*, I, 179-79.
[77] *PL* 30, 124B, *TMPM*, III, 790.

showed forth the aspect and simplicity of that dove which descended on the Lord, indicating the true baptiser in the person of Christ to John. *Cogitis me, 14*[78]

Scepticism about the bodily Assumption did nothing to dampen enthusiasm for the feast day. By the ninth century a highly ritualised procession for the Feast of the Assumption (introduced during the pontificate of Sergius I [687-701]) was being held annually in Rome on the night of August 14/15 during which an icon of the enthroned Christ, dating to the sixth or seventh century, was carried from the Lateran to Santa Maria Maggiore,[79] symbolically meeting with the so-called *Salus populi romani* icon of the Virgin, just as Jesus, according to the apocrypha, had come to meet Mary and accompany her to heaven at her death. This practice spread outside Rome after the year 1000, with processions being held in many parts of Northern Europe, such as Cluny and Worcester, the latter being of particular importance owing to its influence on the composition of Honorius of Autun's († after 1133), *Sigillum sanctae Mariae*, as we shall see.[80]

By the eleventh century three schools of thought existed on the bodily assumption, the pro, the contra, and the uncommitted,[81] though the tide was beginning to turn in favour of the former, in part due to widespread popular belief, as well as the translation of several influential Eastern texts.[82]

Fulbert of Chartres († 1028), though he does not explicitly endorse the belief, notes that according to Christian piety both Mary and the John the Evangelist have been resurrected, a belief that was widely embraced in later

---

[78]*PL* 30, 137C-D.

[79] Other churches may also have been involved en route, certainly Santa Maria Nova. See Corrado Maggioni, *Benedetto il frutto del tuo grembo: due millenni di pietà mariana* (Casale Monferrato: Portalupi, 2000), p. 82

[80] See Gerhard Wolf, *Salus populi romani: Die Geschichte römischer Kultbilder im Mittelalter* (Weinheim: VCH, Acta humaniora, 1990). For documentation on the procession see Hans Belting, *Likeness and Presence: A History of the Image before the Era of Art*, trans. by Edmund Jephcott (Chicago: University of Chicago Press, 1994), pp. 64-73, 311-29, and 498-502. For the route of the procession see the map in Herbert L. Kessler and Joanna Zacharias, *Rome 1300: On the Path of the Pilgrim* (New Haven: Yale University Press, 2000), p. 64. On the procession at Worcester and its relationship to Honorius' *Sigillum* see Rachel Fulton, *From Judgment to Passion: Devotion to Christ and the Virgin Mary, 800-1200* (New York: Columbia University Press, 2002), particularly pp. 267-75. See also her 'Quae est ista quae ascendit sicut aurora consurgens?": The Song of Songs as the *Historia* for the Office of the Assumption', *Medieaval Studies*, 60 (1998), 55-112.

[81] For a list of prominent Churchmen in these three categories see Jean Fournée, 'Les orientations doctrinales', p. 43.

[82] On developments in belief in the Assumption in this period see Henri Barré, 'La croyance à l'assomption'. On the influence of the Greek texts see O'Carroll, *Theotokos*, p. 58. A good example of the sort of popular texts that promoted the belief among the ordinary faithful is the fourth book of influential early thirteenth-century German *Vita Beatae Mariae Virginis et Salvatoris rhythmica*. See below.

centuries.[83] Drawing on the apocrypha he describes the end of Mary's earthly life, and while he is careful to avoid endorsing the veracity of the account, it is clear that this is his intent:

> The most holy Virgin was then buried in the valley of Josephat, where a church was erected in her honour, while St. John was buried at Ephesus. Afterwards, when some pious Christians wanted to see the relics of his Mother, that is, the Mother of the Lord, they found the tomb empty. Looking in the tomb of blessed John instead they found only manna. Therefore Christian piety believes that Christ, God, the Son of God gloriously brought his Mother back to life and raised her above the heavens. In the same way it is believed that blessed John, a virgin and evangelist, merited to participate in her glory in heaven, having served her on earth. *Sermo 5, De Nativitate beatissimae Mariae Virginis*[84]

Peter Damian († 1072) writes along similar lines, again mentioning John, and citing popular piety as justification for the belief:

> Although we do not dare to assert it categorically, it nevertheless seems in conformity with piety to think that the blessed John with all probability has already risen, just as the same is believed of the blessed Mother of God, as both shared virginal integrity. For this reason, it seems good that they should appear equal in sharing the privilege of an anticipated resurrection [...] If, in fact John and Mary, both most blessed virgins, have not risen, why have their bodies not been found in their tombs, given that we can see Peter, Paul and the other apostles and martyrs buried in their tombs? *Sermo 64, De sancto Joanne apostolo et evangelista*[85]

Odilone of Cluny († 1049) does not declare himself openly on the fate of Mary's body, but makes reference to Pseudo-Jerome's *Cogitis me* showing the powerful influence this supposedly authoritative text continued to wield.[86] Godescalcus of Limburg († 1098) is representative of those who choose to affirm the bodily assumption though always with the caveat that this is a pious hope rather than an absolute belief. The reasons he gives for the Assumption are familiar: it is only fitting that Jesus, as a pious Son should honour his Mother, besides which the idea that Mary's body might have been subject to decay is repugnant considering that it was the *locus* of the Incarnation:

---

[83] Nevertheless, he avoids explicitly endorsing the belief. See Graef, *Doctrine and Devotion*, I, 205-06. Paschasius Radbertus mentions the belief in John's resurrection, *Cogitis me*, 2, *PL 9*, 123D-124A.
[84] *PL 141*, 325A-B. See Margot Fassler, 'Mary's Nativity, Fulbert of Chartres, and the *Stirps Jesse*' for a detailed analysis of Fulbert's position on the bodily Assumption.
[85] *PL* 144, 870C-D.
[86] See his *Homily for the Assumption of Mary Mother of God*, 12, *PL* 142, 1027D-1028D, *TMPM*, III, 865-67.

In the heavens the entire choir of the blessed spirits comes out to meet you, singing worthy hymns of praise to you who are leaving the regions of this earthly Egypt. Christ in person visits you here below, freeing the soul of his Mother from the prison of the flesh and rendering you that honour which he commanded children to show to the parents who have generated them. After your body had been buried because of the debt due to death, it is worthy of your Son that it should not have remained buried for long. The clay vessel of your virginal body, made solid by the fire of the Holy Spirit and in which the splendour of the Father wished to assume a body, could not have been corrupted nor undone by putrefaction. And now you rejoice because of the crown of the risen. It is this that the faithful people of the Lord like to believe of you. *Sequentia 'Exulta, exaltata'*[87]

Coming under criticism from opponents of the bodily assumption Godescalcus wrote a pamphlet defending his position entitled *De Assumptione Beatae Mariae et de sequentia 'Exulta, exaltata'*.[88] Indeed he took every opportunity to reassert his position, reaffirming, for instance, in another of his sermons, the various reasons why Mary's body could not have been subject to corruption, among which he includes her numerous merits, her con-corporeality with Christ, the fact that other saints (unnamed) have already been granted the privilege, and, of course, her virginity: 'This more than virginal body could not have been consigned to putrefaction and corruption. Although we do not dare to affirm it, we nevertheless prefer to think that it is reigning in the heavens rather than being hidden among the dead.'[89]

But it was the appearance, some time around the end of the eleventh century, of a treatise on the Assumption, *De assumptione beatae Mariae Virginis*,[90] bearing the name and authority of Augustine, which trumped Pseudo-Jerome and provided what was eventually to prove a decisive impetus in favour of the doctrine. Like Pseudo-Jerome the sermonist rejects the apocrypha as a means of finding out the fate of Mary's body, instead relying on a deeper reading of Scripture and on logical argument, a crucial element that was often lacking in the Eastern quasi-folkloric tradition. The author begins by noting that Scripture remains virtually silent on Mary after the death of Christ, and sounds repeated notes of caution about the care that must be taken in dealing with so great a subject. Nevertheless, offering various examples he points out that it is possible with care and erudition to uncover the deeper, mystical meaning of Scripture which lies hidden beneath the literal. Moreover, he notes, just because Scripture remains silent on something this does not mean that reason cannot deduce something from what it does say. Thus, although there is no mention of Melchisedech's justice, everyone recognises that he was just on the basis of the

---

[87] *AH*, 50, (p.) 343, *TMSM*, III, 65.
[88] See Henri Barré, 'La croyance à l'assomption', pp. 77-80, and *TMPM*, III, 65, n. 1.
[89] *Sermon on the BVM*, *TMPM*, III, 67.
[90] Possibly written by a disciple of St. Anselm, the treatise is to be found in *PL* 40, 1140-1148.

praise he received. Therefore, provided one's deductions accord with reason, it is possible to infer something on which Scripture is not explicit.

Adam returned to dust (Genesis 3. 9), as do we all, but the flesh of Christ, which he took from the Virgin, did not, even though he died as a result of human infirmity. So, if the flesh that he took from the Virgin returned to life, there is at least one exception to the universal law of the corruption of the flesh, concludes the author. He then goes on to speak of Eve and notes that Mary was excepted from the curse of labour pangs (Genesis 3. 16) that God imposed on Eve and all her descendants. If Jesus, making an exception to the laws of nature, wished to preserve Mary's virginity, the author reasons, there is no reason why he should not also have preserved her body from corruption: 'He who, in being born, had the power to leave his Mother a virgin also had the power to preserve her from putrefaction and reduction to dust.'

The principle argument the author then puts forward is that of con-corporeality. Mary was not subject to the corruption of death because of her unique status as the Virgin Mother from whom Christ took on human flesh, and, given that his flesh had been glorified, it was only fitting that hers should be too: 'If, therefore, the Son is the nature of the Mother, it is right that the Mother too should be of the same nature as the Son.' The author then uses the same argument as Pseudo-Jerome, but to opposite effect: in the absence of confirmation from Scripture, it is preferable to believe the best, that is, that Jesus glorified his Mother's body, basing such a belief on a rational interpretation of Scripture, enlightened by faith. He concludes by once again affirming that Christ had the power to raise his Mother's body and that therefore it is right to believe that he did so:

> It is right, therefore, that Mary should rejoice in body and soul with an ineffable joy in her Son, together with her Son, and through her Son. It is right that she should escape the misery of corruption, she who, in giving birth to so great a Son, knew no corruption of her integrity. It is right that she who was pervaded by such an exalted grace should remain forever incorrupt. It is right that she who gave birth to the entire and perfect life of all should live fully. It is right that she should be with him whom she bore in her womb, that she should be next to him whom she generated, nourished, and surrounded with tenderness. Mary is the Mother of God, the nursemaid of God, the most faithful servant of God, and the follower of God. *De assumptione beatae Mariae Virginis, 8*[91]

---

[91] *PL* 40, 1148, *TMPM*, III, 837. See Martin Jugie, *L'Immaculée Conception dans l'Écriture Sainte et la tradition orientale* (Rome: Accademia Mariana, 1952), pp. 282-91 and 360-85, and Henri Barré, 'La croyance à l'assomption' for a fuller treatment of the treatise. See also Graef, *Doctrine and Devotion*, I, 222-23.

Although more and more theologians expressed a favourable opinion on the Assumption in the following centuries as a result of the Pseudo-Augustine,[92] the question was by no means settled. Bernard of Clairvaux, by far the most influential theologian of the twelfth century on Marian matters, maintained a studied ambiguity, never once mentioning the fate of Mary's body in his five sermons on the Assumption.[93] Nevertheless he attributes extreme importance to the Virgin's Assumption, which he says adds to the glory of heaven and seals the alliance of friendship between heaven and earth.[94] She is escorted by the heavenly legions, received by her Son and is seated upon the highest throne, exalted high above all other creatures.[95] All humanity should rejoice at the Assumption of Mary since human nature is raised 'high above the all the orders of immortal spirits', that is, the angels.[96]

With Rupert of Deutz († 1132) and Honorius of Autun († after 1133) come the first complete Marian commentaries on Canticles, which naturally include a reading of the Song as signifying Mary's Assumption.[97] Honorius, writing in the voice of Christ the bridegroom, imagines him coming to bear his Bride away to heaven:

> I shall come with a multitude of the angels to call the Queen of Heaven, who is like a mountain of myrrh (Canticles 4. 6), that is, of martyrs, who are like myrrh, that is, the heights; and like a hill of frankincense, that is, confessors, who are the frankincense, that is, nobility. And I will say these words to her: my beloved, who bore the secrets of the Father, you are all beautiful, because in your singular senses, as I have said, you are gracious, due to the merits of your virtues. And since there is no stain of sin in you, come from Lebanon, that is, from the brightness of virginity, to the joys of heaven. You are my Bride, since I

---

[92] See, for instance, Herbert of Losinga († 1119), *Sermon on the Assumption of the BVM*, *TMSM*, III, 103-5, Honorius of Autun († after 1133), *Sigillum sanctae Mariae*, *PL* 172, 518A, Peter the Venerable († 1156), *Epistola 3*, 7, TMSM III, 262, Amadeus of Lausanne († 1159), *Homilia 7, De B. Virginis obitu*, *PL* 188, 1341A-1342B, Nicholas of Clairvaux († 1176), *In Assumptione beatissimae Mariae Virginis*, *PL* 144, 717B-C, Philipp of Harveng († 1183), *Commentaria in Cantica Canticorum*, *PL* 203, 487D-488D, *TMSM* III, 392-3, Alain of Lille († 1202), *In Cantica Canticorum*, *PL* 210, 74B-C, Oglerius of Lucedio, († 1214), *Tractate in Praise of the Holy Mother of God*, *TMSM*, IV, 63-64. Also, see Graef, *Doctrine and Devotion*, I, 244-47.

[93] For Bernard's sermons on the Assumption, see *SBS*, pp. 166-228.

[94] See *First Sermon on the Feast of the Assumption*, in *SBS*, pp. 166-67.

[95] See *First Sermon on the Feast of the Assumption*, in *SBS*, pp. 168-70.

[96] *Fourth Sermon on the Feast of the Assumption*, in *SBS*, p. 194.

[97] For long it was believed that Rupert was the first to write a complete Marian commentary of Canticles. However more recent scholarship has given the primacy to Honorius. See Valerie Flint, 'The Chronology of the Works of Honorius Augustodunensis', *Revue bénédicte*, 82 (1972), 215-42, and 'The Commentaries of Honorius Augustodunensis on the Song of Songs', *Revue Bénédictine*, 84 (1974), 197-200, and Rachel Fulton, *From Judgment to Passion*, 251-54. Also see Fulton's 'The Virgin Mary and the Song of Songs' (unpublished doctoral thesis, Colombia University, 1994) See also Bride in vol. 2.

am one with the Father, for whom you generated the Son, while remaining a virgin. *Sigillum sanctae Mariae*[98]

Rupert instead, commenting on Canticles 4. 7-8 – 'Thou art all fair, O my love, and there is not a spot in thee. Come from Libanus, my spouse, come from Libanus, come: thou shalt be crowned …' –, imagines the Christ child in dialogue with his Mother foretelling his own future and hers:

> You will leave this body, this shining white body, this virginal body, and you will be crowned before all. […] You will be crowned queen of saints in heaven, and you will be queen of the kingdoms of earth. For wherever it will have been preached concerning the beloved, "you have made him a little less than the angels, and crowned him with glory and honour; and you have given him dominion over the works of your hands" (Psalm 8:6-7), thus it will be preached concerning you, that you, O beloved, may be both the mother of him crowned and in like manner queen of the heavens, by right possessing the whole kingdom of your son, and for this reason kings and emperors will crown you with their crowns. *In Canticum Canticorum, 3, 78-79*[99]

William of Malmesbury (†c. 1143), like many of his fellow Englishmen, is decisively in favour of the bodily assumption, arguing that God's justice could not have allowed Mary's body to become corrupted and that just as the Virgin's grace and merit were superior to all the other saints so God gave her the unique privilege of bodily resurrection: 'For too great is his justice and too great was the grace given to her for her body, that is, the temple of God, to remain in the hope of resurrection, a hope which agitates the ashes of all the saints in their happy anticipation.'[100] He goes on to say that Mary did not possess perfect happiness until she was reunited with her Son in her body so that there should be no doubt that her Son's piety would have prompted him to grant her this favour.

Amadeus of Lausanne († 1159) affirms the bodily Assumption and, like many of before him, associates Mary's efficaciousness as an intercessor with her presence in heaven, close to God:

> Raised up amidst acclamations of joy and praise she is placed on a throne of glory, the first after God, above all the celestial beings. There, having taken on again the substance of her flesh – it is not licit that her body should have known corruption (see Psalms 15. 10) – and having put on a double stole, she contemplates the Man-God in his two natures with the eyes of her soul and of her body with a vision that is of as greater a clarity as is her ardour in comparison to all the other [saints]. Then, directing her gaze of unspeakable charity towards the human race and turning those most merciful eyes, which are

---

[98] *PL* 172, 506D-507A.
[99] Quoted from Rachel Fulton, *Judgement and Passion*, p. 331. See her extensive analysis of Rupert's commentary, pp. 309-50.
[100] *De laudibus et miraculis sanctae Mariae*, TMSM, III, 193.

the light of heaven, towards us, she raises up a universal prayer for the clergy and the people, men and women, alive and deceased. *Homily 7*[101]

Isaac of Stella (†c. 1169) is circumspect, but like Bernard, this does not prevent him from writing with exuberance of Mary's exaltation in a passage that draws heavily on Canticles:

> Today Mary went up from the desert of this world amidst the admiration of the celestial powers who had never seen anyone go up from this world and take her place above all their choirs and their seats. Therefore is it said: 'Who is this that cometh up from the desert, flowing with delights?' (Canticles 8. 5). These delights are the fruits of the virtues. These [virtues], as long as they bud or flower or produce fruits that are still immature, have something bitter, repugnant and disgusting about them. But to those who practice them until the very end they will give a tranquil and most sweet fruit of justice. [...] And since the blessed Virgin Mary, during her earthly life, exceeded all in the flowering of these virtues (for which reason it was at Nazareth that she rightly conceived directly through the intervention of the Holy Spirit),[102] so in that heavenly dwelling, comparable to the house of bread,[103] she is filled with delights more than any of the others and with greater abundance, 'leaning on her beloved' (Canticles 8. 5), whom she felicitously formed, more in her heart than in her flesh, through her faith and her love. *Sermo 52, In Assumptione*[104]

Gerhoh of Reichersberg († 1169) provides some fascinating insights into attitudes towards apocryphal accounts of the Dormition in the prologue to a sermon on the Assumption which he translated from the Greek for some nuns, and which is in reality a collation of various apocryphal texts.[105] Gerhoh comes to the conclusion that the text is admissible since it only contains what he considers to be reliable information, unlike the *Transitus* condemned by Jerome (in reality Paschasius Radbertus). He does not see claims such as the transport of the Apostles on clouds to be outrageous since Scripture speaks of similar occurrences such as in the case of Elijah. Moreover, he notes, the account relies on creditable sources such as those of Dionysius, in his *On the Divine Names*, and Germanus of Constantinople, rather than drawing directly on the discredited apocrypha, and may therefore be considered an orthodox account of the Dormition. What emerges here is a generally favourable disposition towards non-Scriptural sources provided they can be backed up with the authority of the Fathers. The fact that the Patristic texts were themselves apocryphal adds a not

---

[101] *TMSM*, III, 295.
[102] The allusion here is to Jerome's interpretation of Naser as meaning flower. See vol 2.
[103] Another etymological reference, this time to Bethlehem.
[104] *PL* 194.
[105] The prologue and sermon are reproduced by Antoine Wegner in an appendix of his *L'assomption de la Tres Sainte*, pp. 337-40. An Italian translation may be found in *TMSM*, III, 340-44.

inconsiderable irony to the situation. Indeed it may fairly be said that it is unlikely that belief in the bodily Assumption would have made much progress without reliance on these spurious sources. Gerhoh pronounces himself an agnostic when it comes to the question of his own belief in the bodily Assumption, though like many of his fellows he ardently hopes that it is true.

Another factor in the increased interest in the Assumption at this time was the publication of the visions of Elisabeth of Schönau († 1165), by her brother, including several involving the Assumption which she claimed to have had over a period of three years.[106] At first Elisabeth is not given a clear response when she asks if Mary's Assumption was physical but the visions eventually provide a positive answer. Elisabeth's visions, though by no means decisive, were an added element in favour of the bodily Assumption and also had an impact on artistic representations of the event, with Mary's body now being shown ascending upright rather than supine.[107]

Aelred of Rievaulx's († 1167) position is typical of those who were not yet willing to uphold the bodily Assumption definitively but who earnestly hope and believe it to be true:

> And although I do not dare to affirm this to someone who would reject it and inopportunely defend his position, since we do not have at hand any certain witness from Scripture to prove it, nevertheless it is a sweet thing for us to believe that he who can do everything, because of his great love for his Mother, brought not only her soul to heaven but also resuscitated her body so that she could be in his presence body and soul together, and that she received this gift of corporeal immortality that we all hope to receive one day. *On the Assumption*[108]

He provides a number of reasons why this should be so, including the fact that Christ took his flesh from Mary and that she was purified of original sin, concupiscence and any form of illicit desire. He also mentions the fact that some saints' bodies have remained incorrupt despite having been dead for many years and argues that Mary would have been given an even greater privilege than this.

By the late twelfth century the balance had turned more decisively in favour of the Assumption, although the official Church, in the shape of the popes, still remained noncommittal.[109] This is true both of pietistic literature, which was becoming increasingly popular, and the more cerebral offerings of the Scholastics.

---

[106] See *Elisabeth of Schönau: The Complete Works*, trans, and intro. by Anne L. Clark (New York: Paulist Press, 2000).

[107] See Melissa Katz, 'Regarding Mary: Women's Lives Reflected in the Virgin's Image', in *Divine Mirrors: The Madonna Unveiled* ed. by Melissa Katz (Oxford and New York: Oxford University Press, 2001), pp. 19-129 (p. 96).

[108] *TMSM*, III, 324.

[109] Innocent III († 1216), for instance, avoided any pronunciation in either direction. See *TMSM*, IV, 95.

Nicholas of Clairvaux († 1176) is among those who affirm the Assumption of Mary's body, which he describes as 'immaculate'. Where the body of Jesus was raised to heaven through his own will that of Mary was lifted us by 'beatifying grace'.[110] Jesus himself, along with the ranks of the angels, raised up the Virgin exclaiming, 'Thou art all fair, O my love, and there is not a spot in thee' (Canticles 4. 7). Thus it is primarily because of Mary's freedom from sin (which Nicholas attributes to a purification by the Holy Spirit) that she can be raised to heaven in body.

Peter Comestor († 1178) argues in favour of the bodily Assumption, basing his argument on the notion of con-corporeality, that is, the shared flesh of the Virgin and her Son. Interestingly, he does so using the example of a man and woman becoming one flesh in marriage, a reflection of the increasing use of bridal imagery for Mary based on Canticles:[111]

> Man and woman are two in the one flesh, but even more clearly are mother and child of the one flesh. Rightly did the Fathers promulgate decrees, dictated by the Holy Spirit, and issue a law for married couples according to which, if one of the two abandoned the world to consecrate himself to God, then neither could the other stay in the world, because it did not seem lawful to them that the flesh of one single reality should be so violently divided. In like manner the case of the other two needs to be considered: if one part of the virginal flesh is in heaven and the other is returned to the earth, then to one is granted not to see corruption, while the other is dissolved in ashes. *In festo Assumptionis Beatae Mariae 1*[112]

Alain of Lille († 1203), though personally sympathetic, declares that the prerogative of revealing this truth lies with the Virgin alone.[113] Peter of Blois († after 1204) is among the many who were convinced of the truth of the bodily Assumption by pseudo-Augustine. He writes of the shared flesh of Jesus and Mary as the most important reason for the raising up of her body:

> But Christ did not feel that he had fully risen to heaven until he had called to himself she from whose blood and flesh he had taken his body. Christ therefore greatly desired to have this chosen vessel, I mean the body of the Virgin with him, for he had been very pleased with it and had not found anything that would be displeasing to divinity in it. *Sermon 33, For the Assumption*[114]

Absalom von Springiersbach († 1205), instead, works on the principle that it is better to accord Mary the honour of a bodily Assumption even it is not certain than to run the risk of not honouring her enough, the exact opposite position

---

[110] *Sermon on the Assumption*, TMSM, III, 361.

[111] See section on Bride.

[112] *PL* 171, 630C.

[113] The relevant section of Alain of Lille's *In Cantica Canticorum*, PL 210, 74B-C, is cited in *TMSM* III, 509.

[114] *TMSM*, III, 484.

from Bernard of Clairvaux. He cites the words of the Roman missal for the Feast of the Assumption, the *Veneranda nobis*, ('However, she who had given birth from herself to the Saviour of the world could not be kept down by the bonds of death.') as justification for belief in the bodily Assumption.[115]

Martin of León († 1203), who does not hesitate to draw on the apocrypha in his description of Mary, speaks of the Virgin's tomb in the valley of Josephat, although he does not make any comment on the fate of her body. Instead he launches into a laudatory description of her Assumption based on an exegesis of Canticles, in which he makes it clear that he believes her body did not suffer corruption:

> In the Canticle of Canticles the Holy Spirit, admiring her ascent, affirms through the person of the citizens of heaven: 'Who is she that goeth up by the desert, as a pillar of smoke of aromatical spices, of myrrh, and frankincense' (Canticles 3. 6). She ascended from the desert of this world like a pillar of smoke because she was certainly frail and delicate, and tired out by her heavenly penances. In fact, she was no longer living out her existence on earth but in heaven. It is said that the Holy Spirit looked upon this most blessed Virgin with admiration as she was raised above the choirs of angels; it is said that the desert felt abandoned. [...] Again, in the same Canticle of Canticles, the Holy Spirit says with admiration: 'Who is she that cometh forth as the morning rising, fair as the moon, bright as the sun, terrible as an army set in array?' (Canticles 6. 9). The souls of the saints were asking themselves, full of admiration and joy, who she might be, who exceeded even the dignity of the angels. 'Who is she', it says, 'who cometh forth as the morning rising?' Indeed, the ever-Virgin Mary, having left behind the darkness of corruption, shone with the light of incorruption and perpetual immortality in her ascent. 'Fair as the moon', indeed more fair, because the moon waxes and wanes, while she, exempt from the defect of corruption, illuminates the darkness of the Holy Church, and in her the light of blessedness is always present. *In Assumptione sanctae Mariae*[116]

He goes on to explain that she is like the sun because the Sun of justice (Malachi 4. 2) was born of her, and terrible as an army because of the ranks of angels and saints, and affirms that it was most probably the Lord himself who accompanied her in her ascent.

Peter of Poitiers († 1205), disciple of Peter Lombard and chancellor of the University of Paris, and therefore a figure of considerable authority, declares himself decisively in favour of the bodily assumption: 'Christ destroyed death for all, in hope; in reality he did so for himself, [...], for the blessed Virgin, whom we

---

[115] It was not uncommon for these words to be cited as giving authority to the belief. See *Le Sacramentaire Grégorien: Ses principales formes d'après les plus anciens manuscrits*, ed. by Jean Deshusses, Spicilegium Friburgense, 16 (Fribourg, Éditions Universitaires, 1971), Mary Clayton, *The Cult of the Virgin Mary*, p. 53, and *TMSM*, III, 523, n. 7.
[116] *PL* 209, 22C-23D.

believe rose to heaven in her glorified flesh, and also for the sleeping saints [the Hebrew patriarchs] who rose with him' (see Matthew 27. 52).[117]

Sicardus of Cremona († 1215) cites Elisabeth of Schönau in affirming his belief in the bodily assumption:

> The *transitus* of the blessed Virgin is called Assumption by antonomasia. She was first assumed in her soul and later, as is fully believed, she was also assumed in body. Elisabeth of Saxony, a religious woman, bears witness that, forty days after the assumption of her soul, she was also assumed in body. *Mitrale*, 1, 9, 40

He goes on to note that the Assumption is the greatest of the Virgin's feasts, and the only one that involves fasting and an octave, because, like all the saints, it is the day on which they migrated to heaven which is the occasion of greatest joy. He then goes on to comment on the different readings. The Canticle of Canticles is used, he says, because Mary is a figure for the Church who, like her, is a Mother, Virgin and Bride. The Gospel reading of the story of Martha and Mary (Luke 10. 38-42) is to be understood, he says, in its allegorical sense. The town (*castellum*) that Jesus entered when visiting them represents the strength of the Virgin, who did not give in to the temptations of the devil, while Martha and Mary represent the two aspects of life, action and contemplation, in which Mary excelled – a common exegesis of this passage.[118]

Despite the veritable tide of churchmen in favour of the bodily Assumption, Honorius III († 1227), like all the Popes, avoids any definitive statement. Instead he concentrates on describing the awesome majesty of the Virgin as she rose to heaven, which is 'terrible as an army poised for battle' (Canticles 6. 3) and is a source of terror for demons whom Mary continues to combat from heaven.[119]

An apocryphal account of the Assumption is to be found in the highly influential thirteenth-century *Vita rhythmica*, which was the main source for many later vernacular accounts of Mary's life. In abbreviated form, it repeats the story of the angel appearing to the Virgin to announce her impending death, the gathering of the Apostles, and the coming of Jesus to accompany her to heaven. Her soul and body are transported separately, with an interval of three days, to mirror the Resurrection:

> The same Jesus, incarnate Son of God, born of your most holy womb, will descend in order to come personally to you, to receive your soul and transport it to the heavenly realm, where it will be set above the choirs of angels. On the third day after this event, he will bring your soul back down below and, after it has been reunited with your body, he will introduce it to the heavenly kingdom

---

[117] *Sententiae*, 1, 4, 19, *PL* 211, 1207D.

[118] See vol. 2.

[119] See *Second Sermon for the Feast of the Assumption*, *TMSM*, IV, 130-31.

once again, so that together, they [body and soul] will enjoy happiness and be always comforted by the eternal joys. *Vita rhythmica, 4, 7156-7161*[120]

Anthony of Padua († 1231), with his typical ability to read anything into any passage of Scripture, interprets Isaiah 60. 13, 'I will glorify the place of my feet', as foreshadowing the bodily assumption. It is worth quoting a fairly lengthy passage since it will give a taste of the extraordinary way in which Anthony was able to weave together apparently unrelated passages of Scripture to make his point, a style which was extremely popular in his own time but seems decidedly far-fetched today:

> The Lord's 'feet' signify his humanity, of which Moses says in Deuteronomy: 'They that approach to his feet shall receive of his doctrine.' [Deuteronomy 33.3] No-one can approach the Lord's feet unless he first, as Exodus says, 'puts off the shoes from his feet' [Ex 3.5], that is, [removes] dead works from the affections of his heart. Draw near then with bare feet, and you will receive of his doctrine. Isaiah says: 'Whom shall he teach knowledge? And whom shall he make to understand the hearing? Them that are weaned from the milk, that are drawn away from the breasts.' [Isaiah 28.9] Whoever is taken from the milk of worldly desire, and separated from the breasts of greed and lust, will in this life be taught divine knowledge, and in the world to come be found fit to hear the words: 'Come, ye blessed of my Father' [Matthew 25.34]. The 'place of the Lord's feet' was blessed Mary, she from whom he took human nature, the place which he glorified this day when he lifted her above the choirs of angels. From this you may clearly infer that the blessed Virgin was assumed in the body, wherein was 'the place of the Lord's feet'. So the Psalm says: 'Arise, O Lord, into thy resting-place: thou and the ark which thou hast sanctified.' [Psalms 131.8] The Lord arose when he ascended to the right hand of the Father. The ark of his sanctification arose too, when on this day the Virgin Mother was taken up to the heavenly bride-chamber. *Sermon on the Assumption of the BVM*[121]

John de la Rochelle († 1245) interprets Isaiah 50. 1 and Psalm 44 as foretelling the Assumption. Like many others he links the Virgin's Assumption with her efficacy as a protectress of sinners. Her bodily assumption also serves as a reminder and guarantee that all the just will once again be united with their bodies at the end of time:

> 'Arise, arise, put on thy strength, O Sion, put on the garments of thy glory, O Jerusalem, the city of the Holy One.' These words are addressed to the same Virgin Mary to whom 'arise' is said twice because today she has been chosen to

---

[120] *Vita Beatae Mariae Virginis et Salvatoris rhythmica*, ed. by Adolf Vögtlin, Bibliothek des litterarischen Vereins Stuttgart, 180 (Tübingen: Laupp, 1888), p. 240. For extracts from the poem see *TMSM*, IV, 136-145.

[121] *The Sermons of St Antony*, trans. by Stephen Spilsbury, in *The Franciscan Archive* <http://www.franciscan-archive.org/antonius/opera/ant-hd00.html> [accessed 28 March, 2006].

rise up doubly, that is, in body and in spirit, to be raised up, I repeat, from the present life which is almost like a dream. And rightly is she called a city because she is a most secure vault for men who take refuge there. Let no-one think or say to himself that the expression 'gilded mantle' refers to the glory of the soul. It is for this reason that [the Psalmist] adds 'surrounded with variety', as if to distinguish the interior glory, according to what is written: 'All the glory of the king's daughter is within' (Psalms 44. 14). He then adds the external glory when he writes, 'surrounded with variety', for with the covering of gold he wishes to indicate the incorruptibility which bodies will possess in the future, while now they are corruptible. *Sermon 4, On the Assumption*[122]

Richard of St. Laurence († after 1245), citing Canticles 3. 6, 'as a pillar of smoke of aromatical spices', says that it was Mary's nature, as she progressed in grace, to ascend like smoke towards heaven. Whether in her body or not he refuses to speculate on given that the Church has chosen not to pronounce on the question.[123] His agnosticism is important since the *De laudibus* was long attributed to Albert the Great and is published among his works.

Gualtier of Château-Thierry († 1249), a diocesan priest who became chancellor of the University of Paris in 1246, wrote one of the first systematic defences of the corporeal Assumption, though his argument lacks the theological rigour that would characterise some of the Scholastics.[124] Through an extensive exegesis of a bewildering variety of Biblical passages, backed up by references to the Fathers (in reality primarily pseudo-Augustine), he provides a long list of arguments in favour of the Assumption, including the shared flesh of Jesus and Mary, her state of absolute grace and sinlessness, and her dignity as the Mother of God, who would never have allowed his temple to fall into decay. He likens the relationship between Christ and his Mother to that of the Father with the Son: 'But one and the same was the flesh of Christ and the Blessed Virgin from whom Christ took his [humanity], he being consubstantial with his mother in his humanity, just as he is consubstantial with the Father in his divinity.' Another argument that he puts forward is Mary's sinlessness: since the corruption of the body originated in the sin of Adam it is logical to believe that Mary, who was entirely without mark of sin was not subjected to the corruption of the flesh. Interestingly, he also uses the argument that Mary could not be fully occupied with the concerns of humanity if she were separated from her body because her beatitude would not be complete, a position similar to that adopted by Bonaventure a little later.

Stephen of Salley († 1252), an English Cistercian, is representative of a more pietistic strand. Clearly influenced by the apocrypha, he envisions Christ descending from heaven, surrounded by hosts of angels, to transport his

---

[122] *TMSM*, IV, 191.

[123] *De laudibus beatae Mariae Virginis*, 12, 3, 7, *TMSM*, IV, 209.

[124] *Questiones inedite de Assumptione BVM*. See *TMSM*, IV, 210-15. The quotation that follows is on p. 213.

Mother back up to Paradise. There, her role as intercessor is rendered all the more effective by her bodily presence because her Son cannot resist her maternal entreaties.[125] A similar account is to be found in the Dominican, Vincent of Beauvais' († 1264), re-working of the *Pseudo-Melito* in which he writes that as the apostles held vigil at Mary's tomb, 'the Lord Jesus Christ came all of a sudden in great splendour, accompanied by an immeasurable army of angels' and raised her from the dead, after which they both ascended into heaven on a cloud, as the apostles watched.[126]

Bonaventure († 1274) wrote at least five sermons for the Assumption.[127] Although it is clear that his personal belief is that Mary's body was preserved from the corruption of death and was raised to heaven, he is careful to avoid stating this claim in doctrinal terms. He gives the shared flesh of Christ and Mary as one of the principal reasons why her body was not allowed to decay and adds a further justification, saying that her beatitude would not be complete if she lacked her body, which is in line with his teaching that the souls of the saved would not enjoy the fullness of beatitude until they were reunited with their bodies:

> Blessedness would not be complete unless she was personally present and a person is not a soul but a union. It is clear that as a union of body and soul she is there, otherwise she would not have complete enjoyment, because, according to Augustine [*De Genesi ad Litteram*, XII, c. 35, n. 68], 'the souls of the Saints in some way are held to the body by their natural inclination, and not totally centred on God.' *First Sermon on the Assumption of the Blessed Virgin Mary*[128]

Bonaventure's *Third Sermon on the Assumption* is based on an exegesis of 3 Kings 2. 19, 'And the king arose to meet her, and bowed to her, and sat down upon his throne: and a throne was set for the king's mother, and she sat on his right hand.' Here, he portrays Mary's reception into heaven in a manner that is reminiscent of several of the Eastern Fathers and of apocryphal accounts of the Assumption:

> It must be believed totally and doubted in no way that today the Virgin, ascending in solemn procession, is met not only by the King but also by the whole heavenly court. The Angels fly ahead to see their Lady; the Patriarchs come down to see their daughter; the Apostles run to see their teacher; the Martyrs hurry to see the one who encouraged them; married women and widows move eagerly to look on their companion and sister; religious sisters come

---

[125] See *Meditations on the Joys of the Blessed Virgin Mary*, TMSM, IV, 234-35.

[126] *Speculum maius*, TMSM, IV, 251-52. See Robert Maloy, 'The "Speculum historiale" of Vincent of Beauvais and the Marian Works Attributed to St. Ildephonsus of Toledo', *Ephemerides Mariologicae*, 22 (1972), 5-14.

[127] A sixth is almost certainly spurious. See Graef, *Doctrine and Devotion*, I, 288-90.

[128] In *Sermons on the Blessed Virgin Mary*, trans. by Campion Murray, in *Franciscan Friars: Province of the Holy Spirit* <http://www.franciscans.org.au> [accessed 6 January 2006].

together to see their prelate and abbess. […] Whatever reverence the creatures may show it is as nothing compared to the most excellent honour given to her by the Creator. The whole Trinity meets her, not by moving from one place, but by a favourable influence, by a wonderful joy and godlike glory. For the whole blessed Trinity knew you, Mary, spouse of chaste love, palace of a holy indwelling, centre of a wonderful work.

Indeed, in describing the reverence with which she is received by the whole Trinity, and most especially by the Son, whom he later imagines bowing down before her, he goes beyond even the great Byzantine Fathers, and risks giving the impression that Mary is on a par with God. But a closer examination of his teaching reveals that great though her privileges were, all derived from the God-given grace of her divine motherhood.

Bonaventure, in arguing against the Immaculate Conception in his *Commentary on the Sentences*, though he does not directly address the question of the Assumption, does state clearly that Mary underwent death, for to claim otherwise, he says, would suggest that Mary was not subject to the effects of the Fall, or that she subjected herself to death of her own will in order to contribute to the Redemption of humanity, and this, he points out, is true of Christ alone.[129]

Albert the Great († 1280) repeats the well-established argument that it would not be fitting if Mary's body were not in Heaven given that her Son took his flesh from it.[130] On the basis of Aristotelian cosmology he suggests that Mary's body, together with her soul, was assumed to the Empyrean, which is also where Christ resides in his humanity. There too are to be found the embodied souls of those who rose with the Lord (see Matthew 27. 52-53). This rather unusual view was not shared by his fellow Scholastics.

His student, Thomas Aquinas († 1274) believes that Mary was freed from all inclination to sin when she was purified in the womb, and therefore escaped the consequences of the Fall, including the corruption of the body:

> The third curse is common both to man and woman in that both shall one day return to dust. The Blessed Virgin was spared this penalty, for her body was raised up into heaven, and so we believe that after her death she was revived and transported into heaven. *Expositio super salutatione angelica* [131]

---

[129] See *Sent.* III, d. iii, a. 1 and 2.

[130] *In Lucam*, 10, 42, *Alberti Magna Opera Omnia*, XXIII, 90. Also see *TMSM*, IV, 329, Luigi Gambero, 'Il XIII secolo e la fioritura della Scolastica', in *SDM*, I, 774-829 (pp. 817-18), Graef, *Doctrine and Devotion*, I, 274 and 278.

[131] *Exposition on the Angelic Greeting*, trans. by Joseph B. Collins, in *The Catechetical Instructions of St. Thomas* (New York: Wagner, 1939; repr. 2000), pp. 173-80, in *EWTN*, <http://www.ewtn.com/library/SOURCES/TA-CAT-5.TXT> [accessed 21 December 2006]. He also implicitly accepts the Assumption, citing the Pseudo-Augustinian *De assumptione*, in his argument against the Immaculate Conception, *ST*, III, q. 27. a.1.

Conrad of Saxony († 1279), in a work that was often attributed to Bonaventure, has no doubts that Mary's body is in heaven, as is only fitting for the ark that contained God:

> We believe the most holy body of Mary was far removed from this woe of turning to ashes. Her body was the most holy ark of God and it was unfitting for it to suffer corruption, so that she like her Son should be raised up before corruption began. To both the Son and his Mother can be applied the words of the Prophet: Rise up, O Lord, and go to your resting place, you and the ark of your might [Ps 132:8]. This ark was made of incorruptible wood [Ex 25:10] because, as we believe, the flesh of Mary was never subject to corruption. *Speculum Beatae Mariae Virginis, 2*[132]

Bartholomew of Bologna († after 1294) wrote one of the first purely theological works on the Assumption, *Questions on the Assumption of the Virgin*, in which he answers such abstruse points as to whether any time elapsed between the glorification of the Virgin's soul and her body.[133] Nevertheless, he does not work out the precise theology of the doctrine with sufficient rigour and does not provide adequate Scriptural backing.

The pattern established in the twelfth and thirteenth centuries, whereby the vast majority of the faithful along with most churchmen believed in the bodily Assumption but the Church as a body continued to remain agnostic, long prevailed. The reasons for the Church's reluctance to proclaim the dogma officially for so long are complex and lie beyond the scope of the present study. One of the most serious obstacles, however, was lack of agreement on the Immaculate Conception, which forms the subject of the next chapter, since it was difficult to proclaim that Mary had not suffered the corruption of death common to all the children of Adam if the question of her freedom from original sin remained unresolved.

---

[132] Trans. by Campion Murray as *The Angel's Greeting*, in *Franciscan Friars Province of the Holy Spirit* <http://www.franciscans.org.au> [accessed 3 June 2007].
[133] See *TMSM*, IV, 371-378.

Chapter 8 - The Immaculate Conception

Canticles 4. 7:   Thou art all fair, O my love, and there is not a spot in thee.
Luke 1. 28:   Hail, full of grace, the Lord is with thee.
Romans 3. 23:   For all have sinned, and do need the glory of God.
Romans 5. 12:   Wherefore as by one man sin entered into this world, and by
                    sin death; and so death passed upon all men, in whom all have
                    sinned.

The doctrine of the Immaculate Conception states that the Virgin Mary was preserved entirely free from original sin from the instant of her conception through a special prevenient grace, received in view of the merits of her Son in anticipation of the Redemption. The doctrine, which was first set out with theological rigour in the twelfth century, met with considerable opposition from the outset. The principal difficulties in accepting such a claim were the doctrine of Christ's universal Redemption as well as Augustinian teaching on the universality of original sin and the inherent concupiscence of carnal union. How could Mary have been entirely without stain of sin when Christ had not yet redeemed humankind on the Cross, and how could she have remained free from original sin when the very act that gave her life was inherently sinful? Although the solution to these difficulties was already largely provided by Duns Scotus in the early fourteenth century, it is indicative of the controversy surrounding the doctrine that it did not become part of official Catholic teaching until 1854, when Pius IX issued a dogmatic definition in the Papal Bull *Ineffabilis Deus*.[1]

---

[1] Studies on the development of the doctrine are numerous. *The Dogma of the Immaculate Conception: History and Significance*, ed. by Edward O'Connor, (Notre Dame, Ind: University of Notre Dame Press, 1958), remains one of the most comprehensive collections. See also Gabriele M. Roschini, *Maria Santissima nella storia della salvezza*, vol. III, part II, *Il dogma mariano* (Isola del Liri: Pisani, 1969), pp. 9-337. For traditional Catholic thinking on the doctrine see Juniper B. Carol, *Fundamentals of Mariology* (New York: Benziger, 1956), pp. 87-141. A useful summary of the doctrine's development is provided by Sarah Jane Boss, 'The Development of the Doctrine of Mary's Immaculate Conception', in *Mary: The Complete Resource*, ed. by Sarah Jane Boss (Oxford and New York: Oxford University Press 2007), pp. 207-35. For a recent study on the Medieval period see Marielle Lamy's, comprehensive, *L'Immaculée Conception: étapes et enjeux d'une controverse au Moyen Âge (XIIe-XVe s.)*, Collection des Études Augustiniennes, Série Moyen Âge et Temps Modernes, 35 (Paris: Institut des Études Augustiniennes, 2000). Very useful are the various articles appearing in *La "Scuola Francescana" e l'Immacolata Concezione*, Atti del Congresso Mariologico Francescano S. Maria degli Angeli, Assisi, 4-8 dicembre 2003, ed. by Stefano M. Cecchin (Vatican City: Pontificia Academia Mariana Internationalis, 2005), several of which I cite below. On the Fathers see Martin Jugie *L'Immaculée Conception dans l'Écriture sainte et dans la tradition orientale* (Rome: Academia

The Patristic Period

Possibly the earliest writing to suggest, at least implicitly, that Mary's conception was in some way sacred was the second-century *Protoevangelium of St. James*,[2] which tells of the miraculous circumstances of Mary's conception from the sterile Anna (as well as of the extraordinary prodigies and the unique sanctity of her early childhood), thus suggesting that the Virgin was the subject of divine intervention from the very first instant of her existence. The essential lineaments of the story remain unchanged in later accounts such as the *Gospel of the Pseudo-Matthew*, a Latin rendition of the *Protoevangelium* dating to somewhere between the sixth and ninth centuries,[3] the *Life of Mary* attributed to Maximus the Confessor († 662),[4] and the ninth-century *Libellus de Nativitate sanctae Mariae*.[5] In all of these texts great emphasis is placed on the miraculous nature of Mary's conception, which closely resembles that of her Son. Anna and Joachim are greatly distraught at the barrenness of their marriage, which they regard as a

---

Mariana / Officium Libri Catholici, 1952). See also Michael O'Carroll, *Theotokos: A Theological Encyclopedia of the Blessed Virgin Mary* (Collegeville, Minnesota: Liturgical Press, 1982), pp. 179-82; Nancy Mayberry, 'The Controversy over the Immaculate Conception in Medieval and Renaissance Art, Literature, and Society', *Journal of Medieval and Renaissance Studies*, 21 (1991), 207-24, *The Immaculate Conception in the Life of the Church: Essays from the International Symposium in Honor of the 150ᵗʰ Anniversary of the Proclamation of the Dogma of the Immaculate Conception*, ed. by Donald H. Calloway (Stockbridge, MA, John Paul II Institute of Divine Mercy, 2004).

[2] Numbering refers to the version of the *Protoevangelium* in Ronald F. Hock, *The Infancy Gospels of James and Thomas* (Santa Rosa: Polebridge Press, 1995), in *Gospels.net* <http://www.gospels.net/translations/infancyjamestranslation.html> [accessed 5 October 2007]. See his insightful Introduction for one of the best analyses of the text. For an alternative English translation of the text see *The Apocryphal New Testament: A Collection of Apocryphal Christian Literature in an English Translation*, ed. by James K. Elliott (Oxford: The Clarendon Press, 1993), pp. 48-67. For discussion and dating see Mary Clayton, *The Apocryphal Gospels of Mary in Anglo Saxon England* (Cambridge: Cambridge University Press, 1998), Luigi Gambero, *MF*, pp. 33-41, Mary F. Foskett, *A Virgin Conceived: Mary and Classical Representations of Virginity* (Bloomington: University of Indiana Press, 2002), pp. 142-64, and Jean-Daniel Kaestli, 'Le Protoévangile de Jacques en Latin: État de la question et perspectives nouvelles', *Revue d'histoire théologique*, 26 (1996), 41-102. See sections on Virginity Model for further discussion and bibliography.

[3] See vol. 2 for further discussion and bibliography.

[4] See the *Life of Mary*, 3-5, *TMPM*, II, 187-89.

[5] On the dating of the *Libellus* see Margot Fassler, 'Mary's Nativity, Fulbert of Chartres, and the *Stirps Jesse*: Liturgical Innovation circa 1000 and Its Afterlife', *Speculum*, 75 (2000), 389-434 (pp. 400-401) and James, K. Elliott, 'Mary in the Apocryphal New Testament', in *The Origins of the Cult of the Virgin Mary*, ed. by Chris Maunder (London: Burns & Oats, 2008), pp. 57-70 (pp. 61-62). On dating and its spurious attribution to Paschasius Radbertus († 865) see See Rita Beyers, 'De Nativitate Mariae: Problèmes d'origine', *Revue de Théologie et de Philosophie*, 122 (1990), 171-188.

mark of God's disfavour (1). After Joachim has departed for the desert to fast, Anna fears that she will be widowed as well as childless and goes into a garden to pray (2-3). An angel appears to her and gives her the news that she will conceive, telling her that her 'seed shall be spoken of in all the nations', upon which Anna vows to offer the child as a gift to God, should she really conceive. An angel has also appeared to Joachim, who goes to the temple to offer sacrifice and then returns home (4). After nine months the child is born and she soon shows signs that she is especially favoured by God, walking at six months (6). At three she is brought to the temple, which she enters of her own volition and where she dwells, receiving food from an angel, until her betrothal to Joseph (7-9). Although the *Protoevangelium* was never accepted as a canonical text, and was explicitly rejected by some of the Fathers, most notably Jerome, it did exert an influence on official Church thinking on doctrinal matters such as the virgin birth (see chapter on virginity) as well as on the overall perception that Mary had been privileged by God in ways that put her beyond the normal laws of nature. Most importantly, from the perspective of the Immaculate Conception, it introduced the idea that God had played a direct role in Mary's conception, following biblical models such as Anna and Samuel, Sarah and Isaac, Elizabeth and John the Baptist, and Mary herself in the conception of Christ. Two arguments in favour of excepting Mary from the universal inheritance of original sin could be drawn from this account: firstly the action of God in order to bring about her conception would suggest that the conjugal relations of Joachim and Anna were an exception to the postlapsarian norm that the sexual act was inherently concupiscent, even within marriage, since God would not have been present in a sinful act – indeed some versions of the story suggest that Anna conceived, as her daughter would, without sexual intercourse.[6] Secondly, if God had intervened to remove the curse of sterility from Anna, there was no reason why he should not also have acted to preserve Mary from sin.

Though the early Fathers do not even consider the possibility of the Immaculate Conception, they do perceive that Mary needed to be excepted in some fashion from the normal postlapsarian state if she were to become the Mother of God, thereby establishing a fundamental principle concerning Mary's sinlessness. The Fathers believed, with a few notable exceptions, that Mary never actively committed a sin,[7] but this is not to be confused with a freedom from any trace of original sin, which would have eliminated even the inclination towards sin and would have meant that the Virgin had a perfect nature, just like Adam and Eve before the Fall. Broadly speaking, three separate positions may be identified concerning the sinfulness or lack thereof of the Virgin. Some held that the Virgin, although of exceptional purity, was not entirely lacking in minor

---

[6] See Mary Clayton, *The Cult of the Virgin Mary*, p. 4.
[7] The most negative was undoubtedly Tertullian. See *MF*, pp. 62-63, and see the comments below.

faults. Others, beginning with Irenaeus (†c. 202),[8] held that she underwent a purification at the time of the Incarnation. Gregory Nazianzen († 390), for example, writes: 'He was conceived of the Virgin, who had been purified by the Spirit beforehand in soul and in body.'[9] Still others asserted that she was purified either at the time of her conception or at least while still in the womb, though the exact mechanism whereby this took place was not made clear, and that she received a second infusion of grace prior to the Incarnation.

Another, and theologically more significant seed of the doctrine is to be found in Irenaeus' (†c. 202) notion that Mary reversed or recapitulated the actions of Eve.[10] If Mary is the new Eve, just as Christ is the new Adam, as Irenaeus argues, then it follows that Mary must be everything that Eve was not, and more. In fact, for Irenaeus, Mary is much more than a return to the innocent prelapsarian Eve: she is everything that Eve would have become had she not paid heed to the serpent's words. She not only restores human nature to what it had been before the Fall, but actually raises it to a higher, deified level, given that the Word takes flesh from her. If one takes this argument to its logical conclusion, then Mary must be equal, indeed superior to the prelapsarian, sinless Eve. However, the full implications of Irenaeus' teaching were not followed up, in part because the theological apparatus was not sufficiently developed. Moreover, a fundamental obstacle to belief in the Immaculate Conception was the universally accepted doctrine that Christ had come to redeem all of humanity without exception. This issue was particularly thorny for the Latin Church, which was heavily influenced by Augustine's teaching on original sin, and was not to be resolved, as we shall see, until Duns Scotus.

A further element that has led some to conclude that at least some of the Eastern Fathers believed in the Immaculate Conception is the extraordinary praise that is heaped upon the Virgin in any number of their writings, especially following on from the *Theotokos* declaration at the Council of Ephesus (431). Again and again in the Eastern Church, in homilies and hymns, the Virgin's beauty, holiness, and total freedom from any stain of sin are stressed, and she is frequently called the 'Immaculate One'. This is already the case with Ephrem the Syrian (†c. 373), whom some have claimed in the cause of Mary's sinlessness.[11] Yet it would be a mistake to think that the Eastern Fathers are, even implicitly, declaring that the Virgin was free from original sin just because they speak of her purity in so categorical a manner. The Greek Church was largely untouched by

---

[8] See Mary Clayton, *The Cult of the Virgin Mary*, p. 5.

[9] *Oratio 38*, 12, *PG* 36, 325B, *TMPM*, I, 306. All translations, unless otherwise indicated, are mine.

[10] See Georges Joussard, 'The Fathers of the Church and the Immaculate Conception', in *The Dogma of the Immaculate Conception: History and Significance*, ed. by Edward D. O'Connor, pp. 51-86 (pp. 52-54). See also section on Immediate Co-Redemption.

[11] See, for instance, Ignacio Ortiz de Urbina, 'Vale el testimonio de san Efrem en favor de la Immaculada?', *Estudios Eclesiasticos*, 28 (1954), 417-22.

the Augustinian preoccupation with original sin and never explored the question of Mary's sinlessness with the rigorous logic that was to characterise Scholasticism in the West. Instead, the glorification (*doxa*) of Mary in the Greek Fathers was influenced by the notion of deification, that is, that the Incarnation opened the way for humans to unite themselves to God (*theosis*), or to become like God (*homoiosis theoi*), and none more so than the Virgin.[12] Besides which, to speak of Mary in these terms, it was sufficient to believe that she was purified in the womb, in the manner of John the Baptist (or, as some believed, at the time of the Incarnation), rather than at the instant of her conception.

Indeed, in the Greek Church a peculiar dichotomy long persisted between the fulsome, hyperbolic praise that was heaped upon the Virgin and the belief that she was not entirely free from defects, especially her difficulty in accepting her Son's Crucifixion.[13] This idea came from Origen (†c. 254), who interpreted Simeon's words on the sword that would pierce Mary's heart (Luke 2. 35) as a prophecy of her loss of faith when faced with her Son's crucifixion and death:

> And this is what Simon now prophesises, saying, 'And thy own soul a sword shall pierce.' Although you know that you have begotten this child without man's concurrence, and although you have heard Gabriel say. 'The Holy Spirit shall come upon thee, and the power of the Most High shall overshadow thee,' you will be transpierced by the sword of unbelief, you will be struck by the sword of uncertainty, your mind will be torn in two, when before your eyes he, whom you heard called the Son of God and whom you know you begot without the seed of man, is crucified and dies. *In Lucam, 17*[14]

He also argues that since Christ redeemed all, this included Mary ('For all have sinned, and do need the glory of God', Romans 3. 23; 'Wherefore as by one man sin entered into this world, and by sin death; and so death passed upon all men, in whom all have sinned', Romans 5. 12). This was to become the most fundamental objection of the Maculists in the Middle Ages and beyond. A number of the early Church Fathers followed Origen's interpretation,[15] including Basil of Cesaerea († 431), the great Cappadocian father of Eastern

[12] See sections 1, 2 and particularly 3 of *Partakers of the Divine Nature: The History and Development of Deification in the Christian Traditions*, ed. by Michael J. Christensen, Jeffery A. Wittung (Madison, N.J.: Fairleigh Dickinson University Press, 2007).
[13] See Chapter on Immediate Redemption, and see Ermanno Toniolo, 'Gv 19, 25-27 nel pensiero dei Padri, *Theotokos*, 7. 2 (1999), 339-86, Rosa Calì, *I testi antimariologici nell'esegisi dei padri: da Nicea a Calcedonia* (Caltaninsetta: Edizioni del Seminario, 1999), and Tina Beattie, 'Mary in Patristic Theology', in *Mary: The Complete Resource*, ed. by Sarah Jane Boss (Oxford and New York: Oxford University Press 2007), pp. 75-105 (pp. 99-102).
[14] *PG* 13, 1845, translation adapted from Georges Joussard, 'The Fathers of the Church and the Immaculate Conception', p. 55. See also *In Lucam*, 6, 3-4, *PG* 13, 1814-15 and Hilda Graef, *Doctrine and Devotion*, I, 45-46.
[15] See Graef, *Doctrine and Devotion*, I, 45-46.

monasticism, though he softens the language somewhat by speaking of Mary's doubt rather than scandal.[16] Around the same time Cyril of Alexandria († 444) speaks of the events of Calvary as depriving the Virgin of right reasoning, and describes her as a 'simple woman' who was prey to 'absurd thoughts' as she witnessed the Crucifixion:

> What is it then that induced the blessed evangelist to go into trivial detail and mention the transgression of the women? His reason was to show this – that the Passion in its unexpectedness had caused even the mother of the Lord to fall, as it appears, and that the death on the Cross, being extremely bitter, made her depart to some extent from the thoughts that were fitting. [...] For you need not doubt that she admitted into her mind thoughts of the following kind: 'I gave birth to the one who is mocked on the tree. Perhaps in saying that he was the true Son of almighty God he was mistaken.' [...] It is extremely probable that a mere woman, ignorant of the mystery, was deceived into thoughts of this kind. *Commentary on John* [17]

That he is able to write in these terms while elsewhere offering almost boundless praise of the Virgin is indicative both of the deep-rooted misogyny of the time and the lack of an integrated concept of Mary as person and *Theotokos*: when viewed as the Mother of God, she is raised beyond the status of mere woman, yet she may serve as an example of the weakness of her sex when it serves more pastoral purposes. The same negative view of Mary recurs in a hymn by Romanos the Melodist (†c. 560), another figure who is renowned for his praises of the Virgin: 'In fact, when you see your Son nailed to the Cross, O Immaculate One, recalling the words of the angel, the divine conception, and the unutterable miracles, you will immediately begin to doubt. For you this situation will be a sword of suffering.'[18] The *Life of Mary* attributed to Maximus the Confessor († 662) also speaks of Mary's doubt, though according to the author it was only momentary and was instantly assuaged by God.[19] Indeed, Origen's opinion still held sufficient sway over six hundred years after his death for Photius (†c. 897), the archbishop of Constantinople, to feel it necessary to write:

> As to the opinion according to which the sword is that doubt that struck her soul and that led her to ask herself if that crucified man was or was not God,

---

[16] *Epistula* 260, 9, *PG* 32, 965C-968A.

[17] Quoted in Richard Price, 'Theotokos: The Title and its Significance in Doctrine and Devotion', in *Mary: The Complete Resource*, ed. by Sarah Jane Boss (Oxford and New York: Oxford University Press 2007), pp. 56-74 (p. 64). See *PG* 74, 661A-665A. Others that take a negative view: Asterius the Sophist († c. 341), *Homilia 25*, 25, *PG* 55, 555, *TMPM*, I, 259; Ampilochios of Inconium († 398), *Homilia in Natilitaia Jesu Christi*, *PG* 39, 40D-41B; Hesychius of Jerusalem († 451), *Homily on the Hypapante*, 8, *TMPM*, I, 536.

[18] *Hymn of the Hypapante*, 13, *TMPM*, I, 716.

[19] *Life of Mary*, 53, *TMPM*, II, 224.

some have affirmed this to be so. I, however, have never said this. *Ampilochian Questions*, 157[20]

Other Scriptural passages were also sometimes interpreted in a negative light, including Mary's failure to accept the angel's message immediately at the Annunciation (Luke 1. 29-34), and Christ's apparent rebuke of her at the wedding feast of Cana ('Woman, what is that to me and to thee? My hour is not yet come' John 2. 4).[21] Both Irenaeus[22] and Ephrem believe, for instance that Mary acted too hastily in expecting a miracle of Jesus at Cana, the latter adding that Jesus gives Mary a lesson about being too insistent,[23] while Eustathius of Antioch (†c. 337) also sees it as a reproof, inasmuch as Christ, who knew all things, did not require anybody to tell him what was needed.[24] John Chrysostom († 407) is particularly negative in his interpretation of Mary's behaviour at Cana.[25] Her principal interest is to claim glory for herself from her Son's miracle and to impress the wedding guests. Likewise he takes a negative view of Christ's words to those who interrupted his preaching to tell him that his mother and brethren are outside: 'Who is my mother, and who are my brethren? […] Whosoever shall do the will of my Father, that is in heaven, he is my brother, and sister, and mother' (Matthew 12. 47-50. See also Mark 3. 31-35; Luke 19-21). This shows, he says, that Mary did not yet understand who Jesus was and believed that she could tell him what to do. Indeed, he even suggests that Mary did not want to obey Christ because she wanted to assert her maternal authority. However, his purpose is not to criticise Mary, but to put her forward as a model of how one needs to learn to submit to God's will in order to progress spiritually.[26] Similar assessments are offered by a number of the early Fathers, including Severian of Gabala († after 408), Theodore of Mopsuestia († 428) and Severus of Antioch (†c. 538).[27] Theodore writes:

> When the wine ran short, the mother of Jesus said to him, 'They have no wine.' His mother, as is the wont of mothers, pressed him to perform a miracle, wanting to show off the greatness of her son immediately and thinking that the lack of wine was a good opportunity for a miracle. But the Lord said to her, 'Woman, what have you to do with me? My hour has not yet come.' […] In

[20] *PG* 101, 832C.

[21] Many of the Fathers ask themselves why Mary did not immediately accept Gabriel's message, ususlly explaining it in terms of wise caution on the part of the Virgin who wishes to be sure that the vision was not a tricj of the devil such as had deceived Eve.

[22] *Adversus haereses*, 3, 16, 7, *PG* 7, 926A-B.

[23] *Diatessaron*, 5, 1-5, *TMPM*, IV, 85.

[24] *Fragment* 69, *TMPM*, I, 241.

[25] Graef, *Doctrine and Devotion*, I, 74-76.

[26] *In Iohannem*, 21, 1-3, *PG* 59, 129-132, *TMPM*, I, 416-18.

[27] Respectively, *Homily on the Holy Martyr Acacius*, *TMPM,* I 430, *Commentary on John*, *TMPM,* I 442-43, and *Homily 34 on the Nativity*, *TMPM,* I 654.

other words: '[…] I possess the power to work always, whenever and however I choose; even without being pressed by the needs of recipients I am able to display my power. Therefore the excuse you allege of a lack of wine is an insult to me. *Commentary on John*[28]

However, by no means all of the Greek Fathers interpreted Mary's behaviour on these occasions in a negative light. Theodoret of Cyrrhus († 466), for instance, argues that Christ was not rebuking his mother at Cana, but was simply saying that such matters as wine running out were of little concern. He also points out that Jesus' words, 'whosoever shall do the will of my Father, that is in heaven, he is my brother, and sister, and mother' (Matthew 12. 50), could better be applied to his own Mother than anyone else, since her 'virtue surpassed that of all other women.'[29] In fact, Origen himself, notwithstanding his belief that she lost faith at Calvary, sees Mary as a model of humility and believes that she received the seven gifts of the Spirit.[30]

None of these negative views prevented the Eastern Fathers from writing of the Virgin's unique holiness. Of the sixth-century Fathers, the one who comes closest to asserting Mary's absolute freedom from sin is the Syrian Jacob of Serug († 521), who writes of her as having been free from sin, even from childhood, and declares that she was 'alone humble, pure, beautiful and immaculate.'[31] Nevertheless, it is difficult to assert that this is an affirmation of the Immaculate Conception since Jacob does not deal with the question of original sin, at least not in the sense in which it is understood in Western theology from Augustine onwards. Moreover, further on in the homily he speaks of the Virgin being purified in the manner of John the Baptist and Elijah and of the Holy Spirit descending on Mary to purify and sanctify her and to take 'away that ancient sentence of Adam and Eve.'[32] The same is true of Severus of Antioch († 538) who declares, 'She belonged to this earth, in her nature she was part of the human race, and was of the same essence as we, although she was pure from all taint and immaculate',[33] yet speaks in no uncertain terms of Mary's human weaknesses in commenting on Christ's reply to his Mother when she asks him to change the water into wine at the wedding feast of Cana: 'His mother, who nurtured human feelings, and who had pushed him to act out of a love for ostentation, received a correction through the words which he spoke in reply, teaching her that he should carry out such miracles not because of ostentation but at the right time and place.'[34] Romanos the Melodist († c. 560) uses the term 'immaculate' for Mary in several of his hymns. In one, for instance, he has Adam

---

[28] Quoted in Richard Price, 'Theotokos', p. 63.
[29] *Questions and Answers to the Orthodox*, TMPM, I, 588.
[30] See *In Lucam*, 8, 1-6, TMPM, I, 216.
[31] *Homily on the Blessed Virgin Mary Generatrix of God*, TMPM, IV, 146.
[32] TMPM, IV, 153.
[33] *Cathedral Homilies*, 67, TMPM, 648.
[34] *Cathedral Homilies*, 56, TMPM, 654.

declare: 'Here I am at your feet, O Immaculate Virgin Mother, and all of my offspring stand before you, my intermediary.'[35] Yet the same Romanos writes in a hymn for Presentation of the Lord:

> In fact when you see your Son nailed to the Cross, O Immaculate One, recalling the words of the angel, the divine conception, and the unspeakable miracles, doubt will come upon you: for you this situation will be like a sword of suffering. But afterwards God will provide a prompt cure for your heart and an inexhaustible peace to the disciples, he who is the one friend of mankind. *Hymn for the Hypapante*[36]

Towards the end of the sixth century Theoteknos of Livias uses terminology that hints at Mary being free from all sin when, based largely on the *Protoevangelium of St. James*, he writes of the miraculous circumstances of her conception from her previously sterile mother, Anna:

> She was begotten pure and immaculate like the cherubim, she who was from pure and immaculate clay. For while she was still in the loins of her father Joachim, her mother, Anna, received a message from a holy angel in these terms: 'your posterity will be celebrated throughout the whole universe.' For this reason Anna presented her in the temple of the Lord. *Homily on the Assumption of the Holy Mother of God, 6*[37]

Nevertheless, this statement is too fleeting for us to have any certainty about the author's intent. A near contemporary of Theoteknos, Sophronius of Jerusalem († 638) speaks several times of Mary being immaculate even prior to the Incarnation, calling her 'the immaculate Virgin free from all stain', and also describes her as having 'been purified in advance',[38] yet he also refers to her as earning purifying grace in a measure greater than all others, and speaks of her experiencing doubt at the foot of the Cross.[39] One must therefore conclude that while he is clear that Mary was excepted from original sin he is not clear as to the exact moment when this occurred.

The *Life of Mary* attributed to Maximus the Confessor († 662), in speaking of Mary's resolve to remain a virgin, claims that she was entirely free from sin throughout her life, but again, it does not deal with the question of original sin:

> Not only did the Virgin not have any knowledge of the reality of marriage, but she also did not even have the intention of desiring it in her heart, since, from the

---

[35] *Second Hymn for Christmas*, 8, TMPM, I, 710.

[36] *TMPM*, I, 716.

[37] *TMPM*, II, 81.

[38] *Second Oration for the Annunciation of the Mother of God, 25*, PG 87, 3248A.

[39] See *Homily on the Annunciation*, 24 and 25, TMPM, II, 144 and 145, and *Homily for the Hypapante*, 4, 16, TMPM, II, 165.

beginning, she had grown up entirely holy in soul and body. No notion of any passion had ever entered into her heart and mind: she was so much more profound and sublime than all of human nature. It was for this reason that the beauty of her soul attracted the King, Creator of all things. *23*[40]

Those writing towards the end of the Patristic period, such as Germanus of Constantinople († 733), Andrew of Crete († 740), and John of Damascus († 749) were even more effusive in their praise of Mary's purity, speaking of Mary in such extraordinarily glowing terms that it is hard to believe that they did not consider her entirely immaculate. They also write of her role in divinising humanity in such a way that it might seem that they are asserting her absolute freedom from sin. Moreover, by suggesting that the restoration of humanity began with Mary's conception, and not her birth, they would seem to imply that the event itself was in some way sacred.[41] Nevertheless, they should not be understood to be affirming the Immaculate Conception in the Western sense since, as for earlier Eastern Fathers, the theological categories in which they were operating were not the same.

Germanus of Constantinople describes how God came to the aid of Mary's parents and how an angel announced the conception of the Virgin.[42] Andrew also speaks of her absolute purity:

> In fact your flesh does not impede the virtue and the capacity of your spirit since your spirit blows wherever it wills (John 3. 8) inasmuch as it is pure and immaterial spirit: incorruptible and immaculate, a living spirit together with the Holy Spirit, a spirit chosen before all by the divinity of the Only Begotten One. You, according to what was written, 'are beautiful' (Canticles 2. 13), and your virginal body is all holy, all chaste, all habitation of God, so that dissolving into dust is foreign to it. *First Homily for the Dormition of the Holy Mother of God*[43]

In another passage he speaks of Joachim and Anna in terms that suggest that the union that led to the conception of Mary was entirely exceptional: 'Blessed the loins of Joachim from which was deposited an absolutely pure seed! Marvellous the womb of Anna in which a most holy child gradually developed, was formed, and was born.'[44] Here we are a long way from Augustine's doctrine of the inherent libidinousness of intercourse. Heavily influenced by the apocrypha, Germanus is suggesting that Mary's conception was marked by a unique blessing from God so that even the seed of her father was pure.

---

[40] *TMPM*, II, 200.
[41] See chapter on Remote Redemption.
[42] See Andrew, *First Homily on the Dormition, 2* and Germanus *First Homily on the Dormition*, 5-6, Daley, *EPH*, pp. 104-06 and 188-90.
[43] *TMPM*, II, 354. An alternative English translation to may be found in Brian Daley, *Patristic Homilies*, p. 157.
[44] *Homily for the Nativity of Mary*, 2, TMPM, II, 499.

Andrew of Crete writes of Mary's conception in several contexts. In his Canon for the feast of Mary's conception he uses the same type of language as had been used by earlier writers for her nativity. No longer is the beginning of salvation to be dated from the Virgin's birth but from the very instant in which she was conceived: 'Today is announced to us that the treasures of joy will be opened and that an end will be put to the sorrows of malediction, in the holy Conception of the Mother of God.'[45] Speaking of Mary's birth he says that she had already been prepared as a divine abode for her Creator:

> Today the created sanctuary of the Creator of all things has been built, and in an extraordinary way the creature is prepared for the Creator as his divine abode. Nature, which before had been reduced to clay receives the beginning of its divinisation and the dust runs hastily on high towards supreme glory. *First Encomium for the Nativity of the Most Holy Mother of God*[46]

In the same homily he also speaks of her as the 'mystical ephod' – a sacred vestment worn by the High Priest – 'of the divine priesthood,' which grace 'has figuratively weaved with the seed descended from Levi,' and which God 'has coloured red the divine purple with blood descended from David.'[47] In other words, in Mary, God has brought together both the priestly and royal Hebrew lines, and, through grace, he has divinised the resulting weave, in order that the Virgin should be adequately prepared for divine motherhood. Therefore, Andrew believes that Mary, who united the royal and priestly in her person, was perfected by God's grace, but he does not indicate the point at which this occurred. Further on, in a passage that he calls the nub of his homily, Andrew returns to the question of Mary's generation:

> The Redeemer of the human race – as I said – wishing to present a new generation and re-formation, contrary to precedent, just as once he formed the first Adam, having first taken mud from the still virgin and intact earth (Genesis 2. 7), now too, operating his own Incarnation from himself, in the place, as it were, of another soil, chose from all of nature this pure and most immaculate virgin: and the architect of Adam, having once again built in her, from her substance, that which is ours, became the new Adam.

He goes on to explain the extraordinary circumstances of Mary's conception from the sterile Anna, who, like her husband, Joachim, led a virtuous and holy life, praying constantly for the gift of a child. In graphic detail he describes how God intervened that Mary might be conceived:

---

[45] *Ode 1, Troparion 2*, quoted in Cornelius A. Bouman, 'The Immaculate Conception in the Liturgy', in *The Dogma of the Immaculate Conception: History and Significance*, ed. by Edward D. O'Connor, pp. 113-60, (p. 118).

[46] *TMPM*, II, 396.

[47] *First Encomium for the Nativity of the Most Holy Mother of God*, *TMPM*, II, 397.

As a consequence, to them who were invoking and supplicating God with insistence, soon arrived a power that was not slow to reinforce the fecundity of one and the generation of the other; and having strewn the canals of the genital organs, which, until then, had been desiccated, with the humours of insemination, it transformed them from barren to fruitful.

Andrew also states in several passages that Mary was the first to be freed from original sin after the Fall: 'This is Mary, the *Theotokos*, the common refuge of all Christians, the first to be liberated from the original fall of our first parents.'[48] However, he does not indicate precisely when this occurred nor does he specify the manner in which God has brought about this purification, so it is not possible to say that he is affirming the Immaculate Conception, at least in the terms in which it is understood today.

John of Damascus also speaks of Anna's sterility as part of God's providential plan, necessary so that Mary's conception would be perceived to be the fruit of grace rather than of nature. Gambero notes that John uses the term *panámōmomos* (utterly perfect) to describe the seed of which Mary was generated, so he clearly believes that Mary benefited from a special grace from the moment of her conception.[49] In his *De fide orthodoxa*, the first systematic work of theology in the Eastern Church, which was to be an inspiration to the Scholastics, John speaks of Mary being conceived without pleasure and refers to her at the time of the Incarnation as being 'holy and immaculate flesh and blood'.[50] Nevertheless he also speaks of Mary being purified through the action of the Holy Spirit at the time of the Incarnation in order to have the capacity to receive the Word, a passage that Peter Lombard will subsequently quote to deny the Immaculate Conception.[51]

Although it could be argued that Germanus, Andrew and John are implicitly suggesting that the conjugal relations between Mary's parents, Joachim and Anna were grace-filled, and it is clear that they believe that God anticipated the Virgin's future by intervening in her conception and giving her special privileges

---

[48] *Third Homily for the Nativity of Mary, MF*, p. 393.

[49] See *MF*, p. 402. John Janaro, 'Saint Anselm and the Development of the Doctrine of the Immaculate Conception: Historical and Theological Perspectives', *The Saint Anselm Journal*, 3 (2006), 48-56, believes that John's comments 'correspond essentially to the doctrine of the Immaculate Conception' (p. 50, n. 7). However, such a statement is unjustified since John is interested in glorifying the Virgin, like many of his Greek predecessors, and does not take a rigidly theological approach to the question.

[50] *De fide orthodoxa*, 4, 14, *PG* 94, 1160C-D.

[51] *De fide orthodoxa*, 3, 2, *PG* 94, 985B-C. Cornelius A. Bouman, 'The Immaculate Conception in the Liturgy', dismisses these statements, unjustifiably so in my opinion, arguing that they speak merely of an increase of sanctity. But if this were the case, why does John not speak of an increase of grace instead of a purification? Purification necessarily implies that something needs to be removed, not merely that grace is added.

from the outset, the grounds for believing that they were preaching the Immaculate Conception are open to question, as in the case of other Greek Fathers, given the different understanding of original sin with respect to the West.[52] Indeed, the Damascene speaks of Mary being purified by the Holy Spirit prior to the Incarnation, which would suggest that she had some trace of original sin: 'The sanctifying power of the Spirit reposed on her, cleansed her and made her holy.'[53] Likewise Andrew writes in one of his hymns: 'He sanctified your immaculate womb, O Chaste One, he who took flesh from it, the transcendent God, adored in the Triad, who proceeds from the Father, and who is God with the Spirit.'[54] Thus when Germanus addresses the Virgin as the 'wholly immaculate One', and Andrew writes of the extraordinary events surrounding Mary from, and even before, her conception, and speaks of the Virgin's life as being 'without spot of stain, utterly filled with every pure and holy quality, a life such as the world cannot grasp', this does not mean that they were affirming the Immaculate Conception, although it could be argued that such statements laid the groundwork for the doctrine.[55]

The first testaments to the existence of the feast of Mary's Conception, the celebration of which was later to be dogged by controversy in the West, are a canon by Andrew of Crete († 740), mentioned above, to be followed by a homily for the feast by John of Eubea (†c. 750), though it was probably already being celebrated towards the end of the previous century.[56] John also clearly teaches that God intervened directly in Mary's conception, not just in order to render Anna fertile, but to create a new creature, as Martin Jugie observes.[57] According

[52] On this subject see Gambero, *MF*, who repeatedly points out the different conception of original sin in the Eastern Church, for instance, with reference to John of Damascus, p. 402. See also Stephen C. Gulovich's 'The Immaculate Conception of the Blessed Virgin in the Eastern Ecclesiastical Tradition', in *Marian Studies*, 5 (1954), pp. 146-83, and Francis Dvornick, 'The Byzantine Church and the Immaculate Conception', in *The Dogma of the Immaculate Conception: History and Significance*, ed. by Edward D. O'Connor, pp. 87-112.
[53] *First Homily on the Dormition*, 3, Brian E. Daley, *EPH*, p. 185. See also *Exposition on the Orthodox Faith*, 3, 2, *PG* 94, 900, *TMPM*, II, 486, where he writes: 'So then, after the consent of the holy Virgin, the Holy Spirit came upon her, according to the word of the Lord, as the angel had announced, purifying her and giving her the capacity to receive the divinity of the Word and to generate.'
[54] *Canon for the Saturday of Lazarus, Theotokion, Ode V, TMPM*, II, 463-64.
[55] Respectively, *First Homily on the Dormition*, 11, and *First Homily on the Dormition*, 2, Daley, *EPH*, pp. 165 and 105.
[56] *Homily on the Conception of the BVM*, 10, *TMPM*, II, 585. Also see the introduction to the homily p. 583, and see José Antonio Aldama, 'La fiesta de la Concepción de María', *Estudios eclesiásticos*, 36 (1961), 427-49. On Andrew of Crete's canon see Cornelius A. Bouman, 'The Immaculate Conception in the Liturgy', pp. 114-15.
[57] See *L'Immaculeé Conception dans l'Écriture Sainte et la tradition orientale* (Rome: Accademia Mariana, 1952), pp.126-28.

to John, the New Testament begins, not with the conception of Christ, but that of Mary. She differs from her parents, holy though they are, from the outset, as the angel who tells Anna the good news makes clear:

> 'While you are earth, she, instead, is heaven, while you are of the earth, through her, instead, the inhabitants of heaven come. You are truly blessed, because that King of glory, whom Moses could not see, ardently desired the beauty of your daughter. Blessed are you, Joachim and Anna, because you have generated a spiritual paradise, for she is proclaimed all-blessed not only by men, but by the angels.' [...] And, behold, as Anna heard from the angel that *she was to conceive and give birth to an immaculate daughter*, she began to exult joyfully. *Homily on the Conception of the BVM*, 12-13.[58]

He concludes the homily by defending the celebration of the feast, since Christ himself 'built her,' so that he could make his abode in her.[59] Tarasios of Constantinople († 806) also seems to support the Immaculate Conception, and clearly states that there was a divine intervention, when he writes:

> As soon as the angel had given this joyful news, Joachim, exulting, his heart overflowing with joy, went down the mountain while Anna, who had always been sterile, found herself to be with child, neither through will of the flesh, nor the will of man. Then, when after twelve months the pregnancy had run its course, she gave birth to the immaculate Virgin and Mother of God, Mary, the mediatrix of salvation for the whole world. *Homily on the Presentation of Mary in the Temple, 4*[60]

Paradoxically, although Western theology was to throw up far more obstacles to the possibility that God could have preserved Mary free from original sin, most of the Latin Fathers were more reluctant to accept that the Virgin had been guilty of any fault. The one major exception was Tertullian (†c. 230?) who heavily criticizes Mary for her failure to recognise that her Son was the Messiah in his commentary on Matthew 12. 46-50, which tells the story of how Jesus, interrupted in his preaching by the arrival of his Mother and 'brothers', declares that his true mother and brothers are those who do the will of God. Tertullian concludes his analysis by declaring that, 'his estranged mother is a figure of the synagogue, and his unbelieving brethren a figure for the Jews.'[61] Most of the other early Fathers remain silent on the question, an exception being Hilary of Poitiers († 367) who states that the words, 'Who is my mother, and who are my bothers?' do not mean that Jesus is rebuking his Mother but that he is claiming

---

[58] *TMPM*, II, 585, my italics.
[59] *23, TMPM*, II, 592-93. See also 'Temple' in vol 2.
[60] *TMPM*, II, 629.
[61] *De carne Christi*, 7, quoted in Georges Joussard, 'The Fathers of the Church and the Immaculate Conception', p. 66.

kinship to whoever is in communion with him and his Church, while his words to her from the Cross show that he in no way was displeased with her.[62]

Ambrose of Milan († 397) is possibly the single most important figure in changing the course of Patristic Mariology in the West. He accepts none of the negative readings of Mary's behaviour prevalent in the East, instead holding her up as an unqualified model of perfect holiness.[63] What is more, his portrayal of her stoic endurance in the face of the unspeakable agony of Calvary gave an entirely different direction to understanding of Mary's participation in the Passion in the West.[64] It is sometimes held that Ambrose believed Mary to be free of original sin on the basis of the following lines: 'Adopt me however, not from Sarah but from Mary, so that it might be an incorrupt virgin, a virgin by grace free from all stain of sin.'[65] However, as with many of the Greek Fathers, these words could equally well apply if Ambrose believed that the Virgin had been purified after her conception. What is undeniable is that Ambrose was crucial to the establishment of a tradition in the West that Mary had never actually committed a sin.

Equally, Augustine († 430), who nurtured a profound devotion for the Virgin, does not entertain the possibility that she committed any sin, rejecting, for instance, the suggestion that Jesus was rebuking his mother when he asked 'whosoever shall do the will of my Father, that is in heaven, he is my brother, and sister, and mother' (Matthew 12. 50), arguing instead that she was doing the will of God and was therefore included.[66] Indeed he specifically states that Mary was excepted, by a unique gift of God's grace from the general rule of human sinfulness:

> Let us therefore exclude the holy Virgin Mary, concerning whom, out of honour for the Lord, I wish no question regarding sin to be raised; for from him we know what abundance of grace for overcoming sin in every particular was conferred upon her who had the merit to conceive and bear him who most certainly had no sin.' *De natura et gratia, 36, 42* [67]

---

[62] *In Matthaeum*, 12, 24, *PL* 993A-B. However, on another occasion he seems to suggest that Mary was not entirely without fault, where he interprets the sword of Simeon as God's judgement of Mary, though not with reference to any specific fault (*Tractatus super Psalmum 118*, 12, *PL* 9, 523A).

[63] See vol. 2.

[64] See Chapter on Immediate Co-Redemption.

[65] Quoted in O'Carroll, *Theotokos*, p. 180.

[66] See *Epistola* 243, 9, *PL*, 33, 1058.

[67] *PL* 44, 267. All translations, unless otherwise indicated, are from the Latin and Italian texts in S. Aurelii Augustini, *Opera Omnia, Tutte le opere*, ed. by Franco Monteverde, 45 vols (Rome: Nuova Biblioteca Agostiniana and Città Nuova, 1967–), in *Sant'Agostino, Augustinus Hipponensis*, < http://www.augustinus.it/> [accessed 10 November 2008].

This exclusion, which occurs in his refutation of the claims of Pelagius that man was capable of living a sinless life through right use of his will, does not necessarily mean, however, that Augustine believed Mary to be free from original sin, but should be understood in terms of an extraordinary grace that was given to her in order to overcome it.[68] However, he does establish an important principal, namely that Mary was an exception to the general rule and that her preservation from actual sin was due to grace.

In another of his polemical works, written late in life and left uncompleted, he offers a rather convoluted argument against Mary having been entirely free from original sin, in response to the polemical *Ad Florum*, written by the Pelagian bishop Julian, in which he rejects the very notion of original sin:

> I do not say that evil is necessary, but neither did Ambrose. And yet I say that infants are reclaimed from evil, as did Ambrose. And the reason why evil is not necessary is precisely this, that God is able to heal what has been transmitted by nature, and how much more, that which has been added by our free will! I do not say that men are not made free by grace (and God forbid that Ambrose should have said such a thing!), but we say, which you do not wish, that it is only by grace that they are freed, not only in the sense of being forgiven their sins, but also in being kept from temptation. We do not assign Mary to the devil because of the condition of birth but for this: because the condition of birth is resolved by the grace of re-birth. We do not place virginity ahead of marriage as good to evil, but as better to good. *Opus imperfectum contra Julianum, 4, 22*[69]

The exact meaning of these much-discussed lines is not entirely clear, but this much is: Mary was, like all humans, under the dominion of the devil prior to the action of God's grace on her, equivalent to baptism (re-birth). So, although he had excepted Mary from any actual sin through the aid of God's grace in *De natura et gratia* Augustine does not apply the same principle to original sin. In his treatise on the remission of sin Augustine is categorical in stating that only one person, Christ, was born without sin: 'The only one to be born without sin is he whom the Virgin conceived without the embrace of marriage, not by the concupiscence of the flesh but through obedience of the mind.'[70] Further on he

---

[68] Scholars are by no means in agreement on whether Augustine merely excludes Mary from any personal sin or from original sin too, but the preponderance is in favour of the former. See *MF*, p. 226 for a brief review of the question and bibliography. Gambero himself does not believe that Augustine upheld the Immaculate Conception. See also Georges Joussard, 'The Fathers of the Church and the Immaculate Conception', pp. 68-74, for discussion on Ambrose, Jerome and Augustine. He takes a similar position to Gambero on Augustine (p. 70). See also José María Canal, 'San Agustín y el dogma de la Immaculada concepción', *Ephemerides mariologicae* 54 (2004), 361-71.

[69] *PL* 45, 1418. The translation relies in part on Georges Joussard, 'The Fathers of the Church and the Immaculate Conception', p. 72.

[70] *De peccatorum meritis et remissione*, 1, 29, 57, *PL* 44, 142.

reiterates the same point and adds that it was necessary for Jesus to purify the flesh of his Mother:

> He is therefore the only one who, remaining God after he made himself a man, never had any sin and did not assume sinful flesh, although he took on flesh from the sinful flesh of his Mother. As to the flesh he took from his Mother, he either purified it with a view to assuming it, or purified it in assuming it. *De peccatorum meritis et remissione, 2, 24, 38*[71]

On another occasion he writes that although Mary was conceived in the normal way, which transmitted original sin to her, this does not mean that the flesh of Jesus was likewise contaminated, since he was conceived without intercourse:

> Therefore, although Christ's body had its origin in the body of a woman, conceived according to the law of propagation of sinful flesh, nevertheless, not having been conceived in her in the same way in which she had been conceived, his was not sinful flesh but the appearance of sinful flesh. *De Genesi ad Litteram, 10, 18, 32*[72]

In conclusion we may say that since Augustine taught that original sin is transmitted by the male seed as a result of the concupiscence that is inherent in sexual intercourse, Mary could not be free from it. Basing his belief above all on the teaching of Paul (see Romans 3. 23 and 5. 12), he insists that all are marked by the stain of original sin with the sole exception of Christ, and that all are saved only through his redemptive grace: 'No-one is freed from the mass of damnation except in the Redeemer's faith.'[73] Original sin is transmitted through the male seed and infects the soul at its infusion into the body.[74] The logical consequence of this is that only Christ's conception could have been without sin, because it was not a result of a physical union.[75] Mary, instead, could not have been conceived without original sin given that she was the product of the sexual union of her parents, Joachim and Anna. While for Augustine the

---

[71] *PL* 44, 174-175.

[72] *PL* 34, 422.

[73] *De corruptione et gratia*, 7, 11.

[74] See, for instance, *De nuptiis et concupiscentia*, 1, 23, where he allows no wriggle room when he states that 'lust transmits original sin to the child' and that, 'No-one is conceived by a man and a woman without contacting original sin' (1, 35). Augustine toyed with Traducianism, the idea that the soul, and not just the body, was generated not by God through the sexual act, though he made it clear that he was willing to accept the position of the creationists, that the soul was infused directly by God, if the Church should decide that this was so, as indeed it subsequently did when Pope Anastasius II condemned Traducianism in 498.

[75] This belief pervades almost all of Augustine's writings. Among the places where he specifically states that Christ alone was free from original sin, see *De baptismo parvulorum*, 1, 29, 57, *PL* 44, 142.

consequences of original sin were absent in Mary due to the grace of God, this does not mean he believed in the Immaculate Conception since he does not say that grace actually blocked the transmission of the original fault. However, for Augustine this in no way denigrates Mary, nor does it mean that Jesus was born of a less-than-perfect Mother. On the contrary, Mary was even more perfect thanks to the extraordinary grace that she received from God than if she had been in some way been exempt from the transmission of original sin in the first place. Indeed, his intuition that Mary was protected from the consequences of original sin by grace was eventually to become central to the understanding of how Mary was conceived without sin.

A further obstacle arose from Augustine's teaching on the Pauline affirmation that Christ is the one Mediator who died from the Redemption of all (1 Timothy 2. 5). For Augustine, this meant that no-one, not even those who had committed no actual sin and were marked only by original sin, could enter into heaven prior to Christ's redemptive sacrifice on the Cross:

> Therefore, whoever thinks that a human being has existed or exists, or some human beings, who, outside of the Mediator between God and men, do not need remission of their sins, is opposing divine Scripture as the Apostle says: 'Wherefore as by one man sin entered into this world, and by sin death; and so death passed upon all men, in whom all have sinned' (Romans 1. 12). Therefore it would be a godless thing to maintain the opinion that there can be men who are free and saved from sin without the Mediator freeing and saving them. *De perfectione iustitiae, 19, 21*

Therefore, the argument went, if Mary had been free from original sin since conception this would have meant that she could have entered heaven prior to Christ's death if she had died before him, which would have been in direct contradiction to Scripture.

Augustine's teaching on original sin and on the one Mediator was long to prove an obstacle to the doctrine of the Immaculate Conception, with a solution only beginning to emerge in the thirteenth and fourteenth centuries. After Augustine, nothing of major significance was written on Mary's conception in the West for several centuries. Many of the most prominent figures, such as Popes Leo († 461) and Gregory († 604) and Isidore of Seville († 636), ignore the question entirely. Others are ambiguous. Maximus of Turin († after 408), for instance, speaks of 'the original grace' of the Virgin, but without further elaboration,[76] while Ildephonse of Toledo († 667) writes of her being spotless or Immaculate before she conceived Jesus. However, given that he earlier speaks of her purification at

---

[76] Quoted in O'Carroll, *Theotokos*, p. 180. See *The Sermons of Maximus of Turin*, trans. by Boniface Ramsey (New York: Newman, 1989).

the Annunciation,[77] it is likely that his intent here was to affirm her virginal purity rather than her freedom from all trace of sin:

> In the preceding time you were immaculate before God (*in praeterito munda Deo*); in the present time you are completely filled with him, God and man; in a future time you will be she who gave birth to the God-man, rejoicing in your maternity and your virginity, rejoicing in your Son and the preservation of your modesty, faithful to him and to the Spouse. *De virginitate perpetua sanctae Mariae, 12, 1*[78]

Others, such as Cassian (†c. 435) and Fulgentius of Ruspe (†c. 533),[79] simply tow the Augustinian line. Bede († 735) relies heavily on Augustine in his writings on Mary, and expresses the opinion that she had been purified by the Holy Spirit at the Annunciation, a view that necessarily implies that she was marked by original sin, since it had long been accepted that the Virgin had been entirely free of actual sin:

> The Holy Spirit, descending on the Virgin in two ways, shows the efficaciousness of his divine power. For he purified the mind of the Virgin of any foulness of vice – insofar as human fragility allowed it – so that she would be worthy of a heavenly birth. Furthermore, through his intervention alone the holy and venerable body of our Redeemer was formed in her womb. [...] The power of the Most High threw his shadow over the blessed Mother of God, so that, when the Holy Spirit filled her heart, when he made her mistress of all ardour of carnal concupiscence, when he rendered her free of temporal desires, at the same moment he consecrated her mind and her body with heavenly gifts. *In festo Annuntiationis beatae Mariae, 8*[80]

However, Bede did make an important contribution, albeit indirectly, when he argued that John the Baptist had been purified in the womb, a position that Augustine had rejected suggesting instead that he had merely received a momentary grace in order to be able to recognise the Messiah.[81] This inevitably led later commentators to argue that if John the Baptist had been purified in the womb, then no less a grace could have been bestown upon the Virgin.

The Medieval West

Very little distinguishes the early centuries of the Medieval West from the Patristic period when it comes to the Immaculate Conception. Most churchmen continued to hold to the Augustinian position or simply did not pronounce on

---

[77] *De virginitate perpetua sanctae Mariae, 2, 3, PL 96, 61C.*

[78] *PL* 96, 59A.

[79] See respectively *Collatio 22, PL 49, 1232A-C, Epistola 17, 6, 13, PL 65, 458B.*

[80] *PL* 94, 12D-13A.

[81] See Georges Joussard, 'The Fathers of the Church and the Immaculate Conception', pp. 77-79, and Mary Clayton, *Cult of the Virgin*, pp. 15-16.

the matter. Ambrose Autpert (†c. 781), for instance, states with absolute clarity that Mary was free of all sin from the time of her birth, but remains silent on the question of original sin: 'All the faithful know with certainty that the Mother of the Redeemer, from the time of her birth, had never contracted any mark for which she needed to be purified'.[82]

It is Paschasius Radbertus († 865) who gives the first indication that the atmosphere was changing when he writes in a sermon for Mary's nativity that 'she was immune from all original sin' (*ab omni originali peccato immunem*), though this does not necessarily mean that she was never stained by it, as is evident from the remarks that follow on the Holy Spirit purifying her of all stains at the Annunciation, very similar to what John of Damascus had written a century before.[83] In another of his writings, the *Cogitis me*, long attributed to Jerome, Paschasius offers a rather original explanation, inspired in part, perhaps, by a text of Alcuin's († 804) on Mary's virginity,[84] of the purification that the Virgin underwent at the Annunciation, which is not incompatible with belief in the Immaculate Conception. Mary, he suggests, was already entirely pure prior to the Incarnation, but required an additional infusion of grace, which he likens to the purple dye that designated royalty, to take on the entirely unique role that God has planned for her. An analogy might be when a saintly person is appointed to a position of leadership and requires a 'grace of state' in order to carry out his of her new office to perfection:

> Certainly, before this, the womb of the Virgin, although it was pure, incontaminate, free from the contagion of sin, and holy, nevertheless it still was clothed in the baseness of humanity.[85] She, the Virgin was, in fact, as it were, like most pure wool, that is, white according to its natural colour. But when the Holy Spirit came over her, just as wool becomes purple when treated with blood of the oyster and the murex, Mary was transformed into a Mother without conjugal relations. And this because from that moment on she was not to be that which she had been before, but would become authentic purple, since she had been destined properly from above to be the clothing and glory of the High King. And certainly

---

[82] *In Purificatione S. Mariae, 3, PL* 89, 1293B.

[83] *The Parturition of the Virgin, PL* 120, 1372A-B, quoted in Graef, *Doctrine and Devotion*, I, 177. Concerning the apparently contradictory statements of Radbertus on Mary's freedom from original sin see the comments of Mary Clayton, *The Cult of the Virgin*, pp. 22-23, and Leo Scheffczyk, *Das Mariengeheimnis in Frömmigkeit und Lehre der Karolingerzeit*, Erfurter Theologische Studien, 5 (Leipzig: St. Benno-Verlag, 1959), p. 329.

[84] Alcuin uses the same image of Mary as white wool that is dyed purple by the action of the Holy Spirit in order to make her worthy of receiving 'the Eternal Emperor', but relates the whiteness of the wool only to Mary's virginity, not her freedom from all sin. *De fide sanctae et individuae Trinitatis, 3, 14, De Maria Virgine, et incarnatione Verbi Dei, PL,* 101, 46C-D.

[85] The rather ambiguous statement could refer to the stain of original sin, or could simply mean that her flesh had not been infused with the extraordinary grace necessary to conceive a divine Son.

in this way, if we can put it like this, the blessed and glorious Virgin Mary, in order to receive worthily the union of divinity in herself, preserving both natures, even though she had only just become incomparable with all the other virgins that are under the heavens, nevertheless became (when she was filled with grace, when the Holy Spirit descended on her and the power of the Most High spread his shadow over her), richer in merits, more sublime in her divine heights, more beautiful in her holiness, and more glorious in the prerogatives of her merits. *Cogitis me, 7*[86]

Ultimately it was to be the introduction of a number of Marian feasts from the East that would stimulate sustained and serious debate on the question of Mary's sinlessness.[87]   Celebration of the Nativity of the Virgin began in the seventh century,[88] while the feast of the Conception of St. Anne,[89] later known as and the Conception of the Virgin, was also introduced in the East in the seventh century, thus acknowledging, at least implicitly, that the conception of the *Theotokos* was free from sin. It was being celebrated throughout the Byzantine area by the mid-ninth century and was introduced into Eastern-rite monasteries in southern Italy in the tenth and eleventh centuries.[90] The feast of Mary's conception was already being celebrated in the English Church by around the turn of the first millennium, possibly introduced by Irish monks who had considerable contact with the East, or more likely as a result of Benedictine contacts with Eastern-rite monasteries.[91] One of the most important centres for the feast at this time was Winchester where we find one of the first artistic representations in the West of the Conception of the Virgin to Anna in the eleventh-century *Winchester Psalter*.[92] The feast is also mentioned

---

[86] *PL* 30, 129A-B, *TMPM*, III, 796-97.

[87] See Mary Clayton, *The Cult of the Virgin*, pp. 25-51.

[88] For a recent and very rich study of the origins and development of Marian liturgy in the Latin rite, see Margot Fassler, 'Mary's Nativity, Fulbert of Chartres, and the *Stirps Jesse*, particularly, pp. 392-95. See also Tom Brandenbarg, 'Saint Anne: A Holy Grandmother and her Children', in *Sanctity and Motherhood: Essays on Holy Mothers in the Middle Ages*, ed. by Anneke Mulder-Bakker (New York and London: Garland, 1995), pp. 31-65 (p. 36).

[89] Cornelius A. Bouman, 'The Immaculate Conception in the Liturgy', points out that one reason why it was referred to as the conception of Anne rather than Mary was because Greek generally use the term only in the active sense (p. 117).

[90] See Cornelius A. Bouman, 'The Immaculate Conception in the Liturgy', pp. 123-24.

[91] See John Janaro, 'Saint Anselm and the Development of the Doctrine of the Immaculate Conception', p. 49. However the possibility that the feast was celebrated in Ireland at such an early date is contested by Felim Ó Briain, 'Feast of Our Lady's Conception in the Medieval Irish Church', *Irish Ecclesiastical Record*, 70 (1948), 687-704. See also Cornelius A. Bouman's well-argued rejection of the possibility in 'The Immaculate Conception in the Liturgy', pp. 125-27, and his discussion of other possible solutions, including Italian links, pp. 127-30.

[92] See Kristine Edmondson Haney, 'The Immaculate Imagery in the Winchester Psalter', *Gesta*, 20 (1981), 111-18, and more generally on artistic representations of the

in the *Pontificale* of Canterbury and that of Exeter.[93] The suppression of the feast by the Norman Archbishop of Canterbury, Lanfranc, after his appointment to the See in 1070, did nothing to dampen popular devotion and ironically appears to have stimulated theological reflection on the question. It was re-introduced by a nephew of Anselm of Canterbury, Anselm of Bury in 1127, being officially recognised by the English bishops at the Council of London in 1129. The liturgy of the restored feast differed substantially from the old one, in that it was focused more on the Virgin's unique virtue from the moment of conception than on St. Anne's miraculous fertility, which had been the principal feature of both the Eastern and pre-Norman Feast of the Conception.[94] Another disciple of Anselm's, Hugh of Amiens († 1164), together with the Benedictines of Fécamp in Normandy introduced the feast into areas of France, provoking a negative reaction from Bernard of Clairvaux, as we shall see presently. An anonymous sermon, long attributed to Anselm of Canterbury, probably dating from the twelfth century, offers evidence of the powerful devotional motivations behind the promotion of the feast. As with other Marian privileges, it is her divine motherhood that entitles her to such an honour since, according to the sermonist, her conception was necessary for the salvation of the human race, given that the Son originates in his Mother. The sermon also contains accounts of miracles performed by the Virgin to reward those who celebrate her conception.[95] The first, which tells of how the abbot of Ramsay was saved from shipwreck by a mysterious messenger from heaven in return for a promise that

---

Immaculate Conception, Mirella Levi D'Ancona, *Iconography of the Immaculate Conception in the Middle Ages and the Early Renaissance* (New York: College Art Association of America and Art Bulletin, 1957). For the importance of Winchester as a centre of Marian devotion see Rachel Fulton, *From Judgment to Passion: Devotion to Christ and the Virgin Mary, 800-1200* (New York: Columbia University Press, 2002).

[93] See Corrado Maggioni, *Benedetto il frutto del tuo grembo: due millenni di pietà mariana* (Casale Monferrato: Portalupi, 2000), p. 83.

[94] See Edmund Bishop's chapter, 'On the Origins of the Feast of the Conception of the Blessed Virgin Mary', in his *Liturgica Historica: Papers on the Liturgy and Religious Life of the Western Church* (Oxford: The Clarendon Press, 1918), pp. 238-59, A. W. Burridge, 'L'Immaculée Conception dans la théologie de l'Angleterre médiévale', *Revue d'histoire ecclésiastique*, 32, (1936), 570-597, and Jean Fournée, 'Les orientations doctrinales de l'iconographie mariale à la fin de l'époque romane', *Centre international d'études romanes*, 1 (1971), 23-56 (pp. 31-25).

Nicholas Vincent, 'Henry III and the Blessed Virgin Mary', in *The Church and Mary* ed. by Robert N. Swanson, Studies in Church History, 39 (Woodenbridge: Boydell, 2004), pp 126-46 for the history of the feast in England. Also useful are John Janaro, 'Saint Anselm and the Development of the Doctrine of the Immaculate Conception, pp. 49-55, and Barbara Sella, 'Northern Italian Confraternities and the Immaculate Conception in the Fourteenth Century', *The Journal of Ecclesiastical History*, 49 (1998), 599-619 (p. 600).

[95] See Barbara Sella, 'Northern Italian Confraternities', p. 601.

he would have the Feast of the Conception celebrated annually, was circulating widely throughout Europe by the end of the twelfth century.[96]

An important step in removing the obstacle posed by the Augustinian conception of original sin was taken, though not intentionally, by Anselm of Canterbury († 1109). Although Anselm did not accept that Mary was conceived immaculately (indeed the issue had not yet become a subject of debate, at least in the terms in which it was later posited),[97] his theory of original sin opened up new possibilities.[98] His argument that it was the absence of the state of original justice, lost as a result of Adam's disobedience, which was transmitted when a new life was generated, resulting in a will that was easily corrupted, and not any inherent sinfulness transmitted in the male seed, meant that it was possible to overcome the obstacle posed by Mary's natural conception because it decoupled the issue of whether the procreative act was inherently lustful from the question of the means of transmission of original sin. If lust, or the lack of it, was no longer relevant to the processes of transmission of original sin, and it was instead a lack of original justice, then the argument that God could not have participated in an act that was sinful no longer stood and it was now possible to posit that in Mary's case the weakness of will resulting from the absence of original justice was filled by his grace.[99] Effectively, Anselm had offered the first viable alternative to Augustine's teaching on the transmission of original sin, which was of major importance for the question of the Immaculate Conception, though it took several centuries for the full implications of his theory to be worked out. But another statement on the Virgin had a more immediate effect in advancing the argument in favour of her sinlessness: 'It is fitting that that Virgin should shine with a degree of purity greater than which one cannot imagine, to whom God the Father was disposed to give his only Son.'[100] If God gave Mary the greatest possible purity in order for her to be a fitting mother to his Son, it is only one short step to argue that he could have preserved her free from all sin if he so wished (and everything that God willed came to be).[101]

---

[96] See Jean Fournée, 'Les orientations doctrinales', pp. 35-36.

[97] See *Cur Deus homo?*, II, 16, where he argues that she was sanctified in the womb and *De conceptu virginali*, 18, where he states that Mary was of a purity inferior only to God, but stops short of affirming her freedom from original sin (*PL* 158, 451A).

[98] See in particular *De conceptu virginali*, 3, *PL* 158 435B-436D.

[99] On the significance of Anselm's teaching on the transmission of original sin for the eventual formulation of the doctrine of the Immaculate Conception see John Janaro, 'Saint Anselm and the Development of the Doctrine of the Immaculate Conception'. Also see Sarah Jane Boss, *Empress and Handmaid: Nature and Gender in the Cult of the Virgin Mary* (London: Cassell, 1999), p. 130, Graef, *Doctrine and Devotion*, pp. 210-11, and Joseph S. Bruder, *The Mariology of St. Anselm of Canterbury* (Dayton: Mount St. John Press, 1939).

[100] *De conceptu virginali*, 18, *PL* 158, 451A.

[101] See *MLM*, for an assessment of the importance of Anselm's doctrine for the Immaculate Conception (pp. 127-28).

This is precisely what Eadmer of Canterbury († 1124), a disciple of Anselm, argues in what is the first major statement in the West in favour of the Immaculate Conception, the *Tractatus de conceptione b. Mariae Virginis*, which was long attributed to Anselm himself,[102] when he suggests that Mary was sanctified by a special grace at the beginning of her conception:

> If Jeremias was sanctified in his mother's womb as a future prophet of the people, and if John, who was to go before the Lord in the spirit and power of Elias, was full of the Holy Spirit in the very womb of his mother, who will dare to maintain that the singular conciliator of all time, the unique and most sweet cradle of the Son of the all-powerful God was deprived of the grace and illumination of the Holy Spirit in the very first instant of her conception? *Tractatus de conceptione b. Mariae Virginis* [103]

Using the example of a chestnut, which is surrounded by thorns without being touched by them, Eadmer counters the argument that original sin must have been transmitted to Mary because she was conceived naturally by human parents, by using the original example of the chestnut: 'God could prevent the body of Mary from being touched by the thorns of sin, in the same way that the chestnut, surrounded by the spikes of the covering remains immune to their sting.'[104] But why should we believe that this happened? Because if God could do something he would, and therefore he did: '*Potuit plane, et voluit; si igitur voluit, fecit.*'[105] Eadmer's recourse to the argument of convenience – that God could do if he so wished – had previously been used to great effect by the pseudo-Augustine in favour of the Assumption. A further strategy adopted by Eadmer is to appeal to what is known as the *sensus fidei*, the understanding of the faithful, arguing that the people are right in their instinctive desire to honour Mary. Throughout the history of the Church it has been accepted that practices and beliefs that are embraced by large numbers of the people may be of divine inspiration, although it requires the discernment of the Magisterium to determine whether this is in fact so. Such was the case in the popular acclamation of saints and such could still be said to hold true in the matter of Marian apparitions.

---

[102] See G. Geenen, 'Eadmer, le premier théologien de l'Immaculée Conception' in *Virgo Immaculata, De Immaculata Conceptione in epocha introductoria Scholasticae*, Acta Congressus Mariologici-Mariani, V (Rome: Academia Mariana Internationalis, 1955), pp. 90-136. For bibliography on Eadmer see *TMSM*, III, 114-15. See also Boss, *Empress and Handmaid*, p. 127.

[103] *PL* 159, 305A.

[104] *Tractatus*, quoted in Barnaba Hechich, 'La teologia dell'Immacolata Concezione in alcuni autori prescolastici, in *La "Scuola Francescana" e l'Immacolata Concezione*, pp. 141-58 (p. 151).

[105] *PL* 159, 305D.

However, for most theologians, it was still Augustine's teaching on original sin that overshadowed the entire debate.[106] Such is the case with Bernard of Clairvaux († 1153), powerful opponent of the likes of Eadmer, in his authoritative statement in a letter addressed to the canons of Lyons Cathedral, in which he objects strongly to their practice of celebrating of Mary's Conception, which, as we have seen, had spread in England and beyond.[107] He objects that the feast goes against both reason and tradition. How, he asks, basing his arguments almost entirely on Augustine, could it be right to celebrate an inherently sinful act, namely intercourse between Mary's parents?

> The Mother of the Lord, you say, ought greatly to be honoured. You say well, but the honour of a queen loves justice. The royal Virgin does not need false honour, since she is amply supplied with true titles to honour and badges of her dignity. Honour indeed the purity of her flesh, the sanctity of her life, wonder at her motherhood as a virgin, adore her Divine offspring. Extol the prodigy by which she brought into the world without pain the Son, whom she had conceived without concupiscence. Proclaim her to be reverenced by the angels, to have been desired by the nations, to have been known beforehand by Patriarchs and Prophets, chosen by God out of all women and raised above them all. Magnify her as the medium by whom grace was displayed, the instrument of salvation, the restorer of the ages; and finally extol her as having been exalted above the choirs of angels to the celestial realms. These things the Church sings concerning her, and has taught me to repeat the same things in her praise, and what I have learnt from the Church I both hold securely myself and teach to others; what I have not received from the Church I confess I should with great difficulty admit. […]
>
> With no less clearness have I learned in the Church to celebrate the birth of the Virgin, and from the Church undoubtedly to hold it to have been holy and joyful; holding most firmly with the Church, that she received in the womb that she should come into the world holy. And indeed I read concerning Jeremiah, that before he came forth from the womb he was sanctified, and I think no otherwise of John the Baptist, who, himself in the womb of his mother, felt the presence of his Lord in the womb (Luke 1. 41).
>
> The gift, therefore, which has certainly been conferred upon some, though few, mortals, cannot for a moment be supposed to have been denied to that so highly favoured Virgin, through whom the whole human race came forth into life. Beyond doubt the mother of the Lord also was holy before birth; nor is holy Church at all in error in accounting the day of her nativity holy, and celebrating it each year with solemn and thankful joy. I consider that the blessing of a fuller sanctification descended upon her, so as not only to sanctify her birth, but also to keep her life pure from all sin; which gift is believed to have been bestowed

---

[106] See Carlo Balić, 'The Medieval Controversy over the Immaculate Conception up to the Death of Scotus', in *The Dogma of the Immaculate Conception: History and Significance*, ed. by Edward O'Connor, pp. 161-212.

[107] See Marie-Bénédicte Dary, 'Saint Bernard et l'Immaculée Conception: La question liturgique', *Revue Marbillon*, (2002), 219-36.

upon none other born of women. This singular privilege of sanctity, to lead her life without any sin, entirely befitted the queen of virgins, who should bear the Destroyer of sin and death, who should obtain the gift of life and righteousness for all. Therefore, her birth was holy, since the abundant sanctity bestowed upon it made it holy even from the womb.

What addition can possibly be made to these honours? That her conception, also, they say, which preceded her honourable birth, should be honoured, since if the one had not first taken place, neither would the other, which is honoured. But what if some one else, following a similar train of reasoning, should assert that the honours of a festival ought to be given to each of her parents, then to her grand-parents, and then to their parents, and so on ad infinitum? Thus we should have festivals without number. Such a frequency of joys befits Heaven, not this state of exile. It is the happy lot of those who dwell there, not of strangers and pilgrims. But a writing is brought forward, given, as they say, by revelation from on high, as if any one would not be able to bring forward another writing in which the Virgin should seem to demand the same honours to her parents also, saying, according to the commandment of the Lord, Honour thy father and thy mother (Exodus 20. 12). I easily persuade myself not to be influenced by such writings, which are supported neither by reason nor by any certain authority. For how does the consequence follow that since the conception has preceded the birth, and the birth is holy, the conception should be considered holy also? Did it make the birth holy because it preceded it? Although the one came first that the other might be, yet not that it might be holy. From whence came that holiness to the conception which was to be transmitted to the birth which followed? Was it not rather because the conception preceded without holiness that it was needful for the being conceived to be sanctified, that a holy birth might then follow? Or shall we say that the birth which was later than the conception shared with it its holiness? It might be, indeed, that the sanctification which was worked in her when conceived passed over to the birth which followed; but it could not be possible that it should have a retrospective effect upon the conception which had preceded it.

Whence, then, was the holiness of that conception? Shall it be said that Mary was so prevented by grace that, being holy before being conceived, she was therefore conceived without sin; or that, being holy before being born, she has therefore communicated holiness to her birth? But in order to be holy it is necessary to exist, and a person does not exist before being conceived. Or perhaps, when her parents were united, holiness was mingled with the conception itself, so that she was at once conceived and sanctified. But this is not tenable in reason. For how can there be sanctity without the sanctifying Spirit, or the co-operation of the Holy Spirit with sin? Or how could there not be sin where concupiscence was not wanting? Unless, perhaps, some one will say that she was conceived by the Holy Spirit, and not by man, which would be a thing hitherto unheard of. I say, then, that the Holy Spirit came upon her, not within her, as the Angel declared: The Holy Spirit shall come upon thee (Luke 1. 35). And if it is permitted to say what the Church thinks, and the Church thinks that which is true, I say that she conceived by the Holy Spirit, but not that she was conceived by Him; that she was at once Mother and Virgin, but not that she was born of a virgin. Otherwise, where will be the prerogative of the Mother of the

Lord, to have united in her person the glory of maternity and that of virginity, if you give the same glory to her mother also? This is not to honour the Virgin, but to detract from her honour. If, therefore, before her conception she could not possibly be sanctified, since she did not exist, nor in the conception itself, because of the sin which inhered in it, it remains to be believed that she received sanctification when existing in the womb after conception, which, by excluding sin, made her birth holy, but not her conception.

Wherefore, although it has been given to some, though few, of the sons of men to be born with the gift of sanctity, yet to none has it been given to be conceived with it. So that to One alone should be reserved this privilege, to Him who should make all holy, and coming into the world, He alone, without sin should make an atonement for sinners. The Lord Jesus, then, alone was conceived by the Holy Ghost, because He alone was holy before He was conceived. He being excepted, all the children of Adam are in the same case as he who confessed of himself with great humility and truth, I was shapen in iniquity, and in sin hath my mother conceived me (Psalms 52. 6).

And as this is so, what ground can there be for a Festival of the Conception of the Virgin? On what principle, I say, is either a conception asserted to be holy which is not by the Holy Ghost, not to say that it is by sin, or a festival be established which is in no wise holy? Willingly the glorious Virgin will be without this honour, by which either a sin seems to be honoured or a sanctity supposed which is not a fact. And, besides, she will by no means be pleased by a presumptuous novelty against the custom of the Church, a novelty which is the mother of rashness, the sister of superstition, the daughter of levity. For if such a festival seemed advisable, the authority of the Apostolic See ought first to have been consulted, and the simplicity of inexperienced persons ought not to have been followed so thoughtlessly and precipitately. [...] But what I have said is in submission to the judgment of whosoever is wiser than myself; and especially I refer the whole of it, as of all matters of a similar kind, to the authority and decision of the See of Rome, and I am prepared to modify my opinion if in anything I think otherwise than that See. *Letter to the Canons of Lyons*[108]

Such a powerful and passionately argued condemnation of belief in the Immaculate Conception from a figure of the stature and authority of Bernard could not be easily ignored and undoubtedly was a major factor in the Church's reluctance for centuries to come to make any definitive statement on the matter.[109] However, with his closing caveat, that he would defer to the authority of the Church and modify his opinion if Rome decided against him, Bernard

---

[108] Quoted from *Some Letters of Saint Bernard of Clairvaux*, in CCEL <http://www.ccel.org/ccel/bernard/letters.lxviii.html> [accessed 30 January 2009].

[109] See Marielle Lamy, 'L'influence de saint Bernard sur la théologie mariale de la fin du Moyen Âge', in *La Vierge dans la tradition cistercienne, Bulletin de la société française d'études mariales*, 54e session de la S.F.E.M., Abbaye Notre-Dame d'Orval, 1998 (Paris: Médiaspaul, 1999), pp. 193-216, and *Respice stellam: Maria in San Bernardo e nella tradizione cistercense, Atti del convegno internazionale, Roma, Marianum, 21-24 October 1991*, ed. by Ignazio M. Calabuig (Rome: Marianum, 1993).

left an opening that would allow future churchmen to argue that he would have favoured the doctrine had he been in possession of the full facts.

Despite Bernard's categorical condemnation, opinion on the matter remained varied, though not many churchmen were prepared to openly oppose him,[110] the main exception being several English churchmen. Osbert of Clare († after 1158), an English Benedictine, sees no reason why God could not have preserved Mary's flesh free from stain when others such as Jeremiah and John the Baptist had been purified in the womb:

> If God sanctified the precursor John it must be held with all the more reason that she from whose flesh the Saint of saints would take flesh was sanctified at the conception itself. If the birth of the servant is celebrated, how much more reason is there for celebrating the conception of Mary, who, through the action of the Holy Spirit, was entirely filled with grace, enflamed with love, made white by the whiteness of virtue and also purified from bodily stain? What is unusual about it if Almighty God made holy that glorious material of the virginal body at its very conception? *Epistola de festo conceptionis*[111]

Interesting here, as in Eadmer, who obviously inspired this passage, is the shift away from a focus on the purportedly concupiscent actions of Mary's parents in actively conceiving Mary to an interest in how God may have acted in the passive conception of the Virgin, a trend that will continue in the coming centuries.

Outside of England, where the feast already enjoyed popular support, attitudes towards the Immaculate Conception tended to remain more rigid. Gerhoh of Reichersberg († 1169), for instance, an important figure in the German Church, affirms that Mary was born in sin, like the rest of the human race, though he believes that she was protected from actual sin by the Holy Spirit, and was entirely purified by him prior to conceiving the Word.[112]

Nicholas of St. Albans († after 1174), demonstrates once again the strong tradition of the English Church in the promotion of this doctrine. Nicholas believes that Mary was exempt from original sin and filled with the fullness of grace from the instant of the infusion of her soul into her body, since, he argues, it is reasonable to believe that her parents were granted the grace of generating her without concupiscence in view of her future role as Mother of God. He attempts, then, to find a way around the Augustinian insistence on the inherent concupiscence of the sexual act by turning to the apocryphal belief that

---

[110] For a list of the principal works on the subject, many anonymous, in the twelfth century, the majority of which are in favour of the Immaculate Conception, see Barnaba Hechich, 'La teologia dell'Immacolata Concezione', pp. 142-44.

[111] Translated from the passage quoted in Barnaba Hechich, 'La teologia dell'Immacolata Concezione', p. 149. See also Carlo Balić, 'The Medieval Controversy', p. 174.

[112] See *Commentarius in Psalmos*, 1, PL 193, 638D-639A.

an angel told Joachim and Anna that they would conceive a child, which would imply that the act of generating Mary was blessed by God:

> The parents of the Virgin were therefore endowed with an appropriate goodness in their habits and were therefore without doubt worthy of producing such a worthy child. They, at the command of the angel, made licit use of the concupiscent function, so that, without sinning, or sinning only in the mildest of manners, they generated the destroyer of sin. *De celebranda conceptione beatae Mariae contra beatum Bernardum* [113]

But such sloppy reasoning could not be expected to pass muster with more rigorous theologians. Peter Lombard's († 1160) assertion in his highly influential *Sententiae* that Mary was not free from original sin played a key role in what later Scholastics were to write in their commentaries on Lombard. He begins by citing Bernard as authority for the belief that Mary was not free from the stain of original sin and then proceeds in his argument in a manner typical of the Scholastics. The Virgin's flesh, which she gave to Christ, was subject to original sin. In the case of Christ, all traces were removed when the Word united itself to the flesh, though he chose to take on himself the physical consequences of original sin (thirst and hunger, illness, pain, death, etc.). In the case of the Virgin, however, original sin was not removed at the instant of animation. Rather, the Holy Spirit intervened subsequently to remove or neutralise the fomes, or residual effects,[114] of original sin, so that she would be free from any inclination towards sin:

> It can be said and it must be believed, according to the sentence agreed by the saints, that the flesh of Christ, prior to the conception, was subject to sin like the rest of the Virgin's flesh; but by an intervention of the Holy Spirit this flesh was so purified that, when it was united to the Word, it was immune from all contagion of sin, while, instead, the penal consequences [of sin] remained, not out of necessity, but at the will of he who assumed [flesh]. The Holy Spirit intervened with Mary too and completely purged her of sin and freed her from the fomes of sin; either because the Spirit eliminated the fomes in her, as some think, or because he so weakened and exhausted it that afterwards no occasion of sin could exist in her. *III Sententiae*, d. 3, 1 [115]

Richard of St. Victor († 1173) clearly rejects the Immaculate Conception though he does believe that she was purified at her conception and that her incorruptibility is an anticipation of what will hold true for all:

---

[113] *TMSM*, III, 466.

[114] A useful modern analogy for the notion of fomes might be that when one deletes a computer file residual traces nevertheless remain which can be retrieved by a forensic examination of the hard disc.

[115] *PL*, 192, 760.

> In the blessed Virgin Mary human nature received in a certain way the down payment, or firstfruits of its future incorruptibility, that is, the integrity of virginal incorruption. For, in this life one cannot live without corruption. If not, why is human nature not sown without corruption? In effect, the root of our corruptibility began to germinate at the moment of conception. But, in the case of blessed Mary it is rooted out where it seemed to have begun to germinate. [...] Only the Son of this Mother could sing a new song to the Lord: I was conceived without iniquity and my mother conceived me without sin (see Psalms 50. 7). *De Emmanuele, 1, 12*[116]

Odon of Morimond († 1161), like many of his fellows, cites Augustine as authority in asserting that the whole of the human race fell after Adam, Mary included. He affirms, however, that she was purified in the womb and was free from all actual sin.[117] Peter of Poitiers († 1205), disciple of Peter Lombard agrees with his master on the double purification of Mary: 'In the conception, not only was Christ's flesh purified, but also the rest of the Virgin's flesh, in which the fomes of sin was completely extinguished so that henceforth she could no longer sin.'[118] In Spain, his near contemporary, Martin of León († 1203), is emphatic in his insistence that Mary was free from all trace of sin, though he does not specify how or when such a purification came about:

> The most blessed Virgin Mary, defined by the Holy Spirit as all beautiful and without stain, is also declared such by the holy Fathers, something which is not to be believed of any other saint. Opportunely therefore did the Holy Spirit announce in advance that she was without stain because by anticipating her, he purified her totally of sin, freed her from the concupiscence of sin, and cleansed her of every illicit thought, to the point where there was no longer any occasion of sin for her. *In nativitate sanctae Mariae*[119]

Pope Innocent III († 1216) explicitly rejects the Immaculate Conception, opting for the double purification of Mary, firstly in the womb, when her soul was purified from original sin, and then immediately prior to the conception of Christ, when her flesh was freed from the fomes.[120] The position of a later Pope, Honorius III († 1227) is almost identical.[121]

Robert Grosseteste († 1253) is an exception to the rule, showing once again the important role that the English played in promoting Mary's cause. He writes that Mary may have been sanctified at the instant of her conception, though he hedges his bets by saying that the sanctification may have taken place later:

---

[116] *PL* 196, 619D-620A.
[117] *Homily on John 19. 25-27*, *TMSM*, III, 303.
[118] *Sententiae*, 1, 4, 7 *PL* 211, 1165B.
[119] *PL* 209, 25C.
[120] *Sermo 12, In solemnitate purificationis*, *PL* 217, 506B-507C.
[121] See *TMSM*, IV, 119 and *Sermon for the Feast of the Purification*, *TMSM*, IV, 122.

> Either she truly had original sin for a certain time after the infusion of her
> rational soul, but was nevertheless purified before her birth from the womb of
> her mother by an intervention of the Holy Spirit, or she was cleansed and
> sanctified in the very infusion of her rational soul. In this way, there would have
> been a purification, not from a sin which had at one time been present in her,
> but from one which would have been in her if she had not been sanctified in the
> very infusion of her rational soul. *Tota pulchra es* [122]

With the Scholastics, the question of Mary's freedom from sin became more
clearly defined, both in terms of the nature of original sin and its effects, and
the processes involved in the infusion of the rational soul into the body.
Following Aristotle, they taught that each human person upon conception
receives first a nutritive and then a sensitive soul before the rational soul is
infused. Mary could not have been sanctified before the infusion of her rational
soul since it alone is receptive of grace. But, following the objections of earlier
commentators, they argued that to accept that Mary was preserved from
original sin at the instant of the infusion of her rational soul would be to deny
that Christ was the universal redeemer. It is on these grounds that all three of
the major Scholastic theologians of the thirteenth century, Albert the Great,
Bonaventure and Aquinas reject the Immaculate Conception. [123]

Bonaventure († 1274) deals with the question of the Immaculate Conception
at some length in the third book of his *Commentary of the Sentences*. [124] He begins
by asking if the Virgin's flesh was sanctified prior to animation. Citing Bernard's
Letter to the Canons he rejects the possibility, primarily on the basis that it lacked
'existence' (*esse*): it is to the rational soul that the gift of grace is given which in
turn operates on the flesh, and therefore the flesh alone could not have been
the subject of sanctification. Nor could she have been given sanctified flesh by
her parents since that flesh was transmitted to her through 'libidinous coitus'.
Only the Virgin herself conceived in a manner that was entirely free from sin.
However, although he expresses reservations about the celebration of the
Virgin's conception, he avoids an outright condemnation of the practice:

> I believe, however, and I trust, concerning the glorious Virgin, that if someone
> celebrates this feast, not for novelty's sake, but out of devotion to the Virgin,
> without believing anything contrary to what can be elicited from Holy Scripture,
> the blessed Virgin accepts this devotion; and if there is something reprehensible,
> I hope that it will be excused by the just Judge. *Sent. III, d. iii, a.1, q. 1*

---

[122] *TMSM*, IV, 237-38.

[123] See Carlo Balić, 'The Medieval Controversy', pp 189-90.

[124] See *Sent.* III, d. iii, a. 1 and 2. For a detailed analysis of Bonaventure's treatment of
the Immaculate Conception see George H. Tavard, *The Forthbringer of God: St. Bonaventure
on the Virgin Mary* (Chicago: Franciscan Herald Press, 1989), pp. 14-28, from which this
and subsequent quotations are taken, unless otherwise indicated.

Such a hesitant attitude is, at least in part, a reflection of growing observance of the feast since Bernard's time. Question 2 asks 'whether the blessed Virgin's soul was sanctified before contracting original sin.' The lengthy exposition that follows covers all the key questions concerning the Immaculate Conception. On the positive side Bonaventure mentions the positions taken by previous churchmen such as Anselm, Augustine and John of Damascus regarding Mary's freedom from sin. He presents the argument that Mary was freed from original sin at the instant of the infusion of her soul, with sympathy and clarity: 'others were raised after falling; the Virgin was, as it were, supported in the fall itself so that she would not tumble.' Among the counter-arguments that he cites, one of the most telling concerns the Virgin's need of Redemption. If she had no original sin, then either she did not deserve to die (since death was a consequence of original sin), or her death, like her Son's, was sacrificial in nature and thus contributed in some way to salvation, which would contradict the doctrine of Christ's universal Redemption. It is primarily on this basis that he rejects the arguments in favour:

> Since it pertains to Christ's surpassing dignity that he is the Redeemer and Saviour of all, and that he opened the door to all, and that he alone died for all, the Blessed Virgin is not to be excluded from this universality, lest, while the Mother's excellence was increased, the glory of the Son should be lessened. *Sent. III, d. iii, a.1, q. 2*

Thus, Mary's many sufferings in this life were not freely chosen for the redemption of others but were contracted as a result of original sin. Moreover, he points out, returning to the arguments of Question 1, since the existence (*esse*) of the soul, which is to be united to the body, precedes its good existence (*bene esse*), which is to receive divine grace, it is illogical to argue that that Virgin could have been rendered immune to original sin through grace before her ensoulment. Rather, her sanctification took place after the natural being of her soul had been infected with original sin.

He divides Mary's purification into two stages, the first of which most likely took place immediately after the infusion of her soul, enabling her to avoid all sin but leaving the fomes, and the second at the Annunciation, when she was so purified that the inclination towards sin became impossible for her – 'a grace of confirmation in the good'.[125] He makes a similar argument in less technical terms in one of his sermons:

> The glorious Virgin was purified in a double way, namely, internally according to truth, and externally according to what she prefigured; so she needed the grace of baptism or its equivalent because she was conceived in the usual way and so

---

[125] *Sent.* III, d. iii, a. 2. One finds the same belief repeated by his fellow Franciscan, Ubertino of Casale, some years later. (*Arbor Vitae*, I, 8).

contracted original sin; but she did not need a grace of penance because she never committed actual sin. *First Sermon on the Purification of the Blessed Virgin Mary*[126]

Despite Bonaventure's rejection of the Immaculate Conception, he presided over the Chapter of the Franciscans held at Pisa in 1263 which decided to make the celebration of the feast of Mary's conception obligatory for the whole order,[127] a momentous decision which played no small role in the subsequent espousal of the Immaculist cause by many leading members of the order. The explanation for Bonaventure's support is to be found, as we have seen, in his own writings.

Albert the Great's († 1280) principal objection to the Immaculate Conception is the same as that of his fellows, namely that it would contradict Christ's universal Redemption.[128] He also cites Bernard's objections to the feast as grounds for rejecting the doctrine: 'We say that the Blessed Virgin was not sanctified before animation, and the affirmation contrary to this is the heresy condemned by St. Bernard in his epistle to the canons of Lyons.'[129] Like Peter Lombard and Bonaventure he opts for a double purification, the first taking place in the womb which left the fomes of original sin, and the second at the Annunciation.[130] He believes that Mary was sanctified in the womb, most likely immediately after the infusion of her soul: 'She was sanctified in the womb, but on what day and at what hour can be known by no man if not by revelation. It is however more than likely that this happened immediately after the infusion of her soul, rather than being put off until later.'[131] He goes on to discuss the question of the fomes:

> It is necessary to say without prejudice that the *habitus* of the fomes can be considered in two aspects: in its force, that is to say, in the degree to which it inclines towards mortal or venial sin *per se*, or otherwise as a disposition. A habit may pass to action or otherwise may not actualise itself because of habits that are opposed to it, even if these latter are not to be found in the same proximate subject but are found in the same common subject. Moreover, there is a certain disposition which remains even after the habit [has been removed], a disposition that is rather fragile and easily purified. Nevertheless it is sometimes not cancelled out quickly because it is rooted in the subject, that is, deeply rooted, even though it does not influence much.

---

[126] In *Sermons on the Blessed Virgin Mary*, trans. by Campion Murray, in *Franciscan Friars: Province of the Holy Spirit* <http://www.franciscans.org.au> [accessed 20 September 2006]. See also *Second Sermon on the Purification*, where he writes that 'she was sanctified in the womb of the mother immediately after the infusion of her soul and its union with her body and this for our benefit'.

[127] See Corrado Maggioni, *Benedetto il frutto*, p. 85.

[128] *Sent.* III, d. iii, a. 4.

[129] *Sent* III, d. iii, a. 4.

[130] See *Sent.* III, d. iii. a. 6.

[131] *Sent. III* d. iii, a. 5.

Therefore we can say without prejudice that the sanctification of the Virgin in itself eliminated the force that inclines towards mortal and venial sin, but the habit and offence of original sin – according to what the Master [Peter Lombard] and the Damascene [John of Damascus] say regarding this – remained as a non-inclining habit and disposition. In Jeremiah and John [the Baptist] they remained as an inclination towards venial sin, but *per se* not as an inclination towards mortal sin. *In III Sententiae, dist. iii, a. 6*

[…]

Grace does not confirm [in the good] those to whom it is given, but it is also true that in the blessed Virgin it removed the habit which inclines towards evil so that she, in the matter of habit, did not have an inclining habit. *In III Sententiae, dist. iii, a. 9*

Aquinas († 1274) believes that Mary never committed a sin but puts this down to a sanctification in the womb rather than an immaculate conception.[132] He addresses the negative comments of some of the early Greek Fathers concerning the Virgin's behaviour at Cana and Calvary, dismissing Chrysostom's attribution of vainglory to her at Cana as excessive, and rejecting the possibility that she experienced a loss of faith at the Crucifixion arguing instead that she merely wondered at that the enormity of the event.[133] He rejects the Immaculate Conception largely on the same grounds as his fellow Scholastics, although his views on the manner in which original sin is transmitted are more subtle. He believes that original sin is transmitted during intercourse, but not because the sexual act is inherently sinful, which is Augustine's position, but because the human nature which is transmitted through the act is itself fallen. Indeed, he argues, even if God were to intervene to prevent a man from experiencing lust during intercourse, this would not prevent original sin from being transmitted.[134] As with Anselm, this position leaves open the possibility that God could have intervened to preserve the Virgin from sin, since there was nothing inherently sinful in the act that would have prevented him from doing so. Aquinas, however, puts forward several other arguments which he believes militate against acceptance of the Immaculate Conception, his fundamental objection being that if Mary was not marked by original sin then she was not in need of salvation, which would contradict one of the most basic tenets of the faith, namely that Christ was the saviour of all, without exception.[135] He accepts the belief that Mary was

---

[132] For a recent comprehensive treatment of Aquinas' teaching on the Immaculate Conception see Boguslaw Kochaniewicz, L'Immacolata Concezione e la dottrina di San Tommaso d'Aquino', in *La "Scuola Francescana" e l'Immacolata Concezione*, pp. 87-139.

[133] *ST*, III, q. 27, a. 4.

[134] *ST* I-II, q. 81, a. 1 and q. 82, a. 4.

[135] *ST* III, q. 27. a. 2.

sanctified in the womb, pointing out that a similar privilege was granted to Jeremias and John the Baptist, although he, like Albert, makes it clear that her sanctification was of a different order, citing Luke 1. 28 –'Hail, full of grace' – to argue that the Virgin received greater grace than any other creature.[136] On the basis of (pseudo) Augustine's assertion that just because Scripture does not say anything about the Virgin's Assumption this is not sufficient reason to disbelieve it, he argues that it is reasonable to assume that Mary received a special purification in the womb in view of her future role as Mother of the Word. He goes on to dismiss the possibility that she could have been purified prior to animation since she did not yet have a rational soul.[137] Aquinas then turns to the question of the fomes. He maintains that the fomes remained in the Virgin prior to the Annunciation and were only suppressed by a singular infusion of grace, which prevented her from sinning.[138] His response is worth quoting in full since it usefully summarises the various positions taken by his predecessors and also lays out the principal objections to the possibility of an Immaculate Conception with great clarity:

> I answer that, on this point there are various opinions. For some have held that the fomes was entirely taken away in that sanctification whereby the Blessed Virgin was sanctified in the womb. Others say that it remained as far as it causes a difficulty in doing good, but was taken away as far as it causes a proneness to evil. Others again, that it was taken away as to the personal corruption, by which it makes us quick to do evil and slow to do good: but that it remained as to the corruption of nature, inasmuch as it is the cause of transmitting original sin to the offspring. Lastly, others say that, in her first sanctification, the fomes remained essentially, but was fettered; and that, when she conceived the Son of God, it was entirely taken away. In order to understand the question at issue, it must be observed that the fomes is nothing but a certain inordinate, but habitual, concupiscence of the sensitive appetite, for actual concupiscence is a sinful motion. Now sensual concupiscence is said to be inordinate, in so far as it rebels against reason; and this it does by inclining to evil, or hindering from good. Consequently it is essential to the fomes to incline to evil, or hinder from good. Wherefore to say that the fomes was in the Blessed Virgin without an inclination to evil, is to combine two contradictory statements.
>
> In like manner it seems to imply a contradiction to say that the fomes remained as to the corruption of nature, but not as to the personal corruption. For, according to Augustine (*De Nup. Et Concup. i.*), it is lust that transmits original sin to the offspring. Now lust implies inordinate concupiscence, not

---

[136] See *ST* III, 27 where he deals with the question of Mary's sanctification.

[137] *ST* III, q. 27, a. 1 and a. 2 respectively.

[138] He restates this position in his 'Exposition on the Angel's Greeting', trans. by Joseph B. Collins, in *The Catechetical Instructions of St. Thomas* (New York: Wagner, 1939; repr. 2000), pp. 173-80, in *EWTN* <http://www.ewtn.com/library/SOURCES/TA-CAT-5.TXT> [accessed 21 December 2006].

entirely subject to reason: and therefore, if the fomes were entirely taken away as to personal corruption, it could not remain as to the corruption of nature.

It remains, therefore, for us to say, either that the fomes was entirely taken away from her by her first sanctification or that it was fettered. Now that the fomes was entirely taken away, might be understood in this way, that, by the abundance of grace bestowed on the Blessed Virgin, such a disposition of the soul's powers was granted to her, that the lower powers were never moved without the command of her reason: just as we have stated to have been the case with Christ (15, 2), who certainly did not have the fomes of sin; as also was the case with Adam, before he sinned, by reason of original justice: so that, in this respect, the grace of sanctification in the Virgin had the force of original justice. And although this appears to be part of the dignity of the Virgin Mother, yet it is somewhat derogatory to the dignity of Christ, without whose power no one had been freed from the first sentence of condemnation. And though, through faith in Christ, some were freed from that condemnation, according to the spirit, before Christ's Incarnation, yet it does not seem fitting that any one should be freed from that condemnation, according to the flesh, except after His Incarnation, for it was then that immunity from condemnation was first to appear. Consequently, just as before the immortality of the flesh of Christ rising again, none obtained immortality of the flesh, so it seems unfitting to say that before Christ appeared in sinless flesh, His Virgin Mother's or anyone else's flesh should be without the fomes, which is called "the law of the flesh" or "of the members" (Romans 7:23-25).

Therefore it seems better to say that by the sanctification in the womb, the Virgin was not freed from the fomes in its essence, but that it remained fettered: not indeed by an act of her reason, as in holy men, since she had not the use of reason from the very first moment of her existence in her mother's womb, for this was the singular privilege of Christ: but by reason of the abundant grace bestowed on her in her sanctification, and still more perfectly by Divine Providence preserving her sensitive soul, in a singular manner, from any inordinate movement. Afterwards, however, at the conception of Christ's flesh, in which for the first time immunity from sin was to be conspicuous, it is to be believed that entire freedom from the fomes redounded from the Child to the Mother. *ST III, q. 27, a. 3*[139]

Therefore, according to Aquinas, as a result of her initial purification in the womb, Mary was not entirely freed of the inclination towards sin, but these inclinations were fettered to such an extent by the abundance of grace that she received that she never committed a sin, a question that he deals with at greater length in the next article. A second purification took place at the moment of Christ's conception, freeing her of all rebellion of her lower (sensible) nature. The reason that this could not have happened at an earlier stage is that it is

---

[139] *Summa Theologica*, trans. by the Fathers of the English Dominican Province, 2nd edn, rev., 22 vols (London: Burns Oates and Washbourne, 1920), in *The Catholic Encyclopedia, New Advent* <http://www.newadvent.org/summa/4027.htm#article3> [accessed 8 August 2008].

through the power of the Incarnate Christ that all trace of original sin is wiped out. For Aquinas, who believed that the male seed was the active principle in conception, with the mother only passively providing the material, Mary played no active role in the conception of Christ other than the preparation of material: 'The Blessed Virgin did not operate in any active way, being limited to the provision of the material. Nevertheless, she played an active part prior to conceiving, in the preparation of a material adapted to the conception.'[140] It was through the superabundance of grace that she received, which overflowed from her soul into her body, that this preparation took place:

> The Blessed Virgin was full of grace in the overflowing effect of this grace upon her flesh or body. For while it is a great thing in the Saints that the abundance of grace sanctified their souls, yet, moreover, the soul of the holy Virgin was so filled with grace that from her soul grace poured into her flesh from which was conceived the Son of God. *Expositio super salutatione angelica*[141]

Aquinas also comes up with a justification for the toleration of the Feast of the Virgin's Conception by the Roman Church, arguing that the feast really celebrates her sanctification, but since the date of this event is not known, the event is celebrated on her conception.[142]

Conrad of Saxony († 1279), whose *Speculum* was for a long time attributed to Bonaventure, denies that the fomes of original sin remained in Mary. Like Albert he compares her to Jeremiah and John the Baptist:

> First consider, my dearest [reader], the coming forth of Mary in a birth without sin. She can be that vessel of which Proverbs says: 'Take away the rust from silver, and there shall come forth a most pure vessel' (25. 4). The rust was removed from the silver when Mary was purified of original sin in the womb, from which she most certainly came forth as a most pure vessel. Here we have to distinguish between a pure vessel, a purer vessel and a most pure vessel. Anyone who came out of the womb sanctified but having kept in himself the fomes of both mortal and venial sin was a pure vessel, as some say happened to Jeremiah. Anyone who came out of the womb so sanctified that the fomes which causes one to commit mortal sin was extinguished is purer; but the [fomes] of venial sin remain, as happened in the case of John the Baptist […]. Instead the blessed Virgin was a most pure vessel from her birth, since she emerged from the womb so sanctified that in her – so it is believed – no fomes of either venial or mortal sin remained. *Speculum Beatae Mariae Virginis, 13*[143]

---

[140] *ST*, III, q. 32, a. 4.

[141] Trans. by Joseph B. Collins.

[142] *ST*, III, q. 27, a. 2.

[143] *TMSM*, IV, 320, and see the translation by Campion Murrary, *The Angel's Greeting*, in *Franciscan Friars Province of the Holy Spirit* <http://www.franciscans.org.au> [accessed 3 June 2007].

William of Ware (†c. 1305) examines three possibilities concerning Mary's freedom from sin. The first is Henry of Ghent's theory that she was purified at the moment of conception, the second is that she was conceived in original sin and cleansed later, the third, that she did not contract original sin at all. It is the third hypothesis that he sets out to prove. Unlike Scotus, Ware accepts Augustine's teaching on the transmission of sin through the male seed, but he argues that it could have been purified at the moment of insemination. Thus Mary was conceived purified from the impure. It was suitable that God should give Mary the highest possible purity since he was to be born of her, so since he could create a sinless being, he did, the principle of *'potuit decuit, ergo fecit'* already used by Eadmer of Canterbury. Answering the objection that Mary's freedom from sin would mean she did not require the Redemption he says that she required it all the more, not because there was any sin that was in her, but because of what would have been in her, if her Son had not preserved her, an idea akin to Scotus' proposition. He notes that Augustine applies this principle in speaking of Mary Magdalene, saying that there are two kinds of debts – those that are contracted and paid, and those that are not contracted, but could have been.[144]

However, it was John Duns Scotus († 1308) who answered, in typical Scholastic fashion, each of the objections that had been raised by theologians across the centuries, and found a way to get around the Augustinian doctrine on original sin.[145] He begins by rejecting Augustine's teaching on the biological transmission of original sin in favour of Anselm's position that sin resides in the will, not the seed. Original sin is not passed on from infected body to infected soul upon the soul's creation and infusion, but rather is a result of a privation of grace in the soul at the moment of conception due to the sin of Adam and Eve. But, he says, even if sin is transmitted through the seed, there is no reason why God could not have purified Mary at the instant of her conception through an infusion of grace. Grace, he states, is equal in value to original justice, so those who possess grace do not have original sin. Mary, like all the children of Adam, would certainly have lacked original justice at the instant of her conception were it not that in that same instant God sanctified her, so that original sin never touched her. In answer to the

---

[144] See *Questiones disputatae de Immaculata Conceptione B M V*, *TMSM*, IV, 438-48.

[145] *III Sent.* d. 3, q. 1, in *Opus Oxoniense*, XIV, ed. by Vivès, quoted in full in *TMSM*, IV, 450-59. See John Duns Scotus, *Four Questions on Mary*, trans. by Allan Wolter (Santa Barbara: Old Mission, 1988), and Allan Wolter and Blane O'Neill, *John Duns Scotus: Mary's Architect* (Quincy, Ill.: Franciscan Press, 1993), especially pp. 54-84, which provide a summary of the arguments put forward by Scotus as well as the counter-arguments. See also the three articles in *La "Scuola Francescana" e l'Immacolata Concezione*, Barnaba Hechich, 'Il beato Giovanni Duns Scotus: contest storico-teologico', pp. 159-91, Alfonso Pompei, 'Giovanni Duns Scoto e la dottrina sull'immacolata concezione', pp. 193-217, and Stefano M. Cecchin, 'Giovanni Duns Scotus, dottore dell'Immacolata Concezione: alcune questioni', pp. 219-71. Other important studies are to be found in *La dottrina mariologica di Giovanni Duns Scoto*, ed. by Roberto Zavalloni e Eliodoro Mariani (Rome: Antonianum, 1987).

argument that because Mary had suffered from physical ailments and experienced hunger and the like, her body must have been subject to the effects of original sin, he points out that the corruption of the flesh remains for all even after baptism has removed original sin, and adds that God permitted her to undergo physical suffering so that she might gain merit for herself and others. His most original argument was in answer to the objection, raised by Augustine, Thomas and others, that if Mary had not been marked by original sin, she would not have needed redemption, which would directly contradict the fact that Christ was the Redeemer of all. Scotus answers that Jesus did indeed save all, and most especially his Mother, who alone was granted perfect salvation. If he had not saved at least one person perfectly, he would not be the perfect Redeemer. Indeed, she was especially in need of the merits of the Passion, which were anticipated in her case (*praeredemptio*), so that she would never be inhabited by sin, which would have closed off the means of Redemption. This is essentially a closed 'chicken-before-the-egg' argument: if Mary had not been preserved from original sin there could have been no redemption and she could not have been preserved if there had been no redemption. As to how God could have anticipated the redemption in Mary's case, he could do anything and therefore this is what he did.

All the pieces of the theological puzzle were now available, but by no means was the question settled. It would take many centuries of heated debate and sometimes bitter enmities before a consensus emerged. From the time of Scotus onwards the Franciscans almost universally supported the Immaculist cause. Among the more notable figures were Raymond Lull († 1315), who coined the term 'immaculate conception' and is considered the initiator of the Immaculist movement,[146] Pietro Aureoli († 1322), who like Lull, taught at Paris, and Francis of Mayronis († c. 1328). The Dominicans, however, having vowed to adhere to the teaching of Aquinas at the General Chapter of Metz (1313), remained implacably opposed to the doctrine. Although the doctrine came to be generally accepted by the vast majority of the faithful and by most theologians in the coming centuries, the Church did not finally pronounce on the question until the papal bull of Pius IX in 1854 declared the infallible truth of the Immaculate Conception:

> We declare, pronounce and define that the doctrine which holds that the Blessed Virgin Mary, at the first instant of her conception, by a singular privilege and grace of the Omnipotent God, in virtue of the merits of Jesus Christ, the Saviour of mankind, was preserved immaculate from all stain of original sin, has

---

[146] See *TMSM*, IV, 476. See also, Josep Perrarnau i Espelt, 'Raimondo Lullo e la sua teologia sull'immacolata concezione', in *La "Scuola Francescana" e l'Immacolata Concezione*, pp. 273-301, and Fernando Domínguez Reboiras, 'El discurso luliano sobre María', in *Gli studi di mariologia medievale: bilancio storico*, pp. 277-303.

been revealed by God, and therefore should firmly and constantly be believed by all the faithful. *Ineffabilis Deus*[147]

---

[147] Quoted by René Laurentin in 'The Role of the Papal Magisterium in the Development of the Dogma of the Immaculate Conception', trans. by Charles Sheedy and Edward Shea, in *The Dogma of the Immaculate Conception* ed. by Edward O'Connor, pp. 281-307 (p. 312).

ABBREVIATIONS, EDITIONS, TRANSLATIONS

The following abbreviations are used throughout the text:

AH	Dreves, Guido M., Clemens Blume and Henry M. Bannister, eds., *Analecta hymnica medii aevi*, 55 vols (Leipzig: Reisland, 1886-1922; repr. Frankfurt am Main: Minerva, 1961)
EPH	Daley, Brian E., *On the Dormition of Mary: Early Patristic Homilies* (Crestwood, N. Y.: St. Vladimir's, 1998)
Maria	du Manoir, Hubert, ed, *Maria: Études sur la Sainte Vierge*, 8 vols (Paris: Beauchesne, 1949-71)
MF	Gambero, Luigi, *Mary and the Fathers of the Church: The Blessed Virgin Mary in Patristic Thought* (San Francisco: Ignatius Press, 1999)
MLM	Gambero, Luigi, *Maria nel pensiero dei teologi latini medievali* (Milan: San Paolo, 2000)
PG	Migne, Jacques-Paul, ed, *Patrologiae cursus completus, seu bibliotheca universalis, integra, uniformis, commoda, oeconomica, omnium SS. Patrum, doctorum scriptorumque ecclesiasticorum*, Series Graeca, 165 vols (Paris: Migne, 1857-66)
PL	Migne, Jacques-Paul, ed, *Patrologiae cursus completus, seu bibliotheca universalis, integra, uniformis, commoda, oeconomica, omnium SS. Patrum, doctorum scriptorumque ecclesiasticorum qui ab aevo apostolico ad usque Innocentii III tempora floruerunt*, Series Latina, 221 vols (Paris: Migne, 1844-64)
SBS	Bernard of Clairvuax, Saint, *St. Bernard's Sermons on the Blessed Virgin Mary*, trans. by a priest of Mount Melleray Abbey (Devon: Augustine Publishing Company, 1984)
TMPM	Gharib, Georges, and others, eds., *Testi mariani del primo millennio*, 4 vols, (Rome: Città Nuova, 1988–1991)
TMSM	Amato, Angelo and others, eds., *Testi mariani del secondo millennio*, 8 vols (Rome: Città Nuova, 1996–)

Biblical texts are quoted from *The Holy Bible*, translated from the Latin Vulgate, Douay Rheims version (New York: Benziger, 1941). Translations of texts from the *PG*, the *PL*, *TMPM* and *TMSM* are my own unless otherwise stated.

BIBLIOGRAPHY

Albert the Great, Saint, *Alberti Magni Opera Omnia*, ed. by Auguste and Emile Borgnet, 38 vols (Paris: Vivès, 1890-99)

Aldama, José Antonio, 'La fiesta de la Concepción de Maria', *Estudios eclesiásticos*, 36 (1961), 427-49

Alexiou, Margaret, 'The Lament of the Virgin in Byzantine Literature and Modern Greek Folk-Song', *Byzantine and Modern Greek Studies*, 1 (1975), 111-40

————, *Ritual, Religion, and Art: The Ritual Lament in Greek Tradition*, 2nd edn, rev. by Dimitrios Yatromanolakis and Panagiotis Roilos (Totowa: Rowman and Littlefield, 2002)

Alighieri, Dante, *Paradiso*, trans. by John Sinclair, with modifications by Lauren Seem and Robert Hollander (London: Bodley Head, 1948), <http://etcweb.princeton.edu/dante/pdp/index.html> [accessed 5 April, 2006]

————, *La Commedia secondo l'antica vulgata*, ed. by Giorgio Petrocchi, 4 vols (Milan: Mondadori, 1966-67; repr. Florence: Le Lettere, 1994)

Alvarez Campos, Sergius, *Corpus marianum patristicum*, 8 vols (Ediciones Aldecoa, Burgos, 1970-1985)

Amadeus of Lausanne, *Homilies in Praise of Blessed Mary*. Trans. by Grace Perigo, Intro. by M. Chrysogonus Waddell (Kalamazoo: Cistercian, 1979)

Amata, Biagio, 'La "schiavitù mariana" di Idlefonso di Toledo', *Theotokos*, 14 (2006), 57-72

————, 'Intuizioni ambrosiane sulla centralità mediatrice di Maria nel "mysterium salutis"', *Marianum*, 59 (1997), 139-57

————, 'Giovanni 19, 26-27 come prova scritturistica della perpetua verginità di Maria: origine e sviluppo di questa esegesi', in *Arcidiocesi di Capua, XVI Centenario del Concilio di Capua 392-1992*, Atti del Convegno Internazionale di studi Mariologici, Capua 19-24 Maggio, 1992 (Roma, Torre del Greco: Istituto Superiore di Scienze Religiose Capua e Pontificia Facoltà Teologica Marianum, 1993), pp. 107-172

Amato, Angelo and others, eds., *Testi mariani del secondo millennio*, 8 vols (Rome: Città Nuova, 1996-)

Amato, Angelo, 'Il concepimento verginale di Gesù: introduzione a una "quaestio disputata', *Theotokos* 3, (1995), 89-103

Andaloro, Maria, 'I mosaici dell'Oratorio di Giovanni VII', in *Fragmenta picta: affreschi e mosaici staccati del medioevo romano*, ed. by Maria Andaloro and others (Rome: Argos, 1989), pp. 169-77

André, M., *Ombre et splendeur: La foi de la Vierge Mère d'après les écrits de Saint Bernard* (Nicolet, Québec: Centre Marial Canadien, 1954)

Angelidi, Christine, and Titos Papamastorakis, 'Picturing the Spiritual Protector: from Bacharnitissa to Hodegetria', in *Images of the Mother of God: Perceptions of the Theotokos in Byzantium*, ed. by Maria Vassilaki (Aldershot: Ashgate, 2005), pp. 209-17

————, *Pulcheria: la castità al potere (399-455)* (Milan: Jaca, 1998)

Angold, Michael, *Byzantium: The Bridge from Antiquity to the Middle Ages* (New York: St.
        Martin's Press, 2001)

Anselm of Canterbury, Saint, *S. Anselmi Cantuariensis Archiepiscopi Opera Omnia*, ed. by
        Francis S. Schmitt, 6 vols (Edinburgh: Nelson 1946-61; repr.
        Stuttgart: Fromann, 1968)

————, *The Prayers and Meditations of Saint Anselm with the Proslogion*, trans. by
        Benedicta Ward (Harmondsworth: Penguin, 1973)

Anthony of Padua, Saint, *The Sermons of St Antony: The Marian Sermons*, trans. by Stephen
        Spilsbury, in *The Franciscan Archive* <http://www.franciscan-
        archive.org/antonius/opera/ant-hd00.html> [accessed 28 March
        2006]

Apollonio, Mario, 'Il canto XXXIII del "Paradiso", in *Dante nella critica d'oggi: risultati e
        prospettive*, ed. by Umberto Bosco (Florence: Le Monnier, 1965), pp.
        662-673

————, *Jacopone da Todi e la poetica delle confraternite religiose nella cultura preumanistica:
        appunti delle lezioni di letteratura italiana* (Milan: Vita e pensiero, 1946)

Aquinas, Thomas, Saint, *Exposition on the Angel's Greeting*, trans. by Joseph B. Collins, in
        The Catechetical Instructions of St. Thomas (New York: Wagner, 1939;
        repr. 2000), pp. 173-80, in *EWTN*,
        <http://www.ewtn.com/library/SOURCES/> [accessed 20 June,
        2009]

————, *Summa Theologica*, ed. and trans. by Fathers of the English Dominican
        Province, 3 vols (New York: Benzinger, 1947-48)

Aste, Mario, 'Energy of Transport and Ectasy in the Vernacular Characters of Mary's
        Cult in Jacopone's Poetry', in *Maria Vergine nella letteratura italiana* ed.
        by Florinda Iannace (Stony Brook, New York: Forum Italicum,
        2000), pp. 27-37

Atanassova, Antonia, 'Did Cyril of Alexandria Invent Mariology?', in *The Origins of the
        Cult of the Virgin Mary*, ed. by Chris Maunder (London: Burns & Oats,
        2008), pp. 105-25

Atkinson, Clarissa W., *The Oldest Vocation: Christian Motherhood in the Middle Ages* (Ithica:
        Cornell University Press, 1991)

Aubineau, Michel, *Les homélies festales d'Hésychius de Jérusalem*, Subsidia Hagiographica, 59
        (Brussels: Société des Bollandistes, 1978)

————, 'Les écrits de S. Athanase sur la virginité', *Revue d'Ascétique et Mystique*, 31
        (1955), 140-71

Auerbach, Erich, 'Figura', *Archivum Romanicum*, 17 (1938), 320-341

————, 'Typological Symbolism in Medieval Literature', *Yale French Studies*, 9 (1952),
        3-10

————, 'Dante's Prayer to the Virgin and Earlier Eulogies', *Romance Philology*, 3
        (1949-50), 1-26

Augustin, George, 'Les fondements scripturaires de l'intercession de Marie,' *Études
        mariales* 23, (1966), 19-35

Augustine, Aurelius, Saint *Opera Omnia, Tutte le opere*, ed. by Franco Monteverde, 45 vols
        (Rome: Nuova Biblioteca Agostiniana and Città Nuova, 1967–), in
        Sant'Agostino, Augustinus Hipponensis, <http://www.augustinus.it/>
        [accessed 15 February 2008]

Baker, Derek, ed, *Relations between East and West in the Middle Ages* (Edinburgh, Edinburgh University Press, 1973)

Baker, Margaret, 'The Life-Bearing Spring', in *The Origins of the Cult of the Virgin Mary*, ed. by Chris Maunder (London: Burns and Oats, 2008), pp. 127-135

Baldelli, Ignazio, 'La lauda e i Disciplinati', in *Il Movimento dei disciplinati nel settimo centenario dal suo inizio (Perugia, 1260)*, ed. by Lodovico Scaramucci (Spoleto: Panetto & Petrelli, 1962), pp. 338-67

Balić, Karl, 'The Medieval Controversy over the Immaculate Conception up to the Death of Scotus', in *The Dogma of the Immaculate Conception: History and Significance*, ed. by Edward O'Connor, (Notre Dame, Ind: University of Notre Dame Press, 1958), pp. 161-212

—————, 'Die Corredemttrixfrage innerhalb der franziskanischen Theologie', *Franziskanische Studien*, 39 (1957), 218-287

Baltzer, Rebecca A., 'The Little Office of the Virgin and Mary's Role at Paris', in *The Divine Office in the Latin Middle Ages: Methodology and Source Studies, Regional Developments, Hagiography*, ed. by Margot Fassler and Rebecca A. Baltzer (Oxford: Oxford University Press, 2000), pp. 463-85

Bardy, Gustave, 'La doctrine de l'intercession de Marie chez le Pères grecs', *La Vie Spirituelle*, 56, Supplément (1938), 1-37

Barkhuizen, Jan H., 'Proclus of Constantinople: A Popular Preacher in Fifth-Century Constantinople' in *Preacher and Audience: Studies in Early Christian and Byzantine Homiletics*, ed. by Mary B. Cunningham and Pauline Allen (Leiden: Brill, 1998), pp. 179-200

Barnay, Sylvie, 'La foundation viosionnaire des Sanctuaires, un example de politique mariophanique: Notre Dame du Puy', in *Gli studi di mariologia medievale: bilancio storico*, Atti del I convegno mariologico della fondazione Ezio Franceschini con la collaborazione della biblioteca Palatina e del dipartimento di storia dell'università di Parma, Parma 7-8 novembre 1997, ed. by Clelia Maria Piastra (Florence: SISMEL – Edizioni del Galuzzo, 2001), pp. 239-54

—————, 'Le "leggendae" e i "miracula"', in *SDM*, I, 662-72

Barolo, Agostino, *Jacopone da Todi* (Turin: Bocca, 1929)

Baron, Roger, 'La pensée mariale de Hugues de Saint-Victor', *Revue d'ascétique et de mystique*, 31 (1955), 249-71

Barr, Cyrilla, *The Monophonic Lauda and the Lay Religious Confraternities of Tuscany and Umbria in the Late Middle Ages* (Kalamazoo, Mich.: Medieval Institute, Western Michigan University, 1988)

Barré, Henri, 'Antiennes et Répons de la Vierge', *Marianum*, 29 (1967), 153-254

—————, 'L'intercession de la Vierge aux débuts du moyen âge Occidental', *Études mariales*, 23 (1966), 77-104

—————, *Prières anciennes de l'Occident à la Mère du Sauveu: Des origines à saint Anselme* (Paris: Lethielleux, 1963)

—————, 'La nouvelle Ève dans la pensée médiévale, d'Ambroise Autpert au pseudo-Albert', *Études mariales*, 14 (1956), 1-26

—————, Saint Bernard théologien', *Analecti Sacra Ordinis Cisterciencis*, 9 (1953), pp. 92-113

—————, 'Le "Planctus Mariae" attribué a S. Bernard', *Revue d'ascétique de mystique*, 28 (1952), 243-66

_____, 'La croyance à l'assomption corporelle en Occident de 750 a 1150 environ', *Études mariales*, 7 (1949), 63-123

Bathrellos, Demetrios, *The Byzantine Christ: Person, Nature, and Will in the Christology of Saint Maximus the Confessor* (Oxford: Oxford University Press, 2004)

Baudoz, Jean-François, '"Marie, de laquelle est né Jésus" (Mt 1, 16): La virginité de Marie dans la tradition synoptique', in *La virginité de Marie: Communications présentées à la 53e Session de la Société française d'études mariales*, Issoudun, septembre 1997, ed. by Jean Longère (Paris: Médiaspaul, 1998), pp. 9-23

Baun, Jane, 'Discussing Mary's Humanity in Medieval Byzantium', in *The Church and Mary*, ed. by Robert N. Swanson, Studies in Church History, 39 (Woodenbridge: Boydell, 2004), pp. 63-72

Beattie, Tina, 'Mary in Patristic Theology, in *Mary: The Complete Resource*, ed. by Sarah Jane Boss (Oxford and New York: Oxford University Press 2007), pp. 75-105

Beck, Hans George, *Kirche und Theologische Literatur im Byzantinischen Reich* (Munich: C. H. Beck'sche Verlagsbuchhandlung, 1959)

Belting, Hans, *Likeness and Presence: A History of the Image before the Era of Art*, trans. by Edmund Jephcott (Chicago: University of Chicago Press, 1994)

Benedict XVI, Pope, *Ambrogio Autperto*, General Audience, April 22, 2009, <http://www.vatican.va/holy_father/benedict_xvi/audiences/2009/documents/hf_ben-xvi_aud_20090422_it.html> [accessed 2 May 2009]

Benko, Stephen, *The Virgin Goddess: Studies in the Pagan and Christian Roots of Mariology* (New York: Brill, 1993)

Bernard of Clairvaux, Saint, *Some Letters of Saint Bernard of Clairvaux*, in *CCEL* <http://www.ccel.org/ccel/bernard/letters.lxviii.html> [accessed 30 January 2009]

_____, *St. Bernard's Sermons on the Blessed Virgin Mary*, trans. by a priest of Mount Melleray Abbey (Devon: Augustine Publishing Company, 1984)

_____, *The Letters of Bernard of Claivaux*, trans. by Bruno Scott James (London: Burns and Oates, 1953)

_____, *St Bernard's Sermons on the Canticle of Canticles*, trans. by a priest of Mount Melleray, 2 vols (Dublin: Browne and Nolan 1919)

Berschin, Walter, 'Early Medieval Latin Poetry of Mary', in *The Church and Mary* ed. by Robert N. Swanson, Studies in Church History, 39 (Woodenbridge: Boydell, 2004), pp. 112-25

Bertelli, Carlo, *La Madonna di Santa Maria in Trastevere: storia, iconografia, stile di un dipinto romano dell'ottavo secolo* (Rome, Eliograf, 1961)

Besançon, Alain, *The Forbidden Image: An Intellectual History of Iconoclasm*, trans. by Jane Marie Todd (Chicago: University of Chicago Press, 2000)

Besutti, Giuseppe M., (1948-1989), Ermanno M. Toniolo (1990-1993), Silvano M. Danieli (1994-), eds., *Bibliografia Mariana*, 12 vols (Rome: Marianum 1948 –)

Betka, Ursula, 'Marian Images and Laudesi Devotion in the Late Medieval Italy, 1260-1350' (unpublished doctoral thesis, University of Melbourne, 2001)

Bettarini, Rosanna, 'Jacopone da Todi e le Laude', in *Antologia della poesia italiana*, ed. by Cesare Segre e Carlo Ossola, 3 vols (Turin: Einaudi-Gallimard, 1997-99) I

————, *Jacopone e il Laudario Urbinate* (Florence: Sansoni, 1969)

Beumer, Johannes, 'Die Parallele Maria-Kirche nach einem ungedruckten Sermo des Gottfried von St. Viktor', *Recherches de théologie ancienne et médiévale*, 27 (1960), 248-66

Beyers, Rita, 'De Nativitate Mariae: Problèmes d'origine', *Revue de Théologie et de Philosophie*, 122 (1990), 171-188

Bianco, Maria Grazia, 'Riferimenti mariani in Clemente Alessandrino', *Theotokos*, 10 (2002), 33-42

Bisconti Fabrizio, 'La Madonna di Priscilla: interventi di restauro ed ipotesi sulla dinamica decorativa', *Rivista di Archeologia Cristiana*, 72 (1996), 7-34

Bishop, Edmund, *Liturgica Historica: Papers on the Liturgy and Religious Life of the Western Church* (Oxford: The Clarendon Press, 1918)

Bogusz Matula, Stanislaw, *La dottrina mariana nei commentari ai vangeli e nei sermoni di San Bonaventura da Bagnoregio* (Rome: [n. pub.], 2001)

Boitani, Piero, 'The Sibyl's Leaves: A Study of *Paradiso* XXXIII', *Dante Studies*, 96 (1978), 83-126

Bolman, Elizabeth. S., 'The Enigmatic Coptic Galaktotrophousa and the Cult of the Virgin Mary in Egypt', in *Images of the Mother of God: Perceptions of the Theotokos in Byzantium*, ed. by Maria Vassilaki (Aldershot: Ashagate, 2005), pp. 13-22

Bonaventure, Saint, *Collationes de Septem Donis S. Sancti*, in *The Franciscan Archive* <http://www.franciscan-archive.org/index2.html> [accessed 10 August 2005]

————, *Opera Omnia*, ed. by Auguste and Emile Borgnet, 38 vols (Paris: Vivès, 1890-99)

————, *Opere di san Bonaventura*, ed. by Jacques Guy Bougerol, Cornelio Del Zotto and Leonardo Sileo Bougerol, 14 vols (Rome: Conferenza italiana ministri provinciali O.F.M. and Città nuova, 1990-)

————, *Sermons on the Blessed Virgin Mary*, trans. by Campion Murray, in *Franciscan Friars: Province of the Holy Spirit* <http://www.franciscans.org.au > [August 26, 2006]

————, *The Soul's Journey Into God; The Tree of Life; The Life of St. Francis*, trans. by Ewert Cousins (New York: Paulist Press, 1978)

————, *The Works of Bonaventure*, trans. by José de Vinck, 5 vols, (Patterson, NJ: St. Antony Guild Press, 1960-1970)

Boss, Sarah Jane, 'The Development of the Doctrine of Mary's Immaculate Conception', in *Mary: The Complete Resource*, ed. by Sarah Jane Boss (Oxford and New York: Oxford University Press 2007), pp. 207-35

————, 'The Development of the Virgin's Cult in the High Middle Ages', in *Mary: The Complete Resource*, ed. by Sarah Jane Boss (Oxford and New York: Oxford University Press 2007), pp. 149-72

————, ed, *Mary: The Complete Resource* (Oxford and New York: Oxford University Press 2007)

————, *Mary* (London: Continuum, 2004)

_____, *Empress and Handmaid: Nature and Gender in the Cult of the Virgin Mary* (London: Cassell, 1999)

Botte, Bernard, 'Culte et dévotion à la Vierge Marie dans l'ordre monastique aux VIIIᵉ-IXᵉ siècles: Le Calendrier monastique des fêtes liturgiques de la Vierge d'après les « Initia consuetudines benedictinae' de K. Hallinger', in *De cultu mariano saeculis VI-XI*, Acta congressus mariologici-mariani internationalis, Zagreb, 1972 (Rome : Pontificia Academia Mariana Internationalis, 1972), IV, 203-25

_____, 'Le lectionnaire arménien et la fête de la Théotocos à Jerusalem au vᵉ siècle, *Sacris Erudiri*, 2 (1949), 111-22

_____, 'La première fête mariale de la liturgie romaine', *Ephemerides Liturgicae* 47 (1933), 425-430

Bougerol, Jacques Guy, *Introduction to the Works of Bonaventure*, trans. by José de Vinck (Paterson, NJ: St. Anthony Guild Press, 1964)

Bouman, Cornelius A., 'The Immaculate Conception in the Liturgy', in *The Dogma of the Immaculate Conception: History and Significance*, ed. by Edward D. O'Connor (Notre Dame, Ind: University of Notre Dame Press, 1958), pp. 113-60

Branchesi, Pacifico Maria, 'L'ordine dei Servi di Santa Maria e il culto mariano (secoli XII-XV), in *Gli studi di mariologia medievale: bilancio storico*, Atti del I convegno mariologico della fondazione Ezio Franceschini con la collaborazione della biblioteca Palatina e del dipartimento di storia dell'università di Parma, parma 7-8 novembre 1997, ed. by Clelia Maria Piastra (Florence: SISMEL – Edizioni del Galuzzo, 2001), pp. 113-58

Brandenbarg, Tom, 'Saint Anne: A Holy Grandmother and her Children', in *Sanctity and Motherhood: Essays on Holy Mothers in the Middle Ages*, ed. by Anneke Mulder-Bakker (New York and London: Garland, 1995), pp. 31-65

Brenk, Beat, *Die frühchristlichen Mosaiken in S. Maria Maggiore zu Rom* (Stuttgart: Steiner, 1975)

Brock, Sebastian *Bride of Light: Hymns on Mary from the Syriac Churches* (Kottayam: St. Ephrem Ecumenical Research Institute (SEERI), 1994)

Brown, Peter, 'The Notion of Virginity in the Early Church', in *Christian Spirituality: Origins to the Twelfth Century*, ed. by Bernard McGinn and John Meyendorff, World Spirituality, 16 (New York, Crossroads, 1989), pp. 427-43

_____, *The Cult of the Saints: Its Rise and Function in Latin Christianity* (Chicago: University of Chicago Press, 1981)

_____, 'Eastern and Western Christendom in Late Antiquity: A Parting of the Ways', *Studies in Church History*, 13 (1976), 1-23

Bruder, Joseph Simon, *The Mariology of Saint Anselm of Canterbury* (Dayton: Mount St. Joseph Press, 1939)

Buby, Bertrand, *Mary of Galilee*, 3 vols (New York: Alba House, 1994-1997)

Buck, Fidelis, 'The Marian Interpretation of the Song of Songs in the Middle Ages (A.D. 1100-1500)', in *De cultu Mariano saeculis XII-XV: Acta Congressus Mariologici-Mariani,Internationalis Romae anno 1975 celebrati*, 6 vols (Rome: Pontificia Academia Mariana Internationalis, 1979-81), IV (1980), 69-96

Buono, Anthony M., *The Greatest Marian Prayers: Their History, Meaning and Usage* (New York: Alba House, 1999)

Burridge, A. W., 'L'Immaculée Conception dans la théologie de l'Angleterre médiévale', *Revue d'histoire ecclésiastique*, 32, (1936), 570-597

Byer, Anthony, and Judith Herrin, eds., *Iconoclasm* (Birmingham: Birmingham University Press, 1977)

Cacciotti, Alvaro, *Amor sacro e amor profano in Jacopone da Todi* (Rome: Antonianum, 1989)

Calabuig, Ignazio M., and Salvatore M. Perrella, 'Le litanie della Beata Virgine: storia, teologia, significato', *Marianum*, 70 (2008), 103-202

Calabuig, Ignazio M., 'Les sources patristiques de la pensée mariale de saint Bernard', *Estudios marianos*, 64 (1998), 515-39

——, ed, *Respice stellam: Maria in San Bernardo e nella tradizione cistercense*, Atti del convegno internazionale, Roma, Marianum, 21-24 October 1991 (Rome: Marianum, 1993)

Calì, Rosa, *I testi antimariologici nell'esegisi dei padri: da Nicea a Calcedonia* (Caltaninsetta: Edizioni del Seminario, 1999)

Calloway, Donald H., *The Immaculate Conception in the Life of the Church: Essays from the International Symposium in Honor of the 150ᵗʰ Anniversary of the Proclamation of the Dogma of the Immaculate Conception* (Stockbridge, MA, John Paul II Institute of Divine Mercy, 2004)

Cameron, Averil, 'The Cult of the Virgin in Late Antiquity: Religious Development and Myth-Making', in *The Church and Mary* ed. by Robert N. Swanson, Studies in Church History, 39 (Woodenbridge: Boydell, 2004), pp. 1-21

——, 'A Nativity Poem of the Sixth Century A.D.', *Classical Philology*, 74 (1979), 222-32

——, 'Images of Authority: Elites and Icons in Late Sixth-Century Byzantium', *Past and Present*, 84 (1979), 3-35

——, 'The Virgin's Robe: An Episode in the History of Seventh Century Constantinople', *Byzantion*, 159 (1979), 42-56

——, 'The Theotokos in Sixth-Century Constantinople: A City Finds its Symbol', *Journal of Theological Studies*, 29 (1978), 79-108

Campos Alvarez, Sergius, ed, *Corpus Marianum Patristicum*, 8 vols (Burgos: Aldecoa, 1970-85)

Canal, José María, 'San Agustín y el dogma de la Immaculada concepción', *Ephemerides mariologicae*, 54 (2004), 361-71

——, 'María, nueva Eva en Justino, Ireneo, Tertuliano y Agustín', *Ephemerides Mariologicae*, 46 (1996), 41-60

——, 'El oficio parvo de la Virgen de 1000 a 1250', *Ephemerides Mariologicae*, 15 (1965), 464-475

——, 'Dos homilias de Odón de Morimond († 1161)', *Sacris erudiri*, 13 (1962), 377-460

——, 'Oficio parvo de la Virgen: formas viejas y formas nuevas', *Ephemerides Mariologicae*, 11 (1961), 497-525

Capelle, Bernard, *Travaux liturgiques de doctrine e d'histoire*, vol. III, (Louvain: Centre Liturgique Abbaye du Mont César, 1967)

_____, 'La messe gallicane de l'Assomption: Son rayonnement, ses sources', in *Miscellanea Liturgica in honorem L. Cuniberti* (Rome, Edizioni liturgiche, 1948), pp. 33-59

Capelle, Bernard, 'La fête de la Vierge à Jérusalem au ve siècle', *Le Muséon*, 56 (1943), 1-33

Caro, Roberto, ed, *La homiletica mariana griega en el siglo V*, 3 vols (Dayton, Ohio: University of Dayton Press, 1971-73)

Carol, Juniper B., ed, *Mariology*, 3 vols (Milwaukee: Bruce, 1955-1961)

_____, *Fundamentals of Mariology* (New York: Benziger, 1956)

_____, *De corredemptione beatae Virginis Mariae* (Vatican City: Typis Polyglottis Vaticanis, 1950)

Carroll, Michael P., *The Cult of the Virgin Mary: Psychological Origins* (Princeton: Princeton University Press, 1986)

Casagrande, Domenico, *Enchiridion Marianum Biblicum Patristicum* (Rome: Cor Unum, 1974)

Cascante Dávila, Juan María, 'La devoción y el culto a María en S. Ildefonso de Toledo', in *Acta Congressus Mariologici-Mariani Internationalis in Croatia anno 1971 celebrati*, 5 vols (Rome: Pontifica Academia Mariana, 1972), III, 223-48

Casella, Mario, 'Il canto XXXIII del Paradiso', in *Letture Dantesche*, ed. by Giovanni Getto, 3 vols (Florence: Sansoni, 1970), pp. 675-692

Casula, Lucio, 'Natus ex matre virgine': Maria nei sermoni di Leone Magno,' *Theotokos*, 12 (2004), 215-54

Catafygiotou-Topping, Elisabeth, 'Mary at the Cross: St. Romanos Kontakion for Holy Friday,' *Byzantine Studies / Études Byzantines*, 4 (1977), 18-37

Catalani, Luigi, 'Il modello scolastico', in *SDM*, I, 673-99

Cattaneo, E., 'La più antica festa della Madonna e la Chiesa di S. Maria al Circo', *Ambrosius*, 28 (1952), 123-129

Cavadini, John C., *The Last Christology of the West: Adoptionism in Spain and Gaul, 785-820* (Philadelphia: University of Pennsylvania Press, 1993)

Cecchetti, I., 'L'Annunciazione: Il racconto biblico e la festa liturgica', *Bollettino Ceciliano*, 38 (1943), 46-48 and 98-114

Cecchin, Stefano M., 'Giovanni Duns Scotus, dottore dell'Immacolata Concezione: alcune questioni', in *La "Scuola Francescana" e l'Immacolata Concezione*, Atti del Congresso Mariologico Francescano S. Maria degli Angeli, Assisi, 4-8 dicembre 2003 (Vatican City: Pontificia Academia Mariana Internationalis, 2005), pp. 219-71

_____, 'La devozione a Maria in Francesco e Chiara d'Assisi', in *La "Scuola Francescana" e l'Immacolata Concezione*, Atti del Congresso Mariologico Francescano S. Maria degli Angeli, Assisi, 4-8 dicembre 2003, (Vatican City: Pontificia Academia Mariana Internationalis, 2005), pp. 1-54

Christensen, Michael J., and Jeffery A. Wittung, eds., *Partakers of the Divine Nature: The History and Development of Deification in the Christian Traditions* (Madison, N.J.: Fairleigh Dickinson University Press, 2007)

Cignelli, Lino, *Maria, nuova Eva nella patristica greca (sec. II-V)* (Assisi: Porziuncola, 1966)

Clayton, Mary, 'Changing Fortunes: The Cult of the Virgin in Tenth-Century England', in *Gli studi di mariologia medievale: bilancio storico*, Atti del I convegno mariologico della fondazione Ezio Franceschini con la collaborazione della biblioteca Palatina e del dipartimento di storia dell'università di Parma, parma 7-8 novembre 1997, ed. by Clelia Maria Piastra (Florence: SISMEL – Edizioni del Galuzzo, 2001), pp. 87-96

_____, *The Apocryphal Gospels of Mary in Anglo Saxon England* (Cambridge: Cambridge University Press, 1998)

_____, *The Cult of the Virgin Mary in Anglo-Saxon England* (Cambridge; New York: Cambridge University Press, 1990)

_____, 'Feasts of the Virgin in the Liturgy of the Anglo-Saxon Church', *Anglo-Saxon England*, 13 (1984), 209-33

Clayton, Paul B., *The Christology of Theodoret of Cyrus: Antiochene Christology from the Council of Ephesus (431) to the Council of Chalcedon (451)* (Oxford: Oxford University Press, 2007)

Cole, William, 'Theology in Paschasius Radbertus' Liturgy-Oriented Marian Works', in *De cultu mariano saeculis VI-XI*, Acta congressus mariologici-mariani internationalis, Zagreb, 1972 (Rome: Pontificia Academia Mariana Internationalis, 1972), III, 395-431

Conrad of Saxony, *Speculum Beatae Mariae Virginis*, trans. by Campion Murray as *The Angel's Greeting to Mary*, in *Franciscan Friars: Province of the Holy Spirit* <http://www.franciscans.org.au/spirituality/campion/translations.htm> [accessed 13 April 2006]

Constas, Nicholas P., 'Weaving the Body of God: Proclus of Constantinople, the Theotokos and the Loom of the Flesh', *Journal of Early Christian Studies*, 3 (1995), 169-94

Constas, Nicholas P., *Proclus of Constantinople and the Cult of the Virgin in Late Antiquity, Homilies 1-5, Texts, and Translations*, Supplements to Vigiliae Christianae, 66 (Leiden: Brill, 2003)

Cooper, Adam G, *The Body in St. Maximus the Confessor: Holy Flesh, Wholly Deified* (Oxford: Oxford University Press, 2005)

Cooper, Kate, 'Empress and Theotokos: Gender and Patronage in the Christological Controversy', in *The Church and Mary*, ed. by Robert N. Swanson, Studies in Church History, 39 (Woodenbridge: Boydell, 2004), pp. 39-51

_____, 'Contesting the Nativity: Wives, Virgins and Pulcheria's *imitatio Mariae*, *Scottish Journal of Religious Studies*, 19 (1998), 31-43

Coppens, J., 'La prophétie de la "Almah", Is vii: 14-17', *Ephemerides Theologicae Lovanienses*, 28 (1952), 648-78

Copsey, Richard, 'Simon Stock and the Scapular Vision', *The Journal of Ecclesiastical History*, 50 (1999), 652-83

Corsato, Celestino, 'La mariologia in Ambrogio di Milano', *Theotokos*, 11 (2003), 291-336

_____, 'La tipologia "Eva-Chiesa-Maria" nella tradizione patristica prenicena", *Theotokos*, 9 (2001), 153-90

Cothenet, Edouard, 'La virginité de Marie dans les Apocryphes', in *La virginité de Marie: Communications présentées à la 53e Session de la Société française d'études mariales*, Issoudun, septembre 1997, ed. by Jean Longère (Paris: Médiaspaul, 1998), pp. 53-69

Cothren, Michael W., 'The Iconography of Theophilus Windows in the First Half of the Thirteenth Century', *Speculum*, 59 (1984), 308-41

Craig, Hardin, *English Religious Drama of the Middle Ages* (Oxford: The Clarendon Press, 1960)

Cross, Richard, *The Metaphysics of the Incarnation: Thomas Aquinas to Duns Scotus* (Oxford: Oxford University Press, 2005)

Cullen, Christopher M., *Bonaventure* (Oxford: Oxford University Press, 2006)

Cunningham, Lawrence 'Mary in Catholic Doctrine and Practice', *Theology Today*, 56 (1999), 307-18

Cunningham, Mary B., 'The Meeting of the Old and New: The Typology of Mary Theotokos in Byzantine Homilies and Hymns', in *The Church and Mary*, ed. by Robert N. Swanson, Studies in Church History, 39 (Woodenbridge: Boydell, 2004), pp. 52-62

_____, 'Andrew of Crete: A High-Style Preacher of the Eighth Century', in *Preacher and Audience: Studies in Early Christian and Byzantine Homiletics*, ed. by Mary B. Cunningham and Pauline Allen (Leiden: Brill, 1998), pp. 278-86

_____, 'The Mother of God in Early Byzantine Homilies', *Sobomost*, 10 (1988), 53-67

_____, and Pauline Allen, eds., *Preacher and Audience: Studies in Early Christian and Byzantine Homiletics* (Leiden: Brill, 1998)

Custer, John S., 'The Virgin's Birth Pangs: A Johannine Image in Byzantine Hymnography', *Marianum*, 68 (2006), 417-36

da Casale, Ubertino, *Arbor vitae crucifixae Jesu*, ed. by Charles T. Davis (Turin: Bottega d'Erasmo, 1961)

da Todi, Jacopone, *Laude*, ed. and intro. by Gianni Mussini (Casale Monferrato: Piemme, 1999)

_____, *Lauds*, ed. by Serge and Elizabeth Hughes, Classics of Western Spirituality, 30 (New York: Paulist Press, 1982)

_____, *Laude*, ed. by Franco Mancini (Bari: Laterza 1974)

dal Covolo, Enrico, and Aristide Serra, eds., *Storia della mariologia: dal modello biblico al modello letterario* (Rome: Città Nuova and Marianum, 2009)

dal Covolo, Enrico, 'La maternità di Maria nelle definizioni conciliari di Costantinopoli I, Efeso e Calcedonia', in *Fons lucis: Miscellanea di studi in onore di Ermanno M. Toniolo*, ed. by R. Barbieri and others (Rome: Marianum, 2004), pp. 219-28

_____, 'La dottrina mariana di Tertulliano', *Theotokos*, 10 (2002), 17-31

dal Pino, Franco A., 'La presenza della beata Vergine Maria nella vita degli ordini mendicanti (Secolo XIII-XV)', in *SDM*, I, 726-73

_____, 'Culto e pietà mariana presso i frati minori nel medioevo', *Gli studi di mariologia medievale: bilancio storico*, Atti del I convegno mariologico della fondazione Ezio Franceschini con la collaborazione della biblioteca Palatina e del dipartimento di storia dell'università di Parma, parma 7-8 novembre 1997, ed. by Clelia Maria Piastra (Florence: SISMEL – Edizioni del Galuzzo, 2001), pp. 159-92

Daley, Brian E., '"Now and at the Hour of Our Death": Mary's Dormition and Christian Dying in Late Patristic and Early Byzantine Literature', *Dumbarton Oaks Papers*, 55 (2001), 71-89

_____, 'On the Dormition of Mary: Early Patristic Homilies* (Crestwood, N. Y.: St. Vladimir's, 1998)

_____, 'The Hope of the Early Church: A Handbook of Patristic Eschatology (Cambridge: Cambridge University Press, 1991)

Daly, Mary, Pure Lust: Elemental Feminist Philosophy (Boston: Beacon Press 1984)

Daniélou, Jean, Sacramentum futuri: Études sur les origines de la typologie biblique (Paris: Beauchesne, 1950)

Dary, Marie-Bénedicte, 'Saint Bernard et l'Immaculée Conception: La question liturgique', Revue Marbillon, (2002), 219-36

Dattrino, Lorenzo, 'Riferimenti Mariani in Agostino', Theotokos, 12 (2004), 161-68

Davidson, Ivor J., '"Not My Will but Yours be Done": The Ontological Dynamics of Incarnational Intention', International Journal of Systematic Theology, 7 (2005), 178-204

Davidson, John, The Odes of Solomon: Mystical Songs from the Time of Jesus (Bath: Clear Press, 2005)

Davis, Judith M., and F.R.P. Akehurst, ed and trans., Our Lady's Lawsuits in "L'advocacie Nostre Dame" and "La chapelerie Nostre Dame de Baiex" (Tempe, AR : ACMRS, 2011)

Davis, Leo D., The First Seven Ecumenical Councils (325-787): Their History and Theology (Collegeville, MN: Liturgical Press, 1983)

Davis, Stephen, The Cult of Thecla (Oxford: Oxford University Press, 2001)

de Alcántara Martínez, Pedro, 'La cooperación de María en la obra salvífica según el pensamento di Pedro Juan Olivi', in Studies Honoring Ignatius Charles Brady, ed. by Romano Stephen Almagno and Conrad L. Harkins (St. Bonaventure, N.Y.: Franciscan Institute, 1976), pp. 341-55

de Coinci Gautier, Les Miracles de Nostre Dame, ed. by V. Frederic Koenig, 4 vols (Geneva: Droz, 1955-70)

De Fiores, Stefano, Giuseppe Strangio, and Enrico Vidau, Il mistero della croce e Maria, atti del 4 colloquio internazionale di mariologia, santuario di Polsi-San Luca (RC), 13-14 settembre 1999 (Rome: Monfortane, 2001)

de Lubac, Henri, Exégèse médiévale: les quatre sens de l'Écriture, 4 vols (Paris: Aubier, 1959-64)

de Strycker, Émile, La forme la plus ancienne du Protévangile de Jacques, Subsidia Hagiographica, 33 (Brussels: Société des Bollandists, 1961)

de Voragine, Jacobus, The Golden Legend: Readings on the Saints, trans. by William Granger Ryan, 2 vols (Princeton: Princeton University Press, 1993)

Delehaye, Hippolyte, Les origines du culte des martyrs, 2nd edn (Brussels: Société des Bollandistes, 1912)

Delio, Ilia, Simply Bonaventure: An Introduction to His Life, Thought, and Writings (New York: New City Press, 2001)

Denzinger, Henricus Adolfus Schönmetzer, eds., Enchiridion Symbolorum: Definitionum et Declarationum de Rebus Fidei et Morum, 36th edn (Fribourg: Herder, 1965)

Deshusses, Jean, ed, Le Sacramentaire Grégorien: Ses principales formes d'après les plus anciens manuscrits, Spicilegium Friburgense, 16 (Fribourg: Éditions Universitaires, 1971)

Devos, Paul, 'Le date du voyage d'Égérie', Analecta Bollandiana, 85 (1967), 165-94

Di Domenico, Piergiorgio and Elio Peretto, eds., Maria madre di misericordia: monstra te esse matrem, atti del convegno mariologico, Vicenza, Monte Berico (4-8 maggio 1999) (Padova: Messaggero, 2003)

Dobrov, Gregory, 'A Dialogue with Death: Ritual Lament and the θρῆνος Θεοτόκου of Romanos Melodes', *Greek, Roman and Byzantine Studies*, 35 (1994), 385-405

Domínguez Reboiras, Fernando, 'El discurso luliano sobre María', in *Gli studi di mariologia medievale: bilancio storico*, Atti del I convegno mariologico della fondazione Ezio Franceschini con la collaborazione della biblioteca Palatina e del dipartimento di storia dell'università di Parma, parma 7-8 novembre 1997, ed. by Clelia Maria Piastra (Florence: SISMEL – Edizioni del Galuzzo, 2001), pp. 277-303

d'Onofrio, Giulio, 'Il "Mysterium Mariae" nella teologia e nella pietà dell'alto medioevo latino (secoli V-XI)', in *SDM*, pp. 505-66

Donovan, Mary Ann, *One Right Reading? A Guide to Irenaeus* (Collegeville, MN: Liturgical Press, 1997)

Dreves, Guido M., Clemens Blume and Henry M. Bannister, eds., *Analecta hymnica medii aevi*, 55 vols (Leipzig: Reisland1886-1922; repr. Frankfurt am Main: Minerva, 1961)

Dronke, Peter, 'Laments of the Maries: From the Beginnings to the Mystery Plays', in *Idee, Gestalt, Geschichte: Festschrift Fur Klaus von See: Studien zur europäischen Kulturtradition*, ed. by Gerd Wolfgang Weber (Odense: Odense University Press, 1988), pp. 89-116

Druwê, E, 'La médiation universelle de Marie', in *Maria*, I, 417-572

du Manoir, Hubert, ed, *Maria: Études sur la Sainte Vierge,* 8 vols (Paris: Beauchesne, 1949-71)

Dubarle, André-Marie, 'Les fondements bibliques du titre marial de la nouvelle Éve', *Recherches de science religieuse*, 39 (1951), 49-64

Duchesne, Louis, *Liber Pontificalis: Texte, introduction et commentaire*, 2 vols, (Paris: Thorin, 1886-92)

Duffy, Eamon, 'Mater Dolorosa, Mater Misericordiae', *New Blackfriars*, 69, (2007), 210-27

Duhr, Joseph, *The Glorious Assumption of the Mother of God*, trans. by John Manning Fraunces (New York: Kenedy, 1950)

Dunker, P. G., 'Our Lady in the Old Testament – I', in *The Mother of the Redeemer: Aspects of Doctrine and Devotion*, ed. by Kevin McNamara (Dublin: Gill, 1959), 1-12

————, 'Our Lady in the Old Testament – II', in *The Mother of the Redeemer: Aspects of Doctrine and Devotion*, ed. by Kevin McNamara (Dublin: Gill, 1959), pp. 13-29

————, 'Our Lady in the Patristic Age', in *The Mother of the Redeemer: Aspects of Doctrine and Devotion*, ed. by Kevin McNamara (Dublin: Gill, 1959), pp. 42-55

Dvornick, Francis, 'The Byzantine Church and the Immaculate Conception', in *The Dogma of the Immaculate Conception: History and Significance*, ed. by Edward D. O'Connor (Notre Dame, Ind: University of Notre Dame Press, 1958), pp. 87-112

Ebertshäuser, Caroline H., Herbert Haag, Joe H. Kirchberger, and others, *Mary: Art, Culture, and Religion through the Ages*, trans. by Peter Heinegg (New York: Crossroad, 1998)

Edmondson Haney, Kristine, 'The Immaculate Imagery in the Winchester Psalter', *Gesta*, 20 (1981), 111-18

Egeria, *Itinerarium* ed. by Georg Röwekamp (Freiburg: Herder, 1995)

Ellington, Donna Spivey, *From Sacred Body to Angelic Soul: Understanding Mary in Late Medieval and Early Modern Europe* (Washington: Catholic University of America Press, 2001)

Elliott, James K., 'Mary in the Apocryphal New Testament' in *The Origins of the Cult of the Virgin Mary*, ed. by Chris Maunder (London: Burns and Oats, 2008), pp. 57-70

_____, *The Apocryphal Jesus: Legends of the Early Church* (Oxford: Oxford University Press, 1996)

_____, ed, *The Apocryphal New Testament: A Collection of Apocryphal Christian Literature in an English Translation* (Oxford: The Clarendon Press, 1993)

Ephrem, St., *Ephrem the Syrian: Hymns*, trans. Kathleen McVey (New York: Paulist Press, 1989)

Erbetta, Mario, ed, *Gli apocrifi del Nuovo Testamento*, 4 vols (Casale Monferrato: Marietti, 1983)

Ettlinger, Gerard H., *Theodoret of Cyrus: Eranistes* (Oxford: The Clarendon Press, 1975)

Fassler, Margot and Rebecca A. Baltzer, eds., *The Divine Office in the Latin Middle Ages: Methodology and Source Studies, Regional Developments, Hagiography* (Oxford: Oxford University Press, 2000)

Fassler, Margot, 'The First Marian Feast in Constantinople and Jerusalem: Chant Texts, Readings and Homiletic Literature', in *Paths and Bridges, East and West. In Honor of Kenneth Levy*, ed. by Peter Jeffery (Cambridge: Brewer, 2001), pp. 25-87

_____, 'Mary's Nativity, Fulbert of Chartres, and the *Stirps Jesse*: Liturgical Innovation circa 1000 and Its Afterlife', *Speculum*, 75 (2000), 389-434

Fazzo, Vittorio, 'La mariologia di Giovanni Damasceno', *Theotokos*, 15, (2007), 127-36

_____, 'Teologia e spiritualità mariane nelle omelie di Germano di Costantinopoli e di Andrea di Creta', *Theotokos*, 14 (2006), 73-90

Fehlner, Peter Damien, 'I discorsi mariani di san Bonaventura', *Immaculata Mediatrix*, 4 (2004), 17-65

Felici, Sergio, ed, *La mariologia nella catechesi dei Padri (età prenicena)* (Rome: Libreria Ateneo Salesiano, 1991)

Férotin, Marius, ed, *Le Liber Mozarabicus Sacramentorum et les Manuscrits mozarabes* (Paris: Firmin-Didot, 1912; repr. Rome: Edizioni liturgiche, 1995)

Feuillet, André, 'La Vierge Marie dans le Nouveau Testament', in *Maria* VI, 15-69

Finn, Thomas M., *Quodvultdeus of Carthage: The Creedal Homilies: Conversion in Fifth-Century North Africa*, Ancient Christian Writers, 60 (New York: Newman, 2004)

Flint, Valerie, 'The Commentaries of Honorius Augustodunensis on the Song of Songs', *Revue Bénédictine*, 84 (1974), 197-200

_____, 'The Chronology of the Works of Honorius Augustodunensis', *Revue bénédictine*, 82 (1972), 215-42

Foskett, Mary F., *A Virgin Conceived: Mary and Classical Representations of Virginity* (Bloomington: University of Indiana Press, 2002)

Fournée, Jean 'Les orientations doctrinales de l'iconographie mariale à la fin de l'époque romane', *CentreInternational d'Etudes Romanes*, 1 (1971), 23-56

Frénaud, Georges, 'Le culte de Notre Dame dans l'ancienne liturgie latine', in *Maria*, VI, 157-211

Freyer, Alfred, 'Theophilus the Penitent as Represented in Art', *Archaeological Journal*, 92 (1935), 287-333

Fubini, Mario, 'L'ultimo canto del "Paradiso"', in Mario Fubini, *Il peccato di Ulisse e altri scritti danteschi* (Milan & Naples: Ricciardi, 1966), pp. 101-136

Fulton, Rachel, *From Judgment to Passion: Devotion to Christ and the Virgin Mary, 800-1200* (New York: Columbia University Press, 2002)

————, '"Quae est ista quae ascendit sicut aurora consurgens?": The Song of Songs as the *Historia* for the Office of the Assumption', *Mediaeval Studies*, 60 (1998), 55-112

————, 'The Virgin Mary and the Song of Songs' (unpublished doctoral thesis, Colombia University, 1994)

Gaffuri, Laura, 'La predicazione domenicana su Maria (Il secolo XIII), in *Gli studi di mariologia medievale: bilancio storico*, Atti del I convegno mariologico della fondazione Ezio Franceschini con la collaborazione della biblioteca Palatina e del dipartimento di storia dell'università di Parma, parma 7-8 novembre 1997, ed. by Clelia Maria Piastra (Florence: SISMEL – Edizioni del Galuzzo, 2001), pp. 193-215

Gallico, Antonino, 'Riferimenti mariani in Sofronio', *Theotokos*, 15 (2007), 103-25

————, 'Riferimenti mariani in Teodoreto di Cirro', *Theotokos*, 12 (2004), 307-27

Galot, Jean, 'Mary Co-Redemptrix: Controversies and Doctrinal Questions', in *Mary Coredemptrix: Doctrinal Issues Today*, ed. by Mark Miravalle (Goleta, CA: Queenship, 2002), pp. 7-23

————, 'L'intercession de Marie', in *Maria*, VI, 513-550

Gamber, Klaus, *Codices liturgici latini antiquiores*, 2nd ed, 2 vols, Spicilegii Friburgenis Subsidia, 1 (Freiburg: Universitatsverlag 1968)

Gambero, Luigi, 'Il XIII secolo e la fioritura della Scolastica', in *SDM*, I, 774-829

————, 'Maria negli antichi concili', in *SDM*, I, 451-502

————, 'Il contributo di Ambrogio Autperto († 781) all tradizione mariologica della Chiesa', *Theotokos*, 15 (2007), 257-78

————, 'La Madre di Dio nella cristologia di Basileo di Cesarea', *Theotokos*, 11 (2004), 41-72

————, 'Appunti patristici per lo studio della mariologia', in *Gli studi di mariologia medievale: bilancio storico*, Atti del I convegno mariologico della fondazione Ezio Franceschini con la collaborazione della biblioteca Palatina e del dipartimento di storia dell'università di Parma, Parma 7-8 novembre 1997, ed. by Clelia Maria Piastra (Florence: SISMEL – Edizioni del Galuzzo, 2001), pp. 5-17

————, 'Patristic Intuitions of Mary's Role as Mediatrix and Advocate: The Invocation of the Faithful for Help', *Marian Studies*, 52 (2001), 78-101

————, *Maria nel pensiero dei teologi latini medievali* (Milan: San Paolo, 2000)

————, *Mary in the Middle Ages: The Blessed Virgin Mary in the Thought of Medieval Latin Theologians*, trans. by Thomas Buffer (San Francisco: Ignatius Press, 2000)

————, *Mary and the Fathers of the Church: The Blessed Virgin Mary in Patristic Thought* (San Francisco: Ignatius Press, 1999)

Garrido Bonaño, M., 'El servicio a la Virgen en los himnos medievales', *Estudios Marianos*, 51 (1986), 65-76

Garrido, Pablo Maria, 'Elementos marianos presents en los primeros textos escritos Carmelitas medievales', *Marianum*, 64 (2002), 387-406

Gatti, Maria Luisa, *Massimo il Confessore: saggio di bibliografia generale ragionata e contributi per una del suo pensiero metafisico e religioso* (Milan: Vita e Pensiero, 1987)

Gauthier, Marie-Madeleine, *Highways of the Faith: Relics and Reliquaries from Jerusalem to Compostela*, trans. by J. A. Underwood (London: Alpine, 1983)

Gazzini, Marina, 'Bibliografia medievistica di storia confraternale', *Reti Medievali Rivista*, 5 (2004) <http://www.dssg.unifi.it/_RM/rivista/biblio/ Gazzini.htm> [accessed 20 August 2006]

Geenen, G., 'Eadmer, le premier théologien de l'Immaculée Conception' in *Virgo Immaculata, De Immaculata Conceptione in epocha introductoria Scholasticae*, Acta Congressus Mariologici-Mariani, V (Rome: Academia Mariana Internationalis, 1955), pp. 90-136

Gero, Stephen, 'The Infancy Gospel of Thomas: A Study of the Textual and Literary Problems', *Novum Testamentum*, 13 (1971), 46-80

Gharib, Georges, and others eds., *Testi mariani del primo millennio*, 4 vols (Rome: Città Nuova, 1988–1991)

Gherardini, Brunero, 'La corredentrice nel mistero di Cristo e della Chiesa (Monopoli: Vivere In, 1998)

Giannarelli, Elena, 'Gregorio di Nissa: fili mariani', *Theotokos*, 11 (2003), 125-43

Gijsel, Jan and Rita Beyers, eds., *Libri de Nativitate Mariae*, Corpus Christianorum Series Apocyphorum, 9 and 10, 2 vols (Turnhout: Brepols, 1997)

Gil, Juan, 'El tratado "De Virginitate Beatae Mariae" de S. Ildefonso de Toledo', *Habis*, 6 (1975), 153-66

Gilo, Angelo M., 'La Vergine Madre e l'Antico Testamento secondo i primi Padri della Chiesa', *Theotokos*, 9 (2001), 83-128

Graef, Hilda, *Mary: A History of Doctrine and Devotion*, 2 vols (New York: Sheed and Ward, 1963-1965)

————, *The Devotion to Our Lady* (New York: Hawthorn, 1963)

Grego, Igino, 'Il Kathisma o luogo del riposo della Vergine', *Asprenas*, 45 (1998), 231-44

Gregory of Nyssa, *Life of Moses*, trans. by Abraham J. Malherbe and Everett Ferguson (New York: Paulist Press, 1978)

Gregory of Tours, Saint, *Les livres des miracles et autres opuscules de Georges Florent Grégoire, évêque de Tours*, ed. and trans. by Henri Bordier, 4 vols (Paris: Renouard, 1857-1864)

Grillmeier, Aloys, *Christ in Christian Tradition*, trans. by John Bowden, 2nd edn, rev., 2 vols (London: Mowbrys, 1975)

Grosdidier de Matons, José, *Romanos le Mélode et les origines de la poésie religieuse a Byzance* (Paris: Beauchesne, 1977)

Gross, Jules, *The Divinization of the Christian According to the Greek Fathers*, trans. by Paul A. Onica (Anaheim, CA: A and C Press, 2002)

————, *La divinisation du chrétien d'après les pères grecs: Contribution historique à la doctrine de la grâce* (Paris: Gabalda, 1938)

Guarnieri, Anna Maria, *Laudario di Cortona*, (Spoleto: Centro italiano di studi sull'alto medioevo, 1991)

Guitton, Jean, *The Blessed Virgin* (London: Burns Oates, 1952)

Guldan, Ernst, *Eva und Maria: Eine Antithese als Bildmotiv* (Graz and Cologne: Böhlaus, 1966)

Gulovich, Stephen C., 'The Immaculate Conception of the Blessed Virgin in the Eastern Ecclesiastical Tradition', *Marian Studies*, 5 (1954), pp. 146-83

Haffner, Paul, *The Mystery of Mary* (Leominster, Herefordshire: Gracewing, 2004)

Hamilton, Sarah, 'The Virgin Mary in Cathar Thought', *The Journal of Ecclesiastical History*, 56 (2005), 24-49

Hamman, Adalbert, ed, *Early Christian Prayers*, trans. by Walter Mitchell (Chicago: Regnery; London: Longmans and Green, 1961)

Hansbury, Mary, *Jacob of Serug on the Mother of God* (Crestwood, N.Y.: St. Vlamdimir's, 1998)

Hanson, Richard P. C., *The Search for the Christian Doctrine of God: The Arian Controversy, 318-381 AD* (Edinburgh: Clark, 1988)

Hardison, Osborne B., *Christian Rite and Christian Drama in the Middle Ages: Essays in the Origin and Early History of Modern Drama* (Baltimore: Johns Hopkins University Press, 1965)

Harper, John, *The Forms and Orders of Western Liturgy from the Tenth to the Eighteenth Century: A Historical Introduction and Guide for Students and Musicians* (Oxford: The Clarendon Press, 1991)

Harris, Rendel, *The Odes and Psalms of Solomon* (Cambridge: Cambridge University Press, 1909)

Hechich, Barnaba, 'Il beato Giovanni Duns Scotus: contesto storico-teologico', in *La "Scuola Francescana" e l'Immacolata Concezione*, Atti del Congresso Mariologico Francescano S. Maria degli Angeli, Assisi, 4-8 dicembre 2003, (Vatican City: Pontificia Academia Mariana Internationalis, 2005), pp. 159-92

_____, 'La teologia dell'Immacolata Concezione in alcuni autori prescolastici, in *La "Scuola Francescana" e l'Immacolata Concezione*, Atti del Congresso Mariologico Francescano S. Maria degli Angeli, Assisi, 4-8 dicembre 2003, (Vatican City: Pontificia Academia Mariana Internationalis, 2005), pp. 141-58

Hémery, Jean, 'La devotion du people chrétien envers Marie du 8e au 13e siècles' *Cahiers mariales*, 8 (1964), 193-207

Hen, Yitzhak, *Culture and Religion in Merovingian Gaul, A.D. 481-751* (Leiden: Brill, 1995)

Henry, Hugh T., 'Ave Maris Stella,' in *The Catholic Encyclopedia*, ed. by Charles George Herbermann, Edward Pace, and others, 15 vols (New York: Appleton, 1907-12), in *New Advent* <http://www.newadvent.org/cathen/02149a.htm> II (1907) [November 10, 2006]

_____, 'Salve Regina', in *The Catholic Encyclopaedia*, ed. by Charles George Herbermann, Edward Pace, and others, 15 vols (New York: Appleton, 1907-12), in *New Advent* <http://www.newadvent.org/cathen/13409a.htm> XII (1912) [April 6, 2006]

Herrin, Judith, 'The Imperial Feminine in Byzantium', *Past and Present*, 169 (2000), 3-35

Hinnebusch, William A., *History of the Dominican Order: Origins and Growth to 1500*, 2 vols (New York: Alba, 1965-1972)

Hock, Ronald F., *The Infancy Gospels of James and Thomas* (Santa Rosa: Polebridge Press, 1995)

Holum Kenneth G., *Theodosian Empresses: Women and Imperial Dominion in Late Antiquity* (Berkeley: University of California Press, 1982)

Hope, David M., *The Leonine Sacramentary: A Reassessment of its Nature and Purpose* (Oxford: Oxford University Press, 1971)

Hughes, Anselm, ed, *The Portiforium of St Wulstan*, 2 vols, Henry Bradshaw Society, 89–90 (London: Faith Press, 1958–60)

Hunter, David G., *Marriage, Celibacy, and Heresy in Ancient Christianity: The Jovinianist Controversy* (Oxford: Oxford University Press, 2007)

———, 'Helvidius, Jovinian, and the Virginity of Mary in late Fourth-Century Rome', *Journal of Early Christian Studies*, 1 (1993), 47-71

Hurley, Michael, 'Born Incorruptibly: The Third Canon of the Lateran Council (A. D. 649)', *The Heythrop Journal*, 2 (2007), 216-36

Imhof, Paul and Bernd Lorenz, *Maria Theotokos bei Cyrill von Alexandrien* (Munich: Kaffke, 1981)

Iogna-Prat, Dominique, Eric Palazzo, and Daniel Russo, eds, *Marie: Le culte de la Vierge dans la société médiévale* (Paris: Beauchesne, 1996)

Irenaeus, Saint, *The Demonstration of the Apostolic Preaching* (London: Society for Promoting Christian Knowledge; New York: Macmillan, 1920), trans. by J. Armitage Robinson, in *The Tertullian Project* <http://www.tertullian.org/fathers/irenaeus_02_proof.htm> [May 5, 2007]

James, Liz, 'The Empress and the Virgin in Early Byzantium: Piety, Authority and Devotion', in *Images of the Mother of God: Perceptions of the Theotokos in Byzantium*, ed. by Maria Vassilaki (Aldershot: Ashgate, 2005), pp. 145-152

Janaro, John, 'Saint Anselm and the Development of the Doctrine of the Immaculate Conception: Historical and Theological Perspectives', *The Saint Anselm Journal*, 3 (2006), 48-56

Jenner, Henry, 'Mozarabic Rite', in *The Catholic Encyclopedia*, ed. by Charles George Herbermann, Edward Pace, and others, 15 vols (New York: Appleton, 1907-12), X (1911) in *New Advent* <http://www.newadvent.org/cathen/10611a.htm> [accessed 5 July 2007]

Johannson, Ann-Katrin, 'Jalons liturgiques pour une histoire du culte de la vierge dans l'Occident latin (Ve-XIe siècle)', in *Marie: Le culte de la Vierge dans la société médiévale*, pp. 407-39

Johnson, Elizabeth A., 'Marian Devotion in the Western Church', in *Christian Spirituality: High Middle Ages and Reformation*, ed. by Jill Raitt, World Spirituality, 17 (New York: Crossroad, 1988), pp. 392-414

Joussard, Georges, 'Marie à travers la patristique: Maternité divinité, virginité, sainteté', in *Maria* 1, 69-157

———, 'The Fathers of the Church and the Immaculate Conception', in *The Dogma of the Immaculate Conception: History and Significance*, ed. by Edward D. O'Connor (Notre Dame, Ind: University of Notre Dame Press, 1958), pp. 51-86

Jugie, Martin, *L'Immaculée Conception dans l'Écriture Sainte et la tradition orientale* (Rome: Accademia Mariana / Officium Libri Catholici, 1952)

_____, *La mort et l'assomption de la Saint Vierge: Étude historico-doctrinale* (Vatican City: Studi e Testi, 1944)

_____, 'Abraham d'Ephèse: Homélies pour les fêtes de l'Annonciation et de l'Ypapante', in *Patrologia Orientalis* (Turnhout: Brepols, 1907), XVI (1922), 429-441

Jung, Karl, *Four Archetypes: Mother, Rebirth, Spirit, Trickster* (Princeton: Princeton University Press, 1970)

Kaestli, Jean-Daniel, 'Le *Protoévangile de Jacques* en Latin: État de la question et perspectives nouvelles', *Revue d'histoire théologique*, 26 (1996), 41-102

Kamesar, Adam, 'The Virgin of Isaiah 7:14: The Philological Argument from the Second to the Fifth Century', *Journal of Theological Studies*, 41 (1990), 51-75

Katz, Melissa, 'Regarding Mary: Women's Lives Reflected in the Virgin's Image', in *Divine Mirrors: The Madonna Unveiled* ed. by Melissa Katz (Oxford and New York: Oxford University Press, 2001), pp. 19-129

Kelly, John Norman D., *Early Christian Creeds*, 3rd edn (New York: Continuum, 2006)

_____, *Early Christian Doctrines*, 5th rev. edn (New York: Continuum, 2000)

Kessler, Herbert L., and Joanna Zacharias, *Rome 1300: On the Path of the Pilgrim* (New Haven: Yale University Press, 2000)

Klauk, Hans-Josef, *Apocryphal Gospels: An Introduction* (London: Clark, 2003)

Kochaniewicz, Boguslaw, 'L'Immacolata Concezione e la dottrina di San Tommaso d'Aquino', in *La "Scuola Francescana" e l'Immacolata Concezione*, Atti del Congresso Mariologico Francescano S. Maria degli Angeli, Assisi, 4-8 dicembre 2003, (Vatican City: Pontificia Academia Mariana Internationalis, 2005), pp. 87-139

_____, 'Il concepimento e il parto verginale di Maria nella riflessione teologica di san Pietro Crisologo', *Theotokos*, 12 (2004), 197-214

Koehler, Théodore, 'Les principales interprétations traditionelles de Jn. 19, 25-27 pendant les douze premiers siècles', *Études mariales*, 16 (1959), pp. 119-55

Koutrakou, Nike, 'Use and Abuse of the "Image" of the Theotokos in the Political Life of Byzantium (with Special Reference to the Iconocalst Period')', in *Images of the Mother of God: Perceptions of the Theotokos in Byzantium*, ed. by Maria Vassilaki (Aldershot: Ashgate, 2005), pp. 77-89

Kristeva, Julia, 'Stabat Mater', in *The Female Body in Western Culture: Contemporary Perspectives*, ed. by Susan Rubin Suleiman (Cambridge Ma. and London, Harvard University Press, 1986), pp. 99-118

Kuypers, Arthur B., ed, *The Book of Cerne* (Cambridge: Cambridge University Press, 1902)

L'ordine dei Servi di Maria nel primo secolo di vita, Atti del Convegno Storico, Palazzo Vecchio, Santissima Annunziata 23-24 maggio 1986 (Florence: Biblioteca della Provincia toscana dei Servi di Maria, 1988)

Lacoutre, Daniel, *Marie, Médiatrice de toutes grâces: Raisons, enjeux, conséquences* (Saint-Amand, Cher: Béatitudes, 1997)

Lambert, Malcolm, *The Cathars* (Malden, Mass.: Blackwell, 1998)

Lambot, Cyrille, L'homélie du Pseudo-Jérôme sur l'Assomption et l'évangile de la Nativité de Marie d'aprés une lettre inédite d'Hincmar', *Revue Bénédictine*, 46 (1934), 265-82

Lamy, Marielle, *L'Immaculée Conception: étapes et enjeux d'une controverse au Moyen Âge (XIIe-XVe s.)*, Collection des Études Augustiniennes, Série Moyen Âge et

Temps Modernes, 35 (Paris: Institut des Études Augustiniennes, 2000)

_____, 'L'influence de saint Bernard sur la théologie mariale de la fin du Moyen Âge', in *La Vierge dans la tradition cistercienne, Bulletin de la Société Française d'Études Mariales*, 54e session de la S.F.E.M., Abbaye Notre-Dame d'Orval, 1998 (Paris: Médiaspaul, 1999), pp.193-216

Langella, Alfonso, 'La disputa tra Ratramno e Pascasio Radberto sulla verginità di Maria nel parto', *Theotokos*, 16.2 (2008), 39-86

_____, 'Il vangelo di Maria in Giustino martire', *Theotokos*, 9 (2001), 329-52

Lansing, Carol, *Power and Purity: Cathar Heresy in Medieval Italy* (Oxford: Oxford University Press, 1998)

Larson, Atria, 'Passive Instrument and Active Intercessor: Anselm's View of Mary's Role in Redemption', *Cistercian Studies Quarterly*, 41 (2006), 32-50

Lasareff, Victor, 'Studies in the Iconography of the Virgin', *Art Bulletin*, 20 (1938), 26-65

Laurentin, René, 'Singularité significative des textes sur la virginité de Marie et leur omniprésence dans le Nouveau Testament', in *La virginité de Marie: Communications présentées à la 53e Session de la Société française d'études mariales*, Issoudun, septembre 1997, ed. by Jean Longère (Paris: Médiaspaul, 1998), pp. 35-51

_____, 'The Virgin Mary in the Works of St. Anthony of Padua', *Greyfriars Review*, 10 (1996), 47-74

_____, *Marie, mère du Seigneur: Les beaux textes de deux millénaires* (Paris: Desclée, 1984)

_____, 'The Role of the Papal Magisterium in the Development of the Dogma of the Immaculate Conception', trans. by Charles Sheedy and Edward Shea, in *The Dogma of the Immaculate Conception: History and Significance*, ed. by Edward O'Connor, (Notre Dame, Ind: University of Notre Dame Press, 1958), pp. 281-307

_____, L'interprétation de Genèse 3.15 dans la tradition jusqu'au début du XIII siècle', *Études mariales*, 12 (1954), 79-156

_____, 'Le titre de Corédemptrice: Étude historique', *Marianum*, 13 (1951), 399-402

Lausberg Heinrich, *Der Hymnus 'Ave maris Stella'* (Opladen: Westdeutscher, 1976)

Lazar, Moshe, 'Theophilus: Servant of Two Masters. The Pre-Faustian Theme of Despair and Revolt', *MLN*, 87 (1972), 31-50

Leahy, Breandán, *The Marian Profile in the Ecclesiology of Hans Urs von Balthasar* (New York: New City Press, 2000)

Leclercq, Jean, *La femme et les femmes dans l'oeuvre de Saint Bernard* (Paris: Téqui, 1982)

_____, 'Formes anciennes de l'office marial', *Ephemerides liturgicae*, 74 (1960), 89-102

_____, 'Formes successives de l'office votif de la Vierge', *Ephemerides liturgicae*, 72 (1958), 294- 301

_____, 'Dévotion et théologie mariales dans le monachisme bénédictin', in *Maria*, II, 547-78

_____, 'Grandeur et misère de la dévotion mariale au moyen-âge', *La Maison-Dieu*, 38 (1954), 122-35

_____, 'Saint Bernard et la dévotion médiévale envers Marie,' *Revue d'ascétique et mystique*, 30 (1954), 361-75

Lehmann, Leonhard, 'La devozione a Maria in Francesco e Chiara d'Assisi', in *La "Scuola Francescana" e l'Immacolata Concezione*, Atti del Congresso Mariologico Francescano S. Maria degli Angeli, Assisi, 4-8 dicembre

2003, ed. by Stefano M. Cecchin (Vatican City: Pontificia Academia Mariana Internationalis, 2005)

Leonardi, Claudio, 'La Mariologia di Bernardo di Clairvaux nelle "Homiliae in laudibus Virginis Matris"', in *Figure poetiche e figure teologiche nella mariologia dei secoli XI e XII*, atti del II convegno mariologico della Fondazione Ezio Franceschini con la collaborazione della Biblioteca Palatina di Parma, Parma, 19-20 maggio 2000, ed. by Clelia Maria Piastra and Francesco Santi (Florence: SISMEL-Edizioni del Galluzzo, 2004), pp. 129-34

Leroy, François J., *L'homilétique de Proclus de Constantinople*, Studi e Testi, 247 (Vatican City: Biblioteca Apostolica Vaticana, 1967)

Levi D'Ancona, Mirella, *Iconography of the Immaculate Conception in the Middle Ages and the Early Renaissance* (New York: College Art Association of America and Art Bulletin, 1957)

Lietzmann, Hans, *Apollinaris von Laodicea und seine Schule: Texte und Untersuchungen* (Tübingen, Mohr 1904)

Limberis, Vasiliki, 'Hymns to Mary the Mother of God the Theotokos', in *Religions of Late Antiquity in Practice*, ed. by Richard Valantasis (Princeton: Princeton University Press, 2000), pp. 357-63

_____, *Divine Heiress: The Virgin Mary and the Creation of Christian Constantinople* (London and New York: Routledge 1994)

Lipphardt, Walter, 'Studien zu den Marianklagen', *Beiträge zur Geschichte der deutschen Sprache und Literatur*, 58 (1934), 390-444

Livius, Thomas, *The Blessed Virgin in the Fathers of the First Six Centuries* (London: Burns and Oates, 1893)

Longère, Jean, 'Le *Orationes ad sanctam Mariam* e il genere letterario del *Mariale*', in *SDM*, I, 567-89

Louth, Andrew, *St. John Damascene: Tradition and Originality in Byzantine Theology* (Oxford: Oxford University Press, 2002)

Lubich, Chiara, *Maria Trasparenza di Dio* (Rome: Città Nuova, 2003)

Luis, A., 'Evolutio historica doctrinae de compassione B. Mariae Virginis', *Marianum*, 5 (1943), pp. 268-85

Maccarini, Franco, *Jacopone da Todi e i suoi critici* (Milan: Gastaldi, 1952)

MacGregor, Alistair, 'Candelmas: A Festival of Roman Origins', in *The Origins of the Cult of the Virgin Mary*, ed. by Chris Maunder (London: Burns and Oats, 2008), pp. 137-53

Madec, Goulvan, 'Marie, Vierge et Mère selon saint Ambrose et saint Augustin', in *La virginité de Marie: Communications présentées à la 53e Session de la Société française d'études mariales*, Issoudun, septembre 1997, ed. by Jean Longère (Paris: Médiaspaul, 1998), pp. 71-84

Maggioni, Corrado, 'Le feste mariane nell'antichità e nel primo medievo', *Theotokos*, 16 (2008), 127-54

_____, *Benedetto il frutto del tuo grembo: due millenni di pietà mariana* (Casale Monferrato: Portalupi, 2000)

Maguire, Henry, 'Byzantine Domestic Art as Evidence for the Early Cult of the Virgin', in *Images of the Mother of God: Perceptions of the* Theotokos *in Byzantium*, ed. by Maria Vassilaki Aldershot: Ashgate, 2005), pp. 183-193

_____, *Art and Eloquence in Byzantium* (Princeton: Princeton University Press, 1981)

_____, 'The Depiction of Sorrow in Middle Byzantine Art', *Dumbarton Oaks Papers*, 31 (1977), 123-174

Maloy, Robert, 'The "Speculum historiale" of Vincent of Beauvais and the Marian Works Attributed to St. Ildephonsus of Toledo', *Ephemerides Mariologicae*, 22 (1972), 5-14

Mango, Cyril, 'Constantinople as Theotokoupolis', in *Images of the Mother of God: Perceptions of the* Theotokos *in Byzantium*, ed. by Maria Vassilaki (Aldershot: Ashgate, 2005), pp. 17-25

_____, 'The Origins of the Blachernae Shrine at Constantinople', in *Acta XIII Congressus Internationalis Archaeologicae Christinae: Split-Poreč*, ed. by N. Cambi and E. Marin (Vatican City: Pontificio Istituto di Archeologia Cristiana, 1998), 61-76

_____, *The Art of the Byzantine Empire, 312- 1453* (Englewood Cliffs: Prentice Hall, 1972)

Marcel, Richard, 'L'introduction du mot "Hypostase" dans la théologie de l'Incarnation', *Mélanges de science religieuse*, 2 (1945), 5-32, 243-70

Mariscal Chávez, Felipe, *María en las obras de San Isidoro de Sevilla* (Rome: Marianum, 1991)

Maritano, Mario, 'Maria nell'area culturale latina: da Tertulliano († 240 ca) a sant'Ildefonso di Toledo († 667),' in *SDM*, I, 306-27

_____, 'I primi quattro Concili ecumenici in relazione con la mariologia', *Theotokos*, 12 (2004), 3-23

_____, 'I Padri latini e la mariologia nel IV sec.', *Theotokos*, 11 (2003), 215-44

_____, 'Giustino martire e gli eretici negatori della maternità di Maria', *Agustinianum*, 37 (1997), 285-301

Mateo-Seco, Lucas Francisco, 'El título de "Madre de Dios" en la teología de los Padres anteriores a Éfeso', *Estudios marianos*, 68 (2002), 47-68

_____, 'María al pie de la cruz en la patrística griega', *Estudios marianos*, 70 (2004), 71-89

Mathews, Thomas F., and Norman Muller, 'Isis and Mary in Early Icons', in *Images of the Mother of God: Perceptions of the* Theotokos *in Byzantium*, ed. by Maria Vassilaki (Aldershot: Ashgate, 2005), pp. 3-12

Matter, E. Ann, *The Voice of My Beloved: The Song of Songs in Western Medieval Christianity* (Philadelphia: University of Pennsylvania Press, 1990)

Maunder, Chris, 'Mary in the New Testament and Apocrypha', in *Mary: The Complete Resource*, ed. by Sarah Jane Boss (Oxford and New York: Oxford University Press 2007), pp. 11-46

Maximus of Turin, *The Sermons of Maximus of Turin*, trans. by Boniface Ramsey (New York: Newman, 1989)

Maximus the Confessor,, *Maxime le Confesseur: Vie de la Vierge*, ed. and trans. by Michel van Esbroeck, 2 vols (Louvain: Peeters, 1986)

_____, *The Life of the Virgin*, trans. introd. and notes by Stephen J. Shoemaker (New Haven and London: Yale University Press, 2012)

Mayberry, Nancy, 'The Controversy over the Immaculate Conception in Medieval and Renaissance Art, Literature, and Society', *Journal of Medieval and Renaissance Studies*, 21 (1991), 207-24

McCleery, Iona, 'The Virgin and the Devil: The Role of the Virgin Mary in the Theophilus Legend and Its Spanish and Portuguese Variants', in in

The Church and Mary ed. by Robert N. Swanson, Studies in Church History, 39 (Woodenbridge: Boydell, 2004), pp. 147-56

McDonnell, Kilian, 'The Marian Liturgical Tradition', in *The One Mediator, the Saints, and Mary: Lutherans and Catholics in Dialogue* (Minneapolis: Augsburg, 1991), pp. 177-91

McGuckin, John, 'The Early Cult of Mary and Inter-Religious Contexts in the Fifth-Century Church', in *The Origins of the Cult of the Virgin Mary*, ed. by Chris Maunder (London: Burns and Oats, 2008), pp. 1-22

————, 'The Strategic Adaption of Deification in the Cappadocians', in *Partakers of the Divine Nature: The History and Development of Deificiation in the Christian Traditions*, ed. by Michael J. Christensen, Jeffery A. Wittung (Rutherford N.J.: Fairleigh Dickinson Univ Press, 2007), pp. 95-114

————, *St Gregory of Nazianzus: An Intellectual Biography* (Crestwood, N.Y.: St. Vladimir's, 2001)

————, *St. Cyril of Alexandria: The Christological Controversy: Its History, Theology and Texts*, Supplements to Vigiliae Christianae, 23 (Leiden: Brill, 1994)

Meersseman, Gilles Gérard, *Ordo fraternitatis - Confraternite e pietà dei laici nel Medioevo*, in collaboration with G. P. Pacini, 3 vols (Rome: Herder 1977)

————, *Der Hymnos Akathistos im Abendland*, 2 vols (Freiburg: Universizätsverlag, 1958-60)

————, 'Études sur les anciennes confréries dominicaines, III', *Archivium Fratrum Praedicatorum*, 22 (1952), 5-176

Meier, Theo, *Die Gestalt Marias im geistlichen Schauspiel des deutschen Mittelalters* (Berlin: Erich Schmidt, 1959)

Melli, Maria, 'Il mistero della croce in San Massimo il Confessore', in *Il mistero della croce e Maria*, atti del 4 colloquio internazionale di mariologia, santuario di Polsi-San Luca (RC), 13-14 settembre 1999, ed. by Stefano De Fiores, Giuseppe Strangio, and Enrico Vidau (Rome: Monfortane, 2001), pp. 79-95

Meyendorff, John, *Christ in Eastern Christian Thought* (Crestwood, N.Y.: St. Vladimir's, 1987)

Meyer, John R., 'Ambrose's Exegesis of Luke 2, 22-24 and Mary's *virginitas in partu*,' *Marianum*, 62 (2000), 169-92

Michael Kunzler, *The Church's Liturgy*, trans. by Placed Murray, Henry O'Shea and Cilian Ó Sé (London and New York: Continuum, 2001)

Migliore, F. 'La figura di Maria vergine e madre di Dio negli inni di Romano il Melode', *Theotokos*, 15 (2007), 37-76

————, 'Maria Vergine e Madre di Dio nelle opere di Eusebio di Cesarea' *Theotokos*, 10 (2002), 133-70

Migne, Jacques-Paul, ed, *Patrologiae cursus completus, seu bibliotheca universalis, integra, uniformis, commoda, oeconomica, omnium SS. Patrum, doctorum scriptorumque ecclesiasticorum qui ab aevo apostolico ad usque Innocentii III tempora floruerunt*, Series Latina, 221 vols (Paris: Migne, 1844-64)

————, ed, *Patrologiae cursus completus, seu bibliotheca universalis, integra, uniformis, commoda, oeconomica, omnium SS. Patrum, doctorum scriptorumque ecclesiasticorum*, Series Graeca, 165 vols (Paris: Migne, 1857-66)

Miller, Robert J., ed, *The Complete Gospels: Annotated Edition*, 3rd edn (San Francisco: Harper, 1994)

Mimouni, Simon Claude, *Dormition et Assomption de Marie: Histoire des traditions anciennes* (Paris: Beauchesne, 1995)

Miravalle, Mark, *'With Jesus': The Story of Mary Co-Redemptrix* (Goleta, Ca.: Queenship Publishing, 2003)

Mirri, Luciana, 'Maria nell'esegisi di san Girolamo', in *L'esegisi dei padri latini dalle origini a Gregorio Magno*, XXVIII Incontro di studiosi dell'antichità cristiana, Roma, 6-8 maggio 1999 (Rome: Institutum Patristicum Augustinianum, 2000), pp. 573-616

Mitsakis, Kariofilis, 'The Hymnography of the Greek Church in the Early Christian Centuries', *Jahrbuch der Österreichischen byzantinischen Gesellschaft*, 20 (1971), 31-49

Mohlberg, Leo Cunibert, Leo Eizenhöfer, and Petrus Siffrin, eds., *Sacramentarium Veronense* (Rome: Herder, 1966)

Mohlberg, Leo Cunibert, ed, *Missale Gothicum* (Rome: Herder, 1957)

Mone, Franz Joseph, ed, *Lateinische Hymnen des Mittelalters*, 3 vols (Freiburg im Breisgau: Herder, 1853-55; repr. Aalen: Scientia, 1964), II (1854)

Montagna, Davide M., 'La lode alla Theotokos nei testi greci dei secoli IV- VII', *Marianum*, 24 (1962), pp. 453-543

Montanari, Antonio, 'San Bernardo di Clairvaux e la sua scuola', in *SDM*, I, 637-61

———, 'Maria Vergine negli scritti di s. Bernardo di Clairvaux', in *Maria madre del Signore nei Padri della Chiesa*, dizionario di spiritualità biblico-patristica, 41 (Rome: Borla, 2005), pp. 317-52

Moral, Tomas, 'Los benedictinos, la teologia mariana, y el culto a la Madre de Dios', *Cistercium*, 40 (1988), 541-57

Moraldi, Luigi, ed, *Apocrifi del Nuovo Testamento*, 3 vols (Milan: UTET, 1994)

Moralejo, Gaspar Calvo and Stefano Cecchin, *L'Assunzione di Maria Madre di Dio: significato storico salvifico a 50 anni dalla definizione dogmatic*, atti del 1° Forum internazionale di mariologia, Roma 30-31 ottobre 2000 (Vatican City: Pontificia Accademia Mariana Internazionale, 2001)

Moreton, Bernard, *The Eighth-Century Gelasian Sacramentary: A Study in Tradition* (Oxford: Oxford University Press, 1976)

Murray Gasper, Giles Edward, *Anselm of Canterbury and his Theological Inheritance* (Aldershot: Ashgate, 2004)

Musurillo, Herbert, 'The Medieval Hymn *Alma Redemptoris*: A Linguistic analysis', *The Classical Journal*, 52 (1957), 171-174

Navarro Girón, María Ángeles, *La carne de Cristo: el misterio eucarístico a la luz de la controversia entre Pascasio Radberto, Ratramno, Rabano Mauro y Godescalco* (Madrid: Universidad Pontificia de Comillas, 1989)

Neff, Amy, 'The Pain of Compassio: Mary's Labor at the Foot of the Cross,' *Art Bulletin*, 80 (1998), 254-73

Neuman, Erich, *The Great Mother: An Analysis of the Archetype* (New York: Pantheon, 1955)

Neumann, Charles, W., *The Virgin Mary in the Works of Saint Ambrose* (Fribourg, University Press, 1962)

Nin, Manuel, 'Maria nelle liturgie orientali', in *SDM*, I, 424-47

Norelli, Enrico, 'Maria nella letteratura apocrifa cristiana antica', in *SDM*, I, 143-254

———, 'Maria negli Apocrifi', in *Gli studi di mariologia medievale: bilancio storico*, Atti del I convegno mariologico della fondazione Ezio Franceschini con la collaborazione della biblioteca Palatina e del dipartimento di storia dell'università di Parma, parma 7-8 novembre 1997, ed. by Clelia Maria Piastra (Florence: SISMEL – Edizioni del Galuzzo, 2001), pp. 19-63

Norman, Diana, *Siena and the Virgin: Art and Politics in a Late Medieval City State* (New Haven, Conn.; London: Yale University Press, 1999)

Norris, Richard A., *Manhood and Christ: A Study in the Christology of Theodore of Mopsuestia* (Oxford: The Clarendon Press, 1963)

Nyberg, Kathleen N., *The New Eve* (Nashville: Abingdon, 1967)

Ó Briain, Felim, 'Feast of Our Lady's Conception in the Medieval Irish Church', *Irish Ecclesiastical Record*, 70 (1948), 687-704

O'Carroll, Michael, *Theotokos: A Theological Encyclopedia of the Blessed Virgin Mary* (Collegeville, Minnesota: Liturgical Press, 1982)

O'Connor, Edward, ed, *The Dogma of the Immaculate Conception: History and Significance*, (Indiana: University of Notre Dame Press, 1958)

Ogier of Lucedio, *Homilies: In Praise of God's Holy Mother, on Our Lord's Words to His Disciples at the Last Supper.* Trans. and annot. by D. Martin Jenni (Kalamazoo: Cistercian, 2006)

O'Sullivan, Daniel, *Marian Devotion in Thirteenth-Century French Lyric* (Toronto: University of Toronto Press, 2005)

Orbe, Antonio *Antropología de San Ireneo* (Madrid: Biblioteca de Autores Cristianos, 1969)

Ortiz de Urbina, Ignacio, 'Vale el testimonio de san Efrem en favor de la Immaculada?', *Estudios Eclesiasticos*, 28 (1954), 417-22

Ouimet, Aurele, 'Marie et notre Rédemption selon Saint Bernard', *Veillée Mariale*, 41 (1953), 3-61

Palazzo, Eric, *A History of Liturgical Books from the Beginning to the Thirteenth Century*, trans. by Madeleine Beaumont (Collegeville, Minnesota: Liturgical Press, 1998)

Parker, Roscoe, E., 'The Date of the Gospel of Pseudo-Matthew', *PMLA*, 45 (1930), pp. 1266-67

Parlby, Geri, 'The Origins of Marian Art in the Catacombs and the Problems of Identification', in *The Origins of the Cult of the Virgin Mary*, ed. by Chris Maunder (London: Burns and Oats, 2008), pp. 41-56

———, 'The Origins of Marian Art: The Evolution of Marian Imagery in the Western Church until AD 431', in *Mary: The Complete Resource*, ed. by Sarah Jane Boss (Oxford and New York: Oxford University Press 2007), pp. 106-29

Paxton, Frederick S., Christianizing Death: The Creation of a Ritual Process in Early Medieval Europe (Ithaca and London: Cornell University Press, 1990)

Peck, George T., *The Fool of God: Jacopone da Todi* (Alabama: The University of Alabama Press, 1980)

Pegg, Mark Gregory, *A Most Holy War: The Albigensian Crusade and the Battle for Christendom* (Oxford: Oxford University Press, 2007)

Pelikan Jaroslav, *Mary through the Centuries: Her Place in the History of Culture* (New Haven: Yale University Press, 1996)

Peltomaa, Leena, *The Image of the Virgin Mary in the Akathistos Hymn* (Leiden, Boston and Cologne: Brill, 2001)

Pentcheva, Bissera V., *Icons and Power: The Mother of God in Byzantium* (University Park: Penn State Press, 2006)

Peretto, Elio, 'Primi abozzi di riflessione teologica su Maria', in *SDM*, I, 257-62

————, 'Maria nell'area culturale greca: da san Giustino († 165 ca) a san Giovanni Damasceno († 749 ca)', in *SDM*, I, 293-305

Perotto, Lorenzo M., 'La Vergine Maria nel pensiero di uno scrittore del secondo secolo: la mariologia del Protevangelo di Giacomo', *Marianum*, 16 (1954), 228-65

Perrarnau i Espelt, Josep, 'Raimondo Lullo e la sua teologia sull'immacolata concezione', in *La "Scuola Francescana" e l'Immacolata Concezione*, Atti del Congresso Mariologico Francescano S. Maria degli Angeli, Assisi, 4-8 dicembre 2003, (Vatican City: Pontificia Academia Mariana Internationalis, 2005), pp. 273-301

Pertile, Lino, '*Paradiso* XXXIII: l'estremo oltraggio', *Filologia e Critica*, 6 (1981), 1-21

Petersen, William L., 'The Dependence of Romanos the Melodist upon the Syriac Ephrem: Its Importance for the Origin of the Kontakion', *Vigiliae Christianae*, 39.2 (1985), 171-87

Pfaff, Richard W., *Medieval Latin Liturgy: A Select Bibliography* (Toronto: University of Toronto Press, 1982)

Piastra, Clelia Maria, *Gli studi di mariologia medievale: bilancio storico*, Atti del I convegno mariologico della fondazione Ezio Franceschini con la collaborazione della biblioteca Palatina e del dipartimento di storia dell'università di Parma, parma 7-8 novembre 1997, (Florence: SISMEL – Edizioni del Galuzzo, 2001), pp. 193-215

Pieri, Francesco, 'Il concepimento verginale e l'argomento biblico di Is. 7. 14 nell'esegisi di Girolamo, tra polemica ed apologia', *Theotokos*, 11 (2003), 363-84

Pierre, Marie-Joseph, 'La Vierge dans les Odes de Salomon, *Études mariales*, 60 (2003), 119-37

Plenzat, Karl, *Die Theophilus legende in der Dichtung des Mittelalters*, Germanische Studien, 43 (Berlin: Ebering, 1926; repr. Nendlem, Liechtenstein: Krauss, 1967)

Polanco, Fernando Rodrigo, 'La mariologia di sant'Ireneo', *Theotokos*, 9 (2001), 359-400

Pompei, Alfonso, 'Giovanni Duns Scoto e la dottrina sull'immacolata concezione' in *La "Scuola Francescana" e l'Immacolata Concezione*, Atti del Congresso Mariologico Francescano S. Maria degli Angeli, Assisi, 4-8 dicembre 2003, (Vatican City: Pontificia Academia Mariana Internationalis, 2005), pp. 193-217

Potestà, Gian Luca, *Il tempo dell'Apocalisse: Vita di Gioacchino da Fiore* (Roma-Bari: Laterza, 2004)

Power, Eileen, 'Introduction', in Johannes Herolt, *Miracles of the Blessed Virgin Mary*, ed. and trans. by C. C. Swinton Bland (London: Rutledge 1928; repr. New York, Kessinger, 2004), pp. ix-xxxv

Pranger, Burcht, *Bernard of Clairvaux and the Shape of Monastic Thought: Broken Dreams* (Leiden: Brill, 1994)

Price, Richard, 'The *Theotokos* and the Council of Ephesus', in *The Origins of the Cult of the Virgin Mary*, ed. by Chris Maunder (London: Burns and Oats, 2008), pp. 89-103

————, 'Theotokos: The Title and its Significance in Doctrine and Devotion', in *Mary: The Complete Resource*, ed. by Sarah Jane Boss (Oxford and New York: Oxford University Press 2007), pp. 56-74

_____, 'Marian Piety and the Nestorian Controversy', *The Church and Mary*, ed. by Robert N. Swanson, Studies in Church History, 39 (Woodenbridge: Boydell, 2004), 31-38

Raby, F. J. E., ed, *The Oxford Book of Medieval Latin Verse* (Oxford, The Clarendon Press, 1959)

Radford Ruether, Rosemary, *Mary: The Feminine Face of the Church* (London: SCM, 1979)

Rainini, Marco, 'Maria nelle opera di Gioacchino da Fiore († 1202)', in *SDM*, I, 700-25

Rava, Eva Cariota, 'Verginità perpetua e maternità divina di Maria', in *Respice stellam: Maria in San Bernardo e nella tradizione cistercense, Atti del convegno internazionale*, ed. by Ignazio M. Calabuig (Roma, Marianum 21-24 October 1991), (Rome: Marianum, 1993), pp 125-41

Reynolds, Brian, 'L'immagine della Vergine nelle *Laude* del XIII secolo, in relazione alla *Commedia* di Dante' *Fu Jen Studies: Literature & Linguistics*, 43 (2010), 69-93

_____, 'Beyond Beatrice: From Love Poetry to a Poetry of Love', in: *Chivalry and Knighthood in the Middle Ages*, Proceedings of the Fourth Annual Fu Jen Medieval Conference (Taipei: Department of French, Fu Jen University, 2004), pp. 130-192

_____, 'A Beauty that Transforms: The Marian Aesthetics of Dante's *Commedia*', *Fu Jen Studies*, 35 (2003), 61-89

_____, 但丁《神曲》中的女性啟蒙角色 台北;《中外文學》('The Feminine as Clarifier in Dante's *Commedia*'), *Chung Wai Literary Monthly*, 32 (2003), 15-42

Righi, Maria Francesca, 'La presenza della beata Vergine nel rinnovamento cistercense', in *SDM*, I, 618-36

Roberts, Alexander, and James Donaldson, eds., *The Ante-Nicene Fathers: Translations of the Writings of the Fathers down to A.D. 325*, 10 vols, (Buffalo: The Christian Literature Publishing Company, 1885-96; repr. Grand Rapids, MI., Eerdmans, 2001)

Robinson, J. Armitage, *The Demonstration of the Apostolic Preaching* (London: Society for Promoting Christian Knowledge; New York: Macmillan, 1920) in *The Tertullian Project* <http://www.tertullian.org/fathers/irenaeus_02_proof.htm> [accessed 7 May 2007]

Romanos the Melodist, *On the Life of Christ: Kontakia*, trans. with an introduction, by Ephrem Lash (San Francisco: Harper Collins, 1995)

_____, *Kontakia of Romanos, Byzantine Melodist*, ed. and trans. by Marjorie Carpenter, 2 vols, (Colombia, Missouri, 1970)

Rosa, Pietro, 'Aspetti della mariologia di Cirillo Alessandrino e di Nestorio', *Theotokos*, 12 (2004), 255-85

Roschini, Gabriele M., *Maria Santissima nella storia della salvezza*, 4 vols, (Isola del Liri: Pisani, 1969)

_____, *Problematica sulla Corredenzione* (Rome: Edizioni Marianum, 1969)

_____, *Il dottore mariano: studio sulla dottrina mariana di s. Bernardo di Chiaravalle* (Rome: Edizioni Cattoliche, 1953)

_____, *La Regina dell'Universo* (Rovigo: IPAG, 1950)

Rubery, Eileen, 'Pope John VII's Devotion to Mary: Papal Images of Mary from the Fifth to the Early Eighth Centuries', in *The Origins of the Cult of the*

Virgin Mary, ed. by Chris Maunder (London: Burns and Oats, 2008), pp. 155- 99

Rubin, Miri, *Mother of God. A History of the Virgin Mary* (New Haven: Yale, 2009)

Rush, Alfred C., *Death and Burial in Christian Antiquity* (Washington DC: Catholic University Press of America, 1941)

Russell, Norman, *The Doctrine of Deification in the Greek Patristic Tradition* (Oxford and New York: Oxford University Press, 2004)

Salaville, Sévérien, 'Marie dans la liturgie byzantine ou gréco-slave', in *Maria*, I, 249-326

Salgado, Jean-Marie, 'La maternité spirituelle de la Sainte Vierge chez les Pères durant les quatre premiers siècles', *Divinitas*, 30 (1986), 58-61

————, 'La maternité spirituelle de la Sainte Vierge chez les Pères du Ve au VIIIe siècle', *Divinitas*, 30 (1986), 120-60

————, 'La maternité spirituelle de la Sainte Vierge dans la vie de l'Église du IXe au XIe siècle', *Divinitas*, 30 (1986), 240-70

Sansterre, Jean-Marie, *Les moines grecs et orientaux à Rome aux époques byzantine et carolingienne (milieu du VIe s. – fin du IXe s.)* (Brussels: Académie Royale de Belgique, 1983)

Sapegno, Natalino, *Frate Jacopone* (Turin: Baretti, 1926)

Scaramucci, Lodovico, ed, *Il Movimento dei disciplinati nel settimo centenario dal suo inizio (Perugia, 1260)* (Spoleto: Panetto & Petrelli, 1962)

Scaravelli, Irene, 'Teologia e venerazione mariana nella cultura carolingia', *Theotokos*, 16.2 (2008), 15-38

————, 'Per una mariologia carolingia: autori, opere e linee di ricerca', in *Gli studi di mariologia medievale: bilancio storico*, Atti del I convegno mariologico della fondazione Ezio Franceschini con la collaborazione della biblioteca Palatina e del dipartimento di storia dell'università di Parma, Parma 7-8 novembre 1997, ed. by Clelia Maria Piastra (Florence: SISMEL – Edizioni del Galuzzo, 2001), pp. 65-85

Schaff, Philip, ed, Arthur West Haddan, trans., *The Nicene and Post-Nicene Fathers*, First Series, III, (Buffalo, N.Y.: Christian Literature Publishing, 1887), revised and edited for *New Advent* by Kevin Knight, <http://www.newadvent.org/fathers/1301.htm>, [accessed 4 February 2009]

Scheffczyk, Leo, *Das Mariengeheimnis in Frömmigkeit und Lehre der Karolingerzeit*, Erfurter Theologische Studien, 5 (Leipzig: St. Benno-Verlag, 1959)

Schiller, Gertrud, *Iconography of Christian Art*, 2 vols, trans. by Janet Seligman (Greenwich, Conn.: New York Graphic Society, 1971)

Schine Gold, Penny, *The Lady and the Virgin: Image, Attitude, and Experience in Twelfth-Century France* (Chicago: University of Chicago Press, 1985)

Schönau, Elisabeth of, *Elisabeth of Schönau: The Complete Works*, trans, and intro. by Anne L. Clark (New York: Paulist Press, 2000)

Schork, R. J., *Sacred Song from the Byzantine Pulpit: Romanos the Melodist* (Gainesville: University Press of Florida, 1995)

Schuler, Carol M., 'The Seven Sorrows of the Virgin: Popular Culture and Cultic Imagery in Pre-Reformation Europe', *Simiolus*, 21 (1992), 5-28

Scotus, John Duns, *Four Questions on Mary*, trans. by Allan Wolter (Santa Barbara: Old Mission, 1988)

Secor, John R., 'The *Planctus Mariae* in Provençal Literature: A Subtle Blend of Courtly
    and Religious Traditions', in *The Spirit of the Court: Selected Proceedings of
    the Fourth Congress of the International Courtly Literature Society, Toronto,
    1983*, ed. by Glyn S. Burgess and Robert Taylor (Cambridge: Brewer,
    1985), pp. 321-26

Seim, Turid Karlsen, *The Double Message: Patterns of Gender in Luke-Acts* (Nashville:
    Abingdon, 1994)

Sella, Barbara, 'Northern Italian Confraternities and the Immaculate Conception in the
    Fourteenth Century', *The Journal of Ecclesiastical History*, 49 (1998), 599-
    619

Sellers, Robert V., *The Council of Chalcedon: A Historical and Doctrinal Survey* (London:
    SPCK, 1953)

Sensi, Mario, 'I santuari mariani', in *Gli studi di mariologia medievale: bilancio storico*, Atti del I
    convegno mariologico della fondazione Ezio Franceschini con la
    collaborazione della biblioteca Palatina e del dipartimento di storia
    dell'università di Parma, Parma 7-8 novembre 1997, ed. by Clelia
    Maria Piastra (Florence: SISMEL – Edizioni del Galuzzo, 2001), pp.
    217-38

Servants of Mary (Order of Servites)' in *The Catholic Encyclopedia*, IX (New York:
    Appleton, 1910) <http://www.newadvent.org/cathen/
    09750a.htm> [accessed 9 March 2009]

Shepherd, Dorothy, 'An Icon of the Virgin: A Sixth Century Tapestry Panel from
    Egypt', *Bulletin of the Clevland Museum of Art*, 56 (1969), 90-120

Sheridan, Mark, 'Maria nell'area culturale copta', in *SDM*, I, 337-49

Shoemaker, Stephen J., 'Epiphanius of Salamis, the Kollyridians, and the Early
    Dormition Narratives: The Cult of the Virgin in the Fourth Century',
    Journal of Early Christian Studies, 16 (2008), 371-401

———, 'The Cult of the Virgin in the Fourth Century: A Fresh Look at Some Old
    and New Sources', in *The Origins of the Cult of the Virgin Mary*, ed. by
    Chris Maunder (London: Burns and Oats, 2008), pp. 71-87

———, 'Marian Liturgies and Devotion in Early Christianity', in *Mary: The Complete
    Resource*, ed. by Sarah Jane Boss (Oxford and New York: Oxford
    University Press 2007), pp. 130-45

———, *Ancient Traditions of the Virgin Mary's Dormition and Assumption* (Oxford:
    Oxford University Press, 2002)

Simón, Alfredo, 'La presenza della beata Vergine nel rinnovamento promosso da
    Cluny', in *SDM*, I, 593-617

Sissa, Giulia, *Greek Virginity*, trans. by Arthur Goldhammer (Cambridge, Mass.: Harvard
    University Press, 1990)

Smalley, Beryl, *The Study of the Bible in the Middle Ages*, 3ʳᵈ edn, rev. (Oxford: Blackwell,
    1983)

Socrates, *Historia Ecclesiastica*, ed. by Günther Christian Hansen (Turnhout: Brepols,
    2004)

Söll, Georg, *Storia dei dogmi mariani* (Rome: Accademia mariana salesiana, 1981)

Sollier, Joseph, 'Adoptionism' in *The Catholic Encyclopedia*, ed. by Charles George
    Herbermann, Edward Pace, and others, 15 vols (New York:
    Appleton, 1907-1912), I (1907), in *New Advent*,
    <http://www.newadvent.org/cathen/01150a.htm> [30 July 2008]

Sorci, Pietro, 'Maria nelle liturgie latine', in *SDM*, I, 382-421

Southern, Richard William, *St. Anselm: A Portrait in a Landscape* (New York: Cambridge University Press, 1990)

———, 'The English Origins of the "Miracles of the Virgin"', *Medieval and Renaissance Studies*, 4 (1958), 176-216

———, *The Making of the Middle Ages* (New Haven: Yale University Press, 1953)

Springer, Carl P. E., 'The Hymns of Ambrose', in *Religions of Late Antiquity in Practice*, ed. by Richard Valantasis (Princeton: Princeton University Press, 2000), pp. 347-56

Starowieyski, Marek, 'Le titre Θεοτόκος avant le concile d'Ephèse', in *Studia Patristica, XIX: Papers Presented to the Tenth International Conference on Patristic Studies*, ed. by Elizabeth A. Livingstone (Leuven: Peeters, 1989)

Steenberg, Matthew C., 'The Role of Mary as co-Recapitulator in St. Irenaeus of Lyons', *Vigiliae Christianae*, 58 (2004), 117-37

Sticca, Sandro, *The Planctus Mariae in the Dramatic Tradition of the Middle Ages*, trans. by Joseph Berrigan (Athens, GA: University of Georgia Press, 1988)

———, 'The Montecassino Passion and the Origin of the Latin Passion Play', *Italica*, 44 (1967), 209-19

Stroll, Mary, 'Maria Regina: Papal Symbol', in *Queens and Queenship in Medieval Europe: Proceedings of a Conference Held at King's College London, April 1995*, ed. by Anne Duggan (Woodbridge, Suffolk: Boydell Press, 2002), pp. 173-204

Struve Haker, Ricardo, 'Arnoldo de Bonavalle: primer teólogo de la Corredención mariana', *Regina mundi* (Bogotá), 7 (1963), 48-75

Suitner, Franco, *Iacopone da Todi: poesia, mistica, rivolta nell'Italia del Medioevo* (Rome: Donzelli, 1999)

Swanson, Robert N., ed, *The Church and Mary*, Studies in Church History, 39 (Woodenbridge: Boydell, 2004)

Talley, Thomas J., 'The Origin of the Ember Days: An Inconclusive Postscript', in *Rituels: Mélanges offerts au Père Gy, OP*, ed. by Paul de Clerck and Eric Palazzo (Paris: Cerf, 1990), pp. 465-72

Tanner, Norman P., ed, *Decrees of the Ecumenical Councils*, 2 vols (London: Sheed and Ward; Washington D.C: Georgetown University Press, 1990)

Tavard, George H., *The Forthbringer of God: St. Bonaventure on the Virgin Mary* (Chicago: Franciscan Herald Press, 1989)

Thunberg, Lars, *Microcosm and Mediator: The Theological Anthropology of Maximus the Confessor*, 2nd edn (Chicago: Open Court, 1995)

———, 'The Human Person as Image of God: Eastern Christianity', in *Christian Spirituality: Origins to the Twelfth Century*, ed. by Bernard McGinn and John Meyendorff, World Spirituality, 16 (New York, Crossroads, 1989), pp. 291-311

Thurston, Herbert, 'The Origins of the Hail Mary', in *Familiar Prayers: Their Origin and History* (London: Burns and Oates, 1953), pp. 90-114

Toniolo, Ermanno M., 'Akathistos: temi e problemi', *Theotokos*, 15 (2007), 77-102

———, 'Gv 19, 25-27 nel pensiero dei Padri', *Theotokos*, 7. 2 (1999), 339-86

———, ed, *Itinerari mariani dei due millenni*, 4 vols (Rome: Centro di Cultura Mariana 'Madre della Chiesa', 1996-99)

Trembelas, Panagiotis N., *Antologia dell'innografia greco-ortodossa*, (Athens: [n. pub.], 1949)

Trisoglio, Francesco, 'La Madre di Dio in Gregorio di Nazianzo', *Theotokos*, 11 (2003), 91-124

Tsironis, Niki, 'From Poetry to Liturgy: The Cult of the Virgin in the Middle Byzantine Era', in *Images of the Mother of God: Perceptions of the* Theotokos *in Byzantium*, ed. by Maria Vassilaki, (Aldershot: Ashgate, 2005), pp. 91-102

————, 'The Lament of the Virgin Mary from Romanos the Melode to George of Nicodemia' (unpublished doctoral thesis, University of London, 1998)

Utro, Umberto, 'Maria nell'iconografia cristiana dei primi secoli', in *SDM*, I, 353-81

Van Dijk, Ann, 'The Angelic Salutation in Early Byzantine and Medieval Annunciation Imagery', *Art Bulletin*, 81 (1999), 420-36

van Esbroeck, Michel, 'The Virgin as the True Ark of the Covenant', in *Images of the Mother of God: Perceptions of the Theotokos in Byzantium*, ed. by Maria Vassilaki (Aldershot: Ashgate, 2005), pp. 63-68

————, *Aux origines de la Dormition de la Vierge: Études historiques sur les traditions orientales*, Variorum Collected Studies Series, 472 (Aldershot: Ashgate, 1995)

————, 'Le culte de la Vierge de Jérusalem à Constantinople aux 6e–7e siècles', *Revue des études byzantines*, 46 (1988), 181-90

————, 'Les textes littéraires sur l'assomption avant le Xe siècle' in *Les Actes apocryphes des Apôtres: Christianisme et monde païen* (Geneva: Labor et Fides, 1981), pp. 265-88

van Stempvoort, Pieter A., 'The Protoevangelium Jacobi: The Sources of its Theme and Style and their Bearing on its Date', in *Studia Evangelica*, III, part II, ed. by Frank L. Cross (Berlin: Akademie-Verlag, 1959), pp. 413-23

Varanini, Giorgio, Luigi Banfi and others, eds., *Il Laudario di Cortona*, with an introduction and notes by Luigi Lucchi (Vicenza: L.I.E.F., 1987)

Vassilaki, Maria, ed, *Images of the Mother of God: Perceptions of the Theotokos in Byzantium* (Aldershot: Ashgate, 2005)

Vénérable, Pierre le, *Les merveilleux de Dieu*, trans. by Jean-Pierre Torrell and Denise Bouthillier (Fribourg: Éditions universitaire, 1992)

Vergani, Emidio, 'Maria nell'area culturale siriaca nel IV secolo: Efrem il Siro, in *SDM*, I, 328-36

Vincent, Nicholas, 'Henry III and the Blessed Virgin Mary', in *The Church and Mary* ed. by Robert N. Swanson, Studies in Church History, 39 (Woodenbridge: Boydell, 2004), pp 126-46

Vishnevskaya, Elena, 'Divinization as Perichoretic Embrace in Maximus the Confessor', in *Partakers of the Divine Nature: The History and Development of Deification in the Christian Traditions*, ed. by Michael J. Christensen, Jeffery A. Wittung (Rutherford N.J.: Fairleigh Dickinson Univ Press, 2007), pp. 132-45

Viti, Goffredo and Malachia Falletti, 'La devozione a Maria nell'Ordine Cistercense', in *Respice stellam: Maria in San Bernardo e nella tradizione cistercense, Atti del convegno internazionale, Roma, Marianum, 21-24 October 1991* (Rome: Marianum, 1993), pp. 287-348

Vogel, Cyrille, *Medieval Liturgy: An Introduction to the Sources*, trans. and rev. by William G. Storey and Niels Krogh Rasmussen (Washington, DC: Pastoral Press 1986)

Vögtlin, Adolf, ed, *Vita Beatae Mariae Virginis et Salvatoris rhythmica*, Bibliothek des litterarischen Vereins Stuttgart, 180 (Tübingen: Laupp, 1888)

Voisin, Guillaume, *L'Apollinarisme: Étude historique, littéraire et dogmatique sur le début des controverses christologiques au IVe siècle* (Louvain: Van Linthout; Paris: Fontemoing, 1901)

Vona, Costantino, *Omelie mariologiche di s. Giacomo di Sarug* (Rome: Pontificia Univ. Lateranense, 1953)

Waddel, Crisogono, 'La Vierge Marie dans la Liturgie cistercienne', in *La Vierge dans la tradition cistercienne*, Jean Longère 54e session de la Société française d'études mariales, ed. by Jean Longère (Paris, Mediaspaul, 1999), pp. 123-35

Wakefield, Walter and Austin P. Evans, *Heresies of the High Middle Ages*, (New York: Columbia University Press, 1991)

Walker, Alexander, trans, *Gospel of the Pseudo-Matthew*, in *The Ante-Nicene Fathers*, ed. by Alexander Roberts and James Donaldson, 10 vols, (Buffalo: The Christian Literature Publishing Company, 1885-96; repr. Grand Rapids, MI., Eerdmans, 2001), VIII, in *Christian Classics Ethereal Library* <http://www.ccel.org/ccel/schaff/anf08.vii.v.html> [accessed 24 October 2007]

Walker, Caroline Bynum, *Jesus as Mother: Studies in the Spirituality of the High Middle Ages* (Berkeley: University of California Press, 1982)

Ward, Benedicta, *Miracles and the Medieval Mind: Theory, Record and Event, 1000-1215* (Aldershot, Wildwood House, 1987)

Ware, Kallistos, '"The Earthly Heaven": The Mother of God in the Teaching of St. John of Damascus, in *Mary for Heaven*, ed. by William M. McLoughlin and Jill Pinnock (Leominster: Gracewing, 2002), 355-68

⸺, *Mary Theotokos in the Orthodox Tradition* (Wallington: Ecumenical Society of the Blessed Virgin Mary, 1997)

Warner, Marina *Alone of all her Sex: The Myth and Cult of the Virgin Mary* (London: Pan Books, 1985)

Weber, R., 'Ambrose Autpert serait-il l'auteur de l'hymne "Ave maris stella"?', *Revue bénédictine*, 88 (1978), 159-66

Wegner, Antoine, *L'assomption de la Tres Sainte Vierge dans la tradition byzantine du Vie au Xe siècle: Études et documents* (Paris: [n. pub], 1955)

Weinandy, Thomas G., and Daniel A. Keating, eds., *The Theology of St. Cyril of Alexandria: A Critical Appreciation*, (London: Clark, 2003)

Wieck, Roger S., 'The Book of Hours', in *The Liturgy of the Medieval Church*, ed. by Thomas J. Heffernan and E. Ann Matter (Kalamazoo: Medieval Institute Publications Western Michigan University, 2001), pp. 473-513

Wilkinson, John, *Egeria's Travels to the Holy Land*, rev. edn (Warminster: Aris & Phillips; Jerusalem: Ariel, 1981)

Wilmart, André, 'Cinque textes de prière composés par Anselme de Lucques pour la Comtesse Mathilde', *Revue d'ascétique et de mystique*, 19 (1938), 23-72

_____, *Auteurs spirituels et textes dévots du moyen âge latin: Études d'histoire littéraire* (Paris: Bloud et Gay, 1932)

Winston Allen, Anne, *Stories of the Rose: The Making of the Rosary in the Middle Ages* (Pennsylvania: The Pennsylvania State University Press, 1992)

_____, Tracing the Origins of the Rosary: German Vernacular Texts', *Speculum*, 66 (1993), 616-36

Wolf, Gerhard, 'Icons and Sites: Cult Images of the Virgin in Medieval Rome', in *Images of the Mother of God: Perceptions of the* Theotokos *in Byzantium*, ed. by Maria Vassilaki (Aldershot: Ashgate, 2005), pp. 23-49

_____, *Salus populi romani: Die Geschichte römischer Kultbilder im Mittelalter* (Weinheim: VCH, Acta humaniora, 1990)

Wolter, Allan and Blane O'Neill, *John Duns Scotus: Mary's Architect* (Quincy, Ill.: Franciscan Press, 1993)

Wormald, Francis, *The Winchester Psalter* (Greenwich, CT: New York Graphic Society, 1973)

Wright, David F., 'From "God-Bearer" to "Mother of God" in the Later Fathers', in *The Church and Mary*, ed. by Robert N. Swanson, Studies in Church History, 39 (Woodenbridge: Boydell, 2004), pp. 22-30

Young, Frances, *Biblical Exegesis and the Formation of Christian Culture* (Cambridge: Cambridge University Press, 1997)

_____, *From Nicea to Chalcedon: A Guide to the Literature and Its Background* (Philadelphia: Fortress, 1983)

Young, Karl, *The Drama of the Medieval Church*, 2 vols. (Oxford: The Clarendon Press, 1933)

Zannini, P., 'Romano il Melode e le tematiche patristiche greco-siriache su Gv 2, 1-11', *Theotokos*, 7 (1999), 41-65

Zavalloni, Roberto and Eliodoro Mariani, eds., *La dottrina mariologica di Giovanni Duns Scoto* (Rome: Antonianum, 1987)

Zincone, Sergio, 'Maria nell'opera di Giovanni Crisostomo', *Theotokos*, 14 (2006), 31-42

INDEX OF PRIMARY TEXTS CITED